Crystal Reports® 9:
The Complete Reference

About the Author

After more than 10 years as an internal consultant and trainer in a large corporation, George founded his own consulting and training firm, The Ablaze Group, in 1994 (www.AblazeGroup.com). He has trained, consulted, and developed custom software for large and small clients throughout the United States, Canada, the United Kingdom, and Puerto Rico.

George is certified by Crystal Decisions as both a trainer and consultant for Crystal Reports 9, Crystal Enterprise, and Seagate Info. He is a past recipient of the Crystal Decisions *Training Partner of the Year* award.

Prior to his computer career, George was a broadcaster. His voice may still be heard in various national radio and TV commercial and promotional campaigns.

Crystal Reports® 9:
The Complete Reference

George Peck

McGraw-Hill/Osborne

New York   Chicago   San Francisco
Lisbon   London   Madrid   Mexico City
Milan   New Delhi   San Juan
Seoul   Singapore   Sydney   Toronto

The *McGraw·Hill* Companies

McGraw-Hill/Osborne
2600 Tenth Street
Berkeley, California 94710
U.S.A.

To arrange bulk purchase discounts for sales promotions, premiums, or fund-raisers, please contact **McGraw-Hill**/Osborne at the above address. For information on translations or book distributors outside the U.S.A., please see the International Contact Information page immediately following the index of this book.

Crystal Reports® 9: The Complete Reference

567890 DOC DOC 019876543

ISBN 0-07-222519-X

Publisher
    Brandon A. Nordin

Vice President & Associate Publisher
    Scott Rogers

Acquisitions Editor
    Lisa McClain

Senior Project Editor
    Carolyn Welch

Acquisitions Coordinator
    Athena Honore

Contributing Writers
    Brian Norris
    Lauren O'Malley

Technical Editors
    Julia Hennelly, Bobby Kandola, Erik Lemen,
    Daniel Paulsen, Jonathan Wiens

Copy Editor
    Robert Campbell

Proofreader
    Susie Elkind

Indexer
    Claire Splan

Computer Designers
    Apollo Publishing Services
    Tara A. Davis
    Tabitha M. Cagan

Illustrators
    Michael Mueller
    Lyssa Wald

Series Design
    Peter F. Hancik

This book was composed with Corel VENTURA™ Publisher.

For Denise
Four and counting.
And, you've stayed by my side—loyal to the end—
for every one of them.
I Love You.

Contents at a Glance

Part II   Crystal Reports 9 on the Web

Part III   Developing Custom Window Applications

Contents

Part I

Crystal Reports 9 Introduced

Part II

Crystal Reports 9 on the Web

Part III

Developing Custom Window Applications

Acknowledgments

When working on a fourth edition of a book, there's a tendency to become complacent about properly acknowledging those who have helped make this significant piece of work a reality. It's tempting to just paste in the acknowledgements from the previous titles and change a few names. But, there are so many new people this time around who have worked so hard to turn this into a valuable product.

First and foremost, I must offer the most heartfelt thanks to my other Ablaze Group associates! For Contributing Writers Lauren O'Malley and Brian Norris, please accept my gratitude for such great work in such a short timeframe and for so little recompense. To Julia Hennelly, I offer my sincere gratitude for not only an impeccable job at catching my technical gaffes, but for making my "introduction" to Crystal Reports many years ago so pleasant. And, for Jen Boyle, I offer a special Thank You for teaching me yet new stuff about Crystal Reports, as well as being a very, very good, reliable friend.

It goes without saying that many folks at McGraw-Hill/Osborne deserve special recognition. While I got a little nervous by the end of the Acquisitions Editor Shuffle (I hope it wasn't just me!), each associate helped so much with this project. First, thanks to Ann Sellers for getting the project off the ground. And, while the association was short, I still thank Jim Schachterle for a truly professional relationship. And, for Lisa McClain I offer the most sincere thoughts. Your kind and gentle approach during the inevitable panic-at-project-end phase is appreciated more than you'll know. And, so many thanks are due Athena Honore, Bob Campbell, and Editorial Director Wendy Rinaldi. Finally, Carolyn Welch worked so hard to make this title the best it could be. We worked together a little better this time around, didn't we?

Some folks at Crystal Decisions deserve recognition for pulling out all the stops at the last minute to help out. Thanks to Dave Galloway, Mary-Jane Alexander, Matthew Heron, and the Custom Applications Team. One very giving person at Crystal Decisions also warrants special recognition. Megan Risk was so helpful and responsive during the "Oh my God, what's it doing now?" moments—you saved the day on more than one occasion. I'll try to avoid overuse of CAPITAL LETTERS to you in all future correspondence!

And last, but far from least, is an acknowledgement to Dad. Your love and support during this title, and all the rest, is so precious. I Love You. And, Mom, I wish you were here to see this. I'm sure you'd be proud of my use of words and prose the way you taught me.

George Peck, October 2002
author@CrystalBook.com
www.CrystalBook.com

Introduction

O   When I saw the first "technology preview" of Crystal Reports 9 some time prior to commencing writing, I was immediately intrigued with the dramatic changes in its features. By the time Crystal Reports 9 shipped to the general public when I was well into the writing process, it consisted of what I personally consider the most significant upgrade to the tool since version 5. I've tried to explain and demonstrate as much of this new functionality as possible in this title.

First, although it might be an odd statement, let me emphatically tell you that this is *not* a "Complete Reference" on Crystal Reports, at least not from my point of view. If you have ever worked in the publishing industry or taken a marketing class in college, then you'll probably understand why book series are given their names. What I would consider a "complete reference" would take well past a thousand pages to put together—Crystal Reports is that complex of a product. You'd find detailed explanations of each and every function in both syntaxes of the formula language, detailed explanations and examples of all objects, methods, and collections in every programming interface, and exhaustive descriptions of each and every formatting and menu option. Creating such an offering in a single printed piece simply isn't practical.

So, this book is not designed (and never has been) to replace the guides and manuals that accompany Crystal Reports, nor the on-line help that's included with it. If you purchased this book to replace those materials (perhaps you have a bootlegged copy of the software without these items), then you'll probably be disappointed—you won't have all the necessary information you need. Rather, this book has been designed to *supplement* these items with lots of new information, lots of "real world" examples and samples, and as much material as I could muster from my going-on-eight-years of day-to-day experience with the tool.

And, Crystal Reports 9 makes this task a challenge. There are lots of new features in version 9, on top of the plethora of existing capabilities. If you've used this tool for a few years, you'll no doubt find a few things in version 9 right way, such as the repository and custom functions, that bring an "it's about time" response from you. If you are a web developer looking to integrate reports into your web-based applications, you now have an additional option (the Report Application Server). And, if you've recently adopted Visual Studio .NET as your development environment, you'll find additional capabilities added to it if you purchase Crystal Reports 9 Advanced Edition.

Speaking of editions, you'll now find four. While this will probably introduce an additional "confusion level" to deciphering Crystal Reports options, it does give you additional choices when determining what reporting, web integration, and development capabilities you'll want versus the price you want to pay for the software. Just pay careful attention to the features in Standard, Professional, Developer, and Advanced editions (look at www.crystaldecisions.com if you want a detailed comparison) before making your final choice.

And, you'll need to pay careful attention if you'll be adding Crystal Reports 9 into an existing Crystal Reports, Seagate Info, or Crystal Enterprise environment. Because of its new Unicode (multi-language in the same report) capabilities, the Crystal Reports 9 .RPT file format has been changed. And, unlike versions 8.0 and 8.5, it *is not* backward compatible with previous versions. You won't be able to open a version 9 .RPT file in older Crystal Reports versions, applications based on previous versions of the Report Designer Component or other integration methods, Seagate Info, or Crystal Enterprise 8.0 or 8.5. This will need to be carefully considered before you undertake a massive 9.0 upgrade program. (Crystal Enterprise 9, which is not available as of this writing, will support the Crystal Reports 9 file format).

If you've read previous editions of this title, you'll find a similar layout here to those editions. If this is your first purchase of Crystal Reports: The Complete Reference, you'll find the book broken down into three major sections. Part I covers report design techniques that will apply to virtually everybody who uses the tool. Even if your primary needs are integration with web or Windows applications, you'll benefit from knowing different report functions, sections, and design procedures. You'll find in-depth discussions of report design techniques; from your very first simple report using a Report Wizard, to complex reports containing multiple sections, complex formulas with variables, subreports, charts, maps, and much more. Part I will also discuss creative ways to make the most or industry-standard SQL databases with Crystal Reports, as well as exporting your finished reports to various file formats.

Part II is completely dedicated to integrating Crystal Reports with your web applications. From a basic perspective, you'll learn how to simply export your reports to static HTML. For more robust and customizable web integration, read the updated material on using the Report Designer Component with Microsoft Active Server Pages. And, if you want to explore the latest web integration method or move towards Crystal Enterprise integration, you'll want to spend time with the new Report Application Server. Also, Part II goes into great detail on the latest version of Crystal Enterprise (as of this printing), version 8.5.

Part III is for the Visual Basic or Visual Studio .NET developer. In this section, you'll learn about a few updated features in the Report Designer Component for use with Visual Basic. You'll also find very detailed information and examples on working with the most common report properties at run time within your VB applications. You'll also learn about Crystal Reports integration in Microsoft's latest development environment, Visual Studio .NET, including some examples of additional features provided to Visual Studio .NET with Crystal Reports 9 Advanced edition.

Finally, if you've purchased previous editions of Crystal Reports: The Complete Reference, you've found a companion CD-ROM in the back of the book. While you won't find this addition in the back of this title, you will find *more* sample material that was on previous CDs on this book's companion web site. Visit www.CrystalBook.com for lots of sample reports, sample Visual Basic applications, Active Server Pages integration samples with both the Report Designer Component and Report Application Server, and extra chapters on such "legacy" applications as Crystal Dictionaries, the Crystal SQL Designer, and how to develop User Function Libraries in Visual Basic.

And, for a quick rundown of the options available when installing Crystal Reports 9 or the Report Application Server, visit the appendix. This addition to the book talks about the different choices you have when installing the tools.

What's New in Crystal Reports 9

As mentioned earlier, Crystal Reports 9, by all accounts, is a very major upgrade. As such, you'll find new features and user interface changes in most every part of the tool. Of course, some areas expose more changes than others. And, some things haven't been changed at all. But, overall, you'll find lots of new exciting things to learn in version 9.

Major New Functions

What follows is an abbreviated summary of new Crystal Reports 9 features, broken down into several major categories. In most cases, these new features are expanded on elsewhere in the book. When this is the case, a reference to the proper chapter follows mention of the new feature. However, not every new feature is covered in detail later in the book. In these few cases, the feature is mentioned in this section, and you may find more information about it in Crystal Reports documentation.

The Repository   This may be the biggest new feature in the entire release. You can now share critical parts of your reports, such as text objects, bitmap graphics, custom functions, and database connections in "SQL Commands" with other report designers in your organization by was of a shared repository database. A new chapter in the book, Chapter 7, covers this important new feature.

Custom Functions   Previously, the only way to share common formula capabilities among multiple reports, or multiple report designers, was by a simple shared text editor or word processing document, or the use of User Function Libraries. Crystal Reports 9 introduces Custom Functions; pieces of Crystal Reports formula language code that can be shared among multiple formulas in your reports, as well as shared with other report designers in the repository. Custom Functions are covered in a new chapter, Chapter 6.

SQL Commands   Replacing the Crystal SQL Designer tool included with previous versions are new SQL Commands. SQL Commands allow those familiar with Structured Query Language syntax specific to your database server to create flexible, powerful SQL queries that reports can be based on. These SQL Commands can include such complex SQL structures as unions and sub-selects. Chapter 16 covers SQL Commands.

Report Templates   Limited whole-report formatting was available in previous Crystal Reports versions with Styles. Now, Crystal Reports 9 introduces Report Templates: regular .RPT files that can be used to apply whole-report formatting to other reports. Report Templates are covered in Chapter 9.

New Database Query Engine   The core database connection "engine" that Crystal Reports uses to interact with databases has been enhanced. You have greater flexibility to report from multiple, dissimilar databases (such as including a Stored Procedure, PC-based table, and SQL database table all in the same report). You'll also find a redesigned Database Expert that combines database selection and linking in one tabbed dialog box, which eliminates the previous Visual Linking Expert. This new feature is discussed in Chapter 16.

User Interface Enhancements

The Formula Workshop   While the basic Formula Editor you're familiar with in previous versions remains in version 9, a new Formula Workshop has been added to encompass all report formulas in one place. The Formula Workshop is covered in detail in Chapter 5.

New Chart and Map Features   Changes to Charts include more appealing "pastel colors" as a default, and two new chart types (Gantt and Gauge). Also, you can now conditionally set the color of chart elements. Crystal Reports 9 has eliminated the separate Analyzer tab for both Maps and Charts, now allowing customization and editing of individual map and chart elements right in the main Preview tab. Charts are covered in Chapter 12 and Maps are covered in Chapter 4.

Cross-Tab and OLAP Grid Enhancements   Cross-tab objects now include label capabilities, as well as the ability to tabulate running total fields. You can also apply Top or Bottom *N* logic to cross-tabs, only showing a limited set of data. OLAP grids now include the OLAP Analyzer, which allows very interactive OLAP analysis right inside the Crystal Reports Preview tab. Cross-tabs are discussed in Chapter 11 and OLAP Grids are covered in Chapter 18.

Enhanced Formula Language and Debugging Tools   The Crystal Reports 9 formula language has been enhanced somewhat with additional functions. In addition, you can now use Visual Basic-like "predictive typing" to display a list of available functions right as you type your formula. And, you can now debug run time formula errors (such as divide-by-zero errors) with the new Call Stack feature. Check Chapter 5 for information on these new features.

Side-By-Side Installation   Crystal Reports 9 features an entirely new file structure on your hard disk to allow it to be installed side-by-side with a previous Crystal Reports, Crystal Enterprise, or Seagate Info version. For example, if you need to support both version 8.5 and version 9 reports on the same computer, you can now have both versions installed on the same computer.

New Report Wizards   Crystal Reports Wizards replace the older Report Experts. While there are fewer of them than in past versions, their general approach of turnkey report design remains the same. However, the layout of the wizards has changed.

New Explorers   In addition to the now-familiar Field Explorer, new explorers have been added to version 9. The Report Explorer is an example of a new feature that lets you view and format all report objects via a report hierarchy in an "explorer" fashion. The Report Explorer is covered in Chapter 1. And, the Repository Explorer gives you a similar view of the new Crystal Repository (covered in Chapter 7).

New Web Reporting Options

Report Application Server   Crystal Reports 9 Professional, Developer, and Advanced editions include the new Report Application Server (or RAS) for web-based reporting. This new "intro" version of Crystal Enterprise 9 can also be used to host customized web-based applications, similar to the Report Designer Component. RAS is covered in detail in Chapters 20 and 21.

Crystal Enterprise 8.5   The latest version of Crystal Enterprise (as of this printing) is covered in detail in Chapters 22, 23, and 24.

Report Parts and Guided Navigation   Crystal Reports 9 features new web-based report viewers that allow individual parts of reports, as opposed to the entire report, to be viewed in web pages (such as portal pages). In addition, there are enhanced web-based viewers that allow parts of one report to act as hyperlinks to individual parts of other reports. These new features are covered in Chapter 20.

New Web Report Viewers   The Report Application Server includes a new set of pure HTML viewers with enhanced capabilities. These viewers are discussed in Chapter 21.

Microsoft Office Smart Tag Support   You can now link reports or portions of reports to Microsoft Office XP documents with Smart Tags.

Cascading Style Sheet Support   Crystal Reports 9 includes a Cascading Style Sheet (CSS) class area on the Format Editor. By supplying a CSS class name here, you can employ formatting from CSS when you display your reports in HTML.

Java SDK   In addition to an updated COM SDK included in the Report Application Server, you can now develop RAS applications with Java Server Pages.

New Windows Developer Features

Updated Report Designer Component   The Report Designer Component (or RDC) is the one enduring integration component for Visual Basic. Older integration methods, such as the Active X Control or Report Engine API have been relegated to "legacy" status. The RDC, while not exposing all new Crystal Report 9 features, includes support for the new Query Engine and some other new version 9 features. The RDC is covered in detail in Chapter 25.

Visual Studio .NET Enhancements   Although an enhanced version of Crystal Reports is included out-of-the-box in the initial release of Visual Studio .NET, new version 9 functionality will also be added to VS.NET when you install Crystal Reports 9 Advanced Edition. You also will find a RAS SDK for use with VS.NET. Crystal Reports in Visual Studio .NET is covered in Chapter 26.

The
Complete
Reference

Crystal
Reports

Part I

Crystal Reports 9 Introduced

Chapter 1

Getting the Feel of Crystal Reports 9

It's a forgone conclusion that you can find personal computer-based information systems of one sort or another when you walk through most every business—large or small—on any given day. Even organizations that have traditionally relied on mainframes and minicomputers for the lion's share of their computer processing are migrating many of these systems to smaller computers, often utilizing Web-based applications instead.

Along with these new hardware directions, the business world is also quickly adopting buzzwords to describe the new systems. Terms such as *customer relationship management (CRM)*, *enterprise resource planning (ERP)*, and *business intelligence (BI)* are being liberally tossed around more frequently. ERP systems from such vendors as PeopleSoft, Oracle, Baan, SAP, and others are organizing and managing human resources, accounting, inventory, and billing functions for businesses of all sizes. Other, more specialized PC-based applications used in manufacturing, medicine, service businesses, and countless other areas are also in wide use. Continuing a popular trend, many of these systems can now be accessed with a simple Web browser.

Most of these systems all have one core thing in common: an industry-standard database program to manage the data. But after thousands, or often millions, of pieces of data have been put into these databases, how can you extract the right data in a meaningful form? One rule that hasn't changed as computer systems have matured is the necessity to "get out" what you "put in." A tool must exist to extract and summarize all of this data in a meaningful fashion—in a way that allows key decision makers to know what's really happening with their business and how to move forward in the best possible direction.

While these varied information systems may have certain analysis and reporting capabilities "out of the box," many users of database-based systems need more capabilities to create their own specialized views of their centralized data. There is a plethora of query, graphic, spreadsheet, and analysis tools. Still, probably the most often used method of garnering information from corporate information systems is the tried-and-true report. Enter the *database report writer.*

Introducing Crystal Reports 9

With this major upgrade, Crystal Reports remains the market leader and de facto standard for business and corporate report writing. In 1984, a Canadian shipping company wanted to produce custom reports from its accounting system. When the vendor said "We can't help you," the company created Quick Reports, the precursor to Crystal Reports. Crystal Reports' first "bundle" was with that vendor's next version of its accounting software.

Crystal Reports is now bundled with well over 150 leading software packages, including many of the aforementioned ERP and accounting packages from vendors including ACCPAC International, Great Plains Software, and PeopleSoft. Versions of Crystal Reports are also included with various Microsoft packages, including Visual Studio 6, and the latest development environment, Visual Studio .NET.

Crystal Reports is aimed at three general types of users:

■ Casual business users, such as data analysts, executive assistants, and marketing directors, who will design reports around their corporate data to make intelligent business decisions.

■ Information technology professionals, who will use Crystal Reports to integrate sophisticated reporting right inside their own Microsoft Windows programs.

■ Webmasters, who will use Crystal Reports to provide print-quality reports and graphics over their intranets or the Internet.

Figure 1-1 shows the Crystal Reports 9 screen when the program is first started. Note the standard Windows user interface, including different toolbars, pull-down menus, and the Welcome dialog box.

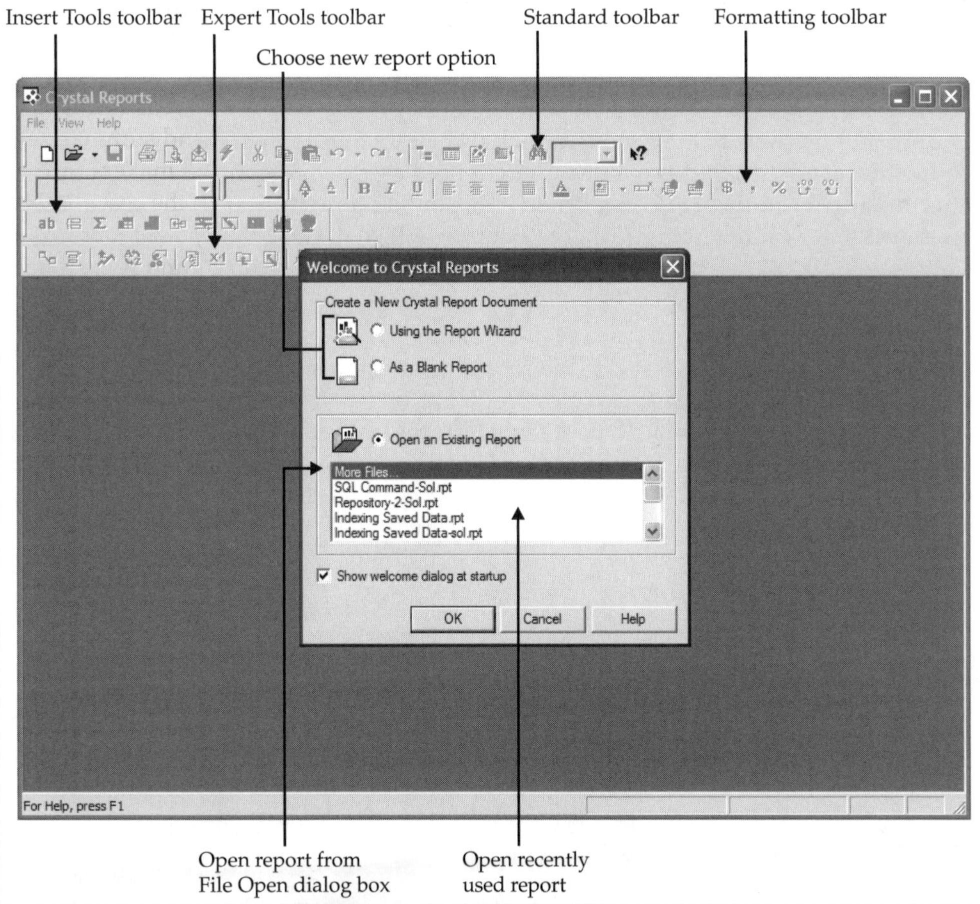

Figure 1-1.   *Crystal Reports opening screen*

When you first start the program, the only two main functions that you'll usually want to perform are creating a new report and opening an existing report. Like most functions in Crystal Reports, these functions can be accomplished in several ways. If the Welcome dialog box appears, you can choose either function from it by using its various radio buttons. If you've closed the Welcome dialog box, you may redisplay it from the Help menu and choose options from there. You may also open an existing report or create a new report with pull-down menu options, keyboard shortcuts, or toolbar buttons, as described later in the chapter.

Crystal Reports Screen Elements

The Crystal Reports screen consists of four main parts you'll want to familiarize yourself with: the pull-down menus, the toolbars, the report design/preview area, and the status bar.

Pull-Down Menus

The pull-down menus are standard Windows-type menus that you can pull down with your mouse. In some cases, you can also use shortcut key combinations (such as CTRL-N to start a new report) to choose pull-down menu options. You'll notice these shortcut key combinations next to their menu options when you pull down the menus. You can also use the standard Windows convention of holding down the ALT key and typing the underlined letter in the menu, and then choosing a menu option by typing another underlined letter from within the menu. For example, you can create a new report (File menu, New option) by typing ALT-F-N.

Toolbars

When you first start Crystal Reports, all four available toolbars are displayed across the top of the screen by default. To selectively turn on or off individual toolbars, choose View | Toolbars from the pull-down menus. The toolbars contain buttons for almost all of Crystal Reports' available functions (some options still require the use of pull-down menu options, but not many). Many of the icons on the toolbars are self-explanatory. In addition, tool tips are available for each toolbar button—just point to a toolbar button with your mouse and wait a few seconds. A small yellow box containing a short description of the toolbar button's function will appear.

Tip
You may "undock" the toolbars from their default positions and place them anywhere you want. Just click the gray line at the left of the toolbar and drag it to the desired location. If you move it left or right within its current location, it will simply move to a different position. If you move it away from the top of the screen, it will become its own "window." If you place it near the edge of the Crystal Reports screen (or back near its original position), it will snap into place along the edge of the screen.

The Standard Toolbar   This toolbar is the first toolbar just below the pull-down menus. It contains the most often used Crystal Reports functions, such as opening and saving report files, printing and exporting the report, undoing and redoing actions, and so on.

The Formatting Toolbar   This toolbar is the toolbar just below the Standard toolbar. You should be familiar with this toolbar if you've used most any office suite type of tool, such as word processors or spreadsheets. This toolbar enables you to change the format (font, size, and alignment) of one or more objects that you have selected on your report.

The Insert Tools Toolbar   The third toolbar is new to Crystal Reports 9 and consolidates functions that were contained on other toolbars in previous versions. This toolbar contains options to insert new objects onto your reports, such as text objects, charts, maps, and cross-tab objects.

The Expert Tools Toolbar   This fourth toolbar is also new to Crystal Reports 9. This toolbar's buttons will display various Crystal Reports "experts" that guide you through various report functions with a tabbed dialog box. Such experts include the Database Expert, Group Expert, and Select Expert.

Report Design/Preview Area

The large gray area in the middle of the Crystal Reports screen is the report design/ preview area. Here, you actually manipulate fields and objects that make up your report. When you want to have a look at the way the report will eventually appear when printed on paper or displayed on a Web page, you can preview the actual report in this area, as well.

You'll soon see that you can choose different views of a report by clicking a number of tabs that will appear at the top of the report design/preview area. When you initially create a report, you see a Design tab, which shows a design view, or "layout," of your report, simply indicating the location of objects in different report sections. When you preview the report, a Preview tab appears, which shows actual data from the database as it will appear in the final report. In addition, as you progress with your report work, you'll see additional tabs for subreports and drill-down views. Simply click the tab you wish to see.

Status Bar

The status bar appears at the very bottom of the Crystal Reports screen. Although you can hide the status bar by unchecking the Status Bar option on the View menu, you'll probably want to leave it displayed, because it contains very helpful information for you as you design and preview reports. In particular, the status bar will show more detailed descriptions of menu options and toolbar buttons. While the short tool tip that appears when you point to a button is handy, it may not offer a good enough description of what the toolbar button does. Just look in the status bar for more information.

Also, the status bar contains more helpful information on its right side, such as how many database records are being used in your report, what percentage of the report processing is finished, and at what location (X-Y coordinates) on the report page a currently selected object is located.

Starting Out: Opening or Creating a Report

To open an existing report, you may use either one of the options from the Welcome dialog box, choosing a recently used report from the list, or choosing the More Files... option. If you've closed the Welcome dialog box, select File | Open, use the shortcut key combination CTRL-O, or click the Open button in the Standard toolbar. A standard file-open dialog box will appear, showing any files with an .RPT extension in the drive and folder. Navigate to any alternate drives or folders to find the existing Crystal Report .RPT file that you wish to open.

To create a new report, choose either the Using the Report Wizard or the As a Blank Report radio button on the Welcome dialog box. Or, if you've closed it, start a new report by choosing File | New, pressing the keyboard shortcut CTRL-N, or clicking the New button in the Standard toolbar.

If you use the As a Blank Report option from the Welcome dialog box, you skip the report wizard and proceed directly to custom report design (see "Using the Blank Report Option" later in the chapter). Any other new report step (the Using the Report Wizard radio button on the Welcome dialog box, or any of the new report options available after closing the Welcome dialog box) will display the *Report Gallery*.

Crystal Reports Gallery

Create a New Crystal Report Document

- ⦿ Using the Report Wizard
- ○ As a Blank Report

Choose a Wizard

- Standard
- Cross-Tab
- Mail Label
- OLAP

Guides the creation of a typical report.

OK   Cancel   Help

There are two general options you can choose from the Report Gallery:

- Create a report using one of the report wizards
- Use the As a Blank Report option for precise control when designing a new report

Using the Report Wizards

The four standard *report wizards* allow you to create "quick and dirty" reports with minimal effort. They're helpful when you want to create a simple report or put together the beginning elements of a more complex report. Choose the wizard that most closely matches the type of report that you want to create. When you make the choice, you'll see a thumbnail view of that type of report appear in the Report Gallery.

To create a simple, general-purpose report (for example, an employee phone list or your last year's sales totals), click Standard to use the Standard Report Wizard (see Figure 1-2). The Standard Report Wizard presents a type of dialog box that's probably familiar to you if you've used other office suites or productivity products. You build your report by choosing options from the different tabbed pages in the dialog box. You advance to the next tab by clicking the tab itself or by clicking the Next button at the bottom of the dialog box.

To create a report with the Standard Report Wizard, follow these steps:

1. First, choose the database tables you want to use for the report using one of the categories from the Available Data Sources list. This list allows you to choose any database Crystal Reports supports, including data connections that you are already connected to from previous reports (from the Current Connections category), that you've used recently (from the History category), and so on. If you need to connect to a database that doesn't reside in any of the initial categories, click the plus sign next to the Create a New Connection category. You'll then see a list of database types that Crystal Reports can connect to, including PC-style "local" databases, client/server databases (such as Oracle or Informix), Crystal SQL Queries (.QRY files), Crystal Dictionaries (.DC5 files), and many other categories (see Chapter 21 for more information on special database types).

2. As you add tables, you'll see them appear in the Selected Tables list. Once you're finished adding tables, click the Next button. You'll be taken to the Link portion of the wizard (provided that you chose more than one table). This area shows you the tables you've chosen in a visual format, allowing you to *link* the tables together, based on common fields. Crystal Reports will *smart-link* the tables automatically, showing you lines indicating the fields and tables that are linked. If these links are correct (in the real world they rarely are), you may leave them as is.

3. If you need to delete a link that Crystal Reports added, click the line that connects the tables, and press the DELETE key to remove the existing link. If you want to delete all existing links, you may click the Clear Links button. You may then create your own link by dragging from the "from" field and table and dropping on the "to" field and table. A line will appear, indicating your new link. Once you've linked the tables correctly, click the Next button at the bottom of the Wizard.

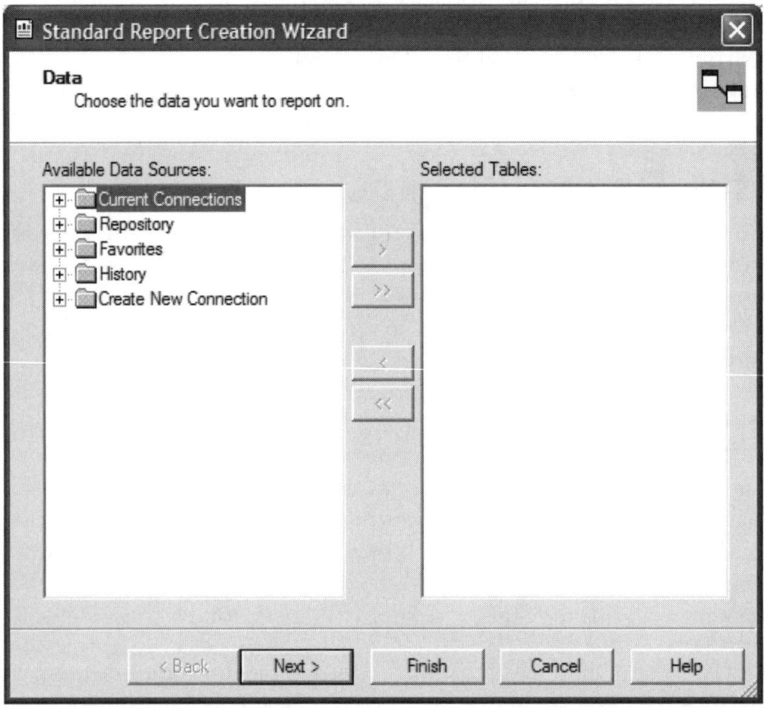

Figure 1-2. *The Standard Report Wizard*

> **Tip** *Linking tables has quite a few fine points. Look for more information in Chapter 16.*

4. Choose the database fields you actually want to appear on your report. You may choose single fields simply by clicking the field name under the Available Fields list. If you want to choose multiple fields, hold down the CTRL key and click. You'll notice that fields are "multiselected" when you click them. To deselect an already selected field, hold down CTRL and click the field name again. To select a range of fields, click the first field in the range. Then, hold down the SHIFT key and select the last field in the range. Both fields, plus all fields in between, will be selected. Then, click the right-arrow button to move your selected fields to the Fields to Display box. If you, per chance, would like to add all fields from the tables to the report, click the double-right arrow.

5. To search for a particular field (in case the tables you chose contain many fields), click the Find Field button under the Available Fields list. You can enter a full or partial field name to search for. If that field is in any tables in the Available Fields list, the field will be highlighted. If you select a field in the field list and then click the Browse Data button, you'll see a sample of actual data from that database field. This may be helpful in determining whether or not this is the correct field to add to your report.

6. If you'd like to change the order in which the fields appear on the report, you can make those changes in the Fields to Display box by choosing the field you want to move and clicking the up or down arrows above the list. When you're finished, click Next to move on.

Tip *This is all the information the Standard Report Wizard needs to display the report. From this point forward, if you don't want to specify any other report features, such as grouping, totaling, charting, or record selection, you may click the Finish button to display the report.*

7. If you wish to have your report contain report groups, choose one or more fields from the Available Fields list on the Group portion of the wizard and click the right-arrow button. *Grouping* puts all report records together on the report whose chosen grouping fields are the same. Grouping is similar to just sorting records, but groups can have subtotals, counts, averages, or other summaries at the end. Grouping is covered in more detail in Chapter 3.

8. If you choose to group the report, the Next button will then display the Summaries section where you'll add an entry in the Summarized Fields list for every group you created previously. This is where you choose subtotals, averages, counts, or other summaries that you want to appear at the end of the group. First, click on the group that you wish to create a summary for in the Summarized Fields list. Then, click the field in the Available Fields list that you wish to summarize for that group and click the right-arrow button. The wizard will choose a default summary type (such as Sum or Maximum) and display it below the Summarized Fields list. If you wish to change the type of summary for the field you just added, choose the different summary function from this drop-down list. Note that you'll see more limited summary types for nonnumeric or noncurrency fields.

9. Clicking Next will display the Group Sorting area of the Wizard, assuming that you have summary fields on your report. Usually, any groups on your report are presented in alphabetical order (for example, Arizona precedes California, followed by Oregon, Texas, and Wyoming). However, if you want to see the "top or bottom five states in order of sales," select the appropriate radio button to show groups in order of the subtotal or summary amount that you choose in the drop-down list, rather than by the name of the group. Click the Next button.

10. The Chart area lets you show your report data graphically in a bar, line, or pie chart. If you choose one of these options, specify the title for the chart, and the fields that the chart should be based on and should use for the size of the bar, wedge, or line. Do this with the Chart Title, On Change Of, and Show options. Chapter 12 explains charting options in more detail.

11. When you click Next, the Record Selection area of the wizard will appear. Use this to limit your report to a limited set of meaningful database records. You likely won't ever want to include every record in the database tables in your report. Many tables contain large numbers of records, and your reports will be much more meaningful if they contain only the relevant set of records. Choose one or more fields to select, and move them to the Filter Fields list by clicking the right-arrow button. When you click a field in the Filter Fields list, an additional drop-down list appears below. You can choose the comparison operator you need in the pull-down list (such as equal to, less than, one of, between, and so on). Then, choose the value you want to compare against in the additional drop-down lists that appear. You may type a comparison value directly in the drop-down list box, or you can click the down arrow in the box to choose from a sample of data that will be read from the database field.

Tip *More detailed information on selecting records is contained in Chapter 8.*

12. Click Next to show the final area of the wizard, the Template area. This area lets you determine the general appearance of your report. When you choose one of the available templates, a thumbnail view of the template appears to the right. If you wish to use an existing Crystal Report .RPT file as a template, click the Browse button to locate that .RPT file. Once chosen, the thumbnail view of that report will also appear to the right.

You may now click the Back button if you wish to move backward through the wizard to make any changes. Once you're satisfied with all your choices, click Finish to show the entire report in the Preview tab.

Once you have created the report using the Standard Report Wizard, you can print it on a printer, export it to another file format, save it to the Crystal Reports .RPT file format, or use any other function that Crystal Reports provides. You can click the Design tab to make any manual adjustments to the report that you wish.

Save the   Send the report
report   to a printer

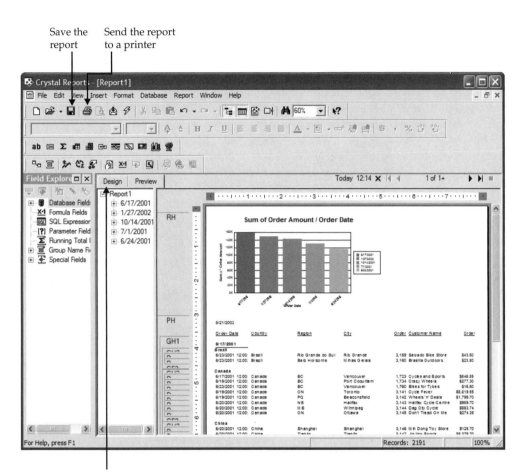

Click the Design tab to make
manual adjustments to the report

Caution   *Unlike previous Crystal Reports versions, Crystal Reports 9 will not allow you to rerun the Report Wizard to make changes to the report you've already created—you must use the Design tab and make manual adjustments. While the Report Wizard does make "quick and dirty" reporting easier than manually creating reports, you'll probably want to familiarize yourself with general report formatting options in the Design tab so that you can modify reports you create with the wizard.*

Using the Blank Report Option

While the report wizards simplify the report design process by presenting a step-by-step approach, they limit your flexibility to create a report exactly as you'd like it to look. You are required to accept the fonts, colors, and layout that the wizard chooses. Group total and summary fields are not labeled, and group fields are repeated over and over again in every report line within the group.

Although it's initially more labor-intensive, using the Blank Report option to create a report gives you absolute control over what you put on your report, where you put it, and how it looks. Even if you use the report wizards, it's important to understand the concepts involved in the Blank Report option, because you'll want to use those concepts to refine most reports that the report wizards create. To use the Blank Report option, click the As a Blank Report radio button on the Report Gallery dialog box when first creating a new report. Then click OK. The Database Expert will appear.

The Database Expert

The *Database Expert,* shown in Figure 1-3, is new to Crystal Reports 9, replacing the previous Data Explorer. This is where you choose the database tables you wish to include in your report. Here, you can select from any database type that Crystal Reports supports, including PC-type "local" databases, such as Microsoft Access, dBASE, Paradox, Btrieve, and others. You can also choose from virtually all popular client/server or SQL databases, such as Microsoft SQL Server, Oracle, Informix, and Sybase. Crystal Reports even supports proprietary data types, such as Web server activity logs, the Windows NT/2000 event log, Microsoft Exchange systems, and XML-formatted data. These data types are all chosen here.

The Database Expert categorizes types of databases, shown as small folder icons with plus signs next to them. Depending on the type of database you want to report on, click the plus sign next to one of the following database categories:

■ **Current Connections** Displays a list of any databases you may already have connected to when working with previous reports.

■ **Repository** Displays a list of any databases that you have added to the new Crystal Reports 9 Repository (the Repository is covered in more detail in Chapter 7).

■ **Favorites** Contains data sources that you've previously added to your Favorites folder—if you use a data source on a regular basis, you may want to add it to the Favorites category to make it easy to find.

■ **History** Shows data sources that you've recently connected to.

■ **Create New Connection** Displays another set of subcategories that show types of databases that Crystal Reports will connect to. The folders that appear here are based on what database connection options you chose when you installed Crystal Reports, as well as on database connection software you may have installed on your computer, such as an existing program that contains an Oracle or Microsoft SQL Server client database driver.

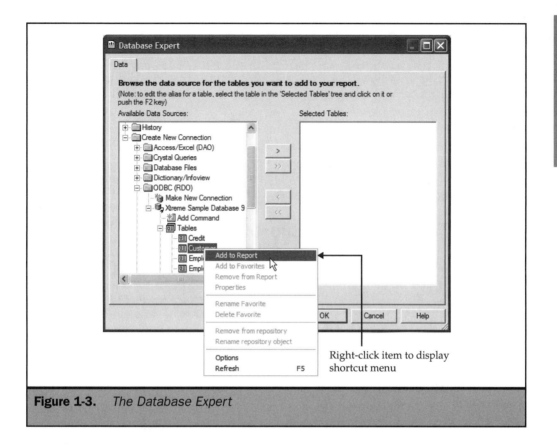

Figure 1-3.   *The Database Expert*

After you click the plus sign next to the category you wish to use, you may see a list of available databases under that category. If you're already logged on to a database in that category, you'll see the database name and all the available tables underneath the database name. Choose the desired database or subcategory. Depending on the category or database you choose, additional dialog boxes will appear, asking you to choose a particular database filename, log in to the database, or choose a database server. Eventually, you'll be able to choose one or more *database tables* that you wish to include in your report.

To add a table to the report, select the table and click the right-arrow button. You can also just double-click the table name. When the table has been added to the report, the table name will appear in the rightmost Selected Tables list. If you add a table by mistake, just select it and click the left-arrow button to remove it—it will disappear from the Selected Tables list. If you want to select and add multiple tables at a time, you may multiselect additional tables by holding down the CTRL key while clicking table names. Or, you may SHIFT-click on two tables to select those two tables, as well as all tables in between. When you've chosen the tables you want to add to the report, click the right-arrow button to add them all at once. And, finally, you may simply add all tables in the Available Data Source list to the Selected Tables list by clicking the double-right-arrow key. Once you've selected all the tables you want to include in your report, close the Database Expert with the Close button.

Tip *There may be several different ways of connecting to the same database. If, for example, you wish to report on a corporate Oracle database, you may connect via ODBC, via OLE DB, or by using a Crystal Reports "native" driver in the More Data Sources category within Create New Connection. If you're unsure of how to connect to your database, check with your database administrator.*

If you choose more than one table for your report, a Links tab will appear in the Database Explorer. You must click this tab to link the tables you've added to your report together. If you don't link tables, you'll be presented with the Links tab when you click OK on the Database Explorer dialog box. Use the Links tab to join or link your tables together. Table linking is discussed in detail in Chapter 16.

The Design Tab and Field Explorer

Once you've chosen and linked tables, Crystal Reports will display the Design tab. This is the "template" view that you use to begin designing the look and feel for your report. The first step to beginning report design is choosing fields for the report from the *Field Explorer*, shown in Figure 1-4. If you don't already see the Field Explorer, you can display it by clicking the Field Explorer button in the Standard Toolbar, or by choosing View | Field Explorer from the pull-down menus. Begin designing your report simply by dragging fields from the Field Explorer and dropping them on the report where you want them to appear.

The Field Explorer contains categories of fields that are available to place on your report. You'll see a plus sign next to the Database Fields category, indicating that more choices are available in that category. Clicking the plus sign next to it will expand the category, showing all the tables you added from the Database Expert. Plus signs next to the table names, as well as next to the Special Fields category, indicate that fields are available below those levels—click the plus sign to see available fields. The other categories of the Field Explorer will not have any plus signs next to them, unless you've opened an existing report that already contains fields of these types. Once you begin creating new formulas, parameter fields, and so on, you'll see plus signs next to these categories as well. Click the plus signs to see available fields in these other categories.

The simplest way to add a field to the report is to drag and drop the field from the Field Explorer to the report's Design tab. When you drag, you'll see an outline of the field object appear on the report as you drag. When you have positioned the field where you want it to appear, simply release the mouse button to drop the field on the report. As an alternative, you may right-click a field and choose Insert to Report from the pop-up menu, select the desired field, and click the Insert to Report button (the first toolbar button) from the Field Explorer toolbar, or just press ENTER. The field will be attached to the mouse cursor, which you can then position to drop the field.

Click to expand field category or
display available fields in table

Checkmark indicates field has been placed on
report or is used in some way with a report feature

Toolbar buttons perform common operations

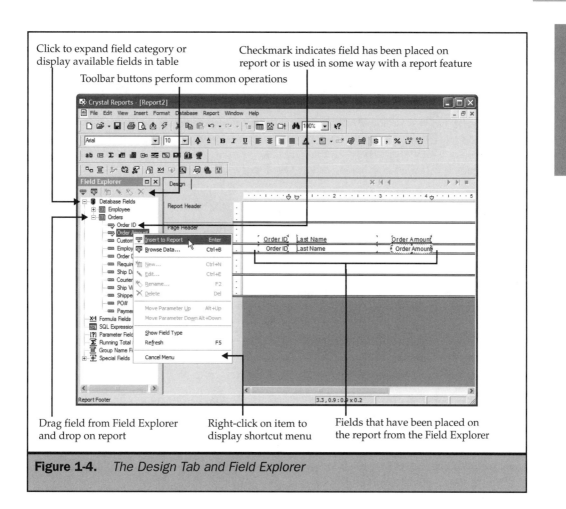

Drag field from Field Explorer
and drop on report

Right-click on item to
display shortcut menu

Fields that have been placed on
the report from the Field Explorer

Figure 1-4.   *The Design Tab and Field Explorer*

You're not limited to dragging and dropping one field at a time to the report. If
you see several fields you'd like to drag and drop at once, use CTRL-click to select or
deselect multiple fields. If you wish to select a range of fields, click the first field in
the range and then hold down the SHIFT key and click the last field in the range. Both
fields, as well as all of those in between, will be selected. After you CTRL- or SHIFT-click
the desired fields, drag and drop them as a group. After you add a field to the report,
you see a small green checkmark next to the field in the Field Explorer. This indicates
that the field is in use somewhere on the report.

Tip

You do not have to leave the Field Explorer docked to the left side of the Crystal Reports window. If you'd like to expand the size of the Design tab so you have more room to work without scrolling, "undock" the Field Explorer by pointing to its title bar area at the top. Then, drag the Field Explorer away from the left of the window until you see the outline of a separate free-floating window.The Design tab will expand to the very left of the Crystal Reports window, and the Field Explorer will now display in its own free-floating window. To redock the Field Explorer, drag it back toward the edge of the Crystal Reports window until the outline of a docked window again appears. You can redock the Field Explorer to the left, bottom, or right of the Design tab.

Report Sections

When you first create a new report, Crystal Reports shows five default sections in the Design tab. Table 1-1 outlines where and how many times each section appears in a report, and the types of objects you may want to place in them.

If you drag a database field into the details section, Crystal Reports places a field title in the page header automatically and aligns it with the database field. If you drag a database field into any other section, no field title will be inserted, even if you drag the field into the details section later—automatic field titles are only created if you drag a field directly into the details section.

Previewing the Report

When you see objects depicted in the Design tab, Crystal Reports is only displaying "placeholders." You'll see the names of fields and objects surrounded by outline

Section	Where It Appears	What to Place in the Section
Report header	Once only, at the beginning of the report	Title page, company logo, introductory information that you want to appear once only at the beginning of the report, charts, or cross-tabs that apply to the whole report
Page header	At the top of every page	Field titles, print date/time, report title
Details	Every time a new record is read from the database	Database fields and formulas that you want to appear for every record
Report footer	Once only, at the end of the report	Grand totals, closing disclaimers, charts, or cross-tabs that apply to the whole report
Page footer	At the bottom of every page	Page numbers, report name, explanations for figures in the report

Table 1-1. *Default Report Sections*

symbols, indicating how wide and tall they are. You won't ever see actual data in the Design tab. To see the report containing real data as it might appear when printed on a printer or exported to a Web page, you need to preview the report.

There are several ways of previewing a report. Choose File | Print Preview or click the Print Preview button on the Standard toolbar to preview the entire report. To preview a limited number of records, choose File | Print | Preview Sample and specify the number of records you wish to see.

When you preview a report, the Preview tab appears next to the Design tab, as shown in Figure 1-5. You can scroll up and down through the report, use the Zoom control to change the Zoom level of the report, and use the page navigation buttons to move through various pages of the report. You can easily move back and forth between the Design and Preview tabs by clicking them.

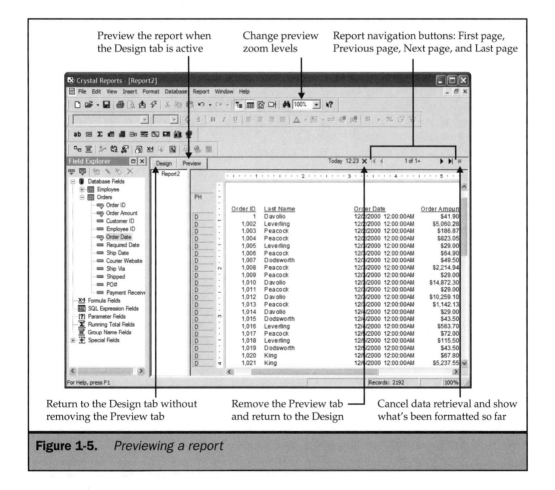

Figure 1-5.   *Previewing a report*

Moving and Sizing Objects

Once you've placed objects on your report, you will probably want to move them around the report as your design progresses. Crystal Reports estimates how much horizontal space is required to display string database fields. This may result in string fields on the report that may appear too narrow or too wide. Also, if you change the font size of an object, you'll usually have to adjust the object size accordingly.

The first step in moving or sizing an object is to select the object. Simply click it. A shaded outline and four blocks appear around the object, indicating that it is selected. Now you can move or size it.

Pointing inside the selected object causes your mouse pointer to turn into a four-way pointer. You can then click and drag the object to a new location with the mouse. If you point at one of the little blue blocks—the *sizing handles* at the top, bottom, left, and right of the object—your mouse pointer turns into a two-way size pointer. Clicking and dragging these handles stretches or shrinks the object. Sizing objects requires very precise accuracy with your mouse! Laptop users with trackpads will probably opt for an external mouse after trying this a few times.

Point inside a selected
object to move it

Point at the desired sizing
handle to resize an object

You're not limited to moving or sizing one object at a time. You can select multiple objects before moving or sizing them. CTRL-click or SHIFT-click to select more than one field or field title. You can also surround multiple objects with an elastic box. Before you start to draw the elastic box, make sure you deselect any already selected objects by clicking an area of the report where there are no objects.

> **Tip** *When the Design tab is displayed, you don't have to use the mouse to move or resize objects. For very fine control of object placement and sizing, use your keyboard's cursor keys. Using the cursor keys by themselves will move selected objects in the direction of the key. If you hold down SHIFT and use the cursor keys, objects will be widened, narrowed, made taller, or made shorter in the direction of the keys.*

Using Guidelines to Move Objects

When you insert a database field into the details section, Crystal Reports inserts two other things automatically. The first, the field heading, appears directly above the field in the page header. What might not be so obvious is the *vertical guideline*. You'll notice a little "upside-down tent" (officially known as a *guideline handle*) in the ruler above the report. The guideline is actually a vertical line extending from the guideline handle all the way down the report. Crystal Reports automatically placed this in the ruler, and it attached the field in the details section and the field heading in the page header to the guideline.

Note   *By default, only the guideline handles are visible when you first install Crystal Reports. If you'd like to see the dashed guidelines themselves in the Design tab, choose View | Guidelines | Design from the pull-down menus. To see guidelines in the Preview tab, choose View | Guidelines | Preview from the pull-down menus. Note that even if you make the latter choice, you'll only see the dashed guidelines in the Preview tab if you click any object to select it in the preview window.*

You may move objects as a group by dragging the guideline handle left or right inside the ruler. All objects attached to that guideline will move at the same time. If you've placed a database field in the details section and an associated field heading in the page header, and you have inserted several group subtotals in groups and grand totals in the report footer, they will typically all be attached to the same guideline. Just move the guideline left or right to move all the objects together.

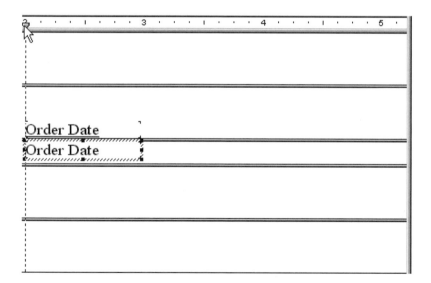

With a little experience, you'll probably quickly develop a love-hate relationship with guidelines. If you have lots of smaller objects positioned closely together on a report, you'll probably give up on the guidelines and just move them by CTRL-clicking or using an elastic box. If you have fewer objects spaced a little farther apart on your report, or lots of aligned objects in several report sections, you'll probably like using the guidelines to rearrange objects. Table 1-2 shows some of the guideline issues that may crop up in your report-design process, along with ways of solving the problems.

Note *If you created the report with a report wizard, you'll see that Crystal Reports inserted horizontal guidelines on the left side of the Design tab. You can add these yourself if you use the Blank Report option. Just click in the side ruler to add a horizontal guideline. Then attach objects to them on the top, bottom, or middle. Move the guideline to move whole lines of objects up or down at the same time.*

What Happened	How Is It Fixed?
You mistakenly dragged a guideline off the ruler when you just wanted to move it left or right. The objects attached to it haven't moved, and the guideline is now gone.	Click the Undo button on the Standard toolbar, or choose Edit	Undo. This will bring the guideline back. If you notice the missing guideline after you've completed other tasks, and you don't want to Undo, just add a guideline back into the ruler by clicking in the ruler; reattach the objects by dragging them to the new guideline.
You selected and moved an individual object or objects with your mouse, but the guideline didn't move with them. Now, when you move the guideline in the ruler, the objects don't move.	You detach an object from a guideline when you move the object in the Design tab. You cannot reattach guidelines to objects by moving the guideline in the ruler. You have to reattach *objects to guidelines* by moving the objects until they snap to the guidelines. You can tell when an object has been reattached to a guideline by looking at the very small red marks on the edge of the object where it's attached to the guideline.
You've resized or moved objects and they now appear to be attached to two guidelines: one on the left and one on the right. When you move either guideline, the objects stretch rather than move.	Resize the objects away from the guideline you don't want them attached to. By resizing, you detach them from one guideline while leaving them attached to the other.
You notice that when you delete objects from the report, the guidelines stay and clutter up the ruler. When you move other objects around on the report, they're always snapping to the stray guidelines.	Remove any unwanted guidelines simply by dragging them off the ruler.

Table 1-2.   *Guideline Issues*

Formatting Objects

When you place objects on your report, Crystal Reports applies default font faces, sizes, colors, and formatting to the objects. You'll usually want to change some of this formatting to suit your particular report style or standards. There are several ways of formatting objects. As you use Crystal Reports, you may find that one way suits you better than another. Also, all formatting options aren't available with every method, so you may need to use a certain one to perform a specific kind of formatting.

Using the Formatting toolbar is the quickest way to apply standard formatting. The Formatting toolbar is similar to other toolbars you may have used in word processors or spreadsheet programs. To format using the Formatting toolbar, first select the object or objects you want to format, and then change their formatting by clicking Formatting toolbar buttons or choosing items in drop-down lists.

Some formatting options, such as formatting a date field to print in a long date format or designating that only one dollar sign should print at the top of each page, aren't available on the Formatting toolbar. These formatting options, along with all the options available on the Formatting toolbar, can be chosen in the Format Editor, as shown in Figure 1-6. To use the Format Editor, first choose the object or objects that you wish to format, and then do one of the following:

- Click the Format button on the Expert Tools toolbar.
- Choose Format Field from the Format menu.
- Right-click the object and choose Format Field from the pop-up menu.

All of these options display the Format Editor. Choose the desired tab on the Format Editor, and make formatting selections by choosing one of the built-in styles, by using a custom style, or by choosing other specific formatting options on the desired tab. Click OK on the Format Editor to apply all the formatting you chose and close the Format Editor.

There are two general ways you can choose formats in the Format Editor—with a default style, or by customizing the style. In particular, you'll notice a selection of predefined formats for most nonstring data types in the Style list. You can just choose one of these default formats from the list. If, however, the exact format you want isn't in the Style list, click the Customize button at the bottom of the Style list. A Custom Style dialog box will appear where you can make more detailed choices about how to

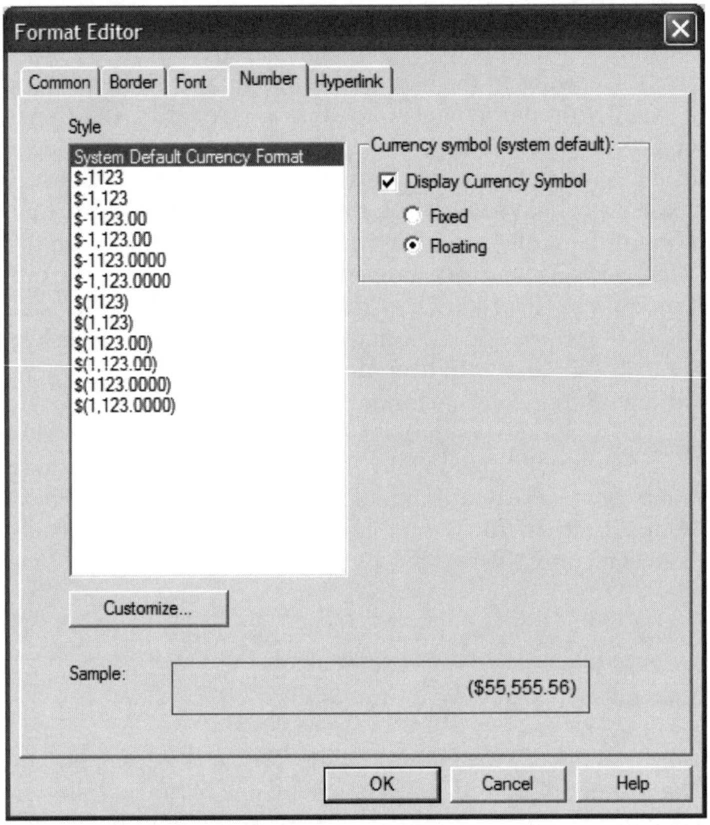

Figure 1-6. *The Format Editor*

format the field. You'll need to use the Customize button to conditionally format some aspects of the field as well (conditional formatting is discussed in Chapter 9).

Custom Style   [X]

| Currency Symbol | Number |

☐ Use Accounting Format

☐ Suppress if Zero   [X·2]   Decimal Separator: [ ] [X·2]

Decimals: [1.00 ▼] [X·2]   ☑ Thousands Separator: [X·2]

Rounding: [0.01 ▼] [X·2]   Symbol: [.] [X·2]

Negatives: [(123) ▼] [X·2]   ☑ Leading Zero   [X·2]

☐ Reverse Sign for Display   [X·2]   Show Zero Values as:

☑ Allow Field Clipping   [X·2]   [<Default Format> ▼]

Sample: [($55,555.56)]

[OK]   [Cancel]   [Help]

Tip   *You can add new objects, or move, size, and format existing objects, just as easily in the Preview tab as in the Design tab. Be careful, though, that you move or size objects accurately in the Preview tab. You may inadvertently move an object from the details section to the page header, or make some similar undesirable move, without realizing it. Formatting objects in the Preview tab is great, but it may be better to size or move them in the Design tab.*

Customizing Crystal Reports Behavior

When you first install Crystal Reports, it behaves in a certain way that should serve most users well. However, you will probably want to customize the behavior of some Crystal Report options. Other software typically has a Preferences or Options menu item to accomplish this. Crystal Reports has two options that work together to control how the program behaves: Options and Report Options, both chosen from the File menu.

Most often, you will use the Options dialog box, shown in Figure 1-7, to change the default behavior of Crystal Reports. For example, to change the default font face and size from Times Roman 10 point to something else, you would click the Fonts tab in the Options dialog box, click the button for the type of object you want to change, and choose a different font or size. To change the default format of date fields from mm/dd/yy to mm/dd/yyyy, you would click the Fields tab in the Options dialog box and then click the Date button.

Caution *Many options you choose here don't change items already placed on the current report, or any existing reports—they will only affect new items added to the report. For example, if you change the default font to 8-point Arial, only new objects that you add to the report from that point forward will take on that new formatting.*

There are a number of options that benefit the new user and make report creation a bit easier. You may want to choose File | Options and set each of the following options to your own personal preference.

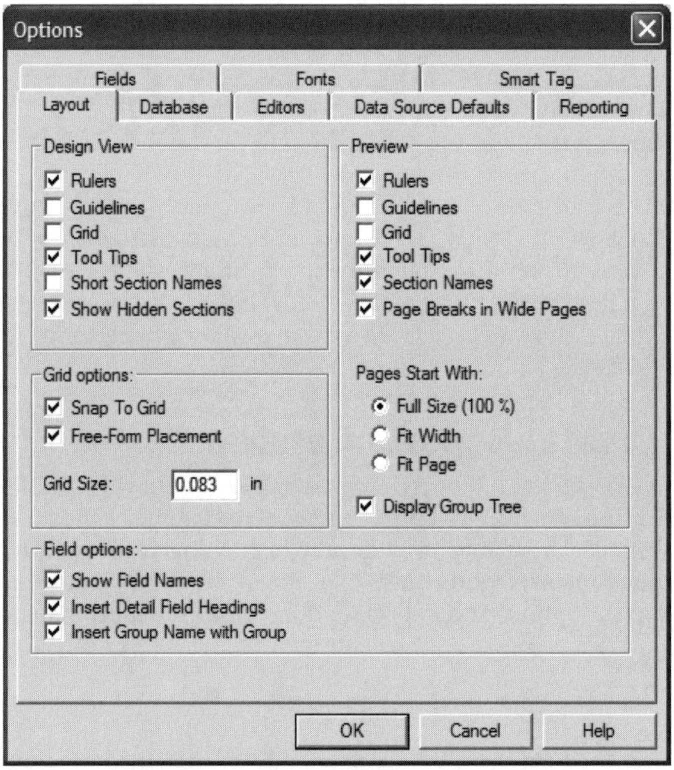

Figure 1-7. *Options dialog box*

The Options dialog box is divided into a series of tabs, each categorizing the various options that are available.

Layout Tab

- **Design View – Guidelines**   You may wish to turn this option on to display dashed guidelines in the Design tab. The majority of report designing should occur in the Design tab, and guidelines can be useful.

- **Design – Short Section Names**   Once you're more familiar with the Design tab, you may turn this option on to give you more design area. This will change the fully spelled section names at the left of the Design tab to smaller abbreviations.

- **Preview – Section Names**   You'll probably want to leave this option in to help you troubleshoot sectional problems when you're in preview mode. This will show abbreviated section names to the left of the Preview tab.

- **Grid Options – Snap to Grid**   Great to turn off when you want to be able to truly use freeform placement of objects. This will allow precise placement without objects snapping to the predetermined grid.

- **Design View – Grid**   If you leave Snap to Grid turned on, this will actually show the grid in the Design tab as a series of dots, so you can see exactly where objects you are moving will snap.

- **Preview –Grid**   You'll probably want to leave this option turned off to improve clarity. You may turn it on if you are moving and resizing objects in the Preview tab and want to see where they will snap.

Reporting Tab

- **Save Data with Report**   Checks the File | Save Data with Report option automatically when you create a new report. This saves data in the Preview tab along with the report design in the report .RPT file. If you don't want this option turned on when you create a new report, uncheck it here in File | Options.

- **Suppress Printing if No Records Selected**   If the particular combination of data and record selection chosen returns no records, this option will suppress printing of every object on the report. If you leave this option turned off and no records are returned, text objects in page/report headers, and other "fixed" objects, will still print.

- **Show All Headers on Drill Down**   Shows all headers above the group being drilled into inside the drill-down tab. See Chapter 8 for information on drill-down reporting.

- **Autosave Reports after x Minutes**   This will automatically save your report files every few minutes, preventing a loss of data if you suffer a power failure or your computer hangs. You may choose how often to automatically save reports. Reports are saved in the drive/folder specified as your Windows "Temp" folder with the file extension .AUTOSAVE.RPT.

■ **Save Preview Picture**   This will automatically save a small "thumbnail view" of your report along with the .RPT file when you save the report (you must preview the report before you save it for the Preview Picture to be saved). This is helpful if you plan on posting the report in Crystal Enterprise (discussed in Section II of the book).

■ **Formula Language**   This feature allows you to choose the default formula language for Crystal Reports formulas. You may change the language used for formulas within each formula, but this allows you to choose the default. Chapter 5 discusses the different formula language options in more detail.

Database Tab

■ **Sort Tables Alphabetically/Sort Fields Alphabetically**   This will sort tables in the Database Expert and fields in the Field Explorer alphabetically, rather than in the order the database returns them. This may be helpful with large databases when you need to find a particular table or field.

■ **Database Server Is Case-Insensitive**   If you check this option, SQL databases that you use (such as Microsoft SQL Server, Oracle, and Informix) will ignore the case of any record selection you may provide. For example, if you supply a record selection or Select Expert comparison value of "USA," the report will still include records if they include "Usa", "usa", or "uSa."

■ **Select Distinct Data for Browsing**   You may notice that browsing for sample data in the Select Expert, in the Field Explorer, and in other parts of Crystal Reports takes a significant amount of time. This is probably because the report is set to Select Distinct Data for Browsing. If you turn off this option, only the first 500 records of the report will be read when browsing, instead of reading records until 500 unique values are retrieved. Although this may not supply as many sample values when browsing, it can be significantly faster.

■ **Perform Query Asynchronously**   Checking this option will allow you to stop a query sent to a SQL database before it begins returning records to the report. You can do this with the Stop button in the Preview tab (the square button to the right of the page navigation buttons). If you leave this option unchecked, you will have to wait until the server completes the query and begins to return records to the report before you may stop report processing.

A subset of items from the Options dialog box appears on the File | Report Options dialog box.

When you create a new report, these options are based on what's chosen in the File | Options dialog box. Later, though, these options can be set to be different than the corresponding File | Options dialog box items. When the report is saved, these options are saved along with the report. The next time the report is retrieved, they will *supersede* the corresponding File | Option items.

The Report Explorer

New to Crystal Reports 9 is the Report Explorer. The *Report Explorer* is a tree-like view of all the sections in your report (Report Header, Details section, Page footer, and so forth) and the report objects within them (database fields, text objects, and so forth). Navigating through the Report Explorer is another way to format or delete individual report objects or entire report sections.

To display the Report Explorer, either click the Report Explorer button in the Standard toolbar, or choose View | Report Explorer from the pull-down menus. The Report Explorer will appear, as shown in Figure 1-8.

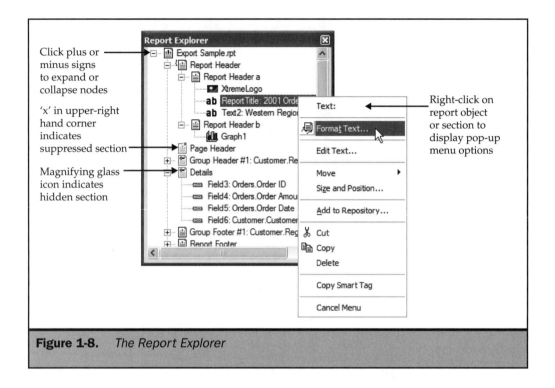

Click plus or minus signs to expand or collapse nodes

'x' in upper-right hand corner indicates suppressed section

Magnifying glass icon indicates hidden section

Right-click on report object or section to display pop-up menu options

Figure 1-8.   *The Report Explorer*

Tip   *As with the Field Explorer, the Report Explorer can be docked to other sides of the Crystal Reports window—not just the left side. You can also move the Report Explorer away from the sides so that it becomes a free-floating window.*

The very top "node" in the Report Explorer represents the report itself—everything else appears within this node. Click the plus sign to expand the report, which will then display a list of report sections (Page Header, Details section, and so forth). If you click the plus sign next to a report section, you'll either be presented with additional sections (if you've created them), or report objects within that section. A different icon will appear for suppressed or hidden sections. And, the type of each report object within a section will also be indicated by a unique icon—a small picture image will appear next to bitmap graphics, the "ab" characters will appear next to a text object, and so on. Report objects will either display their default names, such as "Graph1," or specific names you've given them in the Common tab of the Format Editor (discussed earlier in this chapter, and in more detail in Chapter 9).

If you select a report section, the corresponding gray section name will be highlighted at the left of the Design or Preview tab. If you click a report object, the object will be selected on the Design or Preview tab of Crystal Reports. Once you've selected the section or object to modify, right-click. A pop-up menu will appear giving you several choices, depending on whether you've selected a report section or object (this is the same pop-up menu that you'll see if you right-click on the report object itself or the gray section area in the Design or Preview tab). You may choose, among other things, to format a section (which will display the Section Expert), format a report object (which will display the Format Editor), or delete the object or section. If you wish to format multiple report objects at the same time, you may CTRL-click on more than one object to select them. Then, options you choose from the pop-up menu will apply to all selected objects (note that you can't multiselect report sections).

Remember that you can only work with objects that you've already placed on the report using other methods discussed earlier in the chapter. You can't add new report objects or sections from within the Report Explorer.

| Tip | *More information on formatting sections with the Section Expert is presented in Chapter 10. More detailed information on formatting individual objects with the Format Editor can be found in Chapter 9.* |

Chapter 2

Enhancing Appearance with Text Objects

There are many times during the report design process that you need to just drop some *literal text* into your report. This could be a report title that you place in the report header, a label next to a subtotal in the group footer, or a whole paragraph that you place in the report footer (perhaps explaining the methodology of the report). You can accomplish this with *text objects.*

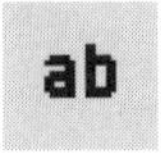

To insert a text object, choose Insert | Text Object or click the Text Object button on the Insert Tools toolbar. You'll see the text object attached to your mouse pointer. Position the mouse where you want the text object to go and click. The text object will be dropped at that location, and you'll be immediately placed in *edit mode.* You'll always know when you're in edit mode because you'll see a flashing cursor inside the text object and a small ruler at the top of the Design or Preview tab, as shown here:

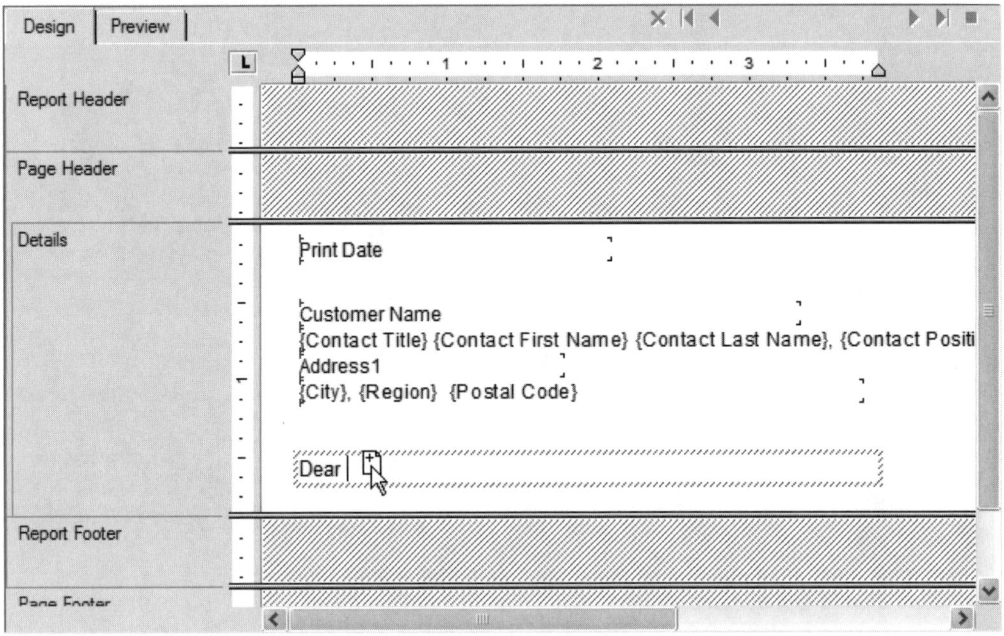

Now, just start typing. The material you type will appear inside the text object. When you're finished, just click outside the text object to save your changes.

There are several ways to edit the contents of an existing text object. To use the "long way," select the text object and then choose Edit | Edit Text from the pull-down menus, or right-click the text object and choose Edit Text from the pop-up menu. The "short way" is simply to double-click a text object, which places you in edit mode. Once in edit mode, use the cursor keys, BACKSPACE key, and DEL key to move around and edit the text.

Caution   *It's commonplace to attempt to exit edit mode by pressing the* ENTER *key. Not only will this not end editing, it will start a new line in the text object. This can often cause the contents of the text object to partially or completely disappear. If you want to put line breaks in your text object, go ahead and press* ENTER, *but make sure you resize the text object when you're finished so that you can see all of your text.*

The Field Heading Text Object

A new feature in Crystal Reports 9 is the *Field Heading Text Object.* In previous Crystal Reports versions, a text object was automatically placed in the page header of the report when you added a field from the Field Explorer to the details section. However, the text object and matching details field weren't "attached"—whenever you would move the field in the details section, the matching text object in the page header would not move.

This behavior is modified slightly in version 9. If you select the matching text object in the page header, you'll now notice that the Crystal Reports 9 status bar indicates that you've selected a Field Heading. While this object can be edited and formatted just like a regular text object, it will now move along with its matching details field—if you move the field in the details section left or right, the field heading will follow. Even if you move the details field vertically to a new section (to the page or report header or footer, for example) and then move the field left or right, the field heading will still move left or right with it.

The only time you may detach the field heading from its associated details field is if you move the detail field out of one section into another *and* move it horizontally at the same time. In this case, the two objects will be separated—the field heading won't follow the original details field anymore. However, to hook the two objects together again, simply move the details field left or right in its new section until it lines up with the field heading. The two will become "reattached."

Combining Database Fields

Simply typing literal text into text objects is a waste of their capabilities! Text objects are powerful elements that can help you create very attractive reports. Consider Figure 2-1, the beginning of a form letter that uses the Customers table from XTREME.MDB (included with Crystal Reports 9). Note the spacing problems with the contact name, city, state, and ZIP code. These lines are composed of separate fields from the Customers table. No matter how much you try or how creative you get sizing and moving these fields, they will not line up properly for every customer. They appear in the same horizontal location in every details section, no matter how wide or narrow the fields are sized.

This type of problem is a dead giveaway that this is a computer-generated letter. Although most consumers are savvy enough to assume that a computer had something to do with the form letters they receive, you don't want to make it obvious. Crystal Reports gives you a better way with text objects.

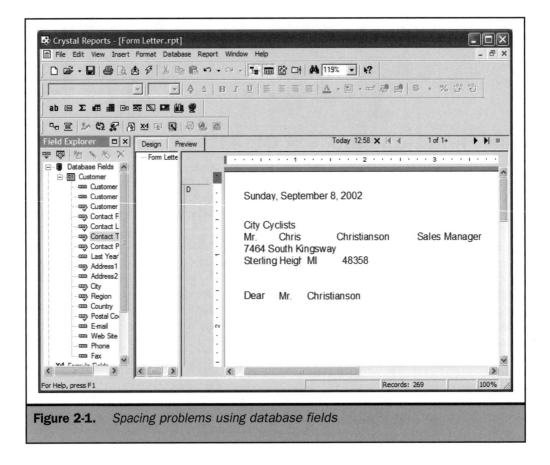

Figure 2-1. *Spacing problems using database fields*

In addition to containing literal text, text objects allow you to combine database fields with literal text. When the text object appears, it automatically sizes the contents of the database fields so that there is no extra space. Figure 2-2 shows the same form letter as Figure 2-1, but a text object is used to combine the database fields with literal text and spaces.

To combine database fields inside a text object, follow these steps:

1. Insert a text object, as described previously. If you need to include any literal text, you may type it either now or after you've inserted the database fields. It doesn't matter whether you leave the text object in edit mode or end editing.

2. From the Field Explorer, choose the field or fields you want to combine in the text object. Drag them from the Field Explorer into the text object. Note that your mouse cursor will change when you move over the text object, and a blinking cursor will appear in the text object at the same time:

3. Before dropping the database field or fields in the text object, look very carefully at the location of the blinking text object cursor. Wherever the cursor is located is where the database field or fields will go when you release the mouse button. Release the button when the cursor is in the proper position.

4. If you were already editing the text object when you dragged the database field into it, it will stay in edit mode. You may now type more literal text or add another database field, if you need to. If the text object wasn't in edit mode, the field will be dropped inside without going into edit mode. If you wish to add more text, double-click the text object to place it in edit mode.

5. When you're finished combining database fields and literal text, end editing by clicking outside the text object.

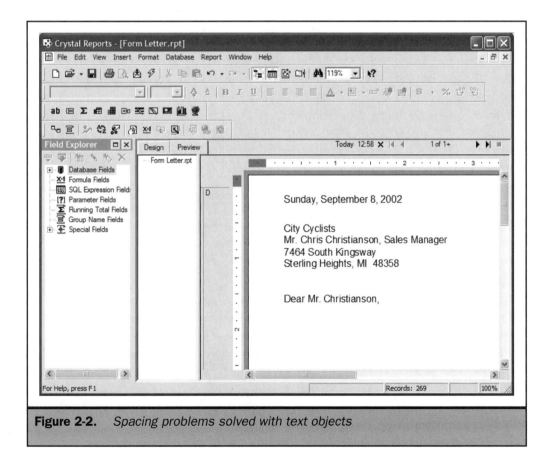

Figure 2-2.   *Spacing problems solved with text objects*

Combining Special Fields

You're not limited to combining database fields inside text objects. You can use *special fields* as well. Special fields are system-generated fields, such as the print date, print time, page number, and total page count. You may place them directly on the report, just like database fields. And, like database fields, they'll give you spacing problems if you try to place them near literal text.

To combine special fields with literal text inside text objects, perform the same steps as for database fields. Just drag the fields from the Special Fields category of the Field Explorer, instead of from the Database Field category. In fact, you can embed any type of field from the Field Explorer in a text object just by dragging and dropping from the desired category.

Figure 2-3 shows the benefits of combining special fields with literal text in text objects.

The following pointers will help you as you combine fields and literal text inside text objects:

- If you place a database or special field in the wrong location inside the text object (suppose you place the Last Name field in between the letters *a* and *r* in the word "Dear"), you can simply use your cursor keys and the BACKSPACE or DEL key to make the correction. In this case, it is easier to just delete the text following the special field, and reenter it before the special field. You may also use CTRL-C to cut text and CTRL-V to paste text inside the text object.

- If you inadvertently drop a subtotal, a summary, a database field, or some other item inside a text object by mistake (it's pretty easy to do, even if you're careful), you have two choices. If you catch the problem immediately, you can choose Edit | Undo, or click the Undo button on the Standard toolbar. The field will move back where it was. However, if you notice that you accidentally dropped a field inside the text object after it's too late to reasonably undo it, edit the text object, click the field that was mistakenly added to highlight it, and press the DEL key. The field will be removed from inside the text object. You will then need to re-create it and place it in its correct position on the report.

The Can Grow Formatting Option

When you combine database fields or special fields inside text objects, you may often find that the text object is no longer wide enough to show its entire contents. Crystal Reports features the Can Grow formatting option that allows a text object to grow vertically, if necessary, to show its entire contents. You may choose this option, as well as change the Maximum Number of Lines option that the text object can grow from the Format Editor.

Special fields and text as separate objects

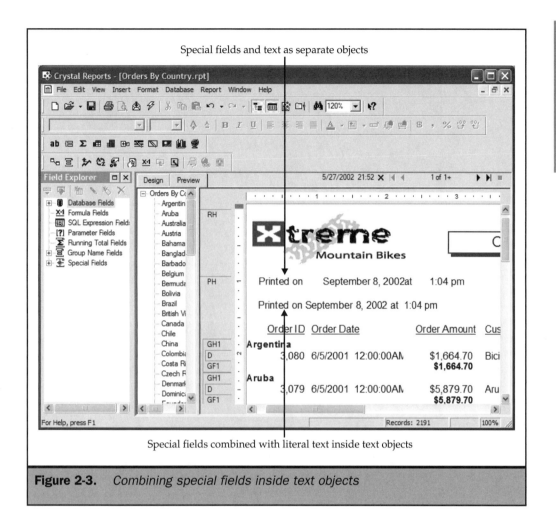

Special fields combined with literal text inside text objects

Figure 2-3. *Combining special fields inside text objects*

Note *In Crystal Reports versions prior to 9, Can Grow was turned on automatically when you combined fields inside text objects.*

To display the Format Editor, use one of these options:

- Select the text object and then select Format | Format Text from the pull-down menus.
- Right-click the text object and choose Format Text from the pop-up menu.
- Click the Format button on the Expert Tools toolbar.

The Can Grow option is found on the Common tab of the Format Editor.

With Can Grow turned on, the text object will automatically grow taller to show all the text inside it. You can specify the maximum number of lines that the text object will grow, or leave the number set to zero for unlimited size. When Can Grow is turned on, the text object will only display as wide as it appears on the report. However, it will word-wrap at spaces in the text, creating additional vertical space up to the maximum number of lines.

This automatic behavior lets you size a text object so that it's only one line high. If the contents of the text object can be displayed in one line, the text object will remain one line tall. If it needs more lines, it will expand only by the amount of vertical space necessary to show the material inside the text object (limited by the maximum number of lines).

Tip *Can Grow is helpful for other types of objects as well, not just text objects. You can set the Can Grow formatting option for string fields and memo fields. This is particularly helpful for "description" or "narrative" types of fields that could contain as little as a few characters and as much as several paragraphs of text. Can Grow isn't available for any type of object other than a text object, string field, or memo field.*

Formatting Individual Parts of Text Objects

You can format a text object as you would any other object, using the Formatting toolbar or Format Editor. When you select a text object and change the formatting, such as setting a color or font size, the entire text object takes on that format. This may be the behavior you want.

However, at other times you may want certain characters or words in a text object to take on different formatting than the rest of the text object. Even more prevalent is a situation in which you need to format individual database fields or special fields that reside *inside* a text object.

For example, when you insert the Print Date special field inside a text object, it takes on the default formatting from File | Options, perhaps an mm/dd/yy format. If you select the text object and display the Format Editor, there is no Date tab in which to choose an alternate date format—this is a text object you're formatting! Similarly, if you've placed a number field inside a text object, you may want to change the formatting to show no decimal places or to add a currency symbol.

To accomplish these types of formatting tasks, you must format individual parts of the text object. This is actually quite simple. Start editing the text object by double-clicking it. You are then free to select individual characters or words by dragging over them with your mouse or by holding down the SHIFT key while using the cursor keys. You can then use the Format toolbar or Format Editor to change the formatting for just those selected characters.

To change the formatting of a database or special field inside a text object, edit the text object and then click the field you wish to format. You'll know you've selected the field when it becomes highlighted inside the text object. You can then use the Format Editor (either from the Format menu or by right-clicking—the number-formatting buttons on the Formatting toolbar won't work here) to change the formatting of the object.

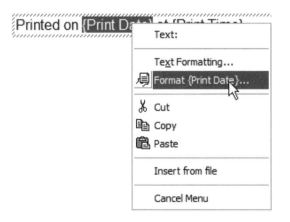

Importing Text from a File

If you have large amounts of text that you want to use in Crystal Reports text objects, you may either type it into a text object directly or copy and paste from the Windows Clipboard. However, data for text objects can also be imported directly from plain text, Rich Text Format (RTF), or Hypertext Markup Language (HTML) files.

To import text into a text object, add a text object as described previously in the chapter (using the Insert menu or toolbar button). If the text object isn't already in edit mode, double-click it to place it in edit mode. Then, right-click and choose Insert from File from the pop-up menu.

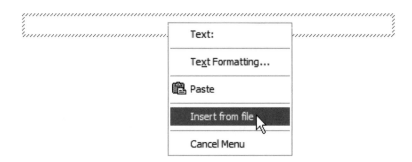

A File Open dialog box will appear. Navigate to the drive and folder where the text, RTF, or HTML file is that you wish to import into the text object. Choose the desired file and click OK. The file will be imported into the text object, alongside any existing text that may already be in the text object. If the text file contains plain text, it will simply be displayed in the text object in the default font style for text objects (set on the Fonts tab of File | Options). If the imported text is in HTML or RTF format, Crystal Reports automatically interprets the embedded font and formatting specifications and includes them in the text object. If you wish to reformat portions of the text object, simply use techniques described previously in the chapter for formatting individual parts of text objects.

Chapter 3

Sorting and Grouping

Whe you first create and preview a report, the report shows details sections in *natural order*. That is, the records appear in whatever order the database sends them to Crystal Reports. This order can vary widely, depending on what database you are using, how you link tables, and other variables.

You'll probably want to control the order in which information appears on your report. An employee listing, for example, isn't very useful if it isn't in alphabetical order. A sales breakdown is probably more helpful if you see your sales figures in a particular order. You're probably interested in a highest-to-lowest sequence of order quantities if you're about to send gifts to your best customers at the holidays. On the other hand, lowest-to-highest sequence is probably more appropriate if you're about to send your marketing department out to talk to lower-performing customers.

Sorting Your Report

If you simply want to reorder your report's details sections into a particular order, you need to *sort* the report. Sorting is useful for simple reports that need to present information in a certain order. To sort a report, choose Report | Record Sort Expert from the pull-down menus, or click the Record Sort Expert button on the Expert Tools toolbar. This displays the Record Sort Order dialog box.

The left Available Fields box shows all the report fields that you've placed on the report, followed by a list of all tables and fields you initially added to the report. If you wish to sort on a field you haven't placed on the report, scroll down through the Report Fields list until you find the list of tables and fields you added to your report. Choose one or more fields to control how you want your report sorted. Simply double-click the field you wish to sort on, or select the field and then click the right arrow button. Either method moves the field to the Sort Fields box on the right. You may then choose between the Ascending and Descending radio buttons to choose the sort order.

An *ascending* sort orders the records alphabetically, A to Z; if the records start with numbers, they will appear before any letters, sorted 0 through 9. In a *descending* sort, the order is reversed. Records appear in Z to A order, followed by any numbers in 9 to 0 order.

You may sort by as many fields as you like—you're not limited to one. This is handy, for example, if you want to sort your customers by state, and within state by customer name. Simply add the additional sort fields to the Sort Fields box and choose the Ascending or Descending for each field. The first field in the list will be the *primary,* or first, sorting field, the second field will be *secondary* (will be used to sort multiple records that have the same primary field), and so forth. If you wish to change the order of sorting priority, select a field in the Sort Fields list and click the up or down arrows above the list to reorder the sort fields. When you click OK, Crystal Reports will sort by the higher (primary) field first, and then the lower fields.

Tip *You can sort just as easily on formula fields (covered in Chapter 5) as you can on database fields. This is often required if you want to customize some aspect of the way records are sorted. Just remember that if you're using a SQL database, such as SQL Server or Oracle, sorting on a formula field makes Crystal Reports sort the records instead of having the database server do the work, which may affect the performance of your report (albeit slightly). This is covered in more detail in Chapter 16.*

Grouping Records

Sorting records is handy for lists or other simple reports that just need records to appear in a certain order. It's more common, however, to want not only to have your report sorted by certain fields, but also to have subtotals, counts, averages, or other summary information appear when the sort field changes. To accomplish this, you must use Crystal Reports *groups*.

When you create a report group, you both sort the records on the report and create two additional report sections every time the group field changes. You may place subtotals, averages, counts, and many other types of summary information in these sections. In addition, grouping your report enables the *group tree,* an Explorer-like window on the left side of the Preview tab. The group tree gives you a quick overview of the organization of your report and enables you to navigate directly to a particular group that you want to see.

To create a report group, you may either choose Insert | Group from the pull-down menus or click the Insert Group button from the Insert Tools toolbar. The Insert Group dialog box appears. It contains two tabs: Common (shown here) and Options (discussed later).

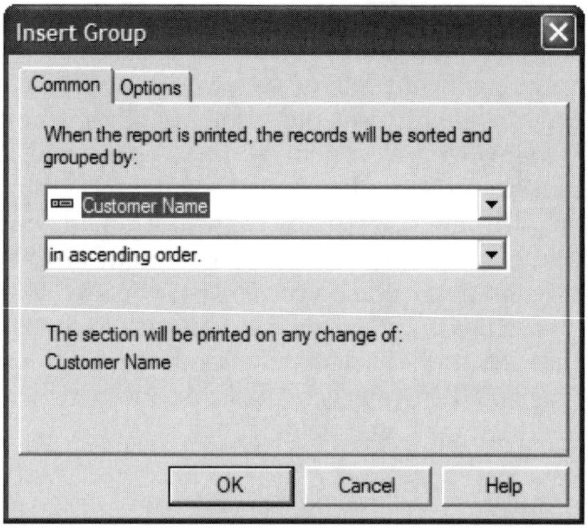

There are two drop-down lists in the Common tab that you use to insert a group. Follow these steps to complete the dialog box:

1. Click the top drop-down list to select the field you want to group on. The list will display fields on your report, as well as other fields in the tables that the report is using. You can group by a field already on the report or by a database field that you didn't put on the report. You can also group by a formula field.

2. Click the second drop-down list to select the order in which your groups will appear on the report. There are four options: *ascending order* shows the groups in A to Z order alphabetically; *descending order* shows the groups in Z to A order; *specified order* lets you create your own groups (described later in this chapter); and *original order* groups records in the order in which they appear in the database. (This last option is an interesting feature, but probably not useful in most reports.)

If you wish to allow Crystal Reports to make "typical" choices for the way groups appear, you may simply click OK now to create the new group. However, if you want to set additional options for the group, click the Options tab.

Make Options tab choices as follows:

1. If you simply want to have the database field itself appear in the groups on the report and the group tree, leave the Customize Group Name Field check box empty. However, if you'd like to customize the way the groups appear (perhaps you'd like a month fully spelled out along with a four-digit year for a date field), click the Customize Group Name Field check box. You can then make additional choices to determine what appears for the group. "Customizing Group Name Fields" appears later in the chapter.

2. Click the Keep Group Together option if you want Crystal Reports to try to keep your groups from breaking at the end of a page. If you leave this option unchecked, the beginning of a group and just a few detail records in the group may print at the bottom of a page, while the rest of the group's detail records and its subtotals may appear at the top of the next page.

3. Click the Repeat Group Header on Each Page option if you think you will have large groups that will span more than a single page. This option will print the group header section (described later) at the top of each page where a group continues. This allows you to look at details sections on subsequent pages and know which group they belong to.

Caution *Clicking Keep Group Together can cause odd behavior if the first group in your report won't fit on a page by itself. In this case, Crystal Reports will detect that it can't fit the group on the first page of the report and will start a new page before it starts printing the group. The result will be a blank first page. If this happens, you may resolve the problem by suppressing the report header section. If you do this but still want material to print at the top of the first page only, create separate Page Header A and B sections, and conditionally format page header A to suppress if the page number is greater than 1. Formatting report sections is described in Chapter 10.*

Figure 3-1 shows the two new sections that are added to the Design tab, the group header and group footer. These sections appear at the beginning and end of every group. Note that Crystal Reports places an object in the group header section automatically.

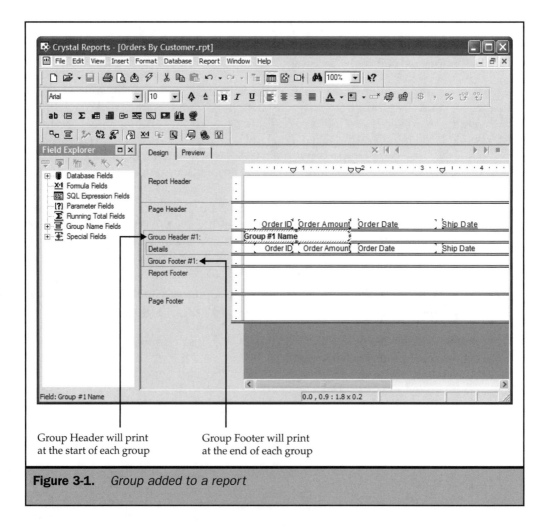

Group Header will print
at the start of each group

Group Footer will print
at the end of each group

Figure 3-1. *Group added to a report*

This *group name* object will automatically print the contents of the field on which the group is based in each group header. The group footer section is empty.

Tip   *You may turn off the Insert Group Name with Group option in File | Options if you don't want Crystal Reports to automatically insert a group name object in the group header when a group is created. If this is turned off, or if you inadvertently delete a group name object, you can insert a group name from the Field Explorer by dragging and dropping a group name object after opening the Group Name Fields category.*

Figure 3-2 shows the Preview tab with the now-active group tree. You can see your groups in an outline form and navigate directly to the beginning of one of the groups

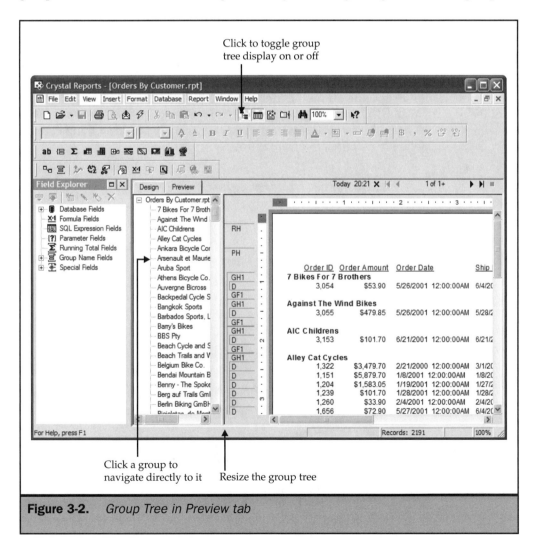

Figure 3-2.   *Group Tree in Preview tab*

by clicking the group in the group tree. You can also turn the display of the group tree on and off by clicking the Toggle Group Tree button on the Standard toolbar.

> **Tip**   *A new feature of Crystal Reports 9 is the Group Expert, discussed in "The New Group Expert" later the chapter. You may also display the Group Expert and add a field to create a new group.*

Manipulating Existing Groups

After you create a group, you may wish to delete it so that only detail records print again without grouping. Or, you may wish to change the field that the group is based on, change the order of the groups from ascending to descending, customize the group name field, or choose one of the formatting options to control the way Crystal Reports deals with page breaks inside groups.

One way to do this is to point your mouse to a group header or footer section in the "gray section area" of the left side of the Design or Preview tab (the section will be abbreviated "GH" and "GF" in the Preview tab). You must point to the group header or group footer for the group you wish to delete, right-click, and choose Delete Group from the pop-up menu. The group header and group footer sections will be removed from the report, along with any objects in them. You may also use the new Group Expert, discussed in the following section, to delete a group.

Group Header #1: Customer.Customer Name - A
Hide (Drill-Down OK)
Suppress (No Drill-Down)
Section Expert...
Change Group...
Hide Section Names
Insert Line
Delete Last Line
Arrange Lines
Fit Section
Insert Section Below
Delete Group
Select All Section Objects
Cancel Menu

There are also several ways to change existing groups by redisplaying the dialog box that appeared when you created the group. You may change the field that the group is based on, change the order of groups (ascending, descending, specified, original), customize the group name field, or select the Keep Group Together or Repeat Group Header on Each New Page option.

As when deleting groups, you may point to the group header or group footer section of the group you want to change in the Design or Preview tab. Then right-click and choose Change Group from the pop-up menu. The Change Group Options dialog box will reappear, where you can change group settings on either the Common or Options tab and then click OK when you're finished. You may also use the new Group Expert, discussed in the following section, to change a group.

Group Header #1: Customer.Customer Name - A
Hide (Drill-Down OK)
Suppress (No Drill-Down)
Section Expert...
Change Group...
Hide Section Names
Insert Line
Delete Last Line
Arrange Lines
Fit Section
Insert Section Below
Delete Group
Select All Section Objects
Cancel Menu

The Group Expert

New to Crystal Reports 9 is the Group Expert, which is designed to let you perform the grouping options described previously in the chapter, such as creating new groups, modifying existing groups, reordering groups, and deleting groups. To display the Group Expert, choose Report | Group Expert from the pull-down menus, or click the Group Expert button in the Expert Tools toolbar. The Group Expert will appear, as shown in Figure 3-3.

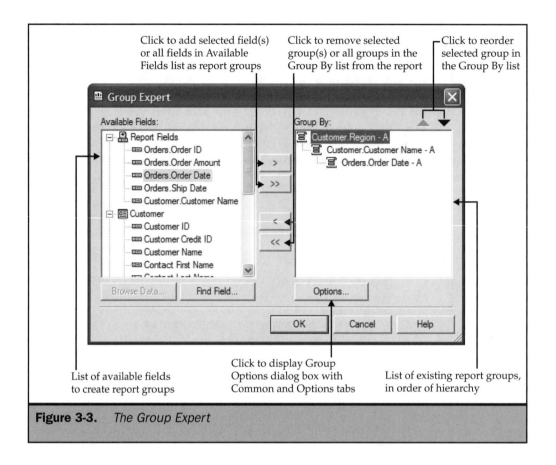

Figure 3-3. *The Group Expert*

Here, you can add a new group to the report by selecting the field from the Available Fields list that you want to use, and clicking the right arrow to add the group. If you have an existing group on the report that you wish to remove, select that group in the Group By list and click the left arrow to remove it. And, if you want to choose options for a group on the report (either a new group you just added or an existing group that was added previously), select the group in the Group By list that you want to modify and click the Options button. The Group Options dialog box will appear. Choose the Common or Options tab and choose or change appropriate options.

If your report contains more than one group (discussed in more detail later in the chapter under "Multiple Groups"), you may wish to change the order in which the groups appear. For example, you may have initially grouped your report first by Customer, and within Customer by Region. If you want to change the order of the groups to be by Region and then Customer, you would select a group in the Group By list and use the up and down arrows above the Group By list to change the order of the groups.

Adding Summaries

So, what's the difference between just sorting the report and creating a group? Not only is the group tree useful with grouped reports, but you now have a section available for subtotals, averages, counts, and other summary functions at the end of each group. Although the group footer is empty when first created, you can insert summary functions into it with ease.

Inserting summaries in your report requires several steps:

Σ

1. Choose Insert | Summary from the pull-down menus, or right-click the field you want to summarize in the Details section and choose Insert Summary from the pop-up menu. To insert a summary, you can also click the Summary button on the Insert Tools toolbar. The Insert Summary dialog box will appear.

2. If you selected a field on the report before you chose an Insert Summary option, that field will be preselected in the Choose Field to Summarize drop-down list. Otherwise, choose the field you wish to total, average, or otherwise summarize, in this list.

3. Choose the summary function (sum, average, and so on) that you wish to use. Then, either choose to insert a grand summary for the entire report (the default) or choose the existing group in which you want to place the summary. If you

wish to create a new group on the report for your summary, click the Insert Group button to create a new group.

4. If you want to create a percentage summary field, click the Show As a Percentage Of check box and choose from the drop-down list the field that you want to show the percentage of (percentage summary fields are discussed in detail later in the chapter). You must choose a report group before you can check this box— Percentage Summaries can't be created in the report footer.

5. If the group you've chosen is a hierarchical group (discussed later in the chapter under "Hierarchical Groups"), you may check the Summarize Across Hierarchy check box to include the summary in all hierarchical groups.

6. Click OK to place the subtotal or summary in the group footer or report footer directly below the detail field that you're summarizing.

7. Since Crystal Reports doesn't label group summaries for you, you should add text objects next to the summaries to indicate what they display. For example, a subtotal won't be confused with an average if you place a text object containing "Subtotal:" next to the subtotal object.

Here are a few pointers to keep in mind when inserting summaries:

- Although Crystal Reports places subtotals and summaries in the group footer or report footer by default, you don't have to leave them there. If you move them to the group header or report header, they'll print the same information, but at the beginning of groups or the report.

- Once a summary or subtotal has been created, you don't have to delete it and insert a new summary if you want to change its function (for example, to change a subtotal to an average). Simply click the subtotal or summary and choose Edit | Summary from the pull-down menus, or right-click the summary and choose Edit Summary from the pop-up menu.

- If you want to insert a summary in one or more group footers and the report footer (to summarize for multiple groups and the entire report), you don't have to use the Insert Summary options over and over for each group and the entire report. Just insert the summary into one group and then copy the summary from that group footer to the other groups or the report footer by using Edit menu options, or just CTRL-dragging the summary from a group footer to copy it to another section.

Note *The method discussed here to copy summaries from one section to another should be of renewed interest to users of Crystal Reports 9. The check boxes allowing you to insert a summary in all groups and for the whole report that were available in previous versions have been eliminated from version 9.*

Table 3-1 shows the different summary functions that are available in Crystal Reports and what each does.

Function	Results
Sum	Returns the subtotal of the chosen field; available only for number or currency fields.
Average	Returns the average of the chosen field; available only for number or currency fields.
Sample Variance Sample Standard Deviation Population Variance Population Standard Deviation	For number of currency fields only, these functions return the statistical result for the group or report values. For detailed descriptions on the specific steps performed to arrive at the results, consult a statistics text or Crystal Reports online help.
Maximum	For number or currency fields, returns the highest number in the group. For string fields, returns the last member of the group alphabetically. For date fields, returns the latest date in the group.
Minimum	For number or currency fields, returns the lowest number in the group. For string fields, returns the first member of the group alphabetically. For date fields, returns the earliest date in the group.
Count	Simply counts the records in the details section and returns the number of records in the group. Although you are required to choose a database field before selecting this option, the Count function will return the same number no matter which field you choose (with the exception of fields that contain null values).
Distinct Count	Similar to the Count function, but returns only the distinct number of occurrences of the field. As opposed to Count, the field you choose in the details section before choosing Distinct Count is very significant. For example, if five records contain the strings Los Angeles, Chicago, Vancouver, Chicago, and Miami, the Count function would return 5, whereas Distinct Count would return 4.

Table 3-1. *Summary Functions*

Function	Results
Correlation Covariance	For number of currency fields only, these functions return the statistical result for the group or report values. When you choose these functions, an additional drop-down list appears where you may choose an additional report field to complete the function. For detailed descriptions on the specific steps performed to arrive at the results, consult a statistics text or Crystal Reports online help.
Median	For number and currency fields only. Returns the median, or middle, number in the group. If there is one number in the group, it is returned. If there are two numbers, their average is returned.
Mode	Returns the most frequently occurring value from all the detail records in the group. For numeric fields, Mode returns the most frequently occurring number. For string fields, Mode returns the most frequently occurring string (for example, with detail records containing five occurrences of FedEx, three occurrences of UPS, and eight occurrences of Parcel Post, Mode would return Parcel Post).
Nth Largest	Returns the third, fifth, or tenth (and so forth) largest value in the group, depending on the value you enter for N. For example, Nth largest, with N equaling 1, returns the largest value in the group. When you choose this function, an additional box appears in which you can enter the value for N. For numeric fields, this function returns the Nth-highest numeric value. With string fields, it returns the Nth value alphabetically (for example, if there are three records containing FedEx and two records containing UPS, Nth largest when N equals 2 will be UPS, and Nth largest when N equals 3 will be FedEx).
Nth Smallest	Returns the third, fifth, tenth (and so forth) smallest value in the group. For example, Nth smallest with N equaling 1 returns the smallest value in the group. When you choose this function, an additional box appears in which you can enter the value for N. This function behaves similarly to Nth highest with both numeric and string fields.

Table 3-1. *Summary Functions* (continued)

Function	Results
Nth Most Frequent	Returns the third, fifth, tenth (and so forth) most frequent occurrence in the group. This is similar to Mode, except that you're not limited to just the *most* frequent occurrence.
Pth Percentile	For number and currency fields only. When you choose this function, an additional box appears in which you can enter a number between 0 and 100 for *P*. This function returns the number that indicates what the percentile is for *P*, based on all the numbers in the group.
Weighted average	For number and currency fields only. This will calculate an average of group or report values, but apply the "weight" of another field to adjust the average. When you choose this function, an additional drop-down list appears where you may choose an additional report field to complete the function.

Table 3-1. *Summary Functions* (continued)

Caution *If the details field that you summarize contains null values (a special database value where the field actually contains nothing, as opposed to a zero or empty string), the summary function won't "count" that record. For example, a Count or Average won't figure the null record into its calculation. If you wish to avoid this problem with the current report, you can convert database null values to zero or empty string values by choosing File | Report Options and clicking Convert Database NULL Values to Default. If you want this to be the default option for all new reports, you can choose the same option on the Reporting tab from File | Options.*

Percentage Summary Fields

Although the default summary functions satisfy most needs for analytical reporting, sometimes you may prefer to calculate percentages rather than whole numbers. For example, if you report groups sales by sales rep within each month, you may want to know both the actual dollars and the *percentage* of revenues each sales rep is responsible for in that month. And, you may also want to calculate the percentage of total sales for the entire year that each month is responsible for. Such an example is shown in Figure 3-4. Crystal Reports 9 features the *percentage summary field,* which creates this type of calculation without the need for a formula.

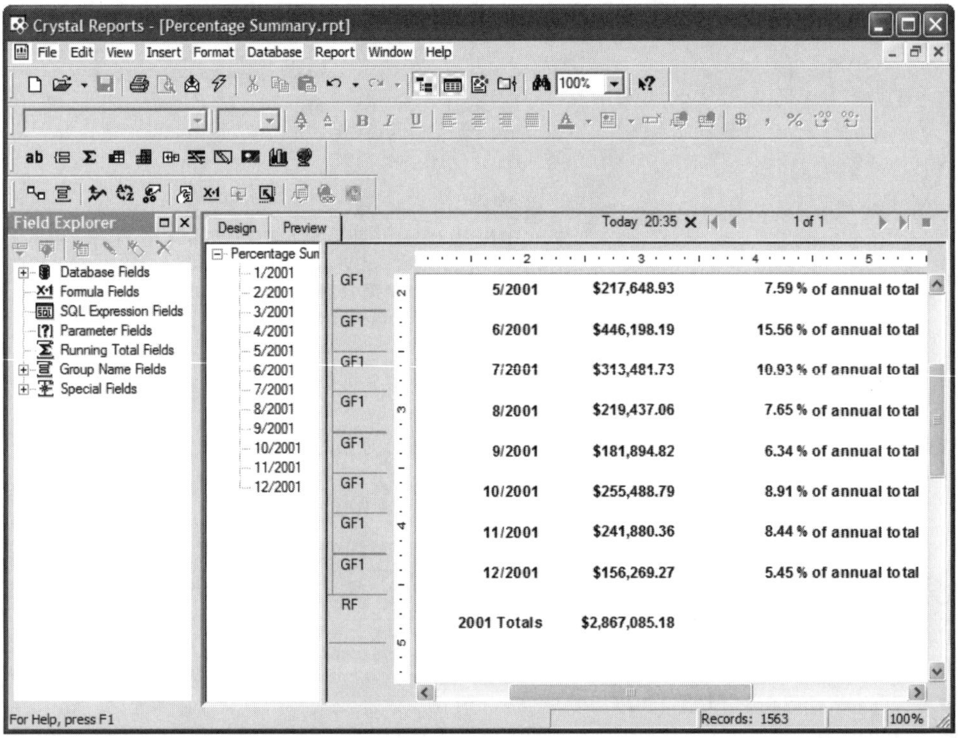

Figure 3-4. *Percentages created with Percentage Summary field*

To create a percentage summary field, follow the steps previously outlined to insert a summary field. Choose the field you want to use to calculate the percentage (the "numerator") and the group in which you want the percentage placed, as though you were creating a regular summary. Then, click the Show As a Percentage Of check box and use the drop-down list to choose the higher-level group or grand total you want used as the "denominator." If you are placing the percentage in the highest-level (or only) group on the report, you'll only be able to choose a grand total for the denominator. Click OK.

Crystal Reports will place a summary field in the group footer of the group you specified. When you preview the report, however, you'll see a percentage number rather than a count, subtotal, or other number. The percentage summary field will already be formatted to display a percent sign.

Multiple Groups

Crystal Reports does not limit your report to just one level of grouping. In fact, many powerful reporting features can be provided to your report viewer by creative use of multiple groups. The key to many sophisticated reporting requirements lies in creative use of formulas (covered in Chapter 5) in conjunction with multiple levels of grouping.

Multiple groups form a report hierarchy, with increasing levels of detailed information being presented by inner groups. For example, a report might be grouped by country first. Within the country group would be a geographic region group (Northwest, Southwest, and so forth), and then a group by state, a group by county or township, a group by city, and finally detail records showing individual customers or orders within that city. Each group has its own group header and group footer sections, and subtotals and summaries can exist for each group.

The group tree handles multiple levels of grouping very elegantly, following the general style of Windows Explorer. Plus signs (expand buttons) are displayed next to groups that can be expanded to display other groups; minus signs (collapse buttons) are shown beside expanded groups that can be collapsed. Figure 3-5 shows a report with multiple groups. Notice that you can navigate through the group tree by clicking the plus and minus signs to open and close group levels. When you find the group you want to see, click the group name in the group tree to go directly to the beginning of that group in the report, no matter how deep the group is in the hierarchy.

To create additional levels of grouping, simply repeat the process described previously for inserting a group, either using the Group Expert or the Insert Group options. The groups will appear in the order that you create them. You can use the Insert Summary options to add subtotals and summaries to the group footer and group header sections.

You may inadvertently create groups in the wrong order. For example, if you wish to have your report grouped by state and then by city, make sure to create the groups in that order. If you create the city group first, followed by the state group, you'll have one group for each city, with whatever state that city is in as a lower-level group. You'd have, for example, a group for Boulder containing a Colorado group. Below that, you'd have a group for Denver containing another Colorado group.

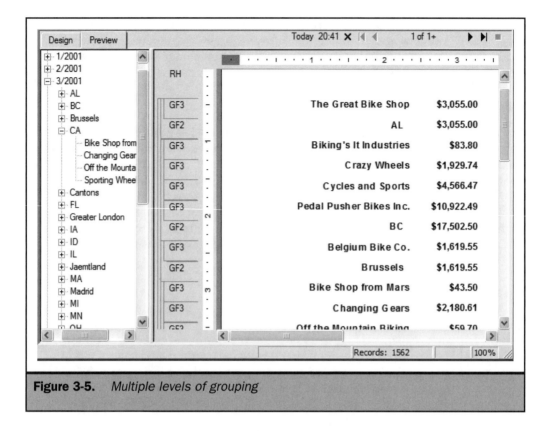

Figure 3-5. *Multiple levels of grouping*

This isn't as much of a problem as it might seem. You don't have to delete groups and reinsert them in the desired order—moving them around is surprisingly easy. Simply return to the Design tab and point to the gray Group Header or Group Footer area on the left side of the screen. Point to the group that needs to be moved, and hold down the left mouse button—the mouse cursor turns into a hand symbol.

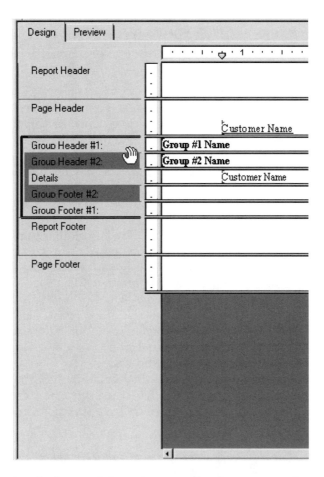

You can now simply drag and drop the group header or group footer on top of the group that you wish to swap it with. When you release the mouse button, the groups swap locations. Don't be confused by the fact that the groups stay numbered in sequential order—the groups have been moved. In the preceding example, simply dropping the state group header (Group Header #2) on the city group header (Group Header #1) will swap the groups. The state group header becomes Group Header #1, and the city group header becomes Group Header #2.

Tip *The new Group Expert also allows you to easily swap the order of groups.*

Specified Order Grouping

Sometimes, you may need data grouped on your report in a special order that the database doesn't offer. For example, the database may contain a state field, but not a field indicating what geographic location the record belongs to (Northwest, Southwest, and so on). One option that may be appropriate for more sophisticated customized grouping is basing a group on a sophisticated formula. However, if your customized grouping is not particularly complicated, *specified order grouping* may be more straightforward. This allows you to create customized groups without having to know the Crystal Reports formula language.

Specified order grouping lets you use a dialog box similar to the Select Expert (discussed in Chapter 8) to create your own groups, based on an existing database field. In the geographic location example used previously, you could create a Northwest group consisting of Washington, Oregon, Idaho, and Montana. The Southwest group could include Nevada, California, Texas, and Arizona. The Northeast group could consist of New York, Maine, Vermont, and New Hampshire. Southeast could include Florida, Alabama, Louisiana, and Mississippi. All the other states not in these four groups could either be ignored, placed in their own individual groups, or lumped together in one final group given a name of your choice, such as Midwest.

To specify your own groups, choose Specified Order in the Group dialog box instead of Ascending or Descending order when you create a new group or change an existing group. When you choose Specified Order, a Specified Order tab is added to the Change Group Options dialog box.

Click the New button to create a new named group. This will display the Define Named Group dialog box, shown next. Type the name the group should have on the report, such as Northwest. Then, using options in the tabs, indicate which records will be included in the group. For example, you may want the Northwest group to include records in which Customer.Region is one of WA, OR, and ID.

If you need to use several different criteria for the named group, you can click the <New> tab and add additional criteria for the group. When you're finished, click OK on the Define Named Group dialog box. The named group will be created and will appear in the list of named groups in the Group Options dialog box. You can now click the New button again to add additional named groups (for example, Southwest, including AZ, CA, and TX).

Tip   *Remember that clicking the <New> tab to create more than one selection tab still only allows you to select by one field—the field your group is created on. The criteria on the tabs will be joined using a logical Or operation—this is different from the Select Expert.*

As you add new named groups, they appear in the Specified Order tab of the Change Group Options dialog box in the order that you created them, *not* in alphabetical order. If you wish to change the order in which the named groups appear on the report, select a named group and use the up or down arrow next to the list of named groups to change its position. The Other group, however, will always be last, no matter what you name it or how you position named groups with the arrow buttons.

After you create at least one named group, the Others tab appears in the Group dialog box. You use this tab to deal with any records that haven't been caught by your specific named groups. You can discard the remaining records, place them in one "catchall" group with the name of your choice, or leave them in their own groups based on the database field. In the geographic example, Northwest, Southwest, Northeast, and Southeast have all been created as named groups. The Others tab is used to lump any regions that weren't otherwise specified into a Midwest group.

You might have noticed the Named Group drop-down list on the Specified Order tab. This list will browse the database, showing you samples of the actual field you're grouping on. If you choose one of these samples, Crystal Reports will create a named group with the same name as the actual database field. This is handy if you want to create the same groups as you would by using Ascending or Descending order, but place the groups in the specific order you desire.

After you create your named groups and click OK on the Change Group Options dialog box, the report will reflect your new grouping. Figure 3-6 shows a report grouped by the five geographic areas described previously. If you wish to change any of your specified grouping options, or remove them altogether so that records appear in their own groups, just use the steps mentioned previously to change an existing group. The Change Group Options dialog box will open, and you can edit your specified groups or change grouping to ascending or descending order, which will remove specified grouping.

Drilling Down on Data

One of the most powerful features of Crystal Reports is its online reporting capability. Although you can print reports on a printer and export them to other file formats, such as Word or Excel, the real power of many reports becomes available only when users can view and interact with them *online*. This means that the user directly views the .RPT file that Crystal Reports creates. This affords two benefits:

■ A user can rerun the report whenever they want, seeing an updated view of the database at that moment.

■ A user can interact with the report by using the group tree and drill-down capabilities.

Various Crystal Reports 9 versions offer online interactive reporting to users in several ways:

■ Giving users their own copy of Crystal Reports, letting them open, view, and modify reports at will

■ Reporting with a Web browser and Crystal Enterprise (covered in Part II, starting with Chapter 20)

■ Including a Crystal Report in a custom Windows application (covered in Part III)

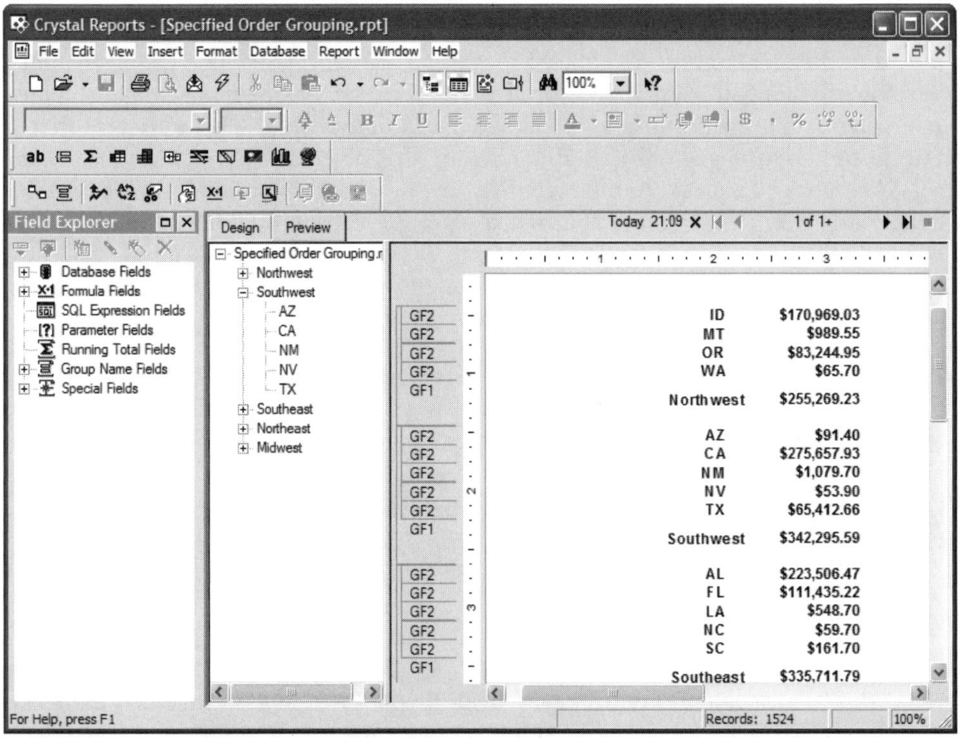

Figure 3-6. *Report with Specified Order grouping*

All of these interactive methods allow a user to *drill down* on data in the report. This technique, a feature that has been carried over from early PC-based decision-support system software, allows a report viewer to initially look at higher-level data. For example, a report might start at the country level. If the viewer sees a subtotal or summary number (or an element in a pie chart or other chart) for a particular country that interests them, they can double-click that number. This will drill down to the next level in the report, possibly the region or state level, where they can see summary numbers for each of those states or regions. If the report is designed with several levels of drill-down ability, the user could then double-click a region that piqued their interest to display all the cities in that region. The drilling down could progress further, allowing users to drill down on cities and finally ZIP codes, where individual detail items at the ZIP-code level would appear.

Crystal Reports automatically sets up a drill-down hierarchy when you create groups. Every group you create can be drilled into, exposing the lower-level group and finally the details section. So, for our drill-down example to work, you would create multiple groups on the report in the following order: country, region (state), city, and finally ZIP code.

After you create groups, you can drill down on the group name (automatically placed in the group header) or any summary or subtotal that you place in a group header or group footer. When you point at these objects, you'll notice that the mouse pointer changes from an arrow to a magnifying glass, called a *drill-down cursor*. This indicates that you can drill down on the group by double-clicking this object. When you double-click, a *drill-down tab* appears next to the main Preview tab, containing the lower-level group or detail data. Every time you drill down, a separate drill-down tab appears.

If you drill down enough times, there won't be enough room to see all the drill-down tabs, along with the main Preview and Design tabs. In this situation, two small arrows appear next to the last drill-down tab. You can click these arrows to move back and forth among the tabs to see tabs that have disappeared off the screen. You can also close any drill-down tab by clicking the red X button next to the page-navigation buttons. This closes the current tab and displays the tab to the left. You can close every tab this way (including the Preview tab), except for the Design tab.

Tip
If you wish to print the report to a printer or export it to another file format, only the material appearing in the current tab will print or export. If you're displaying the Preview tab at the time, the summarized report will print or export. If, however, you have a drill-down tab selected when you print or export, only the material in that drill-down tab will be included.

Figure 3-7 shows a report with several drill-down tabs visible. Notice that there isn't enough room to show all the tabs, so small arrows appear to the right of the last drill-down tab. Also notice that the mouse cursor has changed to a magnifying glass because it is over a group name object.

You can drill down on any report that has at least one group on it, even if all the details sections are showing already. Drill-down ability is really helpful with summary

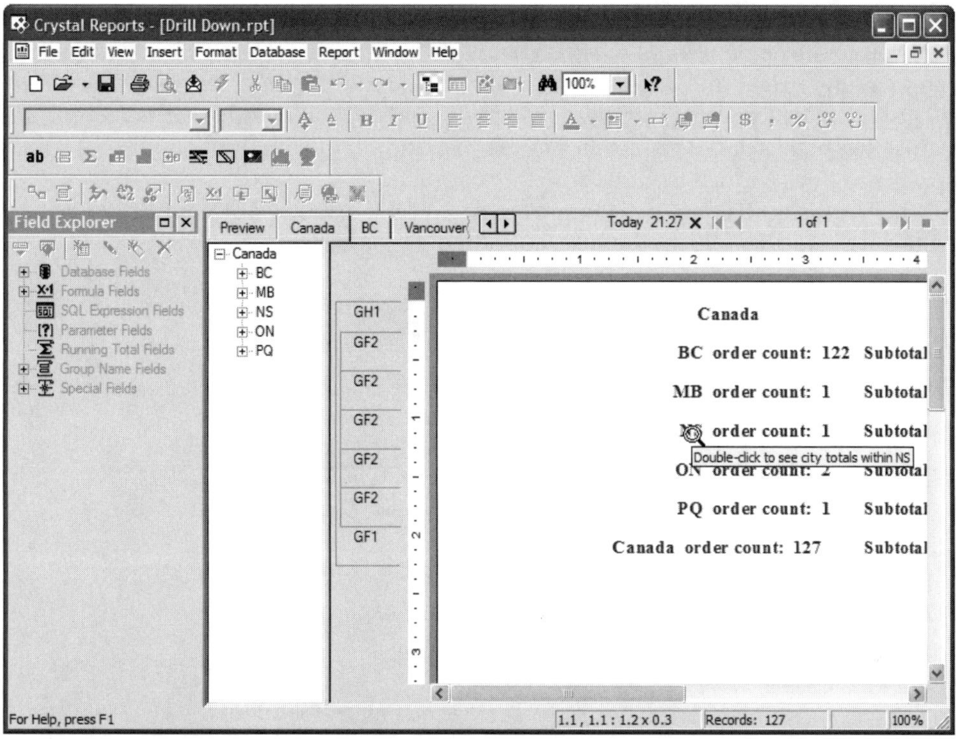

Figure 3-7.   *Drill-down report*

reports that start out showing only high-level data. A viewer will only want to see the lower-level groups and the detail when they drill down. Therefore, you'll want to hide the details section, as well as the lower-level group headers and group footers, to create a truly useful drill-down report. You'll see how to hide or suppress sections in Chapter 10.

> **Tip**   *Controlling detailed drill-down behavior, such as deciding if you want to show all higher-level group headers when you drill down, or whether to show a particular group header in some drill-down tabs, but not others, may require use of Crystal Reports formulas or conditional formatting. A new DrillDownGroupLevel function is available in Crystal Reports 9 to help with this custom drill-down behavior. Look in the Print State category of the Formula Workshop functions tree to find this new function. Formulas are covered in more detail in Chapter 5, and conditional formatting is covered in more detail in Chapters 9 and 10.*

Grouping on Date Fields

When you create report groups based on date fields, you probably don't want a new group to appear every time the date changes from one day to another. You may only want a new group for every week, month, or calendar quarter. You could create a complicated formula that breaks down groups in this manner and groups on the formula, but Crystal Reports provides a much easier way.

When you select a date field to group on, Crystal Reports automatically adds an additional drop-down list to the Insert Group dialog box.

```
Change Group Options                              [X]

 Common | Options |

 When the report is printed, the records will be sorted and
 grouped by:

 [ ▭ Orders.Order Date                        ▼ ]

 [ in ascending order.                         ▼ ]

 The section will be printed:

 [ for each month.                             ▼ ]
 ┌────────────────────────────────────┐
 │ for each day.                       │
 │ for each week.                      │
 │ for each two weeks.                 │
 │ for each half month.                │
 │ for each month.                     │
 │ for each quarter.   ⟍               │
 │ for each half year.                 │
 │ for each year.                      │
 │ for each second.                    │
 │ for each minute.                    │
 │ for each hour.                      │
 │ for AM/PM.                          │
 └────────────────────────────────────┘
```

You can choose how often a new group will be created by selecting the appropriate item from the list. Then click OK. The groups will now appear in the group tree for every month, quarter, year, or whatever period was chosen. The group name in the group header will indicate the beginning date for each group (the first month of the quarter, the first day of the week, and so forth).

Customizing Group Name Fields

The group name field takes on the Crystal Reports default format for the data type of the group field. For example, the default format for date fields is the same as your Windows default date format. Thus, a group name for a calendar quarter group may show up as 1/2001, 4/2001, and so on. What if you prefer the group names to appear as "January, 2001" and "April, 2001"?

You can format a group name field just like any other field or object. Click the group name field and then format it just like any other object (by using the Format menu, by using the Format toolbar button in the Expert Tools toolbar, or by right-clicking and using the pop-up menu). For a group name based on a date field, for example, you can choose how the month and year appear, as well as what character should be used as the separator between them.

However, you'll notice that even when you format the group name field as mentioned here, the group tree will not reflect the change. It continues to use the default formatting regardless of how you format the group name field. Also, you may find situations in which you want to show information for the group that is different from what is actually supplied by the field you group on. For example, you may be grouping by a fiscal month number in a database. You'll want to show the spelled-out month name despite the fact that the group tree and group headers will show the number (1 for January, 8 for August, and so on). Or, you may be grouping by employee number rather than employee name, to avoid the possibility of lumping employee data together for employees that share the same name. But, you still want the report to show the employee name instead of the number.

You may create a formula and group on it instead of the database field to accomplish this type of specialized group display. However, you'll often not get exactly the results you want (in the numeric month example mentioned previously, you will need to add the month number in front of the spelled-out month if you want to still show the months in chronological order). However, Crystal Reports provides the *customized group name field*, which gives you much more flexibility in controlling what the group tree and group header display.

You may customize the group name field when you initially create a group. Or, if you decide later that you'd like to customize the group name field in an existing group, you can change the group by using the Group Expert, or by right-clicking the appropriate group header or group footer gray section name and choosing Change Group from the pop-up menu. Once the Change Group Options dialog box appears, perform the following steps to customize the group name field:

1. Click the Options tab.

2. Click the Customize Group Name Field check box.

3. To choose an alternate database field to display (for example, if you'd like to show an employee name field instead of the employee number field the group is based on), click the Choose from Existing Field radio button and then pick the desired database field in the associated drop-down list.

4. To create a specialized formula to display instead of the field the group is based on, click the Use a Formula As Group Name radio button. Then, click the Conditional Formula button next to the radio button. The group name Formula Editor appears, in which you can create a string formula to display instead of the field the group is based on. For example, to show an employee's last name, a comma, and then the employee's first name, you could create the following formula:

```
{Employee.Last Name} & ", " & {Employee.First Name}
```

Look at Chapter 5 for details on creating formulas.

Grouping on Formula Fields

As your reports become more sophisticated, you'll find more and more often that you won't be able to create the groups you need just from database fields. You may be able to use specified order grouping, but even it is limited by its simple Select Expert—like approach. When your "creative grouping with database fields" runs out of steam, you need to create formula fields and group on them. Creating formula fields is covered in Chapter 5.

Grouping on a formula field is very simple (at least the grouping is, after you create the formula). The formula appears at the end of the list of report fields in the Insert Group or Change Group Options dialog box. Simply choose it as the field you wish to group on.

Although Crystal Reports 9 now allows you to create more than one group based on the same database field, users of previous versions will find a good example of when you might need to group based on a formula field in the geographic grouping case mentioned earlier in this chapter. If you're using an older version of Crystal Reports, suppose you want to first group by geographic location (Northwest, Southwest, and so on), and then within these groups you want to group on individual states or regions. That way, you'll be able to see group totals for both individual states and the higher-level geographic regions.

The problem is this: After you create the specified-order grouping based on the Customer.Region database field for the geographic groups, older Crystal Reports versions won't let you create a second group on the same database field in ascending order for the state groups. If you try to choose a database field that's already been grouped on, the OK button in the Insert Group or Change Group Options dialog box is disabled.

To solve this problem, here's a formula field called @Region that simply returns the Customer.Region database field.

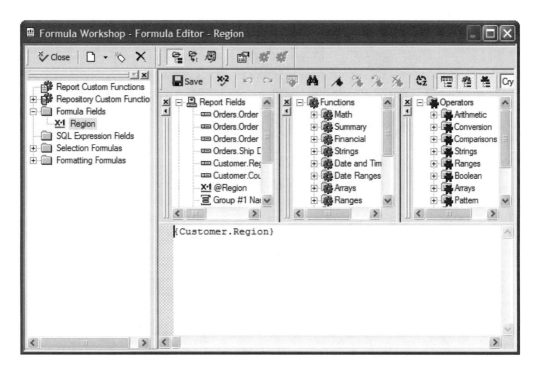

The @Region formula field can now be used instead of the database field to create the second group. Figure 3-6, shown earlier in the chapter, gives an example of two levels of grouping (specified order and regular grouping) using the same field—once directly from the database and once with a formula.

Caution   *Although you gain great flexibility when you group on a formula field, you may lose a little performance along the way. When you group on a database field, Crystal Reports can have the database server (SQL Server, Oracle, and so on) sort records in the proper group order before sending them to Crystal Reports. When you group on a formula field, the server won't be able to sort the records in advance, leaving that for Crystal Reports to do once the records begin to arrive from the server. You may or may not notice any performance degradation, depending on the size of the report and the speed of your computer. If you really want to maximize performance and still have a customized group, you may be able to substitute a SQL expression for a formula as the source for your group. SQL expressions are covered in Chapter 16.*

Top N Reporting

Figure 3-8 shows a typical order summary report by customer name. This is a great drill-down report example—the details section is hidden, and only the summary information for each customer is showing (hiding sections is covered in Chapter 8). This is a good report for the sales manager who is asked, "How did Clean Air Transportation Co. do last year?" All the viewer has to do is click Clean Air Transportation Co. in the group tree to go directly to its summaries.

However, what if the sales manager has ten boxes of Godiva chocolates that she wants to send to her ten best customers? Or, consider the new sales associate who's been assigned the task of visiting the 15 worst-performing customers to try to bolster sales. The report shown in Figure 3-8 is not very useful if you want to find the top 10 or bottom 15 customers. The sales manager and sales associate would be much happier with a Top *N* report.

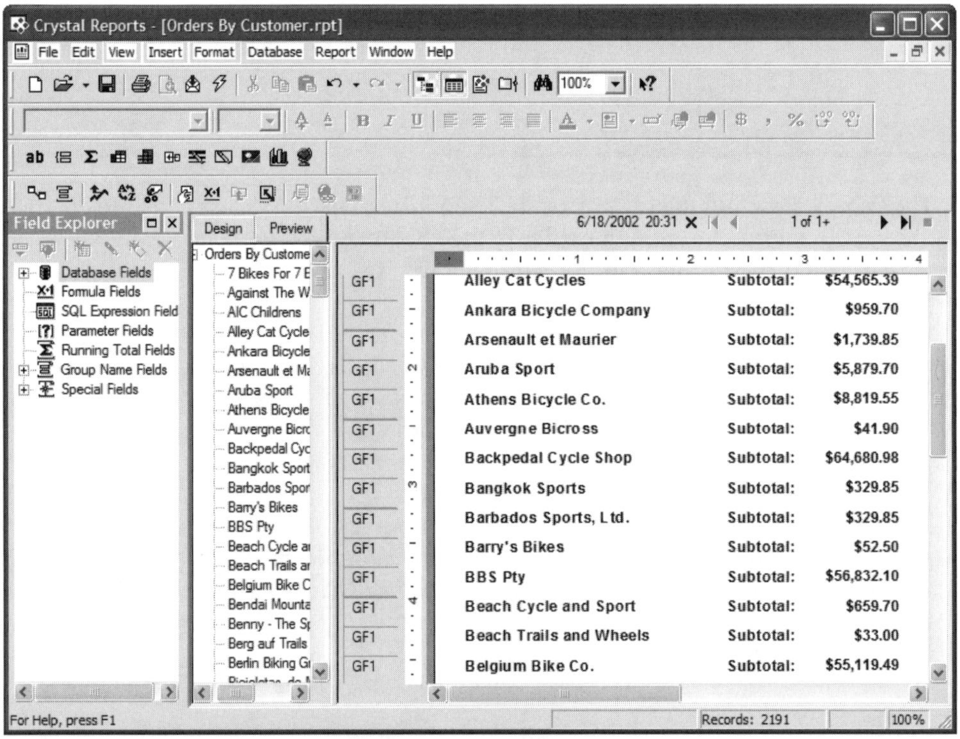

Figure 3-8.   *Order summary by customer*

A Top *N* report lets you sort your groups by a subtotal or summary function (subtotal of order amount, for example), instead of by the name of the group. That way, your groups will appear, for example, in order of highest to lowest sales or lowest to highest sales. In addition, Top *N* reporting enables you to see only the top or bottom *N* groups, where you specify the *N*.

Crystal Reports uses the Group Sort Expert (renamed from the previous "Top N/Sort Group Expert") to reorder your groups by a subtotal or summary. Choose this option from the pull-down menus by selecting Report | Group Sort Expert. You can also click the Group Sort Expert button in the Expert Tools toolbar. Or, finally, if you select a summary or subtotal in a group footer and click the Sort button on the Expert Tools toolbar, the Group Sort Expert will appear instead of the Record Sort Order dialog box.

The Group Sort Expert presents a tab for every group you've created on your report (provided that group has at least one summary created for it). Click the tab for the group that you want to reorder. When you first open the Group Sort Expert, the default setting for the first drop-down list is No Sort. This simply indicates that this group initially will not be a Top *N* group and that groups will appear in the order you chose when you created the groups. If none of the groups on your report have subtotal or summary fields in them, the Group Sort Expert won't be available, as it uses summary fields to sort the groups.

There are several choices available in the For This Group Sort drop-down list, including several new options added to Crystal Reports 9. Choose the desired option from the following choices:

All	Displays all groups on report, but uses one or more summary fields to determine the order of the groups. You have a choice of whether to show groups in ascending order (lowest to highest) or descending order (highest to lowest).
Top N	Displays only the top N (top 5, top 10) groups based on a summary field in order of highest to lowest.
Bottom N	Displays only the bottom N (bottom 5, bottom 10) based on a summary field in order of lowest to highest.
Top Percentage (new to Crystal Reports 9)	Displays the top N percent (top 10 percent, top 25 percent) of groups based on a summary field.
Bottom Percentage (new to Crystal Reports 9)	Displays the bottom N percent (bottom 10 percent, bottom 25 percent) of groups based on a summary field.

When you click the down arrow of the second drop-down list, you see all the summaries you've created for that group (only summaries you created with Insert Summary will be there—you won't see any formulas or other fields). Choose the one that you want the Top N report to be based on. For example, if you want to see the top ten customers according to last year's sales, choose Sum of Customer.Last Year's Sales. If you leave the first drop-down list set to All, all groups will remain on the report, but they will be sorted in ascending or descending order, based on the radio buttons at the bottom of the dialog box. If you want the groups sorted by more than one summary (for example, first by sum of order amount and then by count of order ID), select additional summaries from the drop-down list and choose an ascending or descending sort for each.

Tip   *Using the All option to sort groups in a different order can be a very innovative way to solve unique reporting problems. If you need to create a group based on one field but then have the groups appear in a different order, insert a summary field in the group footer based on the field you want to sort the groups by. Then, using the All option, choose the summary field you created.*

If you are only interested in the Top N, Bottom N, Top Percentage, or Bottom Percentage groups, change the first drop-down list from All to the desired choice. The second drop-down list enables you to select one summary or subtotal to use to sort the groups. Choose the summary you want to use. Once you've done that, type the value of N or the percentage in the appropriate text box. You also have a check box and text box that let you choose whether to include other groups not in the Top or Bottom N or percentage in the report. If you do include them, they will be lumped together in one other group with the name you type. If you want to not increment the N or percentage when group summaries are tied (this may change a top 10 to a top 12 if two of the groups are tied), check the Include Ties check box.

Using the Godiva and worst-performing customer example earlier:

- The sales manager's Godiva chocolate report would be Top N of Sum of Orders.Order Amount, where N is 10 and other groups are not included.

- The sales associate's follow-up visit report would be a Bottom N of Sum of Orders.Order Amount, where N is 15 and other groups are not included.

The following Top N report shows who will be getting chocolates this year:

If you wish to change the report from Top N to Bottom N, change the value of N, or remove the Top/Bottom N sorting altogether and show all of your groups sorted in the order you originally chose, simply redisplay the Group Sort Expert and change the values. Remember that a group will be sorted in its original ascending or descending order if you set the first drop-down list to No Sort.

Caution	*If you create a Top N report and don't include others, any grand totals you place in the report footer will still include all records on the report. If you want to include accurate grand totals in a Top N report, either include others or use a running total instead of grand totals (explained in Chapter 5).*

Hierarchical Groups

Crystal Reports also features *hierarchical groups,* which can be helpful in certain reporting situations where two fields relate to each other hierarchically. A specific example would be an organizational relationship between employees and supervisors, where the database would contain a single record containing both an employee ID and a supervisor ID. Without hierarchical grouping, creating an organizational chart utilizing this data would be difficult. While you could group by supervisor ID to see all the employees that reported to that supervisor, you still wouldn't see any hierarchical levels, where that supervisor would appear underneath *their* supervisor, and so forth.

With Crystal Reports, you may simply choose hierarchical grouping options to indicate the relationship between the two fields in the same set of data, and to specify how much indentation you wish to show between the hierarchies. As an example, you may create a simple report using the Employee table from the XTREME sample database included with Crystal Reports. If you create a group based on Employee ID, you'll simply see one group for each employee in the table. To show the reporting relationship among the employees, choose Report | Hierarchical Grouping Options. This displays the Hierarchical Options dialog box.

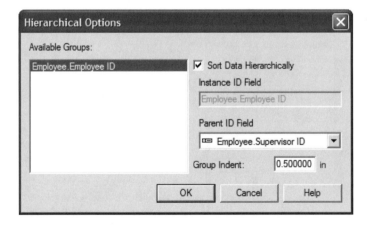

Choose the group (if there is more than one) for which you want to show the hierarchy. Then, click the Sort Data Hierarchically check box and choose the field that relates to the group field in the Parent ID Field drop-down list. Then, type the distance by which you wish to indent the lower-level hierarchies. Click OK.

The report will now create additional occurrences of groups to show the hierarchies created by the relationship of the two chosen fields. Here's an example of hierarchical reporting using the XTREME sample database:

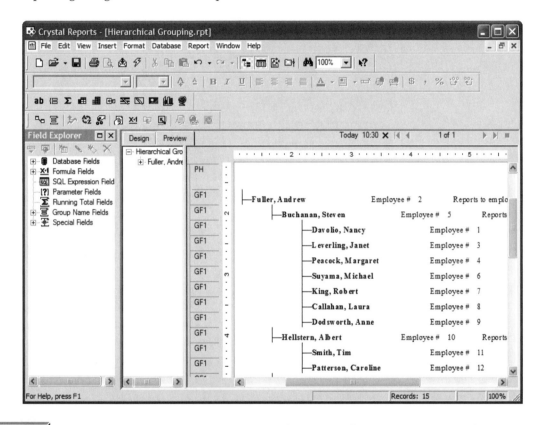

Note   *The lines in this illustration are not created automatically. You may use Crystal Reports' line drawing tools to create this kind of effect. This example also uses a customized group name field, to show the employee name instead of the employee number in the group tree and the report.*

Crystal Reports includes the ability to add subtotals or summaries in hierarchical groups. Once you've created your group hierarchy with the features discussed previously, just use the same Insert Summary feature covered earlier in the chapter to summarize data in hierarchical groups. The Summarize Across Hierarchy check box will appear.

The Complete Reference

Crystal Reports 9

Chapter 4

Creating Geographic Maps

C rystal Decisions retains the Geographic Map feature in Crystal Reports 9, although no major changes in this feature appear. Your reports can include not only textual information (for example, states, cities, and sales totals), but also a colorful map that, for example, plots sales totals by state. Using maps, you can display information in a way that helps to analyze geographical data more easily. In addition to regular groups and details section fields, Crystal Report allows you to create maps based on online analytical processing (OLAP) grids and groups using specified order grouping.

Different Map Types

Crystal Reports provides five different types of maps. The type you should choose depends on the data that you'll be depicting in the map and the way you wish to show it. Table 4-1 discusses the different types of maps and their uses.

Caution *Crystal Reports 9 contains a limited number of maps. If you use a field that Crystal Reports can't resolve to an existing map, the map may not show any meaningful data, or it may show up as a blank area on your report. Crystal Reports mapping modules are provided by a third party, MapInfo. You may also get more information from MapInfo at http://www.mapinfo.com.*

- **Group map** Requires you to use existing groups with their subtotals and summaries for the map. A report grouped by country, for example, can be used to show the concentration of customers by country if you include a summary function that counts customers for each group.

- **Advanced map** Allows you to create a map based on data in the report's details section. You may have a detail report containing a sales figure for each customer. If you include the state each customer is in, you can create an advanced map based on the state and the amount of sales for that state. The map will show how sales compare by state. In effect, the map will group and subtotal your records by state, even if no state group exists on the report. You also would use an advanced map when you need to map multiple values per geographic region (as in the pie chart and bar chart explained in Table 4-1).

- **Cross-Tab map or OLAP map** Plots data from a cross-tab object (covered in Chapter 11) or an OLAP grid (covered in Chapter 18). The cross-tab object must have at least one row or column field that's based on a geographic item, such as a country or state. OLAP grids must have a certain type and organization of dimensions (see "OLAP Maps" later in the chapter for details). Because cross-tabs and OLAP grids can contain multiple summary fields, you can use them to create pie chart or bar chart maps.

Map Type	Description	Uses and Comments
Ranged	Assigns different colors to ranges of numbers. For example, a state that contains over $500,000 in sales would be bright red, a state that contains between $250,000 and $500,000 in sales would be orange, and a state that contains less than $250,000 in sales would be a deep magenta.	Useful for comparing different regions or countries to each other by shade or color. There are four ways to choose how the ranges are colored: **Equal count** Evenly divides the number of map ranges so that an equal number (or as close as possible to an equal number) of mapped values appear in each range. This avoids map views containing almost all one color, which may occur if the data you are mapping is heavily concentrated on the low or high end of the overall range of values. **Equal ranges** Divides the map ranges by the summary numbers being shown on the map. This option assigns equal ranges of summary values, regardless of how many groups or regions make up each range. **Natural break** Also uses the summary numbers to determine map ranges, but bases range breakdowns on the average amounts of the ranges. **Standard deviation** Divides the map ranges such that the middle interval breaks at the average of the summary values. The ranges above and below the middle break at one "standard deviation" above or below the middle.
Dot density	Displays a dot on the map for every occurrence of the item being mapped. A higher concentration of dots appears in areas of the map that have the most occurrences.	Used to show a concentration of activity (for example, quantities or subtotals) in certain states or countries.
Graduated	A symbol (a circle, by default) represents data, and the size of the symbol is based on the concentration or level of the amount: small amounts are represented by small circles, large amounts by large ones.	Shows just one symbol per country, state, etc., but shows a different size depending on the number the map is based on. The default symbol is a circle, but you can choose from other characters, as well as apply special effects (for example, a drop shadow, halo, etc.) to the symbol.

Table 4-1.   *Crystal Reports Map Types*

Map Type	Description	Uses and Comments
Pie chart	Displays a pie chart over the related geographic area.	Only useful when comparing multiple related data points for the same geographic area. A pie chart is better for comparing items against each other, where all items total 100 percent. For example, if you are graphing sales by account rep, grouped by state, you would see a pie chart on each state showing how much of the "state pie" each rep has.
Bar chart	Displays a bar chart over the related geographic area.	Only useful when comparing multiple related data points for the same geographic area. A bar chart is better for comparing items over time, or other comparisons that aren't "piece of the pie" oriented. For example, if you are graphing sales for the past five years, grouped by state, you would see a bar chart on each state comparing the sales for the past five years.

Table 4-1. *Crystal Reports Map Types* (continued)

Adding a Map

To insert a map on your report, choose Insert | Map from the pull-down menus, or click the Insert Map button on the Insert Tools toolbar. The Map Expert appears, containing three main tabs: Data, Type, and Text.

The Data Tab

The Data tab is where you choose the type of map you want to create, as well as the fields and summaries from the report that you want to base your map on.

Group Maps

To create a group map, click the Group button on the Data tab.

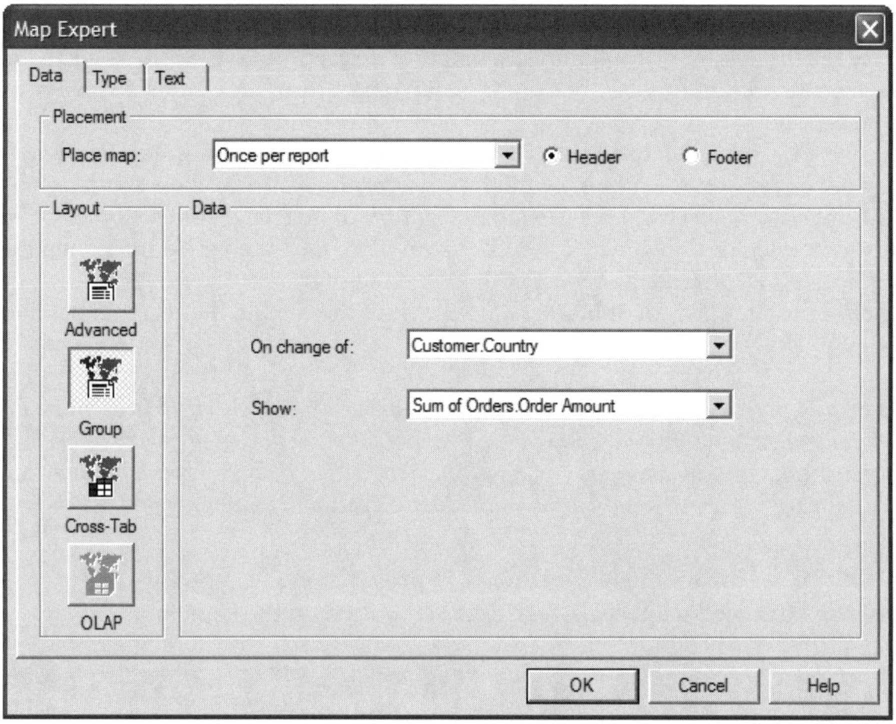

Map Expert

Data | Type | Text

Placement

Place map: Once per report ▼ ⊙ Header ○ Footer

Layout

Advanced
Group
Cross-Tab
OLAP

Data

On change of: Customer.Country ▼

Show: Sum of Orders.Order Amount ▼

OK | Cancel | Help

The Place Map drop-down list lets you choose how often you want the map to appear on the report. The options in this list will vary according to how many groups you have on your report. If you only have one group on your report, the only option available in the drop-down list is Once per Report. If you have more than one group, you also have For Each *Group Field* options for every group, *except* for the bottom-level group, because you must always place a map at least one level higher in your report than the group your map is based on.

For example, if you only have a state group on your report, the only option for a group map is Once per Report, because you must have the map at a level higher than the group. However, if you have a country group, and a region group within the country group, the drop-down list allows you to choose Once per Report or For Each Customer.Country. If you choose this lower country level, you'll have a map appearing in every country group, showing the geographic breakdown *by region* for that country.

You can then choose whether to have Crystal Reports initially place the map in the group or report header or footer, by clicking the desired radio button. After the map has been created initially, you can drag the map object from the header to the footer, or vice versa.

Use the On Change Of drop-down list to choose the geographic group that you want the map to be based on. Continuing with the above example, if you choose once per report then the options are on change of Customer.Country or on change of Customer.Country and Customer.Region. However, if you choose to place the map per country, then the only option in the On Change Of list is Customer.Region.

Choose the summary or subtotal field you want the map to depict from the Show drop-down list.

Tip	*Because Group Maps must be based on a summary or subtotal field in a group, any groups that don't have at least one subtotal or summary field won't show up in the Map Expert. If you only have one group on your report, and it doesn't contain a subtotal or summary field, the Group button in the Map Expert will be dimmed.*

Advanced Maps

To create an advanced map, click the Advanced button on the Data tab.

The Place Map drop-down list lets you choose how often you want the map to appear on the report. The options in this list will vary according to how many groups (if any) you have on your report. If there are no groups, the only option available in the drop-down list is Once per Report. If you have one or more groups, you also have For Each *Group Field* options for every group.

You can then choose whether to have Crystal Reports initially place the map in the group or report header or footer, by clicking the desired radio button. You are also free to drag the map object from the header to the footer, or vice versa, after the map has been created.

The Available Fields list contains all the report, database, and formula fields available for the map. Choose the geographic field that you want your map to use, and then click the right arrow next to the Geographic Field box to choose the field. The same field will also automatically be placed in the On Change Of box. If you wish to just summarize values for the geographic field (for a range or dot density map, for example), simply leave the same field in the two boxes. If, however, you wish to show a pie or bar chart on the map for another field (for example, to show a pie chart in each country comparing states), then choose the field you want to "compare" in the Available Fields list and click the right arrow next to the On Change Of text box. Finally, click one or more fields (using CTRL-click or SHIFT-click) in the Available Fields list that you want summarized in the map. Use the right arrow next to the Map Values box to add them. If you wish to remove a Map Value field or fields, click it in the Map Values box and click the left arrow. If you wish to remove all the Map Value fields, click the double left arrow.

Even though this is an advanced map (based on individual report records in the detail section), Crystal Reports still summarizes values by default, as though report groups exist for the fields you've placed in the Geographic Field and On Change Of boxes. You can choose the summary function (Sum, Average, Count, and so on) you want the map to use when summarizing the detail fields you've added to the Map Values box. Select a field in the box, click the Set Summary Operation button, and choose the function (Sum, Average, Count, and so on) that you wish to use.

Crystal Reports mapping can sometimes be particular about the geographic field you base your map on. For example, if the field contains USA, the map will recognize it. If it just contains US, the map won't recognize it. The same holds true for state names. Two-letter abbreviations and completely spelled state names are recognized, whereas inconsistently abbreviated state names or standard two-letter state names followed by periods may not be recognized. Sometimes you'll need to experiment, and in some cases, you may want to create a formula (discussed in Chapter 5) that changes the way the geographic data is presented, and then base the map on the formula field. Also, Crystal Reports 9 provides the ability to resolve data mismatches that exist between the geographic names that maps recognize and the actual data in the database (see "Resolving Data Mismatches" later in the chapter).

Tip   *If you add a nonnumeric field to the Map Values box, it is automatically summarized with a count function. The only other choice in the Change Summary Operation list is DistinctCount.*

Cross-Tab Maps

To create a cross-tab map, click the Cross-Tab button on the Data tab (this button will be greyed out unless you have a Cross-Tab object in your report).

The Place Map drop-down list will be dimmed, because you must place the map on the same level as the cross-tab (in the same group, once per report, and so forth). You can choose whether to have Crystal Reports initially place the map in the group or report header or footer, by clicking the desired radio button. You can also drag the map object from the header to the footer, or vice versa, after the map has been created.

In the Geographic Field drop-down list, choose the row or column of the cross-tab that contains the geographic field the map will be based on. If you want the cross-tab to be mapped as a pie or bar chart map, choose the other row or column in the Subdivided By drop-down list. In the Map On drop-down list, choose the summary field from the cross-tab that you want depicted. If you have multiple summary fields, you'll have multiple options here.

OLAP Maps

To create an OLAP map, click the OLAP button on the Data tab.

The Place Map drop-down list will be dimmed, because you must place the map on the same level as the OLAP grid (in the same group, once per report, and so forth). You can choose whether to have Crystal Reports initially place the map in the group or report header or footer, by clicking the desired radio button. You can also drag the map object from the header to the footer, or vice versa, after the map has been created.

In the On Change Of drop-down list, choose the dimension of the OLAP grid that contains the geographic field the map will be based on (this may be a "lower-level" dimension; go back and look at the results of your OLAP grid if you're unsure where the geographic data is). If you want the OLAP grid to be mapped as a pie or bar chart map, choose another dimension in the Subdivided By drop-down list.

Note *Cross-tab and OLAP maps aren't available if you don't already have a cross-tab or OLAP grid on the report before you launch the Map Expert. The Cross-Tab and OLAP buttons will be dimmed in the Map Expert in these cases.*

The Type Tab

After you've chosen the data elements for your map, click the Type tab to choose the type of map you want to display. Click one of the following buttons to select a map type:

- **Ranged** Presents options for a ranged map, including how many intervals the map will contain, how the intervals are broken down, the beginning and ending color for the intervals, and whether the map should show empty intervals.

- **Dot Density** Enables you to choose large or small dots for the map.

- **Graduated** Presents the symbol used for the graduated map. A circle symbol is chosen by default, but you can click the Customize button to change the symbol and color and add special effects to the symbol, such as a halo or drop shadow.

- **Pie Chart** Presents options for a pie chart map. You can choose small, medium, or large pies. If you click the Proportional Sizing check box, the pies will be sized according to the quantities contained in the data being mapped: larger quantities create larger pies, and smaller quantities create smaller pies.

- **Bar Chart** Enables you to choose the size of the bars: large, medium, or small.

Tip *You are restricted to either the first three or the second two buttons, depending on how many data elements you've chosen for your map. If you chose only one data element to map, you can use only the Ranged, Dot Density, or Graduated option. If your map contains multiple elements from a detail report, or you chose a Subdivided By item with a cross-tab object or OLAP grid, you can use only the Pie Chart or Bar Chart option.*

The Text Tab

The Text tab lets you customize textual elements, such as the title and legend, which appear with the map. Type in the Map Title box the title you wish the map to display.

Crystal Reports automatically creates a legend for the map. You can choose whether to display a full legend, a compact legend, or no legend at all by clicking the appropriate radio button. If you choose to include a legend, you can display the map-generated legend or specify your own by using the radio buttons and text boxes in the Legend Title section.

After you choose all the necessary options, click OK. Crystal Reports creates the map and places it in the report or group header or footer that you specified. To modify an existing map, simply click the map to select it in either the Design or Preview tab. Then, choose Format | Map Expert from the pull-down menus or right-click the map and choose Map Expert from the pop-up menu.

Drilling Down on Maps

Crystal Reports lets you drill down on Group maps, just like on group names and summaries (discussed in Chapter 3) and on charts and graphs (covered in Chapter 12). When you view a map in the Preview tab, simply point your mouse to the geographic region you wish to look at in more detail. The mouse cursor turns into a magnifying glass. Double-click the desired area of the map to open up a drill-down tab next to the Preview tab. This drill-down tab will contain just the information for the report group represented by that map segment. If you attempt to drill-down on a geographic element that doesn't include any data (perhaps you double-click on a city that's plotted on a map, but there's no group for that city), you'll receive a message indicating the lack of detail data for that city.

To close a drill-down tab, click the red X that appears next to the page navigation buttons on the right side of the preview window. The current tab closes and the next tab to the left is displayed.

Tip *Because an Advanced map is already mapping the lowest level of information on your report, you cannot drill down on this type of map. Nor can you drill down into Cross-Tab or OLAP maps.*

Changing the Map View

While viewing a particular map, you may wish to change your "view" of the map, such as zooming in or out on the map, or panning left, right, up, or down on the map. You may do this by selecting the map you want to change the view of and choosing options from the Map pull-down menu. Or, simply right-click on the map in the Preview tab and choose options from the pop-up menu.

Map:
Map Expert...
🗐 Forma**t** Map...
Move ▶
Si**z**e and Position...
🔍 Se**l**ect Mode
🔍 Zoom **I**n
🔍 Zoo**m** Out
⬌ **P**an
✕ **C**enter Map
Ti**t**le...
🖘 T**y**pe...
🥞 La**y**ers...
▦ Re**s**olve Mismatch...
✔ Map **N**avigator
✂ Cut
🗈 Copy
Delete
Cancel Menu

■ **To zoom in on a map**   Choose the Zoom In option. This will change the mouse cursor to a magnifying glass with a plus sign. Draw an elastic box around the portion of the map you want to zoom in on. The map will resize to show your chosen area.

■ **To zoom out from the map**   Choose the Zoom Out option. This will change the mouse cursor to a magnifying glass with a minus sign. Every time you click on the map, it will zoom out a predetermined level.

■ **To pan left, right, up, or down**   Choose the Pan option. This will change the mouse cursor to an arrow/pan cursor. Hold down the mouse button on the map and move your mouse left, right, up, or down. The map will reposition accordingly.

■ **To recenter the map to its original position**   Choose the Center Map option.

The Map Navigator

Another way to change your view of a map in Crystal Reports 9 is the Map Navigator. When you click on a map to select it in the Preview tab, a smaller "thumbnail" of the map appears in its own window in the lower right of the map. You may drag the Map Navigator by its title bar to move it around inside the map, as well as resize the window by dragging a border of the window.

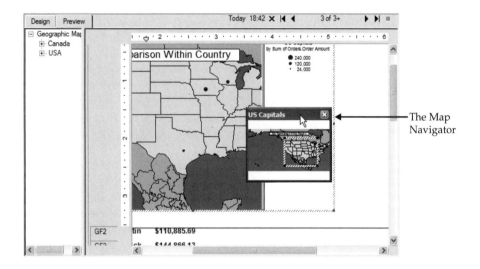

The Map
Navigator

A shaded outline in the Map Navigator shows the portion of the map that you see in the rest of the map view. If you zoom in or out on the map (using the pop-up menu options), the outline shrinks or expands, outlining the zoomed-in portion of the map. You can also use the outline in the Map Navigator to zoom in, zoom out, and pan the view to a particular area of the map. If you point inside the outline, your mouse cursor changes to a four-arrow move cursor; simply drag the outline around to pan to a different area of the map. If you point to a corner of the outline, the mouse cursor changes into a diagonal two-arrow cursor. Drag the corner to expand or contract the outline. This zooms in or out on the map.

You may hide the Map Navigator by clicking the X on its upper right-hand corner. However, if you then deselect and reselect the map, the Map Navigator will return. If you want to turn the Map Navigator display off on a more permanent basis for all instances of maps, you may uncheck the Map Navigator option in the Map pull-down menu or pop-up menu that appears when you right-click on a map.

Note   *The Map Analyzer, an additional view of a map that can appear in its own separate tab beside the Preview tab, has been eliminated from Crystal Reports 9. However, you can view maps in the Map Analyzer in Crystal Reports versions 8 and 8.5.*

Resolving Data Mismatches

One of the serious limitations of geographic maps when they were initially introduced with Crystal Reports 7 was the inability to resolve mismatches of geographic data in the database to what the map would understand. If your database contained, for example, spelled-out state names instead of two-letter abbreviations, the map would not be able to resolve the names to actual states. Crystal Reports 8 and later have improved on this limitation somewhat by allowing you to resolve data mismatches that may cause database data to be improperly mapped, or not mapped at all.

If you suspect that the map may not be interpreting database data correctly, first select the map that you wish to work with in the Preview tab (you can't resolve data mismatches in the Design tab). Then, choose Map | Resolve Mismatch from the pull-down menus or right-click on the map and choose Resolve Mismatch from the pop-up menu. This will display the Resolve Map Mismatch dialog box, with the Change Map tab shown first.

The map definition used to display the particular map you are working with will appear as both the "current map" and will be selected in the Available maps list. If you wish to display a different map definition, scroll through the list of available maps and choose another map. If, however, the mismatch involves a misspelling or misinterpretation of a particular country, state, city, or other geographical field, you'll need to resolve the mismatch on the Resolve Mismatch tab, shown in Figure 4-1 (it may take some time for this tab to appear, as Crystal Reports must build several lists on-the-fly when you choose this tab).

You'll notice that any database values that have already been matched to map values by Crystal Reports will appear in the Match Results list. However, if there are database values that could not be matched, they will appear in the Assign This Field Name list in the upper left-hand corner. And, you'll find a list of all the available geographic values that the map understands in the To This Map Name list in the upper right-hand corner.

To match an unmatched database value to a map value, select the value you want to match in the Assign This Field name list. Then, scroll up and down in the To This Map Name list until you find the substitute data, which you can then select (typing letters on the keyboard will often select items in the list more quickly than using the scroll bar). Click the Match button, which adds the match to the Matched Results list. Each match you create is added to the bottom list, along with all assignments that Crystal Reports made previously. If you decide that you don't want to use an assignment (that either you made or was made automatically), select it in the Matched Results list and click the Unmatch button.

When you're finished assigning values, click the OK button to show the map with the updated mapping assignments.

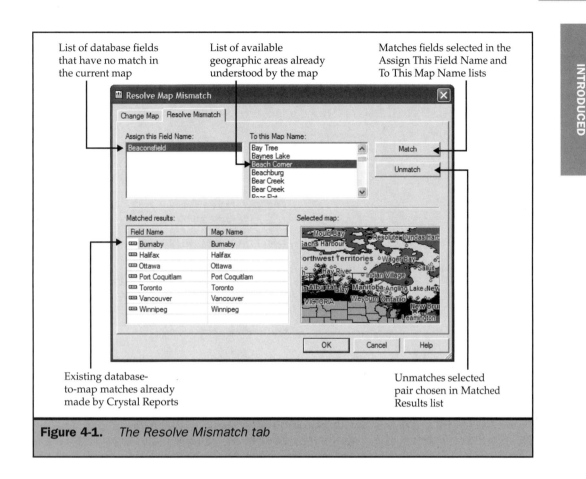

List of database fields that have no match in the current map

List of available geographic areas already understood by the map

Matches fields selected in the Assign This Field Name and To This Map Name lists

Existing database-to-map matches already made by Crystal Reports

Unmatches selected pair chosen in Matched Results list

Figure 4-1. *The Resolve Mismatch tab*

Map Layers

A map is displayed in the Preview tab using *layers*. If you are looking at a USA map, for example, the map may be composed of layers consisting of USA, US Highways, and US Major Cities. You can think of a map layer as a transparency containing just that layer's information that lies on top of the lower layers, which lie on top of the map. By using layers, the map can be displayed showing different levels of detail, usually determined by how far in the map is zoomed. If you are fully zoomed out on the map, you'll only see the states. As you zoom in, you eventually see highways appear across the states. And, as you zoom in even further, you see dots and the names of cities within the states.

Although maps include layers in a default order with default settings, you can choose which layers to display, hide, include, or not include. You can also change the order in which the layers "lie" on the map, and change the zoom level at which layers become visible. To work with map layers, select the map you wish to work with in the Preview tab (you can't work with layers in the Design tab). Then, choose Map | Layers from the pull-down menus, or right-click on the map and choose Layers from the pop-up menu. The Layer Control dialog box is displayed here.

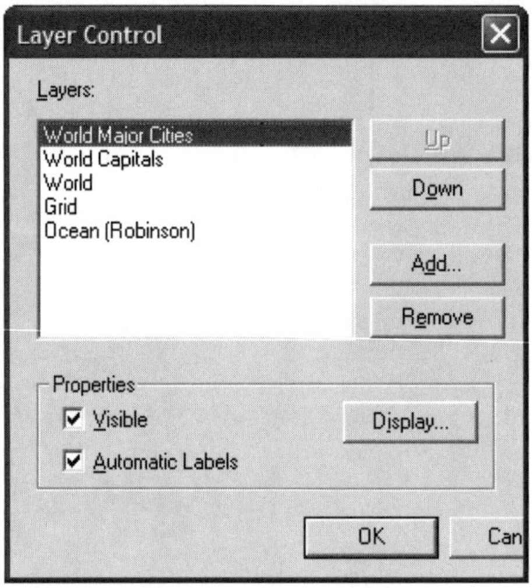

Note   *The Layers dialog box is malformed in the initial release of Crystal Reports 9 but may be repaired in maintenance releases.*

You see all the layers included in the map by default. You can change the order in which the layers appear by selecting an individual layer and then clicking the Up or Down button to change the order of the layers. If you want to hide a layer so that it doesn't show in the map, select the layer and clear the Visible check box. If you decide that you no longer want the layer at all, select it and click the Remove button.

If you later decide you want to redisplay a layer you removed earlier, or you want to add a new layer not already on the map, click the Add button. A File Open dialog box appears. Additional layers are located in \PROGRAM FILES\MAPINFO MAPX\ MAPS. Point to that folder and look for the appropriate .TAB file. After you choose it, it appears in the Layer Control dialog box.

To change the zoom level at which a layer appears, select the layer and click the Display button. The Display Properties dialog box for that layer opens.

If you uncheck Display Within Zoom Range, the layer appears in the map at all times, regardless of the Zoom level. If you leave it checked, you can set the minimum and maximum Zoom levels at which the layer will become visible. After you make your choices, you can zoom in or out on the map to see the layer changes.

Figure 4-2 shows the same map at the same Zoom level with different settings for the US Highways layer.

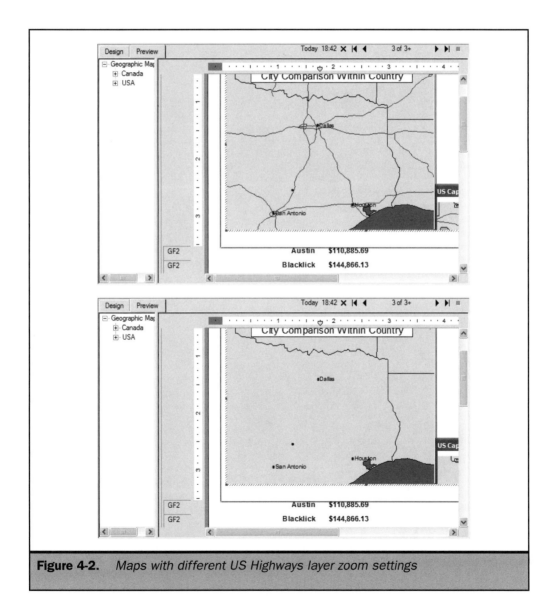

Figure 4-2.   *Maps with different US Highways layer zoom settings*

Chapter 5

Using Formulas

When you first start using Crystal Reports, you'll be able to write some simple reports using data that comes entirely from the database. You simply drag fields from the Field Explorer onto the report, and away you go. However, it won't be long until you find that you want some information to appear on your report that isn't contained in the database. Or, you may find that you want to display a field differently on the report than it appears in the database. For these, and many similar situations, use Crystal Reports *formulas*.

A formula can be thought of as a math calculation or a small piece of computer programming code. If you're not used to them at first, creating formulas can appear to be very complicated. Depending on your background, you may like the fact that some formulas are very much like programming, or this may be one characteristic of formulas that you would prefer not to deal with. Formulas can be as simple or as complex as you want to make them—you can start with simple math computations and, as you get more comfortable, graduate to full Basic-like formulas using Case statements, variables, and other advanced programming techniques. You can even share your formula expertise with your coworkers using new Crystal Reports 9 custom functions (covered in Chapter 6) and the Repository (covered in Chapter 7). Formulas bring the ultimate power and flexibility to Crystal Reports.

You can create formulas with either the Design or the Preview tab displayed, although creating them in the Design tab is probably better because you will have a more accurate idea of where the formulas will really end up when you place them on your report. You may create a new formula or modify an existing formula in two places in Crystal Reports—either the Field Explorer's Formula Fields category or from the new Formula Workshop.

The Formula Workshop

The *Formula Workshop,* new in Crystal Reports 9, is a dialog box that presents a unified approach to examining, creating, and modifying different types of formulas in your reports. With the addition of report custom functions (covered in Chapter 6) and the ability to store functions in the central repository (covered in Chapter 7), the Formula Workshop is a good way to easily access these new features, as well as other formulas used for report calculations and customization, record and group selection, and custom formatting.

To display the Formula Workshop, either choose Report | Formula Workshop from the mail pull-down menus, or click the Formula Workshop toolbar button from the Expert Tools toolbar. The Formula Workshop will appear, as shown in Figure 5-1.

The Formula Workshop consists of a folder "tree" view on the left, a toolbar on the top, and a large area below the toolbar and to the right of the tree view where the

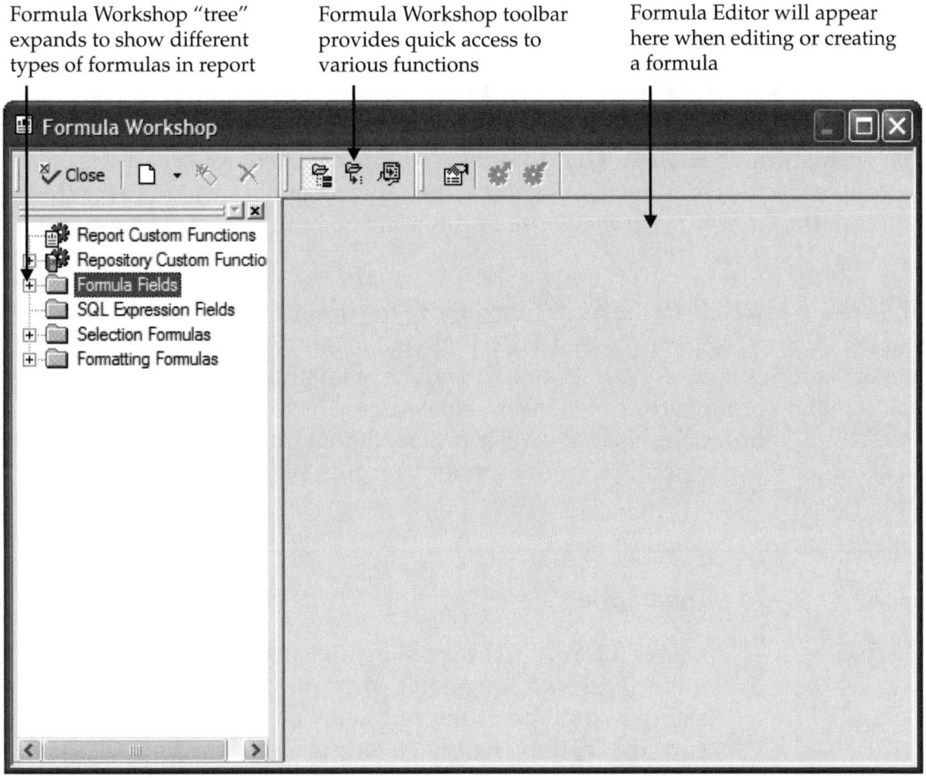

Formula Workshop "tree"
expands to show different
types of formulas in report

Formula Workshop toolbar
provides quick access to
various functions

Formula Editor will appear
here when editing or creating
a formula

Figure 5-1.   *The Formula Workshop*

Formula Expert or Formula Editor (both discussed later in the chapter) will appear
when actually working with a formula.

The tree view contains a list of formula categories available in the Formula Workshop.

- **Report Custom Functions**   "Sharable" functions that can be used by any
  formula in your report (covered in Chapter 6).

- **Repository custom functions**   "Sharable" functions that have been saved in
  the repository to be used by every copy of Crystal Reports connected to the
  repository (the repository is covered in Chapter 7).

- **Formula Fields**   Formulas that you create for use in just this report (covered
  in the rest of this chapter).

■ **SQL expression fields**   Server-based formulas, using the Structured Query Language (covered in Chapter 16).

■ **Selection formulas**   Formulas used to control record and group selection. These are the same formulas created using the Select Expert, or the Report I Selection Formulas pull-down menu options (covered in Chapter 8).

■ **Formatting formulas**   Formulas that set appearance of report objects and sections conditionally. These are the same formulas created using the conditional buttons in the Format Editor and Section Expert (covered in Chapters 9 and 10).

If there are available formulas or functions in the desired category, a plus sign will appear next to that category—just click the plus sign to open up that category and show the available formulas or functions in it. That there is no plus sign next to a category indicates that no formulas or functions in that category have yet been created.

As Table 5-1 shows, the Formula Workshop toolbar at the top of the dialog box provides quick ways to perform more common Formula Workshop options.

Icon	Description
✕✓ Close	Closes the Formula Workshop and any formula you may be currently working on. If you have made changes without saving, you'll be prompted whether or not you want to save the formula before closing. You may also close the Formula Workshop by clicking the X in the window's upper right-hand corner.
or CTRL-N	Creates a new formula. If you click the button directly, you'll create a new formula or function based on the category selected in the tree view. If you click the small down arrow next to the button, you'll be given a choice of type of formula to create. You may also create a new formula by right-clicking the desired tree view category and choosing New from the pop-up menu.
or F2	Renames the formula currently selected in the tree view. Clicking this button will place the formula name in the tree view in Edit mode. You may also rename a formula by right-clicking the formula in the tree view and choosing Rename from the pop-up menu.

Table 5-1.   *Formula Workshop Toolbar Buttons*

Icon	Description
✕ or DEL	Deletes the formula from the Formula Workshop and the report. You may be notified that the formula is being used in the report or that repository function deletions can't be undone and asked to confirm the deletion. You may also delete by right-clicking the formula in the tree view and choosing Delete from the pop-up menu.
	Toggles display of the Formula Workshop tree view on and off.
	Expands or contracts the folder you currently have selected in the tree view. For example, if you have the Formula Fields folder selected, clicking this button will open that category and show all the report formulas within the category. Clicking the button again will close the category, showing just the folder with a plus sign next to it.
	Toggles between showing all Formatting Formula category report objects in the report or only those objects that already contain formatting formulas. For example, if you click this button while viewing the expanded Formatting Formulas category, a limited set of report objects will appear (or none, if there are no existing formatting formulas in the report). This button affects only the Formatting Formulas category in the tree view.
	Toggles between viewing the actual code of a selected custom function or the custom function's properties (such as arguments, author, and so forth). See Chapter 6 for more information on this button.
	Adds the selected report custom function to the repository (see Chapter 7 for more information on adding your own custom functions to the repository).
	Copies the selected repository custom function to the current report. The custom function will then appear in the Custom Functions portion of the Formula Editor functions tree. See Chapter 7 for more information on adding repository custom functions to your report.

Table 5-1.   *Formula Workshop Toolbar Buttons* (continued)

Not all of the toolbar buttons will be enabled all of the time. Certain buttons and their functions are enabled only when an appropriate formula is selected in the tree view. For example, you can't rename custom functions in the repository or click the Delete button when the record selection formula is highlighted.

> **Tip**   *The Formula Workshop toolbar actually consists of three separate toolbars, each of which can be "undocked" from the top of the Formula Workshop window. Just click on the small gray vertical bar to the left of the different parts of the toolbar and drag to a new location.*

You're not limited to using the Formula Workshop to create, rename, and delete formulas. You can also use the Field Explorer. By choosing the Formula Fields category of the Field Explorer, you can access Field Explorer toolbar buttons, right-click pop-up menus, and keyboard shortcuts as well. Accordingly, there are numerous ways to create a new report formula by using the Field Explorer's Formula Fields category or the Formula Workshop. Once you've chosen to create a new formula, you'll be asked to supply a formula name. Remember, you're *not* creating a file on disk when you add a formula, so you don't need to worry about file-naming conventions—the formula is simply stored inside the .RPT file of your report. Your formula names can contain upper- and lowercase letters, spaces, and anything else that makes them descriptive. Use an easy-to-understand formula name—not only does it help you to recognize what the formula is when you look at the list of formulas you've created, but it also is used for the field title when you place a formula in the details section.

In Crystal Reports 9, you now have two buttons available at the bottom of the Formula Name dialog box: Use Expert, and Use Editor. Clicking the Use Expert button will create the formula using the Formula Expert, which is new to Crystal Reports 9. If you choose the Use Editor button, you'll be able to create your formula in the Formula Editor, which is largely unchanged from previous Crystal Reports versions.

The Formula Expert

If, after naming your formula, you click the Use Expert button, the Formula Expert will appear, as shown in Figure 5-2. This expert is designed to help you create a formula without having to use the Crystal Reports formula language. While this sounds tempting to those who may, at least initially, be slightly put off by the Crystal formula language, the Formula Expert immediately introduces one substantial caveat: only formulas using a custom function can be created in the expert. If you want to create a formula using regular Crystal Reports formula language functions or math operators, the Formula Expert won't provide appropriate capabilities. And even if you are using a custom function, the Formula Expert won't allow you to enclose it inside another custom function or use the custom function with any other Crystal Reports formula language syntax. In any situation where you can't use the Formula Expert, you'll need to use the Formula Editor to create your desired formula.

CRYSTAL REPORTS 9
INTRODUCED

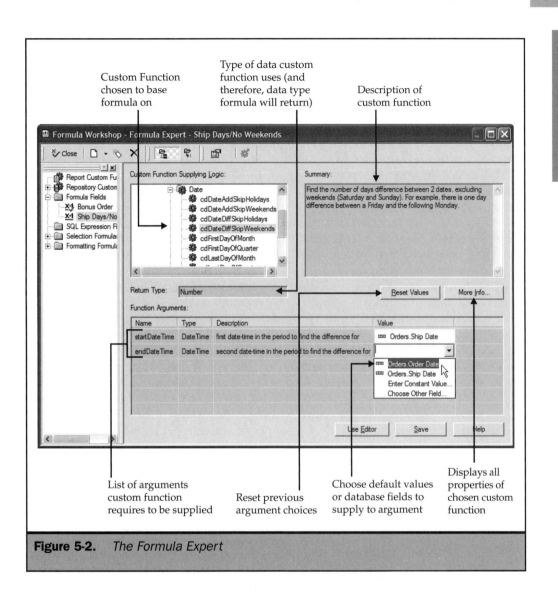

Custom Function chosen to base formula on

Type of data custom function uses (and therefore, data type formula will return)

Description of custom function

List of arguments custom function requires to be supplied

Reset previous argument choices

Choose default values or database fields to supply to argument

Displays all properties of chosen custom function

Figure 5-2.   *The Formula Expert*

The first step in using the Format Expert is to determine the custom function you want to base your formula on. Choose this function in the Custom Function Supplying Logic list. You may choose a function from either the Report Custom Functions category (these are custom functions that are already part of your report) or the Repository Custom Functions category (these are custom functions that reside in the repository you are currently connected to). In either case, click the plus sign next to the desired category and navigate through the tree until you find the desired custom function you wish to use. Once you select that custom function, a description of the function will appear in the Summary area, the data type that the function will return (string, number, and so forth) will appear in the Return Type area, and any necessary parameters or *arguments* that the function requires to be supplied will be added to the Function Arguments area at the bottom of the Formula Expert.

Then, simply choose the database fields, other formula fields, or typed-in values that you want to supply as arguments to the custom function. You may do this by typing in a number, string, date, or other value directly in the Value area for the desired argument. Or, if you click the down arrow to display a drop-down list, you'll see a list of fields you've previously added to the report that match the data type of the argument (for example, if the argument requires a date-time value, only date-time fields that you've previously added to the report will appear in the drop-down list). You may also choose drop-down list options to Enter Constant Value, which will display a separate dialog box where you may choose or type a value (which is just the same as typing the value in directly without clicking the down arrow). You may also select Choose Other Field from the drop-down list, which will display a separate dialog box listing all fields in all database tables that match the data type of the argument.

If you've supplied several values to arguments in the Function Arguments list and wish to discard them all, click the Reset Values button above the Function Arguments list. All previously supplied arguments will be discarded, and you'll need to choose arguments again. If you want more general information on the custom function you've chosen to base your formula on, click the More Info button to see a dialog box showing all the function's properties.

Once you've supplied all the necessary parameters, click the Save button at the bottom of the Formula Expert or the Close button at the upper left of the Formula Workshop. If the formula you're creating in the Expert is based on a function from the repository, you'll be reminded that creating this formula will add the chosen repository custom function (and any other repository functions that it may be based on) to the report. This will be required to use this formula, so click Yes to acknowledge this message.

The formula will be created and added to the Field Explorer, where it may be dragged to your report just like any other field. If you later wish to edit this formula, either right-click the formula in the report's Design or Preview tab and choose Edit Formula from the pop-up menu, choose Field Explorer options to edit the existing formula, or display the Formula Workshop and choose and edit the formula from within it. The Formula Workshop containing the Formula Expert will reappear with the formula already in it. If you wish to see the formula displayed in the Formula Editor instead of the Formula Expert, click the Use Editor button—the formula will be displayed in the Formula Editor instead.

Note   *Creating custom functions that you may base Formula Expert formulas on is covered in more detail in Chapter 6.*

The Formula Editor

If after giving your new formula a name, you click the Use Editor button, the
Formula Editor will appear inside the Formula Workshop, as shown in Figure 5-3.
The Formula Editor looks largely the same as it did in Crystal Reports 8 and 8.5,
with the exception of the Formula Workshop "around it" and a few changes to the
Formula Editor toolbar. It may look a little foreboding at first, but don't worry—
it will soon become second nature to you as you create and edit more formulas.

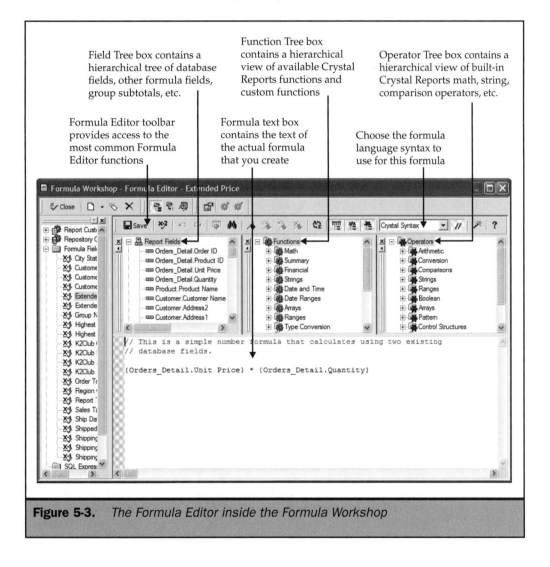

Figure 5-3. *The Formula Editor inside the Formula Workshop*

Tip *If you wish to customize the font face, size, colors, and other appearance options that the Formula Editor uses, select File | Options on the pull-down menus and make your choices on the Editors tab of the dialog box that opens.*

Before you actually create a formula, familiarize yourself with the layout of the Formula Editor. Notice that the Field Tree, Function Tree, and Operator Tree boxes can be closed, resized, moved, and undocked (detached from the main window and put in their own windows). You have a great deal of flexibility in customizing the way the Formula Editor looks. You may also undock the Formula Editor toolbar and move it to another location on the screen.

Tip *If you mistakenly undock and then close the toolbar, you can get it back by right-clicking anywhere in the Format Editor and choosing Show Toolbar from the pop-up menu. You may also press ALT-T.*

When you're working with the Formula Editor, you'll want to familiarize yourself with the toolbar, because you'll need to use it on a regular basis. There are buttons to save the formula you're working on; manipulate bookmarks; hide and show the field, function, and operator trees; and on and on. If you're unfamiliar with a toolbar button's function, point to it with your mouse and wait a second or two—a tool tip for that button will appear. Table 5-2 shows the functions of the Formula Editor's toolbar buttons.

Tip *There are many other shortcut keys you can use while in the Formula Editor. Search Crystal Reports online Help for "Key Controls" within the "Formula Editor" category.*

There are two general approaches to building a formula: type in the parts of the formula directly or double-click in the tree boxes. Once you become more familiar with the Crystal Reports formula language, you will probably create at least some parts of your formula by typing the formula text right into the Formula text box at the bottom of the Formula Editor. For example, simply typing an asterisk when you want to multiply numbers often is easier than clicking around in the Operator Tree box to find the multiplication operator.

Other parts of your formula, however, are best created automatically by double-clicking elements in one of the three tree boxes. For example, to include a database field as part of your formula, just find the field you want to include in the Field Tree box and double-click it. The field will be placed at the cursor position in the Formula text box, using proper formula language syntax.

Using the trees is easy. Simply find the general area of the tree that you are interested in and click the plus sign next to the category that you want to use. All the functions or operators within that category will appear. Double-click the one you want to use and it will be placed at the cursor position in the Formula text box. If you click a function that requires *arguments* (or parameters), such as an UpperCase function that needs to know

Button/Key Combo	Name	Function
🖫 Save or ALT-S	Save	Saves the current formula and closes the Formula Editor (if there is an error in the formula, you will be so notified and given the choice to save with the error or not).
X+2 or ALT-C	Check	Checks the syntax of the formula and reports any errors.
↰ or CTRL-Z	Undo	Undoes the latest action.
↷ or CTRL-SHIFT-Z	Redo	Redoes the latest action.
🔎 or ALT-B	Browse Data	Displays sample data from the database for the selected database field. This button will work only when you've highlighted a database field, not a custom function.
🔍 or CTRL-F	Find/ Replace	Allows searching and replacing for specific characters in the current formula.
⚑ or CTRL-F2	Toggle Bookmark	Places a bookmark at the current line of formula text. If a bookmark is already there, removes it.
⚑ or CTRL-ALT-F2	Next Bookmark	Moves the cursor to the next bookmark in the current formula.
⚑ or SHIFT-F2	Previous Bookmark	Moves the cursor to the previous bookmark in the current formula.
⚑ or CTRL-SHIFT-F2	Clear All Bookmarks	Removes all bookmarks from the current formula.
A-Z or ALT-O	Sort Trees	Sorts the contents of the three Tree boxes alphabetically, instead of in the default logical order.

Table 5-2. *Formula Editor Toolbar Buttons*

Button/Key Combo	Name	Function
or ALT-F	Field Tree	Displays/hides the Field Tree box.
or ALT-U	Function Tree	Displays/hides the Function Tree box.
or ALT-P	Operator Tree	Displays/hides the Operator Tree box.
Crystal Syntax or CTRL-T	Syntax	Chooses syntax (Crystal or Basic) to use for this formula only.
// or ALT-M	Comment/ Uncomment	Adds comment characters (two slashes for Crystal Syntax, an apostrophe for Basic Syntax) to all formula lines that are highlighted. If the lines already are commented, this button removes the comment characters. Lines that are preceded with comment characters are ignored by the formula.
or ALT-X	Use Expert	Displays this formula in the Formula Expert (discussed previously in this chapter and in Chapter 6). If you are displaying a formula not using a "simple" custom function, you'll be warned that displaying the Formula Expert will erase the current formula. Also, this button won't work while you're creating a custom function with the Formula Editor.
?	Help	Displays Formula Editor Help.

Table 5-2.   *Formula Editor Toolbar Buttons* (continued)

what you want to convert to uppercase, the function name and parentheses will be placed in the formula with the cursor positioned at the location of the first argument. You can either type it in or move it to another tree (the field tree, for example) and double-click the field you want to add as the argument. After a while, you'll be able to find the functions or operators you're looking for quickly and create fairly large formulas simply by pointing and double-clicking.

Notice the syntax that Crystal Reports uses when it places objects in the Formula text box (the small formula illustrated in Figure 5-3 is a good example). If you decide to type material into the formula yourself, you'll need to adhere to proper formula language syntax. Table 5-3 identifies special characters and other syntactical requirements of the formula language.

Crystal Syntax	Basic Syntax	Uses
. (period)	. (period)	Used to separate the table name from the field name when using a database field. You must always include the table name, a period, and the field name—the field name by itself is not sufficient.
{} ("curly" or French braces)	{} ("curly" or French braces)	Used to surround database fields, other formula names, and parameter fields. The formula won't understand fields if they're not surrounded by curly braces.
// (two slashes)	' (apostrophe) or Rem	Denotes a comment. These can be used at the beginning of a line in a formula, in which case the Formula Editor ignores the whole line. You can also place two slashes or an apostrophe anywhere in a formula line, in which case the rest of the line will be ignored. You may use the Formula Editor Comment/Uncomment toolbar button to add these characters to multiple selected lines at one time.

" " or ' ' (quotation marks or apostrophes)	" " (quotation marks)	Used to surround string or text *literals* (fixed-string characters) in formulas. With Crystal syntax, you can use either option, as long as they're used in matched pairs. For example:
		
		`If {Customer.Country} = "USA"`
		`Then "United States" Else`
		`'International'`
		
		If you are using Basic syntax, you must use quotation marks only—an apostrophe will be interpreted as a comment.

Table 5-3. *Formula Editor Special Characters*

Crystal Syntax	Basic Syntax	Uses
( ) (parentheses)	( ) (parentheses)	Used to force certain parts of formulas to be evaluated first, as in the following: `({Orders.Amount} + {Orders.Amount}) * {@Tax Rate}.` Also used to denote arguments or "parameters" of built-in functions, as in this example: `UpperCase({Customer.Customer Name}).`
@ ? # %	@ ? # %	Crystal Reports automatically precedes certain fields with these characters. The @ sign precedes formulas, ? precedes parameter fields, # precedes running total fields, and % precedes SQL expression fields. When including these types of fields in a formula, make sure you surround the field with curly braces.
# (pound sign)	# (pound sign)	If you don't include curly braces around a pound sign, Crystal Reports will expect a value appearing between two pound signs that can be converted to a date/time value, as in this example: #2/10/2000 1:15 pm#
, (comma)	, (comma)	Used to separate multiple arguments in functions. For example: `ToText({Orders.Amount},0," ")` Don't add a comma as a thousands separator when using a numeric constant in a formula. For example: `{Orders.Amount} + 2,500` will cause a syntax error.
; (semicolon)	: (colon)	If your formula contains multiple statements, you must separate them with a semicolon in Crystal syntax (putting statements on separate lines without a semicolon will still cause a syntax error). With Basic syntax, you must either put each statement on a separate line or separate multiple statements on the same line with a colon. Note that in Basic syntax, some statements (such as those making up For loops) must be placed on separate lines— separating these statements with a colon will still cause a syntax error.

Table 5-3. *Formula Editor Special Characters* (continued)

Crystal Syntax	Basic Syntax	Uses
ENTER key	_ (space followed by underscore)	In Crystal syntax, you may press ENTER to start a new line in your formula anywhere between a field or function and an operator (don't put new lines or spaces in the middle of field or function names!). Long formulas are more readable on multiple lines. For example:

```
If {Order.Amount} > 5000 Then
    "Qualifies for bonus"
Else
    "Not eligible for bonus"
```

In Basic syntax, you may press ENTER only at the end of a complete statement. If you want a line break in the middle of a statement, you must use a line continuation sequence (a space, followed by the underscore). For example:

```
If {Order.Amount} > 5000 Then
    Formula = _
    "Qualifies for bonus"
Else
    Formula = _
    "Not eligible for bonus"
End If
```

| := (colon followed by equal sign) | = (equal sign) | Used for variable assignment, such as: |

```
NumberVar Quota := 1
```

In Crystal syntax, don't confuse this with the equal sign alone, which is used for comparison:

```
If {Customer.Region} =
"BC "Then" Canadian Customer"
```

In Basic syntax, the equal sign is used for both comparison and assignment, as in:

```
If {Customer.Region} _
    = "BC" Then
Formula = "Canadian Customer"
End If
```

Table 5-3.   *Formula Editor Special Characters* (continued)

Formula Syntax Choices in Crystal Reports

Prior to Crystal Reports 8, formulas could be written in only one formula language. Crystal Reports 9 continues a feature first introduced in Version 8 that allows the choice of two languages or *syntaxes.*

The syntax you use for individual formulas can be chosen with the syntax drop-down list, located at the far-right end of the Formula Editor toolbar. When you choose the desired syntax, you'll notice that the function and operator trees will change, showing all the built-in functions and operators for the chosen syntax. When you check the formula with the Check button, the formula must conform to the syntax chosen in the drop-down list. If, for example, you create a formula that is correct for Crystal syntax and then choose Basic syntax in the drop-down list, you'll probably get an error message if you check the formula. Crystal Reports will not automatically convert from one syntax to the other when you change the syntax drop-down value in an already existing formula.

The choice of syntax is largely one of personal preference. If you are a Basic programmer who often encounters syntax errors with Crystal syntax because you instinctively use Basic, you'll probably be pleased with Basic syntax. If you've used previous versions of Crystal Reports and aren't a Basic programmer, you'll most likely want to continue to use Crystal syntax because you're familiar with it. You don't have to do this at the expense of flexibility, either—virtually all of the Basic-like constructs in Basic syntax are also available in Crystal syntax. You can always choose which syntax to use in each formula that you create (the notable exceptions being record- and group-selection formulas—these can use only Crystal syntax, and you aren't given a choice). You may choose the default syntax for all new formulas by choosing File | Options and clicking the Reporting tab. At the bottom of the dialog box is a Formula Language drop-down list that you use to set the default for all new formulas.

The remainder of this chapter focuses largely on Crystal syntax, showing most examples in the Crystal Reports' "original" formula language. This choice has been made for two reasons:

- If you are using previous versions of Crystal Reports, most of this chapter will still apply to you.

- The Basic language is well documented in many other texts. Since this book is specific to Crystal Reports, language syntax that is specific to Crystal Reports is best documented here.

Any examples or issues that are specific to Basic syntax will be so noted.

New Crystal Reports 9 Formula Auto Complete

If you develop computer programs in certain programming languages or Web pages with certain tools, you may be familiar with auto-completion, which will often anticipate what you are typing and complete portions of your code for you. Crystal Reports 9 now features a limited form of this technology as part of the Formula Editor.

Now, in addition to double-clicking functions in the group tree, you may begin typing portions of your formula directly in the formula text area of the Formula Editor. If you'd like to choose from a list of possible formula functions you can use, press CTRL-SPACE. A list will appear with possible functions you can use.

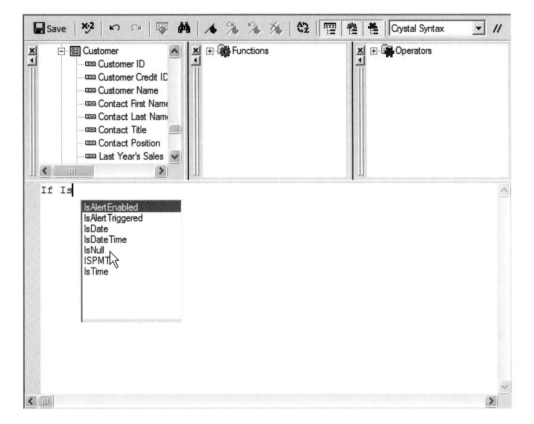

The list of functions you see in the drop-down list will be based on what you've typed so far before pressing CTRL-SPACE. If you've typed enough letters to narrow down the list of available functions to a small group, only the few that fit will appear. If you type CTRL-SPACE with no characters typed beforehand, the whole list of Crystal Reports functions will appear in the drop-down list. And, if you have typed enough characters to narrow the available functions to just one, the drop-down list won't be displayed at all; the complete function name will just be chosen for you.

To choose a function from the drop-down list, use the down-arrow key to choose the desired function and press the space bar or ENTER, or click on the desired function with your mouse. You may also just continue to type, narrowing down the list of available functions as you go. When you get to a single unique choice, the completed function name will be typed for you.

Data Types

As you begin to work with formulas, it's very important to understand the concept of *data types.* Every database field has a certain data type, and every formula you create will result in a single data type. These concepts are important, because if the formula you create doesn't deal with data types properly, you'll get errors when you try to save the formula, or the formula won't give you the result you're looking for. You can't, for example, add the contents of a number field to the contents of a string field with a plus sign—both fields have to be numbers. You can't convert a date field to uppercase characters, because only a string field can be converted to uppercase.

By default, Crystal Reports doesn't display objects in the Design tab by their data types. It shows their names instead. You may prefer to see the data-type representation instead of the field name. To do this, choose File | Options from the pull-down menus and turn off the Show Field Names check box in the Field Options section of the Layout tab. Notice the difference between showing field names and showing data types:

Order ID	Order Amount	Order Date	Courier Website
-5,555,555	($55,555.56)	3/1/1999 1:23:45PM	XXXXXXXXXXXXXXXXXXXXXXXXXX

You may want to turn off Show Field Names when you first start working with formulas. Seeing the data types can help you determine the types of operators and functions that will work with the database fields you're including in your formulas. Also, whenever you *browse* database fields in the Formula Editor, the data type shows up in the Browse dialog box. In the preceding illustration, the fields have the following data types:

- **Order ID**   A *number* data type, which can contain only numbers (along with a period to indicate a decimal point, and a hyphen or minus sign if it's a negative number). You can add, subtract, multiply, divide, and perform other math operations on number data types.

- **Order Amount**   A *currency* data type (available only from certain databases). This is similar to a number data type, but it avoids rounding errors that sometimes occur when performing math operations on number data types.

- **Order Date**   A combined *date/time* data type (again, supported only by certain databases). This can contain a date, a time, or a combination of both. Other databases have date-only data types, and some have time-only data types.

- **Courier Website**   A *memo* data type. The memo data type, like another type called *string*, allows any combination of characters to be placed in the field. However, because letters and punctuation marks can reside in the field, you normally can't perform mathematical calculations with the field.

You may encounter other data types in your databases that aren't shown in this example:

- **Boolean**   Represents data that can have only a true or false value.

- **BLOB**   Designed to contain photos, graphics, or large amounts of plain ASCII text.

Caution   *BLOB (Binary Large Object) fields can be placed on the report only for display. They cannot be used or manipulated inside formulas. They won't even show up in the Formula Editor Field Tree box.*

Creating a New Formula

Creating a simple math calculation is easy. Using the Orders Detail table of the sample XTREME.MDB database included with Crystal Reports, you can calculate the extended price of each order-line item with the following formula.

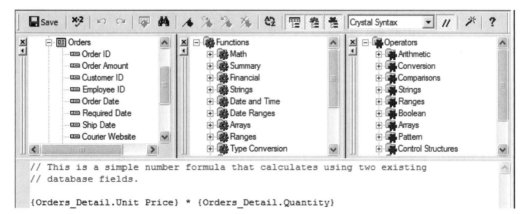

To create this formula, follow these steps:

1. Create a new report using the XTREME.MDB Microsoft Access sample database included with Crystal Reports (you can use the XTREME Sample Database ODBC data source if you choose). Choose the Orders Detail table from this database.

2. Select the Formula Fields category and then click the New button in the Field Explorer toolbar. Or, you may launch the Formula Workshop and create the new formula from there.

3. When asked to name the formula, call it **Extended Price**, and click the Use Editor button.

4. When the Formula Editor appears, double-click the Orders Detail.Unit Price report field in the Field Tree box (you may need to click the plus sign next to the database name to be able to see the Orders Detail table) to add it to the Formula text box. If the field you want to add has already been placed on the report, you will actually find it in the field tree under both the Report Fields section and the database name—there is absolutely no difference if you choose the field from either area.

5. Click the plus sign next to Arithmetic in the Operator Tree box to see all the arithmetic operators that are available. Double-click the multiply operator. (You can save yourself some mouse clicks by typing an asterisk directly in the Formula text box, if you'd like. Although you don't have to put a space before or after the asterisk, the formula is easier to read if you do.)

6. Double-click the Orders Detail.Quantity field in the Field Tree box to place it after the asterisk.

7. If you wish to add a comment explaining the use of the formula (for your own information, or perhaps for others who may be working with your report later), you may precede the comment lines with two slashes, or just type the comment lines, highlight them with your mouse, and click the Comment button in the Formula Editor toolbar.

After you finish the formula, you have several ways to save it and close the Formula Editor and the Formula Workshop. When you first start to use formulas, you'll probably want to check for correct syntax of the formula before you save it. This will ensure that Crystal Reports can at least understand the different parts of the formula and how they are supposed to be calculated or manipulated. Check the formula's syntax by clicking the Check button in the Formula Editor toolbar, or press ALT-C. If Crystal Reports can understand all parts of the formula, a dialog box will appear indicating that no errors were found. (If you've ever written computer programs or used spreadsheet formulas before, though, you know that correct syntax doesn't guarantee that the formula will return the right answer!)

If there is a syntax error in the formula, Crystal Reports will display an error message and highlight the portion of the formula where it stopped understanding it. As you can see here, sometimes these messages may be very descriptive:

or they can be very cryptic:

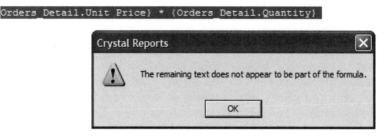

even though both of these examples result from simply forgetting curly braces. You'll learn over time what most error messages indicate and how to resolve them.

Caution *Even though you may not get any syntax errors when you first check the formula after you create it, you may still get an error when the report runs, depending on the actual data in the database. This may happen, for example, if you create a formula that divides two fields, but the "divided by" field returns a zero during a certain record. You'll then get a Can't Divide by Zero syntax error in the middle of the report process. If there's a chance that this type of error may occur given particular data, you'll probably want to add some type of "If {field} > 0 Then..." logic to ensure these types of run-time syntax errors won't occur.*

After you determine that there are no syntax errors, it's time to save the formula. You may either save the formula and remain in the Formula Workshop or save the formula and close the Formula Workshop. To save the current formula and leave the Formula Workshop open to work with another formula, just click the Save button in the Formula Editor toolbar. Or, if you try to create a new formula or edit another formula without first saving the current formula, you'll be asked if you want to save the current formula before you proceed to the next formula.

If you choose to skip the syntax check and immediately save the formula, Crystal Reports will check the syntax anyway. If there is an error, you'll be given the opportunity to save the formula with the error. This makes little sense, because Crystal Reports will stop as soon as you try to run the report and display the error message in the Formula Editor. If you try to save and get a syntax error, correct the error and try to save the formula again. If there are no errors, you'll no longer get a syntax error message and the formula will be saved.

Once the formula has been saved and the Formula Workshop has closed, you will see the formula name under the Formula Fields category of the Field Explorer. You can simply drag and drop the formula on the report, just like a database field. In the case of the Extended Price formula, notice that the formula has taken on the number data type. This occurred because a currency field was multiplied by a number field. The resulting formula will be a currency formula. If you used the ODBC connection to the XTREME database to create this formula, Extended Price will be numeric, as the Microsoft Access ODBC driver converts currency fields to numbers.

New Run Time Debugging Features

As mentioned previously in this chapter, it's possible that an error may occur when the report actually runs but not be detected when you initially create a formula. It's frustrating to create a formula, click the Check button, and receive a "No Errors Found" message, only to have the formula return with an error when the report runs. This situation is known as a *run time error*. Run time errors are often caused by formulas not anticipating the type of data that may be encountered as the report progresses. For example, the formula may perform division on a database field that could possibly return zero for certain records. Or, the formula might extract certain specific characters from a string, only to encounter an error at run time when a record contained a null value for a string or not enough characters to satisfy the formula's requirements.

In previous versions of Crystal Reports, you would receive the error message and the Formula Editor would appear showing the offending formula. However, there would be no indication of what part of the formula was actually causing the error. In Crystal Reports 9, run time errors can be more easily debugged using the new *Call Stack*. If you encounter a run time error, you'll first see the error message indicating what the error is, such as "Divide By Zero," followed by the Formula Workshop showing the offending formula. However, the left-hand tree of the workshop will now show the formulas and functions that led up to the error.

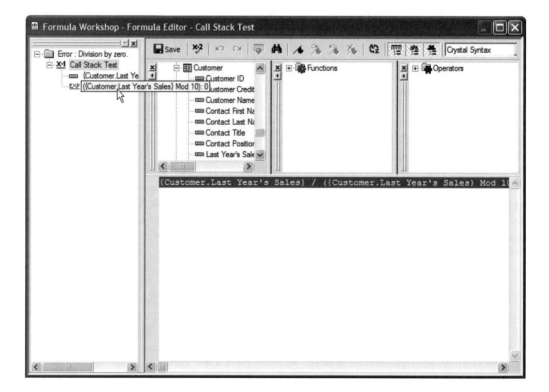

By clicking different entries in the call stack, you can see what the values of variables, functions, and other parts of the formula currently contain. This can be helpful in determining the cause of the error more quickly so that you can supply additional logic to avoid the error in the future.

Editing, Renaming, or Deleting an Existing Formula

After you create a formula, you may wish to change its calculation or add to its function. There are many ways for you to *edit* the existing formula in either the Field Explorer or Formula Workshop. To edit by using the Field Explore, perform any of these steps:

- Select the formula you wish to change and click the Edit button in the Field Explorer toolbar.
- Select the formula you wish to change and press CTRL-E.
- Right-click the formula and choose Edit from the pop-up menu.

Or, you may display the Formula Workshop by clicking the Formula Workshop toolbar button or choosing Report | Formula Workshop from the pull-down menus. You may then expand the Formula Fields category and click the formula you want to edit.

Any of these options will redisplay the Formula Workshop and Formula Editor with the formula in it.

An even quicker method of editing is available after you've placed the formula on your report. In either the Design or Preview tab, click the formula. Notice in the status bar that the formula name is preceded by the @ sign. Crystal Reports automatically adds this symbol to the beginning of all formulas you create. Now that you've selected the formula, simply right-click and choose Edit Formula from the pop-up menu. The formula will reappear in the Formula Editor, ready for you to modify.

If you wish to *rename* a formula, you may do so either from the Formula Fields category of the Field Explorer or the Formula Workshop. If you are using the Field Explorer, begin by selecting the formula you want to rename. Then, you may either click the Rename button in the Field Explorer toolbar or press the F2 key. You may also right-click the formula and choose Rename from the pop-up menu. The name will become "editable"—type the new name and either click outside the formula name or press ENTER. If you've used this formula inside other formulas or elsewhere on your report, Crystal Reports will change the name there, too. To rename a formula in the Formula Workshop, use identical steps to select and rename the formula.

If you select a formula on the report and press the DEL key, you remove that particular occurrence of the formula from the report. However, the formula remains in the Field Explorer and takes up memory and storage space when you save the report. If you're sure you no longer need the formula, delete it entirely. This must be done from the Formula Fields category of the Field Explorer or the Formula Workshop. Select the formula you want to delete and press the DEL key. You can also choose the Delete button from the appropriate toolbar, or right-click the formula name and choose Delete from the pop-up menu. The formula will be removed from the dialog box.

Caution *If you remove a formula that is in use somewhere else on the report, such as in another formula or in a hidden section, you'll be given a warning, because when you delete this formula, other formulas dependent upon it may stop working. In some cases, Crystal Reports won't even allow you to delete a formula if it is being referenced in some other formula in the report. You cannot Undo a formula deletion either, so you may want to save your report first when you get this warning—then go back and delete the formula. That way, you can retrieve the old report from disk if you inadvertently delete an important formula.*

Number Formulas

Probably the most common type of formula is a number formula, such as the Extended Price formula discussed earlier. Number formulas can be as simple as multiplying a database field by 1.1 to increase its amount by 10 percent, or as complex as calculations that include sophisticated statistical math. There is no special procedure required to declare a formula as a "number formula"—the formula simply takes on that data type because of the fields and operators that you use in the formula. As the Extended Price formula, shown here, demonstrates, multiplying a number field by a currency field results in a currency formula:

```
{Orders Detail.Unit Price} * {Orders Detail.Quantity}
```

Many number formulas will use a mathematical *operator*, such as a plus sign, a hyphen or minus sign, an asterisk for multiplication, or a slash for division. You also need to use built-in *functions* that Crystal Reports supplies or custom functions that you create yourself or that others created for you. You'll find all these functions listed in the Function Tree box (you may need to add a custom function to your report from the repository first—see Chapter 7 for more information). When you double-click a function, the function name is placed in the Formula text box with the cursor located in between the opening and closing parentheses. You can then either type in the function's *arguments* or parameters, or double-click other fields or formulas in the Field Tree box to add them as arguments to the function.

For example, if you have a group on the report and want to include a group subtotal in a formula, you would use the Sum function. You'll find that three Sum functions actually are available, with one, two, or three arguments. Here are some examples:

```
Sum({Orders.Order Amount})
```

returns a total of all order amounts for the entire report.

```
Sum({Orders.Order Amount},{Customer.Region})
```

returns a total of just the order amounts in the region group where the formula is evaluated. If the formula was evaluated in the Colorado group, the formula returns the order amount subtotal for Colorado only.

```
Sum({Orders.Order Amount},{Orders.Order Date}, "weekly")
```

returns the order amount subtotal for the current order date group, calculating the subtotal based on a week of orders. Note that this third argument corresponds to the time periods that are available when creating a group based on a date field. (Refresh your memory about date-field grouping by looking at Chapter 3.)

So, you could calculate each order amount's percentage of the region subtotal by using the percentage operator and the Sum function as follows:

```
{Orders.Order Amount} % Sum({Orders.Order Amount},{Customer.Region})
```

There are built-in functions to calculate all the summary-type information discussed in Chapter 3, such as average, subtotal, *P*th percentile, and on and on. By opening the Arithmetic category of functions in the Function Tree box, you'll also find functions to calculate remainders, determine absolute value, and round numbers.

Tip   *If you need to calculate a group subtotal as a percentage of a grand total or higher-level group total, there's no need to create a formula. Instead, use percentage summary fields as described in Chapter 3. However, you'll still need to create a formula as described previously if you want to determine what percentage of a group subtotal a particular detail field is responsible for.*

Order of Precedence

You'll sometimes find situations where you're unsure of the order in which Crystal Reports evaluates a formula's operators. For example, if you wish to add sales tax to an extended price, you might use the following formula, which is supposed to add 8 percent sales tax to the extended price of an order (already calculated in the @Extended Price formula):

```
{@Extended Price} + {@Extended Price} * .08
```

The question of how Crystal Reports calculates this is crucial. Does it calculate the addition operator first and then the multiplication operator, or does it calculate the multiplication operator first and then the addition operator? The results will vary

The Basic Syntax Formula Variable

When you use Crystal syntax, the formula simply returns the results of the last statement in the formula. If the formula consists of only one statement, such as the multiplication in the previous example, the formula returns the results of the multiplication. If the formula contains several statements separated by semicolons, the last statement determines what's returned to the report.

But if you are using Basic syntax, you must keep in mind one slight difference from any Basic-like programming languages you've used. In the Basic computer language, you typically assign and manipulate variables throughout your code. When you wish to display the value of a variable, you use a Print or ? statement or set the value of a text box or other form element to the value of the variable. Because Crystal Reports has no Print statement, you need an alternative method of displaying a value on the report. This is accomplished with the *Formula variable*. The word "Formula" is a reserved word in Basic syntax—you can't use it for any other purpose, such as using it as your own variable name with a Dim statement. By assigning a value to the Formula variable, you determine what the formula returns to the report. You can use the Formula variable over and over within a formula, just like any other variable (as an accumulator, for example). The last occurrence in the formula where a value is assigned to the Formula variable determines what the formula returns to the report. Consider the following Basic syntax formula:

```
' Calculates extended price
Formula = {Orders Detail.Unit Price} * {Orders Detail.Quantity}
If {Customer.Region} = "CO" Then
    ' add 4.25% sales tax to Colorado orders
    Formula = Formula * 1.0425
End If
```

Here, the Formula variable is used like a regular variable (it doesn't even have to be declared with a Dim statement first). It's first used just to calculate the extended price. Then, it's included in an If statement to add sales tax for Colorado orders. If the If statement is true, the existing value of the Formula variable is multiplied by 1.0425 to add 4.25 percent. If the If test fails, the last statement that assigns a value to the Formula variable (the extended price calculation) will be what's returned to the report.

dramatically based on the calculation order. Consider an Extended Price of $100 with addition performed first:

```
100 + 100 = 200
200 * .08 = 16.00
```

or with multiplication performed first:

```
100 * .08 = 8.00
100 + 8.00 = 108.00
```

While your customer might be very pleasantly surprised by the first calculation showing up on their invoice, the second calculation is certainly the correct one. But looking at the formula, you'll notice that the multiplication operator is the second operator. Will it be evaluated second?

The answer is no, based on the *order of precedence*. Although it may sound like a computer concept, order of precedence is actually a concept that you should recall from your ninth grade math class. In this formula, multiplication and division are evaluated first from left to right across the formula; then, addition and subtraction are evaluated from left to right across the formula.

The order of precedence for both Crystal syntax and Basic syntax is as follows:

- Exponentiation (^)
- Negation (–)
- Multiplication, division, left to right (*, /)
- For Crystal syntax only, percent (%) is evaluated at the same time as multiplication and division
- Integer division (\)
- Modulus (Mod)
- Addition and subtraction, left to right (+, –)

Based on this, the formula to add tax to the Extended Price shown earlier will work just fine. But what if, for some reason, you want the addition performed first, not the multiplication. Again, thinking back to ninth grade math, you surround the part of the formula you want evaluated first with *parentheses.* The following formula will perform the addition before the multiplication:

```
({@Extended Price} + {@Extended Price}) * .08
```

Note *If you use one formula inside another formula, as in this example, Crystal Reports calculates the embedded formula first (using the order of precedence) and then calculates the second formula.*

String Formulas

Many times, the database will contain string or text data that is insufficient for your reporting needs. For example, you may want to sort a report by ZIP code, but the database contains ZIP codes only as part of a City_State_Zip field. Or, you may want to write a report to print checks, spelling out the dollar amount in words, using a number or currency field in the database. All of these are applications for a formula that either manipulates or creates string data.

Strings can be *concatenated,* or "tacked together," using the plus sign or the & sign (ampersand). Although the plus operator is the same one used to add numbers, the results will be very different depending on the data type. For example, the formula

```
25 + 7 + 100
```

returns a numeric result of 132. Because all the elements of the formula are numbers, the plus sign will add the numbers together and return a numeric answer.

Contrast that with this formula:

```
"25" + "7" + "100"
```

or

```
"25" & "7" & "100"
```

which returns a string result of 257100. By enclosing the numbers in quotation marks, Crystal Reports interprets the values in the formula as strings, not numbers. When you use a plus sign or ampersand with strings, the result is the concatenation of the individual string elements.

This is very useful for many situations you'll encounter when reporting against databases. The following illustration shows the beginning of a form letter that simply uses database fields on the report.

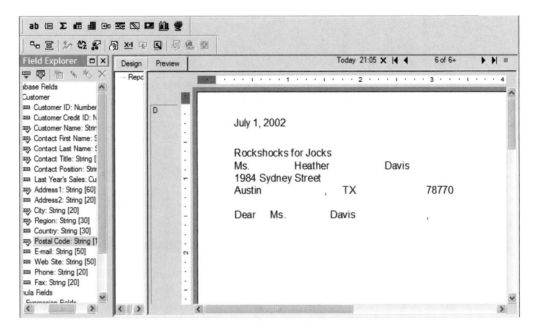

Notice the spacing problems for the contact name, city-state-ZIP line, and salutation. While you may be able to improve the appearance of this report slightly by resizing and moving the individual database fields, you'll never achieve a perfect result. By placing the database fields on the report in fixed locations, the report will never be able to accommodate varying widths of first names, last names, cities, and so on.

The next illustration shows the same report using formulas to concatenate the database fields together.

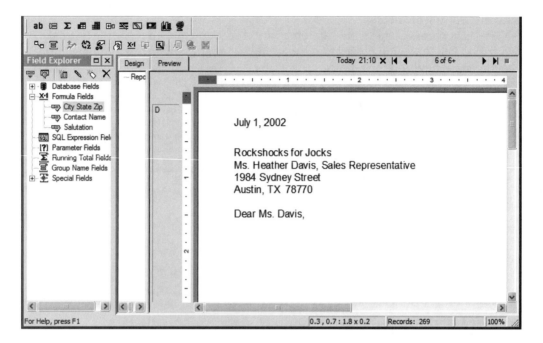

The results are obvious: No matter how wide or narrow names or cities are, they are placed right next to the other items (with a space in between).

While you can conceivably combine these database fields in text objects to accomplish the same result (refer to Chapter 2 if you forgot about text objects), formulas give you a lot more flexibility in how your report looks. For example, you can display only the first initial of a contact name on the report using a formula. You can't do that with a text object.

Concatenating string fields is as simple as using the ampersand (&) operator, as in the following:

```
{Customer.Contact Title} & " " & {Customer.Contact First Name} &
" " & {Customer.Contact Last Name}
```

Notice that a space is hard-coded into the formula using a *string literal,* which is simply a fixed string surrounded by quotation marks. You'll use string literals often in concatenation formulas and If-Then-Else formulas (discussed later in this chapter). So, the literal space in this formula will separate the title from the first name, and the first name from the last name.

You could create a salutation line using several string literals, as follows:

```
"Dear " & {Customer.Contact Title} & " " &
{Customer.Contact Last Name} & ","
```

Notice that the word "Dear" and a space precede the title, a space separates the title from the last name, and a comma follows the last name.

Note   *The ampersand concatenation operator is available in both Crystal and Basic syntaxes. An older concatenation operator, the plus sign (+), is also available in Crystal syntax.*

There are many situations in which you may want to use only certain parts of strings in a formula, not the whole string. For example, you may want to use only a first initial as part of the contact name on a form letter. By following a string field with a number or range of numbers enclosed in square brackets (Crystal syntax) or parentheses (Basic syntax), you can extract certain characters from the string field. This function is known as the *subscript* function. For example, look at this formula in Crystal syntax:

```
{Customer.Contact Title} & " " & {Customer.Contact First Name}[1] &
". " & {Customer.Contact Last Name}
```

Notice that only the first character from the first name will be included in the formula, and a period has been added to the space literal between the first and last names.

Many older database systems contain date information in string fields, because earlier versions of mainframe systems or older database systems did not include a date data type. To allow dates to sort correctly, the year needs to precede the month and day in these fields as well. Thus, it is very common to find January 10, 1999, coded into a string database field as 19990110.

If you want to display the date in an mm/dd/yyyy format to make the date more readable, you could use string subscript operators to pick out the individual parts of the date, add some string literals, and rearrange the date's appearance. Assuming that the hire date in a "legacy" database is an eight-character string field in the form yyyymmdd, this formula will redisplay it as mm/dd/yyyy:

```
{EMP.HIRE_DATE}[5 to 6] & "/" & {EMP.HIRE_DATE}[7 to 8] &
"/" & {EMP.HIRE_DATE}[1 to 4]
```

Notice that the subscript operator can also return a *range* of characters, not just one.

In addition to the subscript operator, there are many built-in string functions that you can use in your formulas. There are functions to return characters from the left of a string, the middle of a string, and the right of a string. Using these, the preceding date formula could be rewritten in Crystal syntax as follows:

```
Mid({EMP.HIRE_DATE},5,2) & "/" & Right({EMP.HIRE_DATE},2) &
"/" & Left({EMP.HIRE_DATE,4})
```

In this case, the Mid function takes three arguments: the field or string to use, the position in the string from which to start reading, and the number of characters to return (there's also a two-argument version of Mid). The Right and Left functions take two arguments: the field or string to use and the number of characters to return.

> **Caution** *Crystal Reports doesn't deal well with formulas that may include a database field containing a null value (a special database value equating to empty, as opposed to zero for a number field, or an empty string for a string/text field). If any part of the formula that you're using contains a null, the entire formula will return null. Use an If-Then-Else formula, along with the IsNull built-in function (described later in the chapter), to deal with potential null situations. Or, you may check the Convert Database NULL Values to Default option by choosing File | Report Options from the pull-down menus to convert any null fields from the database to empty string fields on the report.*

The ToText Function

A crucial built-in function that you will use very often in string formulas is ToText, which is used to convert other data types to a string data type so that you can use them in concatenation or comparison formulas. You can use ToText to convert numbers, dates, times—virtually any other data type—to strings. You need this functionality to avoid the type of problem shown here:

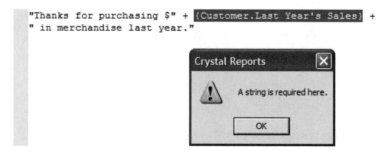

This problem occurs because you can't concatenate a number field onto a string literal (or any other combination of mismatched data types). To convert a number or currency field to a string, such that you can concatenate it to another string, use ToText. The following will solve this problem:

```
"Thanks for purchasing $" + ToText({Customer.Last Year's Sales}) +
" in merchandise last year."
```

That formula will return the following:

```
Thanks for purchasing $32,421.27 in merchandise last year.
```

If you look in the Function Tree box under Strings, you'll see several permutations of ToText, with anywhere from one to five arguments.

Tip	*If you use the ampersand operator (&) to concatenate strings, you reduce your need to use ToText, as this operator performs an automatic conversion if you are mixing data types in your formula. However, if you want to control formatting of the converted values in your formula, you'll still need to use ToText to provide customized formatting.*

While the best place to look for all the ToText details is Crystal Reports online Help, here are a few additional ToText examples:

■ Determine the number of decimal places:

```
"Thanks for purchasing " & ToText({Customer.Last Year's Sales},0)
&
" in merchandise last year."
```

will return

```
Thanks for purchasing $32,421 in merchandise last year.
```

A second number argument to ToText determines how many decimal places Crystal Reports uses when it converts the number or currency field to a text string.

■ Determine the thousands separator:

```
"Thanks for purchasing " & ToText({Customer.Last Year's Sales},0,"")
&
" in merchandise last year."
```

will return

```
Thanks for purchasing $32421 in merchandise last year.
```

A third string argument to ToText determines what thousands separator Crystal Reports uses when it converts a number or currency field to a text string. In this example, the two quotation marks side by side indicate an empty string, so ToText doesn't use a thousands separator.

■ Format date fields:

```
"Your order was placed on " +
ToText({Orders.Order Date},"dddd, MMMM d, yyyy.")
```

will return

```
Your order was placed on Tuesday, July 2, 2002.
```

This version of ToText uses a *format string* as the second argument. The format string (sometimes referred to as a *mask*) uses special characters—pound signs; zeros; decimal points; the letters *d, m, y*; and so forth—as placeholders to indicate how data should be formatted when converted to a string. In this example, the *dddd* characters specify the day of the week to be spelled out fully. *MMMM* specifies a fully spelled month, *d* specifies the day of the month without a leading zero, and *yyyy* specifies a four-digit year. Any characters included in the format string that can't be translated into placeholders (such as the commas and periods) are simply added to the string as literals.

Tip	*It's important to remember that the case of the placeholder characters is significant. When formatting time fields, for example, lowercase h characters indicate hours with a 12-hour clock, whereas uppercase H characters indicate hours with a 24-hour military clock. Apart from that, if you use placeholder characters of the wrong case, Crystal Reports will just include the characters in the resulting string as literals.*

Another built-in function, ToWords, comes in handy when writing checks with Crystal Reports. Consider the following formula:

```
ToWords({PAYROLL.NET_CHECK_AMT})
```

When placed on the report, this formula returns the following for an employee record with net pay of $1,231.15:

```
one thousand two hundred thirty-one and 15/100
```

Picking Apart Strings

In more complex reports, you may wish to pick out only certain parts of strings (the first initial of a name was mentioned previously as an example). Crystal Reports contains many interesting formula functions to handle even more complex "substring" requirements.

For example, you may wish to make use of the ToWords function discussed previously, but not to print checks. If you are printing legal contracts, real estate documents, or bank notes, for example, you may need to print both the numeric and text forms of the same number, as in:

```
This contact expires in thirty (30) days.
```

For the sake of this example, assume that the data indicating the number of "expire days" is contained in a numeric database field. Accordingly, you may try creating a formula to print the previous example. The formula might initially look like this:

```
"This contract expires in " & ToWords({Contracts.Expires}) & " (" &
ToText({Contracts.Expires},0) & ") days."
```

In this example, the ToWords function is used to convert the numeric field to "spelled out" text, and ToText is used to convert the number to a numeric string, with no decimal places.

However, the result of this formula will be:

```
This contract expires in thirty and xx / 100 (30) days.
```

Because ToWords is designed for printing checks, it returns not only the "whole number" part of the numeric field, but the hundredths part as well. For the contract example shown previously, this won't work. How, then, can you create a formula to return just the whole number portion?

If you look closely at ToWords, you'll notice that the whole number portion is always separated from the hundredths portion with the word "and." If you can search through the result of ToWords for the "and" characters, and return just the portion *before* these characters, you will have a successful formula.

Look at this example:

```
"This contract expires in " &
Left(ToWords({Contracts.Expires}),
    InStr(ToWords({Contracts.Expires}), "and") - 1)
& " (" & ToText({Contracts.Expires},0) & ") days."
```

There are several functions and techniques used in this formula that require further explanation:

- **The Left function** The Left function returns a certain number of characters from the left side of another string (and, as you might imagine, there is also an available Right function to return characters from the right side of string). In this formula, the desire is to return the left portion of the words returned by ToWords up until the characters "and" are encountered. So, if ToWords returns "thirty and xx / 100," you may wish to extract the first six characters from the left (up until the "and" is encountered). But how do you determine where the characters "and" are?

■ **The InStr function**   There are several different versions of InStr in the formula language. The version shown in the previous example takes two arguments: the string you want to search, and the "substring" you want to search for within the first string. By supplying the ToWords function as the first argument, and the characters "and" as the second argument, you are asking InStr to find the *numeric position* in "thirty and xx / 100" where the word "and" is. Here the word "and" begins at position 8, which is the numeric result from the InStr function.

So, by using the InStr function within the Left function, you can extract the proper number of characters to get just the whole number portion of the spelled-out number. The only adjustment you must consider is that InStr returns a value of 8, but you want only the first six characters (or seven, if you don't mind having a trailing space). This is why you see the "– 1" subtraction of the value returned by InStr. This will return the leftmost seven characters, including the trailing space, resulting in the characters "thirty " appearing as the spelled-out text.

There are many other built-in string functions that can perform similar functions. Look in the functions tree under Strings, or in online help, for information on other versions of ToText, InStr, Mid, and many others.

Date/Time Formulas

There are many reporting situations in which you need to manipulate date, time, or date/time data types. Most modern PC and SQL databases support some or all of these data types. Although date and time fields don't appear on the report as pure numbers (they often include other characters and words, depending on how they're formatted), they are actually stored by the database and Crystal Reports as numbers. Therefore, it's possible to do mathematical calculations on date fields. There are also built-in date and time functions that return just parts of date and time fields and that convert other data types to date or time fields.

Number of Days Between Dates

When Crystal Reports performs math on date-only fields, the result of the calculation is in whole days. Crystal Reports returns fractional days if fields in the formula are date/time fields. For example, if you subtract a date-only field containing the value May 1, 2002, from a date-only field containing the value May 5, 2002, the result will be the whole number 4. If the fields are date/time fields and the May 1 field contains a time of 12 noon and the May 5 field contains a time of midnight, the result will be the fractional number 3.5.

So, determining how long it took to ship an order is as simple as creating the following formula:

```
{Orders.Ship Date} - {Orders.Order Date}
```

Even though both the database fields in this formula are dates (or date/time if these fields are coming from the sample XTREME database included with Crystal Reports), the result of the formula will be a number—the number of days between the two dates. This formula will return the number of calendar days between the two dates—it uses all days in the calendar. When you perform this type of date arithmetic, you may find fractional days returned, if the date/time fields contain actual time values. This can cause differences between two dates to be "3.5" or "5.75." This can sometimes be difficult if you really want to know just the number of days between two dates, not including time. In these cases, you can use the *Date* built-in function to convert the Date/Time data types to just dates. It may be preferable, for instance, to use the following formula to determine the number of days between two dates:

```
Date({Orders.Ship Date}) - Date({Orders.Order Date})
```

Or, you may also consider using the Round or Truncate function to adjust the numeric result. *Round* (not a Date-related formula function, but helpful in this example) will round a number to a specified number of decimal places—rounding up or down, depending on the fractional value. *Truncate* will simply "throw away" the fractional portion of the result, not rounding in the process. Accordingly, this would also work to avoid fractional dates resulting from time values in the date/time fields:

```
Truncate({Orders.Ship Date} - {Orders.Order Date}, 0)
```

If you wish to exclude weekends from this calculation, it gets a little trickier. Crystal Reports 9 provides the Visual Basic–like function DateDiff in both syntaxes to do more flexible date math. An example of using DateDiff to exclude weekends from this type of calculation can be found in Crystal Reports online Help. Search for "DateDiff function."

You can calculate a date in the future. If, for example, you want to create an accounts receivable report that shows the actual due date of an invoice, the date itself could be calculated by using the invoice date (a date field) and terms (a number field), as follows:

```
{AR.INV_DATE} + {AR.TERMS}
```

Although you don't explicitly define this formula as a date formula, it returns a date data type showing the date on which the invoice is due, provided the terms field contains the number of days required for payment (30, 45, and so forth).

Another function in both Crystal Reports 9 formula syntaxes can be a lifesaver with future and past date calculations. The DateAdd function operates much like its Visual Basic counterpart. For example, to determine a date exactly one month prior to today's date, you would use this formula:

```
DateAdd("m", -1, CurrentDate)
```

The "m" argument indicates an interval of a month. The second argument indicates the number of "time intervals" to add (in this case, a negative one, thereby subtracting a month). The third argument is the date or date/time value to add to (Crystal Reports' *CurrentDate* function returns the date from your PC's system clock). What's particularly powerful about DateAdd is the automatic adjustment for various numbers of days in months and years. For example, if you evaluated this formula on March 31, 2000, it would return February 29, 2000 (there is no February 31, but 2000 was a leap year, therefore resulting in February 29).

> **Tip** *Crystal Reports 9 includes a set of date-related custom functions in the default repository that comes with the software. Many of these custom functions will automatically exclude weekends from date calculations. There's even a custom function you can modify with your own company holidays to exclude these from date calculations, as well as weekends. See Chapter 7 for more information on adding these custom functions to your reports.*

Number of Hours and Minutes Between Times

You can also perform mathematical functions directly on time fields. When you calculate two time fields together, the result is in seconds. For example, the following formula will return the elapsed time, in seconds, between a starting time and ending time field in a college database's course table:

```
{COURSE.EndTime} - {COURSE.StartTime}
```

If the fields containing the time are actually date/time data types, you won't want to return days between the dates, but seconds between the times. In this situation, you'll need to use the built-in *Time* function to return just the time portion of a field. For example:

```
Time({COURSE.EndTime}) - Time({COURSE.StartTime})
```

You may not want the time returned as seconds, but perhaps as hours and minutes, minutes and seconds, or any combination separated with colons. To accomplish this, you have a bit more work to do, but not as much as you might think. Examine the following:

```
Time(0,0,0) + ({COURSE.EndTime} - {COURSE.StartTime})
```

You'll notice that parentheses force the time calculation to be performed first, resulting in the number of seconds between the two times. The Time built-in function (used in a different format in this example) is also being used to return a time data type, using three arguments: hour, minute, and second. The particular time being returned by the Time function is midnight. By adding the seconds between the two times to midnight, you essentially have the number of hours, minutes, and seconds that have elapsed since midnight.

When you place this on your report, you'll see hours, minutes, and seconds, followed by AM or PM (AM if the time difference is less than 12 hours, PM if more, assuming that you're using Crystal Reports' default *hh:mm:ss AM/PM* date format). Now it's simply a matter of using the Format Editor to suppress the AM/PM indicator by choosing 24-hour time display. You can also suppress any combination of hours, minutes, and seconds to show the elapsed time the way you wish.

Tip	*The DateDiff function is not limited to just calculating differences between dates. You can also do time calculations similar to the previous example with DateDiff.*

Month, Day, Year, Hour, Minute, and Seconds Functions

There are many built-in functions to help you use date and time fields. You can use the Month, Day, and Year functions with a date or date/time field as an argument to return just the month, day, or year of the date as a number. Conversely, with the Hour, Minute, and Seconds functions, you can supply a time or date/time field as a single argument and have just the hour, minute, or second of the field returned as a number.

DateValue Function

Two very important functions are DateValue and CDate, both of which are functionally equivalent. The DateValue function is much easier to use than the Date function, which was the only similar option in versions of Crystal Reports prior to Version 8. While there are several variations on DateValue, probably the most intriguing is the variation that accepts one string argument. This string can contain several variations of date-like strings, such as 10/1/99, March 17, 2000, 21 Feb 2003, and so on. Crystal Reports will evaluate the string to determine where the month, day, and year portions reside, returning a "real" date value as the result.

Note	*If you supply a two-digit year to DateValue, Crystal Reports applies a "sliding scale" approach to determining the century. If the two-digit year is between 0 and 29, Crystal Reports assumes the century is 2000. Otherwise, the two-digit year will be converted to the 1900s.*

This greatly simplifies date conversion in Crystal Reports 9. In Crystal Reports versions prior to 8, the Date function required three numeric arguments: year, month, and day. If you needed a date data type to use in comparison formulas or other formulas that worked well with dates, you had to perform fairly involved conversion routines to pick apart a date string. You needed to determine its individual month/day/year parts, convert these to numbers, and supply them to the Date function. For example, if your legacy database contained dates in string fields formatted as "mm/dd/yyyy," you would have used a combination of string subscripts, the ToNumber function, and the Date function to turn them into dates. Examine the following formula:

```
Date(ToNumber({EMP.HIRE_DATE}[7 to 10]),
     ToNumber({EMP.HIRE_DATE}[1 to 2]),
     ToNumber({EMP.HIRE_DATE}[4 to 5]))
```

While this worked, it is now much easier simply to use the following:

```
DateValue({EMP.HIRE_DATE})
```

There may be times when DateValue can't properly evaluate a date string, due to misspellings or other nonconforming string contents in a database field. This is a prime candidate for a run-time formula error. When you check the formula in the Formula Editor with the Check button, you'll get the popular No Errors Found message. However, when the report runs and the formula encounters the nonconforming string value, you'll see the following:

To avoid these run-time errors, use an If-Then-Else statement (described later in the chapter) in conjunction with another function, IsDate, to perform the conversion to a Date value only if the string can be interpreted by Crystal Reports as a date.

Tip   *A number of related Time and DateTime conversion and detection functions are also available in Crystal Reports 9. Look in the functions tree or online Help for DateTimeValue, TimeValue, IsDateTime, and IsTime.*

If-Then-Else Formulas

One of the complaints that's sometimes heard in the competitive community of database report writers is, "Crystal Reports is too complex—it's made for programmers." While this complaint may or may not ring true, there is no doubt that elements of common programming languages can be found in the Crystal Reports formula languages. The first of these programming-oriented features is If-Then-Else logic in formulas. The If-Then-Else combination is the cornerstone of much computer programming code, so once you learn If-Then-Else concepts, you'll be on your way to performing really sophisticated report customization.

If-Then-Else formulas perform a test on a database field, another formula, or some combination of them. Your test can be as simple or as complex as you need it to be—perhaps just checking to see if a sales figure exceeds the $1,000 bonus threshold. Or, you may want to check the number of days a product took to ship, in conjunction with the carrier who shipped the product and the sales level of the customer, to determine if a shipment met your company's shipping goals. If the test passes (returns *true*), the formula will return a certain result. If the test fails (returns *false*), a different result will be returned.

If-Then-Else formulas are created with the following syntax:

```
If <test> Then <result if true> Else <result if false>
```

The test portion of an If-Then-Else formula must use comparison operators found in the Operator Tree box (or a Boolean formula, discussed later in the chapter). You'll find a Comparisons section of the box that, when opened, shows operators that test for equal, less than, greater than, and other combinations of conditions. These can be used in conjunction with And, Or, and Not Boolean operators to combine multiple conditional tests together. Here's a simple If-Then-Else formula that will return a string based on an order amount:

```
If {Orders.Order Amount} > 5000 Then "Bonus Order"
Else "Regular Order"
```

The Order Amount database field is tested to see if its value is greater than 5,000. If the test is true, the formula returns the "Bonus Order" string. Otherwise, the formula returns the "Regular Order" string.

Boolean operators can also be used to combine multiple comparisons together. You can use And, Or, and Not Boolean operators. The preceding formula has been slightly enhanced in the following formula, using a Boolean operator to combine two comparisons:

```
If {Orders.Order Amount} > 5000 And Month({Orders.Order Date} = 12
    Then
    "Holiday Bonus Order"
Else
    "Regular Order"
```

Here, the order amount has to exceed 5,000 *and* the order must have been placed in December for the formula to return Holiday Bonus Order. Orders over 5,000 in other months will still be regular orders. If you change the And to an Or in the preceding formula, then *all* orders in December will be bonus orders, regardless of amount. Orders over 5,000 will also be considered bonus orders the rest of the year.

Data Types in If-Then-Else Formulas

While creating If-Then-Else formulas, you must pay special attention to the data types that you're using in the formula. In the If test of the formula, make sure you use similar data types in each individual comparison operation. For example, if you want to test whether Customer.Country is USA, the test will be

```
If {Customer.Country} = "USA"
```

Since Customer.Country is a string field, you need to compare it to a string literal, enclosed in quotation marks or apostrophes (just quotation marks in Basic syntax). If the field you are testing is numeric, you need to use a number constant, as in the Orders.Order Amount sample shown previously. If you mismatch data types, such as these:

```
If {Orders.Order Amount} > "5000"
```

you'll receive an error.

If you use multiple comparisons separated by Boolean operators, each comparison can have a different data type. For example, if you want to combine the two tests mentioned previously, your formula would start out as follows:

```
If {Customer.Country} = "USA" And {Orders.Order Amount} > 5000
```

In this case, the different data types in the If part of the formula are fine, as long as each "side" of each comparison is of the same data type.

For example, you may have an existing formula on your report, @Ship Days, that calculates the number of days it took to ship an order. But since @Ship Days is a numeric formula, it will display a zero on your report if the order was placed and shipped on the same day. Therefore, you would write the following If-Then-Else formula to show the words "Same Day" on the report if @Ship Days is zero, or to show just the contents of the @Ship Days formula if it is not zero:

```
If {@Ship Days} = 0 Then
    "Same Day"
Else
    {@Ship Days}
```

But if you use the Check button in the Formula Editor to check the syntax of this formula, you'll receive an error:

The problem is that Crystal Reports doesn't know what data type to assign to the formula. If the test returns true, the formula will return a string for the words "Same Day." However, if the test returns false, the formula will return @Ship Days, which is a number. Crystal Reports must assign a data type to a formula when it's first created—it can't wait until the report is running. Therefore, even though the If part of a formula can contain various data type tests, the Then and Else parts must contain the same data types.

Remember the function that converts other data types to strings? The following will solve this problem:

```
If {@Ship Days} = 0 Then
    "Same Day"
Else
    ToText({@Ship Days},0)
```

This result is better, because it doesn't show zero as the number of ship days. But we want to take it a step further to make the report more readable. Look at the enhanced version of this formula:

```
If {@Ship Days} = 0 Then
    "Shipped Same Day"
Else
    "Shipped in " + ToText({@Ship Days},0) + " days"
```

This looks better on the report, particularly if the report isn't a straight columnar report. You might want to put this in a group header for an order, before the individual line items for the order show up in the details section. But there's just one more problem. What will this formula return if it took only one day to ship the order?

```
Shipped in 1 days
```

While this probably won't mean your dismissal from the report development team, why not go one easy step further to make the report look even better? Try the following:

```
If {@Ship Days} = 0 Then
    "Shipped Same Day"
Else
    If {@Ship Days} = 1 Then
        "Shipped in 1 day"
    Else
        "Shipped in " + ToText({@Ship Days},0) + " days"
```

This is an example of a *compound* or *nested* If-Then-Else statement. Notice that you're not limited to one If, Then, or Else clause in a formula. You can make another If statement the result of the first Then, or the result of the first Else, and on and on. There is no specific limit to how many levels you can nest these, but obviously the formula becomes hard to follow after only one or two levels. Also, don't forget that the Else clause isn't required, so when you nest these, you won't have to always have a matching Else clause for every If.

Multiple Actions with One If-Then-Else Statement

You'll notice in all the preceding examples that only one action occurred as the result of the Then and Else parts of the statement. While this is okay for many types of formulas, sometimes you may want several things to happen, particularly when you need to set the contents of several variables as the results of a single Then or Else clause (variables are discussed later in this chapter). In this situation, you can simply repeat the If-Then-Else test several times, with a different result for each Then and Else clause. Just be sure to separate each If-Then-Else statement from the next with a semicolon. For example, to set the contents of several variables in one formula, you might use the following:

```
NumberVar GroupBonus;
NumberVar GroupFollowUpCount;
NumberVar ReportBonus;
NumberVar ReportFollowUpcount;
StringVar GoodCustomer;

If {Orders.Order Amount} > 5000 Then
    GroupBonus := GroupBonus + 1
Else
    GroupFollowUpCount := GroupFollowUpCount + 1;
```

```
If {Orders.Order Amount} > 5000 Then
    ReportBonus := ReportBonus + 1
Else
    ReportFollowUpCount := ReportFollowUpCount + 1 ;

If {Orders.Order Amount} > 5000 Then
    GoodCustomer := {Customer.Customer Name}
```

All of these If statements will be evaluated and the resulting variables will be set. The formula will display the result of the last action in the If statement on the report. In this example, if the Order Amount is over $5,000, all the bonus variables will be incremented by one and the GoodCustomer variable will be assigned the customer name. But because the GoodCustomer variable assignment is the last action that executes, the customer name is what the formula actually displays on the report. If the Order Amount is less than $5,000, then the two FollowUpCount variables will be incremented by one. But because the last statement still tries to set the GoodCustomer variable and fails (and there's no Else clause), the GoodCustomer variable won't be assigned a value and the formula will return an empty string.

If you look at the previous example, you see quite a bit of duplicate typing (the If test is repeated three times). This duplication can be eliminated by creating just one If-Then-Else statement, but supplying several actions to the Then and Else clauses, separating the action statements with a semicolon and surrounding them all with parentheses. Here's the same formula created using this shortened approach:

```
NumberVar GroupBonus;
NumberVar GroupFollowUpCount;
NumberVar ReportBonus;
NumberVar ReportFollowUpcount;
StringVar GoodCustomer;

If {Orders.Order Amount} > 5000 Then
    (GroupBonus := GroupBonus + 1 ;
    ReportBonus := ReportBonus +1 ;
    GoodCustomer := {Customer.Customer Name})
Else
    (GroupFollowUpCount := GroupFollowUpCount + 1 ;
    ReportFollowUpCount := ReportFollowUpCount + 1;
    GoodCustomer := "")
```

Caution	*In the preceding example, you'll need to make sure to include the statement to assign the GoodCustomer variable an empty string in the Else clause. Otherwise, you'll receive the "A String Is Required Here" error. This is because the Then and Else clauses must still return the same data type. Without the GoodCustomer assignment in the Else clause, the Then clause will be returning a string value (a string variable is being assigned) and the Else clause will be returning a numeric value (a numeric variable is being assigned).*

Enhanced Crystal Reports If-Then-Else Options

If the If-Then-Else logic described so far isn't enough to propel you toward (or perhaps away from) a programming career, Crystal Reports includes a bevy of other If-Then-Else possibilities to help you reconsider!

First, the If-Then-Else statements in Basic syntax differ from those Crystal syntax versions described previously. Basic syntax follows the more typical If-Then-Else-EndIf approach familiar to Basic language programmers. In particular, this makes performing multiple actions as the result of a single If-Then-Else statement more straightforward by introducing the End If clause:

```
If <test> Then
   <statement>
   <statement>
   <more statements…>
Else
   <statement>
   <statement>
   <more statements…>
End If
```

Also, you can use the Basic syntax ElseIf clause (don't forget it's one word—no space) to allow nesting of multiple If conditions in one statement:

```
If <first test> Then
   <statements…>
ElseIf <second test> Then
      <second test statements…>
Else
   <statements if first test fails…>
End If
```

Yet another permutation of If-Then-Else logic exists in both Crystal and Basic syntaxes. If you've used Microsoft Office products, such as Microsoft Access, you may be familiar with the IIF *Immediate If* function. This shortened version of protracted If-Then-Else logic is actually a single function, similar to ToText or UpperCase (it appears in the function tree under Programming Shortcuts) that accepts three arguments. The function syntax is as follows:

```
IIF(<boolean expression>, <result if true>, <result if false>)
```

This function can simplify If-Then-Else logic for small, simple formulas, or when you want to perform a "mini" If-Then-Else statement as part of a larger formula. For example, consider the following string formula using traditional If-Then-Else logic:

```
If {Customer.Country} = "USA" Then
    {Customer.Customer Name} + " requires domestic shipping charges"
Else
    {Customer.Customer Name} + " requires international shipping charges"
```

By using the Immediate If function, this can be simplified to the following:

```
{Customer.Customer Name} + " requires " +
IIF({Customer.Country} = "USA", "domestic", "international") +
" shipping charges"
```

Helpful Built-In Functions for If-Then-Else Formulas

If you look in the Function Tree box of the Formula Editor, you'll notice a Print State category. Opening this category shows a variety of built-in functions that you can use in If-Then-Else (and other) formulas to enhance your reporting flexibility. For example, all the Special Fields discussed in Chapter 2, such as Page Number, Total Page Count, Print Date and Time, Record Number, Group Number, and others, are available. There are other special functions that you can use to test for a null database value in the current, next, or last record; to check whether the current database record is the first or last; or to check whether the formula appears in a repeated group header. By using these special built-in functions, you can create formulas that make your reports more intuitive and easier to read.

Here are some examples:

■ IsNull function

```
If IsNull({Customer.Region}) Then
    ""
Else
    ", " + {Customer.Region}
```

The IsNull function is critical if you may encounter null values in database fields that you include in your formulas. By design, a Crystal Reports formula will return a null value if any part of the field contains a null value. If a numeric formula performs addition on a field containing a null value, the formula won't treat the null as a zero and return a numeric result with the rest of the addition—the formula will return a null. If you are performing string concatenation and one of the string fields is null, the whole formula will return null, not the rest of the concatenation.

By using the If-Then-Else test with the IsNull function described previously, you can check whether the region field contains a null value. If so, the formula will return an empty string (denoted by the two sets of quotation marks). Otherwise, the formula will return a comma, a space, and then the region name. This formula can then be concatenated with city and ZIP database fields in another formula to form a city-state-ZIP line. If the region in the database is null, the other formula won't become null.

> **Tip** *Several factors determine whether or not the database will contain null values. In many cases, this is determined by the way the database is initially designed. If you prefer to avoid null values appearing on the report, Crystal Reports allows you to convert them to a "default" format (typically, a zero for number fields and an empty string for string fields). To do this for all new reports in the future, check Convert Database NULL Values to Default on the Reporting tab of the File | Options pull-down menu. Version 9 also has added the Convert Other NULL Values to Default option to deal with other nondatabase values (such as other formulas) that may return null values. To set these options for just the current report, check the same options after choosing File | Report Options from the pull-down menus.*

■ Next function

```
If {Customer.Customer Name} = Next({Customer.Customer Name}) Then
    {Customer.Customer Name} + " continues on next page..."
```

The Next function reads a field in the next record of the database. This formula compares the field in the next record to the same field in the current record. If the values are the same, you know that the same customer will appear in the first record on the next page, and you can note this with a text message. This formula would typically be placed in the page footer.

> | **Tip** | *Notice that there is no Else clause in this formula. Crystal Reports doesn't require an Else clause in an If-Then-Else formula in Crystal syntax. If you leave the Else off and the test returns false, the formula will produce an empty string.* |

- InRepeatedGroupHeader function

```
If InRepeatedGroupHeader Then
    GroupName ({Customer.Customer Name}) + "   - continued -"
Else
    GroupName ({Customer.Customer Name})
```

If you place this formula in the group header of a group with the Repeat Group Header on Each New Page option turned on (this can be set when you create or change a group—see Chapter 3), "- continued -" appears only when the group header is repeated. This also uses the GroupName function to return the group name field for a particular group. An InRepeatedGroupHeader test also comes in handy if you are resetting variables in formulas you are placing in the group header (assuming that you'll always be encountering a new group when the group header prints). Because you don't want to reset your variables in a *repeated* group header, you can condition your variable assignment statement on the value of InRepeatedGroupHeader. You might use something similar to the following:

```
If Not InRepeatedGroupHeader Then GroupBonus := 0
```

Other Crystal Reports Logic Constructs

Many advanced users (particularly those with programming backgrounds) will often find some of the procedural capabilities of high-level computer languages useful when designing reports. If you fall into this category (perhaps you are a Basic programmer), not only will the typical procedural constructs in Basic syntax open up enhanced flexibility for you, but similar logic constructs in Crystal syntax will also make your reporting life easier. Even if you're not a programmer, you'll probably soon find that these features come in handy in the more advanced reporting situations you'll encounter.

The term *logic construct* refers to the features of the Crystal Reports formula language that enable you to go beyond basic If-Then-Else logic. For example, it can be tedious to write long repetitive If-Then-Else formulas to perform tasks such as testing for more than a small number of conditions, picking apart strings, or cycling through multiple-value parameter fields or other arrays. Crystal Reports logic functions such as Select Case, For loops, and Do loops make these tasks much easier. These functions enable Crystal Reports formulas to move closer and closer to a full procedural language, such as Visual Basic.

Select Case Statement

Select Case is very similar to its Visual Basic counterpart. It provides a much simpler and cleaner approach to testing for multiple conditions and returning appropriate results—those complex If-Then-Else statements can now be replaced with more readable and easy-to-maintain logic.

Look at the following compound If-Then-Else statement:

```
If {@Ship Days} = 0 Then
    "Shipped Same Day"
Else
    If {@Ship Days} = 1 Then
        "Shipped in 1 day"
    Else
        "Shipped in " + ToText({@Ship Days},0) + " days"
```

This is a relatively simple formula that checks whether the @Ship Days formula returns a 0 or a 1, returning a different string value in each case. If neither of these conditions is true, a catchall Else clause displays another string value. While this particular example isn't particularly complicated, it could quickly become much more difficult to interpret and maintain if more than two conditions have to be tested for.

Select Case is much better suited to this type of logic. Consider the following:

```
Select {@Ship Days}
    Case 0:
        "Shipped Same Day"
    Case 1:
        "Shipped in 1 day"
    Default:
        "Shipped in " + ToText({@Ship Days},0) + " days"
```

You may choose Select Case from the Control Structure category of the Formula Editor Operator Tree or simply by typing the correct syntax. Begin with the word "Select" followed by a database field, formula, or other expression. Then, supply multiple Case clauses, each testing the value of the Select expression (make sure the value you supply to each Case clause is the same data type as the Select expression). If you want to have the formula return the same result for several different values of the Select expression, you may separate the values after the Case clause with commas and include the To operator to supply a range of values. After the Case clause, supply a colon (don't use a semicolon—this isn't the end of the statement) and then supply the expression you want the formula to return if the Select value equals the Case clause. Remember that all expressions that result from a Case clause must be the same data type—you can't have one Case clause return a string and another Case clause return a number. After the Case clauses have been defined, you may supply an optional Default clause, followed by a colon, and the expression you want the formula to return if none of the Case clauses match the Select value.

For Loop

Basic programmers have always enjoyed the capability to loop through fragments of program code over and over to perform repetitive logic. This also becomes helpful in certain reporting situations (if, for example, you need to cycle through a multiple-value parameter field or iterate through a number array).

Crystal Reports includes the ubiquitous For loop in both syntaxes (except there's no Next clause in the Crystal syntax version). The For loop uses a counter variable to keep track of how many times a specified piece of logic has been cycled through. The For clause sets both the beginning and ending values of the counter variable. The optional Step clause tells the For statement how to increment the counter variable (the default is 1 if the Step clause is left out). The For statement is closed off by the word "Do," followed by one or more statements enclosed in parentheses (use a semicolon to separate more than one statement within the parentheses). The statements inside the parentheses will be executed once for every increment of the counter variable.

The following formula displays all the entries a user has chosen in the multiple-value Region parameter field:

```
NumberVar Counter;
StringVar Message := "Regions Chosen: ";

// cycle through all members of the multi-value
// ?Region parameter field
For Counter := 1 to Count({?Region}) Step 1 Do
(
    // build the Message variable, along with comma/space
    Message := Message & {?Region}[Counter] + ", "
);

// strip off last comma/space added by the loop
Left(Message, Length(Message) - 2)
```

First, this formula declares two variables: Counter to increment the For loop, and Message to accumulate the parameter field values (look at the next section of the chapter for information on using variables). The For loop then cycles Counter from 1 to the number of elements in the parameter field (returned by the Count function). For each loop, Counter is used to retrieve the next element of the parameter field and accumulate it, along with a comma and a space, in Message. The final statement of the formula, which is not associated with the loop, strips off the last comma and space that were added inside the last occurrence of the loop.

Note	*Although Crystal Reports 9 now allows string formulas and variables to return up to 64K of characters (only 254 characters could be returned by strings prior to version 9), good formula logic dictates adding a test in this formula that uses the Exit For statement to exit the For loop if the Message variable exceeds approximately 64,000 characters in length. If the loop tries to accumulate more than 64K characters in the variable, a run-time error will occur.*

While Do Loop

A looping construct similar to the For loop described previously can be used to repeat statements while a certain condition is met. Whereas the For loop uses a counter variable to determine how many times the loop executes, the While Do loop evaluates a condition before each occurrence of the loop and stops if the condition is no longer true. This construct is similar to Do and While loops used in Visual Basic and other procedural languages.

The following listing is a formula that sets a variable to a phone number database field and then uses a While Do loop to look for hyphens in the variable. As long as a hyphen exists in the variable, the Do loop will execute a statement to "pick out" the hyphen, leaving behind only the pure numbers from the phone number. When there are no more hyphens in the variable, the While condition will fail and the statement after the closing parenthesis of the While Do loop (the variable name, which will display the number without the hyphens) will execute.

```
StringVar NewPhone := {Customer.Phone};

While Instr(NewPhone,"-") > 0 Do
(
    NewPhone := Left(NewPhone, Instr(NewPhone,"-") - 1) &
    Right(NewPhone, Length(NewPhone) - Instr(NewPhone, "-"));
);

NewPhone
```

Using the Join and Split Functions to Avoid Loops

While the previous code is a great For loop example, there's actually another built-in formula function that negates the need for the variable declarations, the looping logic, and the removal of the training comma/space when creating a single string containing multivalue parameter field entries. Look at the following code:

```
"Regions chosen: " + Join({?Region}, ", ")
```

This formula uses the *Join* function, similar to its Visual Basic counterpart, which takes all the *elements* of the array supplied in the first parameter (a multivalue parameter field actually is an array), concatenates them together, and optionally separates each with the string supplied in the second parameter. Join performs the same thing as all the looping logic and variable manipulation demonstrated earlier, with one simple function.

Conversely, you may wish to take a string value or variable that contains multiple strings separated by a common delimiter (such as a slash) and create an array of string values. You could create a loop that cycles through the string one character at a time, looking for the delimiter (the slash), and performing complex logic to extract the substring and add it to an array. But the *Split* function, like its equivalent in Visual Basic, will perform all this logic for you automatically. Look at the following code fragment (this is not a complete formula):

```
StringVar array Regions;
Regions :=
Split("Northwest/Southwest/Northeast/Southeast/Midwest", "/")
```

The second line of code will populate the Regions array variable with five elements by looking through the string and separating the five substrings that are separated by slashes.

But, don't forget your looping capabilities just yet—the Join and Split function work only with string values. If you have a multivalue parameter field that is designated as a number, date, or other nonstring type, you'll still need to use loops to extract the individual elements. And if you want to build a nonstring array, you may need to use loops as well, as Split works only with strings.

Although this is a good example of how a While Do loop can cycle while a condition is true, it's a fairly complex process for the relatively simple "search and replace" function that it performs. For a more streamlined formula, you can use the Crystal Reports 9 Replace function, as in the following example:

```
Replace({Customer.Phone}, "-", "")
```

In this case, the Replace function makes use of three parameters: the first being the string field or value that you want to modify, the second being the character or characters you want to search for, and the third being the character or characters you want to replace the search characters with.

Note   *The previous logic construct examples are presented in Crystal syntax. Basic syntax logic constructs are very similar, if not identical, to their Visual Basic counterparts. Just remember that you must use at least one instance of the Formula intrinsic variable in Basic syntax to return a result to the report.*

Boolean Formulas

The one remaining type of formula that you may need to create is the *Boolean formula*, which can return just two values: true and false. You can think of a Boolean formula as just the "test" part of an If-Then-Else formula. When the formula is evaluated, it ultimately returns only one of the two states.

Here's a simple Boolean formula:

```
{@Ship Days} > 3
```

In this formula, the existing @Ship Days formula (a number formula) is tested to be greater than 3 (indicating a shipping exception). It either is or isn't greater than 3! If it is greater than 3, the formula returns a true value—if it's not, the formula returns a false value.

When you then place this formula on your report, it will appear with a Boolean data type. If you have Show Field Names turned off in File | Options (discussed earlier in the chapter), then you'll see the formula show up with the word "True" in the Design tab. If you format the field, you'll notice a Boolean tab in the Format Editor that lets you choose how you want the true/false values to appear on the report.

Although you may occasionally find Boolean formulas helpful when they're actually placed on the report, you'll probably use them much more often as a cornerstone for other formulas. For example, the Boolean formula shown previously indicates that Xtreme Mountain Bikes considers orders that took longer than three days to ship as exceptions. But, Xtreme really wants to break down the shipping exception rule according to Last Year's Sales. If the customer purchased more than $50,000 in merchandise last year, the three-day shipping exception will apply. However, if a customer purchased less, a six-day shipping exception applies.

This requires a *compound* Boolean formula, such as

```
({@Ship Days} > 3 And {Customer.Last Year's Sales} > 50000)
Or {@Ship Days} > 6
```

which uses a combination of And and Or operators, along with the comparison operators, to create a more complex Boolean formula. What's important to remember, though, is that the ultimate result will still be either true or false. You can make a Boolean formula as complex as you want, using combinations of comparison operators along with And, Or, and Not operators, but in the end, only true or false will result.

Tip   *Notice the parentheses around the first part of this compound Boolean formula. They ensure that both @Ship Days is less than 3 and Last Year's Sales is greater than $50,000 before "Or'ing" the @Ship Days greater than 6 test. Although this may make the formula more understandable, it is optional. Crystal Reports considers all Boolean operators (And, Or, and Not) equally in the order of precedence (discussed previously in this chapter). That is, it evaluates them equally as it travels through the formula from left to right.*

There are several benefits to creating Boolean formulas in this fashion:

- After you create a complex Boolean formula, you can include it in other formulas as the test part of an If-Then-Else formula, as in the following:

```
If {@Shipping Exception} Then
    "*** Shipping Exception ***"
Else
    "Shipped Within Goal"
```

This makes the second formula much easier to read and understand.

- By using the Boolean formula throughout the report, you eliminate the need to retype the complex Boolean test repeatedly, thus reducing the chance of errors. Even more important, you have only one formula to change if the report requirements change down the road. For example, if you use the @Shipping Exception formula as the cornerstone for 50 other formulas in your report, and you later decide to reduce the Last Year's Sales qualification from $50,000 to $35,000, you have only *one* formula to change on your report, not 50. All the rest will follow the change.

- You can use the Boolean formula in advanced record selection (covered in Chapter 8) and conditional formatting (covered in Chapter 9) to limit the report to certain records or to have certain objects on the report appear with different formatting.

Tip   *Crystal Reports' online help is a wealth of wisdom on formula concepts and built-in functions. You'll find samples of every built-in function and many sample formulas that you can use as building blocks for your reports. Just click the Index tab within online help and type in the formula language function or statement you want help with. Then, pick the function from the list to see the help material for that function.*

Variables in Formulas and Evaluation Times

As a general rule, formulas contain their value only for the duration of one database record. If you put a formula in the details section, it will evaluate every time a new record is processed and put its result in the details section. If you put a formula in a group footer, it will be evaluated when each group footer prints. In every case, the formula will not "remember" anything from the previous record or previous group footer. Once the next record or footer comes along, the formula evaluates completely "from scratch."

Sometimes, though, you may need a formula to remember material from record to record or from group to group. You may want to accumulate some value as the report progresses so that you can print a total in a group footer or report footer. For example, you may want to check the value of a subtotal in a group footer. If it exceeds a certain threshold, you may want to increment a counter so that you can show how many groups exceeded the threshold at the end of the report.

To accomplish this, you need to somehow store information from record to record or from group to group. This can be accomplished by using *variables*. A variable is simply a "placeholder" that Crystal Reports sets aside in the computer's memory. As the report progresses from record to record or from group to group, your formula can refer back to the variable or change its contents. You can then use the variable in other formulas or display its accumulated contents in a group or report footer.

Note   *Crystal syntax and Basic syntax use different statements to maintain variables. Just like in Microsoft Visual Basic, Crystal's Basic syntax requires use of the Dim statement to declare a variable before use. And as when working in Visual Basic, you can either assign a data type to a variable when you Dim it, or simply assign a value to it after you have used Dim without a data type (and the variable will automatically take on the data type of the value you assign it). Because of this similarity to Visual Basic, Basic syntax variables won't be discussed here, as they are well documented in Visual Basic texts. The rest of the discussion on variables applies to Crystal syntax.*

Declaring a Variable

The first step in any formula that uses a variable is to *declare* the variable. This sets aside a specific amount of memory for the variable, based on its data type. You'll find variable declarations listed in the Operator Tree box of the Formula Editor under Variable Declarations.

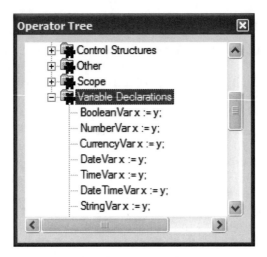

Notice that a different variable declaration statement exists for each Crystal Reports data type. You must consider in advance what kind of data your variable is going to hold, and declare the correct type of variable accordingly. If, for example, you want to keep track of a customer name from record to record, and the customer name field in the database is a string data type, you need to declare a string variable to hold the information.

You must also give each variable a name. You can give it any descriptive name you wish, provided it doesn't contain spaces or conflict with another Crystal Reports formula language *reserved word*. You can't, for example, use variable names such as Date, ToText, or UpperCase—these are reserved by the formula language for its own built-in functions (you'll know if your variable names are reserved words by looking at their color in the Formula Editor—Crystal Reports turns all reserved words blue).

To declare a variable, type the variable declaration followed by the variable name, such as this example:

```
NumberVar BonusAmount;
```

This declares a number variable called BonusAmount that can later be assigned a numeric value. The semicolon at the end of the statement separates this statement from the next one in the formula (presumably a statement to assign or test the contents of the variable).

If you wish to use more than one variable in the formula, you may declare them together, again separated by semicolons. For example:

```
NumberVar BonusAmount;
StringVar BonusCustName;
DateVar DateBonusReached;
```

Tip *You may be used to assigning variables in other programming languages. Remember that Crystal Reports treats variables differently. You must declare a variable in each formula where you want to refer to the variable. However, even if you declare a variable and assign it a value in one formula, and then declare it again in a formula that appears later in the report, it will retain the value from the first formula. Unlike in many other languages, declaring a variable more than once in Crystal Reports does not reset its value to zero or empty (with the exception of local variables, as described in the following section). These considerations apply to both syntaxes, Crystal and Basic. Even if you're used to using the Dim statement only once in Visual Basic, you must use it with Basic syntax in every formula where you want to refer to a variable. If the variable has been declared with a Dim statement in another formula, declaring it again will not reset its value.*

Variable Scope

The whole idea and benefit of variables is that they retain their values as the report progresses from record to record or from group to group. So, for variables to be of real benefit, they need to keep their values throughout the report process. And because you may have several formulas that you want to refer to the same variable, you need to be able to refer to a variable in one formula that was already declared and assigned a value in another.

Exactly how long and where a variable keeps its value is determined by the variable's *scope*. If a variable has a narrow scope, it will retain its value only in the formula where it is initially declared—any other formula that refers to a variable with the same name will be referring to a brand new variable. If a variable has a wide scope, its value will be retained for use not only in other formulas, but also in subreports within the main report. (Subreports are covered in Chapter 13.) The following are three additional words you can place in front of your variable declarations (or use in place of the Dim statement in Basic syntax) to determine the variable's scope.

Local	The variable remains in scope only for the formula in which it is defined. If you declare a variable with the same name in another formula, it won't use the value from the first formula.
Global	The variable remains in scope for the duration of the entire main report. You can declare a global variable in one formula, and another formula will be able to use the contents placed in the variable by the first formula. Global variables, however, are not visible in subreports.
Shared	The variable not only remains in scope for the duration of the entire main report but can also be referred to in formulas in subreports. You can use shared variables to pass data around the main report, back and forth between the main report and subreports, and from subreport to subreport.

Add these keywords in front of variable declarations to determine their scope, as follows:

```
Local NumberVar BonusAmount; //will only be visible in this formula
Global StringVar BonusCustName; //available to the whole main report
Shared DateVar DateBonusReached; //available to main and subreports
```

Tip *If you leave off the variable scope keyword in Crystal syntax, the default scope for a variable will be global—it will be available to other formulas in the main report, but not to subreports. If you use the Dim statement in Basic syntax, the default scope for the variable will be local—it will be available for use only in the rest of the formula where it's declared. If you don't want to use the default scope, make sure you always add the proper scope keyword. And, make sure you add the keyword to the declaration in every formula that will be using the variable!*

Assigning a Value to a Variable

After you declare a variable, it won't do you much good if you don't assign a value to it. You may want to use it as an accumulator, to "add one" to it each time some condition is met for the database record. You may want to assign a string value to it, concatenating additional string values onto the variable as records progress. You then might display the value of the accumulated variable in the group footer, and assign the variable an empty string in the group header to start the whole process over again for the next group.

Tip *If you declare a variable but don't assign a value to it, it takes on a default value based on its data type. Numeric and Currency variables default to 0, string variables default to an empty string, Boolean variables default to false, and Date variables default to a "0/0/00" date. Date/Time and Time variables have no default value.*

Crystal syntax provides two instances in which you can assign a variable a value: at the same time the variable is declared or on a separate line later in the formula. In either event, you must use the assignment operator, consisting of a colon followed by an equal sign, to assign a value to a variable. This is important—it's easy to get confused and just use the equal sign by itself. The equal sign works only for comparison—you must place a colon in front of the equal sign to make assignment work properly unless you are using Basic syntax, in which case the equal sign by itself is used for both assignment and comparison. Here's a Crystal syntax example of assigning a variable a value on a separate line:

```
WhilePrintingRecords;
NumberVar CustomerCount;
CustomerCount := CustomerCount + 1
```

Here, the CustomerCount variable is declared on the first line (terminated with a semicolon) and assigned on the second line. In this particular formula, the CustomerCount variable will keep its value from record to record, so it will be incremented by one every time the formula executes.

If you want to reset the value of the CustomerCount variable in a group header, you need to reset it to 0. Here's a Crystal syntax example of how to declare and assign a variable at the same time:

```
NumberVar CustomerCount := 0;
```

Here, the variable is declared, followed by the assignment operator and the value to assign the variable. In this example, placing this formula in the group header will reset the CustomerCount variable at the beginning of each group.

> **Tip** *Notice that a semicolon doesn't have to appear in the last line of a formula, because it is used to separate one statement from another. If your formula only declares and assigns a variable, you don't need the semicolon at the end of the declaration/assignment statement.*

You don't have to assign a value to a variable every time the formula executes, nor do you need to assign the same value every time. Creative use of logic constructs, such as If-Then-Else or Select Case, along with variable assignment, provides report flexibility that rivals that of many programming languages. Look at the following formula, which declares and conditionally assigns several variables:

```
CurrencyVar BonusAmount;
StringVar HighestCustName;
DateTimeVar DateBonusReached;

If {Orders.Order Amount} > BonusAmount Then
    (HighestCustName := {Customer.Customer Name};
     DateBonusReached := {Orders.Order Date};
     BonusAmount := {Orders.Order Amount})
```

Look at this formula closely. Assuming it's placed in the details section, it keeps track of the highest order amount as the records progress. When an order exceeds the previous high amount, the customer who placed the order and the date the order was placed are added to variables. Then, the new high order amount is assigned to the bonus amount. The following are some important points to note about the formula:

- There are multiple variable assignments separated by semicolons inside the parentheses. They will all execute, but only the last statement will determine how the formula appears on the report. In this example, the last statement uses a currency data type, so the formula will appear on the report as currency.

■ If you are keeping track of the bonus amounts, dates, and customer names for a certain group, such as a region or country, make sure to reset the variables in the group header. If you fail to reset the variables, and the next group doesn't have an order as high as the top value in the previous group, the previous group's values will appear for the following group as well.

■ If you want to keep track of quotas or similar values for both group and report levels (for example, you want to see the bonus customer for each region and for the entire report), you'll need to assign and maintain two sets of variables: one for the group level that is reset in the group header and one for the report level that's not reset.

Displaying a Variable's Contents

In the preceding example, you saw how to accumulate values in variables in the details section, and how to reset them by assigning them a value of 0 in the group header (or in another area of the report). You also need to have a way to show exactly what's contained in a variable on the report, or to use the variable's value in a formula some other way.

To show the contents of a variable, you simply need to declare it. If the formula contains no other statements, declaring the variable will also return it as the formula value. For example, you might place the following formula in the group footer to show the customer who reached the bonus in the region group:

```
StringVar HighestCustName
```

You neither need to place any other statements in the formula to show the value of the variable nor even need the semicolon at the end of the declaration line—it's the last line in the formula.

You may have situations in which you want to show the contents of a variable but are using other statements to assign the variable in the formula. In that case, just declaring the variable won't display it, because the declaration statement won't be the last line in the formula. In this situation, just add the name of the variable as the last line of the formula. This will then display the contents of the variable when the formula executes. Here's an example:

```
CurrencyVar BonusAmount;
StringVar HighestCustName;
DateTimeVar DateBonusReached;

If {Orders.Order Amount} > BonusAmount Then
    (HighestCustName := {Customer.Customer Name};
     DateBonusReached := {Orders.Order Date};
     BonusAmount := {Orders.Order Amount});

HighestCustName
```

This formula performs the test and variable assignments as before, but the last line of the formula simply shows the HighestCustName variable, a string variable. So, this formula shows up with small *x*'s in the Design tab (if Show Field Names is turned off in File | Options), and the contents of the HighestCustName variable will be shown whenever the formula executes.

You can go even one step further by testing and assigning variables and then using them later in other calculations or concatenations. Here's another permutation of this formula:

```
CurrencyVar BonusAmount;
StringVar HighestCustName;
DateTimeVar DateBonusReached;

If {Orders.Order Amount} > BonusAmount Then
    (HighestCustName := {Customer.Customer Name};
     DateBonusReached := {Orders.Order Date};
     BonusAmount := {Orders.Order Amount});

"As of this order, the amount to beat is " & ToText(BonusAmount) +
" set by " & HighestCustName & " on " &
ToText(DateBonusReached,"M/d/yy")
```

This formula not only declares variables, it also conditionally assigns them and then concatenates and displays them, converting them to text as necessary.

Evaluation Times and Report Passes

As you may have gathered by this time, formulas that contain variables are affected by where they are placed physically on the report. If you want to check values and assign variables during record-by-record processing, you must put the formula in the details section. If you want to show the accumulated totals for each group, you place a formula in the group footer to show the total variables. To reset the variables for the next group, you need to place the formula that resets them in the group header.

However, just placing the formulas in these sections doesn't necessarily guarantee that they will actually evaluate in that section or during the logical "formatting" process of the report (during which a group header prints, then the details section for that group prints, then the group footer prints, and so on). Consider the following example. Figure 5-4 contains a report that calculates a "running total" using a variable. The variable accumulates the order amounts in each details section as the report progresses.

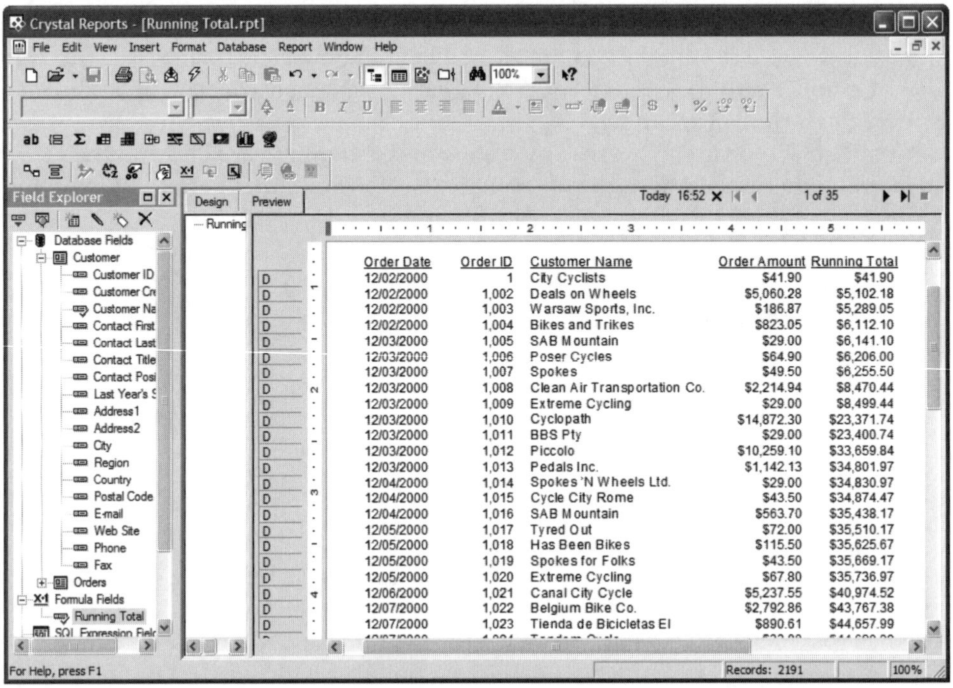

Figure 5-4.   *Running total using a variable*

As you can see, the report is a simple detail report—there are no groups. The running total is accumulating the orders as the report progresses. The formula contains the following variable assignment:

```
CurrencyVar MonthlyTotal := MonthlyTotal + {Orders.Order Amount}
```

In Figure 5-5, the report is grouped by Order Date, using "for each month" grouping. In this situation, the desire is to reset the running total for each month, as the viewer evaluates each month on its own. Accordingly, the running total variable "MonthlyTotal" must be reset in each group header with the following formula:

```
CurrencyVar MonthlyTotal := 0
```

However, even when this formula is placed in the group header of the report, the desired result is not achieved.

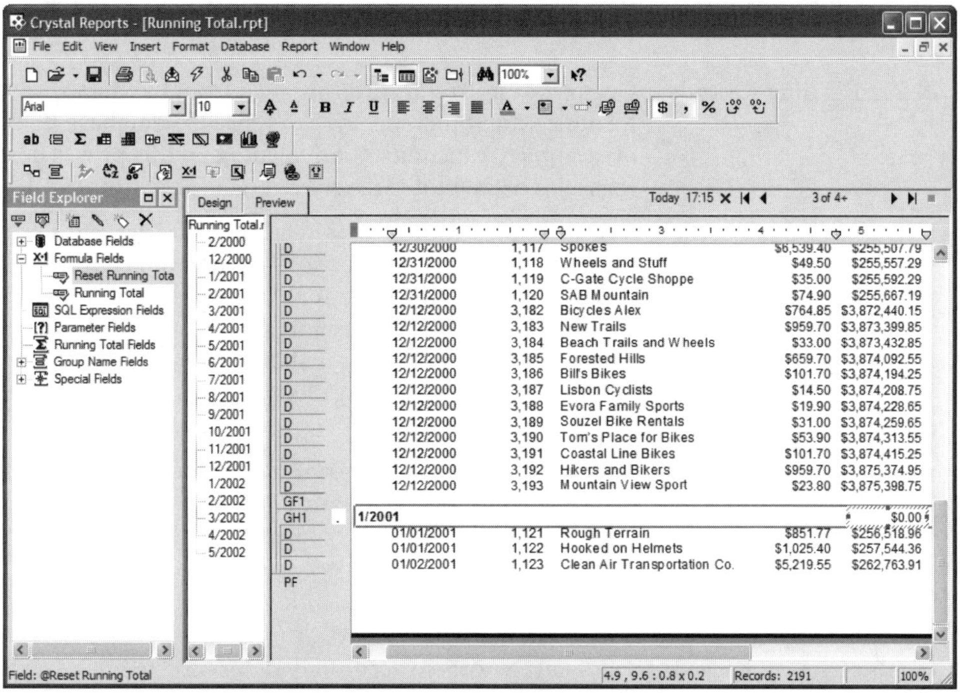

Figure 5-5. *Formula in group header to reset running total doesn't work*

Notice that not only did the running total not get reset to zero from the group header, but that it's showing a *lower* value than it was in the previous group. Why does adding a group result in the oddities with the running total? This happens because the formula is accumulating the running total at a different time from when it's actually displaying it on the report, and because the formula to reset the running total is evaluating at yet another time during report processing.

The formula to accumulate the running total is calculating while records are being read from the database, not when records have been grouped and are actually being printed or formatted. Also, the formula that resets the running total is actually being processed only once, at the very beginning of report processing, not when each group header prints. These formulas are said to be calculating in different *report passes* than the pass that actually formats the report. So, the running total has already been calculated for every record before Crystal Reports sorts the records to be placed in groups. Besides, the running total is actually being reset to zero only once before anything else happens on the report.

Crystal Reports generally breaks down its report processing into the following three passes, during which certain types of formulas automatically evaluate.

Before Reading Records   Occurs before any records are read from the database. If formulas don't include any references to database fields or summary functions, they calculate in this pass. These formulas are sometimes referred to as *flat* formulas.

While Reading Records   Occurs as records are being read from the database, but before any record selection, sorting, or grouping is performed. Formulas that include references to database fields, but don't contain any subtotal or summary functions, are calculated in this pass. These formulas are often called *first pass* formulas.

While Printing Records   Occurs after records have been read and are being formatted for display or printing. Sorting and grouping occurs during this pass. Formulas that include sum, average, or other summary functions are included in this pass. These formulas are often called *second pass* formulas.

In most cases, you can trust Crystal Reports to accurately determine in which pass it needs to evaluate a formula. The glaring exception, however, is when a formula uses variables. If a formula simply declares a variable, or declares the variable and assigns it a literal or constant value, Crystal Reports evaluates that formula in the Before Reading Records pass, because it makes no reference to database fields or summary functions. If you assign a variable a database value, Crystal Reports evaluates that formula in the While Reading Records pass (the formula will become a first pass formula). Only if you have some type of summary or subtotal function in the formula will Crystal Reports automatically evaluate the formula in the While Printing Records pass (the formula then becomes a second pass formula).

This default behavior can cause very strange results, as the previous running total example illustrates. The formula to accumulate the running total makes reference to the Order Amount database field and therefore evaluates in the first pass (WhileReadingRecords). This accumulates the running total just fine before the report was grouped. However, when the report was grouped by the Order Date, records appeared on the report in a different order than they were read from the database, resulting in the running totals no longer appearing in a logical order. And to complicate matters even further, the formula that resets the running total variable makes no references to database fields at all, so it becomes a flat formula (BeforeReadingRecords) and processes only once at the very beginning of report processing, instead of at the beginning of every group.

When you use variables in a formula, you may need to force the formula to evaluate in a different pass than it would by default. You do this by changing the formula's *evaluation time.* To do this, add an evaluation-time statement as the first statement in the formula. Look in the Formula Editor Function Tree box and you'll notice an Evaluation Time section. Open that section to see several evaluation-time statements that should now be mostly self-explanatory.

To force the formula that accumulates the running total to the second pass, where it will calculate the running total correctly after the records have been grouped, add the WhilePrintingRecords evaluation-time statement to the formula, as follows:

```
WhilePrintingRecords;
CurrencyVar MonthlyTotal := MonthlyTotal + {Orders.Order Amount}
```

Caution   *Don't get confused if you can't insert a subtotal, summary, or grand total on a second pass formula. When you click this type of formula in the details section, no subtotal, summary, or grand total options will be available on the pull-down or pop-up menus, because subtotals, summaries, and grand totals are calculated in the WhilePrintingRecords pass. If the formula is already evaluating in that pass, you can't create a summary or grand total on it.*

Now, to ensure that the formula that resets the running total actually happens when the groups are being formatted, instead of one time only at the beginning of the report, force it to the WhilePrintingRecords pass as well.

```
WhilePrintingRecords;
CurrencyVar MonthlyTotal := 0
```

The one evaluation-time function that may not be self-explanatory is EvaluateAfter, which takes one argument: the name of another formula. This forces one formula to evaluate after another formula when they evaluate in the same pass and are in the same section of the report. Because Crystal Reports automatically evaluates formulas that contain other formulas in the proper order, you'll use this function very rarely. However, it may be necessary to use it with formulas that contain variables.

When Crystal Reports evaluates two formulas that contain the same variable in the same section of the report, the order in which it will evaluate them is not predictable. One example is if you place two formulas in a group footer. The first formula shows the values of the variables (assuming that those values have been set in other formulas in the details section):

```
WhilePrintingRecords;

CurrencyVar BonusAmount;
StringVar HighestCustName;
```

```
DateTimeVar DateBonusReached;
"The highest order of " + ToText(BonusAmount) +
" was placed by " + HighestCustName + " on " +
ToText(DateBonusReached,"M/d/yy")
```

The second resets the variables to zero or an empty string to prepare for the next group:

```
WhilePrintingRecords;

CurrencyVar BonusAmount := 0;
StringVar HighestCustName := "";
DateTimeVar DateBonusReached := DateTime(0,0,0);
```

Because there's a chance that the formula that resets the variables will evaluate before the formula that shows them, you have two choices. First, and probably most logical, is simply to move the formula that resets the variables to the group header. That way, the variables will be reset when a new group begins, after they have been displayed in the previous group footer. Or, if there is some logical reason why both formulas must exist in the group footer, you can use EvaluateAfter in the formula that resets the variables, as follows:

```
EvaluateAfter ({@Bonus Show});

CurrencyVar BonusAmount := 0;
StringVar HighestCustName := "";
DateTimeVar DateBonusReached := DateTime(0,0,0);
```

By placing EvaluateAfter as the first statement in the formula, you force the reset formula to evaluate after the display formula. Because you are forcing this formula to evaluate after a formula that's in the second pass, there's no need to include WhilePrintingRecords in this formula.

Tip   *As you begin to add formulas that calculate and reset variables, you may find quite a few instances of things appearing in details and group header sections that show zeros or other unnecessary information. You can't delete the formulas from these sections, because then they won't evaluate properly. To hide them, just click Suppress on the Common tab of the Format Editor. You'll then see them on the Design tab, but not on the Preview tab or any other report output.*

When Not to Use Variables

It's fairly common to learn how to use certain "spiffy" features of a tool, and then to use them to excess! Variables have that potential. Although they are fast and, if used judiciously, don't consume significant extra memory or resources, they can sometimes be "overkill." If you find a use for variables, first look closely at your report to see whether an easier, quicker way exists to accomplish the same task.

Figure 5-6 is an example of a report that counts orders that exceed a $1,000 bonus level. The number of orders needs to be shown both at the group level and at the end of the report.

Using variables to accomplish this requires the creation of several formulas. Two variables are also required: one to accumulate the bonus order count for each group and one to count for the whole report. Following are the formulas.

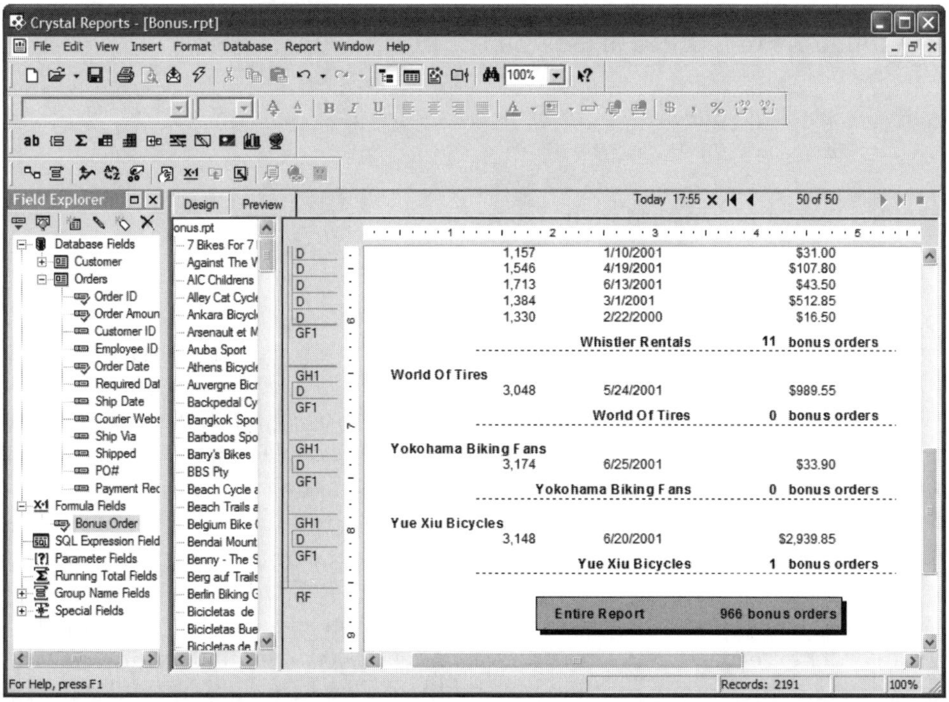

Figure 5-6.   *Over $1,000 Bonus report*

@Bonus Calc is placed in the details section and suppressed:

```
WhilePrintingRecords;
NumberVar CountCustomer;
NumberVar CountReport;
If {Orders.Order Amount} > 1000 Then
    (CountCustomer := CountCustomer + 1;
     CountReport := CountReport + 1)
```

@Show Group Bonus is placed in the group footer:

```
WhilePrintingRecords;
NumberVar CountCustomer;
"This customer had " + ToText(CountCustomer,0) + " bonus orders."
```

@Reset Group Bonus is placed in the group header and suppressed:

```
WhilePrintingRecords;
NumberVar CountCustomer := 0;
```

@Show Report Bonus is placed in the report footer:

```
WhilePrintingRecords;
NumberVar CountReport;
"This report had " + ToText(CountReport,0) + " bonus orders."
```

While this will work, there is a much simpler way to accomplish the same task with just one formula using no variables. Create a single formula, place it in the details section, and suppress it. It will simply consist of the following:

```
If {Orders.Order Amount} > 1000 Then 1
```

When you place this in the details section, it will return a number constant of 1 when an order exceeds $1,000. If an order is under $1,000, the number formula will return 0 (because the formula is numeric and there is no Else clause, it will return 0 if the If test fails). You then simply need to insert a group subtotal and a report grand total on the formula to calculate group and report totals.

The result: the same totals with much less effort. This simple technique of assigning a formula a value of 1 if a test is passed can become the cornerstone for a lot of statistics-type reports you may have to write.

You may also be able to save time by using running total fields instead of formulas with variables. The running total report earlier in the chapter that illustrates evaluation times is a perfect example. In this type of report, there's no need to create formulas to calculate the running total. Running total fields are covered later in this chapter.

Tip	*Many of the types of formulas illustrated in this chapter are included in a sample report on this book's accompanying Web site. Look at www.CrystalBook.com for FORMULAS.RPT to see how these, and similar formulas, are implemented.*

User Function Libraries

Crystal Reports has been designed as an *extensible* reporting tool. With respect to formulas, that means that you can develop your own functions to add to the Function Tree box if Crystal Reports doesn't provide one that you need. In Crystal Reports 9, this capability has been enhanced with custom functions that you can create directly in your report, or add to the repository to be shared with other Crystal Reports users (custom functions are covered in Chapter 6).

However, previous versions of Crystal Reports didn't feature custom functions. But it was still possible to create your own functions that would appear in the Formula Editor. This capability remains with Crystal Reports 9. Look at the built-in functions that appear under the Additional Functions category.

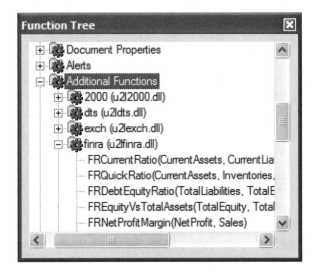

The functions in this category aren't really "built-in." These functions are being supplied to Crystal Reports by *user function libraries (UFLs)*. The UFL is supplied to Crystal Reports by an external dynamic link library developed in another programming language. You can write your own custom functions using a Windows programming language, such as C++ or Visual Basic, and have them appear in this section of the Function Tree box.

For example, you could write a function that calculates the number of business days between two dates you supply, excluding any weekends and company holidays that are contained in an external database. Or, you might write a UFL that reads a value from an external piece of proprietary measurement equipment and supplies a value to your report.

The filename that supplies the UFL appears as a category in the Additional Functions list—you may click the plus sign next to the filename to see the available functions supplied by that file. As with other functions, double-click the function name and supply the necessary arguments inside your formula.

> **Tip**   *Although the need for external UFLs is probably greatly reduced by Crystal Reports 9 custom function and repository capabilities, you may still need to use them to connect to external databases, external equipment, or any other capability that is not provided by the Crystal Reports formula language (which is what Crystal Reports 9 custom functions use). Information on creating User Functions Libraries with Visual Basic can be found on this book's Web site. Look at www.CrystalBook.com.*

Running Total Fields

In certain situations, the use of formulas with variables (discussed earlier in the chapter) is inevitable. However, many of the examples shown previously can actually be accomplished without even creating a formula. If you need to accumulate, display, and reset running totals, you will probably prefer the *running total field*. A running total field can be inserted just like a database field. It gives you great flexibility to accumulate or increment values as the report progresses, without the need for formulas or variables.

Figure 5-7 shows a Top *N* report (discussed in Chapter 3) that shows regional subtotals for the top five regions in the U.S. This particular Top *N* report does not include Others. As mentioned in Chapter 3, this causes the report grand totals not to agree with the sum of all the group totals. The grand totals are based on all report records, not just those that fall into the top five groups. Using running total fields is the perfect answer to this problem.

All new running total fields are created from the Field Explorer. First, select the Running Total Fields category in the Field Explorer. Click the New button in the Field Explorer toolbar or right-click the Running Total Fields category and choose New from the pop-up menu. You may also select an existing field in the Details section, right-click, and choose Insert | Running Total from the pop-up menu. The Create Running Total Field dialog box appears, as shown in Figure 5-8.

Start by giving the running total field a name (if you don't like the default name given by Crystal Reports). It can contain mixed-case characters and spaces and won't conflict with formula or database field names. Crystal Reports will precede the running total field name with a pound sign (#).

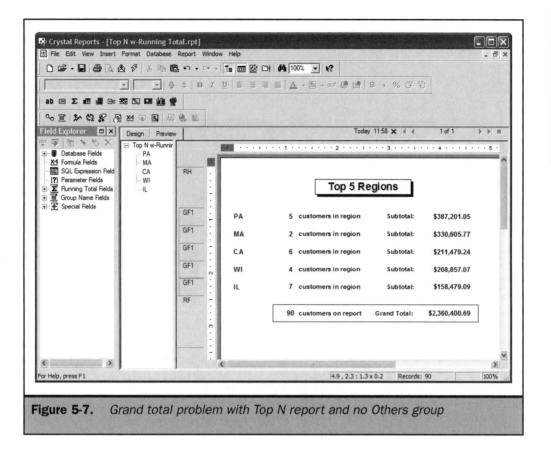

Figure 5-7.   *Grand total problem with Top N report and no Others group*

If you select a detail field and use the right-click method to insert the running total field, the field you choose will already appear in the Field to Summarize drop-down list, and a default summary function will appear in the Type of Summary drop-down list. If you're creating a new running total field from the Field Explorer, choose the report, database, or formula field that you want to use to calculate the running total by selecting the field in the Available Tables and Fields list and clicking the right arrow next to the Field to Summarize box. Choose the type of calculation you want to use from the Type of Summary pull-down list. If you just want to increment the running total by one for certain records, use the Count or DistinctCount summaries (depending on how "unique" the field you are summarizing is), along with any field from the report that won't contain null values. Nulls don't increment counts. Other functions available in running totals are the same as those available for summaries. Look back at Chapter 3 for a detailed description of available summaries.

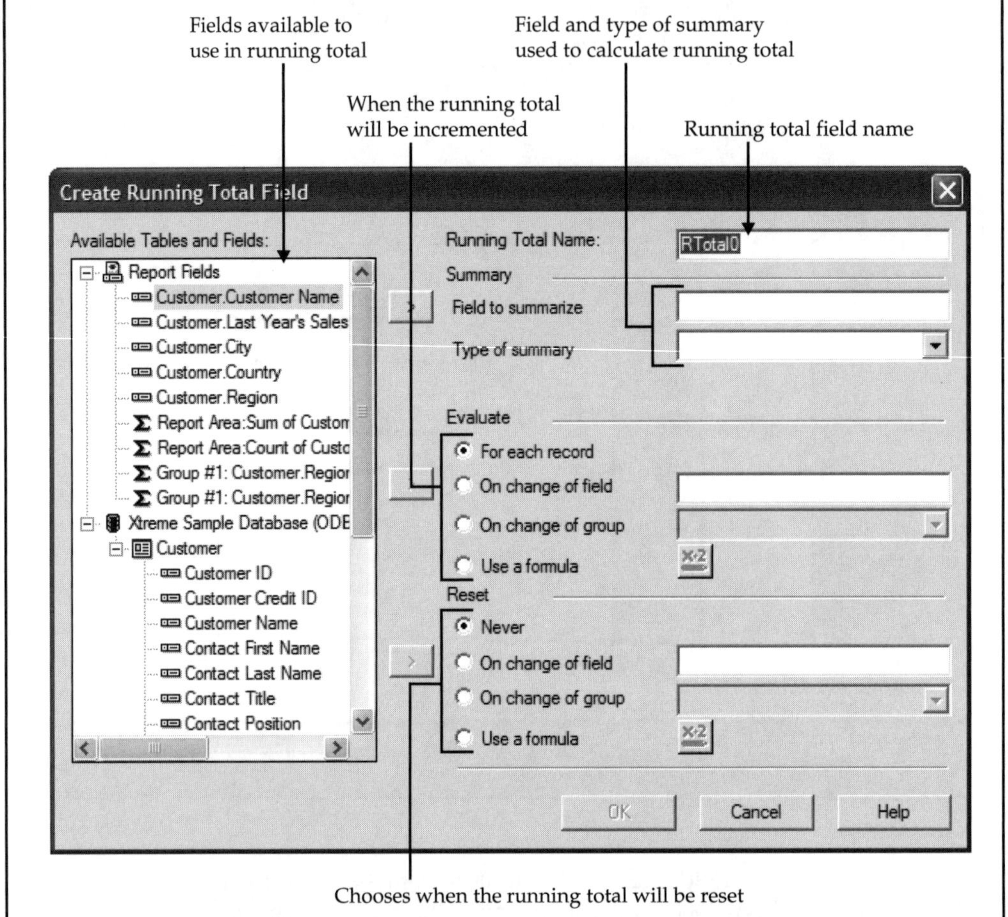

Fields available to
use in running total

Field and type of summary
used to calculate running total

When the running total
will be incremented

Running total field name

Create Running Total Field

Available Tables and Fields:

- Report Fields
  - Customer.Customer Name
  - Customer.Last Year's Sales
  - Customer.City
  - Customer.Country
  - Customer.Region
  - Report Area:Sum of Custom
  - Report Area:Count of Custo
  - Group #1: Customer.Region
  - Group #1: Customer.Region
- Xtreme Sample Database (ODE
  - Customer
    - Customer ID
    - Customer Credit ID
    - Customer Name
    - Contact First Name
    - Contact Last Name
    - Contact Title
    - Contact Position

Running Total Name: RTotal0

Summary

Field to summarize

Type of summary

Evaluate

- For each record
- On change of field
- On change of group
- Use a formula

Reset

- Never
- On change of field
- On change of group
- Use a formula

OK   Cancel   Help

Chooses when the running total will be reset

Figure 5-8. *Create Running Total Field dialog box*

Choose when you want the running total to increment, by making choices in the Evaluate section. Then, choose when you want the running total to reset, by making choices in the Reset section. If you select a field in the Available Tables and Fields list and then click the arrow next to the On Change of Field radio button, the running total will increment or reset every time a new value appears in that field. If you click the On Change of Group radio button, you can then choose an existing report group in the pull-down list. The running total will increment or reset every time the chosen group changes. If you click the Use a Formula radio button, you can then click the Formula button next to it. The Formula Editor will appear, in which you can enter a Boolean formula that will trigger when the running total field is incremented or reset.

Click OK when you've completed the Create Running Total Field dialog box. The running total will now appear in the Field Explorer and can be dragged and dropped on the report just like a database field. If you'd like to edit, rename, or delete the running total field, you have these choices in the Field Explorer. You can also right-click a running total field in either the Design or Preview tab and choose Edit Field Object from the pop-up menu.

To solve the problem with the Top *N* report without "Others," simply create two running total fields: one to calculate the number of customers:

and one to calculate the sale grand total:

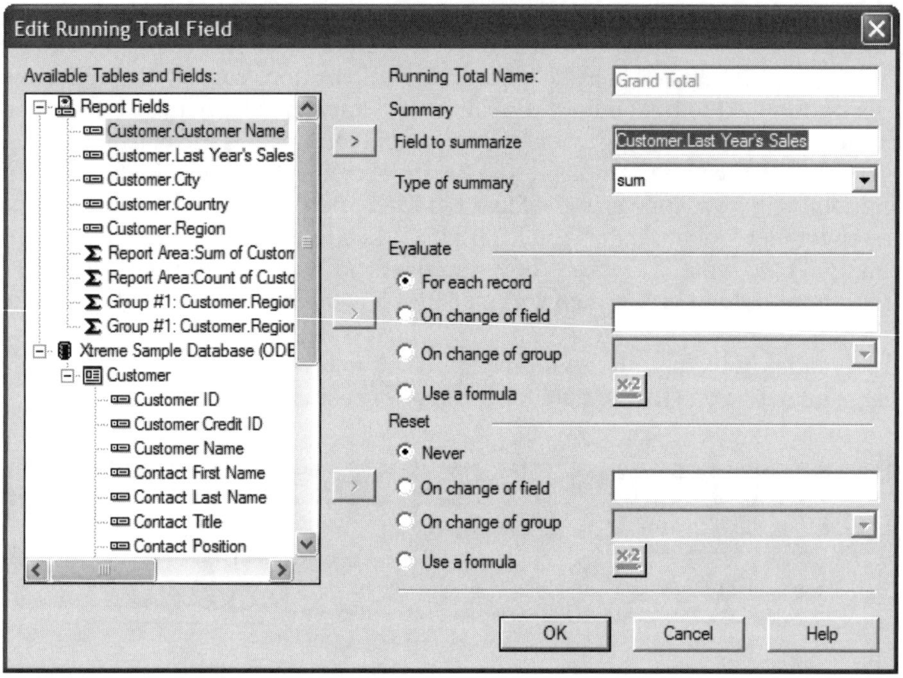

Place these running totals in the report footer instead of grand totaling the fields from the details section. Because running totals evaluate only during the While Printing Records pass, the extra records in the Others group won't be included in the report footer. Figure 5-9 shows the correct totals now displayed on the Top *N* report.

Caution *Because running total fields are calculated in the While Printing Records pass of the report, you cannot create running total fields based on second-pass formulas.*

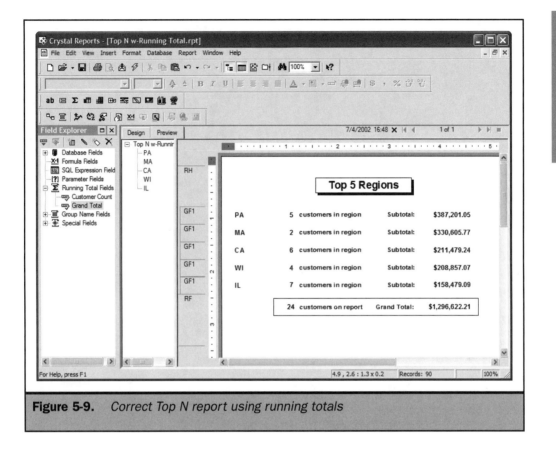

Figure 5-9.   *Correct Top N report using running totals*

Chapter 6

Creating Custom Functions

175

One of the most often heard questions from Crystal Reports users is, "How can I share a formula I write with other reports or with other Crystal Reports users?" Often, too, a report designer will find a set of formula logic that is particular to their type of business or type of reports that must be used over and over again in many other formulas. The question then becomes, "Is there any way of reducing the need to type these same parts of the formula over and over again?"

In previous versions of Crystal Reports, the solutions to these questions typically weren't very elegant. Some users would open two reports side-by-side, reduce the size of the windows inside the Crystal Report designer, and drag a formula from one report to another. Others would open a report, edit a formula, copy the contents to the clipboard, and paste the contents to a new formula. Or, a user might copy the contents of a formula in a report, close the first report, open a second report, create a new formula, and paste the formula text from the first report into the Formula Editor. Still others would keep their own "library" of formulas in a text file or word processing document, cutting and pasting between various formulas in various reports and this document on a regular basis.

With Crystal Reports 9, this has all been made much easier. This latest version features the ability to create your own "reusable functions," called *custom functions*, that not only can be used over and over again in different formulas in the same report, but can be added to the new Crystal Reports repository for use in other reports and for use by other Crystal Reports users.

Custom Functions Defined

A custom function is very similar to a regular function you will already find in the function tree of the Crystal Reports Formula Editor (learn more about formulas in general and the function tree in Chapter 5). For example, the built-in ToText function in the Crystal Reports formula language will convert from, for instance, a numerical data type to a text data type. The built-in Left function will return a certain number of characters from the left side of a string value. And the built-in Round function will round a numeric value to a specified number of decimal places.

But what if you have a special need in your company to use a function that's not included as part of the built-in Crystal Reports functions? You may, for example, need to calculate the number of business days between two dates, excluding weekends and company holidays. Or you may want to calculate a discount for customers in a large number of formulas. However, you want to base this discount on several factors, including the size of the order amount, the number of orders the customer placed last year, and the length of time they have been a customer. While you can most probably make use of Crystal Reports' extensive formula language to create these special formulas, making use of the logic over and over again in more than one formula, or sharing the logic with other report designers, is where a custom function becomes really useful.

Available custom functions (either that you built after creating the report, or added from the repository) will appear in the Formula Editor just like built-in functions. However, custom functions appear in their own Custom Functions area of the function tree, as shown in Figure 6-1.

CRYSTAL REPORTS 9
INTRODUCED

Available custom functions are listed
in the Formula Workshop tree

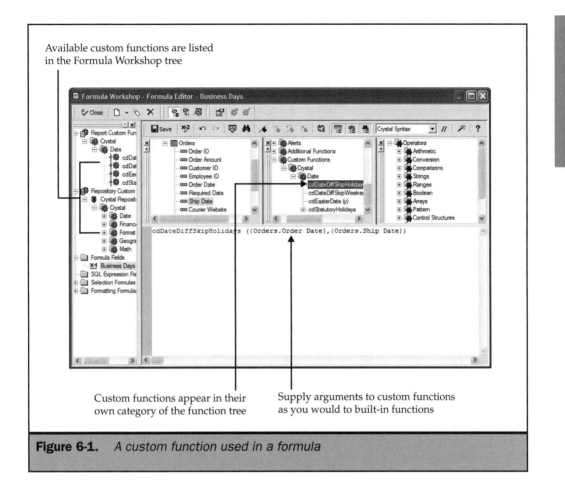

Custom functions appear in their
own category of the function tree

Supply arguments to custom functions
as you would to built-in functions

Figure 6-1.   *A custom function used in a formula*

A custom function can accept parameters or arguments, just like a regular function (arguments are discussed in more detail later in the chapter). And as with regular functions, you can use the custom function over and over in as many formulas as you desire. If the core logic of your custom function changes (perhaps business holidays or a discount percentage tier change with the new year), changing the custom function in its one location will be reflected in all formulas that make use of that function—you won't have to edit each and every formula to change the formula logic.

Creating Your Own Custom Functions

While Crystal Reports 9 ships with a "starter set" of custom functions in its default repository, you'll probably soon discover a use for your own. Creating a custom function is very similar to creating a Crystal Reports formula—most of the typical built-in functions and operators otherwise available in regular formulas are available for your use in a custom function (Chapter 5 covers formula creation in more detail).

There are two ways to create a new custom function: base it on an existing formula or create it from scratch.

Extracting Custom Functions from Existing Formulas

If you have an existing formula in a report that contains the "core" set of logic that you wish to use for your custom function, you may base your custom function on it by *extracting* the custom function from the formula. Do this by performing these steps:

1. Launch the Formula Workshop by clicking the Formula Workshop button in the Expert Tools toolbar, or choosing Report | Formula Workshop from the pull-down menus.

2. In the Formula Workshop tree, right-click the Report Custom Functions category and choose New from the pop-up menu. You may also just click the Report Custom Functions category to select it and click the New button in the Formula Workshop toolbar, or click the down arrow next to the New toolbar button and choose Custom Function from the drop-down list.

3. Type in a name for your custom function. Choose a name within the naming limitations discussed later in this chapter.

4. Click the Use Extractor button to base your custom function on an existing report formula. The Extract Custom Function from Formula dialog box will appear, as shown in Figure 6-2.

5. Make any desired changes to arguments that are substituted for database fields in the original formula. You may also add descriptive text to the function definition that will appear when you use the function in the Formula Expert (discussed in Chapter 5).

6. If you wish to change the original formula to use the function, check the Modify Formula to Use New Custom Function check box.

7. Click the Enter More Info button to supply optional items, such as default argument values and other descriptive text.

8. Click OK to save the new custom function.

Custom Function Arguments

One of the first adjustments you'll need to make when creating custom functions, as opposed to formulas, is handling function arguments. An *argument* is a parameter that you create within your function to accept a value from the formula that calls it. It then uses this value (possibly along with other arguments that are also supplied) to perform some calculation or logic and return a result to the calling formula.

If you think of Crystal Reports built-in functions, most require that you supply arguments when you use them in formulas. For example, if you use the ToText function to convert a number, date, or other nonstring data type to a string, you must supply at

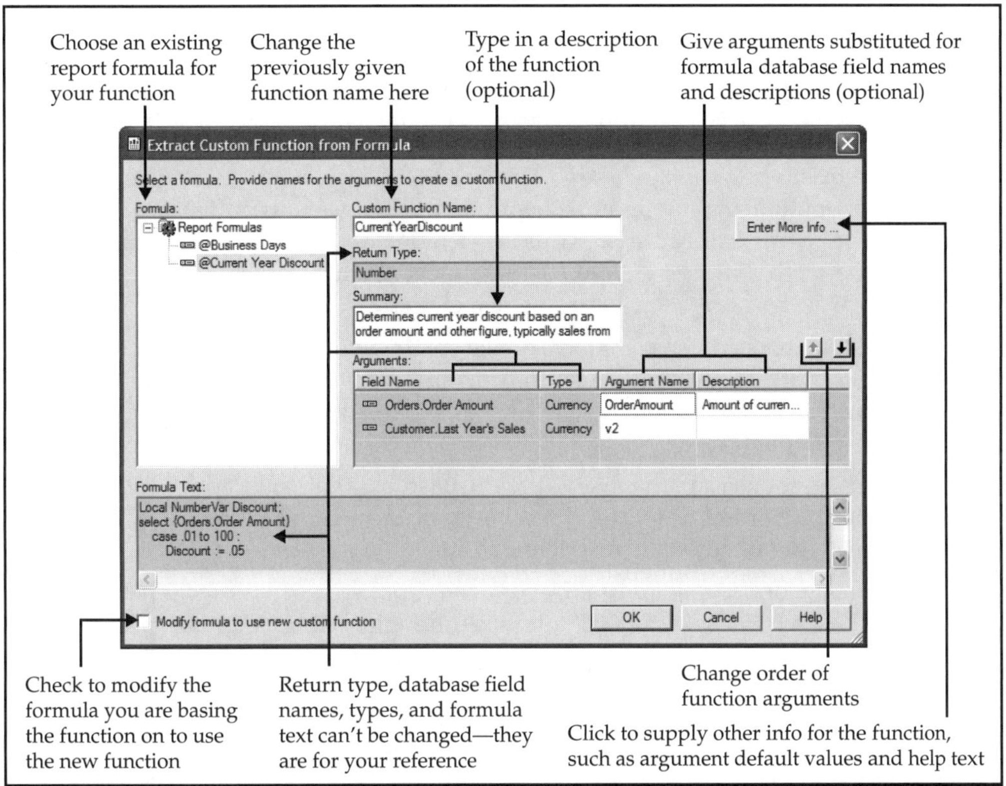

Choose an existing report formula for your function

Change the previously given function name here

Type in a description of the function (optional)

Give arguments substituted for formula database field names and descriptions (optional)

Extract Custom Function from Formula

Select a formula. Provide names for the arguments to create a custom function.

Formula:
- Report Formulas
  - @Business Days
  - @Current Year Discount

Custom Function Name:
CurrentYearDiscount

Return Type:
Number

Summary:
Determines current year discount based on an order amount and other figure, typically sales from

Enter More Info ...

Arguments:

Field Name	Type	Argument Name	Description
Orders.Order Amount	Currency	OrderAmount	Amount of curren...
Customer.Last Year's Sales	Currency	v2	

Formula Text:
```
Local NumberVar Discount;
select (Orders.Order Amount)
    case .01 to 100 :
        Discount := .05
```

☐ Modify formula to use new custom function   OK   Cancel   Help

Check to modify the formula you are basing the function on to use the new function

Return type, database field names, types, and formula text can't be changed—they are for your reference

Change order of function arguments

Click to supply other info for the function, such as argument default values and help text

Figure 6-2. *Creating a custom function based on a formula*

least one argument: the nonstring value to be converted. And the Left function, which returns a certain number of characters from the left side of a larger string, requires you to supply two arguments: the string to retrieve a subset of characters from, and the number of characters to retrieve. In cases of built-in functions, arguments you supply must conform to specific data types. The single-argument ToText example requires a string argument to be supplied. The Left function requires a string argument and a number argument.

When you create your own custom functions (by either extracting logic from an existing formula or creating the function from scratch), you must consider if your function will need to accept arguments from the calling formula, how many arguments your function requires, what data types the arguments will be, and if you want to supply one or more default values for each argument.

When extracting a custom function from a formula, such as the function illustrated in Figure 6-2, the number and data types of arguments in your function are automatically

Custom Function Naming Limitations

You are more restricted in choosing names for your custom functions than you are for formulas. Because custom functions appear in the Formula Editor's function tree alongside all the built-in functions, there are several limitations:

- Custom function names must begin with a letter—you can't start a function name with a number. Also, you can include only letters, numbers, and the underscore character in your custom function name—other special characters (such as the % or # signs) cannot be included.

- Custom function names cannot contain spaces—you can use only underscores to separate a multiword custom function name. However, you can use mixed upper- and lowercase letters to help delineate multiword custom function names.

- You cannot use a name that is already used by a Crystal Reports built-in function. For example, you'll receive an error message if you try to create a custom function named ToText or Left.

- You may notice that Crystal Decisions—supplied custom function names include a two-character "cd" prefix. Although adding your own prefix is certainly not required, it may be a handy way of identifying a certain group of custom functions. Prefixing custom function names may also help avoid naming conflicts with other custom functions contained in the repository, as well as conflicts with built-in function names.

determined by the number of unique database fields included in the original formula. In the example shown in the figure, the original formula the custom function is based upon contains two database fields: {Orders.Order Amount} and {Customer.Last Year's Sales}. When the custom function is extracted from this formula, the database fields are removed from the function and replaced with two arguments, both of which require currency data types (the data types of the original database fields) to be supplied.

The arguments that the extract process identifies are listed in the Arguments list of the Extract Custom Function from Formula dialog box. You'll see the original database fields that are being replaced with arguments, the data type of the argument (both of these columns are for your information and can't be changed), the name of the argument in the custom function, and the description of the argument. By default, the extract process will number arguments successively from the number 1, preceding the argument number with the letter v.

If you simply wish to allow the default v-numbered arguments to remain, you may ignore this section of the Extract Custom Function from Formula dialog box. However, in that case, the function illustrated in Figure 6-2 would appear like this in the function tree of the Formula Editor:

```
CurrentYearDiscount(v1, v2)
```

It's more likely that you will want arguments in your custom function to be more meaningful, perhaps replacing v1 with OrderAmount, and v2 with PreviousSaleAmount. To accomplish this, rename the v1 and v2 argument names in the dialog box. You may optionally add descriptions to each argument that will appear in the Formula Expert (described in Chapter 5).

The More Info Button

When you extract a custom function from a formula, you'll notice the Enter More Info button on the Extract Custom Function from Formula dialog box. If you click this button, the Custom Function Properties dialog box appears.

The shaded areas of this dialog box are just for reference—they can't be changed here. The Summary and Argument descriptions are interchangeable with those in the Extract Custom Function from Formula dialog box—changing the descriptions of the function and arguments in either place will change it in the other. However, the Category, Author, Display in Experts check box, argument default values, and help text can be changed only on this dialog box.

Category   If you look at the custom functions Crystal Decisions supplies with Crystal Reports, you'll notice that they are categorized in a hierarchy several levels deep (for example, the cdDateDiffSkipHolidays custom function is within the Date category, which is within the Crystal category). You may set up categories and hierarchies for your own custom functions. Do this by specifying the category in the Category text box. If you wish to build a hierarchy for the categories, separate the category names with slashes. For example, placing a function in the Sales/Orders category will show a Sales entry in the Formula Workshop tree with a plus sign. When you click the plus sign, the Orders subcategory will appear with the CurrentYearDiscount custom function in it.

Author   This is, in essence, a comment field that you can either leave blank or fill with text of your choice (probably the name of the person who developed the custom function). This value will appear only when you edit the custom function or use it in the Formula Expert. This text won't be available in the Formula Editor.

Display in Experts   This check box determines whether or not the custom function will appear in the list of available functions when using the Formula Expert (covered in Chapter 5). If you uncheck this box, then you'll see the custom function in the function tree of the Formula Editor, but not in the list of available custom functions when using the Formula Expert.

Argument Default Values   For certain arguments, such as those that may accept department codes, months of the year, or other common values (the order amount/ previous period sales examples here probably don't fall into this category), you may wish to supply a list of one or more default values that a user can choose from when they use the custom function in the Formula Expert. To supply these, click the Default Values box for the argument that you want to set the defaults for. This will display the Default Values dialog box.

Here, you may type in a default value that you want a user to be able to choose; then click the Add button. This will add the value to a list in the lower part of the dialog box. If you want to add additional values, type them in and click the Add button. If you wish to remove a value that's already been added, choose it in the lower list and click the Remove button. And if you wish to change the order of the default values you've already added, choose the value in the list that you wish to move and click the up or down arrow to the right of the list.

When you click OK, the default value list will be added to the custom function and will appear in the argument list on the original Custom Function Properties dialog box.

Help Text   Clicking the Help Text button will simply display yet another dialog box where you can type in free-form text describing the custom function, providing more detail on its arguments or return value, or other helpful information. This help text will be visible only when editing this function later, or using it in the Formula Expert. This text won't be available in the Formula Editor.

Caution *There are certain requirements an existing report formula must meet to be used as the basis for a custom function. For example (and this list is not all-inclusive), the formula cannot contain any evaluation time functions (such as WhilePrintingRecords), any summary functions used with database fields (such as Sum({Orders.Order Amount})), or any variables scoped other than Local. If you attempt to extract a custom function from such a formula, you'll either receive an error message indicating that the formula can't be used, and explaining why, or a function that may not perform the way you expected it to. You may either copy the formula to the clipboard and paste it into the Custom Function Editor when creating the function from scratch (making modifications to the copied formula to allow it to work as a function), or edit the report formula (perhaps explicitly setting variable scope to Local), and then extract the function from the updated formula.*

Creating Custom Functions from Scratch

There may be times when an existing report formula isn't available as the basis for your custom function. Also, you may have a need for a custom function that is more sophisticated than an existing formula, or the existing formula might contain elements that prohibit it from being used as the basis for a custom function (it may use global variables, evaluation time, or other limiting features). In these cases, you will want to create a custom function "from scratch" using the Custom Function editor.

In this case, the steps for initially creating the custom function are the same. Create and name the new custom function in the Formula Workshop, as described previously in the chapter. However, in the Custom Function Name dialog box, click the Use Editor button to display the Custom Function Editor inside the Formula Workshop, as shown in Figure 6-3.

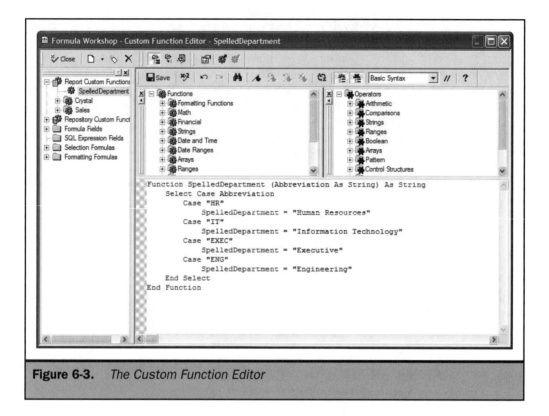

Figure 6-3.   *The Custom Function Editor*

The Custom Function Editor is almost identical to the Formula Editor discussed in detail in Chapter 5. The difference is that the field tree, containing a list of database fields, is not visible. And the function tree, which contains a list of built-in Crystal Reports functions, contains a slightly reduced set of built-in functions. This variance is because custom functions are designed to be independent of any particular report they are placed in; you can't include database fields in a custom function—there would be no way of ensuring these fields would be available when the function is called from another report. You are also prevented from including the limited set of built-in functions (such as Evaluation Time, Print State, and others) because of the "stateless" nature of a custom function.

> **Tip**   *Even though the function tree contains a reduced set of options, it will still display a Custom Function category where you can choose another existing custom function to use in the current custom function.*

You may now just create the custom function logic by double-clicking built-in functions in the function tree and operators in the operator tree. You may, of course, type in these items yourself, as well as associated formula code. And as with the Formula Editor, you can check the syntax of your custom function before saving by clicking the Check button in the toolbar or typing ALT-C.

Syntax Choices and Requirements

When you create a custom function, you have the choice of both Crystal Reports formula languages (or syntaxes) just like you do when creating a report formula. Choose the desired syntax from the drop-down list toward the right of the Custom Function Editor toolbar. The function tree and the operator tree will adjust the chosen syntax. You'll also see a slight difference in the formula text that is automatically added by Crystal Reports.

The basic premise of creating a custom function directly in the Custom Function Editor is to design a formula to accept any necessary values passed into the function from the calling formula; perform evaluations, calculations, If-Then-Else tests, and so forth within the custom function; and return a value back to the calling formula. If you have created functions in a programming language, such as Visual Basic, then this should be a fairly straightforward process. If you haven't programmed in a programming language in the past, then getting the "hang" of custom function creation may take some time. But, if you're familiar with Crystal Reports formulas in general, you should be able to apply your existing knowledge to custom function creation pretty quickly.

Here is an example of a Basic Syntax custom function that returns the spelled-out name of a company department based on an abbreviated name passed in as an argument.

```
Function SpelledDepartment (Abbreviation As String) As String
    Select Case Abbreviation
        Case "HR"
            SpelledDepartment = "Human Resources"
        Case "IT"
            SpelledDepartment = "Information Technology"
        Case "EXEC"
            SpelledDepartment = "Executive"
        Case "ENG"
            SpelledDepartment = "Engineering"
    End Select
End Function
```

The basic (no pun intended) layout of a Basic syntax function is formula code within a Function and End Function block. The Function statement declares the name of the function (the same name you used when you created the function), a list of any arguments and data types the function should accept (a string argument named Abbreviation in this case), and the type of data the function will return to the calling formula (the data type "As" portion is optional—if you don't include it, the data type the function returns will be determined by the data type you assign to the function name later inside the function).

The last statement within the Function–End Function block that assigns a value to the function name will determine what the function returns to the calling formula. In this case, the function uses a Select Case construct (from the Control Structures category of the operator tree) to test for various values of the passed Abbreviation argument, setting the function name to a string literal based on the value of the argument.

Here is the same function in Crystal syntax:

```
Function (StringVar Abbreviation)
Select Abbreviation
    Case "HR" :
        "Human Resources"
    Case "IT" :
        "Information Technolgoy"
    Case "EXEC" :
        "Executive"
    Case "ENG" :
        "Engineering"
```

In this case, there is no Function–End Function block—all the formula text included in the function is implicitly considered to be within this "block." The argument being passed to the function is included in parentheses immediately after the Function keyword, preceded by the data type that the argument is assigned (data type keywords are the same as those for declaring variables—see the Variable Declarations section of the operator tree for proper spelling). Similar to the Basic syntax example, the last statement inside the function to evaluate will determine what the function returns to the calling formula. In this example, the Case statement that matches the passed argument will return a string value to the calling formula.

Complex Data Types and Optional Arguments

In the preceding examples, the custom function accepted a single "simple" string value as an argument and returned a single simple string value as a result. However, you may have more complex custom functions that need to deal with more than one argument, or complex data types, such as array and range values. While using the extract function, discussed earlier in the chapter, can create custom functions with multiple arguments, it can't create functions that accept or return complex data types. To accept range values or arrays as arguments, or pass similar data types back to the formula, you must use the Custom Function editor.

You also may create a special kind of argument in the Custom Function editor called an *optional argument*. By placing the Optional keyword in front of an argument name, you specify that the formula calling the function does not have to supply this argument. If the formula does supply the argument, it will override the default value for the argument that you must supply if you declare an argument as optional.

For example, if you create the following as the *first* line of a Basic syntax function,

```
Function DaysBetweenDates _
(BDate As Date, Optional EDate As Date = CurrentDate)
```

you will be able to call the function in a formula using one *or two* arguments, as the second argument is optional. If you call the function using two arguments, both will be supplied to the function. If you call the function using only one argument, that argument will be supplied as the BDate argument and the current date from the computer's system clock (CurrentDate is a built-in function) will be supplied as the second argument. Adding optional arguments will create multiple occurrences of the function in the function tree to indicate the ability to call the function with multiple arguments. For example, the single custom function created with the Function statement illustrated previously will appear in the function tree twice.

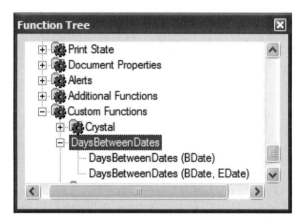

Optional arguments are declared in Crystal syntax with the Optional keyword as well, but with the standard Crystal syntax data type spellings and colon-equal operator used to assign the default value.

```
Function (DateVar BDate, Optional DateVar EDate := CurrentDate)
```

Tip *Finer points on Crystal and Basic syntax when used in custom functions, such as how to declare complex data types in arguments and syntax differences between custom functions and report formulas, can be found in Crystal Reports online help. Search for Custom Functions | Basic Syntax or Custom Functions | Crystal Syntax.*

Modifying Existing Custom Functions

Once you've created a custom function, you may wish to change it later. One of the benefits of custom functions over copying and pasting the same formula logic over and over again in multiple formulas is that all formulas based on a custom function will automatically reflect the change made in the one custom function. As such, a great deal of effort can be eliminated by sharing custom functions in the repository (custom functions in the repository is covered later in this chapter and in Chapter 7) and making a single change to the repository. The change will automatically be reflected in all formulas in all reports that make use of that function.

If you've added the custom function just to one report, you may change a custom function in the same way you would change a formula: select it in the Formula Workshop and make changes directly to the formula text in the Custom Function Editor. When you save changes, any formulas using the function will immediately reflect the change.

Note   *Even though you were able to initially extract a custom function from a formula using a dialog box, you will need to make changes to the custom function in the Custom Function Editor. Once you've saved any custom function, even by extracting it from a formula, editing must be done in the Custom Function Editor.*

If you've added custom functions to your report from the repository, you'll notice that the Custom Function Editor formula text area is disabled for editing when you select the custom function in the Formula Workshop tree. This is because you have not disconnected the custom function from the repository. In order to change the contents of a repository-based function, you must *disconnect* the function—this is similar to "checking out" the function from the repository.

To disconnect a custom function from the repository, right-click the function you wish to edit in the Formula Workshop tree (this must be a function in the Report Custom Functions category—you can't disconnect or edit a custom function that hasn't first been added to the report). Choose Disconnect from Repository from the pop-up menu. You'll notice two changes: first, the custom function can now be edited in the Custom Function Editor, and second, the small icon appearing next to the custom function name in the Formula Workshop tree will no longer display the small "linked" icon.

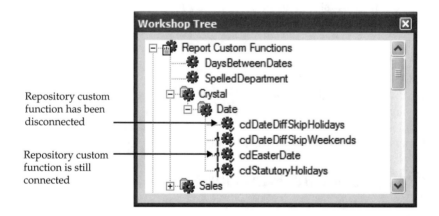

You may not only edit the formula text of an existing custom function, but the summary, author, category, and other nonformula items that you specified when first creating the function. With the function you wish to edit displayed in the Custom Function Editor, click the Toggle Properties Display button in the Formula Workshop toolbar, or right-click the function name in the Formula Workshop tree and choose Toggle Property Display from the pop-up menu. The Custom Function Editor will be replaced with a dialog box summarizing all the other properties that can be set for the function. Make any necessary changes on this screen and click the same toolbar button or use the same pop-up menu choice to toggle back to the Custom Function Editor.

Once you've made changes to the custom function and saved the changes, you may wish to add your new custom function to the repository for sharing with other reports or users, or else you will probably want to "reconnect" the custom function back to the repository with changes. The following section describes how to add a custom function to the repository.

Sharing Custom Functions with Other Users

One of the huge new benefits of Crystal Reports 9 is the ability to share custom functions you create not only with other reports you may design, but with reports that other Crystal Reports users design as well. This is accomplished by saving the custom function or functions you wish to share in the repository. And if you've disconnected a custom function from the repository to change it, you'll most probably want to save the updated function back to the repository again. The steps to add a new custom function to the repository for the first time, or to update a custom function that you disconnected, are the same, and there are actually three different ways to accomplish the same thing:

- Right-click the custom function you wish to add to the repository in the Formula Workshop tree. Select Add to Repository from the pop-up menu. You'll be prompted to choose which repository you wish to add the function to. If the function already exists (you disconnected it earlier), you'll be prompted to confirm that you want to overwrite the existing repository function.

- Select the custom function you wish to add to the repository in the Formula Workshop tree. Click the Add to Repository button in the Formula Workshop toolbar. You'll be prompted to choose which repository you wish to add the function to. If the function already exists (you disconnected it earlier), you'll be prompted to confirm that you want to overwrite the existing repository function.

- Simply drag the custom function you wish to add to the repository from the Report Custom Functions category of the Formula Workshop tree to the Repository Custom Functions category. This will automatically add the function to the selected repository. If the function already exists (you disconnected it earlier), you'll be prompted to confirm that you want to overwrite the existing repository function.

Caution   *You may not be able to add a custom function to the repository—either a new custom function you created yourself, or a custom function you disconnected from the repository to edit. Depending on how your copy of Crystal Reports is connected to your company's central Crystal repository, you may not have the right to modify the repository. If you get an error message when attempting to add a custom function to the repository, contact your system or database administrator to verify that you have the right to modify the repository. Chapter 7 discusses various database connections and security methods that control who can and cannot update the repository.*

Using Custom Functions in Your Formulas

Once you've created a custom function, either for use in just the current report, or to be shared from the repository, using the function in a formula is easy. You may create a formula that makes use of the function with the Formula Expert (covered in detail in Chapter 5). Or, if you create a formula with the Formula Editor, custom functions you've created in the current report will appear in the Custom Functions category of the function tree.

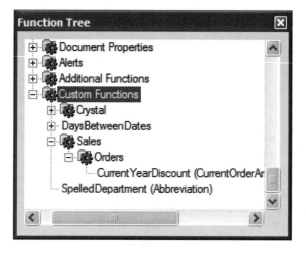

Custom functions in the repository, however, won't automatically appear in the function tree unless you add them to the report first. To add a repository custom function to the report, expand the Repository Custom Functions category of the Formula Workshop until you find the custom function that you wish to use. Select the function you wish to add and click the Add to Report toolbar button in the Formula Workshop toolbar. You can also right-click the function name in the Formula Workshop tree and choose Add to Report from the pop-up menu. And finally, you may simply drag the custom function you wish to add to the report from the Repository Custom Functions category to the Report Custom Functions category of the Formula Workshop tree.

If the custom function you choose to add to the report calls other custom functions as well (remember, one custom function can call another), you'll be notified that additional custom functions will be added as well. The custom functions will now appear in the Custom Functions category of the function tree for you to add to formulas.

Chapter 7

The Repository

One of the most often heard questions asked by users of previous versions of Crystal Reports (especially users in larger organizations) was "Can I share parts of this report with other users or other reports?" While some use of creative copying and pasting to shared word processor or text files might have provided a piecemeal answer to this question, the general response was usually "No."

Well, Crystal Reports 9 has finally changed this. With Crystal Reports 9's new repository, several types of report objects can now be stored in a central database that can be shared among other reports and other users. Not only does this greatly reduce the need for repetitive report design steps, it also affords a simple, centralized way of automatically updating common portions of shared reports.

Note   *The repository is **not** included in Crystal Reports 9 Standard Edition. If you wish to make use of the repository, you must purchase the Professional, Developer, or Advanced edition.*

The Repository Defined

Simply put, the Crystal Reports *repository* is a common place where report objects can be stored. Once you store a report object in the repository, it's available to be added to other reports you create. If you connect to a shared repository that other users in your organization also share, objects you add to the repository are available to other Crystal Reports users, and objects they add are available to you.

The repository actually stores all of its items in a standard relational database. When you first install Crystal Reports, a Microsoft Access database is installed by default. You may create another database to use as the repository instead of the default Access database. You'll probably find that a shared repository maintained on an industry standard client/ server database will be immensely helpful in shared reporting environments in an organization. Even if you have just a few report designers who share a common repository, the benefits of shared report design and automatically updated report objects will soon become evident.

You make use of the repository in Crystal Reports with the *Repository Explorer*, a separate frame (or "un-dockable" dialog box) inside the report designer, similar to the Field Explorer.

The Repository Explorer shows the repository categorized into folders. Although the sample repository that ships with Crystal Reports shows folders for specific types of objects (text objects, bitmaps, SQL commands), you don't have to organize folders this way—you may put any type of object that the repository supports into any folder. You may add any of the objects in the repository to appropriate areas of your report.

The repository supports four types of Crystal Reports objects:

- **Text objects**   Standard text objects containing static text (no embedded fields)
- **Bitmaps (pictures)**   Bitmap pictures, such as logos, photos, and signatures
- **Custom functions**   Functions or "subroutines" that can be used inside report formulas. Note that repository custom functions appear only in the Formula Workshop, not in the Repository Explorer
- **SQL commands/queries**   Server-based SQL commands that reports can be based upon

Text objects and bitmaps can simply be dragged from the Repository Explorer onto the report, just as you would drag and drop fields from the Field Explorer. Repository custom functions must be added to report formulas from within the Formula Workshop (covered in Chapter 5), and repository SQL commands must be added to the report from within the Database Expert (SQL commands are covered in more detail in Chapter 16).

Creating a Shared Repository

While the repository that ships with Crystal Reports 9 is helpful in getting a feel for how the repository works, it solves only half the "How can I share things among reports and among report designers" question. Because the default repository is stored in a local Microsoft Access database on your local computer, you can share repository objects within all your own reports, but not with other report designers within your organization. To do this, you must use a shared repository stored on a client/server database, such as Microsoft SQL Server, Oracle, Informix, or IBM DB/2.

If you using Crystal Reports in an organization with a centralized Information Technology department, they may have already set up a shared repository for you. However, if you are in charge of setting up the shared repository *in* the corporate IT department, or if you are in a smaller organization without such a department, you may be required to set up the shared repository yourself. This isn't as hard as it might seem.

The first step is choosing which database you wish to host the shared repository on. It's doubtful that this database will be the busiest in your organization, so you can probably safely choose a database system that already contains other production databases, or a smaller database used for less-critical applications. No particular database software or hardware is necessary—as long as you can connect to the database with a standard ODBC (Open Database Connectivity) connection, the database should work properly for your shared repository.

The steps to setting up and configuring the shared repository are fairly straightforward:

1. Create an empty database on the database server.

2. Configure an ODBC data source on each PC running a copy of Crystal Reports that will connect to the shared repository.

3. Modify the orMap.ini file on each PC to refer to the ODBC data source you created in step 2.

Create an Empty Database

The steps necessary to create a new empty database on the database server that will host the shared repository vary according to the database. If you are familiar with the database you are configuring, there is no particular magic required to create the repository database. No particular naming conventions are required for the database—you'll match the database name up to the repository name in the ODBC Administrator and the orMap.ini file. There is no need to create any tables or fields in the database, as the first copy of Crystal Reports to connect to the repository will create these for you.

When determining how to size the database, consider how many report objects you think may be ultimately added to the database. While no hard and fast sizing guidelines exist, consider that the repository will ultimately consist of six tables that make up the contents of the repository. These tables won't contain any abnormally large or complex data structures but will probably vary in size, to a certain extent, according to the size of report objects you add to them (a 1MB full-page bitmap will probably require more space in the repository than a one inch by one inch black and white logo).

If your database supports automatic sizing, you'll probably want to start at a "small" size (say, 10–15MB) and allow the database to grow if necessary. If you must specify a fixed size for the database, you may wish to size a bit larger and watch the actual allocated database space as the repository begins to grow in size.

Configure the ODBC Data Source

Once the new repository database has been defined, you must configure each PC that will connect to the shared repository with an ODBC connection to the database. This is accomplished with the ODBC Administrator (available from the Windows Control Panel). It's probably best to choose a System DSN (Data Set Name), as it can be shared by all users who log in to the particular computer that you're configuring. Choose the appropriate database driver to match the database system you created the shared repository database on. You may specify any name you wish for the ODBC DSN, as long as it doesn't conflict with an existing DSN.

Configure any additional parameters necessary for your particular database. Note that this ODBC connection will need at least read access to the database, and most probably write access, if you want users to be able to add items to, and update items in, the shared repository.

Note

More detailed steps for creating ODBC data sources are found in Crystal Reports online help, or in standard Windows or database documentation.

Modify orMap.ini

Crystal Reports uses a specifically located text file to "point" to the correct ODBC DSN for the shared repository. This file, **orMap.ini**, is located in **\Program Files\Common Files\Crystal Decisions\2.0\bin**. Edit it with a standard text editor, such as Notepad.

```
orMap.ini - Notepad

File  Edit  Format  View  Help

# Syntax:
#
# <repository name>=<real data source name>
#
# Please note that <repository name> cannot contain these special characters
- # " { } ; /
# Any entry that contains such will be ignored.
# Also, this file is saved with UTF8 encoding. This allows <repository name>
to be of unicode characters.
#
Crystal SQL Repository=MS SQL Crystal Repository
```

Notice the existing entry for the included Access repository. To add the entry for your new shared repository, either add a pound sign in front of the current definition (which will comment out the line), or delete the line entirely. Then, add a new line in the form:

```
Repository Name in Crystal = ODBC Data Source Name
```

For example, the illustration presented previously would create a shared repository appearing as "Crystal SQL Repository" in the Crystal Reports Repository Explorer from an ODBC data source named "MS SQL Crystal Repository."

Caution

Ensure that only one uncommented line exists in orMap.ini. If you add an additional definition and leave the original as-is, Crystal Reports won't know which repository to connect to and may behave erratically. Also, make note in the orMap.ini comments about reserved characters that can't be included in your repository name.

Controlling Repository Permissions

When using a shared repository, as with other shared database connections, you may wish to limit the ability to update or delete repository objects to a certain set of key users, while permitting the rest of those sharing the repository to just add existing repository items to their reports. There is nothing special required in Crystal Reports to do this—you will simply set database permissions for different users.

If the shared repository database you create is secure, users will need to log on to the repository database when they try to access the repository. For example, attempting to display the Repository Explorer when connected to a secure database will result in the following:

You must enter a valid database user ID and password in order to log on to the repository. The repository database can be set up with several different user IDs, each with various permissions to add or modify records, or to just read records. You may, perhaps, wish to create two different user ID/password sets and distribute them to appropriate users. For example, you might create the user ID "ITReportDeveloper," which would have full database permissions, allowing users to add, update, and remove items from the repository database. However, the ID "ReportEndUser" would allow only read access to the repository database, thereby allowing users only to add existing repository items to their reports but not add, update, or delete items in the repository.

Tip   *Note that denying write/update/delete capabilities to certain repository users will still allow them to "detach" objects from the repository and change them once they've been placed on the report. Read-only users won't, however, be able to update the repository with their changed objects.*

Adding To/Updating the Repository

Once you've created your own repository database and pointed your copies of Crystal Reports to it, you'll need to begin to populate it with shared objects. And while it's not required, you'll probably gain more usability with the repository if you organize the repository into folders.

Creating Folders

You may create as many folders in the repository as you like. And you're not limited to creating a single level of folders—you may create subfolders within other folders to build a hierarchy for repository objects. Once you've created your folder structure, you can place text objects, bitmap graphics, or SQL commands in the folders (custom functions are placed in a separate part of the repository reserved just for themselves—they won't appear in the Repository Explorer).

To create a folder, launch the Repository Explorer by clicking the Repository Explorer button in the Standard Toolbar, or choose View | Repository Explorer from the pull-down menus. If you have not placed any objects in the repository as of yet, you'll simply see the name you gave the repository appear in the Repository Explorer identified with a disk icon. Select the repository name, right-click, and choose New Folder from the pop-up menu. A folder will be added to the repository with the default name of "New Folder," and you'll be placed immediately into edit mode, where you can type your own name for the folder. Type the new folder name and press ENTER or click elsewhere with your mouse.

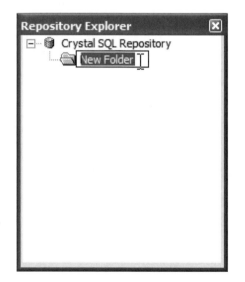

If you wish to create additional folders, you may create top-level folders by repeating the previous steps (just make sure you've selected the repository name prior to right-clicking). If you wish to create a subfolder below an existing folder, select the higher-level folder first. Then, right-click and choose New Folder from the pop-up menu. You'll see a lower-level folder within the higher-level folder you right-clicked, again with the default name of New Folder, which you can rename immediately.

If you wish to rename a folder you've already added, select the folder you wish to rename and then hold the mouse button down on the folder for an few seconds. You may also select the folder and press F2, or right-click the desired folder and choose Rename from the pop-up menu. In all cases, the folder name will go into edit mode and you can type a new name for the folder.

Deleting folders is similarly straightforward. First, you must delete all objects and subfolders within the folder—if you try to delete a folder that contains something else, you'll receive an error message. Select the folder you wish to delete and simply press the DEL key. You may also right-click the desired folder and choose Delete from the pop-up menu.

| Caution | *Deleting folders, like deleting individual objects in the repository, cannot be undone. Make sure the object or folder you want to delete is no longer needed before you delete it. The only recourse you'll have after a deletion is restoring a backup copy of the repository database.* |

Adding and Deleting Items

You may add report objects to the repository at any time, even if you haven't yet created any folder structure (moving objects into or among folders will be discussed later in the chapter). The method for adding an object to the repository is dependent on the type of object you wish to add.

Text Objects or Bitmap Graphics

A text object or bitmap graphic can be added to the repository by simply dragging and dropping it from the Design or Preview tab of the report into the Repository Explorer. If you wish to place the object into a particular folder, drag and drop the text object or bitmap on top of the folder you wish to add it to. You may also add a text object or bitmap by right-clicking the desired object and choosing Add to Repository from the pop-up menu. A dialog box will appear asking you to supply additional information for the object.

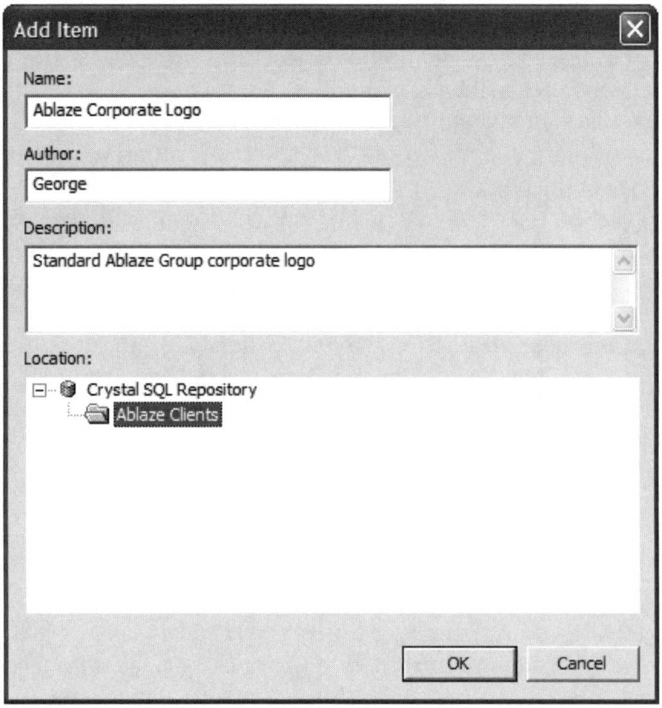

Add Item

Name:
Ablaze Corporate Logo

Author:
George

Description:
Standard Ablaze Group corporate logo

Location:
- Crystal SQL Repository
  - Ablaze Clients

OK   Cancel

Specify a name for the object to appear in the repository (note that you can't include a few special characters in your object names, such as the pound sign, curly braces, the backslash, and others—if you try, you'll receive an error message). Make sure you don't use a name already used for another repository object (you'll be warned if you do this and will overwrite the repository object with the same name if you proceed). Although this is not required, you can also add an author name and description for your entry. If you choose the pop-up menu method to add the object, you'll also be presented with the repository's folder hierarchy at the bottom of the Add Item dialog box. If you wish to place the object in a folder, choose the folder where you want to place the new object. If you select the name of the repository instead of a folder, the object will be placed directly under the repository name in the Repository Explorer.

If you wish to rename an object you added to the repository previously, you may simply select the object and then hold the mouse button down for a few seconds.

The object will go into edit mode, where you can type in a new name (you'll receive an error if you try to use a name of another object) and press ENTER or click away from the object name. The object will be renamed.

If you initially place an object in a particular folder (or in no folder, but right below the repository name itself), you may move it to another location with a simple drag-and-drop operation. Select the object you wish to move and hold your mouse button down. Then, drag the object on top of its new preferred location (a folder if you wish to move the object to that folder, or the repository name if you wish to move the object out of a folder and place it right below the repository name). When you drop the object in its new location, it will then appear where you dropped it.

Deleting a text object or bitmap from the repository is similar to deleting folders. Just select the object you want to delete and press the DEL key. You may alternatively right-click the object and choose Delete from the pop-up menu. And as with folders, deleting text objects or bitmaps can't be undone. Make sure you really want to delete the object from the repository before proceeding. Note that deleting an object from the repository won't delete it from reports that had originally made use of it. It will still remain in those reports, but it won't be available to add to any new reports.

> **Note** *If you delete an object from the repository that may be part of existing reports, users will receive an error message when they open the report and attempt to "Update Repository Objects." The object on the report will then appear as it did when the report was last saved.*

Custom Functions

Add custom functions to the repository from the Formula Workshop. With the Formula Workshop displayed, select the custom function you wish to add to the repository and click the Add to Repository button. You may also right-click the custom function name and choose Add to Repository from the pop-up menu. And you may also simply drag the custom function name from the Report Custom Functions category of the Formula Workshop to the Repository Custom Functions category (drop on top of the repository name). If you use the toolbar button or right-click methods, you'll be prompted to choose the repository you want to add the custom function to (and since you can have only one repository in Crystal Reports, you'll have only one choice).

> **Note** *You won't be prompted for a folder to place the custom function in. The folder structure discussed earlier applies only to text objects and bitmaps. Custom functions are placed in a separate area of the repository just for them. If you assigned categories to your custom functions when you created them, the categories will be retained when you place the custom function in the repository.*

Deleting a custom function from the repository is similar to deleting folders, text objects, or bitmap images. Simply expand the Repository Custom Functions category of the Formula Workshop, select the custom function that you wish to delete, and press the DEL key. You may alternatively right-click the custom function name and choose Delete from the pop-up menu. In either case, you'll be warned that deleting a custom function from the repository can't be undone. Confirm that you want to delete the function and it will be permanently removed from the repository. Note that deleting an object from the repository won't delete it from reports that had originally made use of it. It will still remain in those reports, but it won't be available to add to any new reports.

Tip   *The sample repository shipped with Crystal Reports 9 contains a few sample text objects, SQL commands, and bitmaps. These are for demonstration only and will be of little or no use to you when designing your own reports. There are, however, some useful custom functions supplied with the Crystal Repository that you may find of use in your own reporting tasks. You may wish to add these to a report, change orMap.ini to point to your custom repository, and then add the custom functions in the report back into your own repository.*

SQL Commands

Add SQL commands to the repository in the Database Expert (creating SQL commands is discussed in more detail in Chapter 16). You may add the SQL command to the repository either when you first create it or later, when you edit the SQL command. In either case, add the command to the repository by checking the Add to Repository check box in the Add Command or Modify Command dialog box.

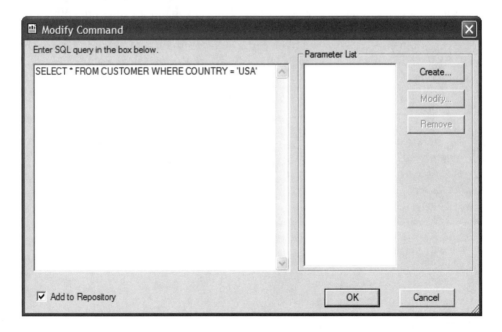

Once you check this option and click OK, you'll be presented with a dialog box asking you to name the object and choose a location in the repository for the object (SQL commands can be stored in the same folder structure you set up in the Repository Explorer). You may optionally specify the author, as well as changing the description for the SQL command to something other than the SQL statement that makes up the command (which is placed in the description text box by default). When you click OK, the SQL command will be added to the repository. It will appear in the Repository section of the Database Expert.

> **Note**   *You'll also be able to see SQL commands in the Repository Explorer alongside text objects and bitmaps—they'll just be displayed with a different icon. However, you won't be able to just drag and drop them to the report as you can text objects or bitmaps. You can, however, rename and delete SQL commands from the Repository Explorer using the same techniques described for text objects and bitmaps.*

You may rename a SQL command you added to the repository either in the Repository Explorer or in any of the data-related dialog boxes where the repository is available (such as the Database Expert). The process is identical in all situations. Select the object, hold down the mouse button for a few seconds to put the object in edit mode, and make the change. You may also right-click and choose Rename from the pop-up menu.

Deleting a SQL command from the repository can similarly be done in either the Repository Explorer or any of the repository-equipped data-related dialog boxes. However, the steps are slightly different in the Repository Explorer than they are in the other dialog boxes. In any situation, you may right-click the SQL command name and choose Delete from the pop-up menu. You may also select the SQL command you want to remove from the repository and press the DEL key, but only in the Repository Explorer. Note that deleting an object from the repository won't delete it from reports that had originally made use of it. It will still remain in those reports, but it won't be available to add to any new reports.

> **Caution**   *Depending on permissions that you are granted with the repository database, you may be unable to add or delete items from the repository. If you receive an ODBC error message when trying, contact your database manager for permission to update the repository database.*

Adding Repository Items to Reports

Once you've added objects to the repository as outlined earlier in the chapter, you, along with other users sharing the same repository, will want to add the items to reports. Repository versions of text objects, bitmap graphics, custom functions, and SQL commands are added in different places throughout Crystal Reports.

Text Objects or Bitmap Graphics

Add these items to your report from the Repository Explorer (which can be displayed by clicking the Repository Explorer button in the Standard toolbar or with the View | Repository Explorer pull-down menu item). Simply expand any folders to reveal the text objects and bitmaps that are available. If you want to see properties for a repository object, select the object and choose Properties from the pop-up menu. A small dialog box will appear showing various pieces of information about the object.

To add the object to the report, simply drag it from the Repository Explorer to the report. As when dragging and dropping fields from the Field Explorer, an outline will appear as you drag. When you've reached the desired position for the object, release your mouse button. The text object or bitmap graphic will be placed on the report.

Tip   *Don't be alarmed when you are unable to format or resize objects you add to the report from the repository. These objects are "connected" to the repository and can't be edited, resized, or formatted until they have been "disconnected." This is discussed later in the chapter.*

Custom Functions

Make use of repository custom functions in the Formula Workshop. You may add a custom function to the report from the repository directly, which will place it in the Formula Editor's function tree for use like built-in Crystal Reports functions. Alternatively, you can use the Formula Expert to create a formula based on a custom function from the repository.

To add a custom function to the report directly, so that it appears in the Formula Editor's function tree, begin by displaying the Formula Workshop. You may do this by clicking the Formula Workshop button in the Expert Tools toolbar, or by choosing Report | Formula Workshop from the pull-down menus.

Expand the Repository Custom Functions category of the Formula Workshop until you find the custom function that you wish to use. Select the function you wish to add and click the Add to Report toolbar button in the Formula Workshop toolbar. You can also right-click the function name in the Formula Workshop tree and choose Add to Report from the pop-up menu. And finally, you may simply drag the custom function you wish to add to the report from the Repository Custom Functions category to the Report Custom Functions category of the Formula Workshop tree.

Since a repository custom function can potentially call other custom functions within the repository, you may be asked to confirm the addition to the report of other custom functions. Once you do this, all custom functions you've added from the repository will now appear in the Custom Functions category of the function tree for you to add to formulas.

Tip *More details on creating formulas with the Formula Expert and using custom functions in formulas can be found in Chapters 5 and 6.*

SQL Commands

Add repository-based SQL commands to your report from the Database Expert, the Set Location dialog box, or another data-related dialog box that you typically use to add database tables to the report. In these dialog boxes, you'll see a Repository folder that you can expand to see the folder structure that has been set up in the repository. Expand the folders to reveal SQL commands that are located in the repository. An example of the Database Expert is shown here:

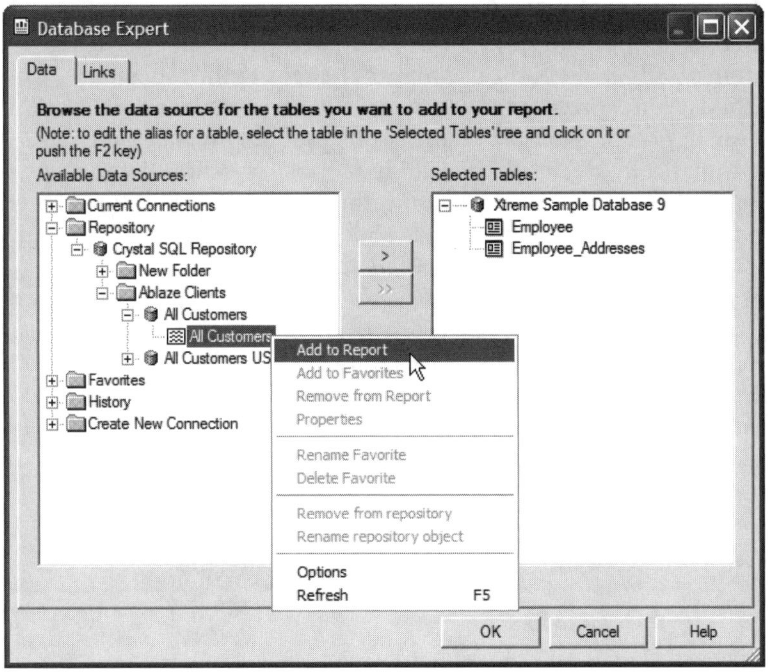

Choose the SQL command that you want to add to the repository. You may then click the right arrow to add the selected repository SQL command to the report, right-click the command and choose Add to Report from the pop-up menu, or just drag the command from the left side of the Database Expert to the right side. Similar procedures will add SQL commands to the report from the repository in other data-related dialog boxes.

Changing Repository Items on Your Report

As indicated earlier in the chapter, you may become confused once you add an object from the repository to your report. This might occur if you attempt to change the format of a text object you added from the repository, resize a bitmap graphic you added from the repository, or change the text of a SQL command or custom function that's been added to the repository. In all these case, you'll discover that the objects are "locked" or set to a read-only status—you won't be able to make these kinds of changes.

This behavior is by design. In order to ensure that the repository controls the appearance and behavior of these objects, they remain *connected* to the repository once you've added them to the report. As long as they're connected, the repository will control their appearance and size (in the case of text objects and bitmap graphics), or their text (in the case of SQL commands and custom functions). Probably the most obvious clue that an object is connected is the inability to change it. However, in some dialog boxes, you'll also notice a small vertical-bar icon next to the object's name, which will indicated that the object is connected to the repository.

The main benefit of leaving objects connected to the repository is to allow them to be updated automatically if anybody else makes changes to the repository. For example, if you have added a common company logo and slogan to your report using a repository-connected bitmap graphic and text object, you'll probably want all reports using those objects to automatically reflect changes to the repository should your logo or slogan change. In order to ensure consistency with this behavior, individual changes to the objects once they've been added to reports shouldn't be allowed.

Tip *To ensure connected objects will be updated when you initially open your reports, you must make one of two choices. By choosing File | Options from the pull-down menus and checking the Update Connected Repository Objects When Loading Report option on the Reporting tab, you ensure all reports automatically update connected objects when opened. If you only want to update connected objects on a report-by-report basis, leave this global option off and instead check the Update Repository Objects check box on the Open File dialog box when opening a Crystal Report.*

To change this behavior and manually make changes to objects you've added from the repository, you must *disconnect* them from the repository. Begin by right-clicking the object. In the case of text objects or bitmap graphics, right-click directly on the object in the Design or Preview tabs. For SQL commands or custom functions, right-click the command or function name in their respective dialog boxes. From the pop-up menu, choose Disconnect from Repository. Notice that you may now resize or reformat text objects or bitmap graphics, as well as changing the contents of SQL commands or custom functions. Also, you'll notice the previously mentioned vertical bar "connected" icon is no longer visible.

Be aware, though, that these objects will now behave as though you just added them to the report—they won't be automatically updated by the repository any more. Using the company logo and slogan example mentioned previously, if you disconnect the objects from the repository and save the report, they won't reflect any repository changes the next time you open the report.

Updating Repository Versions of Objects

Continuing with the company logo and slogan examples referred to previously in this chapter; what if you are in charge of updating the repository copies of the company logo and slogan? Or you may have a company-wide custom function that requires changing for a new fiscal year or a new bonus program. In these situations, you must add the object from the repository to your report, make changes, and update the repository with the changed object.

As mentioned previously, you can't edit or modify an object that's connected to the repository. This may cause confusion if you are required to update the repository copy of an object. To get around this confusion, consider the steps required to update the repository copy of an object:

1. Add the object to a report from the repository.

2. Disconnect the object from the repository.

3. Make necessary changes to the object.

4. Save the object back to the repository with the same name as the original object.

Step 4 will exhibit behavior that is slightly different than the first time you added the object to the repository. When you attempt to add an object to the repository with the same name, you will be warned that an object already exists and given the opportunity to update the version in the repository with the version that you're saving. If you choose to do this, the old repository object will be replaced and its version number will be incremented by one (you can see the version number in the properties dialog boxes for repository objects).

Once you've performed these steps, note that the updated object you just added back to the repository will once again be connected—you won't be able to change formatting or contents. To make future changes to the object, you must once again disconnect it from the repository.

Caution *As with deleting and adding repository objects, you must have permission to update objects in the repository as well. If you attempt to update a repository object and get an ODBC error message, consult your database manager about obtaining permission to update the repository database.*

Chapter 8

Analyzing with Advanced Selection Criteria

reating a simple report is as quick as choosing tables, dragging and dropping fields on the report, and clicking the Preview button. However, if you only perform those few steps, you may have a much larger report show up than you bargained for! One important step missing is *record selection*. If you don't enter some record selection criteria, every record that exists in the tables you choose will appear on the report.

In the case of a small PC-type database with, say, 1,000 records, this won't be terribly time- or resource-intensive. However, if you're connected to a large SQL database with potentially millions of records, the consequences of not including record selection will probably be felt on your network, and they will certainly be felt on your desktop PC. Since Crystal Reports needs to store the data that makes up a report somewhere, you may run out of memory or temporary disk space in such a situation. Regardless of these concerns, your report will be terribly slow, and probably not very useful, if you have that many records on the report.

Virtually all reports will need record selection criteria. You may want to limit the report to only USA customers, only orders placed in 2001, or only invoices that are more than 30 days past due. Record selection criteria can be used to limit your report to any of these sets of records. In any event, it's very wise to apply your record selection criteria early on in your report design process—certainly *before* you preview or print the report!

The Select Expert

Crystal Reports includes the *Select Expert* to help you create useful record selection criteria. You can use the Select Expert for simple, straightforward record selection, and as a starting point for more sophisticated record selection. The Select Expert can be run from the Record Selection section of any of the report wizards, or after you have chosen and linked tables using the Blank Report option. In either case, you'll want to make sure to use it before you preview the report.

To use the Select Expert while using one of the report wizards, choose at least one table in the Data section, and, if necessary, link the tables in the Link section (table linking is covered in more detail in Chapter 16). Then progress through the other sections until you reach the Record Selection section, which looks like this:

If you are using the Blank Report option to create a report, you must initially select and link tables. Once the Design tab appears, you can either immediately run the Select Expert or add fields to the report before running the Select Expert. Again, you'll want to run the Select Expert before you preview the report.

Run the Select Expert by clicking Select Expert in the Expert Tools toolbar. You can also choose Report | Select Expert from the pull-down menus. If you have already added fields to the report and want to use one of them from the Design tab or Preview tab for record selection, select the field on the report before you start the Select Expert. You can also right-click your selected field and choose Select Expert from the pop-up menu. In each case, the Select Expert will start with a tab already created for the chosen field.

Caution   *You may use this feature unintentionally. If you start the Select Expert and see a tab for a field that you don't want to select on, just click the Delete button on the right side of the expert to delete the current tab. Then click the <New> tab or the New button to choose the correct field to select.*

If this is the first time you've run the Select Expert, and you haven't chosen an existing report field, you'll see a Choose Field dialog box listing all report and database fields. You'll also see this dialog box if you are already displaying the Select Expert and click the <New> tab or the New button to add additional criteria.

Click the report or database field that you want your record selection to be based on. If you want to see sample data from the database for that field, click Browse. Once you're satisfied with the field you want to use for record selection, select it and click OK. The Select Expert will appear with a tab for that field.

Once you've chosen a field to select on, you'll see an additional pull-down list with the default of Is Any Value. You will use this list to choose the comparison operation you want to use for your record selection. The pull-down list will reveal all the comparisons you can use to select records; it may vary somewhat based on the type of field you've chosen for record selection. Table 8-1 explains the different operators that may appear in the pull-down list. Note that the pull-down list will contain the operators discussed in the table, as well as operators like them except that they begin "Is Not." As you might

Operator	Description
Is Any Value	This is the same as having no selection criteria at all. Is Any Value means it doesn't matter what's in the field—all records will be included in the report.
Is Equal To	The field must be exactly equal to what you specify.
Is One Of	You can specify more than one item to compare to by adding multiple comparison items to a list. If the field is exactly equal to any of them, the record will be included.
Is Less Than	The field must be less than the item you're comparing to. If you are comparing numbers, the field must be smaller numerically. If you are comparing dates, the field must be an earlier date. If you're comparing strings, the field must be lower in the alphabet. If you choose the Less Than Or Equal To option, the field can be equal to or less than what you're comparing to.
Is Greater Than	The field must be greater than the item you're comparing to. If you are comparing numbers, the field must be larger numerically. If you're comparing dates, the field must be a later date. If you're comparing strings, the field must be higher in the alphabet. If you choose the Greater Than Or Equal To option, the field can be equal to or greater than what you're comparing to.
Is Between	Allows you to select two items to create a comparison range. The field must be between the two items, or equal to one of them. Is Between uses the same type of comparison as is used with Is Less Than and Is Greater Than: numbers compare numerically, dates compare chronologically, and strings compare alphabetically.

Table 8-1.   *Select Expert Comparison Operators*

Operator	Description
Starts With	Allows you to specify "leading" characters to compare to. If the first characters in the field equal the specified characters, the record will be returned. If you want to perform several Starts With comparisons, you can add multiple criteria to a list. This operator will only appear when you are using a string field.
Is Like	You can look for partial text matches using wildcard characters to search for records that contain particular characters or groups of characters. When you specify your comparisons, you can use a question mark to indicate that one character in the field at that position can contain anything. You can use an asterisk to indicate that the rest of the field from that point on can contain anything. If you want to perform several Like comparisons, you can add multiple criteria to a list. This operator will appear only when you are using a string field.
Is In the Period	Allows you to compare a date field to a group of built-in date ranges, such as the last week, last month, last quarter, current year, etc. These built-in ranges are all based on the system clock of your computer when you run the report. This operator will appear only when you are using a date field.
Is True	Includes records where the field equates to true. This operator will appear only when you are using a Boolean field.
Is False	Includes records where the field equates to false. This operator will appear only when you are using a Boolean field.
Formula	Allows you to enter any Boolean formula using the Crystal Reports formula language. Similar to the Show Formula button in the lower-right corner of the Select Expert.

Table 8-1.   *Select Expert Comparison Operators* (continued)

imagine, choosing the "Not" version of the operator will include all records where the condition is *not* true, instead of where the condition is true.

Once you've chosen a comparison operator in the pull-down list, the Select Expert will change based on the selection you've made. If you've chosen an operator that only compares to one item (such as Equal To, Less Than, or Greater Than), one additional pull-down list will appear. If you've chosen an operator that can compare to multiple items (such as One Of, Like, or Starts With), a pull-down list will appear, along with a multiple-item box. You can add and remove items from the multiple-item box by clicking the Add and Delete buttons that appear next to the box.

The new pull-down list allows you to choose the item you want to compare the field to in either of two ways: you can type it directly or choose it from the pull-down list. You can simply type the literal item you want to compare to directly in the pull-down list.

If you click the arrow on the pull-down list, the Select Expert will browse the database and list a few sample items from that database field. You may choose one of the items in the pull-down list for comparison.

If the comparison operator you've chosen allows multiple entries, you can add an item you've typed to the multiple-item box by clicking Add. If you choose a browsed database item from the pull-down list, it will be added to the multiple-item box automatically. In either case, you can remove an item from the multiple-item box by selecting it and then clicking Remove.

Note that you can choose *Is Not* versions of the comparison operators as well. This will, in essence, *reverse* the selection criteria you've chosen. If, for example, you chose a country field, selected the Is Not Equal To operator, and specified "USA" as the item to compare to, your report will now include records for every country *except* the USA.

The Select Expert does not limit you to comparing just one field. Once you have added one database field, you can click the <New> tab or the New button. This will redisplay the Choose Field dialog box, from which you can pick another field to compare to. Once you pick this field, a new tab will display in the Select Expert, enabling you to create another comparison. You may create as many tabs and comparisons as you need.

Tip   *Crystal Reports applies a logical AND to all the tabs in the Select Expert—all the criteria have to be true for a record to be selected. If you would rather have a logical OR applied to some or all of the tabs (so that if any one of them is true, but not all of them, a record is returned), you must manually edit the selection formula created by the Select Expert. This is discussed later in this chapter in "Manipulating the Record Selection Formula Directly."*

Refreshing the Report Versus Using Saved Data

When you preview a report on the screen for the first time, Crystal Reports has to actually read the database and perform record selection, and only thereafter can it format and display the report. To enhance future performance while you work with the report, Crystal Reports creates a set of *saved data*. This saved data consists of the records that were retrieved from the database, which are then kept either in memory or in temporary files on your hard drive. If you perform simple formatting changes, move fields around, or make other minor modifications that won't require the database to be requeried, Crystal Reports will use the saved data every time you preview the modified report, thus improving performance. If you add new fields to the report, Crystal Reports knows it has to requery the database, and it does so without prompting. You may notice a bit of a wait (or maybe a long wait, depending on your database) while it runs the new query.

But when you change record selection criteria, Crystal Reports doesn't know whether or not it needs to requery the database. You will be given the option to Refresh or Use Saved Data. The choice you make is dependent upon whether you widened or narrowed the selection criteria. If you *narrowed* your selection criteria so that the new selection criteria can be completely satisfied with the existing saved data, you can choose to use the saved data. Since the database doesn't have to be requeried, the changes will appear very quickly in the Preview tab.

If, however, you *widened* the selection criteria so that the saved data won't contain all the records you're specifying, you need to refresh the report so that the database can be requeried. Choosing to use saved data in this situation will result in your report showing too few (if any) records, even though they actually exist in the database. However, the requery will take time to perform. If you make the wrong choice and end up with too few, or no, records, you can refresh the report manually by clicking the Refresh button in the Standard toolbar, pressing the F5 key, or choosing Report | Refresh Report Data from the pull-down menus.

When you save a report, you have the option to store the saved data in the .RPT file. If you include the saved data, the report will immediately display the Preview tab showing the saved data the next time you open the .RPT file—no database requery will be required. However, this will also make the .RPT file larger (sometimes significantly so), since it has to keep the saved data along with the report design.

Tip *Even if you open a report with saved data, the saved data will be discarded and only the Design tab will appear if the Discard Saved Data When Loading Reports option is checked on the Reporting tab of File | Options.*

To choose whether or not to save data, check or uncheck File | Save Data with Report from the pull-down menus, and then resave the report after making your choice. You can also make the choice with the appropriate check box on File | Report Options. If you wish to set default behavior for this option for all new reports in the future, turn on or off the Save Data with Report option on the Reporting tab of File | Options.

Record Selection with Date Fields

Many reporting requirements can be satisfied by creatively using date fields in record selection. Crystal Reports provides a good selection of built-in date ranges you can use to compare to, or you can use other operators to compare date fields. When you choose a date field in the Choose Field dialog box, the Select Expert makes the In the Period comparison operator available. If you choose this operator, another pull-down list containing Crystal Reports' built-in date ranges appears.

By using these built-in ranges, you can create a report that will return, say, only orders in the previous month by comparing to the LastFullMonth. What's particularly appealing about using built-in date range functions is the "self-maintenance" of the report. When you use the LastFullMonth range, for example, the report will always use the system clock in your computer to include orders from the previous month, no matter when the report is run. You don't have to manually change the date range every month.

There may be times, however, when you have to manually enter a date range for record selection. If, for example, you want to see all orders for 2001, you need to specify those dates manually. There is no built-in *X* Years Ago date range. In this case, you choose the date field you want to select on (for example, Order Date) and use a Between comparison operator to indicate orders between January 1, 2001, and December 31, 2001. You can enter a beginning date of 1/1/2001 and an ending date of 12/31/2001.

> **Tip** *Previous versions of Crystal Reports were pickier about how you entered date or date/time values. You often had to use somewhat cryptic Date or DateTime functions from the Crystal Reports formula language, or surround your date or date/time values with pound signs. Crystal Reports 9 has removed many of these obstacles, generally allowing you to type in free-form dates as you wish. However, you'll still receive error messages if you type in dates that Crystal Reports isn't sure about, such as dates that include only a two-digit year.*

If you're selecting on a Date/Time field, supplying just a date, as opposed to a date and time, will work, but Crystal Reports will automatically assume times on or after midnight of the first date. However, only records that include times of exactly midnight for the second date will be included—any times of even one second after midnight for the second date won't be included. Therefore, make sure you include a time value alongside a date value if you want to select records based on some time other than midnight.

Manipulating the Record Selection Formula Directly

When you create record selection criteria with the Select Expert, it actually creates a formula using the Crystal Reports formula language behind the scenes. For most simple record selection criteria, you won't have to worry about manipulating this formula directly. Also, by using the Select Expert directly and not manipulating the actual formula that it creates, you will often maximize performance, particularly when using SQL databases.

However, there are times when the Select Expert itself won't provide enough flexibility for the record selection you need to accomplish. Consider the following scenario—you have two fields on their own tabs included in the Select Expert: Region Is Equal to CA, and Order Amount Is Greater than 2500.

Since the Select Expert performs a logical AND between the tabs, what do you do if you want to see all orders from California, regardless of the order amount, as well as orders from any other state over $2,500?

In this case, the Select Expert doesn't provide sufficient flexibility to create this type of special record selection. Thus, you must use a *record selection formula*. The Select Expert creates a record selection formula automatically as you add tabs and selection criteria. You can modify the formula it creates in one of three ways:

- By clicking the Show Formula button on the Select Expert itself
- By choosing Report | Selection Formulas | Record from the pull-down menus
- By displaying the Formula Workshop (discussed in more detail in Chapter 5) and choosing Record Selection in the Selection Formulas category

Tip *If you know you'll need extra features that the Select Expert doesn't provide, you can skip it entirely and create your record selection formula right in the Formula Editor or Formula Workshop. Choose Report | Selection Formulas | Record from the pull-down menus or choose Record Selection in the Formula Workshop's Selection Formulas category to create the formula this way.*

In the scenario previously mentioned, you need to change the relationship that exists between the two criteria from an And to an Or. This is a simple process that you can apply either right from the Select Expert or by using the Formula Editor. To use the Select Expert, simply click Show Formula.

You can now modify the formula created by the Select Expert to show you all California orders, regardless of amount, and other orders over $2,500. Notice that the Select Expert has placed the And operator between the two parts of the selection formula. Simply position the cursor in the formula and change the And to Or, and then click OK.

Tip *If you click Show Formula in the Select Expert and then decide you want to use the full-featured Formula Editor, just click the Formula Editor button in the expanded Select Expert dialog box. The formula will be transferred to the Formula Editor, where you can modify or enhance it.*

Since you will ultimately be using the Crystal Reports formula language for your record selection, most of the features of the language are available for record selection. In this situation, it may be preferable to edit the selection formula in the Formula Editor so that you can see and use all the built-in functionality. The formula that the Select Expert created will appear when you choose Report | Selection Formulas | Record from the pull-down menus.

You can modify this formula to your heart's content, provided that the ultimate finished formula is a Boolean formula—it will ultimately just return true or false (refer to Chapter 5 for more information on Boolean formulas). The formula will be evaluated for each record in the database. If the formula evaluates to true, the record will be included in the report; otherwise, the record will be ignored.

Case Sensitivity with Record Selection

A question that you will probably ask yourself fairly quickly when using record selection is, "Is it case sensitive?" In other words, if you ask to see records where the country is "USA," will a record be returned if the database field contains mixed-case characters, such as "Usa"?

Case sensitivity is generally ignored when using SQL databases and PC databases via ODBC, as well as certain PC-style databases using a direct database driver. Although this case insensitivity is the default behavior "out of the box," be sure to check the Database Server Is Case-Insensitive option in the File | Report Options dialog box to affect the current report, or check the same option on the Database tab of File | Options to set the default for all new reports you create in the future. Even if this option is checked, some databases and ODBC drivers may not support case insensitivity with Crystal Reports. It's best to run a test with your own database to make sure you're retrieving all desired records with your record selection.

Note   *If you modify the formula the Select Expert created, or you create your own formula, running the Select Expert again is fine. However, if the Select Expert is unable to fully interpret the formula you created, you'll see slightly different behavior for one or more tabs. You may see a tab with a field set to Is Formula and part of the selection formula showing in the third list box. You may also see a message indicating that the formula uses a "composite expression" and prompting you to edit the formula directly.*

Limiting Data with a Group Selection Formula

When you use the Select Expert or create a record selection formula with the Formula Editor, you affect the way Crystal Reports initially selects data from the database. Record selection occurs during the *first pass* of the report, before data has been sorted or grouped. Because of this, you can't use record selection to limit your report, say, to groups where the total sales exceeds $100,000—the record selection occurs before these totals are calculated (see Chapter 5 for a discussion of report passes).

You may also want to use an existing report formula in record selection. However, if you use the WhilePrintingRecords function or a summary function in the formula, it will evaluate in the report's *second pass* and won't show up in the Field Tree box when you create a record selection formula. Again, the record selection occurs during the first pass, and second-pass formulas can't be used.

If you want to limit the report according to group subtotals or summaries, or somehow limit the report using second-pass formulas, you must use a *group selection formula* instead of a record selection formula. You may actually create a group selection formula inadvertently and not even know it. If you use a subtotal or summary field you create on your report in the Select Expert (perhaps you choose the Sum of Customer.Last Years

Sales instead of the Customer.Last Years Sales database field itself), you will be using group selection instead of record selection.

You may also create a group selection formula from the Select Expert by clicking Show Formula and then clicking the Group Selection radio button. If you want to make use of a typed-in formula, you have two choices: Select Report | Selection Formulas | Group from the pull-down menus or Group Selection in the Selection Formulas category of the Formula Workshop. You can now create a Boolean formula to limit records using group summaries or second-pass formulas.

One word of caution: Group selection occurs *after* the group tree, subtotals, and grand totals have been calculated. This can lead to apparent inaccuracies on your report. For example, look at the report shown in Figure 8-1.

You'll notice that the group tree shows many more regions than actually appear on the report. It doesn't take a math degree to see that the grand totals don't quite add up. Don't forget that selection of a summary or subtotal field in the Select Expert will create a group selection formula instead of a record selection formula. You may see this kind

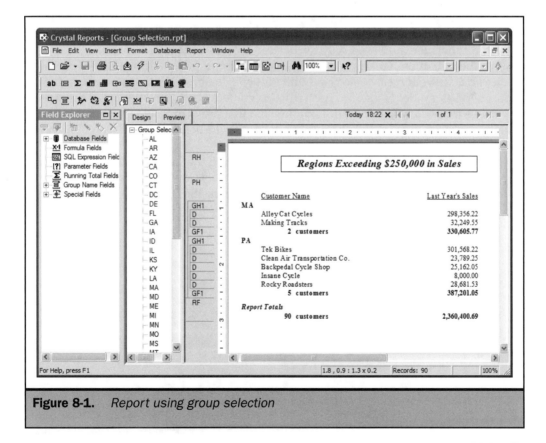

Figure 8-1.   *Report using group selection*

of odd behavior and not fully understand why. Look back at the Select Expert to see if your selection is based on a subtotal or summary field.

This report applies a group selection formula to limit the report to groups where the sum of Last Year's Sales exceeds $250,000. This group selection is applied after the group tree and grand totals have been created. Although there is no way to change the group tree in this situation, you can correct the totaling problem by using running totals instead of grand totals. Look at Chapter 5 for information on running total fields.

Performance Considerations with Record Selection

In many cases, record selection is the most time-consuming portion of the report process, particularly with larger databases. If you're using a PC-style database located on a local or network hard drive, Crystal Reports performs the record selection itself, reading every record in the database and keeping only those that match. If you are using a server-based database (such as SQL Server or Oracle), Crystal Reports will attempt to create a WHERE clause in the query that's sent to the database server, which will cause the database server to perform the query and send only the desired records to Crystal Reports.

In either situation, you'll probably see overall improved performance if you use *indexed fields* for your record selection (with PC-style databases, this is often very critical). Indexed fields are fields that are specially designated when the database is designed. The field's index stores all the values in the field in a presorted state that makes it much faster to select records based on the field. To determine if a field is indexed, you may wish to consult the database designer.

You can also see which fields are indexed by using the Links tab of the Database Expert. Click the Database Expert button on the Expert tools toolbar, or choose Database | Database Expert from the pull-down menus. Then, click the Links tab (you must have added at least two tables to your report to see it).

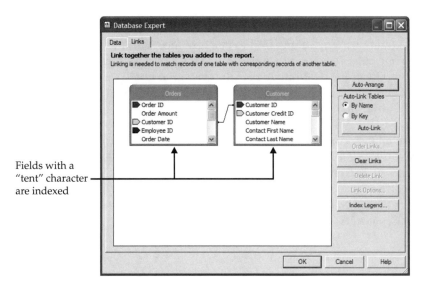

Fields with a "tent" character are indexed

You'll notice a small "tent" character appearing next to every indexed field (the different colors you may see are generally insignificant to record selection, as long as you select on a field with the symbol). Make note of the indexed fields and attempt to use them in record selection. If the field you need to select on is not indexed, and record selection appears very sluggish, you may wish to consult the database designer about adding an index for that field.

Tip   *Crystal Reports versions prior to 9 did not show the tent characters when using SQL databases. Crystal Reports 9 now displays index designations for popular SQL databases, as well as PC-style databases. However, depending on the database driver you are using, you still may not see the "tent" index designators in some instances.*

Finally, double-check the setting of the Use Indexes or Server for Speed option. To check the option for the current report, look in the File | Report Options dialog box. If you wish to check the option for all new reports in the future, look for the option on the Database tab of File | Options. If this is turned off, Crystal Reports won't use field indexes at all.

SQL databases (or PC-style databases accessed via ODBC) present a different set of performance considerations when compared to performance with PC-style databases. As a general reporting rule, you want to always have the database server perform the record selection (via the aforementioned WHERE clause), if at all possible. This can typically be accomplished by using only the Select Expert to create selection criteria—using the Formula Editor makes it entirely too easy to introduce functions that Crystal Reports can't move to the database server. Also, making changes to what the Select Expert creates with an Is Formula operator or the Show Formula button may seriously degrade database server record selection performance. As with PC-style databases, make sure the Use Indexes or Server for Speed option is turned on in File | Report Options.

Tip   *More in-depth discussion and examples of performance issues, including record selection, are found in Chapter 16.*

Chapter 9

Making Your Reports
Visually Appealing

Crystal Reports, as a Windows-based report writer, has many features that can help you create eye-catching, visually effective reports. You can often use Crystal Reports to create reports right from the database, whereas you formerly had to use a word processor or page publishing program to create such reports. The next time you're tempted to export database records to a text file and merge them in a word processing or page publishing document, use some of the techniques covered in this chapter and save the extra work.

You may consider using geographic maps (discussed in Chapter 4) and charts and graphs (discussed in Chapter 12) as visual elements to make your reports more appealing. But even using just the textual elements of Crystal Reports can be very creative. Not only can you use a variety of fonts and typefaces in your reports, you also can set object foreground and background colors, choose unique borders on all four sides of objects, add drop shadows, and use other graphical features. You can include bitmap pictures on your report, either reading them directly from the database (if the database you're using supports and includes them) or adding graphics files right into a report section. You can draw lines and boxes around the report to highlight important portions. You can use Report Alerts to trigger a message when a certain condition is met, as well as highlight portions of the report that met that condition. And new to version 9, you can choose a predefined set of object and report formatting and apply it to other reports in one step by use of templates.

General Formatting

Crystal Reports gives you considerable flexibility in customizing the appearance of objects that you place on your report, such as database fields, text objects, and formulas. By using various formatting options for these objects, you can change many aspects of their appearance, such as font face, size, color, alignment, and more. The most basic type of formatting is known as *absolute formatting*, in which you simply select the object and make formatting changes with the Formatting toolbar or the Format Editor. In either case, the change applies to all occurrences of the object on the report—if you format a field in the details section absolutely, that field will appear the same every time it prints.

The Formatting Toolbar

The quickest way to format one or more objects on the report is to select the object or objects you want to format and then choose options from the Formatting toolbar. To choose a single object, just click it with the mouse. To choose multiple objects to format at once, CTRL-click or SHIFT-click on more than one object. You'll notice that all objects you've selected will have a shaded outline around them. Then, click buttons in the Formatting toolbar to format the selected objects. Table 9-1 outlines each Formatting toolbar button.

Button	Function
`Times New Roman` **Font Face**	Choose a different font face (such as Arial, Times Roman, etc.) from the drop-down list
`10` **Font Size**	Choose the font size, in points, from the drop-down list, or enter a value directly in the box
A **Increase Font Size**	Increase the font size (each click of this button increases the font size by one point)
A **Decrease Font Size**	Decrease the font size (each click of this button decreases the font size by one point)
B **Bold**	Format object using bold emphasis
I **Italic**	Format the object using italic letters
U **Underline**	Add an underline to the object
Left Align	Align text to the left of the object's defined width
Center Align	Align text to the center of the object's defined width
Right Align	Align text to the right of the object's defined width
Full Justify (new in version 9)	Align on both the left and right side of the object's defined width. This provides "fully justified" text, similar to that often found in newspaper columns.
A **Font Color** (new in version 9)	Change font color. If you click the button itself, it will set the font color to that displayed on the small line in the button. If you click the down arrow, a dialog box will appear giving you a choice of colors. Once you choose a color that becomes the default color for the button, you will see the small line in the button change color.

Table 9-1.   *Formatting Toolbar Options*

Button	Function
Outside Borders (new in version 9)	Add border lines on sides of object. If you click the face of the button, all four sides of the object will initially be given a border. If you click the face of the button again, the borders will be turned off. If you click the down arrow, a subset of buttons will appear, which allow you to choose combinations of left, right, top, or bottom borders, all, or none.
Suppress (new in version 9)	Will toggle display of the object on and off. This is equivalent to clicking the Suppress check box on the Common tab of the Format Editor.
Lock Format (new in version 9)	Will toggle ability to change other formatting properties on the object. If formatting is locked, all other formatting options, including width and height, will be disabled. This is equivalent to clicking the Read Only check box on the Common tab of the Format Editor.
Lock Size/Position (new in version 9)	Will toggle ability to change the width or height, or to move the object. This is equivalent to clicking the Lock Position and Size check box on the Common tab of the Format Editor.
Currency	Will toggle display of a currency symbol (the symbol chosen as the default currency symbols in the Windows Control Panel) with the object. This button will be enabled only if all objects you've selected are currency or numeric fields.
Thousands Separator	Will toggle display of a thousands separator (the symbol chosen as the default thousands separator in Windows Control Panel) within the object. This button will be enabled only if all objects you've selected are currency or numeric fields.
Percent Sign	Will toggle display of a percent sign on the right side of the object. This option actually adds a currency symbol, but it changes the symbol to the percent sign and the position to the right side of the object. This button will be enabled only if all objects you've selected are currency or numeric fields.

Table 9-1.   *Formatting Toolbar Options* (continued)

Button	Function
.00 **Increase Decimals**	Increases the number of decimal places displayed. For example, if the object is displayed as $121.22 and this button is clicked, the number might display as $121.223. This button will be enabled only if all objects you've selected are currency or numeric fields.
00. **Decrease Decimals**	Decreases the number of decimal places displayed. For example, if the object is displayed as $121.22 and this button is clicked, the number will display as $121.2. This button will be enabled only if all objects you've selected are currency or numeric fields, and if at least one decimal place is already showing.

Table 9-1.   *Formatting Toolbar Options* (continued)

The Format Editor

Although Crystal Reports 9 has added more formatting options to the Formatting toolbar than in previous versions, there are still quite a few formatting options that you can't perform with toolbar buttons. For these formatting requirements, you must use the Format Editor. The *Format Editor* is not an "editor" per se, but a tabbed dialog box that displays a varying set of tabs, depending upon the data type of the object you're formatting.

To display the Format Editor, select objects as described earlier in this chapter and then choose one of the following options:

- Choose Format | Format Text, Format | Format Field, or Format | Format Objects from the pull-down menus (the choice of Text, Field, or Objects is determined by the number and data type of objects selected before you choose the option)

- Right-click the selected object and choose Format Text, Format Field, or Format Objects from the pop-up menu

- Click the Format toolbar button in the Expert Tools toolbar

The tab that displays in the Format Editor will vary, depending on the data type of the object you're formatting. For example, if you selected one or more date/time fields before displaying the Format Editor, the Date/Time tab will initially display. Number fields will result in the Number tab displaying, and string fields or text objects will cause the Paragraph Formatting tab to initially display. If you select multiple objects of varying data types, the Common tab will display by default, and you'll be able to change only formatting options that apply to all objects you've selected—any data type–specific options will be unavailable until you select one or more objects with a common data type.

In some of the Format Editor tabs (such as the Number tab or Date/Time tab), you'll be able to choose from predefined formatting "styles" that appear in a list. These styles provide more commonly used formatting styles that you may select with one mouse click. If, however, you'd like to use some combination of formatting that these styles don't provide, a Custom Style button at the bottom of the Format Editor will display additional dialog boxes where you can format individual pieces of the field, such as the leading day-of-week for a date field, or the currency symbol for a number or currency field.

Most Format Editor options are fairly self-explanatory in terms of the data type being formatted. For those options that aren't self-explanatory, Crystal Reports online help will provide additional information. Also, additional discussion of various Format Editor options can be found throughout this book in sections and chapters relating to the different types of fields being formatted.

The Highlighting Expert

While the absolute formatting options on the Format Editor will solve many reporting needs, you'll soon find that you may wish object formatting to change according to the data being displayed. This is called *conditional reporting*, which lets you change the appearance of objects depending on their contents or the contents of other fields, objects, or formulas. Although the possibilities of conditional formatting are limited only by your imagination and creativity, some immediate uses of conditional reporting that may come to mind are the following:

- Showing sales figures in red if they fall below a predefined level
- Using a different font to highlight long-time customers
- Adding a border around an invoice number if it's past due
- Showing a report title that's different on the first page than on the rest of the pages
- Graphically indicating with file-folder icons whether a case file has been opened or closed

Probably the simplest conditional formatting tool with Crystal Reports is the *Highlighting Expert*, which lets you arrange that the appearance of a field will change when a certain condition is met. If a sales figure falls below a preset goal for the department, you can have it stand out with a white font color on a red background. Or, you can change the border on a Days Overdue formula that exceeds, say, 60 days.

To use the Highlighting Expert with a field, select the field you want to change. Start the Highlighting Expert by clicking the Highlighting button on the Expert Tools toolbar, choosing Format | Highlighting Expert from the pull-down menus, or right-clicking the object and choosing Highlighting Expert from the pop-up menu. Figure 9-1 shows the Highlighting Expert.

The idea of the Highlighting Expert is to allow conditional formatting of a field without intricate knowledge of the Crystal Reports formula language. By using the drop-down lists in the dialog box, you choose a series of conditions (by clicking the New button multiple times), and choose specific formatting for each condition. Begin by clicking the New button to add a new condition. Then, choose the field you want to use in a comparison test from the first drop-down list in the Value Of section of the dialog box

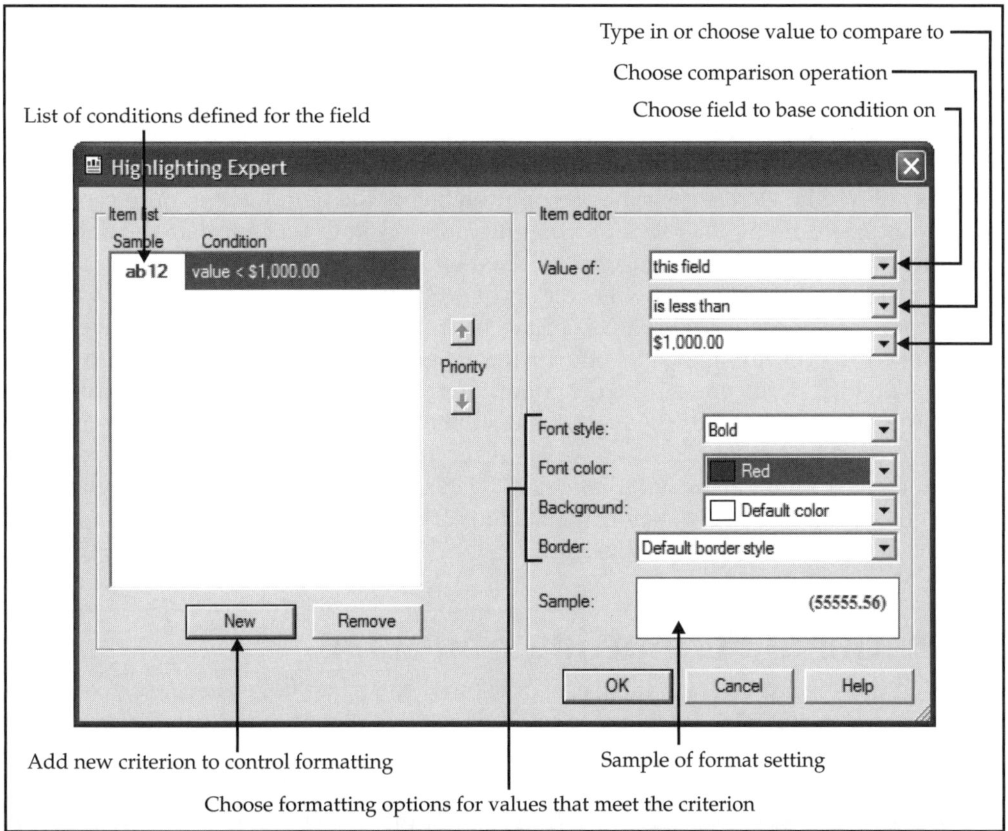

Figure 9-1. *The Highlighting Expert*

(Crystal Reports 9 now allows you to choose any field on the report, not just the field you are highlighting for this test). Then, choose a comparison operator in the second drop-down list. You'll find most of the standard comparison operators you've used in formulas or in the Select Expert, such as Less Than, Greater Than, Equal To, Not Equal To, and so forth. After making this choice, enter a constant value to compare to in the third drop-down list (you can also click the drop-down arrow and choose a value from the sample data in the list). Finally, choose any combination of font and background styles, colors, and border styles you want the field to display if the comparison is true.

For example, to format the sales figure to show up as white text on a red background if it falls below the preset sales figure of $1,000, choose "this field" in the first drop-down list, choose a comparison of Less Than, type **1000**, and then choose a Font Color of White and a Background of Red. You will see a sample in the Sample box in the lower right of the Highlighting Expert, as well as to the left of the now-created condition in the Item List box on the left. When you click OK, the field will show white text on a red background for any sales figures less than $1,000.

You may want to set up multiple conditions if you want more than one formatting option displayed. To expand on the previous example, suppose you want to show bonus sales (over $5,000) in blue, in addition to the existing red background for those that fall below $1,000. Just click the New button below the Item List box. You can enter a new condition and another set of formatting options. Both will apply to the field.

You may have two conditions that conflict with each other. For example, you could have a condition that formats field contents over $1,000 in red, and another that applies blue formatting for contents over $5,000. Since both conditions would satisfy the over-1000 condition, will everything over $1,000 (including anything over $5,000) be in red? It depends on the *priority* you assign the conditions. If the over-1000 condition is higher in the Item List box, everything over $1,000 will be in red. However, if the over-5000 condition is set higher, then it has priority—everything over $5,000 will be in blue. Then, the second item in the list (the over-1000 item) will be tested, placing anything over $1,000 in red. To change priority, click the condition you want to move and then click the up or down Priority arrow.

Conditional Formatting Formulas

The Highlighting Expert is a simple and quick way to format fields, because you don't have to know the formula language to use it. However, the trade-off is in flexibility. As your reports become more sophisticated, sometimes the Highlighting Expert won't provide all the flexibility you need. Even though the Highlighting Expert is greatly improved in Crystal Reports 9, you may need to apply formatting other than just color and borders. Or, you may need to perform a more complex test than can be done with the comparisons that are in the expert. For these situations, you need to use *conditional formatting formulas*. Conditional formatting formulas use the Formula Editor to create one or more conditions to determine how the object appears.

Absolute Versus Conditional Formatting

Before you learn how to set formatting conditionally, it's important to have a fundamental grasp of absolute formatting, which simply refers to applying normal formatting to objects with the Format Editor. This type of formatting, described earlier in the chapter, makes use of the Formatting toolbar or the Format Editor to apply the same formatting to all occurrences of the field. If you right-click an object and choose Format Field from the pop-up menu, the Format Editor will appear. You can then click the Font tab to change the font face, style, size, or color. If you change the color of the font to Red, *all* occurrences of the object on the report will be red. If you click the Border tab and select the Drop Shadow check box, *all* occurrences of the object will have a drop shadow. This is the process of absolute formatting.

The first rule to follow when it comes to conditional formatting is determining whether to use the Formatting toolbar or the Format Editor. While you can perform absolute formatting with either the Formatting toolbar or the Format Editor, you can set up conditional formatting only with the Format Editor—the Formatting toolbar won't work.

As you approach conditional formatting, it's important to distinguish between two types of Format Editor formatting properties: *multiple-choice* properties and *on-off* properties. On the Font tab, Font and Color are good examples of multiple-choice properties. You can click a drop-down list and choose from any one of several fonts or colors. An example of an on-off property is Drop Shadow on the Border tab, which just has a check box: it can only be turned on or off. Whether a formatting property is multiple choice or on-off determines the type of formula you'll use to set it conditionally. Multiple-choice properties are conditionally formatted with If-Then-Else formulas, while on-off properties are conditionally formatted with Boolean formulas.

> **Tip** *You need to be familiar with the Crystal Reports formula language to use conditional formatting effectively. To refresh your memory, look for information on If-Then-Else and Boolean formulas in Chapter 5.*

To set formatting conditionally, click the Conditional Formula button that appears on the Format Editor next to the property that you want to format.

This will display the *Format Formula Editor* inside the Formula Workshop (essentially the same Formula Editor discussed in Chapter 5, but with a new title and without the Formula Workshop tree on the left), shown in Figure 9-2. Notice that you can set conditional formatting with either Crystal or Basic syntax by making your choice from the Syntax drop-down list. If you are formatting a multiple-choice property, all the available options for the property appear at the top of the Function Tree box. If, for example, you are conditionally formatting the Color property, you'll see all the available colors listed. If you're formatting a border, you'll see the different available line styles.

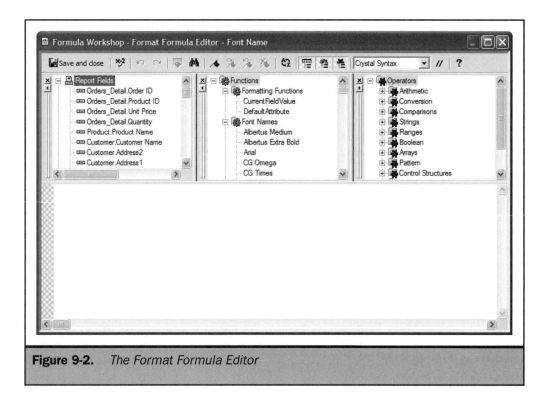

Figure 9-2. *The Format Formula Editor*

Use an If-Then-Else formula to determine the formatting of the object. Your formula can be as simple or as complex as you need. For example, you may have a formula to set font color that is as simple as the following:

```
If {Customer.Last Year's Sales} > 5000 Then Blue Else Black
```

or a formula to set a bottom border as complex as this:

```
If {Orders.Order Amount} > 5000 And {Orders.Ship Via} = "Fedex" Then
    DoubleLine
Else
    If {Orders.Order Amount} > 1000 And {@Ship Days} < 3 Then
        SingleLine
    Else
        NoLine
```

Tip *You may type formatting values, such as color or line type, into the formula directly (as in the previous examples). You may also double-click on values shown in the Functions box of the Formula Editor. If you double-click, the prefix "cr" will appear in front of the formatting value in the formula. Either the value name by itself, or the value name preceded by "cr" is acceptable.*

You can use any type of simple or compound If-Then-Else formula, as long as the results of every Then and Else are one of the available formatting properties in the Function Tree box.

When you have finished with the formula, you can use the Check button to check for correct syntax of the formula, or save the formula and close the Format Formula Editor with the Save and Close button. The Format Editor will remain on the screen. Notice that the Conditional Formula button changes from blue to red, and the pencil character inside the button points at a different angle. This indicates that a conditional formula is set for this property.

To change the existing formula, click the Conditional Formula button again and change the formula that appears in the Format Formula Editor. To delete conditional formatting and return to absolute formatting (or no formatting at all), just highlight and delete the whole conditional formula. Then, click the Save and Close button. You'll notice that the Conditional Formula button has returned to a blue color with the pencil pointed in its original direction.

Note   *While most conditional formulas must use a built-in formatting function for the Then and Else clauses of your formula, the Size property is a little different from other properties. In this case, the result of your conditional formula must be a number, which will indicate the font size to be used.*

If you're formatting an on-off property, the general procedure for conditional formatting is the same. But when you click the Conditional Formula button next to the property, you won't see any additional functions in the Function Tree box of the Format Formula Editor, because you can't use an If-Then-Else formula to format this property. Because the property can have only one of two states, on or off, you must format it with a Boolean formula that can return only one of two results: true or false.

To add a drop shadow to Customer Name fields of customers who have last year's sales greater than $100,000, start by right-clicking the Customer Name field. Choose Format Field from the pop-up menu, choose the Border tab, and click the Conditional Formula button next to the Drop Shadow property. When the Format Formula Editor appears, type in the following Boolean formula:

```
{Customer.Last Year's Sales} > 100000
```

The Boolean formula will evaluate to only one of two states: true or false. If the formula returns true, the formatting property will be turned on and the field will have a drop shadow around it. If the formula returns false, the property will be turned off and the field won't have a drop shadow.

You may be curious about how conditional formatting and absolute formatting interrelate. Consider the following scenario. You choose an absolute color of Red on the Font tab of the Format Editor and click OK. Of course, every occurrence of the field will be red. You then return to the Format Editor and, without changing the absolute formatting, click the Conditional Formula button next to the Color property and add the following formula:

```
If {Customer.Last Year's Sales} > 50000 Then Blue
```

Note the missing Else clause. Remember that Crystal Reports does *not* require an Else clause in an If-Then-Else formula. In a regular formula, if the If test fails and there's no Else clause, the formula returns an empty string, zero, or other default value based on the data type of the formula. But what color will the font take on here if there's no Else clause and absolute formatting is set to red?

Contrary to what might seem logical, when the If test fails in this case, the font will show up in black type, despite the absolute formatting of red. This is by design—if conditional formatting is applied, absolute formatting is ignored. If the conditional formula fails (and there's no condition to "catch" the failure, like an Else clause), the Windows Control Panel default color or format for that type of object will be used. Be careful with this if you don't use Else clauses, especially if you're formatting background colors. A font color of black isn't necessarily problematic, but a background color of black will often cause your report to look like someone plastered electrical tape all over it!

The exception to this rule, and a way to combine absolute and conditional formatting, is to use the DefaultAttribute function, located in the Formatting Functions category of the Function Tree box in the Format Formula Editor. If you use this function with the Then or Else clause, the formula will use the setting from the absolute formatting property. Hence,

```
If {Customer.Last Year's Sales} > 50000 Then Blue
Else DefaultAttribute
```

will show sales figures over $50,000 in blue and others in red (provided that the absolute color chosen in the Format Editor is red). If you change the absolute color, then figures over $50,000 will still show up in blue, but the rest will take on whatever color you specified as absolute.

Tip *If you've applied conditional formatting to a field that's also being formatted with the Highlighting Expert, the Highlighting Expert will take precedence. Only if it doesn't change the formatting of a field will conditional formatting be visible.*

Creative Use of the Suppress Property

If you search through the Format Editor, you'll notice that virtually all formatting properties can be set conditionally. One of the most flexible is the Suppress property on the Common tab. You may consider that absolutely setting the Suppress property is of limited usefulness. (Why even bother putting the object on the report if you're just going to suppress it?) There are some good reasons for suppressing the object; for example, a formula that sets a variable to zero in a group header has to be physically placed in the header to work properly, but you don't want zeros showing up at the top of every group.

There are many more situations in which *conditionally suppressing* an object can be useful. Here are some examples, and the corresponding Boolean formulas you will apply to the Suppress property:

■ **Placing the word "continued" in a repeated group header**   In Chapter 3, the repeated group header was introduced. If you select this option in the Group Options dialog box, a group header section will repeat at the top of a page if a group continues from the previous page. Indicating that this group continues from the previous page adds readability to your report. Place a text object that contains the word "continued," or something similar, in the group header close to the Group Name field. You must now suppress it if it is *not* in a repeated group header. Conditionally suppress the text object with the following Boolean formula:

```
Not InRepeatedGroupHeader
```

Tip   *When you conditionally suppress an object, you use a Boolean formula; when your formula returns true, the object will be suppressed. So, you may have to think "backward" when conditionally suppressing.*

■ **Showing a bonus message only for certain records**   You may want a report to indicate that a certain record (for example, a certain order or a certain salesperson) has exceeded a predefined goal amount. Simply create a text object that displays something like "Congratulations! You've exceeded the sales goal." Again, you have to think about when you *don't* want the text object to appear, not when you do. Assuming a $10,000 sales goal, conditionally suppress the text object with the following Boolean formula:

```
{AccountRep.Sales} <= 10000
```

■ **Showing a different heading on page 2 and later**   You may want to have a larger report title, perhaps including the company logo and a large font, on page 1 of the report. However, every other page needs to contain a smaller title without the logo, and perhaps include the word "continued." If you put the large title in the report header, you'll only see it at the beginning of the report. Putting the smaller title in the page header, on the other hand, will result in it showing up on every page, including page 1. Create the text object that contains the smaller title and place it in the page header along with any column headings or other objects you want to appear on every page, but conditionally suppress the text object containing the title with the following Boolean formula (PageNumber is a built-in function from the Print State category of the Formula Editor Function Tree box that returns the current page number):

```
PageNumber = 1
```

Tip   *You can also create string formulas that provide roughly the same functionality as these examples and place them in appropriate report sections. However, to minimize potential "formula clutter," it sometimes may be preferable to just create text objects and conditionally suppress them.*

Special Fonts, Graphics, and Line Drawing

As mentioned at the beginning of the chapter, Crystal Reports is a true Windows report writer. This means that it can use most of the fonts and graphical capabilities of Windows.

Using Special Fonts

Don't hesitate to use symbol fonts that are installed on your computer. In particular, the Symbol and Wingdings symbol fonts are included as part of Windows and should be available to most "target" systems that will be running your report.

Caution   *Don't forget that any fonts you use when designing your reports must also be present on the machine that runs your reports if you expect the report to look identical on both machines. Using Times Roman, Arial, Symbol, and Wingdings fonts, at a minimum, is pretty safe, because they are installed by default on all Windows systems.*

Both Symbol and Wingdings fonts contain typographical symbols instead of letters and numbers. Although you type letters and numbers into a text object or formula formatted with a text font initially, you'll see them replaced with the symbol characters once you change the font from a text font to one of the symbol fonts. You'll need either a font table (typically available from Windows Control Panel) or a little extra time to experiment and figure out what symbols display when you type certain letters, numbers, or special characters.

Figure 9-3 shows a report using the Wingdings font. In this example, the following formula is being displayed on the report next to the order amount, formatted using the Wingdings font:

```
If {Orders.Order Amount} < 1000 Then
    "L"
Else
    If {Orders.Order Amount} > 1000 And
       {Orders.Order Amount} < 2500 Then
       "K"
    Else
       "J"
```

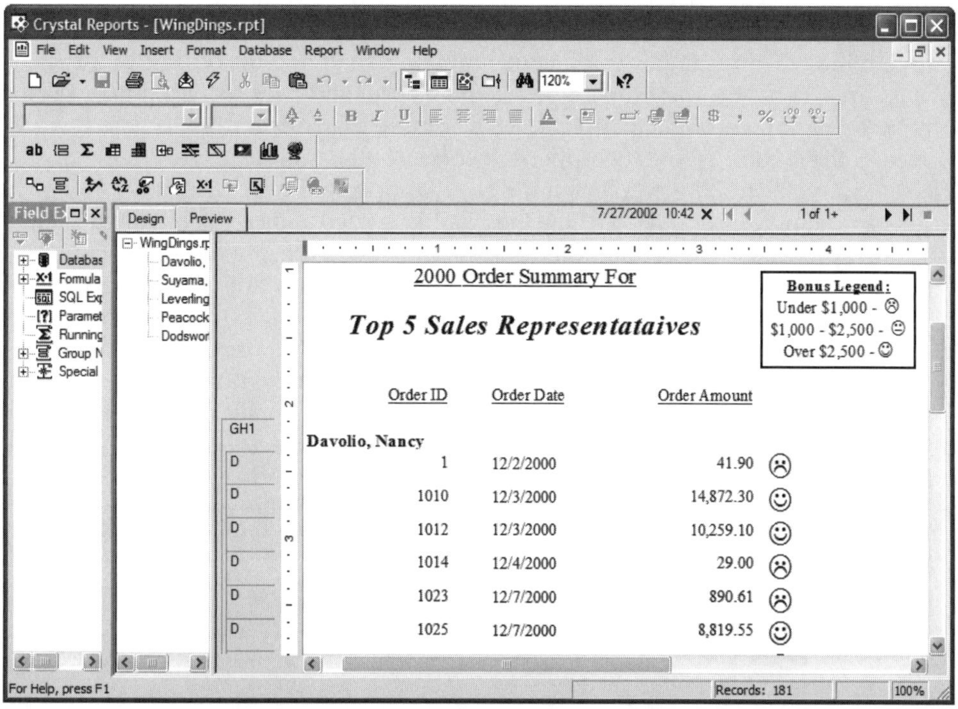

Figure 9-3. *Report using symbols as well as text*

Using Bitmap Graphics

If you are planning to create reports that approach the quality of output from page publishing programs, you'll soon have a need to use *bitmap graphics* in your reports. Bitmap graphics are common graphics files most often associated with the Web (such as .JPG files) or Windows paint program files (such as .BMP and .PCX, and .WMF files). You may have a company logo that you want included on the title page of the report. Or, you may want to add a smaller graphical element, such as an icon, to another section of the report.

To insert a bitmap graphic, first make sure you are displaying the Design tab. Although it's possible to add a graphic while viewing the Preview tab, this is risky, because you won't always be sure which report section the graphic will end up in. Click the Insert Picture button on the Insert Tools toolbar, or choose Insert | Picture from the pull-down menus. A familiar File Open dialog box will appear, asking you to choose a bitmap format file. Navigate to the necessary drive and folder, and the dialog box will show any files at that location that can be added to the report. Choose the correct file and click OK.

An outline will appear alongside your mouse cursor. Drag the outline to the section of the report where you want the graphic to be placed, and click the left mouse button to drop it there. If the graphic happens to cover more than one report section, it will be dropped in the section where the upper-left corner of the outline is when the mouse is clicked. Once you drop the graphic, you'll see it appear in the Design tab.

You have complete control over how the graphic is sized and cropped. You can simply drag the graphic to a new location on the report, or resize it using the sizing handles on the sides and corners. You can also position the graphic (or any other object on the report, for that matter) with the Object Size and Position dialog box. Select the object that you want to position, right-click, and choose Size and Position from the pop-up menu. You can also choose Format | Size and Position from the pull-down menus.

To format the graphic more precisely, you can use the Format Editor. Make sure the graphic is still selected. Then, click the Format button in the Expert Tools toolbar, right-click the graphic, and choose Format Graphic from the pop-up menu; or choose Format | Format Graphic from the pull-down menus. The Picture tab allows you to specify exact cropping and scaling specifications.

Tip

Only common bitmap graphic formats are supported in Crystal Reports. It will not recognize specialized formats, such as Adobe Photoshop, or vector formats (other than Windows Metafile), such as those from CorelDRAW or Adobe Illustrator. If you wish to use these graphics in a report, you need to convert them to common bitmap formats with another program before adding them to your report. And if you wish to include graphics from Web pages, you must use .JPG format—Crystal Reports won't recognize .GIF files.

Although using symbol fonts, such as Wingdings, is very powerful, you are limited to what is included in the font itself. Also, the symbols are generally simple two-dimensional images and can be displayed only in a single color. Wouldn't it be nice if you could use smaller bitmap files, such as icon-like graphics that look more three-dimensional and include several colors, on your report?

Because you can suppress bitmap files conditionally, just like other objects, you have real power and flexibility in creating visually appealing and interesting reports using bitmap graphics. Figure 9-4 shows a report with unique icons indicating the status of an order. Orders that have been shipped (or are "closed") have a closed file folder next to them. Open orders (not shipped) have an open file folder next to them.

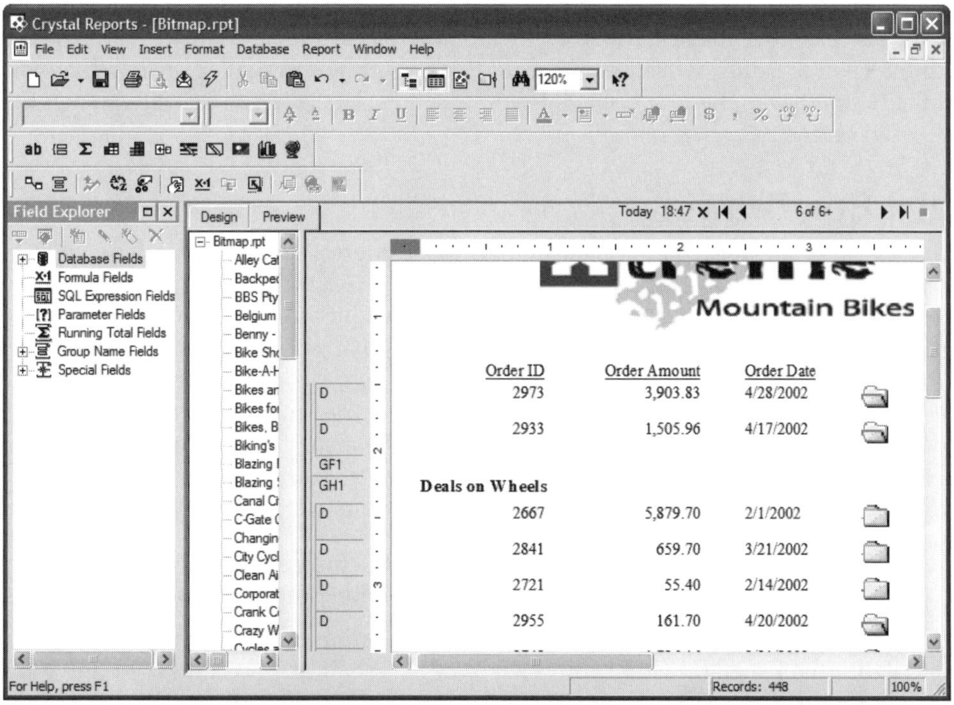

Figure 9-4. *Using bitmap files formatted conditionally*

This report uses a technique that could be called *mutually exclusive suppression*. There are two different bitmap files on the report: an open-file bitmap and a closed-file bitmap. They are placed right on top of each other in the details section. They are conditionally suppressed in such a way that only one will ever be displayed at a time. In this case, they are suppressed using the Shipped field (a Boolean field that returns true or false) from the XTRME Sample Database Orders table.

The open-file bitmap is conditionally suppressed using this formula:

```
{Orders.Shipped}
```

while the closed-file bitmap is conditionally suppressed using this formula:

```
Not {Orders.Shipped}
```

Because of this, only one bitmap will ever be visible at a time.

The success of this technique depends on Crystal Reports allowing multiple objects to be placed right on top of each other. You have the ability to do this with any text or graphic object whenever and wherever you choose. Just make sure you implement some technique similar to this to prevent them from splattering all over each other. You can also use the Move to Back, Move Backward, Move Forward, and Move to Front options from the Format pull-down menu or from the pop-up menu that appears when you right-click an object. These options determine which objects have "priority" when they are placed on top of each other.

Line and Box Drawing

You can use the Border tab on the Format Editor to control lines on all four sides of individual objects. While this lets the individual objects stand out by having lines or boxes appear around them, you may want more flexibility to have groups of objects highlighted with boxes or to have lines stretch partially or completely across sections.

Crystal Reports lets you use line and box drawing tools to create these boxes and lines. To create a line or box, ensure that you have the Design tab chosen. Inserting lines or boxes in the Preview tab may give you undesirable results if you don't put them in the right section.

To add a line or box to your report, perform these steps:

1. Click the Insert Line or Insert Box button in the Insert Tools toolbar. You can also choose Insert | Line or Insert | Box from the pull-down menus.

2. When you make either of these choices, your mouse cursor changes to a pencil. Point the pencil to where you want to begin the line or box and hold down the left mouse button.

3. Drag the line or box to its ending position and release the button. Notice that you can draw only perfectly vertical or horizontal lines—diagonal lines can't be drawn.

The line or box will appear on the report, complete with sizing handles. You can now drag or resize the line or box just like any other object. You may also format the line or box with the Format Editor (using options from the Format pull-down menu, or by right-clicking the line or box and choosing Format from the pop-up menu). You can choose the color, size, and style of the line or box, along with other options (Crystal Reports allows you to create rounded boxes, for example). Figure 9-5 shows a report that uses a horizontal line to delineate group footers, and places a filled, rounded box around report totals.

Tip   *You can draw lines and boxes that traverse multiple report sections. This is handy if you want to have a single box enclose a column starting in the page header and ending in the page footer, including all the sections in between. However, this can sometimes result in odd behavior if, for example, you start a line in the page header but end it in the details section or a group footer. If your lines or boxes traverse sections, make sure you preview the report to check that you get the desired results.*

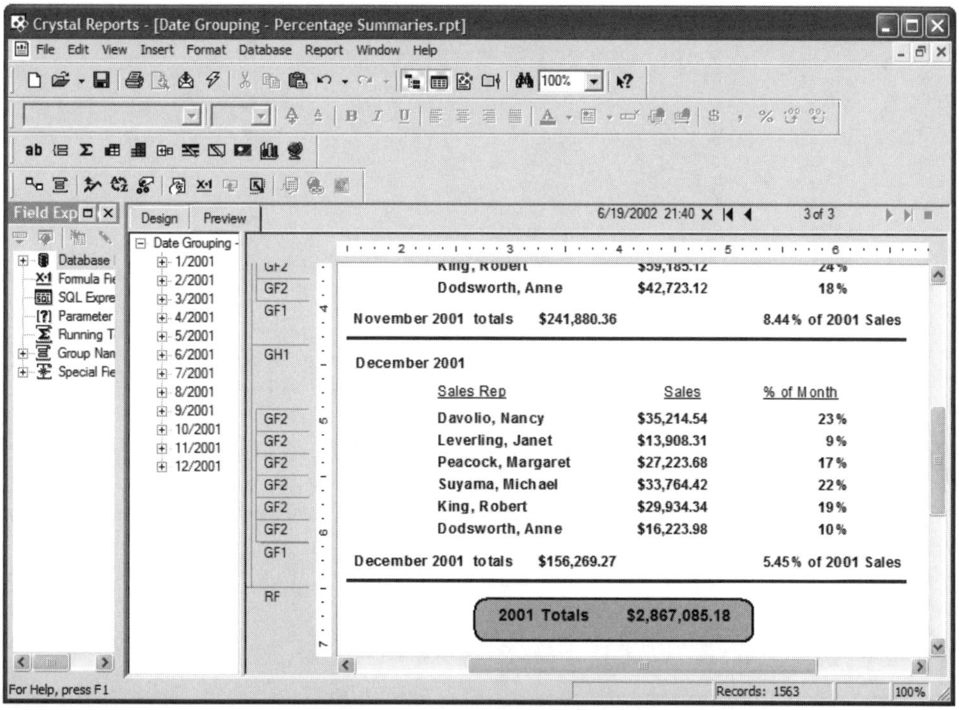

Figure 9-5.   *Line and box drawing*

Text and Paragraph Formatting

Crystal Reports includes various text formatting features that enhance reporting capabilities. Some are designed for use with foreign-language versions of the report writer (such as Japanese), while others simply provide enhanced functionality for more reporting situations.

A subtle feature that may not be immediately noticeable is *fractional point sizes* for fonts. If you use the Point Size drop-down list either in the Format toolbar or from the Font tab of the Format Editor, you'll see that only whole-number point-size values are available. However, if you click inside the drop-down list, you can then type values directly into the drop-down list, rather than choosing predefined numbers. If you want to use a 10.5 point size instead of a whole number, simply type **10.5** and press ENTER. You may type in sizes in ½-point increments (10.5 will work, but 10.25 will round to 10.5).

You'll also notice a *Text Rotation* option on the Format Editor Common tab. This allows you to rotate objects based on TrueType or built-in printer fonts to 90 degrees (sideways from bottom to top) or 270 degrees (sideways from top to bottom). Just choose the desired rotation from the drop-down list. You'll probably need to adjust the height and width of the now-rotated text to properly show all the material in the object.

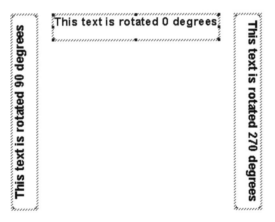

Tip *You can make innovative use of text rotation by using multiple report sections and the Underlay section formatting option, described in Chapter 10. For example, by placing a rotated text object in Page Header b (which is formatted with the Underlay option), you can have vertical text flow down alongside the rest of your report on every page. This technique can be helpful for replicating special forms, for example.*

Format Editor Paragraph Formatting Tab

If you format a string or memo database field or a text object, Crystal Reports presents an additional *Paragraph* tab on the Format Editor, as shown in Figure 9-6. Use these options to determine how multiple lines of text or data will be formatted:

■ **Indentation—First Line**   Indicates the amount of space the first line in each paragraph will be indented. The first line of the text or any line after a carriage return is considered the first line of a paragraph.

■ **Indentation—Left**   Indicates the amount of space that the entire field will be indented from the left side of the object.

■ **Indentation—Right**   Indicates the amount of space that the entire field will be indented from the right side of the object.

■ **Spacing—Line Spacing**   Adds vertical blank space between each line in the paragraph. Choose the Multiple option to choose a multiple of the normal spacing (for example, two times normal spacing). Choose the Exact option to choose a specific point size for line spacing (for example, 5 points).

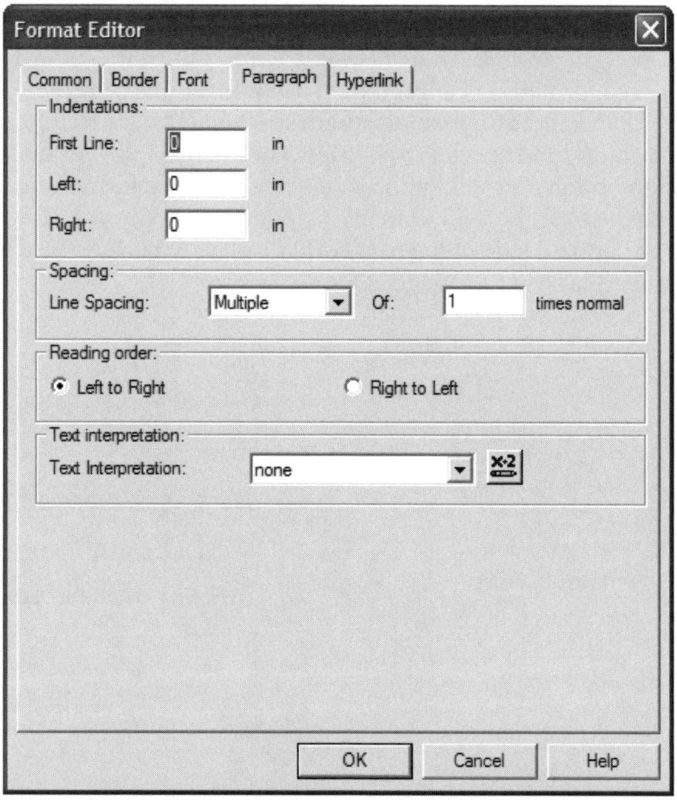

Figure 9-6.   *Paragraph Formatting tab on Format Editor*

- **Spacing—Of *x* Times Normal** Specifies the associated number for the Multiple or Exact Line Spacing option.

- **Reading Order** Specifies whether the text in the object that's being formatted will be read from left to right, or right to left. This option generally applies to non-English versions of Crystal Reports, and while it doesn't reverse the display of characters that make up a field, it does rearrange placement of punctuation marks that appear at the end of fields.

Using HTML and RTF Text Interpretation

Figure 9-6 also shows the *Text Interpretation* drop-down list on the Paragraph Formatting tab (you'll see this option only with string or memo database fields—not with text objects). Available options in this drop-down list are None (the default), HTML Text (Hypertext Markup Language), and RTF Text (Rich Text Format). HTML text is often associated with the Web—Web pages are encoded in HTML. RTF is a standard text format that is interchangeable between most popular word processors and page publishing programs.

If you leave the default Text Interpretation option of None chosen, Crystal Reports simply displays the value from the database as it actually appears in the database. If the field contains special formatting codes, they'll just appear on the report directly. If your database string or memo fields contain text with special HTML or RTF formatting codes to describe fonts, colors, and special formatting, choose the appropriate HTML or RTF Text Interpretation option. Crystal Reports will convert these formatting codes into actual typeface, point size, color, and formatting options. Notice how a Text Interpretation setting of None (as opposed to a setting of HTML) displays a database field that's encoded using the Hypertext Markup Language.

```
<HTML>
<HEAD>
<META
HTTP-EQUIV="Content-Type"
CONTENT="text/html;
charset=windows-1252">
<META NAME="Generator"
CONTENT="Microsoft Word
97">
</HEAD>
<BODY>

<I><FONT
FACE="Arial"><P>Now</I> is
the time for all
```

Now is the time for all good men to come to the aid of their country.

Tip *For a list of specific HTML tags that Crystal Reports interprets, search online help for "Paragraph Formatting tab."*

Report Alerts

In addition to some of the conditional reporting features discussed elsewhere in this chapter, Crystal Reports allows you to highlight records that meet a requirement using Report Alerts. *Report Alerts* enable you to set up a condition that Crystal Reports checks for every time you refresh the report (by clicking the Refresh button in the Standard toolbar, by selecting Report | Refresh Report Data from the pull-down menus, or by pressing the F5 key). Report Alerts can also be used to highlight desired conditions when reports are scheduled with the Crystal Enterprise Web-based reporting system (covered in Part II of this book).

While you've always been able to conditionally format report sections and objects in terms of a condition, you might not have always known which customers, sales reps, months, and so forth had "triggered" this condition without going through the report page by page looking for the conditionally formatted sections. Now when a report with Report Alerts defined runs, a separate dialog box will pop up if any of the conditions on the report have been met. You can then click a button on the dialog box to display a separate tab (similar to a drill-down tab) that shows only report records that meet the alert condition.

To work with Report Alerts, choose Report | Create Alerts from the pull-down menus. The Create Alerts dialog box will appear, as shown in Figure 9-7. If any existing alerts have already been created in the report, they'll appear inside this dialog box. If you wish to modify any existing alert, select it in the dialog box and click the Edit button.

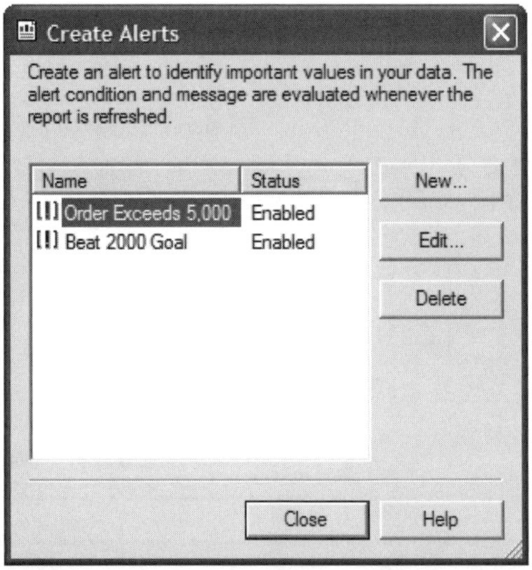

Figure 9-7.   *The Create Alerts dialog box*

To delete an existing alert, select it and click the Delete button. If there are no alerts in the report yet, the dialog box will be empty.

To create a new alert, click the New button. The Create Alert dialog box will appear, as shown in Figure 9-8. At a minimum, you must specify the name of the Report Alert in the Name text box, and the condition that will trigger the alert by clicking the Condition button. You may optionally type a message that will appear when the alert is triggered in the Message text box, or customize the message with a string formula you create by clicking the conditional formula button. Clicking the Condition button will display the Formula Editor, where you enter a Boolean formula that determines when the alert will be triggered (see Chapter 5 for information on Boolean formulas). If you wish to temporarily disable the alert without deleting it entirely, deselect the Enabled check box.

For example, you may wish to create a simple report showing orders that were placed. If the order amount exceeds a certain level ($5,000, for example), you wish to trigger a report alert. Create the report as you usually would and then create a new Report Alert. Give the alert a name of your choosing (perhaps "Order Exceeds 5,000"), type any message you want to appear when the alert is triggered, and then click the Condition button. Enter a Boolean formula to indicate what records should trigger the alert, such as

```
{Orders.Order Amount} > 5000
```

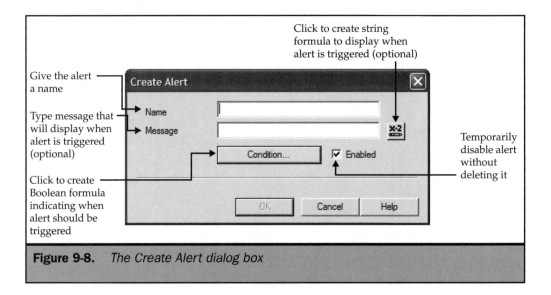

Figure 9-8. *The Create Alert dialog box*

Once you've saved the alert, simply refresh the report. If any order amounts in the report exceed $5,000, you'll receive an alert dialog box indicating that the alert has been triggered.

To see a separate tab showing all report records with orders that exceed $5,000, just click the View Records button. A separate tab (similar to a drill-down tab, discussed in Chapters 3 and 10) will appear showing just the relevant records.

You don't have to just base Report Alerts on database fields, as in the previous example. You can also base report alerts on summaries or subtotals in group footers (although you can't base Report Alerts on WhilePrintingRecords or "second pass" formulas). For example, you may prefer to create a parameter field (discussed in Chapter 14) to prompt the user for a customer total threshold. You can then create a Report Alert that will be triggered if an order subtotal in a customer name group footer exceeds the value supplied by the parameter field. In this situation, the Boolean formula used to trigger the alert will look something like this:

```
Sum ({Orders.Order Amount}, {Customer.Customer Name}) >
{?Report Alert Threshold}
```

Basing Report Formulas or Conditional Formatting on Report Alerts

While it's helpful to see a dialog box showing that a Report Alert has been triggered, and see a separate tab of report items that triggered the alert, you may appreciate the additional power afforded to your formulas by Report Alerts as well. Three functions exist in the formula language in Crystal Reports to support alerts: *IsAlertEnabled*, *IsAlertTriggered*, and *AlertMessage*. Each of these new functions takes one parameter, the name of a previously created report alert:

- **IsAlertEnabled**   Returns a true or false value, depending on the state of the Enabled check box in the Create Alert dialog box (shown in Figure 9-8 earlier in the chapter). If the alert is enabled, then this function will return true. Otherwise, it will return false.

- **IsAlertTriggered**   Returns a true or false value, depending on whether the record the formula is evaluating for triggers the alert or not. For example, if you create a formula containing the IsAlertTriggered("Order Exceeds 5,000") function, the function will return true for records with order amounts greater than $5,000, and false for records with order amounts equal to or less than $5,000.

- **AlertMessage**   Returns the message specified for the Report Alert. This is either the "hard-coded" message that was typed into the Message text box when the alert was created, or the results of the message string formula that was created with the alert.

For the previously discussed customer subtotal example, you may wish to create a formula that displays a message in group footers that trigger the alert. The formula might look similar to this:

```
If IsAlertTriggered ("Beat 2000 Goal") Then
    GroupName ({Customer.Customer Name}) & " beat the 2000 goal"
```

You may also wish to highlight the entire group footer with a different background color if the group triggered a Report Alert. You can use these new formula functions in conditional formatting formulas, as well as report formulas. For example, you could conditionally set the background color of the Customer Name Group Footer to aqua by using the Section Expert. The conditional formula would be similar to this:

```
If IsAlertTriggered ("Beat 2000 Goal") Then crAqua Else crNoColor
```

Note *For complete information on formatting sections and the Section Expert, refer to Chapter 10.*

New Crystal Reports 9 Templates

Versions of Crystal Reports prior to 9 included a feature when using the Report Experts to preformat a report using a report style. The report styles would format certain sections of the report with prechosen formatting options, such as fonts, font sizes, and colors. Oftentimes, the question would arise, "Can I create my own styles?" The answer was "No." Well, Crystal Reports 9 has changed that.

Crystal Reports 9 introduces Report Templates. *Report Templates* are just existing .RPT files that are used to format other reports. The Style tab on the report wizards (which replaced Report Experts) has been replaced with the Template section, where you can choose a template to apply to the report being created in a wizard.

To apply a template from a report wizard, simply select one of the predefined templates in the Available Templates list. When you choose one of the templates in the list, a thumbnail view of the template is shown in the Preview section of the Report Wizard. You may also choose another .RPT file to use as a template by clicking the Browse button. This will launch a standard open file dialog box, where you can navigate to the existing .RPT file you wish to use as a template.

Once you've chosen the report, it will be added to the template list, where you may select it to control the formatting of the new report. If the report you added has a value in the File | Summary Info Title field, it will appear as the name of the template. And if the Save Preview Picture check box is checked in the File | Summary Info dialog box of the report you just added, the preview of the report will appear in the Preview area of the report wizard.

Note *Any .RPT files you add to the template list won't remain in the list the next time you use the report wizards. You'll need to navigate to the report with the Browse button again if you want to use it as a template.*

The Template Expert

If you want to apply a template to a report you've already created (either with a report wizard or without), you can use the Template Expert to apply a template or undo the previous application of a template. To display the Template Expert, either click the Template Expert toolbar button in the Expert Tools toolbar, or choose Report | Template Expert from the pull-down menus. The Template Expert will appear, as shown in Figure 9-9.

The Template Expert looks very similar to the Template section of the report wizards, with a few additional features. As with the report wizards, you can pick a template from the list to add to your current report. When you select a template in the list, a preview of the template will appear in the Preview area of the Template Expert. And you may also click the Browse button to add an existing .RPT file to the template list to use to reformat the current report.

However, the Template Expert includes a few more features that don't apply to the report wizards. In particular, if you've already applied a template and aren't satisfied with its results (and this is a real possibility—templates can dramatically change the formatting of your report), you can undo the template application by clicking the Undo the Current Template radio button in the Template Expert. This is the only way to undo a template application—the Undo feature on the Edit menu or the Undo toolbar button won't undo a template application. If you've already undone a template and wish to redo it, you may either choose it in the template list again or click the Re-Apply the Last Template radio button. It's important to remember that the Undo and Redo features will be available only during the current Crystal Reports session. If you apply a template, save the report, and then exit Crystal Reports, you'll be stuck with the template's formatting when you next reopen the report.

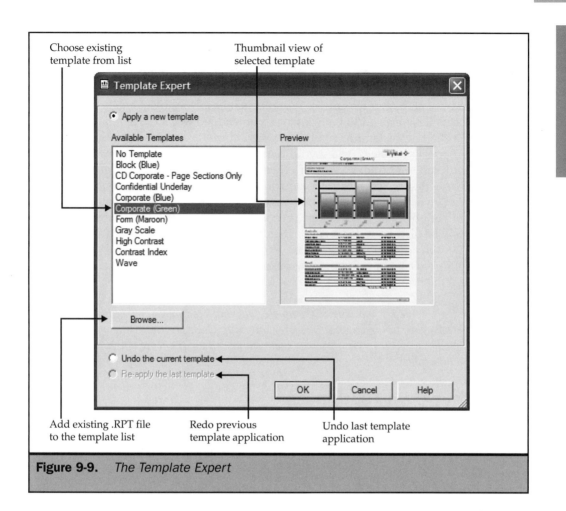

Choose existing
template from list

Thumbnail view of
selected template

Add existing .RPT file
to the template list

Redo previous
template application

Undo last template
application

Figure 9-9.   *The Template Expert*

Tip

The predefined templates in the Template Expert are supplied by existing .RPT files. By default, Crystal Reports looks in \Program Files\Crystal Decisions\Crystal Reports 9\Templates for template reports. If you wish to change the location that Crystal Reports uses to populate the Template Expert, you must change the Registry key HKEY_LOCAL_MACHINE/Software/Crystal Decisions/Crystal Reports/ Templates/TemplatePath. Ensure you are familiar with manipulating Registry settings before attempting this change.

Once you've chosen a template to apply to your current report, the report's formatting will change, often drastically. How Crystal Reports applies all the individual object and section reporting of the source template to your current report is not necessarily predictable—you'll want to experiment with several templates to see how they affect formatting. However, as a general rule, Crystal Reports will compare report objects and report sections between the template and the current report, applying many of the formatting properties of both report sections and individual objects in the template to the current report. If, for example, the template report contains two details sections (Details a and Details b) and the current report contains only a single details section, the current report will have an additional details section added when the template is applied. If you have a chart in the template but not in your current report, a chart will be added when the template is applied. And if your template contains ten details section fields formatted with different colors, you can generally expect the template's formatting to be applied to the first ten objects in the details section of your current report.

If you plan on using a template, you probably won't want to do a great deal of formatting to your original report before you apply the template—your pretemplate formatting will be discarded. If you are generally pleased with a report's formatting, you would be well advised to save the report before applying templates. While the Undo capability exists in the Template Expert, you'll want to play it safe in case you may not want to permanently accept a template's formatting changes.

| Tip | *You are not limited to applying one template to a report, but may apply as many as you'd like by following the previous steps more than once. These multiple template applications will "blend" together to form a report that combines the formatting options from all templates applied.* |

Creating Your Own Templates

As was mentioned previously, templates are merely other Crystal Report .RPT files whose formatting is copied to the current report. While the few sample templates that are already provided by Crystal Decisions are acceptable for exploring the capabilities of adding templates, you'll probably want to develop a set of templates that conform to your company's "look and feel," perhaps including a company logo, preferred font face and size, and various object and section formatting standards that you wish to commonly apply to reports.

You may want to begin by just picking some already-created "standard" reports that approximate the look and feel you desire. You can then experiment with using them as templates. You may wish to save them in a temporary folder and modify the original reports to make better use of them as templates. Once you've modified the existing "template" reports to meet your needs, you may add an appropriate name to the Title field in the File | Summary Info dialog box, as well as checking the Save Preview Picture check box in the same dialog box. Then, preview the report (this is required to generate the preview picture) and save the report into the template directory. That report will now appear as a template in the Template Expert and Report Wizard Template section.

You may also wish to create a new report from scratch to act as a template. Crystal Reports 9 includes a new feature, the Template Field, to help in this endeavor. A *Template Field* is a special kind of field you can add to a report to act as a placeholder for a report object when applying the template to the main report. A Template Field doesn't initially display any data—it just contains formatting information that is carried over when the template is applied to the main report. To insert a Template Field, choose Insert | Template Field Object from the pull-down menus. An object outline will be placed on your mouse cursor. Drag the object to its desired location on the report and click to drop it. The Template Field will be added to the report.

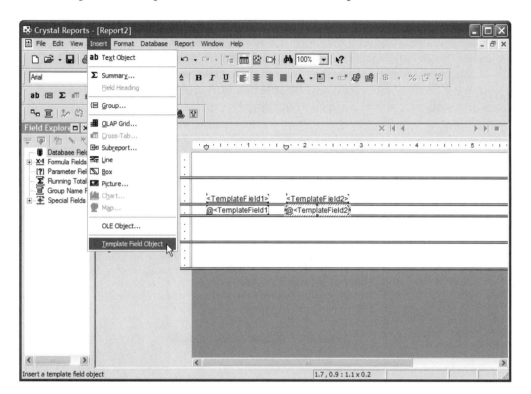

You now select the Template Field and format it with any of the methods discussed earlier in this chapter. However, you'll notice one unique difference between Template Fields and regular database fields when you format them with the Format Editor: tabs for every possible data type will appear in the Format Editor when formatting a Template Field. This additional Template Field flexibility lets you set up formatting for various target report fields that you may use with this template report. For example, if you're not sure whether the first field in the details section of the target report will be a string, number, or date, you can use the Paragraph tab, the Number tab, and the Date and Time tab to set formatting for the Template Field. When the Template Field is used to apply formatting in the target report, the formatting you've chosen in the appropriate tab will filter to the target fields.

When using Template Fields in a template report, it may be difficult to see what the actual target report formatting may look like. This is because Template Fields, by default, aren't connected to any database fields. As such, they won't show any data if you try to view your template report in the Preview tab. However, you can set Template Fields to display a value in the Preview tab by using the Formula Workshop. Notice that when you add a Template Field to the report, a corresponding formula is added to the Field Explorer. If you edit the Template Field formulas (editing formulas is discussed in detail in Chapter 5), you can change the formula to return something other than ten spaces, which are initially returned by the formula by way of the Space(10) function. You may replace the Space(10) function with a database field from the Field Tree, or another function from the Function Tree that will return data. When you display the template report in the Preview tab, you'll now be able to more accurately determine how the resultant formatting will be applied in the target report.

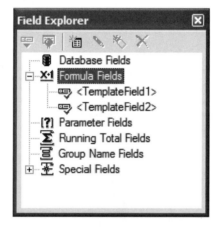

Once you've used Template Fields to create the template report, supply a name for the template in the Title field of File | Summary Info. You may also wish to check Save Preview Picture, preview the template report (which is required to save the preview picture), and then save the template report to the folder where other template reports are located. You will then see the new template appear the next time you need to apply a template with the Template Expert or in the report wizards.

Tip *A detailed chart discussing how objects and report sections in templates interact with the main report can be found in Crystal Reports online help. Search help for "templates, considerations."*

Chapter 10

Using Sections and Areas

In previous chapters, you learned how to change the appearance of individual objects on the report, such as by changing the color of a field or adding a drop shadow to a text object. However, you also have the ability to format *entire sections* of your report. Just a few of the section formatting options available to you are to

- Add a gray background to every other details section
- Format a group header so that every group starts anew on its own page
- Create multiple columns in your details section for labels
- Add a light-colored watermark graphic in its own page header section that appears behind the rest of your report

Formatting Sections with the Section Expert

There are several ways to change the appearance of an entire report section. You'll often just want to change the *size* of a section. Consider this "single-spaced" report:

Customer Name	City	Region	Last Year's Sales
City Cyclists	Sterling Heights	MI	$20,045.27
Pathfinders	DeKalb	IL	$26,369.63
Bike-A-Holics Anonymous	Blacklick	OH	$4,500.00
Psycho-Cycle	Huntsville	AL	$52,809.11
Sporting Wheels Inc.	San Diego	CA	$85,642.56
Rockshocks for Jocks	Austin	TX	$40,778.52
Poser Cycles	Eden Prairie	MN	$10,923.00
Spokes 'N Wheels Ltd.	Des Moines	IA	$25,521.31
Trail Blazer's Place	Madison	WI	$123,658.46
Rowdy Rims Company	Newbury Park	CA	$30,131.46
Clean Air Transportation Co.	Conshohocken	PA	$23,789.25

Notice the details sections appearing very close to each other. Maybe you'll just want to "double-space" the report. However, there is no double-space, space-and-a-half, or any similar function available in Crystal Reports. Instead, you choose how tall you want a section to be by using one of several techniques.

The simplest technique is simply to drag the bottom border of a section down to make the section taller. Point to the line at the bottom of the section you want to resize—the mouse cursor will turn into two lines with up and down arrows. This section-sizing cursor indicates that you can drag the section border down to make a section taller, or drag the border up to make the section shorter.

When you simply make the details section taller, the white space that's exposed becomes the "double-space" when you re-preview the report, as shown here:

| Preview | | | | Today 10:33 ✕ |◀ ◀ | 1 of 1+ | ▶ ▶| ▪ |

	Customer Name	City	Region	Last Year's Sales
D	City Cyclists	Sterling Heights	MI	$20,045.27
D	Pathfinders	DeKalb	IL	$26,369.63
D	Bike-A-Holics Anonymous	Blacklick	OH	$4,500.00
D	Psycho-Cycle	Huntsville	AL	$52,809.11
D	Sporting Wheels Inc.	San Diego	CA	$85,642.56

Although this is the most straightforward way to resize a section, you have other options available. By right-clicking in the gray section name on the left side of the Design tab, you display the section pop-up menu. For example, right-clicking the details section brings up this menu:

> Details
>
> Hide (Drill-Down OK)
> Suppress (No Drill-Down)
>
> Section Expert...
>
> Show Short Section Names
>
> Insert Line
> Delete Last Line
> Arrange Lines
> Fit Section
>
> Insert Section Below
>
> Select All Section Objects
>
> Cancel Menu

This pop-up menu contains four additional features for resizing sections, as listed here:

Insert Line	Adds an additional horizontal guideline to the section ruler on the left side of the section. If the section isn't tall enough to show the additional guideline, the section grows taller.
Delete Last Line	Removes the bottom guideline in the section and shrinks the size of the section proportionally. If you choose this option and a report object is attached to the guideline that you would remove, you'll receive an error message.
Arrange Lines	Rearranges any horizontal guidelines in an even fashion. If there aren't enough horizontal guidelines to fill the section, additional guidelines will be added.
Fit Section	Automatically shrinks the size of the section to the bottommost object in the section. If there are any horizontal guidelines below the bottom object, they are removed before the section is resized.

Although you may sometimes use the Insert Line, Delete Last Line, or Arrange Lines option from the section pop-up menu, you'll most likely find Fit Section the only useful option. It's particularly useful if the section is very tall (perhaps you've deleted a large map, chart, or picture from the section and all the white space it took up is still there), and you want to shrink it without having to scroll down to find the bottom section border.

The Section Expert

Whereas the Format Editor is used to format individual objects, you use the *Section Expert*, shown in Figure 10-1, to format entire sections of your report. The Section Expert has a large number of options for formatting individual report sections. Using these options provides a high level of flexibility for your reports.

The Section Expert can be displayed in several ways. You can click the Section Expert button on the Expert Tools toolbar, choose Report | Section Expert from the pull-down menus, or right-click in the gray area of the section you wish to format and choose Section Expert from the pop-up menu. If you choose the toolbar button or menu option, the first section will be highlighted in the Section Expert. If you right-click in the gray area of a section and use the pop-up menu, that particular section will be highlighted.

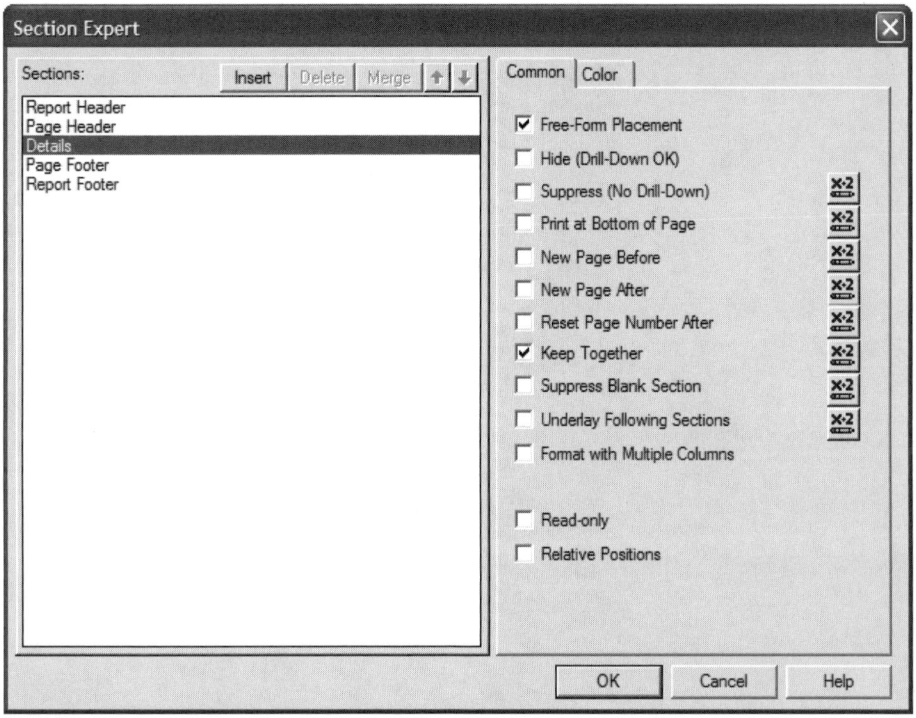

Figure 10-1.   *The Section Expert*

By selecting different sections of the report in the Section Expert, you can view and set formatting properties for the section. Note that the properties will vary slightly, some new properties may appear, and some won't be available, depending on which section you select. For example, the New Page Before property doesn't make much sense for a page header section, so it will be grayed out when a page header is selected. And if you select the Page Footer section, an additional "Reserve Minimum Page Footer" option will appear. Table 10-1 explains the different section formatting properties available in the Section Expert's Common tab.

Caution   *Don't confuse the Keep Together section property and the Keep Group Together group property on the Options tab of the Change Group dialog box. Keep Together in the Section Expert just prevents the particular section from splitting over two pages; whereas Keep Group Together will attempt to keep the group header, all details sections, and the group footer for the same group from printing across multiple pages.*

Property	Function
Free-Form Placement	Allows objects to be moved freely throughout the section without snapping to horizontal guidelines. If it is turned off, horizontal guidelines are added to the left of the section and objects snap to them when moved.
Hide (Drill-Down OK)	Hides a section and all objects in it. However, if the section is within a higher-level group and that group is drilled into, this section *will* appear in the drill-down tab.
Suppress (No Drill-Down)	Suppresses a section and all objects in it. If the section is within a higher-level group and that group is drilled into, this section *will not* appear in the drill-down tab, even though a drill-down tab will appear.
Print at Bottom of Page	Prints the section at the bottom of the page. Typically used for invoices, statements, or other, similar reports that require a group footer with a total to print at the bottom of the page, regardless of how many details sections print above it.
New Page Before	Starts a new page before printing this section. Useful in a group header if you want each group to start on its own page.
New Page After	Starts a new page after printing this section. Useful in a group footer if you want the next group to start on its own page.
Reset Page Number After	Resets the page number back to 1 after printing this section. Useful in a group footer if you want each group to have its own set of page numbers, regardless of the total number of pages on the report. Also resets the Total Page Count field.
Keep Together	Prevents Crystal Reports from putting a page break in the middle of this section. For example, this would avoid having the first few lines of a multiple-line details section appear on the bottom of one page and the last few lines appear on the next page.
Suppress Blank Section	Suppresses the entire section if all the objects inside it are blank. Useful in situations where you want to avoid white gaps appearing in your report if all the objects in a section have been conditionally suppressed or suppressed "if duplicated."
Underlay Following Sections	Prints the section, and then all following sections print right on top of the section. Useful for printing maps, charts, or pictures alongside data or underneath the following sections.

Table 10-1.   *Section Expert Common Tab Formatting Properties*

Property	Function
Format with Multiple Columns	Creates multiple newspaper- or phonebook-style columns. The Layout tab will appear when this property is checked. This is only available when the details section is chosen.
Reserve Minimum Page Footer	Reserves only enough vertical space to show the largest page footer section (if you have added multiple page footers, such as Page Footer a, Pager Footer b, and so on, and have conditionally suppressed them). If you have multiple conditionally suppressed page footers and don't check this option, Crystal Reports will leave enough vertical space for all the combined page footers, even if they are not all displayed.
Read Only (new in version 9)	Prevents formatting, moving, or sizing of all objects in the report section. This is, in essence, the same as selecting all objects in the section and using the Lock Format and Lock Size and Position options from the Formatting Toolbar or Format Editor.
Relative Positions (new in version 9)	When selected, this will automatically move any objects that are placed to the right of a cross-tab or OLAP grid in the section, based on the size of the cross-tab or OLAP grid. For example, if you place report fields or text objects to the right of a cross-tab, the cross-tab may very well print right over the top of the other object, as it grows horizontally to match the data it shows. By checking this option, you ensure that any objects to the right of the cross-tab or OLAP grid will automatically move right to avoid being overprinted.

Table 10-1. *Section Expert Common Tab Formatting Properties* (continued)

You'll also notice Conditional Formula buttons for many properties on the Common tab. These properties can be set conditionally with a Boolean formula, if necessary. There are many uses for both absolute and conditional properties on the Common tab. Here are some common examples.

Starting a Group on Its Own Page

Checking New Page Before in a group header or New Page After in a group footer (but not both) will cause each group to start on a new page. There is one problem with setting this property absolutely—you can end up with "stranded" pages. If you set New Page Before on a group header, you'll often encounter a stranded first page, because the report header will print and Crystal Reports will skip to the next page before printing the first group header. Conversely, if you set New Page After on a group footer, you'll often encounter a stranded last page, because the last group footer will be followed by a page break before the report footer prints.

To avoid these pitfalls, you have two choices:

- Suppress the report header and/or report footer if you have no data in them to show.
- Set the New Page Before or New Page After properties conditionally.

If you have material in the report header or report footer that you want to print on the same page as the first group header or last group footer, you must do some conditional formatting. To avoid a stranded first page, you can use a conditional formula to set the New Page Before property only on the second and subsequent groups—the first group will stay on the first page with the report header. Since the first group header will print at the same time the first record is printing, you can use the following Boolean conditional formula for New Page Before:

```
Not OnFirstRecord
```

To avoid a stranded last page, you want a new page after every group footer *except the last one*. Since the last group footer will only occur on the last record of the report, you can use this conditional formula for New Page After:

```
Not OnLastRecord
```

Printing an Invoice Total at the Bottom of the Page

You may be creating invoices grouped by invoice number, or statements grouped by customer number. You want the invoice or statement total, located in the group footer, to print at the bottom of the page, regardless of how many detail records print. Crystal Reports' normal behavior is to print the group footer immediately following the last detail record. If there are only a few invoice items or statement lines, the total will print high up the page, right after the last detail line. If you want the total to print at the bottom of the page in this situation, check the Print at Bottom of Page property for the group footer.

Starting Page Numbers Over for Each New Group

You might have a large report grouped by department that you want to "burst" apart
and distribute to each individual department. Initially, you'll want to make sure to use
the New Page Before property with the group header or the New Page After property
with the group footer so that you won't ever have the end of one department appearing
on the same page as the beginning of the next.

However, you also don't want to confuse those who may look at page numbers on
later groups in the report. Even though a page may be the first one for the IT department,
it will probably have a much larger page number than 1. Simply check the Reset Page
Number After property for the department group footer. Page numbers will then start
over at 1 for each department.

Changing Color for Entire Sections

The Color tab in the Section Expert, shown in Figure 10-2, lets you change the background
color for an entire section, separate from any color formatting that individual objects in
the section may have.

If you check the Background Color property, you can then choose from various
colors from the color palette below it. This will set the background color for the entire
section. This lets you highlight entire sections with different colors, if you choose—for
example, a report with the group footer section showing a different background color:

Platou Sport	Stavanger	Rogaland	$201,000.00
Platou Sport	Stavanger	Rogaland	$201,000.00
Platou Sport	Stavanger	Rogaland	$201,000.00
Platou Sport	Stavanger	Rogaland	$201,000.00
		Platou Sport total	**$1,005,000.00**
Poser Cycles			
Poser Cycles	Eden Prairie	M N	$10,923.00
Poser Cycles	Eden Prairie	M N	$10,923.00
		Poser Cycles total	**$21,846.00**
Psycho-Cycle			

Page 10

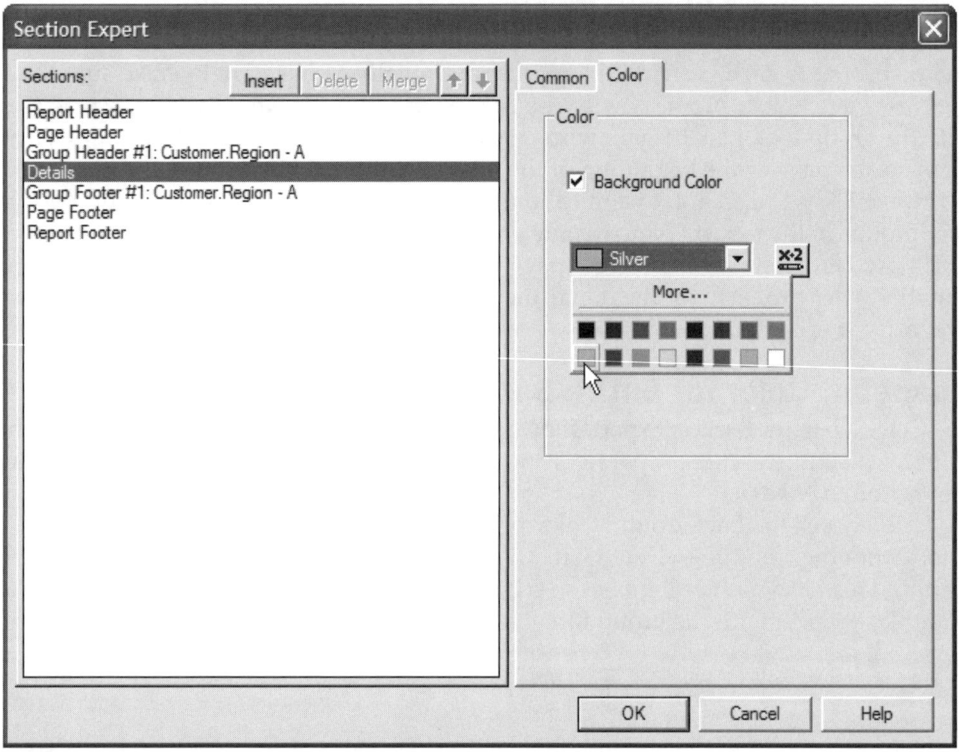

Figure 10-2.   *Setting the background color for a section*

Notice the Conditional Formula button on the Color tab. This lets you set the background color conditionally, which can be helpful if you want to base a background color on some particular condition.

Creating a "Banded" Report

Mainframe reports often were printed on "green bar" or "blue bar" paper with alternating shades of color and white. This was designed to make columns of numbers easy to follow across the page. Now that many PC-based reports are printed by laser printers on plain paper, you must create your own "banded" reports if your reports would benefit from this kind of look.

Simply giving the details section a silver background color isn't visually appealing, as shown here:

Cycles and Sports			
Cycles and Sports	Vancouver	BC	$38,199.10
Cycles and Sports	Vancouver	BC	$38,199.10
Cycles and Sports	Vancouver	BC	$38,199.10
Cycles and Sports	Vancouver	BC	$38,199.10
Cycles and Sports	Vancouver	BC	$38,199.10
Cycles and Sports	Vancouver	BC	$38,199.10
		Cycles and Sports total	$229,194.57
Cyclist's Trail Co.			
Cyclist's Trail Co.	Sterling Heights	MI	$15,937.96
Cyclist's Trail Co.	Sterling Heights	MI	$15,937.96
Cyclist's Trail Co.	Sterling Heights	MI	$15,937.96
Cyclist's Trail Co.	Sterling Heights	MI	$15,937.96
Cyclist's Trail Co.	Sterling Heights	MI	$15,937.96
Cyclist's Trail Co.	Sterling Heights	MI	$15,937.96
Cyclist's Trail Co.	Sterling Heights	MI	$15,937.96
Cyclist's Trail Co.	Sterling Heights	MI	$15,937.96

However, setting every other details section to silver provides a good way to help report readers follow columns of material across the page. You can set the background color conditionally to accomplish this. Use the following conditional formula:

```
If RecordNumber Mod 2 = 0 Then Silver Else NoColor
```

This uses several built-in Crystal Reports functions. The Mod function (which performs Modulus arithmetic) divides one number by another but returns the *remainder* of the division operation, not the result of the division. The RecordNumber built-in function simply counts records consecutively, starting at 1. Therefore, *every other* record number, when divided by 2, will return 0 as the remainder. This will alternate the details section background color for every record.

Cycles and Sports			
Cycles and Sports	Vancouver	BC	$38,199.10
Cycles and Sports	Vancouver	BC	$38,199.10
Cycles and Sports	Vancouver	BC	$38,199.10
Cycles and Sports	Vancouver	BC	$38,199.10
Cycles and Sports	Vancouver	BC	$38,199.10
Cycles and Sports	Vancouver	BC	$38,199.10
		Cycles and Sports total	$229,194.57
Cyclist's Trail Co.			
Cyclist's Trail Co.	Sterling Heights	MI	$15,937.96
Cyclist's Trail Co.	Sterling Heights	MI	$15,937.96
Cyclist's Trail Co.	Sterling Heights	MI	$15,937.96
Cyclist's Trail Co.	Sterling Heights	MI	$15,937.96
Cyclist's Trail Co.	Sterling Heights	MI	$15,937.96
Cyclist's Trail Co.	Sterling Heights	MI	$15,937.96
Cyclist's Trail Co.	Sterling Heights	MI	$15,937.96
Cyclist's Trail Co.	Sterling Heights	MI	$15,937.96

You can make modifications to this formula to shade more than just every other line. If you want *every two* lines shaded, you could change the formula slightly:

```
If RecordNumber Mod 4 In [1,2] Then Silver Else NoColor
```

This divides the record number by 4 and checks for remainders of 1 or 2. This will be true for every two records. The result is shown here:

Cycles and Sports			
Cycles and Sports	Vancouver	BC	$38,199.10
Cycles and Sports	Vancouver	BC	$38,199.10
Cycles and Sports	Vancouver	BC	$38,199.10
Cycles and Sports	Vancouver	BC	$38,199.10
Cycles and Sports	Vancouver	BC	$38,199.10
Cycles and Sports	Vancouver	BC	$38,199.10
		Cycles and Sports total	$229,194.57
Cyclist's Trail Co.			
Cyclist's Trail Co.	Sterling Heights	MI	$15,937.96
Cyclist's Trail Co.	Sterling Heights	MI	$15,937.96
Cyclist's Trail Co.	Sterling Heights	MI	$15,937.96
Cyclist's Trail Co.	Sterling Heights	MI	$15,937.96
Cyclist's Trail Co.	Sterling Heights	MI	$15,937.96
Cyclist's Trail Co.	Sterling Heights	MI	$15,937.96
Cyclist's Trail Co.	Sterling Heights	MI	$15,937.96
Cyclist's Trail Co.	Sterling Heights	MI	$15,937.96

You probably get the general idea of how this works. You can now modify the formula in any number of ways to change the way background shading works.

Tip *When setting the background color of a section, as well as background colors for individual objects, you may want to use NoColor instead of White to indicate a normal color. By using White, you will have solid white colors that can sometimes look unpleasant in combination with other solid colors. If you use NoColor, you often achieve a certain amount of transparency that will look better when mixing colors on the report or when using watermarks (discussed later in the chapter).*

Creating Summary and Drill-Down Reports

A *details report* shows every individual detail record in the database. This may often be preferable for certain listings or smaller transaction-type reports. Often, however, a viewer will only want to see subtotals, counts, averages, or other summary information for certain groups on the report. The details information used to arrive at those summaries isn't as important. This calls for a *summary report*.

In its simplest form, a summary report is a report with one or more groups with the details section hidden or suppressed. Consider Figure 10-3, a details report of orders, grouped by customer.

This shows every order for the customer, with order count and order amount subtotals appearing in the group footer. While this may be useful for a report viewer concerned about individual orders, the sales manager or account representative may often just be interested in the summary information for each customer—just the *bottom line*. All the order details just get in the way of their analysis.

In this case, simply hiding or suppressing the details section will create a much more meaningful report for these viewers. You can hide or suppress the details section from the Section Expert. As a shortcut, there are Hide and Suppress options available right in the section pop-up menu, as well. Just right-click the gray details section name at the left of the Design or Preview tab and choose Hide (Drill-Down OK) or Suppress (No Drill-Down) from the pop-up menu.

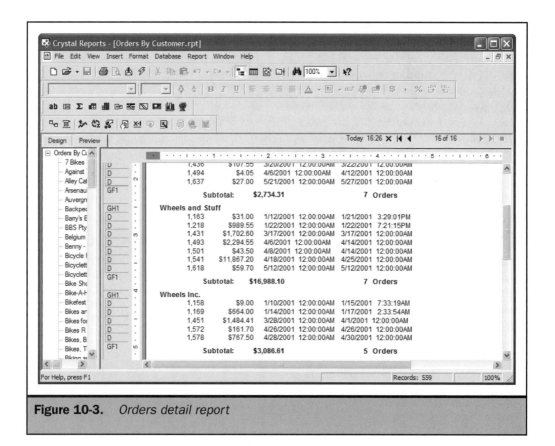

Figure 10-3. *Orders detail report*

The details section will simply disappear from the Preview tab, while the group header and footer still show up. Figure 10-4 shows the resulting summary report, which is much more succinct and meaningful to a viewer looking at the big picture.

If you later want to change your report back to a details report, you need to have the details section reappear. Just display the Section Expert by using the toolbar button or pull-down menu option. Select the details section and turn off the Hide or Suppress property. You can also display the Design tab and right-click the gray area to the left of the screen where the details section is hidden or suppressed. To redisplay the details section, choose the opposite of the Suppress or Hide option you initially set.

> **Tip** *You can choose how a hidden or suppressed section appears in the Design tab. Choose File | Options from the pull-down menus and look for the Show Hidden Sections option in the Design View section of the Layout tab. If this is checked (the default), hidden or suppressed sections will still appear in the Design tab, but they will have gray shading. If you turn this option off, they will only show the bottom border of the hidden or suppressed section in the Design tab.*

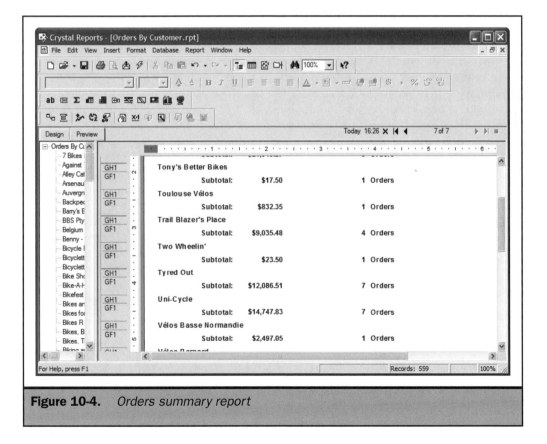

Figure 10-4. *Orders summary report*

Choosing whether to hide or suppress a section determines whether or not you want a report viewer to drill down into the section. Also, note that the Suppress property can be conditionally set in the Section Expert, while the Hide property cannot.

Drill-Down Reports

One of the most powerful features of an online reporting tool like Crystal Reports is interactive reporting. You may be creating a report to distribute to a large audience via a Web page in Crystal Enterprise or Crystal Reports 9 RAS (covered in Part II), or as part of a custom Windows application (covered in Part III). A truly useful report will initially present viewers with higher-level summary or total information. If the viewer sees a number or other characteristic of the report that interests them, you want them to be able to drill down into just that particular area.

Note *Drill-down is an interactive feature only applicable to viewers looking at a Crystal Report in its "native" format. Drill-down isn't available in any reports exported to another format, such as Word or Excel. And obviously, drill-down isn't a feature that applies to reports printed on paper!*

In its simplest form, a drill-down report can be created by hiding the details section (hence, the Drill-Down OK notation alongside the Hide property) in a report that has one or more groups. When you point at the group name field, or a subtotal or summary object in a group header or footer, you'll notice your mouse cursor change to a magnifying glass, or *drill-down cursor*. When you double-click, a separate drill-down tab will appear, showing the group header, footer, and details sections for that group. You can then navigate to the main Preview tab to see the summary report, or back to individual drill-down tabs to see the details information. You can double-click in the Preview tab as many times as you want in order to create additional drill-down tabs.

More complicated drill-down reports can be created by using multiple levels of grouping, along with creative use of section hiding. Figure 10-5 shows a drill-down report containing a details section and three groups: country, region, and city. Initially, the report just shows countries and their totals. If you drill down on a country, you'll find region subtotals for that country. Drilling down on a region will show city totals. And finally, drilling down on a city total will show individual orders placed from that city.

Tip *Make note of the Show All Headers on Drill Down option. When you turn this option on (it's off by default), your report will display all higher levels of group headers when you drill into a group, instead of showing just the previous level of group headers. Choose this option for the current report only by selecting File | Report Options. To choose the option for all new reports in the future, set the option on the Reporting tab after choosing File | Options.*

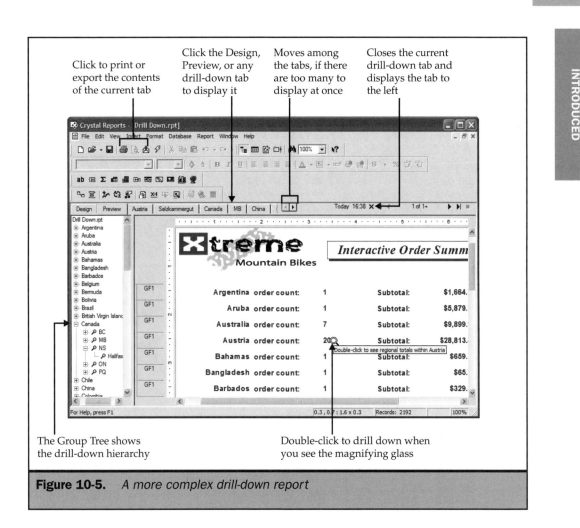

Click to print or export the contents of the current tab

Click the Design, Preview, or any drill-down tab to display it

Moves among the tabs, if there are too many to display at once

Closes the current drill-down tab and displays the tab to the left

The Group Tree shows the drill-down hierarchy

Double-click to drill down when you see the magnifying glass

Figure 10-5.   *A more complex drill-down report*

If you're interacting with a report, it's important to remember what will print or export if you click the Print or Export button on the Standard toolbar, or choose File | Print or File | Export from the pull-down menus. Only what's shown in the current drill-down tab (or Preview tab) will print or export. If you want to just print one drill-down tab, choose the drill-down tab and then click the Print button. If you want to print all the summary information in the main Preview tab, make sure it's selected before you print or export. If you want to print or export both summary and details information *in the same report,* you must either display the details section and print from the Preview tab, or create a separate report more appropriate for printing.

Creative Use of Column Headings and Group Headers in Drill-Down Reports

If you leave Crystal Reports' default column headings in the page header and simply hide or suppress lower-level group headers in your drill-down reports, you may get undesirable results when the viewer sees the initial Preview tab.

Column Heading Problems   The first problem will be the appearance of column headings in the Preview tab above the first group header, but with no matching detail records. But when you eventually drill down to the details level, the page header won't appear, so the viewer won't see the column headings.

There are two ways of resolving this problem, depending on how many levels of grouping exist on the report. If you only have one level of grouping, perform the following steps:

1. Move the column headings from the page header to the group header, either above or below the group name field (or remove the group name field altogether), depending on how you want the drill-down tab to appear.

2. Copy the group name field from the group header into the group footer.

3. Hide the group header along with the details section.

This way, the summary report will just show one line per group until you drill down. Then, the group header (containing the column headings) will appear inside the drill-down tab, along with the details sections.

However, if you have more than one level of grouping, the previous technique won't work properly—you'll see the column headings appear over and over again at the last group level. In this case, use this approach:

1. Create a second details section (Details b) and move the column headings into it.

2. Swap Details b and Details a so that the column headings are on top of the details section that contains database fields.

3. Select the text objects that comprise the column headings. You may multiselect them with CTRL-click or an elastic box. Using the Format Editor, choose the Suppress if Duplicated formatting option.

4. Using the Section Expert, choose the Suppress Blank Section formatting option for Details a.

This technique, while a little more time-consuming, provides perfect results. When the lowest level of grouping appears, there will be no column headings (because they've been moved to the details section). But when you drill down to the details level, the column headings only show up once at the top of the drill-down tab, because of the Suppress if Duplicated/Suppress Blank Section formatting combinations.

Repeating Group Headers   If you simply choose the Hide (Drill-Down OK) formatting option on group header sections, your report may suffer from extra sets of group headers that appear when you drill down. For example, if you drill down into a country group to see all the regions within the country, the region group header will print before every group footer. To solve this problem, you may try to suppress the region group header so that it will never show up. However, when you then drill into a region group to see cities within the region, the region group header won't print at the top of the list of cities.

In theory, you'd like the region group header to show up when you've drilled into the region group to see cities, but *not* show up when you're looking at the region group at its summary level. But, what conditional formula can you use to suppress the region group header so that it only shows up when there isn't a country group header there as well?

In previous versions of Crystal Reports, a complex process of creating formulas with variables and using the variables in the Section Expert was the only option. However, Crystal Reports 9 has introduced the *DrillDownGroupLevel* function to the Crystal Reports formula language. This function allows you to test for a certain drill-down level and conditionally suppress a group header (or perform any other functions or calculations, for that matter), based on the level of the drill-down. Making use of this new function to conditionally suppress group headers will allow you the ultimate control over your report behavior when the viewer drills down.

Using the previous Country/Region/City drill-down scenario as an example, you suppress the region group header (Group Header 2) conditionally so that it won't appear when you drill down to the country level, but will appear when you drill down to the region level. This is simply a matter of using this formula to conditionally suppress Group Header 2:

```
DrillDownGroupLevel = 1
```

This will suppress the group header when a Country drill-down occurs (level 1), but will not suppress when a Region drill-down occurs (level 2). You may also use the DrillDownGroupLevel function to determine if the main Preview tab is being displayed. If the DrillDownGroupLevel function returns a zero, no drill-down is occurring at all.

Examples of the drill-down techniques discussed here can be found in a sample report on this book's companion Web site. Look for the Drill Down.RPT sample report at www.CrystalBook.com.

Using Tool Tip text (under the common section of the Format Editor) can help a viewer determine what will happen when they double-click an object. By creating a string formula with the Tool Tip text Conditional Formula button in the Format Editor, you can give a viewer more information about what the object contains. The tool tip illustrated in Figure 10-5 comes from the following Tool Tip text Conditional Formula added to the summary field in the Country group footer:

```
"Double-click to see regional totals within " &
    GroupName ({Customer.Country})
```

Multiple-Column Reports for Labels and Listings

Crystal Reports is designed to replace much of the repetitive printing that you may have used a word processor for in the past. Immediate uses include form letters and mailing labels. You can also use the multicolumn feature of Crystal Reports to create newspaper-style columns in your reports. If you have just a few fields that you'd like to print in columnar form, the Section Expert provides the necessary section formatting.

To create mailing labels in Crystal Reports, choose the Mail Label Wizard in the Report Gallery when first creating a new report. This brings up the Mailing Labels Report Creation Wizard. This wizard takes you step by step through the process of choosing the table and fields that make up your mailing label, and choosing from a predefined list of continuous-feed and laser printer labels. Figure 10-6 shows the section of this wizard where you may select predefined labels or make fine adjustments to label specifications.

Since there is no similar expert for creating newspaper-style reports, you have to create such reports using the Blank Report option and the Section Expert. Recall from Table 10-1 one of the Section Expert's formatting properties, Format with Multiple Columns. This property is only available for the details section—it won't even appear in the Section Expert if you have any other section selected. Once you check this property, the Layout tab appears in the Section Expert, as shown in Figure 10-7.

On the Layout tab, you determine the specifics of the columns you want to create. Although you might expect to see a "number of columns" setting, this is actually determined by page margins (set with File | Page Setup), the width of the details section, and the horizontal gap between details. For example, if you have quarter-inch margins with standard letter-size paper in portrait orientation, you'll have 8 full inches of printable space. If you choose a details-size width of 2.5 inches and a horizontal gap of a quarter inch, you'll have three evenly spaced columns with a quarter inch on all sides.

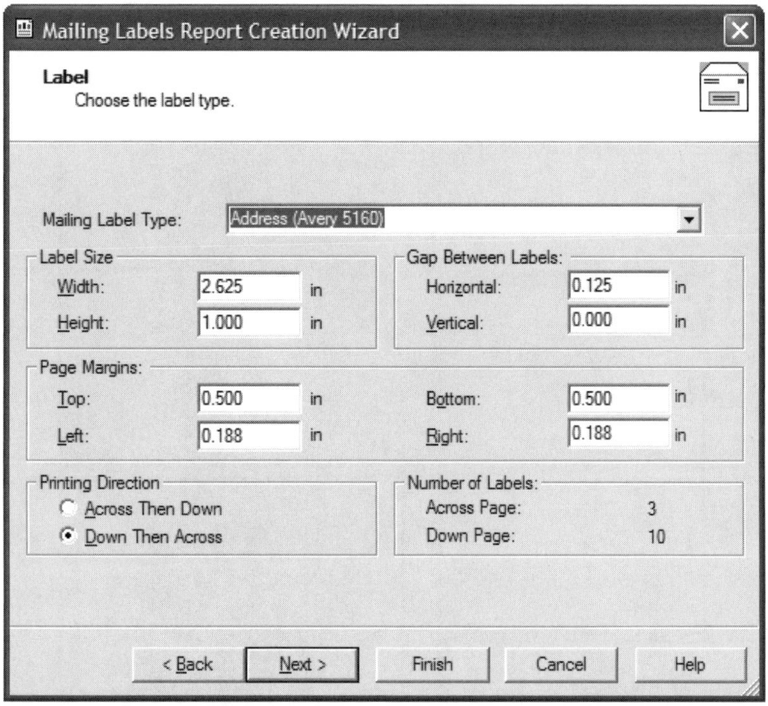

Figure 10-6. *Mail Label Report Creation Wizard*

When you choose to format the details section with multiple columns, the Design tab changes slightly. You'll notice that the width of the details section's bottom border shrinks to equal the width you set in the Layout tab. The other sections of the report retain the full width of the page.

The exception to this rule occurs when you check the Format Groups with Multiple Column check box on the Layout tab. In this case, all group headers and footers take on the same width as the details section. This can make a marked difference in the appearance of your report, depending on the size of your groups. As a general rule, not formatting groups with multiple columns will cause smaller groups to print only in

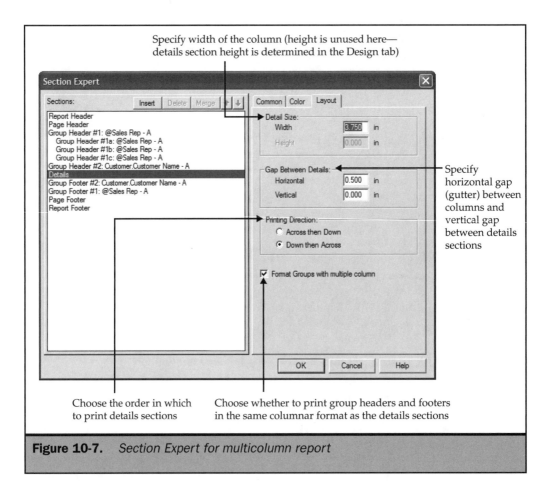

Specify width of the column (height is unused here—details section height is determined in the Design tab)

Specify horizontal gap (gutter) between columns and vertical gap between details sections

Choose the order in which to print details sections

Choose whether to print group headers and footers in the same columnar format as the details sections

Figure 10-7.   *Section Expert for multicolumn report*

one column on the left side of the page. Usually, the only small groups that print across multiple columns are ones that start at the bottom of the page. Figure 10-8 shows the difference. You'll typically experience more predictable behavior by formatting groups with multiple columns.

Using Multiple Sections

To be precise, the five default sections that first appear in a new report, and any additional group headers and footers that are added later, are referred to as *areas*. This is in contrast to the term "section," which really refers to "subareas." Because Crystal Reports lets you create multiple occurrences of the same area, such as multiple details or multiple group headers, each of the individual occurrences is called a *section*. Creating multiple sections can be accomplished from the Section Expert or by using the pop-up menu that appears when you right-click in the gray area on the left side of the screen.

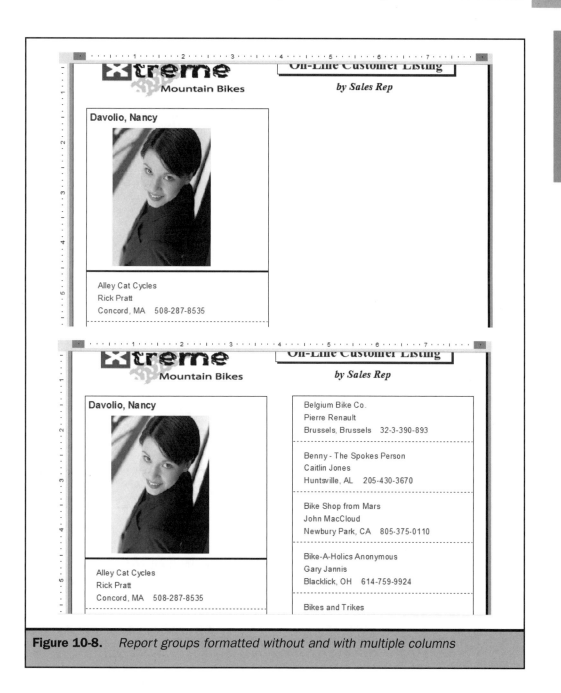

Figure 10-8.   *Report groups formatted without and with multiple columns*

To insert an additional details section, for example, right-click in the details gray area on the left side of the Design tab and choose Insert Section Below from the pop-up menu. Or, from the Section Expert, select the area that you wish to duplicate and click

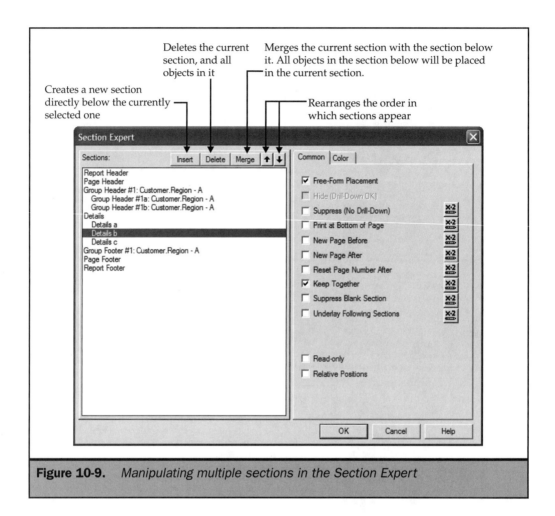

Deletes the current section, and all objects in it

Merges the current section with the section below it. All objects in the section below will be placed in the current section.

Creates a new section directly below the currently selected one

Rearranges the order in which sections appear

Figure 10-9. *Manipulating multiple sections in the Section Expert*

the Insert button. You'll see the details area split into two sections: Details a and Details b. Once you've created multiple sections in an area, the pop-up menu (shown here) and Section Expert (shown in Figure 10-9) take on a great deal of additional capability.

Details b
Hide (Drill-Down OK)
Suppress (No Drill-Down)
Section Expert...
Show Short Section Names
Insert Line
Delete Last Line
Arrange Lines
Fit Section
Insert Section Below
Merge Section Below
Delete Section
Select All Section Objects
Cancel Menu

Tip *You can also rearrange the order in which sections appear right in the Design tab. Simply point to the gray section name on the left of the screen, hold down the mouse button, and drag the section you wish to move—the mouse cursor will change to a "hand." Drop the section in its new location in the same area. Although the section contents will swap, the consecutive lettering will not change—the first section will still be lettered a; the second, b; and so on.*

You can insert as many sections in an area as you wish—there can be Details a, b, c, d, and on and on (when Crystal Reports runs out of letters, it starts doubling them up, as in "Details ab"). Any area can consist of multiple sections. Nothing prevents you from having three report headers, five details sections, two group footer #1s, or any other combination.

Once you've created the multiple sections, you can add objects to any of the sections. You can even add the same object to some, or all, of them. When the report prints, the sections will simply print one right after the other, with the objects showing up one below the other. Probably the biggest question you have right now is, "What's the benefit of multiple sections anyway? Everything just prints as though it were in one bigger section!"

Figure 10-10 is a great example of the benefit of multiple sections. This shows a form letter based on the Customer table from the sample XTREME Mountain Bike database included with Crystal Reports. Notice that the letter consists of three different details sections. Details a contains the Print Date, Customer Name, and Address 1; Details b contains Address 2; and Details c contains the rest of the letter. When you preview the report, it just shows the details sections one on top of the other, as though everything were in one big details section.

But look at the letter for Pathfinders. Notice the empty line that appears when there is no Address 2 database field. This behavior, again, is identical to what you'd expect if you had put all the objects in one tall details section.

Here's the benefit: you may *conditionally suppress* individual sections—in this case, Details b—so that they appear or disappear according to your specifications. To eliminate the blank line that appears when there's nothing in Address 2, format Details b with Suppress Blank Section. If the objects contained in it all contain empty values (as is the case with Pathfinders), the section will not appear at all. You can also use the Conditional Formula button next to the Suppress property to suppress according to any condition you need.

These techniques, and others that make good use of multiple sections and conditional formatting for form letters, are illustrated in the sample Form Letter.rpt report. Find it on this book's companion Web site at www.CrystalBook.com.

| Tip | *The more you work with areas and sections, the more you may notice the large amount of space the area and section names take up on the left side of the Design tab. If you wish to have more space for actual report objects, you can change the way Crystal Reports shows section names. Choose File | Options and check Short Section Names in the Design View section of the Layout tab. You can also right-click in a gray section name in the Design tab and choose Show Short Section Names from the pop-up menu. "Report Header" will now be abbreviated "RH," "Page Header a" will become "PHa," and so on. You'll now have more room to work with actual report objects.* |

Figure 10-10.   *Multiple details sections*

Conditionally Suppressing Sections

You may think that conditional suppression is only useful when you have multiple sections. Actually, there may be times when you want to control the appearance of just a single section. Using the Conditional Formula button next to the Suppress property lets you supply a Boolean formula to determine when the section appears or doesn't appear. Consider the following examples.

Printing a Bonus Message for Certain Records

You are designing a list of orders by a salesperson. You want a bonus message and a "lots o' money" graphic to appear below the order if it exceeds $2,500. However, if the order doesn't exceed the bonus level, you *don't* want the large blank space to appear where the graphic and message are located. If you just use the Format Editor to conditionally suppress the graphic and text object containing the message, they won't appear, but the empty space still will.

Simply create a Details b section and place the graphic and text object in it. Then, suppress Details b when the bonus isn't met, using the following conditional formula for the Suppress property:

```
{Orders.Order Amount} < 2500
```

Figure 10-11 shows the result.

Printing a Different Page Header on Page 2 and Later

You may wish to print a title page or other large page header on page 1 of the report, perhaps containing a logo and large formatted title. However, on subsequent pages of the report, you want a less flashy header with smaller type and no graphic. You want column headings and the print date and time to show up on all pages of the report, including the first.

This presents a special reporting problem. The flashy page header can simply be put in the report header section. It will then appear only on the first page. However, if you put the smaller report title in the page header along with the column headings and other information, it will appear on page 1 along with the report header. You can use the Format Editor to suppress the object containing the smaller header, but then extra white space will appear on page 1.

The solution is to create a second page header section. Put the smaller report title in Page Header a and put the column headings and print date/time in Page Header b. Then, conditionally suppress Page Header b so that it won't show up on page 1. Here's the conditional formula, which uses the PageNumber built-in function:

```
PageNumber = 1
```

CRYSTAL REPORTS 9
INTRODUCED

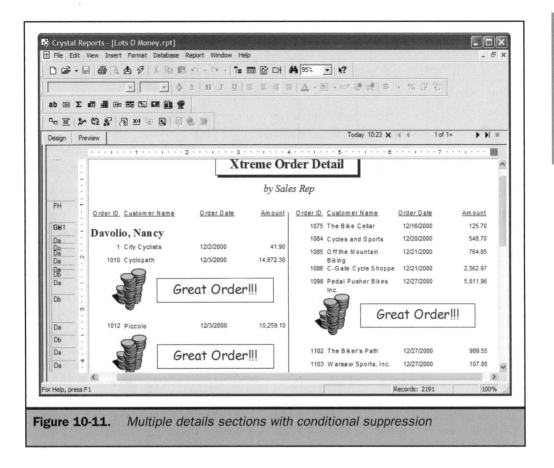

Figure 10-11.   *Multiple details sections with conditional suppression*

Printing Odd and Even Page Headers or Footers

You may be printing your report on a "duplex" laser printer that can print on both sides of the paper. Or, you may want to photocopy your report from one to two sides and place it in a three-ring binder or other bound format. Crystal Reports lets you create separate odd and even page headers and footers to add a real page-published look to your report.

Simply create separate Page Headers a and b (and, perhaps, Page Footers a and b). Place the appropriate material in each section and position it properly for odd/even appearance. Now, conditionally suppress the sections. The sections containing the material for odd page numbers will be suppressed for even page numbers with the following conditional formula:

```
PageNumber Mod 2 = 0
```

Also, the sections containing the material for even page numbers will be suppressed for odd page numbers with the following conditional formula:

```
PageNumber Mod 2 = 1
```

These formulas use the PageNumber built-in function illustrated previously. In addition, they use the Mod function, which will indicate whether a page number is even or odd (even page numbers divided by 2 return a remainder of 0, and odd page numbers return a remainder of 1, as explained earlier in the chapter).

Underlaying Sections

The Section Expert includes the Underlay Following Sections property. As described in Table 10-1, this property prints the underlaying section in its usual position but prints the following sections right over the top. Initially, this may seem of limited usefulness. How readable will a report be if sections are printing right over the top of earlier sections?

Look at Figure 10-12 to get an idea. This report includes a large, light "Draft" graphic that has been placed in the page header. When Underlay Following Sections is checked for the page header in the Section Expert, all the other sections will print right over the top of the page header, creating the watermark effect.

If you want to include column headings in the page header, along with the watermark, you experience a problem. The watermark will be underlaid as you desire, but so will the column headings! The solution, as you might expect, is to add a Page Header b. Place the watermark graphic in one page header section and format it to Underlay Following Sections. Place the column headings in the other page header section and don't underlay it. Which page header you place the objects in will determine whether or not the column headings are underlaid. If you put the watermark in Page Header a (which is formatted to Underlay Following Sections) and the column headings in Page Header b (not underlaid), the watermark will underlay the column headings. If you choose the other way around, the column headings won't be underlaid.

Note   *When you underlay a section, all sections will print over the top of it, until Crystal Reports comes to its "companion" section, which will not underlay it. For example, if you underlay a page header, all sections will print on top until Crystal Reports gets to the matching page footer. If you underlay Group Header b, all other sections will print on top until the report hits Group Footer b, which will not be underlaid.*

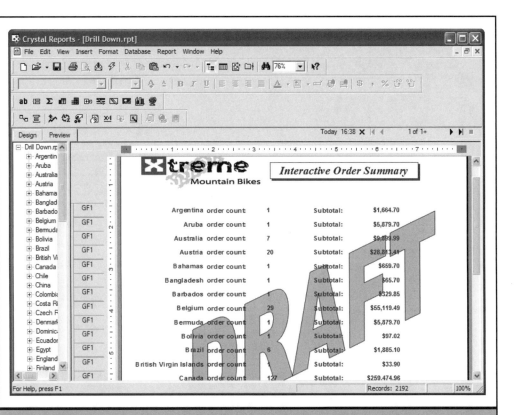

Figure 10-12.   *Using Underlay Following Section to print a watermark*

You can also use the Underlay Following Sections feature to place maps or charts beside the data they refer to, rather than on top or bottom of the related data. Figure 10-13 shows a report containing a chart. Notice that the chart appears alongside the data that the chart refers to, rather than above. The chart is contained in a second report header (Report Header b), but the chart object has been moved to the right of the section, and the report header section is formatted to Underlay Following Sections.

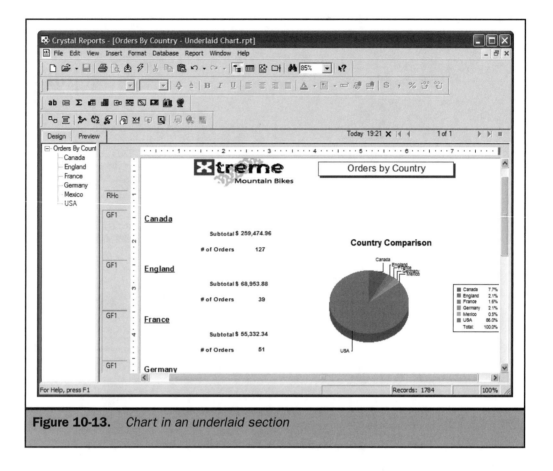

Figure 10-13. *Chart in an underlaid section*

Placing the chart in Report Header b permits the report title and logo to remain in Report Header a (which isn't underlaid) so that the report title and logo aren't also underlaid along with the chart.

Chapter 11

Analyzing with Cross-Tabs

Database report writers and spreadsheet programs are typically considered to be two completely separate products. The database report writer sorts and selects data very well, while the spreadsheet is great for analyzing, totaling, and trending in a compact row-and-column format. Crystal Reports provides a tool that, to a limited extent, brings the two features together: the *cross-tab object*. A cross-tab is a row-and-column object that looks similar to a spreadsheet. It summarizes data by using at least three fields in the database: a row field, a column field, and a summarized field. For each intersection of the row and column fields, the summarized field is aggregated (summed, counted, or subjected to some other type of calculation).

Consider two common summary reports. The first summary report shows total sales in dollars for each state in the United States. The second report shows total units sold by product type. If a marketing analyst wanted to combine these two reports to more closely analyze both sales in dollars by state and units sold by product type, you would be limited in what you could offer with the standard grouped summary report.

You can create a report, similar to that shown in Figure 11-1 (initially grouped by state, and within state grouped by product type), that provides the information the

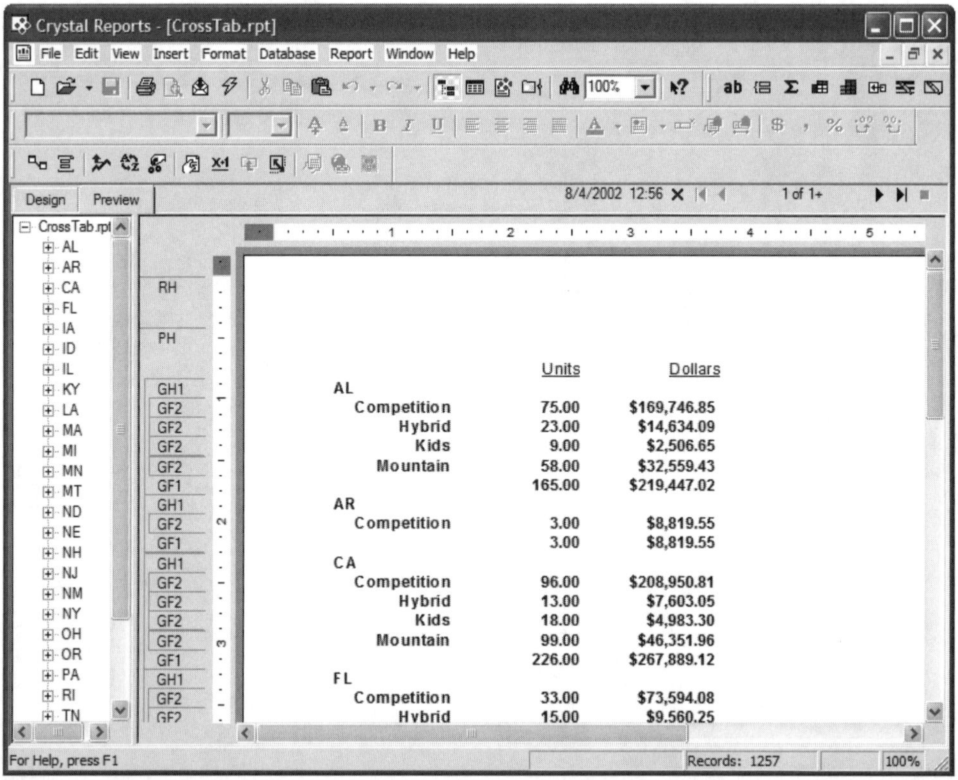

Figure 11-1.   *Standard summary report with two groups*

analyst desires. But if the analyst wanted to compare total mountain bikes sold in the country with total kid's bikes sold in the country, this report would make the process very difficult. Product type is the inner group, so there are no overall totals by it. Also, comparing Alabama totals with Illinois totals would be difficult, because they would be several pages apart on the report.

This scenario is a perfect example of where a cross-tab object would be useful. A cross-tab is a compact, row-and-column report that can compare subtotals and summaries by two or more different database fields. Whenever someone requests data to be shown by one thing and by another, it's a cross-tab candidate. Just listen for the "by this and by that" request. Figure 11-2 will probably be much more useful to the analyst.

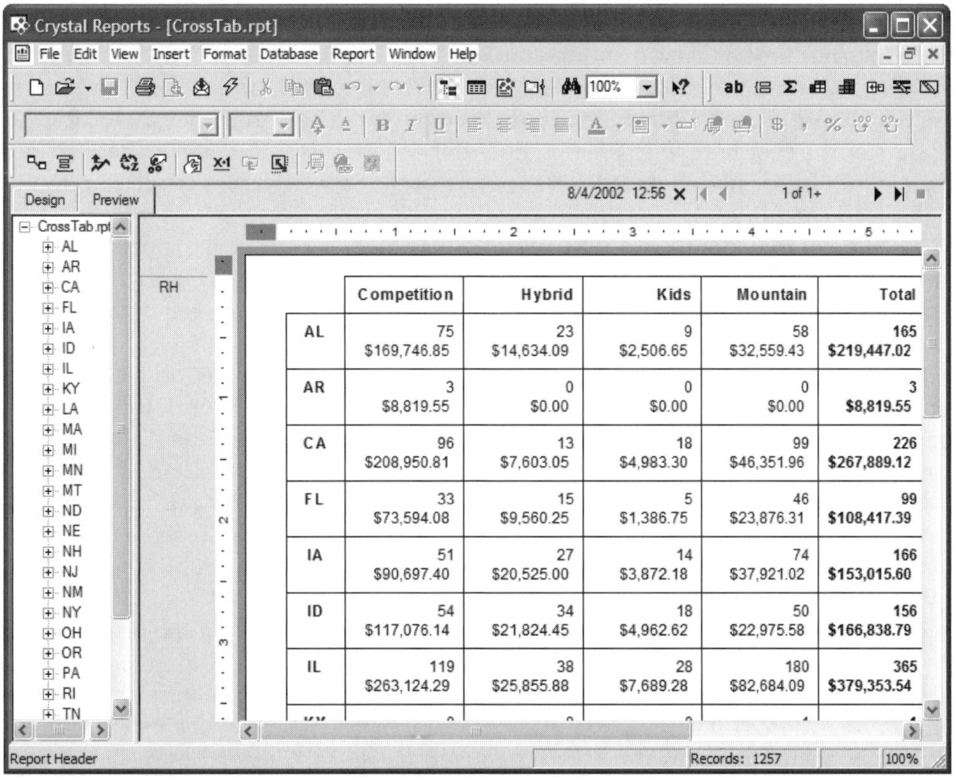

Figure 11-2. *Cross-tab showing units/dollars by region and by product type*

Creating a Cross-Tab Object

When you look at a cross-tab, it's tempting to think of it as an entire report unto itself, much as an Excel spreadsheet is entirely independent. In fact, a cross-tab is just an object that resides in an existing report section. Even when you choose the Cross-Tab Wizard from the Reports Gallery, Crystal Reports just creates a cross-tab object and puts it in the report header. You can create more than one cross-tab per report, if you wish. In fact, you can even copy an existing cross-tab and put it in several different sections of the same report. It's just an object, like a text object, map, or database field.

A cross-tab can exist by itself on a report (as evidenced by the Reports Gallery Cross-Tab Wizard), or it can be placed on a report that already contains fields in the details section, as well as one or more groups. The report can be completely functional in every respect before the cross-tab is added—the cross-tab just gets dropped in.

The first step in creating a cross-tab is to ensure that the tables you've chosen and linked for your report contain enough data to populate the cross-tab. If, for example, you want to look at order totals for the years 1995, 1996, 1997, and 1998 by state, make sure you choose tables that include the order amount, the year the order was placed, and the state of the customer who placed the order. While this may seem rather obvious, you may not have enough data to adequately populate your cross-tab if you don't think ahead carefully.

You may or may not want to use actual report fields as cross-tab fields. If the fields are already on the report, you can add them to the cross-tab object. Or, if you've added, completely different fields to the report, you can still base the cross-tab on other fields that exist in the tables you chose when creating the report.

You can use the Cross-Tab Reports Creation Wizard from the Report Gallery, or add a cross-tab to an existing report you've already created. To begin with the Cross-Tab Report Creation Wizard, simply choose it from the list of Wizards in the Reports Gallery when creating a new report. In addition to the familiar Data, Link, Chart, and Record Selection dialogs seen in other report wizards, the Cross-Tab Wizard displays a Cross-Tab row/column dialog and a Grid Style dialog similar to those discussed in more detail as we cover the Cross-Tab Expert. (You may notice that some features of the Expert are slightly different or not available in the Wizard.)

If you've already created another report using another Expert or the Blank Report option, you may insert a cross-tab object whenever you want. To create a cross-tab object, it's best to select the Design tab first. Although you can place a cross-tab on the report in the Preview tab, you may not be able to accurately tell where it's being placed. In the Design tab, there's no question. Click the Insert Cross-Tab button on the Insert Tools toolbar, or choose Insert | Cross-Tab from the pull-down menus. The Cross-Tab Expert dialog box will appear, as shown in Figure 11-3.

The Cross-Tab Expert dialog box has three tabs: Cross-Tab, Style, and Customize Style. The Cross-Tab tab is used to define the database fields or formulas that make up the rows and columns of the cross-tab. The Style tab lets you choose a predefined formatting style for the grid on the cross-tab. And, the Customize Style tab displays a large number of custom formatting options to precisely control the appearance of the cross-tab.

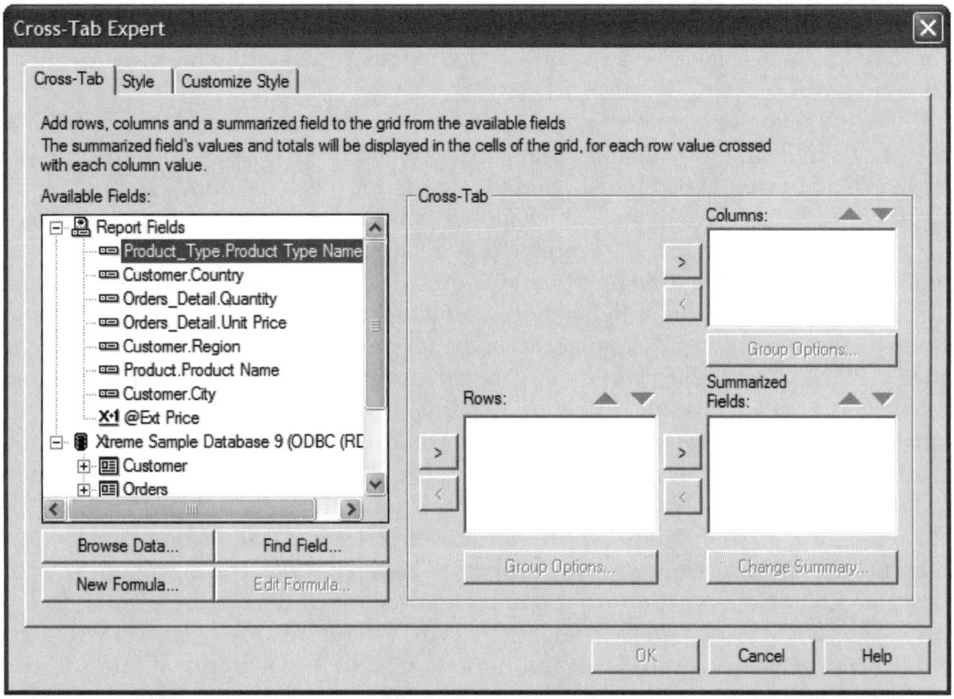

Figure 11-3.   *The Cross-Tab Expert dialog box*

The first step to creating a cross-tab is to define the fields that will make up the row, column, and summarized fields in the cross-tab. This is done with the Cross-Tab tab. Look through the Available Fields box to find the fields you want to use for the cross-tab's row and column fields. Just drag your chosen field from the Available Fields box and drop it on the Rows or Columns box. You can also select the field in the Available Fields box and click the right arrow button beside the Rows or Columns box. If you don't want to scroll the Available Fields box to find your field, you can click the Find Field button and type all or part of the field name in the resulting dialog box. The first field name containing that string will be highlighted in the Available Fields box.

In addition to identifying row and column fields, you'll need to choose the field you want summarized in each *cell* (the intersection of each row and column). This will typically be a number or currency field, such as Quantity Sold or Order Amount, but it doesn't have to be. If you choose a number field, the default summary type will be a sum (subtotal) of the field for each cell. If you choose a field with another data type, the default summary type is a count of the number of occurrences of the field for each row/column combination. Drag the field to be summarized from the Available Fields box to the Summarized Field box, or select the field and click the right arrow next to the Summarized Fields list. If you need a different summary type, use the Change Summary button. Edits to the summary operation are discussed in more detail later in this chapter.

If you'd like to use an existing formula for a row, column, or summarized field, just select the formula in the Available Fields box. If you'd like to create a new formula or edit an existing formula before using it in the cross-tab, click the New Formula button or Edit Formula button, either of which launches the Formula Editor, where you can create or edit the formula. The formula will then appear in the Available Fields box, from which you can drag it to the Rows, Columns, or Summarized Field box.

If you're not concerned initially about doing any customized formatting for your cross-tab object, you're ready to place it on the report (formatting options on the other two tabs of the Cross-Tab Expert dialog box are discussed later in the chapter). When you click OK on the Cross-Tab Expert dialog box, you are returned to the report, with a small object attached to your mouse cursor. You can drop the cross-tab object in the report header or footer, or in a group header or footer. Cross-tabs can't be placed in the details section or in a page header or footer—you'll get a "no-drop" cursor (a circle with a line through it) if you try to position the cross-tab in these sections.

Drop the cross-tab below any other objects in the section, such as summaries, group names, or text objects. Although the cross-tab will appear relatively small in the Design tab, when you actually preview or print the report, the cross-tab will grow both horizontally and vertically to accommodate all of its rows and columns. If there are other objects below or to the right of the cross-tab, it will print right over the top of them. When you drop the cross-tab, the small object on the mouse cursor turns into a larger cross-tab object, showing a layout of the row, column, summarized field, and row and column totals.

When you preview the report, Crystal Reports will cycle through the database several times to properly calculate the totals for all row and column combinations—you may note some extra time required to do this. The cross-tab will then appear in the section where you placed it (as seen in Figures 11-2, 11-4, and 11-5).

The section in which you place a cross-tab is critical in determining the data that the cross-tab will encompass. If you place a cross-tab in the report header or footer, only one occurrence of the cross-tab will appear on the report (remember, the report header and footer appear only once, at the beginning and end of the report, respectively). This cross-tab will encompass all the data on the report. If you place a cross-tab in a group header or footer, you get as many cross-tabs on your report as there are groups, each encompassing only data for that group.

Figure 11-4 shows the same report as Figure 11-2, using the XTREME.MDB sample database included with Crystal Reports. This cross-tab includes product names as the rows, and cities as the columns. Notice that all cities in all states show up in the cross-tab.

Contrast this with Figure 11-5, which is the exact same cross-tab object that's just been moved to a state group footer. Now there will be a cross-tab on the report for every state group, but each cross-tab will contain data only for that particular group. If you choose to, you can copy the cross-tab object between a group header or footer to the report header or footer and actually see cross-tabs for individual groups, as well as an all-encompassing cross-tab for the whole report.

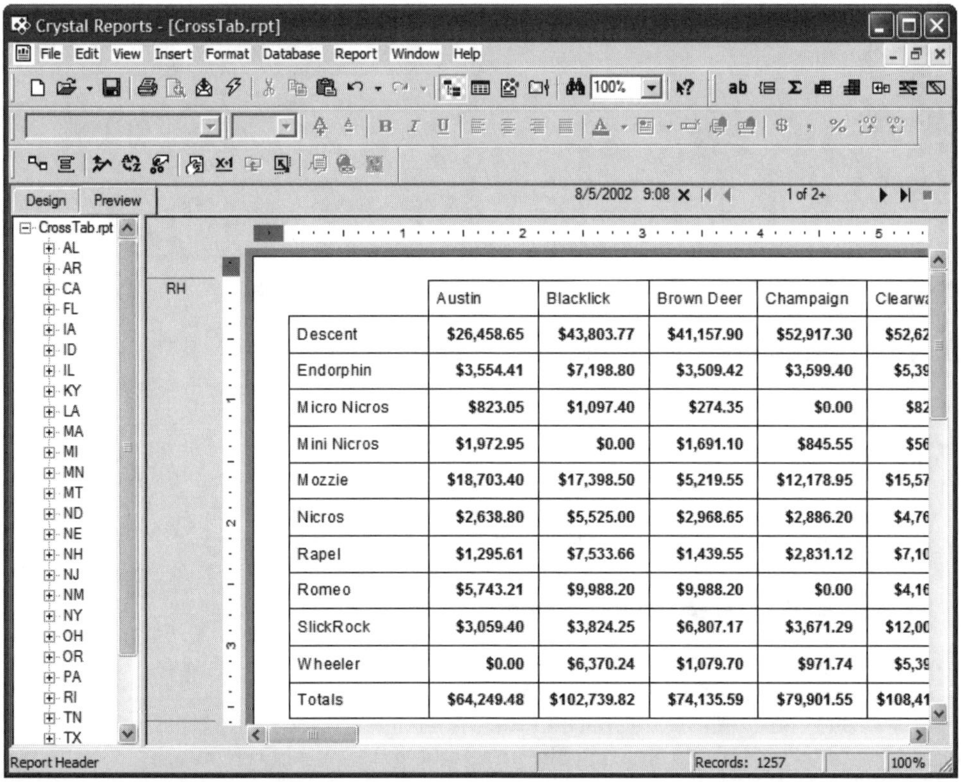

Figure 11-4. *Cross-tab in report header*

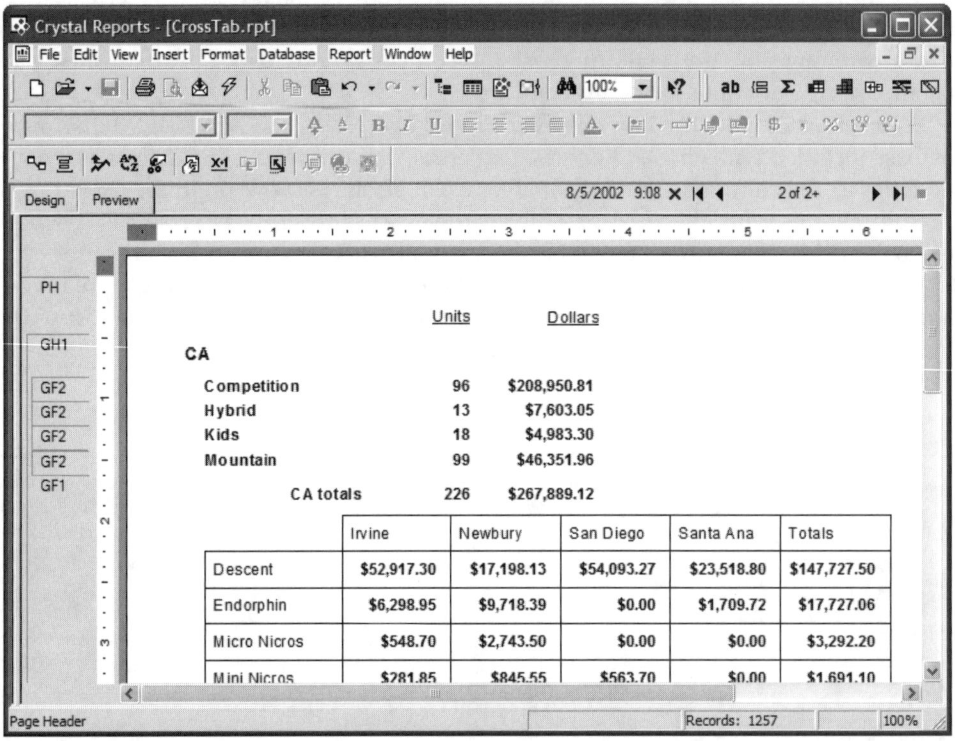

Figure 11-5. *Cross-tab in group footer*

Note   *If you created the cross-tab through the report creation Wizard, you have no groups, even though the row and column fields of a cross-tab are treated as if they were grouped. (You can see this in Figure 11-6, where the group tree is empty.) You would have to insert a group on the field desired, if you want a cross-tab in each group footer.*

Editing an Existing Cross-Tab

After you create a cross-tab and drop it on your report, making changes to it is easy. You must first select the entire cross-tab object, not just one of its individual objects, by clicking either the small white space in the upper-left corner of the cross-tab (above the first row and to the left of the first column) or the grid lines between cells. You'll know you've selected the entire cross-tab if the status bar displays Cross-Tab: you can select the cross-tab in either the Design tab or the Preview tab.

After you select the cross-tab that you want to modify, choose Format | Cross-Tab Expert from the pull-down menus, or right-click and choose Cross-Tab Expert from the pop-up menu. This simply redisplays the Cross-Tab Expert dialog box, allowing you to change row, column, or summarized fields on the Cross-Tab tab, or format cross-tab styles with the Style tab or the Customize Style tab.

You can also *pivot* the cross-tab, which simply refers to swapping the rows and columns around so that what used to be the row will now be the column, and vice versa. Choose Format | Pivot Cross-Tab from the pull-down menus, or right-click the selected cross-tab object and choose Pivot Cross-Tab from the pop-up menu.

Creative Use of Grouping and Formulas

As discussed previously, Crystal Reports chooses a default calculation for the summarized field when it creates the cross-tab. If you choose a number or currency field for a summarized field, Crystal Reports will use the Sum function to subtotal the numbers in each cell. This typically is what you want for this type of field (for example, the total sales figure for Green Bikes in the USA). If you use any other type of field (string, date, Boolean, and so forth), Crystal Reports will default to the Count function to count the occurrences of the particular summarized field for each row / column combination.

You are, however, completely free to change the function that Crystal Reports assigns to the summarized field. If you want to see the average sales figure in each cell instead of the total figure, it's easy to change. In either the Design or Preview tab, click the object in the cell (the intersection of the row and column). The status bar will indicate that you've selected Sum or Count of <summarized field>. Change the summary operation to any other available summary by choosing Edit | Edit Summary from the pull-down menus or by right-clicking and choosing Edit Summary from the pop-up menu. This brings up the Edit Summary dialog box:

You can change the field that's summarized, if desired, or just the summary operation itself. If you've used a nonnumeric field for the cross-tab summarized field, you can change the summary operation from Count to Minimum, Maximum, Distinct Count, or any other summary function that is available for nonnumeric fields. You can also choose to express the summary as a percentage of another total or summary. These options are similar to how you can change the summary operation with existing group summaries and subtotals, as discussed in Chapter 3. In fact, the cross-tab in essence groups database records for every row/column combination, creating the summary or subtotal field for each cross-tab "group." Chapter 3 has more information on available summary functions and what they calculate.

Note
No matter how hard you try or how creative you might be, cross-tab cells cannot contain anything but numbers created from summary functions. Reports such as calendars, schedules, or other row/column reports may look like potential cross-tabs. However, to have some textual information at the intersection of the rows and columns, you need to design the report using other techniques. Cross-tabs are strictly for numeric analyses.

Changing Cross-Tab Grouping

Because Crystal Reports uses a procedure to create cross-tabs that's similar to its procedure for creating groups, you have some of the same flexibility to change the way the cross-tab is organized. You can change a cross-tab "group" when first creating the cross-tab or when editing an existing cross-tab through the Cross-Tab Expert. In the Cross-Tab tab, select the row or column field you want to change, and then click the Group Options button. The Cross-Tab Group Options dialog box appears.

The Common tab allows you to change the field on which you're grouped, as well as the order in which the group is displayed. For a nondate field, there are three order choices:

- **Ascending Order**   Shows the cross-tab row or column in A to Z order.
- **Descending Order**   Shows the cross-tab row or column in Z to A order.
- **Specified Order**   Lets you create custom rows or columns, based on the contents of the database field you chose for the row or column. This works identically to Specified Order Grouping, discussed in Chapter 3.

On the Options tab, the Customize Group Name Field check box, radio buttons, and formula button work identically to the same options in the Change Group dialog box discussed in Chapter 3. You may customize the appearance of the text that displays in the row or column of the cross-tab with these options.

Note *Any grouping on the main report doesn't change when the cross-tab row/column fields or their group options are changed. You can see this when you compare Figure 11-2, where the cross-tab is a direct illustration of the report's grouping by region, and Figures 11-4 and 11-5, in which the cross-tab summarizes cities rather than regions, but the region grouping is intact.*

If the row or column field is a date field, time field, or date/time field, the Cross-Tab Group Options dialog box offers additional options that give you even greater flexibility, similar to creating report groups with similar fields.

The pull-down list under "The column will be printed:" gives you a choice of how often you want a new row or column to appear in the cross-tab. Choices include every day, every week, every two weeks, every hour, every minute, and so on. Again, these are identical to the date/time grouping choices discussed in Chapter 3.

The pull-down list under "The value printed for the column will be:" gives you two choices: the first date in the period and the last date in the period. If you choose the first-date option with, say, a quarterly date period for 1997, the cross-tab will show 1/97, 4/97, 7/97, and 10/97. If you choose the last-date option, the cross-tab will show the exact same data in the cells, but the dates will be 3/97, 6/97, 9/97, and 12/97.

To give you a better idea of the flexibility that date group options provide, look at Figures 11-6 and 11-7, both showing cross-tabs based on the same date field. Figure 11-6 shows weekly date grouping with the first-date option.

Figure 11-7 shows the same cross-tab, but with the order date grouped quarterly with the last-date option.

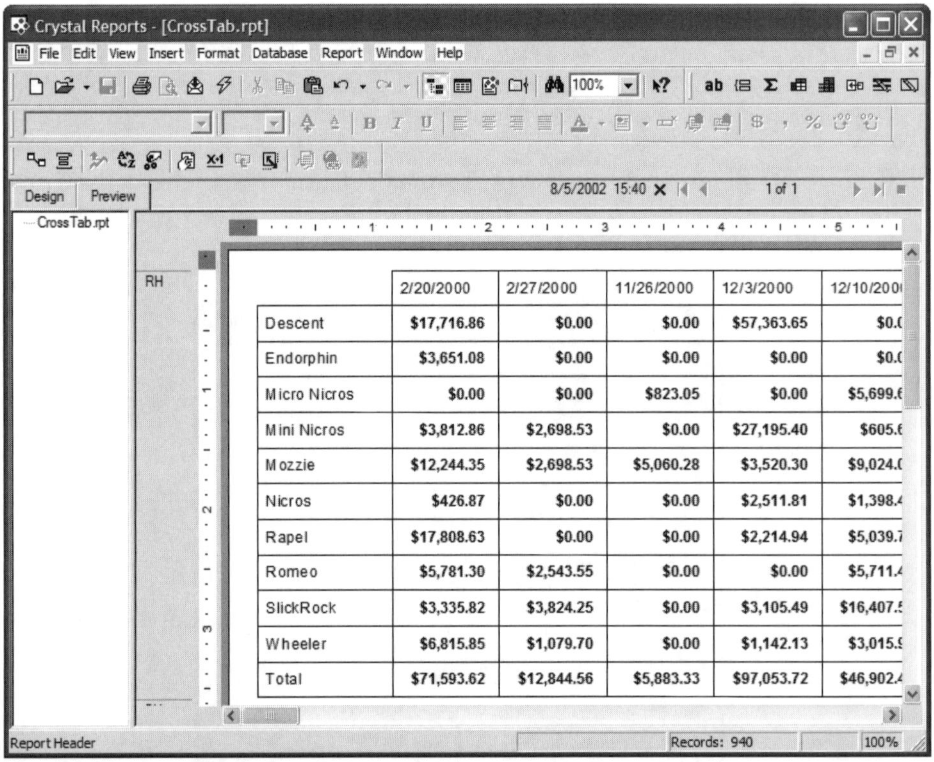

	2/20/2000	2/27/2000	11/26/2000	12/3/2000	12/10/200(
Descent	$17,716.86	$0.00	$0.00	$57,363.65	$0.(
Endorphin	$3,651.08	$0.00	$0.00	$0.00	$0.(
Micro Nicros	$0.00	$0.00	$823.05	$0.00	$5,699.8
Mini Nicros	$3,812.86	$2,698.53	$0.00	$27,195.40	$605.8
Mozzie	$12,244.35	$2,698.53	$5,060.28	$3,520.30	$9,024.(
Nicros	$426.87	$0.00	$0.00	$2,511.81	$1,398.4
Rapel	$17,808.63	$0.00	$0.00	$2,214.94	$5,039.7
Romeo	$5,781.30	$2,543.55	$0.00	$0.00	$5,711.4
SlickRock	$3,335.82	$3,824.25	$0.00	$3,105.49	$16,407.5
Wheeler	$6,815.85	$1,079.70	$0.00	$1,142.13	$3,015.9
Total	$71,593.62	$12,844.56	$5,883.33	$97,053.72	$46,902.4

Figure 11-6. *Cross-tab date field with weekly first-date group options*

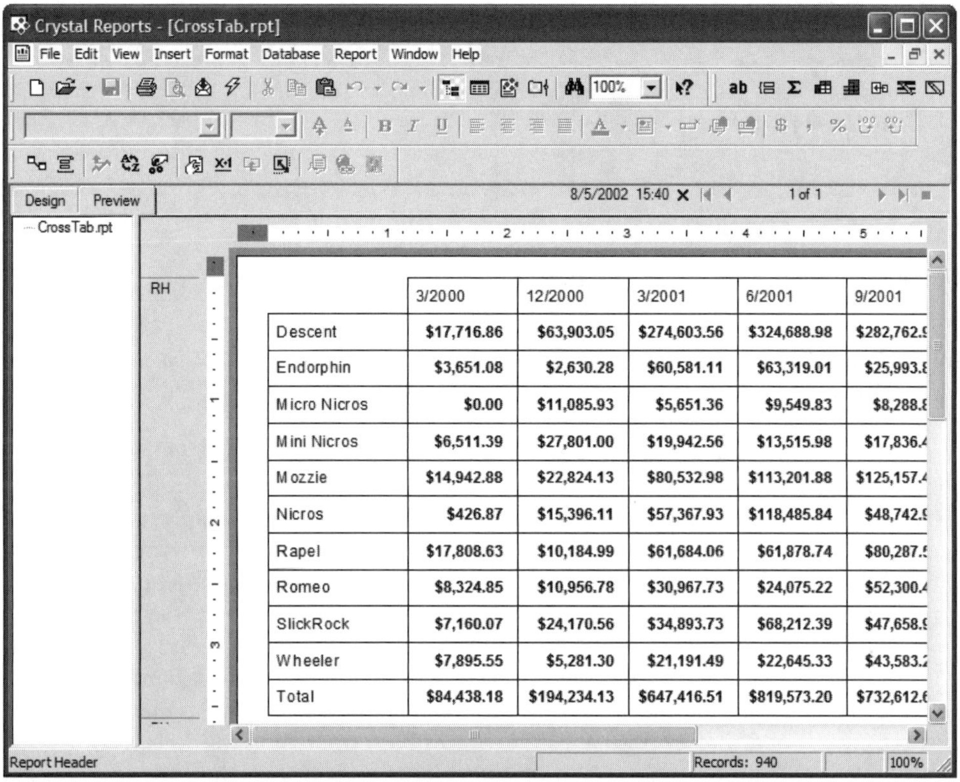

Figure 11-7. *Cross-tab on date field with quarterly last-date group options*

Using Formulas in Cross-Tabs

Even with the powerful grouping options and the ability to change the summary function used to calculate cell values, you may not always be able to display material in a cross-tab exactly the way you want using just the database fields in the Available Fields box. You are completely free to use formulas in your cross-tabs as a row, column, or summarized field. You can create the formulas in advance with the Formula Editor, or click the New Formula button right in the Cross-Tab Expert dialog box to display the Formula Editor. After you create the formula, it will appear in the Available Fields box under the Report Fields category. Simply drag it to the Rows, Columns, or Summarized Field box.

Caution *Because cross-tabs are calculated during the first report pass (WhileReadingRecords), you cannot use second-pass formulas in cross-tabs. You can use only formulas that calculate during the first pass. However, you can base a chart or a map on a cross-tab, because cross-tabs are processed before charts and maps. See Chapter 5 for a discussion on report passes.*

Multiple Rows, Columns, and Summarized Fields

The Rows, Columns, and Summarized Field boxes in the Cross-Tab Expert dialog box obviously are more than one field tall. Yes, that means that you can add more than one database field or formula to any of these cross-tab sections. It's important to understand, though, how this will affect cross-tab behavior and appearance.

Probably the simplest place to start is with multiple summarized fields. If you add more than one field to the Summarized Field box, the cross-tab will simply calculate the additional summary or subtotal in each cell. You could, for example, use Product Name as the row, Region as the column, and *both* Quantity and Price as summarized fields. The cross-tab would simply include two numbers in each cell—the total quantity and total price for that particular product and region.

You can even add the same field to the Summarized Field box more than once and choose a different summary function for each occurrence, using the Change Summary button. You could, for example, add both the Quantity and Price fields to the Summarized Field box again, and then choose a different summary operation for these summaries, such as Average. Alternatively, you might add them as Sum functions again, but this time choose the Percentage Of summary function for the second occurrence of the summed fields.

In the Edit Summary dialog box, when you select the Show As a Percentage Of option, you are given a choice between the Row total and the Column total as the target comparison number. In this example, the sums will be shown as a percentage of the column totals, so the resulting cross-tab shows four numbers in every cell: total quantity, total price, percentage of total quantity for the quarter, and percentage of total price for the quarter. It's interesting to note that the Row totals also display their percentage of the column totals, so the report is very effective as an analysis of each product by quarter:

	3/2001	6/2001	9/2001	12/2001	Total
Competition	156 25.08 % $167,529 26.11 %	171 27.49 % $175,377 27.33 %	159 25.56 % $158,857 24.76 %	136 21.86 % $139,874 21.80 %	622 100.00 % $641,637 100.00 %
Hybrid	54 21.18 % $16,622 20.28 %	37 14.51 % $11,682 14.25 %	83 32.55 % $28,029 34.20 %	81 31.76 % $25,621 31.26 %	255 100.00 % $81,953 100.00 %
Kids	35 24.65 % $4,169 22.51 %	28 19.72 % $3,850 20.78 %	39 27.46 % $5,534 29.88 %	40 28.17 % $4,971 26.84 %	142 100.00 % $18,523 100.00 %
Mountain	166 22.77 % $37,066 21.49 %	210 28.81 % $50,226 29.12 %	179 24.55 % $42,551 24.67 %	174 23.87 % $42,642 24.72 %	729 100.00 % $172,486 100.00 %
Total	411 23.51 % $225,386 24.64 %	446 25.51 % $241,134 26.37 %	460 26.32 % $234,971 25.69 %	431 24.66 % $213,109 23.30 %	1,748 100.00 % $914,599 100.00 %

If you had instead asked for the percentages against the Row totals, it would be an analysis of how each product compared to others each quarter.

Adding multiple fields to the Rows or Columns boxes causes a little different behavior that you need to understand. Whereas multiple summarized fields simply calculate and print in the same cell, multiple row or column fields don't just print over and over, side by side. When you add multiple fields to these boxes, you create a *grouping relationship* between the fields. Consider a cross-tab in which you add the Product Type field as the first row field, and the Product Name field as the second row field. Crystal Reports will create a group hierarchy by Product Type, and within that, by Product Name. The resulting cross-tab would look like this:

		3/2001	6/2001	9/2001	12/2001	Total
Competition	Descent	$274,603.56	$324,688.98	$282,762.94	$197,962.14	1,080,017.62
	Endorphin	$60,581.11	$63,319.01	$25,993.85	$33,129.29	**$183,023.26**
	Mozzie	$80,532.98	$113,201.88	$125,157.48	$94,772.95	**$413,665.29**
	Total	**$415,717.65**	**$501,209.87**	**$433,914.27**	**$325,864.38**	1,676,706.17
Hybrid	Romeo	$30,967.73	$24,075.22	$52,300.44	$60,115.98	**$167,459.37**
	Wheeler	$21,191.49	$22,645.33	$43,583.23	$30,743.11	**$118,163.16**
	Total	**$52,159.22**	**$46,720.55**	**$95,883.67**	**$90,859.09**	**$285,622.53**
Kids	Micro Nicros	$5,651.36	$9,549.83	$8,288.81	$9,339.10	**$32,829.10**
	Mini Nicros	$19,942.56	$13,515.98	$17,836.49	$17,182.50	**$68,477.53**
	Total	**$25,593.92**	**$23,065.81**	**$26,125.30**	**$26,521.60**	**$101,306.63**
Mountain	Nicros	$57,367.93	$118,485.84	$48,742.91	$75,395.97	**$299,992.65**
	Rapel	$61,684.06	$61,878.74	$80,287.56	$56,247.45	**$260,097.81**
	SlickRock	$34,893.73	$68,212.39	$47,658.93	$47,295.02	**$198,060.07**
	Total	**$153,945.72**	**$248,576.97**	**$176,689.40**	**$178,938.44**	**$758,150.53**
Total		**$647,416.51**	**$819,573.20**	**$732,612.64**	**$622,183.51**	2,821,785.86

Notice that rows are created for both the "inner" and "outer" groups—each product name has its own row within its product type, and each product type has its own subtotal row. And, at the end of the cross-tab is a grand total row for everything.

You can set up this multiple-field group hierarchy for either rows or columns. Also, you can include as many fields as you want in the Rows box and the Columns box (although it won't make much sense if you go beyond two or three levels).

Here's a portion of the resulting cross-tab:

				AL				AR		C/
		3/2001	6/2001	9/2001	12/2001	Total	6/2001	Total	3/2
Competition	Descent	0 $0	11 $32,338	7 $20,579	6 $17,639	24 **$70,556**	3 $8,820	3 **$8,820**	$45,
	Endorphin	3 $2,700	4 $3,419	2 $1,800	0 $0	9 **$7,919**	0 $0	0 **$0**	$5,
	Mozzie	0 $0	2 $3,480	6 $9,917	5 $8,699	13 **$22,096**	0 $0	0 **$0**	$5,
	Total	3 **$2,699.55**	17 **39,237.49**	15 **32,295.81**	11 **26,338.35**	46 **$100,571**	3 **$8,819.55**	3 **$8,820**	56,480
Hybrid	Romeo	3 $2,247	1 $791	2 $1,498	1 $832	7 **$5,369**	0 $0	0 **$0**	
	Wheeler	2 $1,080	2 $1,080	0 $0	0 $0	4 **$2,159**	0 $0	0 **$0**	$1,
	Total	5 **$3,327.06**	3 **$1,870.43**	2 **$1,498.24**	1 **$832.35**	11 **$7,528**	0 **$0.00**	0 **$0**	$1,079
Kids	Micro Nicros	0 $0	1 $274	3 $823	0 $0	4 **$1,097**	0 $0	0 $0	

> **Note**   *What section of the report you place the cross-tab in is particularly important when you are using multiple row or column fields. If you create a cross-tab that's based on Country, and then Region, you'll see different behavior depending on where you put the cross-tab. If you put it in the report header or footer, you'll have rows or columns for each country, and all the regions within those countries. However, if you have already grouped your report by country, and you place the cross-tab in a country group header or group footer, you'll then have one cross-tab for every country. However, that cross-tab will have only one country row or column in it, followed by any regions within that country. If you find cross-tabs at group levels with only one high-level row or column, there's not a great deal of benefit to using multiple row or column fields in that cross-tab.*

If you plan to use multiple row or column fields, choosing fields that have a logical, groupable relationship with each other is crucial. You may think of this relationship as being *one-to-many.* The Product Type/Product Name relationship is a good example—every one product type has many product names. Country/Region is another good example—every one country has many regions.

Placing two fields in the Rows or Columns boxes that don't have this relationship will cause an odd-looking cross-tab. For example, if you add Customer Name and Address fields to the same row or column box, you'll simply see the customer name row or column, immediately followed by a single address row or column. The summaries in each will be exactly the same, because there's no logical one-to-many relationship between the fields. (The exception would be if a single customer had more than one office location—then this would be a valid multiple-field cross-tab example.)

> **Note**   *You may yearn for a cross-tab that allows multiple row or column fields that don't act as groups. You might, for example, want to see Actual $, Budget $, Variance $, and Variance % all as separate column fields that just calculate and print side by side. Sorry, but any time you add multiple fields to the Rows box or Columns box, Crystal Reports displays the fields in a grouping hierarchy from top to bottom.*

Reordering Fields in the Rows, Columns, or Summarized Field Boxes

The multiple fields you add to the Rows box or Columns box not only have to have a logical relationship, they also need to appear in the box in the right order. Using the previous Country/Region example, Country must be the first field in the box, followed by Region. If they're added the other way around, then each region will appear first, followed by a single row or column containing numbers from the country the region is in.

If you happen to add fields to the Rows, Columns, or Summarized Field boxes in the wrong order, you can reorder them by one of two methods: either click one of the fields and then click the up or down arrow for that box to move it up or down, or click and drag a field in any of the boxes and drop it in a different location in the box.

Customizing Cross-Tab Appearance

So far, this chapter has concentrated on the basic steps required to create cross-tabs, on grouping options, and on some of the finer points of multiple row, column, and summarized fields. In all of these examples, the resulting cross-tab object looks fairly plain. In keeping with the ability of Crystal Reports to create publication-quality reports, you have numerous options available to help you improve the appearance of your cross-tab reports.

The most basic type of formatting options for cross-tabs lies in the individual cross-tab objects themselves. A cross-tab actually consists of a series of individual objects. The best way to see this is to look at a cross-tab in the Design tab.

	Column #1 N	Total
Row #1 Name	Order Amount	Order Amount
Total	Order Amount	Order Amount

Notice the row and column name fields, which are similar to group name fields in a regular report—they display the database fields that make up the row and column headings. The Total text objects indicate the subtotal and total rows and columns. These are standard text objects—simply double-click them to change their contents, if you wish. And, in the actual cells, notice the subtotal or summary functions that calculate the cross-tab totals.

Each of these individual objects can be resized or formatted to change the appearance of the cross-tab. For example, if a column in the cross-tab isn't wide enough to show its contents, the contents will just be cut off, or *truncated*. Examine the following cross-tab:

	3/2001	6/2001	9/2001	12/2001	Total
Descent	########	########	########	########	#########
Endorphi	########	########	########	########	#########
Micro	$5,651.36	$9,549.83	$8,288.81	$9,339.10	$32,829.10
Mini	########	########	########	########	$68,477.53

Notice that the row labels are being truncated. Also, note that many of the cells contain pound signs, indicating that the cells aren't wide enough to show all the data in them. (Remember that if Allow Field Clipping is turned on, you won't see pound signs when numbers are truncated.)

Although you may be tempted to look on one of the tabs of the Cross-Tab Expert dialog box for some sort of column width setting, you simply need to select the individual object that makes up the column and resize it. This can be done in either the Design or Preview tab. Simply select the object, noting that all other similar cells are selected as well. Then, point to the desired *sizing handle* (one of the small blue blocks on all sides of a selected object) until the mouse cursor changes to the two-way sizing cursor. Then, simply resize the object to its desired width.

	1/2000	10/2000	1/2001	4/2001
Active Outdoors	$308.00	$9,762.67	$13,482.96	$43,83
Active Outdoors	$1,266.15	$6,403.89	$58,214.00	$39,09
Descent	$23,612.06	$96,033.66	$370,455.42	$526,09
Endorphin	$3,651.08	$12,416.79	$74,866.88	$110,46
Guardian "U"	$0.00	$35.00	$6,105.66	$6,77
Guardian ATB	$0.00	$2,362.97	$3,135.00	$6,56
Guardian Chain	$0.00	$157.30	$5,905.56	$1,28
Guardian Mini	$149.50	$4,933.86	$3,795.34	$13,18
Guardian XL "U"	$0.00	$19.90	$2,366.92	$14,21
InFlux Crochet	$0.00	$1,202.05	$11,608.25	$3,53
InFlux Lycra	$8,531.10	$3,934.32	$4,025.16	$7,93

Tip *If the summarized values in your cross-tab are just too large to fit into a tidy grid, there is also a function you can use to abbreviate thousands or millions with the standard "K" or "M" notation. See "Conditionally Formatting Cross-Tabs" later in this chapter.*

You can format the individual pieces of the cross-tab just like any other text object or number field, using either the Formatting toolbar or the Format Editor. You can change the object's color, font face and size, horizontal alignment, or any other standard formatting option. If you choose one of the summary or subtotal objects in the middle, you can choose one of the default formatting styles, or choose a custom style to specify the number of decimal places, whether to include a thousands separator or currency symbol, or any other formatting option available to numeric or currency fields. If you base a row or column on a date or time field, you can choose how the field is displayed—month/year, month/day/year, hour:minute, hour:minute:second, or any other variation provided by the Format Editor.

Tip

You can select multiple objects in a cross-tab by using CTRL*-click. You can then format them all at the same time with the Formatting toolbar or the Format Editor. The elastic box method doesn't select multiple objects in a cross-tab, but it does select the entire cross-tab.*

The Style Tab

When you select a cross-tab object and choose Format | Cross-Tab Expert or right-click and choose Cross-Tab Expert from the pop-up menu, the Cross-Tab Expert dialog box will appear. Two tabs in this dialog box control formatting: Style and Customize Style. The Style tab lets you choose from several predefined formatting styles for the cross-tab object.

The Original option simply displays the cross-tab object with no special formatting—this is the original formatting option when a cross-tab is first created. You may choose from any of the predefined styles in the list. When you click a style, a sample of the style appears in the right side of the Style tab. Then, just click OK. The cross-tab will be formatted according to the built-in style you chose.

Caution	*Crystal Reports behaves somewhat oddly when using the Style tab on the Cross-Tab Expert dialog box. Even if you haven't chosen any customized settings, you'll always receive a warning that you'll lose customized settings when you choose one of the built-in styles. And if you return to the Style tab later after choosing one of the built-in styles, the Custom setting will be highlighted, not the built-in style you chose before.*

The Customize Style Tab

For very specific formatting of a cross-tab object, you need to use the Customize Style tab on the Cross-Tab Expert dialog box. This tab contains advanced cross-tab options that more precisely control cross-tab behavior. The Customize Style tab is shown in Figure 11-8.

If you've already chosen one of the built-in styles on the Style tab, you'll see the settings for that built-in style when you choose the Customize Style tab. For example, you'll see background colors for each row or column item that the built-in style selected. If the built-in style shows totals before rows and columns instead of after, you'll see those options chosen. If you haven't chosen one of the built-in styles, or you want to change some of the settings that the built-in style selected, you may choose the various options in the Custom Style tab. The various options are explained in Table 11-1.

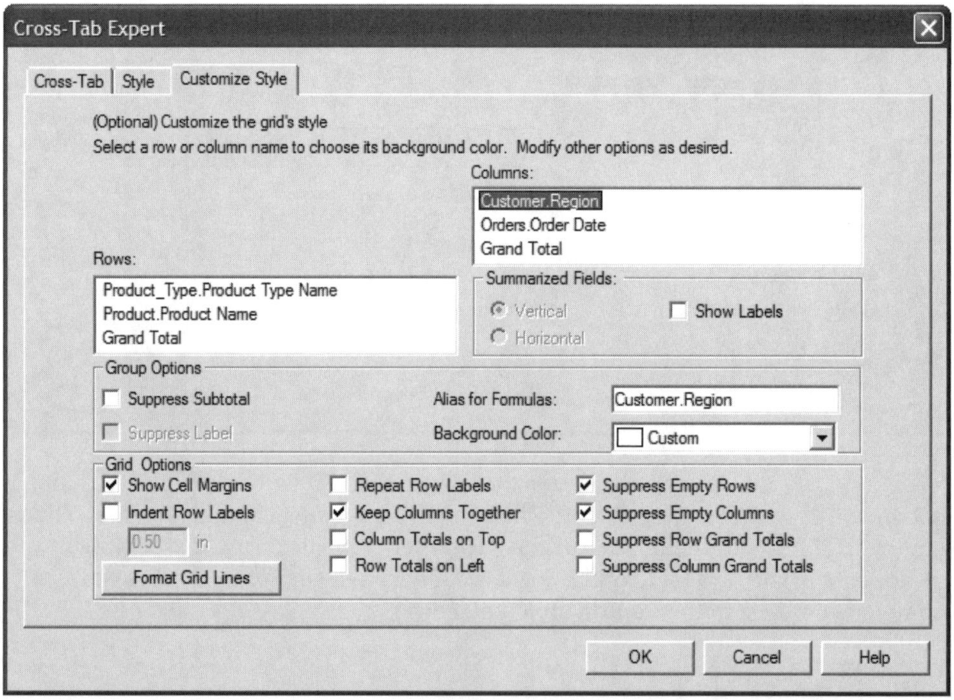

Figure 11-8. *The Customize Style tab of the Cross-Tab Expert dialog box*

Option	Description
Customize Grid's Style	
Rows list	Select the row that you want to format. If you've added multiple row fields, you'll see each row field listed. You can also choose separate formatting options for the row grand total.
Columns list	Select the column that you want to format. If you've added multiple column fields, you'll see each column field listed. You can also choose separate formatting options for the column grand total.
Summarized fields (new in version 9)	When you have multiple fields summarized, you can choose whether to display them in a vertical stack (this is the default) or horizontally side-by-side. The Show Labels option prints the summarized field name(s) in the column header area (you can't customize the labels here, but can edit them in the Design or Preview tabs just like text objects). Figure 11-9 shows the horizontal summaries with labels.
Group Options	
Suppress Subtotal	If you select this option, the subtotal row or column (depending on what's selected in the Rows or Columns list) won't appear. In this case, the cross-tab still shows the hierarchical grouping relationship among the multiple row or column fields, but the subtotals for the selected field won't appear. This option is available only for higher-level fields when you've chosen multiple row or column fields—the option is disabled if you select the lowest-level (or if you added only one) row or column field.
Suppress Label	If you choose the Suppress Subtotal option, this option becomes enabled. Checking this option will completely eliminate the field you chose from the row or column. The grouping hierarchy will remain, but the higher-level group won't appear at all in the cross-tab. If you have also checked Indent Row Labels (described later in this table), this option will be checked and you can't change it.

Table 11-1.   *Customize Style Tab Options*

Option	Description
Alias for Formulas	Used to refer to an entire row or column when performing conditional formatting on the cross-tab. See "Conditionally Formatting Cross-Tabs" later in the chapter.
Background Color	Sets the background color for the entire row or column that's chosen in the Rows or Columns list. This color is independent of any individual cell colors you may choose by selecting an object in the cross-tab and using the Format Editor.
Grid Options	
Show Cell Margins	Pads cells with white space on all sides. Turning this option off will place cells right next to each other.
Indent Row Labels	Checking this option will indent the label for the chosen row from the left of the cross-tab. You may specify how much to indent the row in the text box after the Indent Row Labels check box. This is typically used to highlight a hierarchical grouping relationship when you've added multiple row fields to the cross-tab.
Format Grid Lines button	Displays the Format Grid Lines dialog box (described later in the chapter) to customize where and how grid lines appear in the cross-tab.
Repeat Row Labels	If Keep Columns Together is checked, this option will repeat the row labels when a cross-tab exceeding the width of the page is printed on two or more pages.
Keep Columns Together	Prevents columns from being cut in half when a cross-tab exceeding the width of the page is printed.
Column Totals on Top	Displays column totals on top of the actual columns containing the data being totaled, rather than at the bottom of the columns.
Row Totals on Left	Displays row totals to the left of the actual rows containing the data being totaled, rather than on the right of the rows.

Table 11-1. *Customize Style Tab Options* (continued)

Option	Description
Suppress Empty Rows	Rows with no data will not appear in the cross-tab.
Suppress Empty Columns	Columns with no data will not appear in the cross-tab.
Suppress Row Grand Totals	Prevents row grand totals from appearing in the cross-tab.
Suppress Column Grand Totals	Prevents column grand totals from appearing in the cross-tab.

Table 11-1. *Customize Style Tab Options* (continued)

Several of the options on the Customize Style tab, particularly the Repeat Row Labels and Keep Columns Together options, dictate how a cross-tab appears when printed on paper. This is significant because Crystal Reports displays cross-tabs differently in the Preview tab than it will print them on a printer. Even if the cross-tab width exceeds the width of the page, the Preview tab will show the entire cross-tab across the screen. You can continue to scroll farther right to see the rest of the cross-tab.

When Crystal Reports prints the cross-tab on paper, however, it must add page breaks if the cross-tab exceeds the width of the printed page. You can control how Crystal Reports formats the cross-tab across multiple pages with the options in the Customize Style tab. When you display the cross-tab in the Preview tab, you can see where Crystal Reports will insert page breaks when the cross-tab is printed on paper. In Figure 11-9 notice that the page break occurs between columns (it's not running right through the numbers of a column) and that the row labels are repeating after the page break. This is the result of turning on both Keep Columns Together and Repeat Row Labels.

Formatting Grid Lines

Crystal Reports provides the ability to customize grid line appearance, including which grid lines appear and how they look. Customize the grid lines by clicking the Format Grid Lines button in the Grid Options area of the Customize Style tab. The Format Grid Lines dialog box will appear, as shown in Figure 11-10.

You may simply choose to not show any grid lines at all by unchecking the Show Grid Lines option. Or to control individual grid lines, you may either select the grid line you want to customize in the grid line list or actually click a particular line in the grid lines diagram at the top of the dialog box. Then, choose individual options for the grid line in the Line Options portion of the Format Grid Lines dialog box.

Adding Legends to Cross-Tabs

If you add multiple summarized fields to a cross-tab, it may not be clear to your viewer what the numbers mean—they may be totals, averages, or counts. The Show Labels option, shown in Figure 11-9, is effective with one or two summaries, but the labels can be hard to fit in the column headers, and with more than two summarized fields it's unwieldy.

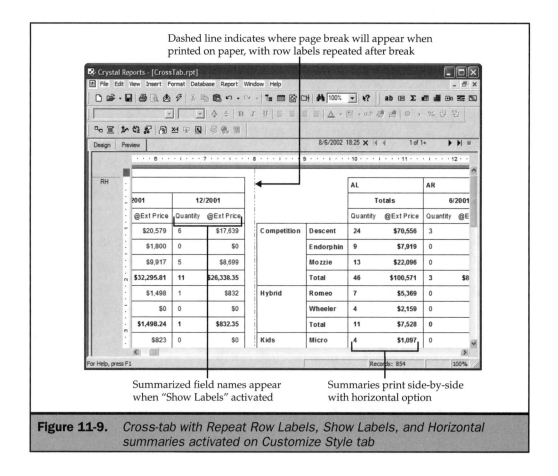

Figure 11-9. *Cross-tab with Repeat Row Labels, Show Labels, and Horizontal summaries activated on Customize Style tab*

Although Crystal Reports does not have a legend capability for cross-tabs, you can create your own legends using text objects and, optionally, with filled-box drawing. Here is a multiple-summary cross-tab with a legend.

Units Sold ☐
Units % of total ■
Amount Sold ☐
% of total sales ■

	3/2001	6/2001	9/2001	12/2001	Total
Competition	156	171	159	136	622
	25.08 %	27.49 %	25.56 %	21.86%	100.00%
	$167,529	$175,377	$158,857	$139,874	$641,637
	26.11 %	27.33 %	24.76 %	21.80 %	100.00 %
Hybrid	54	37	83	81	255
	21.18 %	14.51 %	32.55 %	31.76%	100.00%
	$16,622	$11,682	$28,029	$25,621	$81,953
	20.28 %	14.25 %	34.20 %	31.26 %	100.00 %
Kids	35	28	39	40	142
	24.65 %	19.72 %	27.46 %	28.17%	100.00%
	$4,169	$3,850	$5,534	$4,971	$18,523
	22.51 %	20.78 %	29.88 %	26.84 %	100.00 %
Mountain	166	210	179	174	729

Text objects have simply been placed in the same report section as the cross-tab so that they appear in the upper-left corner of the cross-tab. The small white area in the cross-tab above the first row and to the left of the first column can be placed right over the top of the text objects. The summary fields have been formatted to show in a different color, and small filled boxes of the same color have been drawn with the box-drawing tool (discussed in Chapter 9).

Conditionally Formatting Cross-Tabs

You may wish to conditionally format cross-tab cells, depending on their contents. *Conditional formatting* (discussed in more detail in Chapter 9) is the process of changing the appearance of a cross-tab cell based on its contents. You may wish to highlight certain cells that exceed a certain sales goal or shipping level; you can change the color, shading, or border of just those cells.

Select the summary or subtotal object that you want to conditionally format. Then, choose Format | Highlighting Expert from the pull-down menus, or right-click the cell

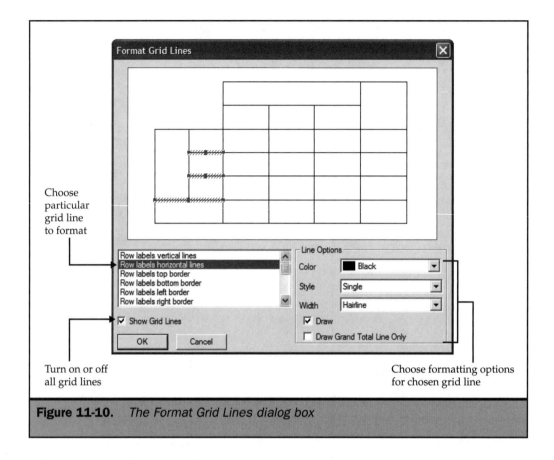

Choose particular grid line to format

Turn on or off all grid lines

Choose formatting options for chosen grid line

Figure 11-10. *The Format Grid Lines dialog box*

and choose Highlighting Expert from the pop-up menu. You can choose Highlighting Expert conditions and formats to highlight certain cells.

You can also use conditional formulas. After selecting a summary or subtotal object in the cross-tab, display the Format Editor by choosing options from the Format pull-down menu or by right-clicking and choosing options from the pop-up menu. You can click a Conditional Formula button anywhere on the Format Editor to set that formatting property conditionally.

What Is CurrentFieldValue?

When you choose to use conditional formulas instead of the Highlighting Expert, you must be careful about the tests you use to conditionally format cross-tab summaries. Since the summaries are calculations based on database fields, but are not actually the database fields themselves, you can't just test a database field to conditionally format the cross-tab. And contrary to what you see if you've placed subtotals or summaries in a group footer, you won't see the summaries or subtotals that make up the cells in the field list of the Formula Editor.

You must test the built-in CurrentFieldValue function when conditionally formatting cross-tabs. CurrentFieldValue, as its name suggests, returns whatever the cell or "field" being tested contains. You can, therefore, use a conditional formula similar to the following to apply a silver background color to cross-tab subtotals that exceed $50,000:

```
If CurrentFieldValue > 50000 Then Silver Else NoColor
```

Figure 11-11 shows a cross-tab with this formatting.

Another use for the CurrentFieldValue is to allow a field to be abbreviated when it is too large. A custom function that can be added from the Crystal Repository, cdFormatCurrencyUsingScaling, can replace large numbers with abbreviation strings

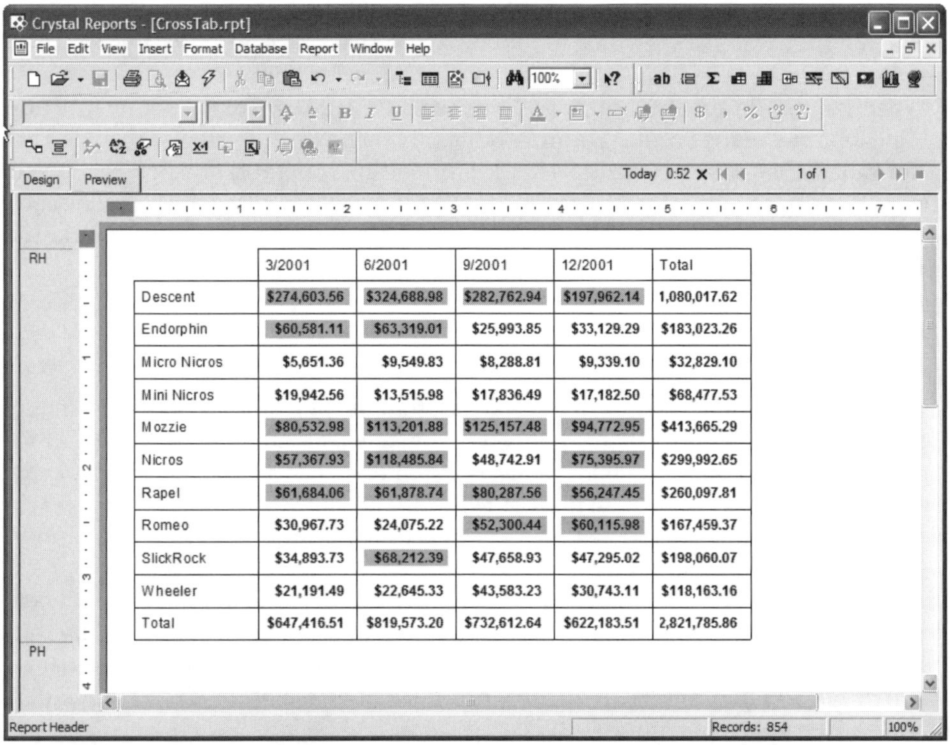
Crystal Reports - [CrossTab.rpt]
File Edit View Insert Format Database Report Window Help
Design Preview
Today 0:52
1 of 1
RH
3/2001 6/2001 9/2001 12/2001 Total
Descent $274,603.56 $324,688.98 $282,762.94 $197,962.14 1,080,017.62
Endorphin $60,581.11 $63,319.01 $25,993.85 $33,129.29 $183,023.26
Micro Nicros $5,651.36 $9,549.83 $8,288.81 $9,339.10 $32,829.10
Mini Nicros $19,942.56 $13,515.98 $17,836.49 $17,182.50 $68,477.53
Mozzie $80,532.98 $113,201.88 $125,157.48 $94,772.95 $413,665.29
Nicros $57,367.93 $118,485.84 $48,742.91 $75,395.97 $299,992.65
Rapel $61,684.06 $61,878.74 $80,287.56 $56,247.45 $260,097.81
Romeo $30,967.73 $24,075.22 $52,300.44 $60,115.98 $167,459.37
SlickRock $34,893.73 $68,212.39 $47,658.93 $47,295.02 $198,060.07
Wheeler $21,191.49 $22,645.33 $43,583.23 $30,743.11 $118,163.16
Total $647,416.51 $819,573.20 $732,612.64 $622,183.51 2,821,785.86
PH
Report Header
Records: 854
100%

Figure 11-11. *Cross-tab conditional formatting with CurrentFieldValue*

according to your specifications. The formula is placed as the Display String formula on the Common tab of the Format Editor for the summarized field, and it looks like this:

```
cdFormatCurrencyUsingScaling(CurrentFieldValue,1,"K","M")
```

The first argument of the function pulls the current field value, the second argument establishes how many decimal places you wish to include in the abbreviation (e.g., abbreviate $165,783.05 as "$165.8K" or "$165.78K"), and the third and fourth arguments are the strings you wish to display for thousands and millions placeholders. To use the cdFormatCurrencyUsingScaling function, the function must be added to the report. See Chapter 7 of this book for a discussion of adding custom functions from the repository.

What Are GridRowColumnValue and the Alias for Formulas?

Using the CurrentFieldValue function described in the preceding section, you can set conditional formatting in the cross-tab only based on the value of the current cell. However, you may also want to set conditional formatting based on the row or column that the cell is in, not just the value in the cell. Crystal Reports provides this capability using two functions, GridRowColumnValue and Alias for Formulas.

When you conditionally format a cell, notice the GridRowColumnValue function in the Functions box of the Format Formula Editor. By using this function with an If-Then-Else formula (when setting a multiple-choice formatting property) or a Boolean formula (when setting an on/off formatting property), you can determine which row or column the cell is in and format accordingly. Consider the following Boolean formula that conditionally sets the Drop Shadow property on the Format Editor Border tab:

```
GridRowColumnValue("Customer.Region") = "CA"
```

The result is shown in Figure 11-12. Notice that only cells under the CA column have drop shadows applied to them. By supplying an *alias name* as the parameter for the GridRowColumnValue function, you can determine which row or column the formula will refer to. In this scenario, Customer.Region is supplied as the alias name. So the GridRowColumnValue for the Region column is tested. If the value of the column is CA, the drop shadow is applied.

By default, each row or column's alias is the field or formula name of the row or column (without the curly braces). If you want to change the alias name to something more meaningful (perhaps just the field name instead of the entire table/field name combination), you may change it on the Customize Style tab of the Cross-Tab Expert dialog box (refer back to Figure 11-8).

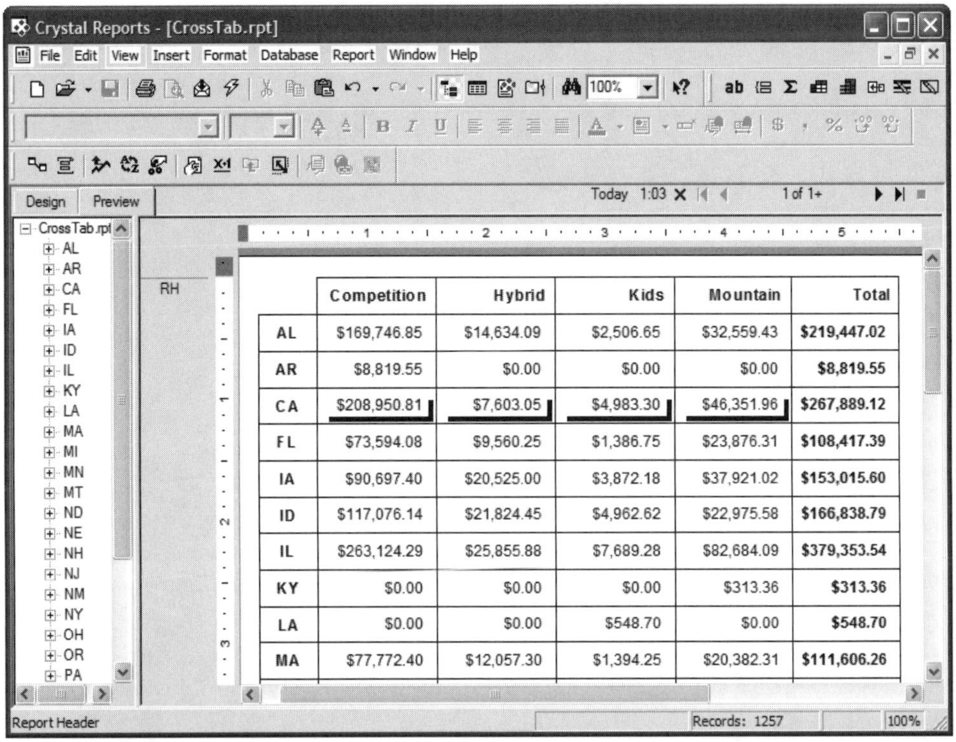

Figure 11-12.   *Cross-tab conditional formatting with GridRowColumnValue*

Select a row or column field in the Rows or Columns list. Then, type a new value in the Alias for Formulas text box. You may then use the new text you typed as the parameter for the GridRowColumnValue function to refer to the row or column.

Caution   *As much as you might like to, you cannot drill down on a cross-tab object. If you include a cross-tab in a summary report, you can drill down on the summary report groups, but not on the cross-tab.*

Chapter 12

Creating Charts

Crystal Reports 9 continues the tradition of a rich charting capability. This complements Crystal Reports' complete formatting capabilities for textual information. Not only can you create attractive, meaningful text-based reports, you can present the information graphically as well. Using Crystal Reports charting and graphing capabilities, you can see your database data presented in colorful bar charts, pie charts, three-dimensional area charts, and in many other ways (three additional chart types have been added to version 9). These charts can be seen in the Preview tab right inside Crystal Reports, on Web reports, included in reports exported to other external file formats, or printed on a black-and-white or color printer.

In addition to the new chart types added to version 9, the Analyzer (the separate tab and toolbar just for viewing and manipulating charts and maps in previous versions) has been eliminated. Now you can do all chart formatting and modifications *in-place*—that is, without having to display a separate tab, use any separate pull-down menus, or click any separate toolbar buttons. All chart formatting can be done right on the chart in the main report design or preview tabs.

There are some very fundamental questions you should initially ask before you add a chart to a report. Either you or your reporting audience should answer these questions satisfactorily before you proceed:

■ Will my viewers really benefit from a graphical representation of the data?

■ What kind of chart best matches the information to be shown?

While it's tempting to load up reports with lots of pretty, colorful charts, they aren't always an appropriate way to get across the "message" of the report. But for the many instances when a chart will add value to a report, you have a great number of charting options available to you.

Types and Layouts of Charts

Once you've decided to use a chart, you have two general choices to make about how you'll create your chart: what type of chart to use and how the chart will be laid out. The *chart type* refers to what the chart will look like—whether it will show the data in bars, lines, a pie, or some other graphical representation. The *chart layout* refers to the data that will be used to make up the chart, whether it comes from the details section, group summaries, or a cross-tab or OLAP grid (OLAP reporting is discussed in Chapter 18).

Chart Type

The first choice to make is which type of chart best represents the data to be charted. Although some types may be prettier than others, you again need to consider what type of chart will add real meaning to the data, allowing the viewer to get the most benefit from the report. Table 12-1 discusses the main types of charts available in the

Chart Type	Usage
Bar	Shows a series of bars side by side on the page, which is effective for showing how items compare to each other in terms of volume, size, dollars, etc., and may also be effective in plotting growth over time.
Line	Shows trends over time, particularly for multiple groups of data.
Area	Similar to a line chart, except that the area below the line is filled in with a color. Like the line chart, it is helpful for showing trends over time, but for just one or a few groups of data.
Pie	A circle with colored slices for each item, which is good for showing which item is the biggest "piece of the pie." The pie chart represents percentages for each item and is effective for small to moderate numbers of items.
Doughnut	Similar to a pie chart, showing who has the biggest bite of the donut. The only difference from a pie chart is that the doughnut has a hole in the middle, where the grand total for the chart is displayed.
3-D riser	A three-dimensional version of the bar chart. You can choose what shape you want for the bars—a cone, a pyramid, etc. Because this chart is three-dimensional, it can show multiple groups of data side by side.
3-D surface	A three-dimensional version of the area chart; it shows multiple groups of data in a three-dimensional view.
XY scatter	Plots data as points on two axes, allowing you to see if a correlation exists between the individual items.
Radar	Looks a little like a radar screen, with concentric circles expanding from the center. Each group of data is drawn as a line from the center to the outside of the chart, with the subtotal of that group displayed on the line in its relative location.

Table 12-1. *Crystal Reports Chart Types*

Chart Type	Usage
Bubble	Very similar to an XY scatter chart, plotting individual points within two axes, but provides more quantitative information by varying the size of the plotted points as well.
Stock	Similar to a bar chart in that it displays side-by-side bars. However, all the bars don't start at the bottom of the chart. Both the tops and bottoms of the bars are based on data supplied. This chart is helpful for viewing minimum and maximum financial data, such as stock prices.
Numeric Axis (new in version 9)	While this actually isn't a new chart "type," it is a new way of creating bar, line, or area charts (discussed previously in this table). A Numeric Axis chart allows you to use a numeric value or date/time field as the X-axis value for the charts.
Gauge (new in version 9)	A gauge chart shows values much as a gauge on an auto dashboard shows the amount of fuel left or the speed of the automobile—a needle points to the value represented by the chart. One gauge appears for each group or single "on change of" value. If there are multiple "on change of" values, multiple needles appear in each gauge.
Gantt (new in version 9)	This is the quintessential "project schedule" chart, showing one bar for each "task," plotting the start and end date. This chart type can only be used with an Advanced Chart (no Group charting is available), and two date or date/time fields must be used with the chart.

Table 12-2.   *Crystal Reports Chart Types* (continued)

Crystal Reports Chart Expert and where they are best used. When you begin to use the Chart Expert, you'll notice that each of these main chart types actually has several variations.

Chart Layout

In addition to the type of chart, you have a choice as to what data the chart will represent. *Cross-Tab charts* and *OLAP charts* are fairly easy to understand—they graph data in existing cross-tab objects or OLAP grids on your report. A *Group chart* graphs data contained in subtotal or summary fields in existing group headers or footers. An *Advanced chart* graphs data in the details section. Your choice of which to use will be based on your individual report design and the way you want to graphically display the data.

It's particularly important to understand the difference between a Group chart and an Advanced chart, and to know where they can be placed on a report. Consider the following illustration:

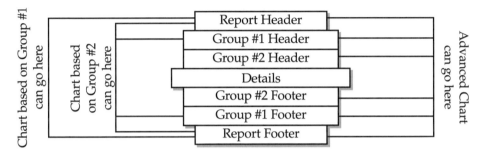

In essence, a chart must always be placed *at least one level higher* than the data it's graphing. An Advanced chart must be placed in a group header or footer or the report header or footer. A Group chart must be placed in a group header or footer of a higher-level group (if there is one), or the report header or footer. Because of the one-level-higher requirement, you can *never* place an Advanced chart or Group chart in the details section—cross-tab and OLAP charts can't go there either.

Cross-Tab and OLAP charts don't fit the one-level-higher scenario. Because they depict data in a specific cross-tab or OLAP grid, they make sense only if they're in the same section as the cross-tab or OLAP grid they're based on. If you base a chart on a cross-tab or OLAP grid, you'll be able to drop it only in the same section. If you later move the cross-tab or OLAP grid to another report section, the chart will automatically move along with it.

Where you place a chart determines the data that it depicts. If you create an Advanced chart and place it in a group header, it will depict just the details sections for that group—a different chart will appear for each group. If you place the same Advanced chart in the report header or footer, it will depict data for the entire report. You'll see the same behavior for a Group chart. If you place it in a higher-level group, it will graph data only for subgroups within the group where it is located. If you place the Group chart in a report header or footer, it will include data for all groups on the report.

Creating Charts with the Chart Expert

You can create a limited set of chart types within the Standard, Cross-Tab, or OLAP Report Wizards from the Report Gallery. To get full charting capabilities, you'll need to use the Chart Expert after you've created a report, either with the Blank Report option or after you've finished using one of the wizards. If you're using one of the report wizards, you will eventually arrive at a Chart section that contains a reduced set of charting options.

If you've already created a report with a wizard and simply want to add a chart to it, or if your report is designed with the Blank Report option, you can display the Chart Expert in one of two ways. Either click the Insert Chart button on the Insert Tools toolbar or choose Insert | Chart from the pull-down menus. The Chart Expert will appear.

The Chart Expert is a tabbed dialog box that gives you tremendous flexibility for designing your charts. You specify chart options by progressing through the Chart Expert's five tabs: Type, Data, Axes, Options, and Text (of which only three are visible if Automatically Set Chart Options is checked).

The Type Tab

When the Chart Expert first appears, the Type tab will be displayed, as shown in Figure 12-1.

First, choose the general type of chart (such as pie, bar, or area) that you want to use from the list. When you make a general choice, you typically see a more specific set of

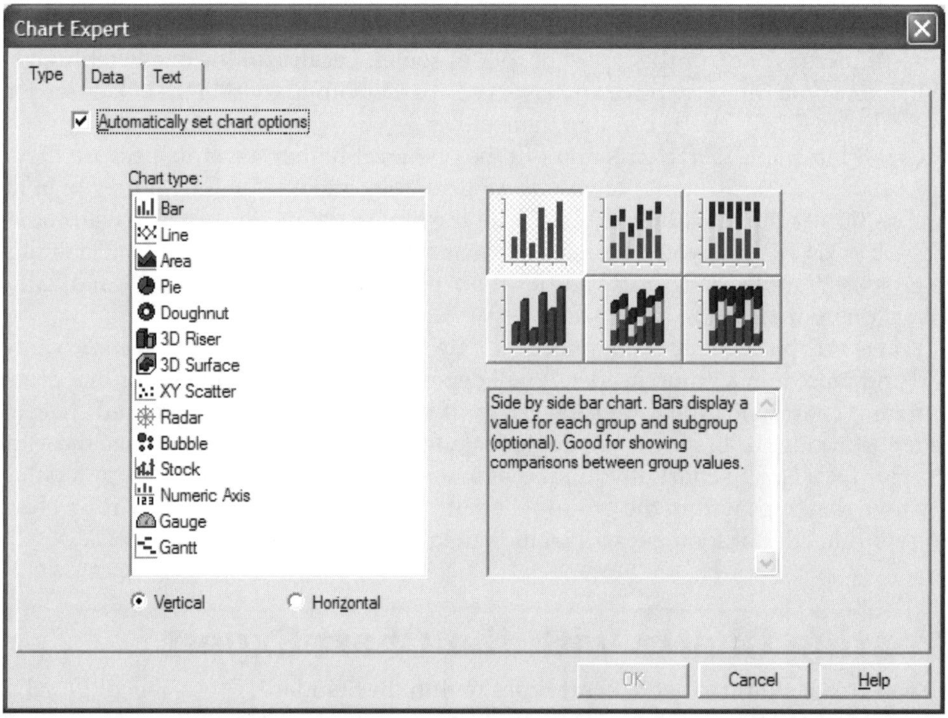

Figure 12-1. *The Chart Expert Type tab*

choices, shown as thumbnails on the right. To use the specific type of chart, click the thumbnail that best represents what you want to use. You'll see a description of the layout and uses of the chart in the scroll box below.

Certain chart types give you a choice of horizontal or vertical direction. If you choose vertical with a bar chart, for example, the bars will grow out of the bottom of the chart. If you choose horizontal, they will spread from the left of the chart toward the right.

If you check Automatically Set Chart Options, the Axes and Options tabs (discussed later in the chapter) will disappear from the Chart Expert and default settings for items on those tabs will be chosen. If you don't like the default settings or need to customize some settings on the Axes or Options tabs, uncheck this option. The tabs will return to the Chart Expert, where you may choose your custom settings.

The Data Tab

The Data tab is where you choose the layout for the chart—whether it will be an Advanced, Group, Cross-Tab, or OLAP chart. You also use the Data tab to select the actual database or formula fields you want Crystal Reports to use when creating your chart, to choose where you want the chart placed, and to specify when you want the chart to "change" graphically (when you want a new bar or pie slice to be created, when you want a new point plotted on the line, and so on).

Begin by choosing the chart layout you want to use. The following four buttons on the left side of the Data tab may or may not be enabled, depending on other elements in your report:

- ■ **Group**   Available only if at least one group has been created on your report.
- ■ **Advanced**   Always available, although it is the default button only if nothing else is available.
- ■ **Cross-Tab**   Available only if one or more cross-tab objects already are on the report. If you have more than one cross-tab but haven't selected the cross-tab you want to chart first, this button will be disabled.
- ■ **OLAP**   Available only if one or more OLAP grids already are on the report. If you have more than one OLAP grid but haven't selected the grid you want to chart first, this button will be disabled.

The only parts of the Data tab that remain constant regardless of the button you choose are the Place Chart drop-down list and the Header and Footer radio buttons. The Place Chart drop-down list lets you choose where on the report you want Crystal Reports to initially place your chart. Again, depending on the chart type you use, the choices here will be different. Group charts can be placed in a higher-level group or in the report header and footer. Advanced, Cross-Tab, and OLAP charts can be placed in a group or report header or footer. Choose Once per Report or For Each *group* from the drop-down list. Then click the radio button that corresponds to where in the report you want the chart placed—the header or footer.

The rest of the Data tab will change based on the chart layout button you click.

Group

A Group chart will graph data from fields in an existing report group. You have to have at least one group defined, with at least one subtotal or summary field, before you can use this button. Figure 12-2 shows the Data tab when the Group button is clicked.

The On Change Of drop-down list lets you choose when you want the graph to start a new element. If, for example, you choose Customer.Country, a new bar will show up in a bar chart for every country. Or for another example, if you choose Employee.Last Name, a new slice in a pie chart will appear for every employee.

The On Change Of drop-down list's contents change in correlation with what you choose in the Place Chart drop-down list. In essence, the On Change Of drop-down list shows you one or two levels lower than where you're placing your chart. For example, if you choose to place the chart Once per Report, the On Change Of drop-down list will

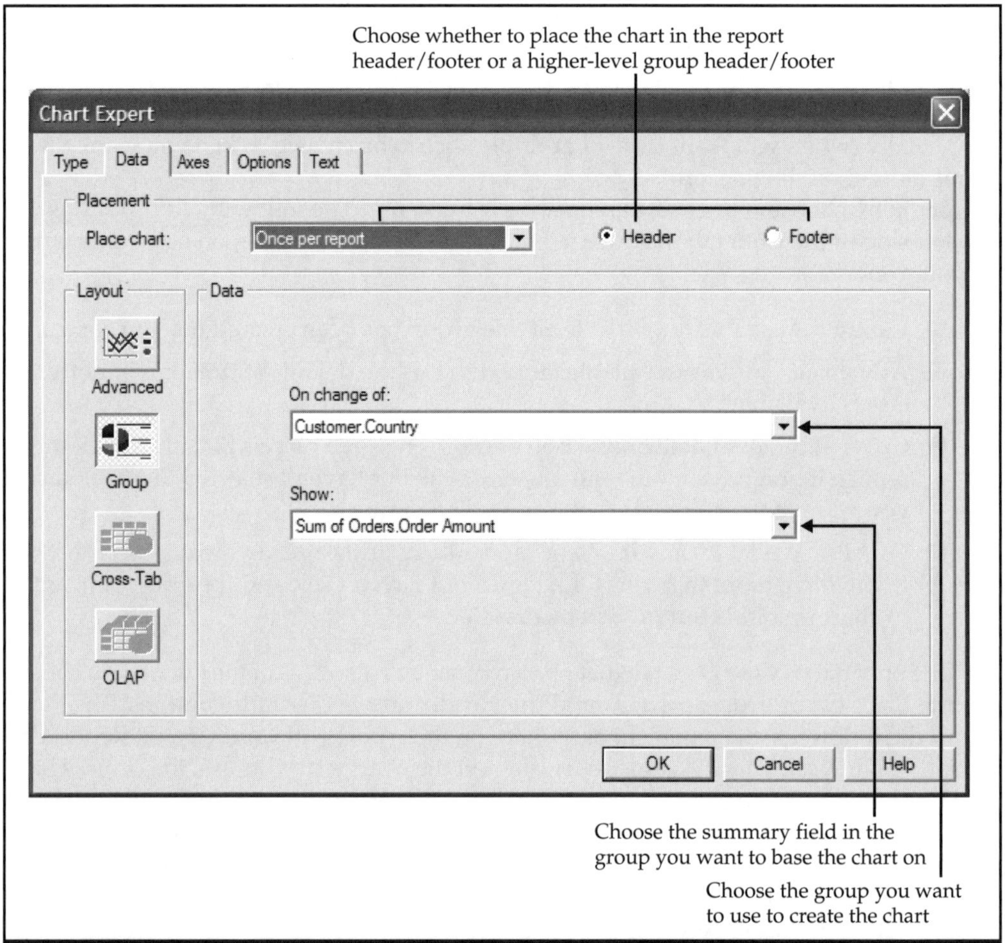

Choose whether to place the chart in the report
header/footer or a higher-level group header/footer

Chart Expert

Type | **Data** | Axes | Options | Text

Placement

Place chart: [Once per report ▾]   ⦿ Header   ○ Footer

Layout | Data

Advanced

Group

Cross-Tab

OLAP

On change of:
[Customer.Country ▾]

Show:
[Sum of Orders.Order Amount ▾]

[OK]   [Cancel]   [Help]

Choose the summary field in the
group you want to base the chart on

Choose the group you want
to use to create the chart

Figure 12-2.   *Data tab for Group button*

show the highest-level group on the report. If there is more than one group, it will also show an additional option of showing the highest-level group and the next-highest-level group. If you choose to place the report in a group, On Change Of will show the next two lower-level groups, and so on.

Here's an example of what shows up in the On Change Of drop-down list when the chart is placed Once per Report and there are country and region groups on the report:

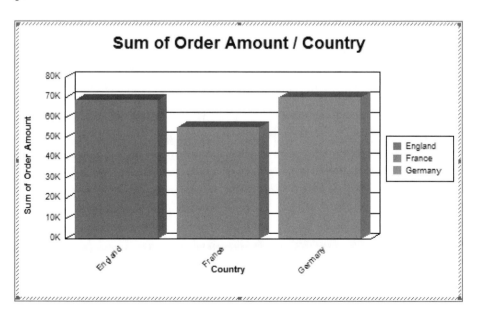

If you choose a single group, your chart will just summarize the values in that group, as shown here:

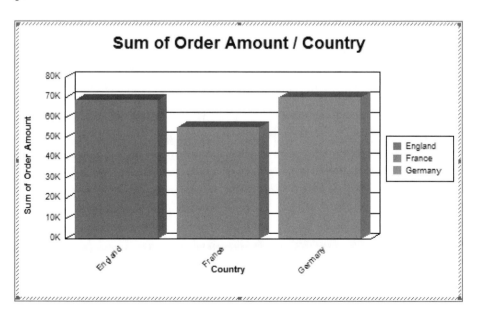

If you choose the two-group option, Crystal Reports actually creates multiple sections of the chart—the first section based on the first group, each containing individual chart elements based on the second group, like this:

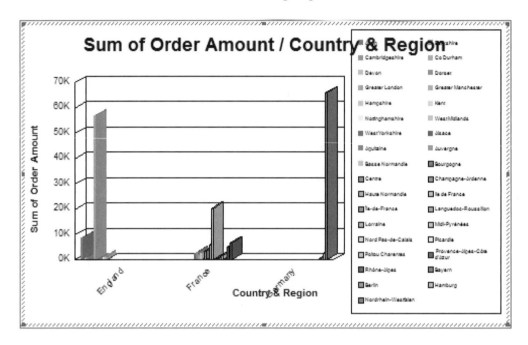

The Show drop-down list lets you choose what makes up the chart element. If, for example, you create a bar chart with On Change Of set to Customer.Country, and Show set to Sum of Orders Detail.Order Amount, you'll see a new bar for every country. The bar's height or width (depending on whether you chose a horizontal or vertical bar chart) will be based on the subtotal of Order Amount for the group.

The Show drop-down list is populated according to what subtotal and summary fields you place in the group header or footer of the group chosen in On Change Of. For a group graph to work, you must have at least one summary or subtotal for the group—if you don't, the Group layout button won't even be available.

Advanced

An Advanced chart graphs data from the details section of your report. Although you can create an Advanced chart even if you have groups defined, it won't be affected by the groups at all. Figure 12-3 shows the Data tab when the Advanced button is clicked.

This rather busy dialog box lets you choose data from the report or database to create a chart (fields don't have to be used on the report to be used to create the chart). Because several different fields in the database can affect the chart's appearance, a little more forethought is required when using this dialog box.

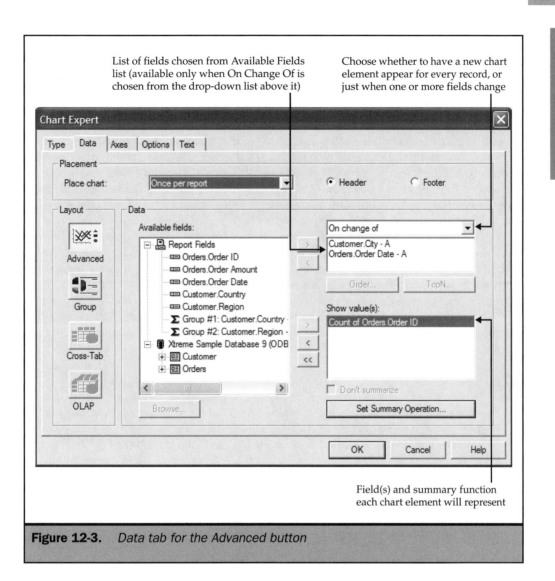

List of fields chosen from Available Fields list (available only when On Change Of is chosen from the drop-down list above it)

Choose whether to have a new chart element appear for every record, or just when one or more fields change

Field(s) and summary function each chart element will represent

Figure 12-3. *Data tab for the Advanced button*

The Available Fields list shows report, formula, subtotal/summary, running total, and database fields in the report. You can select any of these fields that you need for creating your chart (except summary/subtotal fields, which can be used only in the Show Value(s) list). If you're unsure what kind of data is in a field, select it and click the Browse button to see a sample of database data. Once you're ready to use a field as either an On Change Of or Show Value(s) field, select the field and click the right arrow next to the box where you want the field placed. It will be copied to the box on the right.

The drop-down list in the upper right gives you three choices: On Change Of, For Each Record, and For All Records. The choice you make here determines how often a new chart element (bar, pie slice, and so on) will appear in the chart.

If you choose For Each Record, a new element appears in the chart for every record in your details section. This may be useful for very small tables that have only a few records in them. However, if your database has more than a few records, making this choice will probably render a chart that's too crowded to be of any real value. If you choose For All Records, you essentially create a *grand total* chart, showing just one element that displays a total of all records on the report. If you choose the For All Records choice, the box below the drop-down list remains empty—you won't be able to add any fields to it from the Available Fields list. An improvement in version 9 lets you add one field from the Available Fields list if you choose For Each Record—this field will label each chart element.

By choosing On Change Of in the drop-down list and choosing one or more fields from the Available Fields list (except group summary or subtotal fields), you can create a chart that summarizes values for each record. This option basically creates an invisible group on your report and creates a new chart element every time the chosen field changes. For example, if your report contains no groups but you choose On Change Of Customer.Country, your chart will have a new element appear for each unique country that appears in the database. Whatever field you add to the Show Value(s) list will be summarized or subtotaled by country, and the result will be used as the value for the chart.

| Tip | *You can choose one or two fields to add to the On Change Of list. This works like the Group chart option, described previously, in which you can choose to show the highest-level group and the next-highest-level group. If you choose one field, the chart will contain only one section with all the elements located in it. If you choose two fields, the chart will be broken into side-by-side sections, with the first-chosen field making up the first section. Then, individual elements for the second field will appear within each of the sections based on the first field.* |

Although there isn't an actual group on the report, Crystal Reports is creating an "invisible" group to base your chart on. You have control over the way the Chart Expert uses these groups. The TopN and Order buttons control this. If you click the TopN button, you'll see the Group Sort Expert dialog box, in which you can choose to include only the top N, bottom N, Top N Percentage, or Bottom N percentage groups in your chart, and choose which number to use for N.

Group Sort Expert

Analyze report or chart results by taking the Top N or Sort of totals.

Customer.Country | Customer.Region

For this group sort

Top Percentage ▾   based on   Count of Orders.Order ID ▾

Where Percentage is: ☐ Include Others, with the name:

75   Others

                                        ☐ Include ties

[OK]   [Cancel]   [Help]

If you click the Order button, you'll see the Chart Sort Order dialog box with a
drop-down list containing Ascending, Descending, Specified Order, and Original Order
options. You may choose to show the chart elements in A to Z order, Z to A order, or
using specified grouping (and, if you recall from Chapter 3, although Original Order
is an option, it's probably of little use). If the chosen field is a date, time, or date/time
field, you can choose how often you want a new chart element to appear (monthly,
weekly, every minute, hourly, and so on). Refer to Chapter 3 for information on Top N,
Specified Order grouping, and grouping on date/time fields.

Chart Sort Order

Common

When the report is printed, the records will be sorted and
grouped by:

▭ Orders.Order Date ▾

in ascending order. ▾

The section will be printed:

for each month. ▾

[OK]   [Cancel]   [Help]

Once you've chosen a field in the On Change Of box to determine when a new chart element will appear, you can add a field or fields to the Show Value(s) list to indicate which values Crystal Reports will use to size the chart element. If you add multiple fields to this list, the chart will contain multiple bars, lines, and so forth—one for each field you add to the list.

If you add a number or currency field to this list (and you haven't chosen For Each Record in the top drop-down list), Crystal Reports automatically uses the Sum function to subtotal the field for each invisible group. If you choose another type of field, Crystal Reports automatically uses the Count function. If you wish to change the summary function (for example, to graph the average sales amount instead of the total), you can select the field you want to change in the Show Value(s) list and click the Set Summary Operation button. A dialog box will appear with a drop-down list containing the available summary functions for that type of field. Choose the summary function you want used to size the chart element. The Percentage Summary Field option for group summaries, discussed in Chapter 3, is also available here. By checking the Show As a Percentage Of check box, you can choose a higher-level group total or grand total, and chart elements will display the percentage of the higher totals that each of the invisible group totals represents.

If you choose For Each Record in the top drop-down list, Crystal Reports will display a new chart element for every record on the report—no invisible group will be created. In this case, any fields you add to the Show Value(s) list won't be summarized—whatever value the fields return for each record will be charted. In previous versions of Crystal Reports, if you chose On Change Of in the top drop-down list and the invisible groups were created, you could specify that one or more values in the Show Value(s) list *not* be summarized, by selecting the field and checking Don't Summarize Values. While this check box still appears in the Advanced chart options for version 9, it's always grayed out and can't be used.

Cross-Tab

The Cross-Tab button is available only if you have one or more cross-tab objects on your report. If you have only one cross-tab object, this button will be enabled even if you haven't selected the cross-tab first. However, if you have more than one cross-tab, you must select the cross-tab that you want to chart *before* you start the Chart Expert (Chapter 11 discusses cross-tab objects). Figure 12-4 shows the Data tab when the Cross-Tab button is clicked.

The On Change Of drop-down list includes the two outer fields you chose for your cross-tab row and column; if you used multiple row and column fields, only the first row or field can be used. Crystal Reports will create one chart element (bar, pie slice, and so on) for each occurrence of this field in the cross-tab.

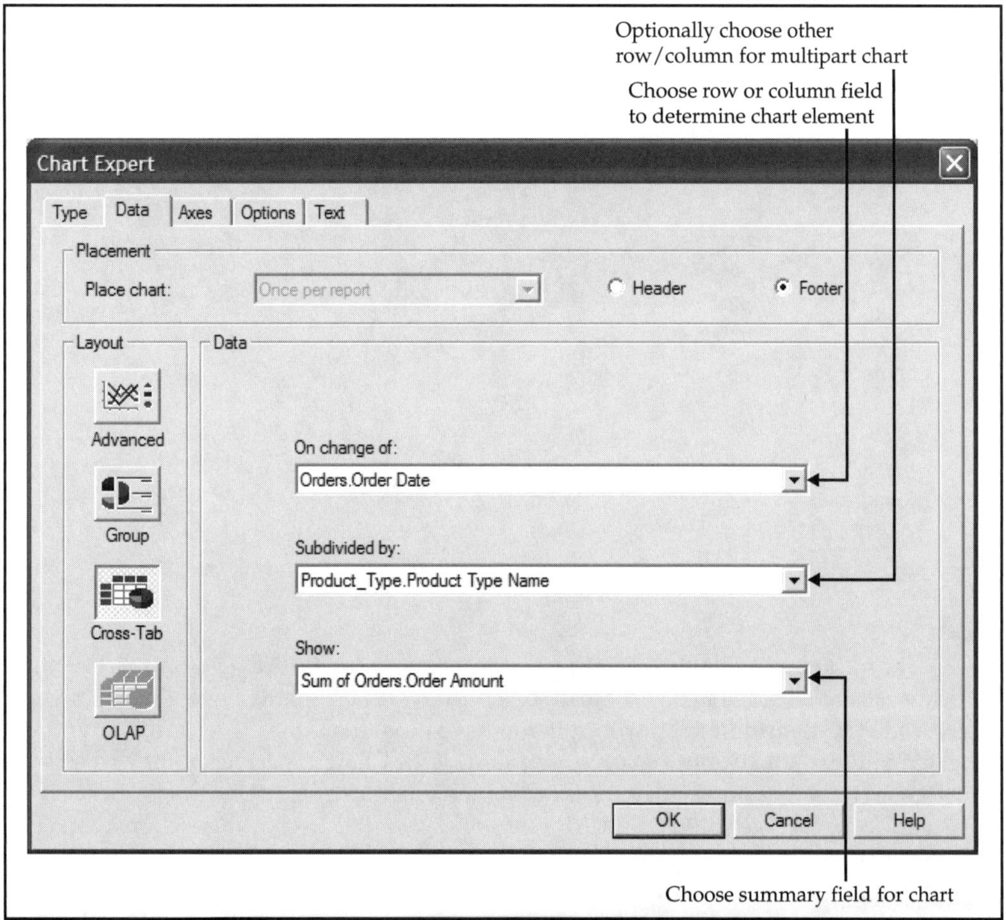

Figure 12-4. *Data tab for the Cross-Tab button*

The Subdivided By drop-down list is initially set to None. If you leave it this way, the chart will create only one series of chart elements, based on the field in the On Change Of drop-down list. If, however, you want to create two series of elements for side-by-side comparison, or if you're using a 3-D riser or 3-D area chart and want to see multiple elements three-dimensionally, choose the other row/column field in the Subdivided By drop-down list.

The Show drop-down list shows the summary field or fields you placed in your cross-tab. Choose the field that you want to use in your chart. This field determines the size of the chart elements (height of a bar, size of a pie slice, and so forth).

The following illustration shows the resulting 3-D riser chart for the Data tab shown in Figure 12-4:

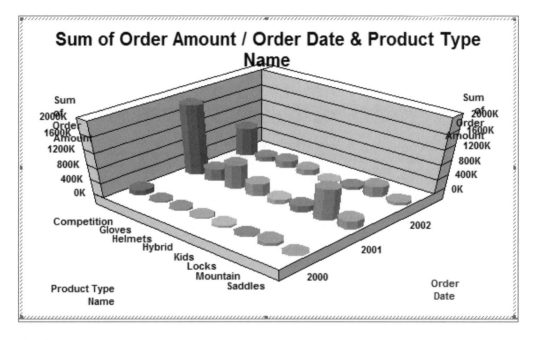

OLAP

The OLAP button is available only if you have one or more OLAP grid objects on your report. If you have only one OLAP grid, this button will be enabled even if you haven't selected the OLAP grid first. However, if you have more than one OLAP grid, you must select the grid that you want to chart *before* you start the Chart Expert (Chapter 18 discusses OLAP reporting). Figure 12-5 shows the Data tab when the OLAP button is clicked.

Creating a chart based on an OLAP grid is very similar to creating a chart based on a cross-tab. There are just a couple of differences between the two. There is no summary field to choose (OLAP grids display only one value, so there is no choice to make). Also, the dimension hierarchy of your OLAP grid may be a little different than the multiple row/column fields you added to a cross-tab object.

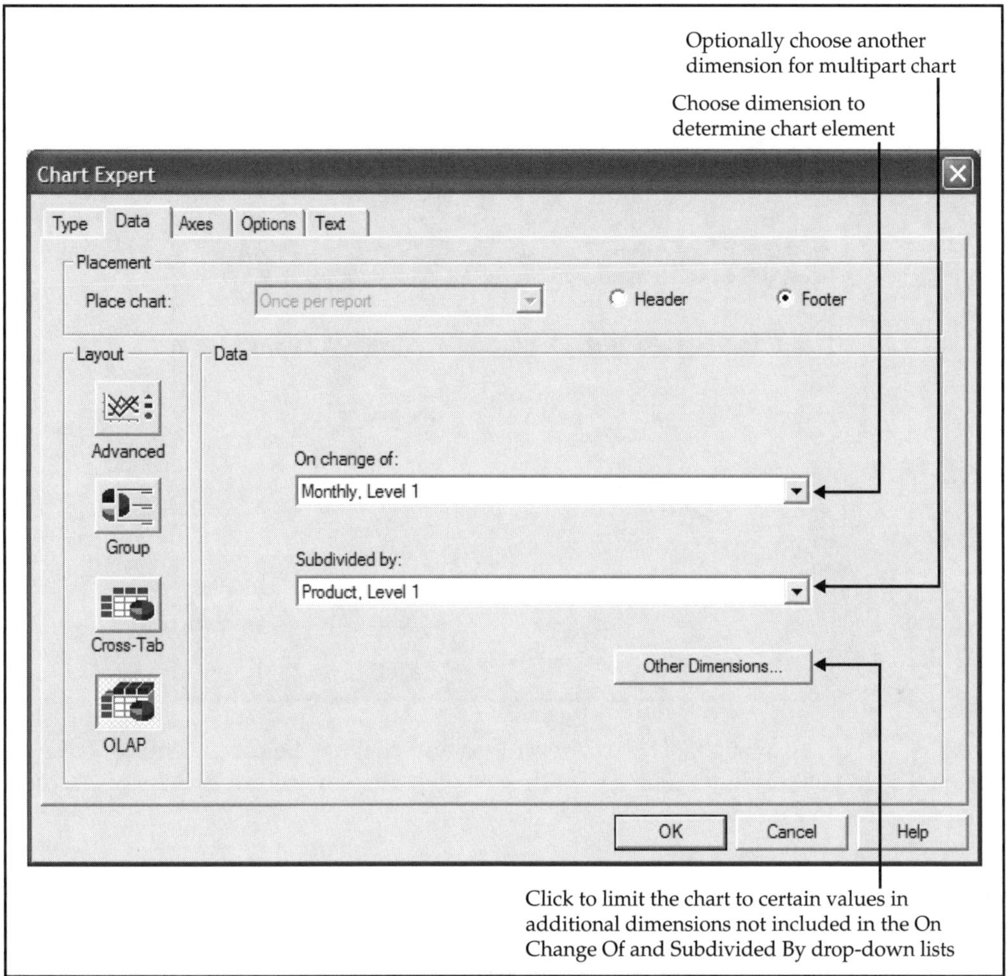

Optionally choose another
dimension for multipart chart

Choose dimension to
determine chart element

Chart Expert   ⊠

Type | Data | Axes | Options | Text |

Placement

Place chart: Once per report   ▼   ○ Header   ⊙ Footer

Layout   Data

🔲 Advanced

🔲 Group

🔲 Cross-Tab

🔲 OLAP

On change of:

Monthly, Level 1   ▼

Subdivided by:

Product, Level 1   ▼

Other Dimensions...

OK   Cancel   Help

Click to limit the chart to certain values in
additional dimensions not included in the On
Change Of and Subdivided By drop-down lists

Figure 12-5.   *Data tab for the OLAP button*

Choose a dimension on which to base the chart from the On Change Of drop-down list. A new chart element will be created for every occurrence of this dimension. If you leave the Subdivided By drop-down list set to None, the chart creates only one series of chart elements, based on the dimension in the On Change Of drop-down list. If, however, you want to create two series of elements for side-by-side comparison, or if you're using a 3-D riser or 3-D area chart and want to see multiple elements three-dimensionally, choose another dimension in the Subdivided By drop-down list. You can choose a next "deeper" level dimension here if you've created multiple levels of dimensions in your OLAP grid.

Depending on how many dimensions your OLAP grid contains, and how the fields that make up the dimension relate to each other (their *hierarchy*), you may need to filter the chart to just certain field values in a dimension. To do this, click the Other Dimensions button in the lower right of the Data tab. This displays the Format Other Dimensions dialog box, where you can choose the particular subdimension of the OLAP grid that you want the chart filtered by.

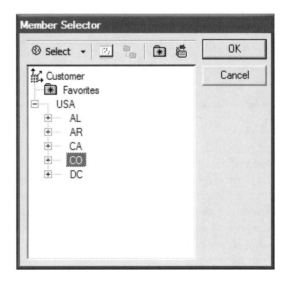

Click one of the available Other Dimensions and click the Select a Member Value button. The Member Selector dialog box appears, with the dimension hierarchy displayed in an Explorer-like fashion.

Navigate through the dimension hierarchy and choose a level that you want to limit the chart to. For example, if you navigate down from USA and choose CO, your OLAP chart will just contain totals for the Colorado region in the OLAP grid.

Tip   *You can experiment with OLAP grids and charts by using a sample OLAP cube file installed with Crystal Reports. Create an OLAP grid (using the steps described in Chapter 18) based on the Crystal Analysis Server cube file Program Files\Crystal Decisions\Crystal Reports 9\Samples\En\Databases\Olap Data\Xtreme.hdc. Note that you must have included the OLAP Data data access type when you installed Crystal Reports in order to create an OLAP grid. You can then create a chart based on this OLAP grid.*

The Axes Tab

The Axes tab will appear if you leave the Automatically Set Chart Options check box unchecked on the Data tab. The Axes tab gives you complete control over how Crystal Reports displays the X, Y, and Z (if you're using a 3-D chart) axes of the chart. Figure 12-6 shows the Axes tab.

By making choices in the Axes tab, you can control how Crystal Reports displays axes on your charts. The *axes* are the areas of the chart that describe or depict the data values in the chart. If, for example, you have a bar chart in which each bar represents sales volume for a salesperson, the bottom of the chart where each salesperson is listed is called the *group axis* (also sometimes called the *X axis*). The left side of the chart where the numbers representing the volume appear is called the *data axis* (sometimes called the *Y axis*), as shown here:

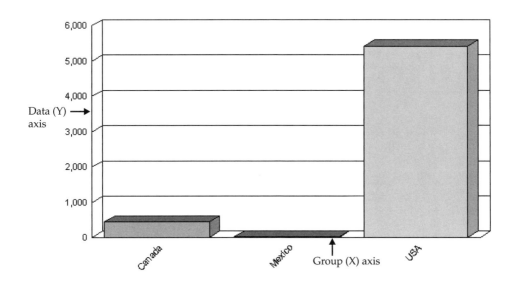

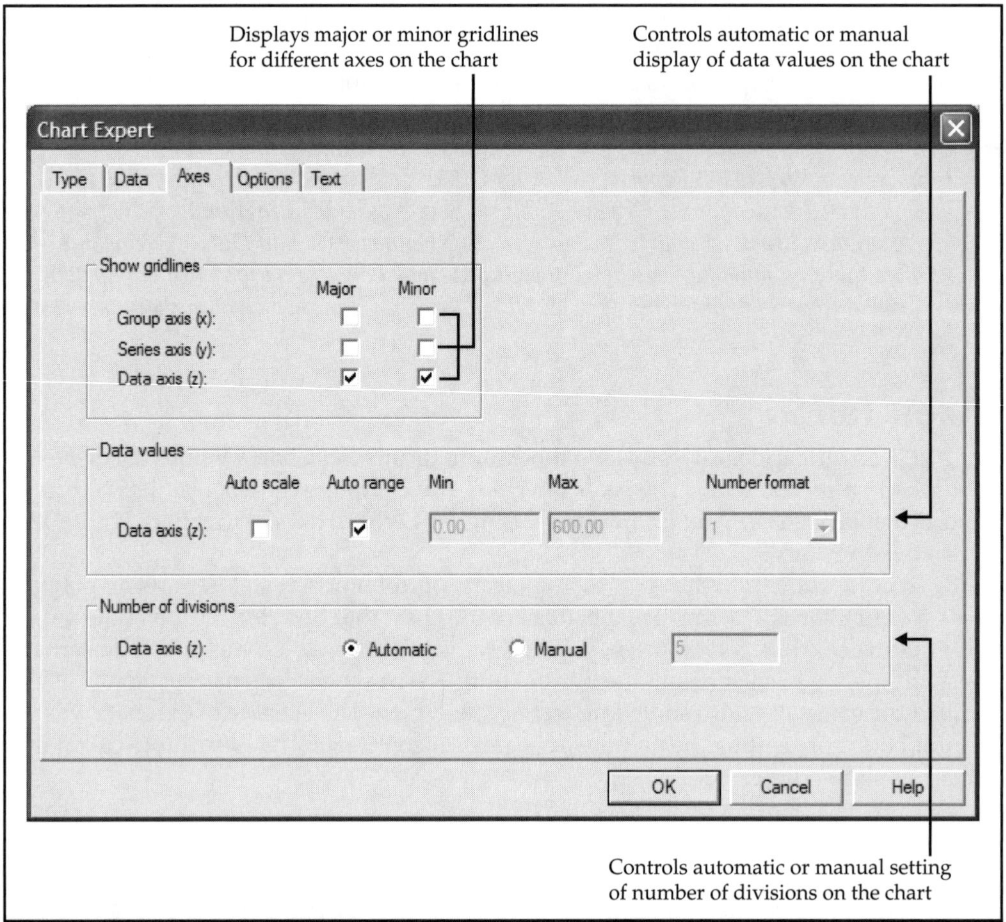

Displays major or minor gridlines for different axes on the chart
Controls automatic or manual display of data values on the chart
Chart Expert
Type
Data
Axes
Options
Text
Show gridlines
Major
Minor
Group axis (x):
Series axis (y):
Data axis (z):
Data values
Auto scale
Auto range
Min
Max
Number format
Data axis (z):
0.00
600.00
1
Number of divisions
Data axis (z):
Automatic
Manual
5
OK
Cancel
Help
Controls automatic or manual setting of number of divisions on the chart

Figure 12-6. *The Axes tab*

If you are using a 3-D chart, the data axis is the Z axis, and a new axis called the *series axis* is the Y axis, like this:

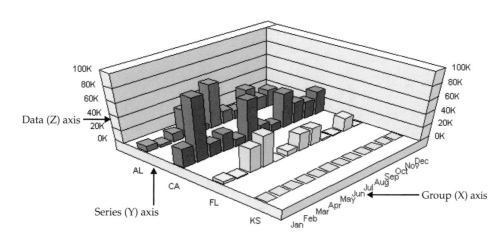

Click the Major or Minor check boxes to add gridlines to the chosen axes. *Major gridlines* fall directly in line with the axis labels that Crystal Reports assigns to the axis. *Minor gridlines* appear in between the axis labels and work only for numeric labels. Depending on the type of chart you're using, you may not notice any difference between major and minor gridlines. Also, some charts will always have a group axis gridline, regardless of what you choose on the Axes tab.

If you leave the Auto Range check box for the Data Values option on, Crystal Reports automatically formats the chart according to the number of elements it includes. If you wish to customize this, you can turn off the Auto Range option and add starting and ending values for the axes, as well as choose the number format (decimals, currency symbols, and so on) to use for the labels. If you choose a certain number format, such as a currency symbol, and then recheck Auto Range, the axes will be automatically renumbered, but the number format you chose will stay in place. The Auto Scale option affects the beginning numeric value that the data axis starts with. If you choose Auto Scale, Crystal Reports uses the values of the chart elements to choose an appropriate starting number for the data axis.

If you leave the Number of Divisions set to Automatic, Crystal Reports will create a predefined number of labels and gridlines for the data axes. Clicking the Manual radio button and specifying a number in the text box will create your specified number of divisions, along with labels and gridlines, for the data axes.

> **Note**
> *Not all of the options on the Axes tab will necessarily apply to the style of chart you are using. For example, a pie chart doesn't use any axes options. If the chart you've chosen doesn't use axes, the tab won't even appear in the Chart Expert.*

The Options Tab

The Options tab will appear if you leave the Automatically Set Chart Options check box unchecked on the Data tab. The Options tab allows you to customize general options for your chart, such as whether to display it in color or black and white, whether to show a legend and where to place it, and other options. The Options tab will change based on the type of chart you've chosen. Figure 12-7 shows the Options tab for a bar chart.

> **Tip**
> *If you're printing your reports on a black-and-white printer, it may be preferable to leave the chart in color and let the printer assign gray tones to the chart elements. These may actually look better than the ones Crystal Reports assigns. Experiment to determine what works best with your particular printer.*

The Data Points section lets you choose whether you want labels or numbers to appear on your chart elements. If, for example, you choose Show Label with a pie chart, each of the slices of the pie will be labeled with the item that the slice refers to. If you choose Show Value with a bar chart and choose a number format of $1, you'll see the actual dollar amounts (with no decimal places) appear above each bar.

The Marker Size and Marker Shape drop-down lists let you choose how markers look on a line chart. *Markers* are the points on the line chart that are connected by the lines.

The Show Legend check box determines whether or not a legend appears on your chart. The *legend* is the color-coded key that indicates what the elements of your chart refer to. You can also choose where to place the legend with options in the Placement drop-down list. You might want legends for a pie chart with no labels, for example. However, if you are using a bar chart with labels already appearing along the bottom of the chart, a legend is redundant and should be turned off.

The Text Tab

The Text tab, shown in Figure 12-8, allows you to assign text to different parts of your chart, and change the appearance of these text items. You can add a chart title, subtitle, and footnote. Also, you can place titles on the group, data, and series (or data2) axes of your chart.

By default, the Auto-Text check boxes are all selected and the text boxes next to them are dimmed. You'll notice that Crystal Reports has added titles into certain items

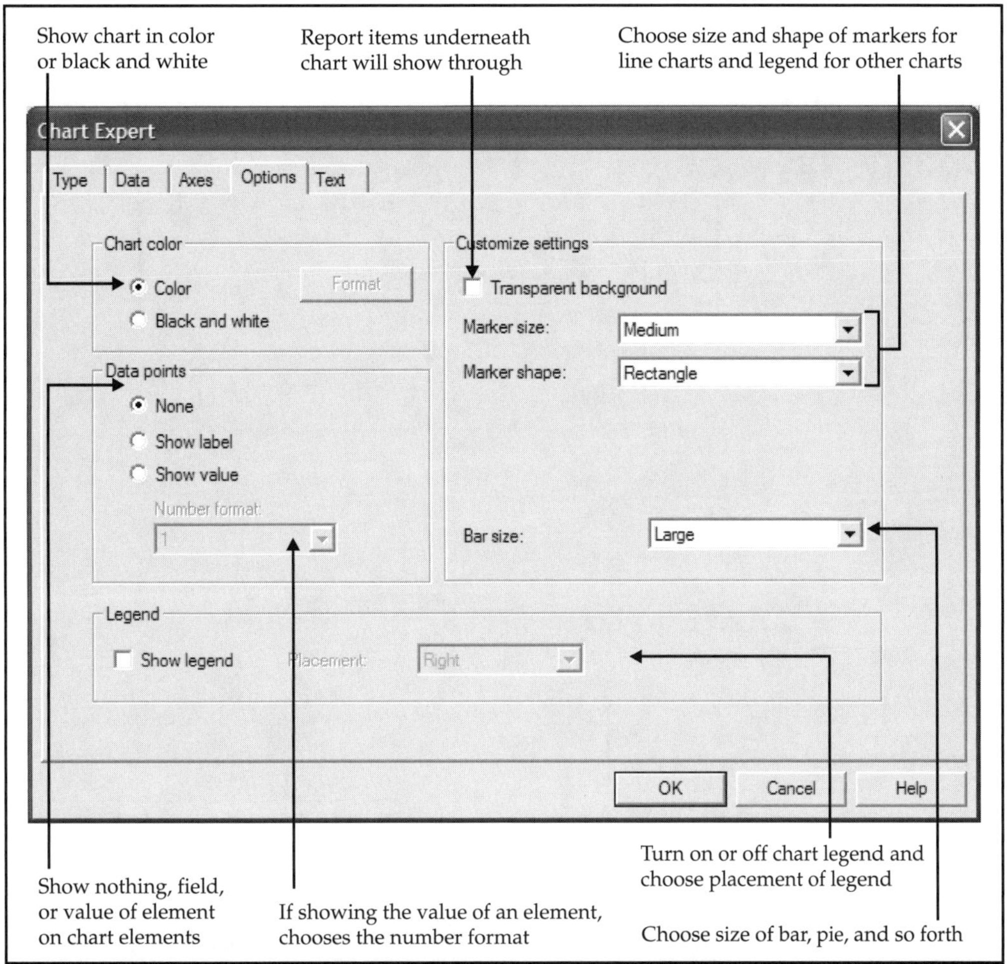

Show chart in color or black and white

Report items underneath chart will show through

Choose size and shape of markers for line charts and legend for other charts

Chart Expert

Type | Data | Axes | Options | Text

Chart color
- (•) Color   [Format]
- ( ) Black and white

Customize settings
- [ ] Transparent background
- Marker size: [Medium ▾]
- Marker shape: [Rectangle ▾]

Data points
- (•) None
- ( ) Show label
- ( ) Show value
- Number format: [1 ▾]

Bar size: [Large ▾]

Legend
- [ ] Show legend   Placement: [Right ▾]

[OK]   [Cancel]   [Help]

Show nothing, field, or value of element on chart elements

If showing the value of an element, chooses the number format

Turn on or off chart legend and choose placement of legend

Choose size of bar, pie, and so forth

Figure 12-7. *The Options tab*

automatically, depending on the data that the chart is based on. If you don't wish to use Crystal Reports' default titles on the chart, uncheck the Auto-Text check box for the desired title and then type the material you want to appear on the chart in the associated text boxes on the Text tab. If you leave a text box blank, that title won't appear on the chart.

To change the appearance of the different items, select the item you want to change in the list on the lower right of the Text tab. Then, click the Font button to choose the

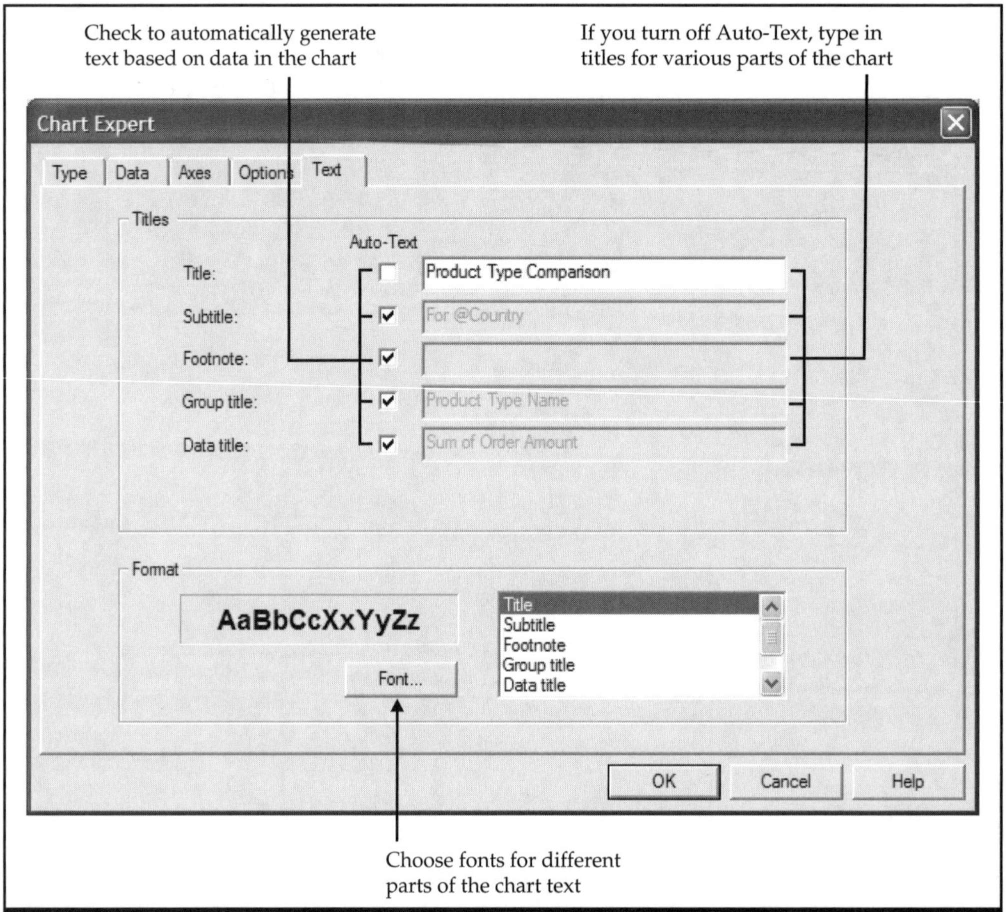

Check to automatically generate
text based on data in the chart

If you turn off Auto-Text, type in
titles for various parts of the chart

Chart Expert ⊠

| Type | Data | Axes | Options | Text |

Titles

Auto-Text

Title: ☐ Product Type Comparison

Subtitle: ☑ For @Country

Footnote: ☑

Group title: ☑ Product Type Name

Data title: ☑ Sum of Order Amount

Format

AaBbCcXxYyZz

Font...

| Title |
| Subtitle |
| Footnote |
| Group title |
| Data title |

OK | Cancel | Help

Choose fonts for different
parts of the chart text

Figure 12-8. *The Text tab*

font face, size, and appearance for that item. A sample of the font you choose appears
in the shaded box above the Font button.

Figure 12-9 shows a chart with all the labels set. You can see where each of the
labels appears on a typical chart.

Placing and Sizing Charts

Once you complete all the information on the Chart Expert and click OK, Crystal Reports
places the chart in the upper-left corner of the header or footer section you chose. Unlike
other objects you add, it won't initially be attached to your mouse cursor allowing you
to drop it where you wish. If other objects are already in the section, the chart is placed

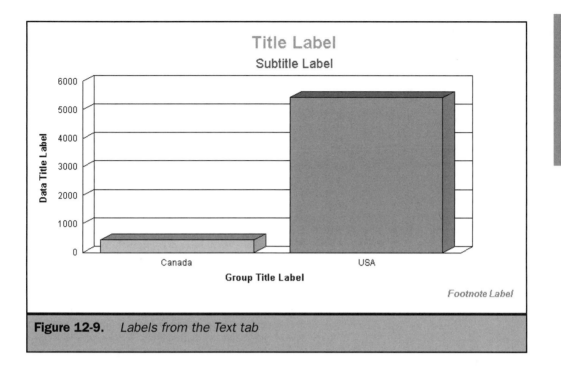

Figure 12-9. *Labels from the Text tab*

on top of them (the Transparent Background option on the Chart Expert's Options tab allows objects underneath the chart to show through).

When the chart is placed, it remains selected, however. You'll notice the shaded outline and sizing handles around the chart. You can now drag it to another location in the same section, or move it to another section on the report. You can also resize the chart by using the sizing handles, or move and resize the chart by choosing Format | Size and Position from the pull-down menus, or by right-clicking the chart and choosing Size and Position from the pop-up menu.

Remember that where you place a chart determines the data that it displays. If you place an Advanced or Group chart in the report header or footer, it will display data for the whole report. If you place the chart in a group header or footer, the chart will appear for every group, showing data for only that particular group. Cross-Tab and OLAP charts display the data from the particular objects they're based on. If you place a cross-tab object and matching chart in a group header or footer, the cross-tab and chart will display data only for the group they're in. Since OLAP grids don't change with their location on the report, a matching OLAP chart won't change if you move it.

Cross-Tab and OLAP charts are always in the same section as their matching cross-tab object or OLAP grid object. You may have an OLAP grid in the report footer and its matching chart in the report header, but if you try to move the chart into a group header or footer, it won't work. And if you then move the OLAP grid from the report footer to a group footer, the chart will automatically move to the matching group header.

> **Tip** *If you create a chart based on, say, a Region field, but years appear in the Design tab, don't be surprised. The charts that appear in the Design tab are "dummy" charts that don't depict actual data in the database. When you preview the report, however, you will see live data depicted in the chart.*

Placing Charts Alongside Text

When you first create a chart in a section, it's placed in the upper-left corner of the section by default. If the chart is in a report or group header, the chart will print before the rest of the report or the group, because the section containing the chart prints first. Sometimes, you may want a chart to appear *alongside* the data it's referring to. Typically, this might be an Advanced chart that you've placed in a group header. Instead of having the chart print by itself, followed by the details that belong to the group, you may want the chart to print alongside the details sections.

By using the Underlay option in the Section Expert, you can format the group header section to underlay the following details sections, thereby printing the chart alongside the other items. For this to work effectively, you need to size and move the details section objects so that they won't be overprinted by the chart. Then, move and size the chart so that it will appear to the side of the details section objects. Using the Section Expert, choose the Underlay Following Sections option for the section containing the chart. If there is a group name, column headings, or other information in the group header that you *don't* want to be underlain, you need to create a second group header section for the chart that you underlay. Format it to use the Underlay feature and format the first group header containing the textual information with Underlay turned off. See Chapter 10 for more information on multiple sections and the Underlay feature.

Figure 12-10 shows a chart placed in a Group Header with Underlay Following Sections turned on.

Modifying Existing Charts

Once you've created a chart, you may wish to change it. Perhaps you prefer to see a pie chart instead of a bar chart. Or, you may want to change the titles that appear on the chart. You may even want to change the chart from an Advanced chart to a Group chart, or vice versa.

First, select the chart you want to change in either the Design or Preview tab. Then, choose Format | Chart Expert from the pull-down menus, or right-click the selected chart and choose Chart Expert from the pop-up menu. The Chart Expert will reappear, and you can make any desired changes before clicking OK.

Zooming In and Out on Charts

You may zoom in and out on a limited number of chart types. If you have created a Bar or Line chart, you'll notice additional options available on the pop-up menu when you

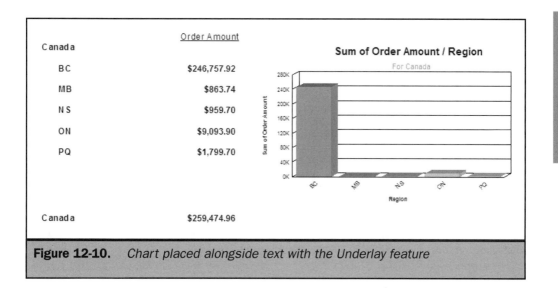

	Order Amount
Canada	
BC	$246,757.92
MB	$863.74
NS	$959.70
ON	$9,093.90
PQ	$1,799.70
Canada	$259,474.96

Figure 12-10. *Chart placed alongside text with the Underlay feature*

right-click the Chart: Select Mode (selected by default) and Zoom In. You may also select a chart and use the Zoom options from the Chart pull-down menu.

If you choose the Zoom In option, your mouse cursor will change to a magnifying glass with a plus sign. While you may be tempted to just click somewhere inside the chart expecting to zoom in, you must actually hold down your mouse button and draw an elastic box with the mouse. When you release the mouse button, the chart will zoom in to the area you surrounded. You may continue to highlight additional areas to zoom in further on the chart.

To zoom back out, right-click the chart and choose Zoom Out from the pop-up menu, or choose the associated option from the Chart pull-down menu. The mouse cursor will change to a magnifying glass with a minus sign. Just click anywhere on the chart to zoom back out.

When you're finished zooming in or out on a chart, choose Select Mode from the chart pop-up or pull-down menus. Your mouse cursor will return to its default "four-arrow" state so that you can select the chart to move or resize it on the report.

Note *Zoom and pan options were available on an Analyzer toolbar and Analyzer pull-down menu in previous versions of Crystal Reports. The Analyzer view and its related toolbars and menus have been eliminated from Crystal Reports 9. You may make all the previous Analyzer choices on either Chart pop-up menus or the Chart pull-down menu in version 9.*

Drilling Down on Charts

If you create a Group chart, you'll notice the mouse cursor change to a magnifying glass when you point to a chart element. This drill-down cursor indicates that you can double-click a chart element that you're interested in to drill down on the chart. When you drill down on a chart element, another tab appears next to the Preview tab for the particular group you drilled down on. Drill-down allows your report viewer to interact with charts, much as they interact with group footer and group header subtotal and summary fields.

By creative use of Group charts and hiding of details and group header/footer sections, you can create a very visually appealing interactive report for use in online reporting environments. You could, for example, create a large Group pie chart and place it in the report header, along with grand totals and text objects. You might add a text object that directs the viewer to double-click a pie slice for more information. You may also set Tool Tip text for the chart, prompting the viewer to double-click the slice they're interested in. Select the chart and right-click, choosing Format Chart from the pop-up menu. Then, use the Conditional Formula button to add Tool Tip text.

To add even more interactivity, you could add lower-level Group or Advanced charts in the report's group headers or footers, hiding them with the Section Expert. When the user drills down on the higher-level chart in the report header, a drill-down tab showing a more detailed chart will open. You can create drill-down levels until the user eventually reaches details sections to see low-level transaction data.

Get more information about creating multiple groups, drill-down, and hidden sections in Chapters 3 and 10.

Tip   *Drill-down is available and useful only when viewing a report in its native format. Viewers can drill down on reports displayed right on the Preview tab of Crystal Reports, by using a report integrated with a custom Windows application, or by using Crystal Reports Web-based viewers, including Crystal Enterprise (discussed in Part II of this book). Drill-down doesn't work with reports exported to other file formats, such as Word and Excel. Obviously, drill-down won't be effective with printed reports.*

Finer Points of Chart Formatting

In Crystal Reports 8 and 8.5, you had to use a separate chart view known as "Analyzer view" to perform detailed chart formatting. In Crystal Reports 9, the Analyzer is gone and you can perform all chart formatting directly in the Design or Preview tabs. Now, not only can you view charts in the Preview tab alongside other report elements around them, but you can perform *in-place* formatting of charts as well.

Caution   *While in-place chart formatting reduces the number of steps required to format individual chart elements, it also makes it easier to inadvertently move or resize an individual chart element when you mean to move or resize the entire chart. Pay close attention to what has been highlighted (the entire chart, or an individual chart element) before you move or resize with your mouse.*

One of the first new options with Crystal Reports 9 that you should become familiar with is the *Auto Arrange Chart* option. Once you've selected a chart, you may choose this option either from the Chart pull-down menu or by right-clicking on the chart and choosing it from the pop-up menu. This option will use default placement, sizing, and formatting for chart elements. If you haven't done any individual element formatting since you've created the chart, this option very well may not do anything at all. However, if you've changed positions of certain items (such as the chart title, legend, or axes titles), you may see them snap back to other positions that you didn't intend. Don't worry too much about this behavior—if you don't like the changes that Auto Arrange makes to the chart, you may undo its effects with Edit | Undo from the pull-down menus, the Undo toolbar button in the Standard toolbar, or by pressing CTRL-Z.

New Version 9 Conditional Formatting

While you can pick individual chart elements, such as an individual pie wedge, or an individual bar, and change the color (discussed later in the chapter under "Changing Colors and Shades of Chart Elements"), your change will always affect the same wedge or bar in each chart, regardless of what the value of that element is. In other words, if you change the pie wedge for Colorado, which happens to be the second wedge in the chart, to a light blue color, the second wedge in the chart will be light blue no matter what data populates the chart. If the data changes so that Colorado becomes the fourth wedge, the second wedge will still be formatted as light blue.

Crystal Reports 9 has introduced *Conditional Formatting* to the Chart Expert. This option, which is available only for certain chart types, is available by clicking the Format button in the Color section of the Options tab (see Figure 12-7). This button, which will be enabled only if the chart type allows conditional formatting, will display the Chart Color Format Expert, shown in Figure 12-11.

This dialog box is similar to the Highlighting Expert used to conditionally format textual elements on the report (the Highlighting Expert is discussed in Chapter 9). By choosing either the "On Change Of" field that the chart is based on or the summary field used to determine the weight of the chart element, you can conditionally set the color of the chart element.

For example, Figure 12-11 shows a condition set up to change the color of the chart element (in this case, the wedge of a donut chart) to Teal if the value shown by the wedge exceeds $100,000. To set this condition, click the New button, which will add a new condition to the Item list. Then, choose the field you want to base the condition on and the comparison operator (such as equal to, greater than, and so forth) in the first two drop-down lists of the Value Of section. Type the value you want to compare to in the text box in the same section. Then, choose the color you wish the chart element to display if the condition is true from the color list on the lower right. Any chart elements that meet the condition will be given the chosen color.

You may add as many conditions as you wish by clicking the Add button multiple times. If you have multiple conditions that may conflict, such as a condition that looks for a value between 100 and 1,000, and another condition that looks for a value greater than 500, you can set the priority of the conditions by using the up and down arrows at the top of the item list. Conditions toward the top of the item list take priority.

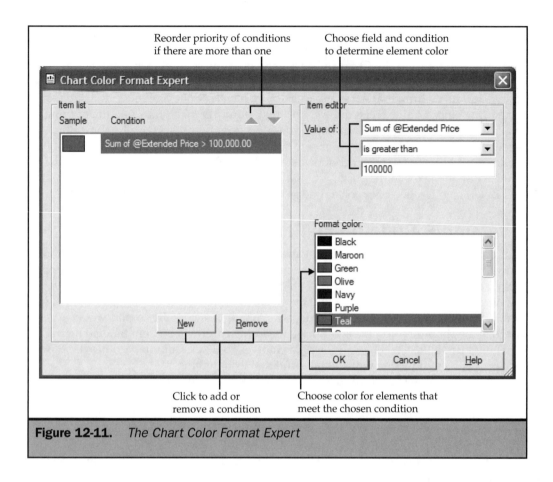

Figure 12-11.   *The Chart Color Format Expert*

Once you click OK on the Chart Color Format Expert and then click OK to close the Chart Expert, the chart will apply the chosen color to elements that meet the condition, regardless of which actual element (second, fifth, and so forth) appears.

Customizing Charts with Chart Options

While you can control a good deal of chart formatting from within the Chart Expert, there will probably be many times when you wish to have more detailed control over chart appearance. Crystal Reports allows you either to select individual elements of the chart (such as the title, individual bars or pie wedges, the legend, and so forth) and apply formatting to them, or to make more specific changes that affect the overall chart appearance.

To perform generalized formatting on the entire chart, choose Chart | Chart Options from the pull-down menus or right-click the chart and choose Chart Options from the pop-up menu. A submenu will appear with various chart-formatting options.

Depending on the type of chart you're using and the formatting option you choose, different dialog boxes will appear with different options. Some dialog boxes can be quite complex, with both vertical and horizontal sets of tabs to provide a wide array of options.

Notice the thumbnail miniature picture of the chart in the dialog box. As you make changes to the dialog box, you'll see the changes immediately reflected in the thumbnail. When you click OK, the chart will reflect the changes.

Tip   *Any changes you make to a chart using Chart Options will apply to only that one instance of the chart back on the Preview tab. If, for example, you choose a chart in the Canada group header and customize it with Chart Options, the other charts in the USA and Mexico group headers won't be affected. If you want to have these changes propagate to all other chart instances, right-click the chart and choose Apply Changes to All Charts from the pop-up menu, or choose Chart | Apply Changes to All Charts from the pull-down menus.*

Various customization options are available, depending on the type of chart you've chosen, the number of data elements the chart is showing, and so forth. Some of the more useful capabilities are discussed in the following sections.

Changing Colors and Shades of Chart Elements

When you create a chart in the Chart Expert, your only choices on the Options tab for affecting chart colors are the Color and the Black and White radio buttons (a new Format button has been added for conditional color selection—this is covered earlier in this section).

By choosing the Color radio button, you have no control over what individual colors or shades the chart elements will have. The ability to completely customize element colors and shades is a feature available with Chart Options.

Begin by selecting the element you wish to color. This can be an individual bar, pie slice, or line. Note that it may look as though you've selected only a part of an element—for example, just one side or just the top of the bar. Whenever you change the color, however, it will apply to the entire element.

To change the color of the element, right-click and choose Chart Options | Selected Item from the pop-up menu, or choose Chart | Chart Options | Selected Item from the pull-down menus. The Formatting dialog box appears, as shown in Figure 12-12.

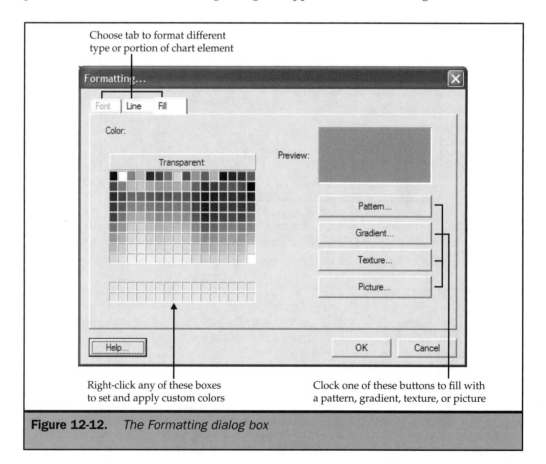

Figure 12-12. *The Formatting dialog box*

You change not only the color of the chosen chart element, but also the pattern displayed in the element. By default, all charts created with the Chart Expert contain solid colors. However, you may want to replace the solid color with a graduated color, a pattern, or maybe even a picture. You may change the solid color to use for the element by choosing a predefined color from the palette. If you want to use a color that's not in the standard palette, right-click one of the gray boxes below the standard palette. A Custom Color dialog box appears, in which you can choose a custom color. Then, click the button you just modified to apply the custom color to the chart element.

To apply a pattern, gradient, or texture, or to fill the chart element with a picture, choose one of the corresponding buttons on the right side of the Formatting dialog box. For example, clicking the gradient button displays a dialog box showing preset color gradients. If you click the Advanced Options button, the gradient dialog box displays an extra section that lets you design your own gradients.

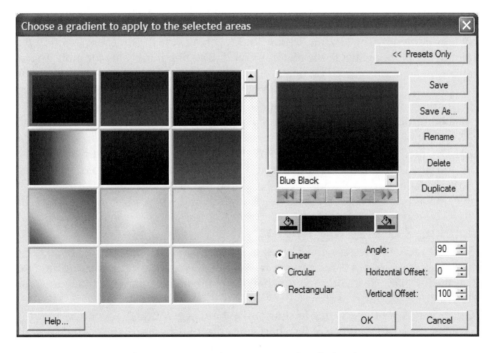

Either choose one of the preset gradients or use the dialog box options to customize your own gradient. When you click OK, the solid color previously appearing in the Formatting dialog box will be replaced by the selected gradient.

Click OK on the Formatting dialog box to apply your selected color, pattern, gradient, or picture to the chart element.

Tip	*Often, gradients and patterns, or even certain solid background colors, can add visual appeal if applied to the whole background of the chart. To do this, select the entire chart, making sure no individual chart elements are selected. Then, right-click or use the Chart menu options to format the selected item. Color and gradient/pattern options you choose will then apply to the chart background.*

Customizing and Moving Chart Titles, Labels, and the Legend

When you add a title, labels, and legend to your chart with the Options and Text tabs of the Chart Expert, Crystal Reports places them in specific locations, using specific colors and alignment. If you choose to display a legend on your chart, you have only a few predefined locations on the Options tab where you can place it. Also, if you choose the Auto Arrange Chart option discussed earlier, chart elements will be repositioned to default locations.

However, chart titles and labels are all objects that you can select by pointing and clicking within the chart in either the Design or Preview tab. Once you've selected an object (as denoted by the "sizing handle" blocks on all sides), you can reposition the text simply by pointing inside the text frame and dragging it to a new location. To resize the object, position the cursor on one of the sizing handles and narrow or stretch the object. Then, use the Chart Options | Selected Item options described earlier to display the Formatting dialog box. You may choose alternate colors, fonts, alignment, and other text-related options on the Font tab of the Formatting dialog box.

If you want to move the legend to a specific place on the chart, just drag it (you can't resize it) to its new location. You can actually select and format three different parts of the legend: the frame, the textual items, and the symbols. Select each piece and use the Formatting dialog box to change them. Note that if you change certain properties of the symbol, the associated chart element (bar, pie slice, and so forth) changes along with it.

Changing 3-D Viewing Angles

Some of the more impressive chart types that Crystal Reports can create are 3-D charts. There are several types of 3-D charts, some of which actually chart only one data item, such as the 3-D bar, pie, and doughnut charts, and others that chart two data items, such as 3-D riser and 3-D surface charts.

Once you create these types of charts, you have a great deal of control over the three-dimensional appearance of the chart. For example, if you choose a single doughnut chart, Crystal Reports gives it a certain 3-D appearance by default. Using choices from Chart Options, you can completely change the viewing aspects of the chart. To make these selections, choose Chart Options | General from the pop-up or pull-down menu. The Chart Options dialog box will appear.

Chart Options...

General | Layout | Data Labels | Numbers | Look | Display Status

Pie Tilt: ——J———— 20

Pie Depth: —J———————— 34

Pie Rotation: ——J—— 90

Explode Pie: J———————— 0

Country Comparison

Hole Size: ——————J— 69

Restore All Slices

Help... | OK | Cancel

The General tab contains various sliders and spin boxes that allow you to change all visual aspects of the 3-D doughnut chart.

Dual-data-item 3-D charts, such as the 3-D riser and 3-D surface charts, have even more "whiz-bang" 3-D capabilities. Not only can you choose from a variety of viewing angles right on the Chart Expert's Options tab when you create the chart, but you also can perform almost unlimited 3-D customizations using Chart Options.

Select the 3-D riser chart you want to adjust. Then, choose Chart Options | Viewing Angle from either the pull-down or pop-up menus. The Choose a Viewing Angle dialog box appears. If you click the Advanced Options button, the dialog box displays an extra section that lets you completely customize the viewing angle, rather than just choosing presets, as shown in Figure 12-13.

This dialog box offers numerous options for changing the 3-D appearance of the chart. You can simply choose from any of the 12 built-in angles by clicking one of the 12 boxes on the left side of the dialog box, or choose from a large number of saved angle definitions by clicking the drop-down list or forward/backward buttons below the main thumbnail. You can also manually change all kinds of 3-D viewing aspects of the chart by making manual adjustments on the Rotate, Pan, Walls, and Move tabs. You'll see the main thumbnail in the middle of the dialog box change as you choose alternative viewing options.

You may be confused by the prompt to name and save a viewing angle that you've customized when you click OK. If you make manual changes to the viewing angle with options on the tab, rather than choosing one of the built-in presets or named angles,

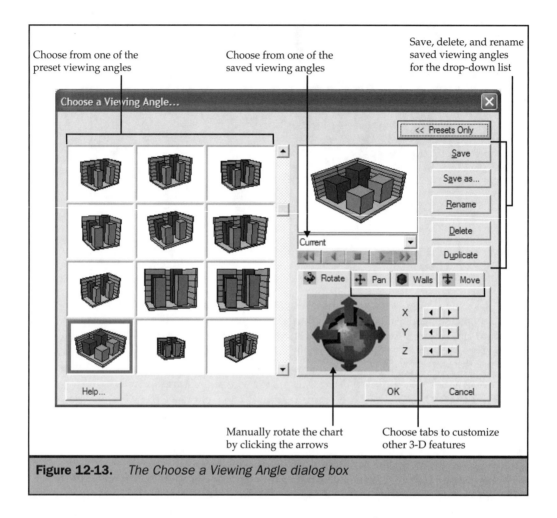

Choose from one of the preset viewing angles

Choose from one of the saved viewing angles

Save, delete, and rename saved viewing angles for the drop-down list

Manually rotate the chart by clicking the arrows

Choose tabs to customize other 3-D features

Figure 12-13. *The Choose a Viewing Angle dialog box*

you'll be prompted to save the settings before you apply them. While you can replace an existing named angle, or create a new one, before you actually apply the viewing angle to the chart, you don't have to. Just click the Cancel button on the Enter 3D Viewing Angle Preset name dialog box. The changes will still be applied to the chart.

Choosing Additional Chart Types

Although the Chart Expert contains many different types and variations of charts (bubble, scatter, and so forth), the Format Chart option contains even more (provided you selected the Custom Charting option when you installed Crystal Reports). To look at the available additional chart types, select the chart that you want to potentially apply a new chart type to. Then, choose Chart Options | Template from either the pull-down or pop-up menu. The Choose a Chart Type dialog box will appear.

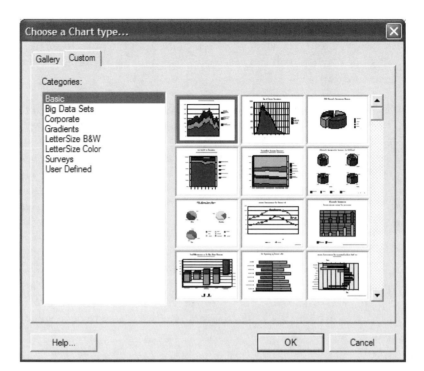

This dialog box contains two tabs: the Gallery tab and the Custom tab. The Gallery tab mostly contains the standard chart types that you find in the Chart Expert. You can choose some variations of these with the various options that appear, and then view the results of your choices in the thumbnail at the top of the Gallery tab.

If you click the Custom tab, you'll see a list of chart categories on the left. When you click each category, a large assortment of chart thumbnails from within that category appears on the right. Scroll down through the different thumbnails until you find a custom chart type that appeals to you. Select it and click OK. The new chart type will be applied to the selected chart. If you want to customize the look of the chart further, use any of the techniques discussed earlier in the chapter.

Note *You must have chosen the Custom Charting option when you installed Crystal Reports for these additional chart types to be available. If they're not available, rerun Crystal Reports setup and choose the Custom Charting option.*

Saving and Reusing Chart Templates

If you have a particular set of Chart Option settings you'd like to use on more than one chart, you can save the settings in a chart *template*. You can then apply the template to another chart that you create or edit.

To save a template, make any desired changes to your chart, such as changing label positions, element colors, perhaps the legend position, and any other settings you want to make. Then, either choose Chart | Save as Template from the pull-down menus or right-click on the chart and choose Save as Template from the pop-up menu. A Save As dialog box will appear where you can give your chart a name (the template will be saved with a .3tf file extension).

Tip   *By default, templates are saved in \Program Files\Common Files\Crystal Decisions\ 2.0\ChartSupport\Templates\User Defined folder. If you need to delete a user-defined template, use Windows Explorer to navigate to that folder and delete the templates (or you can delete them directly from the Save Template As dialog box when saving a new template). If you wish to point your copy of Crystal Reports to an alternate location for Chart Templates, use the Registry Editor and look for the ChartSupport key in HKEY_LOCAL_MACHINE/ Software/Crystal Decisions/9.0/Crystal Reports/ ChartSupportPath. Use the Registry Editor only if you are sure how it works.*

To apply the saved template to a new chart, use the steps described in the preceding section, "Choosing Additional Chart Types." Notice that the last category on the Custom tab is *User Defined.* When you choose that category, the collection of thumbnails consists of all the templates you've saved. Choose the thumbnail that you wish to apply to your current chart. When you click OK, the template settings will be applied to the existing chart.

Chapter 13

Using Subreports

As you become more sophisticated in your report designing abilities, you will find at times that it's difficult, if not impossible, to create certain kinds of reports. For example, you might want to create one of the following:

■ A single-page Company Condition report that contains an accounts receivable summary in the upper left, an accounts payable summary in the upper right, a payroll expense summary in the lower left, and a sales summary in the lower right. At the bottom of the report, you'd like some grand totals for each of the summary reports.

■ A listing of orders by customer for the month that also has a summary of the top five products sold during the month, regardless of customer.

■ A sales report grouped by state, with a list of all credit granted in the same state in the group footer.

■ A report based on a PC-style database that you can't properly link because of the lack of indexed fields.

■ A report that contains a report title, logo, and company information from a separate Company Information table in the database that doesn't contain any field that can be linked to other fields in other tables.

In each of these cases, you can't create the report using traditional Crystal Reports methods. The first three instances are prohibitive because a report, by nature, can use only a single result set, or a single group of fields returned all at once, from the database. The fourth instance exhibits Crystal Reports' requirement that PC-style databases be linked using indexed fields. And the fifth instance (a fairly common situation), exhibits the problem encountered when there are no common fields that can be linked between the two tables.

Crystal Reports provides an innovative way to deal with these types of reporting challenges. *Subreports* allow you to solve these problems by, in essence, placing one report inside another report. A subreport is simply another report that appears inside the original *main report* as an object. Even though both reports have separate layouts and separate Design tabs, they appear together in the same place. The main report is created initially, after which one or more subreports are added to the main report.

Each subreport is designed separately, based on its own database tables and fields. You can preview each subreport in its own Preview tab, format individual objects in each subreport, and create unique selection criteria for the subreport. However, when you return to the main report's Preview tab or print the main report, the subreports will be processed and printed at the same time, appearing inside the main report.

The following are the two main types of subreports:

■ **Unlinked subreports**   Have no tie-in to the main report at all—they exist completely on their own and don't typically communicate with the main report. The Company Condition report mentioned previously falls into this category. Each of the unlinked subreports stands on its own and won't change along with any controlling field in the main report.

■ **Linked subreports**   Are controlled by the main report. The subreport will "follow" the main report, returning only a certain set of records based on the main report's controlling field or fields. The subreport containing sales by state followed by matching credit, mentioned previously, is an example of a linked subreport. When the state group changes in the main report, the subreport will return only records for that particular state.

You can also choose when subreports are processed by the main report. *In-place* subreports process at the same time as the main report and return their results at the same time. *On-demand* subreports appear in the Preview tab only with a placeholder and don't process until a viewer double-clicks them. This improves the performance of the main report, because all the subreports don't have to be processed at the same time as the main report.

Unlinked Subreports

The most straightforward subreport is an unlinked subreport. An unlinked subreport can be thought of as a completely separate report that just shows up on the main report—there's no connection at all. The subreport has its own layout, its own database connection, and its own selection criteria. It is not affected at all by what appears on the main report.

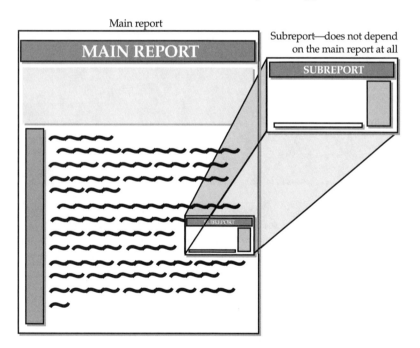

Note *Crystal Reports will not create another .RPT file when you create a subreport. Even though you will see another Design tab with separate tables and record selection, the subreport definitions are all contained in the main .RPT file.*

To create an unlinked subreport, you must first create or open at least the skeleton for the main report, and then use the Insert Subreport function to create or identify a subreport. Although you can insert a subreport on the report in the Preview tab, you may not be able to accurately tell where it's being placed, so it's best to be in the Design tab when you add a subreport.

Start to create the subreport by clicking the Insert Subreport button on the Insert Tools toolbar, or by choosing Insert | Subreport from the pull-down menus. The Insert Subreport dialog box will appear.

The Insert Subreport dialog box contains two tabs: Subreport and Link. The Link tab, discussed later in the chapter in "Linked Subreports," is used to create a linked subreport. The Subreport tab contains two radio buttons, Choose a Report and Create a Subreport, and one check box, On-Demand Subreport (on-demand subreports are discussed later in this chapter). If you've already created another report that you would like to import as a subreport now, you can click the Choose a Report radio button and type in the path and filename of the existing report, or use the Browse button to navigate to the existing report. When you click OK, a subreport object outline will be attached to your mouse cursor. Place the subreport object in the desired location on the main report. As soon as you place the subreport, you'll notice that another Design tab will appear. If you click it, you'll find the report layout for the report you just imported.

If you wish to create a new subreport from scratch, click the Create a Subreport radio button and give the subreport a descriptive name in the Report Name text box. Remember that you are not creating a new .RPT file when you create a subreport, so the subreport name doesn't have to conform to file-naming conventions. It should be descriptive of the subreport, because the name will appear on the main report Design tab wherever the subreport object is placed. Notice that once you enter a name, the only button that becomes enabled is the Report Wizard button. The OK button at the bottom of the dialog box is still dimmed. This indicates that you must use the Report Wizard to create at least a minimal portion of your subreport. (Once you close the Report Wizard and return to the Insert Subreport dialog box, the OK button will be enabled.) When you click the Report Wizard button, the Standard Report Creation Wizard appears.

Don't forget that one of the powerful features of subreports is the ability to create reports based on entirely different databases and tables. You can select completely different databases, tables, and fields than are used on the main report. New in Crystal Reports 9, you don't have to complete any of the dialogs in the Wizard in order to click Finish and place the subreport on the main report—you can have a completely empty subreport as a placeholder while you work on other things—but usually you would choose options in at least the Data and Fields dialogs. All of the same dialogs available in the Standard Report Creation Wizard when creating a main report are available when you're creating a subreport, including Grouping, Summarizing, Group Sorting (TopN), Chart, Record Selection, and Template. You can refine your subreport before you click Finish, or enter minimal information and plan to work in the subreport Design tab directly.

When you've selected your desired options in the Wizard and clicked Finish, you'll be returned to the Insert Subreport dialog box. Notice that the OK button is now enabled, because you have created enough of a report in the Wizard. When you click OK, you will be returned to the main report Design tab, and a box-like subreport object will be attached to your mouse cursor. Drop the object by clicking in the report section of the main report where you want the subreport to appear. Choose this section carefully; it typically makes no sense for an unlinked subreport to appear more than once in the main report. For example, if you place the subreport in the details section, the same unlinked subreport will appear over and over again, once for each details record. You'll typically place an unlinked subreport in a report header or footer, unless you want it to repeat on more than one page.

Tip   *Don't forget the Underlay formatting option on the Section Expert (discussed in detail in Chapter 10). You can, for example, easily create a second page header section for your subreport object and format the second page header to Underlay Following Sections. That way, your subreport will print alongside—not on top of—any data on the main report.*

When you place your subreport in the main report Design tab, it simply shows up as a box with the subreport name centered inside it. Notice, however, that another Design tab labeled with the subreport name now appears alongside the main report Design tab. If you click the new tab, the subreport Design tab will appear.

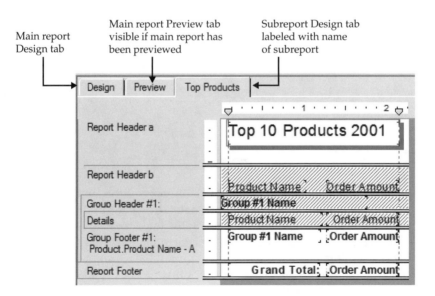

You can now move, resize, reformat, and otherwise modify objects in the subreport just as you would in the main report. The subreport will present its own Data and Field Explorers, allow a separate set of formulas to be created, and allow you all the flexibility you have on the main report. However, the subreport Design tab has one limitation: You cannot add another subreport to it—subreports can be created only one level deep.

Caution   *Since subreports can be only one level deep, an existing report that already contains subreports will not include the subreports when it is imported from the Insert Subreport dialog box. The main report will be imported into the subreport Design tab, but the lower-level subreports won't show up. You may need to modify the imported report to make up for the empty space that appears where the subreport used to be.*

You can even preview a subreport in its own Preview tab. With the subreport Design tab displayed, preview the report using the Preview toolbar button, the Refresh button, the F5 key, or the pull-down menu options. A separate Preview tab for the subreport will appear next to the subreport Design tab.

The preview tab will have the subreport name followed by the word Preview.

When you now preview the main report, you'll see the subreport where you placed it. By default, subreports are surrounded by a border, so you'll see a box around the subreport.

If you do not want to see a box around the subreport, right-click the subreport object and select Format Subreport. On the border tab, you can remove all or some of the border.

If the subreport is not entirely visible (it may be partly off the right side of the page, or it may be overwriting main report data if you set it to Underlay Following Sections), return to the main report Design tab and reposition or resize the subreport object. If you don't have sufficient room in the subreport Design tab to properly place objects, return to the main report Design tab and resize the subreport object. The subreport Design tab's width is determined by the subreport object's width in the main report.

Tip   *You may save a subreport in its own .RPT file to use elsewhere or on its own. Select the subreport object in the main report Design or Preview tab and choose File | Save Subreport As, or right-click the subreport object and choose Save Subreport As from the pop-up menu.*

Drilling Down on Subreports

You have the same flexibility for drill-down reporting in subreports as you do in the main report. If you design a subreport with grouping, hidden sections, or charts, you can drill down in the subreport, too.

When you first preview the main report, the subreport will appear inside it. If you point to the subreport, you'll notice the mouse cursor change to a magnifying glass, indicating drill-down capability. When you double-click the subreport, it will be displayed in its own Preview tab (but no actual subreport drill-down will occur). If you've designed the subreport to allow drill-down, you'll notice the mouse cursor displaying a drill-down cursor again in the subreport Preview tab. If you then double-click again, additional drill-down tabs will appear for groups you've created in the subreport.

If Crystal Reports runs out of room to display all the tabs, two small left-right arrows will appear to the right of the group of tabs. You can use the arrows to cycle through the tabs from the left or right. If you wish to close some of your drill-down tabs, click the red X next to the page navigation controls. This will close the tab you are currently viewing and display the tab to the left. Figure 13-1 shows an unlinked subreport with more tabs than can be displayed at once.

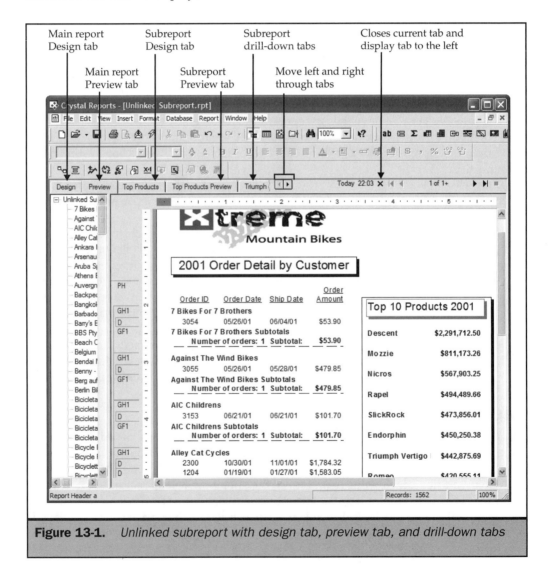

Figure 13-1. *Unlinked subreport with design tab, preview tab, and drill-down tabs*

Tip *When you add a subreport to the main report, a Design tab for the subreport is created automatically. You can close the subreport Design tab by clicking the red X button. To redisplay a subreport Design tab, display the Design tab for the main report and then double-click the subreport object, or select the subreport and choose Edit | Edit Subreport from the pull-down menus, or right-click the subreport object and choose Edit Subreport from the pop-up menu.*

Linked Subreports

A linked subreport is handy when you want to have multiple records from one database appear after multiple related records from another database. A report that shows all sales in a region, followed by all credits in a region, fits this category. The subreports follow along with the main report.

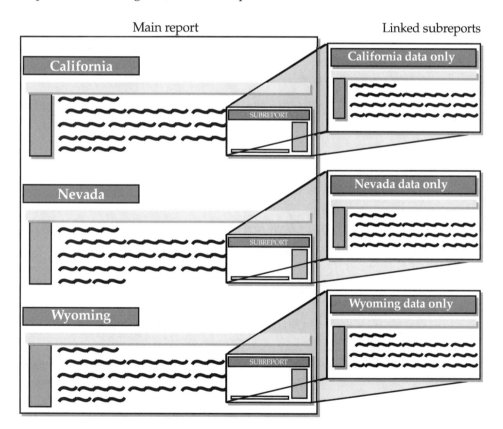

A linked subreport is also required if you have a report based on a PC-style database that requires linking to a field that's not indexed. Since a linked subreport can show matching records based on a nonindexed field, you can create reports using a linked subreport that you would normally be unable to create.

The initial steps for creating a linked subreport are the same as creating an unlinked subreport. Use the Insert Subreport toolbar button or menu options to create a subreport. Then, import an existing report or create a new subreport with the Subreport Expert. However, before you click OK in the Insert Subreport dialog box, click the Link tab. This will display the Subreport Links dialog box, shown in Figure 13-2, in which you can choose how to link the subreport with the main report.

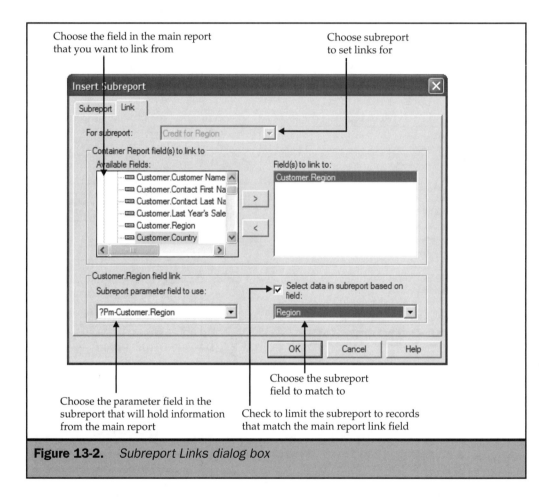

Figure 13-2. *Subreport Links dialog box*

Tip	*If you inadvertently click OK in the Insert Subreport dialog box before linking, you can still link the subreport after you place it in the main report. You can also choose to change links for an existing linked subreport or link a previously unlinked subreport. Choose Edit	Subreport Links from the pull-down menus, or right-click the subreport object and choose Change Subreport Links from the pop-up menu.*

If you are linking directly from the Link tab on the Insert Subreport dialog box, the For Subreport drop-down list will be dimmed—you will be setting links for the subreport you are currently creating. If you are linking a subreport already on the main report, you can choose the subreport you want to set links for (don't forget—there can be more than one subreport on a main report).

The Available Fields list shows fields and formulas available in the main report. Select the field from the list you want to link from, and add it to the Field(s) To Link To list by clicking the right arrow button. If you later decide you don't want to link on that field, select it in the Field(s) To Link To list and remove it with the left arrow button.

Once you've added a main report field to link on, three additional options appear at the bottom of the Subreport Links dialog box. The Subreport Parameter Field To Use drop-down list contains any parameter fields you have created in the subreport (see Chapter 14 for information on parameter fields). In addition to any that you have created, Crystal Reports will create a parameter field consisting of the main report field prefixed with Pm-. If you want to link the subreport so that it shows only matching records for the main report field, just leave this automatically created parameter field selected.

The general approach of linked subreports is to limit the subreport to records that match the linking field from the main report. If this is the behavior you want, make sure Select Data in Subreport Based on Field is checked. Then, use the drop-down list below the check box to choose the field in the subreport that you want to use to limit records (Crystal Reports will automatically show any subreport field that has the same field name as the main report linking field). If you want to use more than one field to link the main report to the subreport, just add additional fields to the Field(s) To Link To list and match them up to the corresponding subreport fields.

Clicking OK closes the Subreport Links or Insert Subreport dialog box and creates the links between the main report and the subreport. If you're just creating the subreport, it will be attached to your cursor and you'll need to place it on the report in a section that makes sense for the link and data you've designed. A subreport link is based on two concepts: passing data from the main report into a subreport parameter field and creating a record-selection formula in the subreport based on the parameter field. This way, every time the main report runs the subreport, it places the value of the main report linking field in the parameter field, which is used to select records for the subreport.

Because of this method of subreport linking, whenever you try to preview a linked subreport on its own, you'll see a prompt similar to this:

This indicates that the value for the parameter field is not being passed from the main report and you need to provide it. Type a valid value for the linked field (such as a state abbreviation, customer number, department code—whatever value is appropriate for the linked field) and click OK. The subreport Preview tab will appear showing just the records that you specified.

When you preview the main report, it will pass data to the subreport via the parameter field every time the subreport is processed; the subreport will use the parameter field in its record-selection formula and will return the limited set of resulting records to the main report. Figure 13-3 shows the customer/credit report mentioned previously, with the credit subreport appearing in the state group footer.

Linking Based on Formula Fields

If you use the Database Expert (discussed in Chapter 16) to link tables together in the main report, you can link only by database fields. This may be a problem if a field in one table doesn't exactly match the data type or organization in another table. For example, you may want to link two tables together based on a First/Last Name field because there is no other common number field or other linkable field. The problem,

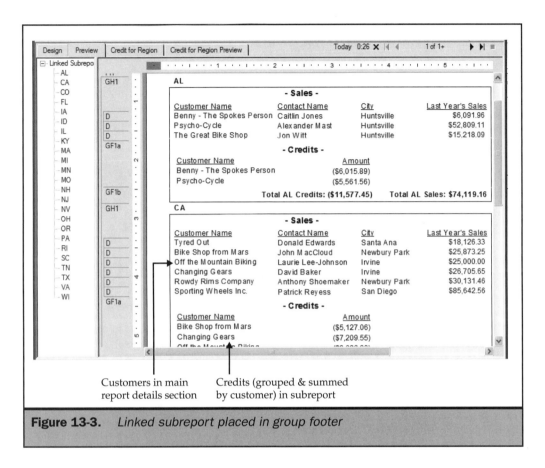

Customers in main report details section

Credits (grouped & summed by customer) in subreport

Figure 13-3. *Linked subreport placed in group footer*

however, might be that the fields are separated into individual First and Last Name fields in one table, and contained in a single Name field in the other table. The link will never work in the Database Expert because of the differences in the data layout.

One of the benefits of using subreports is their ability to link based on a formula field, instead of just using database fields. By creating a subreport, you can link the two tables together. The key is to use a formula to concatenate the individual First and Last Name fields together into one combined formula field. Once you've created the formula in the report that contains the separate Name fields, the Name formula field will appear in the Subreport Links dialog box and you can choose it as a From or To linking field.

Note *Chapter 5 discusses concatenating string fields and other formula-creation techniques.*

Format Editor Common Tab and Subreport Tab

There are a number of settings and features you can use to further format and control subreport objects in the Format Editor. On the main report Design or Preview tab, select the subreport object. Then, display the Format Editor by clicking the Format button in the Expert Tools toolbar, or by choosing Format | Format Subreport, or by right-clicking the subreport object and choosing Format Subreport from the pop-up menu. The Format Editor appears with the Common tab open.

If you will have more than one subreport in your main report, you may wish to change the default Object Name from "Subreport1" to a more meaningful name. This will help you distinguish between the subreports when using the Report Explorer and when defining hyperlinks to specific report parts.

Tip   *Don't use the Supress check box for a subreport unless you truly don't want it to run at all. Unlike a suppressed formula field (which will still calculate but won't display), a suppressed subreport does not process and will not generate values to pass to the main report. If you need to suppress a subreport from displaying, you will need to go to the subreport Design tab and hide or suppress every section of the subreport. Then, in the main report, shrink the subreport object size until the top and bottom handles are together. The subreport will still run and pass values as if it were visible.*

The Can Grow option is checked on, by default, whenever you create a subreport. This allows for variable amounts of data returned for each run of the subreport, and normally should be left on.

On the Subreport tab of the Format Editor, there are additional features to help you in displaying and controlling subreports. Most of the options on the Subreport tab apply to on-demand subreports, which are discussed later in this chapter; however, three of the options bear further discussion here: Subreport Name, Re-import When Opening, and Suppress Blank Subreport.

Format Editor				⊠

Common	Border	Font	Subreport

Subreport options :

Subreport Name: Credit for Region

☐ On-demand Subreport

On-demand Subreport Caption   X·2

Subreport Preview Tab Caption   X·2

☐ Re-import When Opening

☐ Suppress Blank Subreport

Sample:

Subreport

OK	Cancel	Help

If you'd like a more user-friendly name to display on the Preview and Design tabs for the subreport, or perhaps a better abbreviation, you can change the Subreport Name here. The change applies as soon as you close and reopen those tabs, and it applies to both in-place and on-demand subreports.

The Re-import When Opening option is available only for subreports that were imported, rather than created, during the Insert Subreport dialog. When you import an existing report as the subreport, Crystal Reports does not create a real-time link to the original .RPT file. The report design characteristics of the existing report are just added to the main report and then "forgotten." If you later make changes to the original report that you imported, the changes won't be reflected here. However, Crystal Reports provides the ability to automatically or manually update (reimport) the subreport to reflect any changes to the original .RPT file.

To manually reimport a subreport that has had changes made to the original .RPT file, right-click the subreport object on the main report Design tab. Choose Re-import Subreport on the pop-up menu. The .RPT file that was used to originally import the subreport will be read again, and any changes will now be reflected in this report.

To have Crystal Reports automatically update imported subreports every time the main report is opened, format the subreport by selecting the subreport object in the main report Design tab or Preview tab. Then, either use the Format menu or right-click the subreport object and choose Format Subreport, which will display the Format Editor. On the Subreport tab, check the Re-import when Opening check box. You may also set this option globally by choosing File | Options and then checking the Re-import Subreports when Opening Reports option on the New Report tab.

Caution *The automatic reimport option will cause problems if the original .RPT file is missing, if changes have been made to it for other purposes, or if the main report/subreports have been maintained with database changes but the original subreport .RPT file hasn't. And if you reimport a subreport, any changes you made to the subreport design will be overwritten by the updated subreport. You won't be warned that your changes are going to be overwritten, and you cannot undo the import. If you realize that you've overwritten subreport changes that you wanted to keep, close the report without saving it. Then, reopen the report.*

It's interesting to note that even if you use the Save Subreport As function to save a copy of a subreport you've modified perfectly, you can't tell Crystal that from now on you want to import the subreport from that new .RPT file. The subreport will always "remember" the original file it's importing from. You would have to delete the subreport altogether and perform the Insert Subreport again, this time browsing to the new file.

The last option on the Subreport tab of the Format Editor is Suppress Blank Subreport. This option evaluates the subreport and if it returns no records, it suppresses the display of the report, including any titles and text objects. However, note that the blank subreport object still takes up room in its section of the main report, and any values passed from the subreport are not updated. The section on "Handling Empty Subreports" later in this chapter describes steps to correct these display issues.

On-Demand Versus In-Place Subreports

By default, a subreport will process *in-place* as soon as Crystal Reports encounters it during main-report processing. Therefore, if you place a subreport in a group footer and preview the report, the subreport will process every time Crystal Reports comes to a group footer. If the report contains 75 groups and you click the last page-navigation button, 75 subreports will have to be processed before you see the page.

Depending on subreport size, database speed, or any of a number of other factors, this subreport processing may present a prohibitive performance problem. That's why Crystal Reports provides the *on-demand* subreport. An on-demand subreport simply exists as a placeholder on the main report, but it doesn't process as the main report progresses. Only when you drill down on the subreport placeholder by clicking it does the subreport actually process and appear in its own Preview tab.

There are two ways to denote a subreport as on-demand versus in-place. When you first create the subreport, check the On-Demand Subreport check box in the Insert Subreport dialog box. Or, you may change the settings for the subreport on the Subreport tab of the Format Editor. Check On-Demand Subreport to make the currently selected subreport on-demand. Now, when you preview the main report, only a placeholder outline will appear where the subreport would be. When the viewer double-clicks the placeholder, the on-demand subreport will process and appear in its own Preview tab.

Caution *Since data is not saved in on-demand subreports, you may wish to avoid them if you distribute a report to a viewer who doesn't have access to the database. Even if a viewer opens a report with File | Save Data with Report checked, on-demand subreports will have to connect to the database to be shown.*

There are two helpful text options that make on-demand subreports more intuitive and interactive. The On-Demand Subreport Caption and Subreport Preview Tab Caption properties also exist on the Format Editor's Subreport tab. Both of these properties are

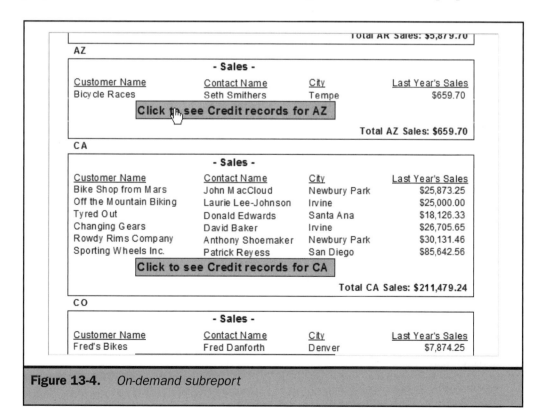

Figure 13-4. *On-demand subreport*

set via Conditional Formula buttons, which allow you to create a conditional string formula that determines what appears inside the subreport placeholder in the main report and in the subreport Preview tab, respectively.

Since both are conditional formulas, you can use the complete Crystal Reports formula language to create a string formula to display. This gives you the flexibility to include actual database data in the formulas. For example, to prompt the user to double-click a subreport placeholder to see credit information for a particular state, you could enter the following formula for the On-Demand Subreport Caption:

```
"Click to see Credit records for " + GroupName ({Customer.Region})
```

To show the state name in the Preview tab for the particular on-demand subreport that a viewer chooses, you could use the following conditional formula for the Subreport Preview Tab Caption:

```
GroupName ({Customer.Region}) + " credits"
```

Tip   *The Subreport Preview Tab Caption works with either on-demand or in-place subreports when in-place subreports are previewed by double-clicking on them. (If you ask to preview an in-place subreport by clicking Preview or Refresh, the subreport name is used on the Preview tab.) The On-Demand Subreport Caption will be available only if you check On-Demand Subreport.*

You can use other options on the Format Editor to choose the font face, size, and color; the border style; and the background color that appear on the placeholder. By using these formatting options creatively, you can make an on-demand subreport placeholder look clickable. Also, in the Preview tab of the main report, when you mouse-over an on-demand subreport, the cursor changes to the standard Windows hand, which denotes a clickable object.

Figure 13-4 shows the resulting main report Preview tab. Notice that several subreports have been double-clicked and their Preview tabs have been customized.

Caution   *If you are passing data back to the main report from a subreport (discussed later in the chapter), making the subreport on-demand will prevent the data from being passed back when the main report runs. Since the subreports aren't processing as the main report runs, there's nothing for them to pass back!*

Passing Data Between Main Reports and Subreports

In addition to passing a linking field to a subreport from a main report to limit the subreport's record selection, you may want to pass data from a main report to a subreport for other purposes. Or, you may want to pass data from a subreport back to the main report to use in summary calculations or similar functions. You can pass data to a subreport from the main report by using a parameter field. Crystal Reports also provides the *shared variable,* which allows you to pass data back and forth between main reports and subreports.

Passing data to a subreport from the main report but not having the subreport use it in record selection is fairly straightforward. Display the Subreport Links dialog box, as explained earlier in this chapter. Choose a linking field from the main report and add it to the Field(s) To Link To list. This will automatically add a parameter field prefixed with Pm- (all parameter fields automatically begin with a question mark) to the Subreport Parameter Field To Use drop-down list. Now, simply uncheck Select Data in Subreport Based on Field.

Uncheck to create a linked
parameter field that doesn't
change subreport record selection

These steps will create the Pm-parameter field in the subreport and pass data to it, but the parameter field won't be used for subreport record selection. Then, just use the parameter field in subreport formulas or place it on the subreport for display, as desired. For example, if you added a parameter for the summary field for the last year's sales by region figure in the sample report, your subreport would "know" the region's sales subtotal even though the subreport is not grouped by region. You could then add, in the footer of the subreport, a formula that compared the credit sum for the region and the sales sum for the region, and conditionally display appropriate text.

Note *Chapter 14 discusses how to use parameter fields in your reports.*

Using shared variables is a consistent way to pass data back and forth between the main report and one or more subreports, or even from subreport to subreport. You'll need to create formulas that declare the same shared variable in both the main report and the subreport. You can assign the variable a value in the subreport and then read the contents of the variable in the main report. Or, you can assign a value in the main report and read it in the subreport.

Here's an example of a formula in a subreport that places the sum of a currency field into a shared variable:

```
WhilePrintingRecords;
Shared CurrencyVar CreditTotal := Sum ({Credit.Amount})
```

Here's the corresponding formula in the main report that retrieves the value of the shared variable:

```
WhilePrintingRecords;
Shared CurrencyVar CreditTotal
```

The final step in using shared variables is determining when and where a reset formula is needed, to reset the shared variable to zero. This is necessary because, for example, if you are passing the credit total from the subreport to the main report, and your data set includes regions that have no credit records, the subreport won't run and therefore doesn't change the shared variable. The main report will still be "remembering" the value of the variable from the previous region. You need a formula to reset the shared variable to zero for each new region:

```
WhilePrintingRecords;
Shared CurrencyVar CreditTotal := 0
```

After you place this formula on the main report (in the region group header, for this example) and verify that it's producing the correct results, you can use the Format Editor to suppress it so that the zeros don't display.

For more information on assigning and using variables, and other formula topics, refer to Chapter 5.

> **Note** *Because subreports process after formulas in the main report processing cycle, you must take special steps to retrieve the contents of a shared variable set in a subreport. For example, if you place both the subreport and a formula to retrieve the contents of a shared variable set in that subreport in a group footer, you'll notice odd behavior. Typically, you'll find that the formula returns the value of the shared variable from the previous group, instead of the current group. This is because the subreport is setting the value of the shared variable after the formula to retrieve the variable has already processed. To resolve this problem, insert an additional section (for example, a Group Footer #1 b) as described in Chapter 10. Then, place the formula that retrieves the value of the shared variable in the second section (Group Footer #1 b), while leaving the subreport in the first section (Group Footer #1 a). The formula that retrieves the contents of the shared variable will not retrieve the value from the correct corresponding subreport.*

Handling Empty Subreports

When you link subreports, there may be situations in which the subreport won't retrieve any records that match the linking field from the main report. Typically, this will just result in a subreport showing up without any details sections. If there are column headings or other information in other sections, they will appear with zeros for subtotals.

There are two graceful ways to handle empty subreports: suppress them and any related totals, or display an informational message denoting the lack of data.

If you want to suppress the blank subreport altogether, check that option on the Subreport tab of the Format Editor. For this solution to work effectively, the subreport should reside alone in its section (e.g., GF2a or GH1b); then you can go to the Section Expert, as discussed in Chapter 10, and choose Suppress Blank Section. The main report will appear seamless where the subreport is blank.

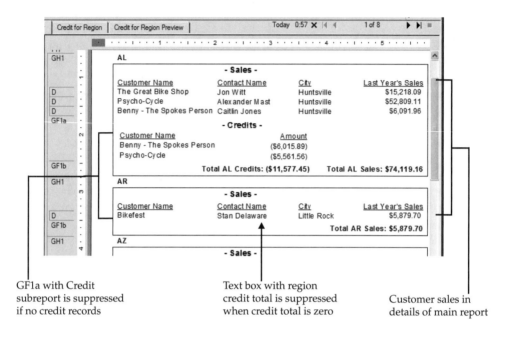

GF1a with Credit subreport is suppressed if no credit records

Text box with region credit total is suppressed when credit total is zero

Customer sales in details of main report

Note that if you're displaying any formulas with values passed from the subreport, they will be zeros on the main report, and you'll want to conditionally suppress them. For example, if there is a text box with the subreport credit totals, those totals will be zero when the subreport is blank. To conditionally suppress that text box in the main report, select the text box and request Format Text by any method to get the Format Editor. On the Common tab, click the formula button for Suppress, and enter any formula that will activate suppression when the subreport values are zero. In this example, @CreditTotal Var is the name of the formula containing the shared variable discussed previously.

```
{@CreditTotal Var} = 0
```

When the formula returns zero, the text box (and its embedded formula result) is suppressed.

You may prefer to display an informational message instead of suppressing the blank subreport, similar to what's shown in Figure 13-5.

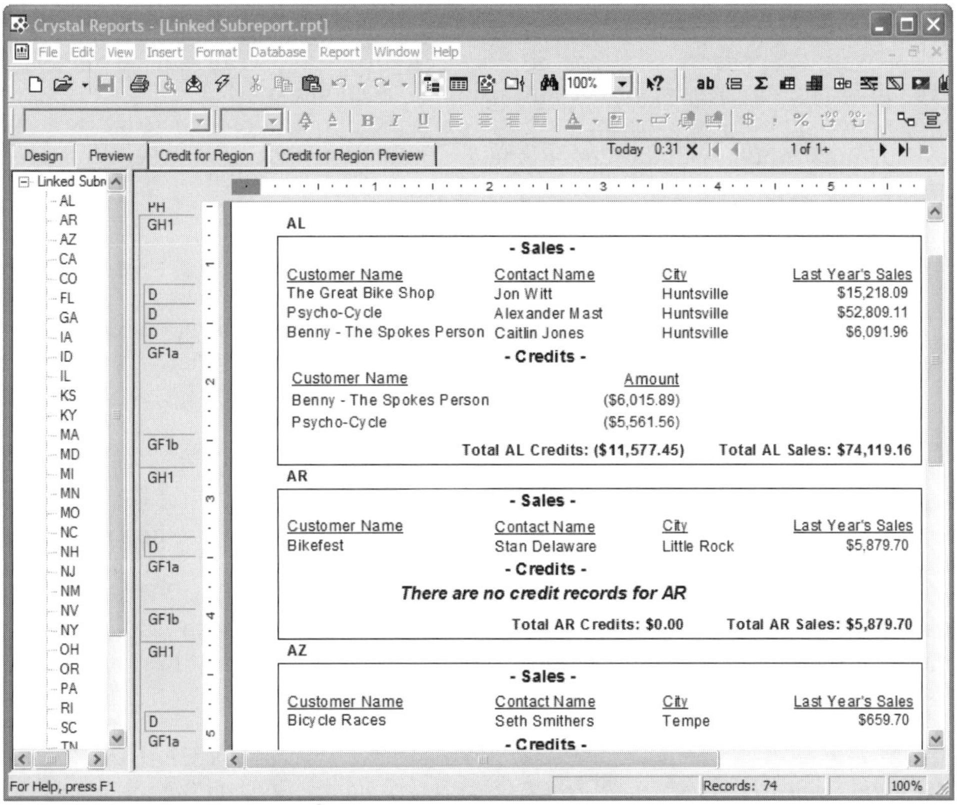

Figure 13-5. *An empty subreport showing an informational message*

This is accomplished by conditionally suppressing different sections of the subreport, based on a condition indicating the presence or absence of details records. Look at the Design tab for the subreport.

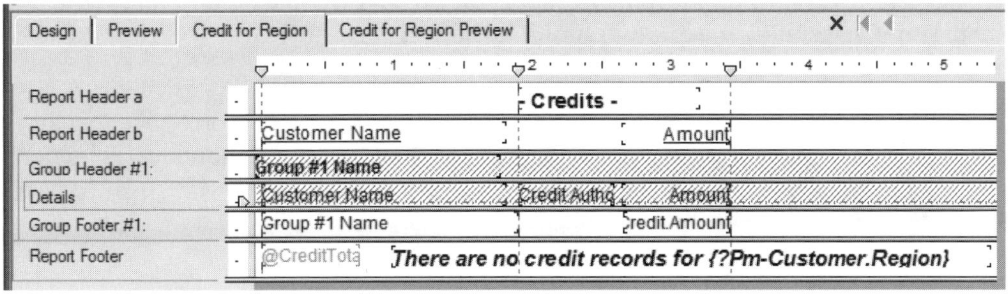

The report header and details sections contain objects that you want to appear if the subreport will return records. The report footer contains the object (the text message) that you want to appear if the subreport doesn't return records. This can be controlled by conditionally suppressing all sections using the Section Expert.

Conditionally suppress the section containing the informational message by adding the following formula with the Conditional Formula button next to the Section Expert's Suppress property:

```
Not IsNull({Credit.Credit Authorization Number})
```

Then, conditionally suppress the sections that contain the actual subreport data with the following conditional formula applied to the Suppress property:

```
IsNull({Credit.Credit Authorization Number})
```

Don't forget—you are conditionally *suppressing* these sections, not displaying them, so you may need to think backward. If the subreport is empty because no records were returned based on the linked field from the main report, the Credit Authorization Number will be null. In this case, you'll want to suppress the actual subreport data but not the informational message. If data is returned, then the Credit Authorization Number will contain data and will not be null. In this case, you want to suppress the informational message but not the actual subreport data.

Tip　*You can use this technique for all of your Crystal Reports, not just subreports. If you might potentially have main reports that return no records, you can display an informational message in them. See Chapter 10 for more information on conditionally formatting sections.*

Performance Considerations

Subreports create potential performance problems for your reporting projects. Here are some tips to help maximize performance for your report viewer. Obviously, these considerations are more important if a viewer will be viewing a report online using Crystal Reports or as an on-demand report on the Web with Crystal Enterprise. If a report is being printed or exported, subreports affect performance as well, but the user won't be staring at the screen waiting for them.

- Use on-demand subreports if you can. That way, a viewer won't have to wait for many subreports to process. Viewers can double-click the individual subreports they want to see when they want to see them.

■ If you are creating a linked subreport, try to base the link on an indexed field in the subreport. This will cause record selection in the subreport to occur substantially faster. If the subreport is based on an ODBC or SQL database, make sure you are keeping as much of the SQL query on the server as possible (see Chapter 16 for SQL database performance considerations).

■ If you are linking subreports with formula fields, try to keep the formula field in the main report and use a database field in the subreport. Using formula fields in the subreport, particularly with subreports based on SQL databases, will move part or all of the subreport query off the server, impeding performance.

CRYSTAL REPORTS 9
INTRODUCED

Chapter 14

Viewer Interaction with Parameter Fields

If you are designing reports to distribute to a viewer audience that may not be familiar with Crystal Reports or the Select Expert, you will soon have the need to prompt the viewer for values that affect record selection, conditional formatting, or some other ad hoc information. This becomes even more crucial when the viewer doesn't actually have a copy of Crystal Reports but wants to view a report presented in some "turnkey" fashion, such as an on-demand report run on the Web with Crystal Enterprise (discussed in section II of this book). In these situations, the viewer won't have the ability to make changes with the Select Expert anyway.

The ideal solution for these types of ad hoc reporting requirements would be to present the viewer with a dialog box prompt, preferably including a choice of default values or a range of values, to help the user enter the correct values for the prompt. The response the viewer provides could then be passed to the Select Expert to customize record selection and formatting, and the values the viewer supplied could also be included on the report to indicate what data makes up the report.

This ideal solution is made possible by *parameter fields*, prompts that are presented to the viewer when he or she refreshes the report. The value the viewer provides is then passed on to the Select Expert, report formulas, or conditional-formatting formulas to customize the way the report appears, based on the viewer's response. The viewer doesn't have to know how to enter selection criteria or conditional formulas to customize the way the report behaves.

Consider the following report:

This report uses three fields in record selection:

- **Order Date**   Filtered with a Between selection criterion to include orders that were placed during 2001 (between January 1 and December 31).
- **Region**   Filtered with a One Of selection criterion to include orders placed from AL, AR, AZ, CO, CT, and DC.
- **Customer Name**   Filtered with a Like selection criterion to include customer names that contain the string *Bik*.

These criteria are hard-coded into the Select Expert, and a text object appears in the report header to indicate the restrictions.

The difficulty comes when you want the person reviewing the report to be able to easily change these criteria whenever the report is refreshed. The way this report is currently designed, the viewer must have the ability to alter record selection (and know enough about its intricacies to be able to change it). That person also must be able to edit the text object that displays what records are included. Even in this case, it's time-consuming to change this information every time the viewer wants to change these options. Parameter fields are the answer.

Using parameter fields is, at minimum, a two-step process. The third step is optional:

1. Create the parameter field.
2. Use the parameter field in record selection.
3. Place the parameter field on the report, perhaps embedded in a text object, to indicate what is included on the report.

Creating a Parameter Field

Parameter fields are created from the Field Explorer, which can be displayed when either the Design or Preview tab is selected. You can click the Field Explorer button in the Standard toolbar, or choose View | Field Explorer from the pull-down menus. If the Field Explorer is already displayed, just click the plus sign next to the Parameter Fields category to show existing parameter fields.

If there are parameter fields in the report already, you can edit them by selecting the desired parameter field and clicking the Edit button on the Field Explorer toolbar. You can also rename or delete existing parameter fields with the Rename and Delete buttons on the toolbar. If there are no existing parameter fields, or if you wish to create a new parameter field, ensure that the Parameter Fields category of the Field Explorer is selected (click it), then click the New button. You can also right-click the Parameter Fields category of the Field Explorer and choose New from the pop-up menu. The Create Parameter Field dialog box appears, as shown in Figure 14-1; the various fields and options are described in Table 14-1.

Choose a name for your parameter field. It can be the same name as other database or formula fields, because Crystal Reports distinguishes parameter fields by preceding

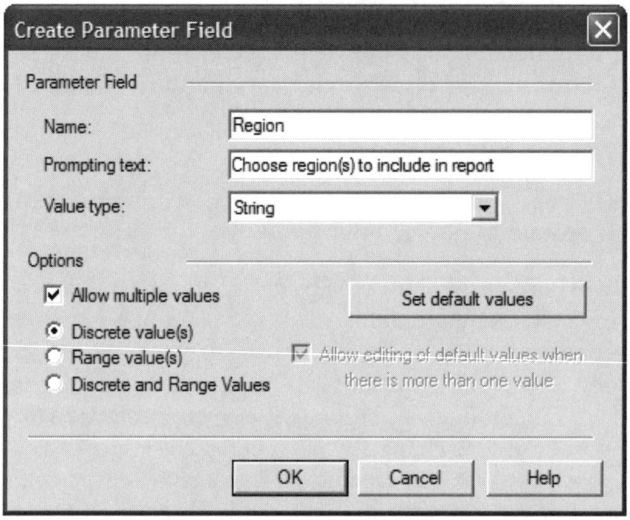

Figure 14-1. *The Create Parameter Field dialog box*

the parameter field name with a question mark. Choose a descriptive yet reasonably short name for your parameter field.

Although not absolutely required for parameter fields, you'll want to enter the message that will appear in the Supply Parameter Field dialog box when a viewer is prompted to provide the value. The message is entered in the Prompting Text field and should be easy to understand and helpful to the user, such as "Enter the state code (2 characters only) for this report." The prompting text can be up to 254 characters long, although prompting text that long will probably look unsightly when the parameter value is prompted for. Crystal Reports will word-wrap the prompting text when the viewer is prompted, if the prompting text won't all fit on one line.

Choose a value or data type for the parameter field from the Value Type drop-down list. This is a crucial step, as it determines how your parameter field can be used in record selection, formulas, and conditional formatting. For example, if you are planning on using the parameter field to compare to a string database field in the Select Expert, choose a String value type. If you are going to limit the report to a certain date range, based on a date/time field in the database, choose a DateTime value type.

These are the only items that are actually required for using a parameter field. However, there are many features in Crystal Reports that enhance the flexibility of parameter fields.

You can set up a *pick list* that provides one or more default values for a viewer to select. You can allow the viewer to select a from/to *range of values*, which is helpful for

Field or Option	Description
Name	Name of the parameter field being created.
Prompting Text	Descriptive text that appears when the viewer is prompted for the parameter value.
Value Type	Data type to assign to the parameter field.
Allow Multiple Values	Check this box to allow more than one value to be assigned to the parameter field.
Discrete Value(s) Range Value(s) Discrete and Range Values	Choose between a single parameter field value, a beginning and ending value range, or a combination of both. You may choose Discrete and Range Values only if you check Allow Multiple Values. If you then choose Discrete and Range Values, you'll be able to enter a combination of one or more discrete (single) values and range (from/to) values.
Set Default Values	Displays the Set Default Values dialog box (described later in the chapter).
Allow Editing of Default Values When There Is More Than One Value	Check this box to allow the viewer to type values into the parameter field, even if the values are not in the drop-down pick list.

Table 14-1. *Create Parameter Field Dialog Box Options*

selecting beginning and ending date ranges. And if you are using a string parameter field, you can set minimum and maximum lengths for the parameter field, or use an *edit mask* to force the viewer to enter the string in a certain way. These features are selected in the Set Default Values dialog box. To display this dialog box, shown in Figure 14-2, click the Set Default Values button. The various options for this dialog box are described in Table 14-2.

Note *The Set Default Values dialog box will change, depending on the value type you choose for the parameter field, and whether you choose discrete or range values. You'll find options on this dialog box that are appropriate for the settings you choose on the Create Parameter Field dialog box.*

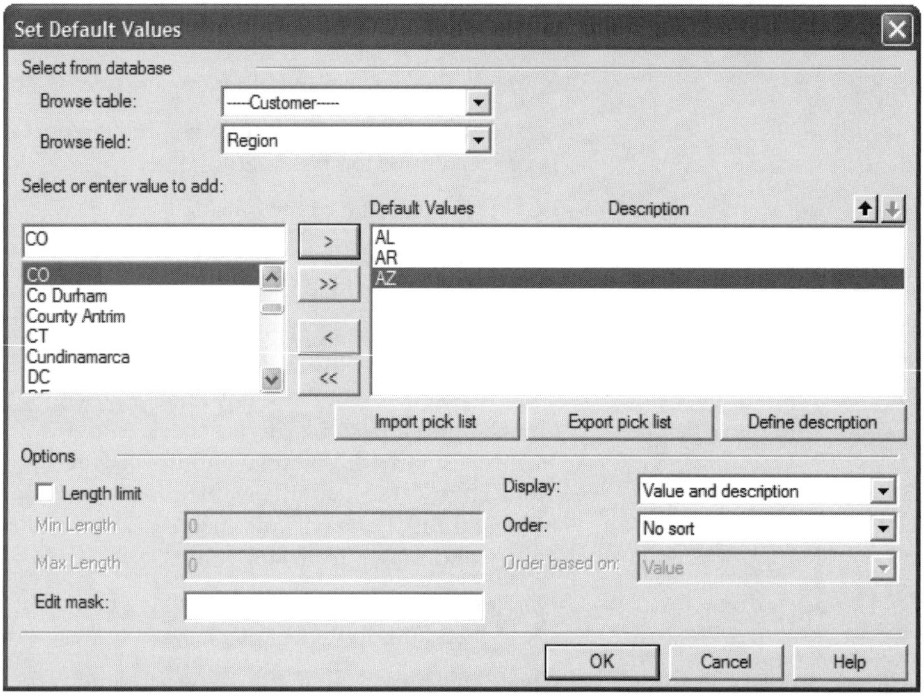

Figure 14-2. *Set Default Values dialog box*

Field or Option	Description
Browse Table	Choose a database table to help provide default values.
Browse Field	Choose a database field to help provide default values. You will only see a list of fields that match the data type that you defined for your parameter field.
Select or Enter Value to Add	Type a value to be added to the Default Values list or select a value from the database with the scrolling list. You can select one value using the single arrow or all values using the double arrow.
Default Values	List of values that will appear in the parameter field's pick list.
Up/Down arrows	Use the up and down arrows above the upper-right corner of the Default Values list to change the order that the default values will appear in when the viewer displays the pick list.

Table 14-2. *Set Default Values Dialog Box Options*

Field or Option	Description
Import Pick List Export Pick List	Imports an ASCII text file into the default values list or exports the values you've already added to an ASCII text file that can be used with other reports. If you have added a description it will also be exported and then can be imported into other reports.
Define Description	Displays a dialog box allowing you to type a description for the parameter field value that's currently selected. This is helpful when you are using coded fields for the parameter field and want the report viewer to see a description of the coded value.
Length Limit	Check this box to limit the length of data that can be added to the parameter field (will appear only with string parameter fields).
Min Length Max Length	If Length Limit is selected, enter the minimum and maximum lengths for the value to be entered into the parameter field (will appear only with string parameter fields).
Range-Limited Field	Checking this box allows the values a user enters into the parameter field to be forced to be within a certain range of values (will appear only with numeric or date/time parameter fields).
Min Value/Max Value or Start Date-time/ End Date-time	Enter the minimum and maximum values or beginning and ending dates/times that a user will be allowed to enter for the parameter field (will appear only with numeric or date/time parameter fields).
Edit Mask	Control how information can be entered into the parameter field (will appear only with string parameter fields). You can not define both a length limit and an edit mask. If you enter an edit mask, the length limit dialog will be grayed out.
Display	If you enter descriptions for parameter fields, determines whether both the value and the description or just the description appears when prompting for the parameter field.
Order	Choose whether not to sort the default values (leaving them in the same order you entered them here) or to sort them in ascending or descending order when prompting for the parameter field. An alphabetic sort of the numbers 1 to 25 would be: 1,10,11,12,13,14,15,16,17,18,19,2,20,21,22,23,24, 25,3,4,5,6,7,8,9.
Order Based On	If you choose a sort order, determines whether the order is based on the parameter field value or description.

Table 14-2.   *Set Default Values Dialog Box Options* (continued)

Setting Up a Pick List

If you don't add any default values when you first create a parameter field, the viewer will have to type in the value for the parameter field. While this sometimes may be desirable, it requires that the viewer know enough about the parameter field and the way the report and database are designed that they can type the value correctly. They may make a mistake by misspelling a name or entering an incorrect code for the field. By creating a pick list, you can let the viewer choose from a predefined list of default values.

The pick list presented to the viewer will be the set of values contained in the Default Values list (refer to Figure 14-2). You can add items to this list by typing them in the text box under the Select or Enter Value to Add label and clicking the right arrow next to the text box.

Or, you can choose a database table and field to choose values from. To do this, choose a table and field in the Browse Table and Browse Field drop-down lists. This will fill the list under the Select or Enter Value to Add label with sample data from the database. You can then select an item in the list to place in the text box. Then by clicking the right arrow, you can add the selected item to the Default Values list. If you want to add all the sample database values, click the double right arrow. If you decide you don't want some existing values to be included in the pick list, you can remove specific items by selecting them in the Default Values list with the left arrow, or you can remove all the values by clicking the double left arrow.

Caution *While it might be a nice feature for a future Crystal Reports release, choosing a Browse Table and Browse Field in the Set Default Values dialog box will not automatically populate the parameter field's pick list with live database data whenever the viewer is prompted for the value. This table and field combination is used only to provide a list of sample values for you to manually add to the Default Values list. If the database later changes, the pick list won't reflect the changes unless you manually edit the parameter field and add new values to the Default Values list.*

You can force the viewer to choose only values from the pick list by unchecking the Allow Editing of Default Values check box back in the Create Parameter Field dialog box. If you leave this option checked, the viewer will be able to select an entry from the pick list or type in their own entry.

There are additional features that improve flexibility with pick lists. You can add descriptive values to hard-to-remember codes, as well as import or export ASCII text files that contain the values that appear in the Default Values list. You'll soon find situations in which you're using a parameter field to limit record selection based on a coded field.

Perhaps you have one-letter codes to indicate colors of products; for instance, B equates to black, L to blue, R to red, and G to green. If you'd prefer that the report viewer not have to remember these codes, but be able to choose the actual colors, define a description for the single-letter default values. Then, even though the user chooses Blue, the parameter field will supply the letter *L* to the Select Expert. Do this by selecting the default value you want to add the description to and then clicking the Define Description button.

If you have a large number of default values (and potentially descriptions) that you'd like to add to your pick list, you may want to import a pick list file. When you click the Import Pick List button, you are presented with a standard File Open dialog box that asks you to select the ASCII text file containing your pick list data. When you choose the appropriate pick list text file and click OK, the Default Values list will be populated with the data from the text file. If you wish to create a pick list file from the existing values that you've already added to the Default Values list (to use in another report, for example), click the Export Pick List button. A standard File Save dialog box will appear in which you can specify the filename for the pick list file.

Pick List File Format

If you wish to create pick list files on your own, using Notepad or some other programmatic option, such as a custom Visual Basic program, you need to know the particular file format that Crystal Reports requires for pick lists. A sample Region Pick List.TXT file that can be used with a pick list looks like this.

At a minimum, you simply need to type in the parameter field default values you want to appear in the pick list and press ENTER after each (or have your program follow each value with a carriage return/line feed combination). If you wish to add descriptions for the values, press the TAB key between the parameter field value and the description (if you're programmatically creating the pick list, a tab character can be added by inserting an ASCII value of 9).

You may optionally add one or two *directives* at the top of the file. Directives are words that control how Crystal Reports will display the pick list—showing either values and descriptions or descriptions only—and how to sort the pick list. Begin a directive with four percent signs, followed by the name of the directive. Directive names are **Sort** and **ShowDescOnly**. Then, press the TAB key and type in a value for the directive.

The Sort directive accepts four values:

aa	Sort the pick list in ascending order using an alphabetical sort.
ad	Sort the pick list in descending order using an alphabetical sort.
na	Sort the pick list in ascending order using a numeric sort.
nd	Sort the pick list in descending order using a numeric sort.

The **ShowDescOnly** directive accepts two values:

1	Show Descriptions only. However, the actual code matching up to the chosen description (the value) will be provided to the report.
0	Show Values and Descriptions. Will show both the code and descriptions for the code.

> **Tip** *Crystal generally treats the first item in a pick list as a default value that is used if the viewer doesn't make a selection for that parameter when prompted. It may help the viewers if the first pick item for every parameter is the most commonly used criterion, especially if there are a lot of parameters in a report.*

Responding to Parameter Field Prompts

Once you've created a parameter field, you will be prompted for it the first time you preview the report after the parameter field has been created. The Enter Parameter Values dialog box will be displayed.

If you haven't entered any default values or created a pick list, the viewer will need to type their response to the prompt. If you've created a pick list, the prompt will be a drop-down list from which one of the predefined values can be selected. If you have created more than one parameter field for the report, only one Enter Parameter Values dialog box will appear, but each parameter field will appear in the list. Click the parameter field you want to select.

Tip *Typically, parameter fields will appear in the Enter Parameter Values dialog box in the order you created them. If you'd like to change the order in which they appear, return to the Parameter category of the Field Explorer and select the parameter field you wish to move. In earlier versions of Crystal Reports, you can reorder the parameter fields with the small up and down arrow buttons in the upper right of the Explorer box. In Crystal Reports 9, you can use ALT-arrow keyboard combination, or right-click and select Move Parameter Up or Move Parameter Down from the pop-up menu.*

When you refresh the report, the Refresh Report Data dialog box will ask whether to use the currently set parameter field values or to prompt for new values. If you use the current values, the database will be reread with the current values in the parameter fields. If you choose to prompt for new values, the Enter Parameter Values dialog box will appear again, and you'll need to specify new values for all parameter fields. When you refresh the report and select Prompt for New Parameter Values, you'll need to resupply all parameter values. The information you had placed in them previously won't be retained.

Value Type Considerations

The value type you choose for your parameter field determines how the parameter field can be used in the rest of the report. If, for example, you need to compare a parameter field to a date database field, you'll need to use a date parameter field. The value type will also determine how the report viewer must respond to the parameter field prompt.

String and number/currency parameter fields are fairly straightforward. In the case of strings, a viewer can respond with any combination of letters, numbers, or special characters. For numbers, only the numbers 0 through 9 and a minus sign can be used—other characters will result in an error message. Using date, time, date/time, or Boolean parameter fields will introduce some new features and limitations.

| Tip | *Ranges and edit masks can be used to limit or format what a viewer can enter into a parameter field. These special features are discussed later in this chapter.* |

Dates and Times

You'll often want to use date or time parameter fields to limit your report to certain date or time ranges. You can choose value types of Date, Time, or DateTime. You can build a pick list for these value types just as you can for number or string fields. And if you leave Allow Editing of Default Values checked in the Create Parameter Field dialog box, you'll be able to choose dates or times other than those in the pick list.

When you are prompted for a date or time parameter field, a few special features are available to you.

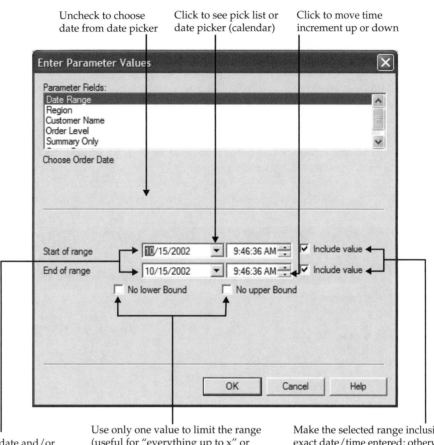

Uncheck to choose date from date picker

Click to see pick list or date picker (calendar)

Click to move time increment up or down

Type in date and/or time values directly

Use only one value to limit the range (useful for "everything up to x" or "x and everything higher")

Make the selected range inclusive of exact date/time entered; otherwise, ends at prior increment

If you didn't check Allow Editing of Default Values... when you created the parameter field, you'll only be able to click the drop-down list and choose from the pick list. If you did check Allow Editing of Default Values... when you created the parameter field, you can just type a date and/or time value into the prompt.

Preformatted dates and times will appear in the dialog box—just type the correct date and time over any existing default value. If no pick list or default has been specified, the current date and time will appear in the prompt. These can be left as they are, or you can use them as a guide for typing in the correct values.

If a pick list is available, click the down arrow to see the available values in a drop-down list. There may also be a Pick from Defaults check box available if Allow Editing of Default Values was checked when the parameter field was created. If you uncheck this option, or if there is no pick list, the pick list will not be available, and any DateTime values will split into separate boxes.

If you are working with a time value, there will be increment and decrement arrows to the right of the time value. Use these to increment the selected hour, minute, or second up or down. If you are working with a date value, the down arrow will show the *date picker*, which is a small calendar from which you can choose the desired date.

Boolean Parameter Fields

You may find a Boolean parameter field helpful when using record selection based on a Boolean database field or when conditionally formatting according to a parameter field value. A Boolean parameter field, like a Boolean formula (discussed in Chapter 5), can contain one of only two values: true or false.

When you choose a value type of Boolean in the Create Parameter Field dialog box, the dialog box changes to accommodate the special features of a Boolean parameter field, as shown in Figure 14-3. Specify the Name of the field and the Prompting Text for the parameter field just as you would for other parameter fields. You can also choose a True or False default value, as well as specify descriptions for the values, by clicking the Set Default Values button.

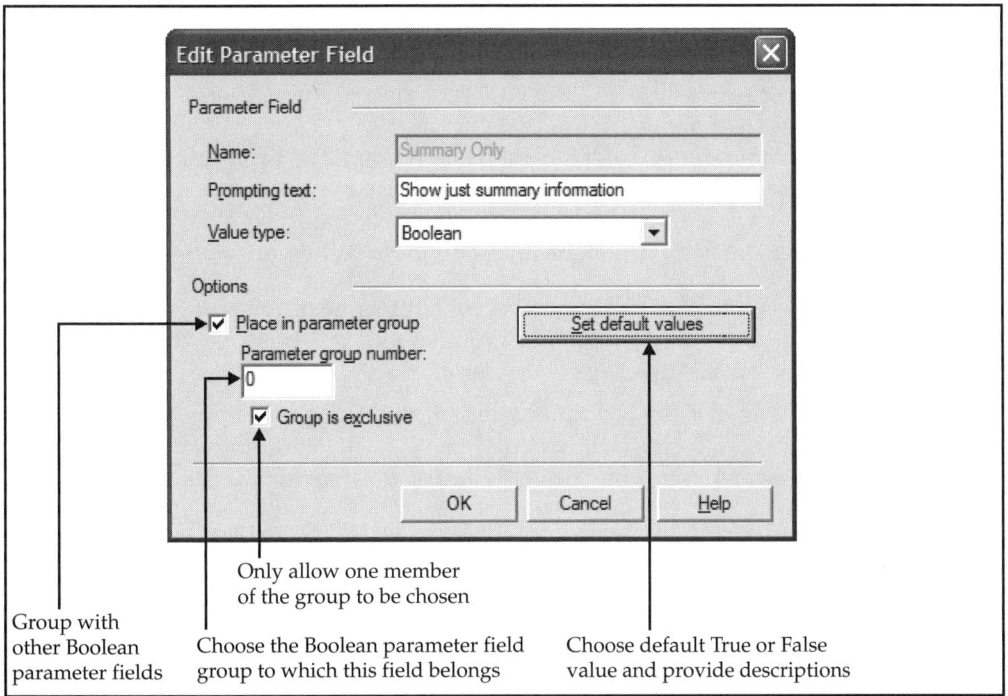

Figure 14-3.   *Special features of a Boolean parameter field*

The Options section is different for a Boolean parameter field. If you check the Place in Parameter Group check box, you will add this parameter field to a grouping of one or more other Boolean parameter fields. Boolean parameter field groups allow you to simulate the "radio button" behavior you see in Crystal Reports and other Windows applications. Since you can have more than one group of parameter fields, use the Parameter Group Number text box to specify a group number for this parameter field.

If you check Group Is Exclusive, only one parameter field in a group can be chosen at a time in the drop-down list. The chosen field will return true, and all others will return false. If you don't check Group Is Exclusive, you will be able to click the Add button to choose more than one member of the group. Each chosen parameter field will return true, while others not chosen will return false.

For example, you might create seven Boolean parameter fields. The first, a choice between Summary or Details, won't be placed in a group; three of them will be assigned to group number 0 and the group will be exclusive, allowing the viewer to choose between three different sort field options; the remaining three will be assigned to group number 1, which will not be exclusive, allowing the viewer to choose to group the report by up to three different fields.

The first parameter field will appear on its own when the prompting dialog box appears. It will offer a Discrete Value box with a choice between True and False, with whatever descriptions you assigned to those values when setting default values for the parameter. There will be two other Boolean parameters in the prompting dialog box:

- **Group #0**   Contains a drop-down list containing the prompting text for the three parameter fields placed in the first group—you can choose only one of these three parameters because the group is exclusive.

- **Group #1**   Includes the prompting text for the last three parameter fields. You may choose one *or more* of these parameter fields by choosing it and clicking the Add button. Any parameter fields added this way will be set to True.

The following illustration shows a prompt for a nonexclusive Boolean parameter field group.

Exclusive group parameter offers drop-down list
of all parameters in group; only one can be chosen

Add selected parameter to
list (nonexclusive group only)

Nongroup parameter offers True or False choice only

Enter Parameter Values   ☒

Parameter Fields:

| Region |
| Customer Name |
| Summary Only |
| Group #0 |
| Group #1 |

Select and add group parameter fields which have True values.

Boolean Parameter   [Orders that have shipped ▼]   Add

| Orders that have shipped |
| Orders that are paid |
| On Back Order |

Boolean parameters with True value

| Orders that have shipped | Delete

OK   Cancel   Help

Nonexclusive group parameter offers
drop-down list of all parameters in
group; any or all can be added

Delete selected parameter from
list (nonexclusive group only)

Any parameters added to the list will return True when the report runs.

If you create an exclusive group, the Add and Delete buttons, as well as the list box below the drop-down list, won't appear. You'll be able to choose only one of the parameter fields in the drop-down list. It will return true, while all others in the group will return false.

Using Parameter Fields in Record Selection

Probably the most common use for a parameter field is in report record selection. By creating a parameter field and using it with the Select Expert or a record-selection formula, you can prompt the viewer to provide variable information when the report runs, and have the report record selection reflect the viewer's choices.

After creating the desired parameter fields, use the toolbar button or pull-down menu option to start the Select Expert. Add a selection tab for the database field you want to compare to the value the viewer enters into the parameter field. In the operation drop-down list, choose the appropriate operation for the parameter action you need, e.g., "is equal to" for a region selection parameter, "greater than" for a sales or order threshold parameter, "is like" for a string-matching name parameter. It's not always intuitive, though: you'll usually use "is equal to" when you're matching to a ranged or multiple value parameter (not "is between" or "is one of"). When you choose the drop-down list to see sample database values, you'll see parameter fields of the same data type in the list. Choose the correct parameter field.

Caution *Only parameter fields of the same data type as the database field will show up in the Select Expert. If you don't see the parameter field you expect in the Select Expert, it wasn't created with the same data type as the database field you are using. Change the value type of the parameter field and rerun the Select Expert.*

If you use the Formula Editor to edit the record-selection formula, you'll see all parameter fields (regardless of data type) in the Field Tree box. Choose the parameter field you want to use in the record-selection formula. The formula may look something like this:

```
{Customer.Region} = {?Region}
```

Make sure you choose a parameter field of the same data type, or use functions to convert the parameter field to the correct data type. If you try, for example, to compare a numeric parameter field to a string database field, you'll receive an error in the Formula Editor.

Displaying Parameter Fields on the Report

One of the other major benefits of using parameter fields is that you can place them on your report just like database or formula fields. Whatever value the viewer placed in them before the report ran will appear on the report. By creatively using parameter fields, you can have a customized report that changes record selection and shows the values used in record selection on the report.

To place a parameter field on the report, drag and drop it from the Field Explorer just as you would a database or formula field. Depending on the value type of the parameter field, you can format it using all the usual Format toolbar or Format Editor features discussed earlier in this book. You can also combine parameter fields with other fields and literal text inside text objects (as discussed in Chapter 2). A text object combining a parameter field looks like this in the Design tab:

> Orders over {?Order Level} are highlighted

and will use the value supplied by the viewer when the report runs:

> Orders over $2,500.00 are highlighted

Tip	*Only single (discrete) parameters are effectively displayed this way. To display multiple values or ranged values, you must create a formula that extracts the whole set or range of values the user has entered. Solutions for these cases are discussed in the Special Parameter Features discussion later in this chapter.*

Special Parameter Field Features

Parameter fields have become increasingly sophisticated as new versions of Crystal Reports have been released, particularly versions 7 and 8. For example, a viewer can choose multiple values for a single parameter field to allow One-Of types of record selection. Parameter fields can be specified to include entire ranges of values, so a viewer can, for example, include all orders placed between January 1, 2001, and December 31, 2001. Also, string parameter fields can be limited to certain lengths (for example, no less than three nor more than six characters) or limited to certain formats with edit masks.

Multiple Values

Often, you may want to be able to choose more than one value for a parameter field and have the report recognize the multiple values in record selection. You may, for example, want to initially specify only one region for a report and later run the same report including ten different regions. If you're not using parameter fields, you'll need to change the Select Expert operator from Equal To to One Of and select the multiple regions.

By clicking the Allow Multiple Values check box in the Options section of the Create Parameter Field dialog box, you allow multiple entries to be added to a parameter list— you, in essence, turn the parameter field into a single object called an *array* that contains more than one value. Even if you choose an Equal To operator in the Select Expert with a multiple-value parameter field, all the values in the array will be included in record selection. When you are prompted for a multiple-value parameter field, you can use the Add and Delete buttons to add or remove multiple values. The values that are added to the list can be either chosen from a pick list or typed in the text box and then added with the Add button (typing values is dependent upon the setting of the Allow Editing of Default Values... check box in the Create Parameter Field dialog box).

Caution *If you add a multiple-value parameter field to your report to display selected values, only the first value will actually appear on the report, even though all values will be used by the Select Expert. Use array functions in a formula, such as the Join function, to retrieve all the values in the parameter field. The Join function is described in detail in Chapter 5.*

Range Values

Crystal Reports provides *range-value* parameter fields, which allow you to create just one parameter field that can contain both low and high values. When this parameter field is supplied to the Select Expert with the Equals operator, it effectively supplies both the low and high values and changes the operator to Between.

To create a range-value parameter field, click the Range Value(s) radio button in the Create Parameter Field dialog box (this is the opposite of a discrete-value parameter field, which doesn't contain high/low values). This will change the way the parameter field prompt appears when the report is refreshed.

There are now two prompts to choose or enter values: the Start of Range prompt and the End of Range prompt. These two prompts behave the same way a single prompt would behave, being based on pick list creation, allowing editing of default values, and so forth. However, when the viewer clicks OK, both prompts will be supplied to the Select Expert or record-selection formula, and all records between and including the selected values will be returned.

Normally, range-value parameter fields are "inclusive"; that is, the values returned to the report *include* the two values that are specified in the Enter Parameter Values dialog box. If you uncheck Include Value, however, the chosen value *will not* be included in the range. For example, if you choose the number 300 as the Start of Range and leave Include

Value checked, any records including the number 300 will be included in the report. If you uncheck Include Value, anything over 300 will be included, but not 300 itself.

There are also No Lower Bound and No Upper Bound check boxes to allow you to make the range an open-ended range. If you leave both boxes unchecked (the default), the range will be limited to the finite values you enter as Start of Range and End of Range. If you check No Lower Bound or No Upper Bound (you can't select both), the corresponding range value will be discarded and the range will include only the other value. For example, if you specify a range of 100 to 1000, checking No Lower Bound will discard 100 and return records where the value is simply less than 1000 (or less than and including 1000 if you leave Include Value checked). Checking No Upper Bound will return records exceeding 100 (or equal to or greater than 100 if you leave Include Value checked).

If you add a range-value parameter field directly to your report to display selected values, the parameter field will not show anything, because the parameter field is actually a range value. A *range* value is a single object (in this case, the parameter field) that actually contains the entire range of values specified by the parameter field. If you just put the object on the report by itself, Crystal Reports won't return a value, because it's not sure which value in the range you want to return. You can use range functions in the Formula Editor to return the first or last entries in the range. For example, the following formula will display the starting and ending dates of a date-range parameter field:

```
"Orders between " + ToText(Minimum({?Date Range}),"M/d/yyyy") + " and " +
ToText(Maximum({?Date Range}),"M/d/yyyy")
```

The Minimum and Maximum functions return the first and last entries in the range, respectively. The ToText function turns the date values from the array into strings.

However, when either No Lower Bound or No Upper Bound is selected for a date range, the corresponding Minimum or Maximum value is displayed oddly—it may appear to return a nonsensical or blank value. To display a more helpful message, you can use a formula to evaluate the date and display text in place of the min or max date:

```
local datetimevar dMinDate := minimum({?Date Range});
local datetimevar dMaxDate := maximum({?Date Range});
local stringvar sMinDate := totext(dMinDate,"M/d/yyyy");
local stringvar sMaxDate := totext(dMaxDate,"M/d/yyyy");

if Year(dMinDate) = 0 then "From first order to " + sMaxDate
else
if Year(dMaxDate) = 0 then "From " + sMinDate + " to newest order"
else
"From " + sMinDate + " to " + sMaxDate
```

| Note | *The usage of variables, and other techniques used in this formula, is explained more fully in Chapter 5.*

If, in addition to checking the Range Value(s) check box, you click the Allow Multiple Values check box in the Create Parameter Field dialog box, the parameter field will allow entry of multiple range values, or an *array of ranges.* For example, you could choose to see orders placed between January 1, 2000, and March 31, 2000; January 1, 2001, and March 31, 2001; and January 1, 2002, and March 31, 2002. When you are prompted for a range-value parameter field that allows multiple values, a list will appear in which you can add multiple ranges.

Different values can be specified in the Start of Range and End of Range areas and added to the list with the Add button. If you want to delete an existing range, select it in the list and click the Delete button.

This single parameter field, when supplied to the Select Expert or record-selection formula, will effectively change the selection operator to Between *and* One Of at the same time.

> **Caution**   *The Minimum and Maximum array functions demonstrated earlier behave a little differently with combination range/multiple-value parameter fields and combination range and discreet value/multiple value parameter fields. In these cases, you may use the Minimum and Maximum function, as well as an array subscript (a number inside square brackets after the parameter field name), to extract the beginning and ending values of different elements of the array.*

Controlling Parameter Field Data Entry

One of the issues Crystal Reports users face is how to best customize the user interface for "turnkey" report users—those that aren't familiar with the intricacies of Crystal Reports. In an ideal world, the user interface will contain business rules, limits, and customized formatting to guide an end user through proper choices of parameters. While this ideal world is best provided with a customized "front end" program developed, perhaps, in Visual Basic, Crystal Reports still gives the report developer a fair amount of control over how end users can enter data into parameter fields.

Limiting Entry to Certain Ranges of Values

For parameter field types, except string and Boolean, you can limit the range of entries that a viewer can supply. By checking Range Limited Field in the Set Default Values dialog box, you can specify a beginning and ending value for the range in the controls that become enabled below the check box. When the viewer is prompted for the parameter field, they will be unable to enter values that are below the beginning range or above the ending range.

An added feature of range limiting is the group of default values that can be added to the parameter field. When you range-limit a parameter field and choose a database table and field to help populate the Default Values list, only database items that fall within the specified range can be added to the Default Values list. If you use the double right arrow to add all browsed database values to the list, only those that fall within the beginning and ending ranges will be added. If you have already supplied values that are outside the range, then when you click OK, you will be told that you will lose some default values; say OK to limit default values to be within your range.

When a viewer is prompted to supply a range-limited number or currency parameter field, they will receive an error message if they type in a value outside the range. If the range-limited parameter field is a date, time, or date/time field, the viewer will not be able to even type dates or times outside the range. The date picker will display only dates that fall within the range.

Minimum and Maximum Lengths

If you create a string parameter field, the Length Limit check box appears in the Set Default Values dialog box. By checking this option, a Min Length and a Max Length text box are enabled below the check box. You can specify the minimum and maximum number of characters that must be supplied when responding to the parameter field's prompt. If you enter too few or too many characters, an error message will appear.

Enter Parameter Values

Parameter Fields:

Date Range
Region
Customer Name
Order Level
Summary Only

Enter region(s) to include

Insert Parameter Field

⚠ The maximum length for this field is 2.

OK

Discrete Value   Alabama ▾   Add

Value

Delete

OK   Cancel   Help

If you supply a length limit, you are also restricted from adding any default values to the pick list that fall outside the minimum and maximum lengths.

Edit Masks

The most flexibility for controlling string parameter field entry comes from *edit masks*. An edit mask is a string of characters that controls many different aspects of data entry. One example might be an edit mask that allows only two uppercase characters to be entered (perhaps for a state abbreviation). Another example would be an edit mask that sets up the parameter field to accept data in a social security number format, accepting only number characters, and automatically adding hyphens between the third and fourth characters and between the fifth and sixth characters.

The key to using edit masks is learning the correct use of masking characters. These are listed in Table 14-3. Note that not only is the character you use significant, but so is the *case* of the character—uppercase and lowercase versions of the same character perform different masking functions.

So, an edit mask of (000) 000-0000 when used with a phone number parameter field will require entry of the area code and phone number portions, and will include the parentheses, space, and hyphen in the parameter prompt to format the entry. The resulting content of the {?Phone} parameter value will include the literal characters, so if used for record selection it will find only phone strings formatted with exactly those

Character	Usage
A	Requires entry of an alphanumeric character.
a	Allows an alphanumeric character to be entered, but doesn't require it.
0 (zero)	Requires a digit between 0 and 9 to be entered.
9	Allows a digit between 0 and 9 or a space to be entered, but doesn't require it.
#	Allows a digit, space, or plus or minus sign to be entered, but doesn't require it.
L	Requires entry of a letter between A and Z to be entered.
?	Allows a letter between A and Z to be entered, but doesn't require it.
&	Requires entry of any character or space.
C	Allows entry of any character or space, but doesn't require it.
>	Automatically converts any subsequent characters to uppercase.
<	Automatically converts any subsequent characters to lowercase.
\	Causes the next character to be included in the parameter field prompt (and resulting value) as a literal—helpful if you want to actually include masking characters in the parameter field.
. , : ; - / ( ) or any character not listed in this table	These characters will be included in the parameter field prompt and value as literals—they will appear in the parameter field exactly as typed.
Password	Causes characters typed in the parameter field to be displayed with asterisks instead of their actual characters; the actual characters are passed to the report.

Table 14-3. *Parameter Field Masking Characters*

literals, e.g., (204) 949-6053. If the phone number string in the database is stored as 204-949-6053, it would not match the parameter value with the parentheses, but an edit mask of 000-000-0000 would find it.

An edit mask of Password will replace characters typed in the parameter prompting field with asterisks. This is commonly used for entry of passwords or other sensitive information to prevent the information from being learned by someone looking at the screen. When the viewer clicks OK, the actual characters typed will be passed to the report as the parameter value.

If you enter an edit mask for a parameter before creating your defaults for the viewer's pick list, when you hit the double right arrow button to send all the possible values to the defaults list, it only sends the ones that match the edit mask. For example, an edit mask of >LL used for the Region field parameter sends only the two-character uppercase codes to the defaults pick list, but not all the spelled-out regions in the Xtreme sample database. It can be used to quickly select only the correctly formatted entries from a larger imported pick list.

Conditional Formatting with Parameter Fields

Parameter fields can be used to customize other parts of the report, not just record selection. If a viewer wishes to highlight orders over a certain amount, they can specify the amount in a parameter field and use the parameter field to set conditional formatting. If they wish to see summary data instead of details data, they can respond to a Boolean parameter field that is used to suppress the details section. Basically, any place you can do conditional formatting, you can base it on parameter fields just as easily as you can on database or formula fields.

Highlighting Data Based on Parameter Fields

Once a parameter field has been created, it can be used for conditional formatting just as easily as any database or formula field. As with any parameter field, you need to consider the value type used to create the parameter field. For example, you might wish to prompt the viewer for an order amount threshold so that you can highlight orders over that amount in red. If the Order Amount field in the database is contained in a currency data type, you'll need to either create the parameter field with the currency data type or do some data-type conversion in the conditional formula.

A currency parameter field will prompt the viewer to enter an order amount threshold. Then, you can use two conditional formulas: one for the background color of the details section and one for the font color of the order amount and customer name fields. The details section background color can be formatted to show in silver if the order exceeds the parameter field, as follows:

```
If {Orders.Order Amount} > {?Order Level} Then Silver Else NoColor
```

The following conditional formula, when applied to the font color of both the order amount and customer name, will display the fields in red if the order amount exceeds the threshold:

```
If {Orders.Order Amount} > {?Order Level} Then Red Else Black
```

Figure 14-4 shows the result when a threshold of $1,000 is supplied to the parameter field prompt.

Caution *Since the Highlighting Expert allows you only to compare to actual database values to set formatting conditionally, the Highlighting Expert will not work with parameter fields. You must use the Conditional Formula buttons that appear in the Format Editor if you wish to conditionally format with parameter fields.*

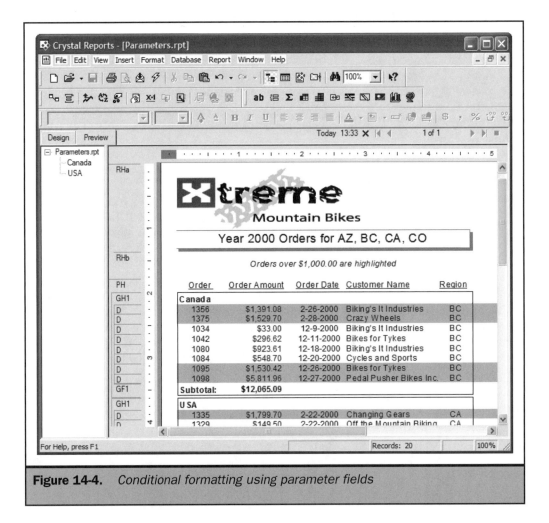

Figure 14-4. *Conditional formatting using parameter fields*

Conditionally Suppressing Based on Parameter Fields

Use a parameter field just like a database or formula field to conditionally suppress individual objects or sections. Since the Suppress property requires a Boolean formula when being set conditionally, you can create a Boolean parameter field and supply it as the sole part of the Boolean formula, or you can create a Boolean formula by using a comparison operator with another type of parameter field.

You could, for example, create a Boolean parameter field called Summary Only that returns a true or false value based on the viewer's choice. By simply supplying the Boolean parameter field as the only item in a section or object's Suppress conditional formula, you could control whether the details section or a page header section containing column headings for the details section appears or doesn't appear.

When prompted for this parameter field, the viewer could select a True or False option for the Summary Only parameter field. You could then place this parameter field directly in the Suppress conditional formula for the details section. If the Summary Only parameter were true (indicating that the viewer wants a summary-only report), the details section would be suppressed. You could also suppress the page header section that contains column headings for the details fields.

A Password parameter can be used to conditionally format a sensitive data field, such as Salary, to suppress if {?Password} does not equal a certain value. Since the password is masked by asterisks when the viewer enters it, it's protected from inadvertent "over-the-shoulder" viewing, and only people who enter it correctly will see the sensitive data. Note, however, that anyone with access to the report and to the Crystal Reports Designer can simply view the conditional formatting formula to determine the password value required, so the password edit mask is not, in itself, a security measure for sensitive data.

Using Parameter Fields with Formulas

There will be many situations in which you need to prompt for a parameter field in a certain way or choose a particular value type for a parameter field so it will work properly with record selection. However, you might want to display the parameter field on the report in a different way, perform some calculation based on the parameter field, or otherwise manipulate the parameter field in a formula. Or, you may want to provide some variable information to a formula, such as a sales tax rate. By setting up a parameter field to prompt for the tax rate, it's very easy to run the report for different states or cities that have varying sales tax rates.

When you create a parameter field, it will appear in the Formula Editor's Field Tree box under Report Fields. It can be added to a formula just like a database field or another formula. Just remember the value type you choose when creating the parameter field—you must use it correctly inside the formula to avoid type-mismatch errors. You may need to use ToText, ToNumber, or other conversion functions.

Using a Parameter Field for Partial Text Matches

A handy capability of the Select Expert is the Like operator that can be used when selecting records based on string database fields. Like allows you to supply *wildcard characters*, such as the question mark (?) and asterisk (*) to indicate single-character and whole-field matches, respectively. For example, supplying a Select Expert operator of Like with the literal *?eor?e* would return George, Jeorge, Jeorje, or Georje. Using the Like operator with an asterisk in the literal *Je** would return Jean, Jenny, Jennifer, and Jerry.

> **Note** *A more complete discussion of record selection is contained in Chapter 8.*

By allowing question marks and asterisks to be included in parameter fields, and by using the Like operator in the Select Expert, you give your report viewer great flexibility in choosing only the records they want to see. However, if you want a meaningful message to appear on the report indicating what the user has chosen, you'll need to use a formula to display different information than the parameter field actually supplies to the Select Expert.

Consider a parameter field called Customer Name that will prompt the viewer to add question marks or asterisks for partial-match searches:

If you wish to place a descriptive message in the page header indicating which customers have been chosen, you can create the following formula:

```
If {?Customer Name} = "*" Then
    "All Customers"
Else
    If Instr({?Customer Name},"?") > 0 or
        Instr({?Customer Name},"*") > 0 Then
        "Customers matching the pattern " + {?Customer Name}
    Else
        "Customer: " + {?Customer Name}
```

This formula simply uses the Customer Name parameter field as you would another database or formula field in an If-Then-Else statement. If the parameter field contains only an asterisk, it will return all records, so the formula returns "All Customers." Otherwise, if the parameter field contains at least one asterisk or question mark (the Instr function will return the location of the first occurrence of the character, or zero if there isn't any occurrence), the formula indicates that the report is based on a partial pattern. Finally, if there are no asterisks or question marks at all, the report will be returning an exact text match to the parameter field, and this formula indicates that.

To make it easy for the report to default to all customers without the viewer knowing or remembering to enter an asterisk in the prompt, you may wish to add it as a default value for the parameter prompt, with the description All Customers.

Note   *If you make further use of this type of parameter field in the Select Expert, remember that you'll need to use the Like operator, instead of Equal To, to ensure the selection works with the asterisk.*

Using a Parameter Field to Change Sorting or Grouping

You may often wish to have a report viewer choose the report sorting or grouping on the fly. Since a parameter field can't actually return a database or formula-field name itself, you need to create a formula based on the parameter field, and use that formula as the sort or group field in the report.

You could, for example, create a parameter field called Group By that prompts for grouping by Country, Region, or City. These would be the only three options, as the viewer will not be allowed to edit the default values. The prompt for this parameter field would look like this:

Because the parameter field will contain only the string Country, Region, or City, you can't use the parameter field directly as a sort or group field. You need to create a formula based on the parameter field and supply it as the sort or group field. Look at this formula:

```
If {?Group By} = "Region" Then {Customer.Region}
Else
If {?Group By} = "City" Then {Customer.City}
Else {Customer.Country}
```

This will actually return a different database field based on the parameter field's value. Then, this formula can be supplied as the grouping or sorting field, and the group or sort will change according to the viewer's response to the parameter field.

Tip	*You may pay a slight performance penalty when you use this method with SQL or ODBC databases. Since the sorting or grouping will be done with a formula field and not directly with a database field, the ORDER BY clause won't use this formula, requiring Crystal Reports to actually sort the data once it arrives from the database server.*

Using a Parameter Field to Control Top N Reporting

Top N reporting (covered in more detail in Chapter 3) accepts a "hard-coded" value for *N*. That is, if you want to see the top five groups, or the bottom ten groups, you must choose Top N or Bottom N and type an actual "5" or "10" into the Group Sort Expert dialog box.

There may be instances, however, where you desire to supply the value of *N* with a parameter field. You'll soon discover, though, that there's no way to place a parameter field value in the Group Sort Expert text box for *N*. If you try to type the parameter field in manually (starting with the curly brace), you won't achieve success—the text box only accepts numbers. While you may be convinced that this renders Top N via a parameter field only a "dream," some creative reporting techniques can still be used to achieve the same goal.

To approximate the same behavior, perform the following steps:

1. Rather than choosing Top N or Bottom N in the Group Sort Expert dialog box, choose Sort All. Then, choose the summary field you want to use to control top or bottom N grouping in the "based on" drop-down list, and choose Descending

order to show "Top N" values (high to low), or Ascending order to show "Bottom N" values (low to high).

2. Create a parameter field to accept the value of *N* from the report viewer. The parameter field should be set as a number value type.

3. Conditionally suppress all group sections (such as the group header and footer) that you don't want to appear for any groups other than *N*. Do this by adding the following formula using the conditional suppression button in the Section Expert (assuming that your parameter field is named {?Top N Months}). Note the use of the GroupNumber function from the Print State category of the Functions box in the Formula Editor—this function returns a sequential number for each group displayed on the report.

```
GroupNumber > {?Top N Months}
```

The result will be groups appearing in Top or Bottom *N* order (depending on whether you chose Descending or Ascending order in the Group Sort Expert), with groups being suppressed if the GroupNumber function exceeds the value of the parameter field.

While this technique will, in effect, allow Top *N* reporting with a parameter field, it introduces an additional challenge if you want to show grand totals at the end of the report for only the Top or Bottom *N* groups. As conditional suppression occurs **after** grand totals or running totals in the Crystal Reports processing cycle, you can't use them to calculate totals for only the Top or Bottom *N* groups displayed in this manner. Instead, you will need to create your own "manual" running total formulas, utilizing variables.

Tip   *Chapter 5 contains more information on creating formulas with variables. Also, an example of this technique, including a proper totaling formula, can be found on the book's companion Web site (www.CrystalBook.com). Look for Top N-w Parameter Field.rpt.*

Chapter 15

Exporting Reports

419

When you save a Crystal Report, your report file is saved on disk with an .RPT extension. This Crystal Reports native format can be used only with another copy of Crystal Reports, with Crystal Enterprise, or with a Web-based application using a native Crystal Reports programming interface (discussed in Part II of the book), or with a customized Windows application (discussed in Part III of the book). Since everyone who might ever need to view a report probably won't have their own copy of Crystal Reports, there are many ways to *export* a report to a different file format for use with such products as Microsoft Word, Microsoft Excel, Acrobat Reader, and others. You can also export your reports in HTML format for viewing in a Web browser. Furthermore, you can attach these differently formatted files to e-mail messages or place them in a Lotus Notes database or a Microsoft Exchange public folder.

Although exporting is a handy way of distributing reports to non-Crystal Reports viewers, your exported reports are *static,* meaning they contain a picture of the database as it existed when the report was exported. As soon as the database changes (perhaps the second after the report was exported), the report becomes outdated. If your viewers have their own copies of Crystal Reports, they can solve this problem by opening and refreshing the report, but this also means that they can *change* the report. This solution also assumes that your viewers know enough about Crystal Reports to be able to open and refresh a report.

If your viewers do not have their own copies of Crystal Reports and do need real-time data reporting, you may want to consider implementing Crystal Enterprise to allow real-time running of reports in a Web browser. (See Part II for more information.) Or, you may be able to provide your report viewers with a copy of Seagate Analysis, which will allow them to open reports and run them directly against the database in real time.

| Note | *Previous versions of Crystal Reports allowed creation of compiled reports—stand-alone programs that allowed reports to be run in real time without a copy of Crystal Reports. However, Crystal Reports 9 has removed this functionality. And, no compiled reporting "add-in" for Crystal Reports 9 is available from the Crystal Decisions Web site.* |

The examples in this chapter are based on a report, shown in Figure 15-1, containing both text and a chart placed beside the text with the Underlay feature. In addition, some of the text contains special formatting, such as drop shadows. The report also contains additional graphical elements, such as line and box drawing.

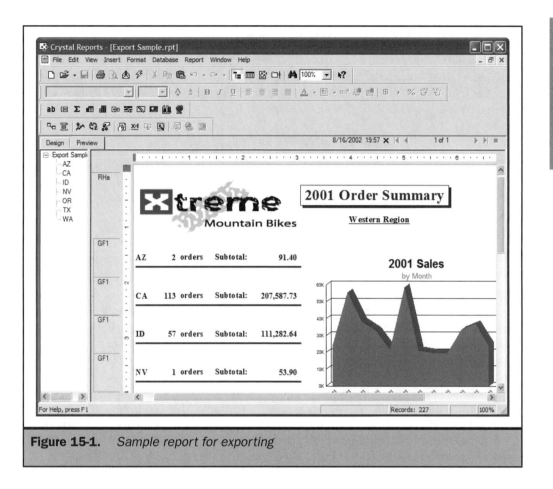

Figure 15-1.   *Sample report for exporting*

Exporting Reports to Office Applications

You'll often wish to convert or export a report you've designed to a popular office file format, such as Excel, Word, WordPerfect, or Acrobat Reader. With Crystal Reports, this is as simple as choosing an option from the File menu. You can also export the file to a temporary location and immediately launch the application you want to use to view the file, provided it's installed on your PC.

Exporting to Different File Formats

To export a file, first open the report you wish to export. Refresh and preview the report, if necessary, to ensure that it contains the most up-to-date data from the database. Then, click the Export button on the Standard toolbar or choose File | Export. The Export dialog box will appear.

You have two simple choices to make for your export: the file format of the export, and the destination of the export. The Format drop-down list lets you choose from the large number of file formats to which Crystal Reports will export. You can choose from several different ASCII or "straight-text" formats, several versions of Microsoft Excel, Microsoft Word, Acrobat Reader, and others.

The Destination drop-down list lets you choose how you want the report exported: to a disk file, attached to an e-mail message, placed in a Microsoft Exchange public folder, or launched in an application on your workstation. If you choose Disk File, the Choose Export File dialog box will prompt you for the folder and filename to export to. Choose a folder and type a filename, if the default folder and filename aren't sufficient.

Caution   *If your report contains several drill-down tabs or subreport Preview tabs, ensure that the tab you want exported is selected before you begin exporting. Whatever appears in the current tab (and all pages generated by that tab) is what will be exported by Crystal Reports.*

Figure 15-2 shows the sample report from Figure 15-1 after it has been exported to a Microsoft Word document.

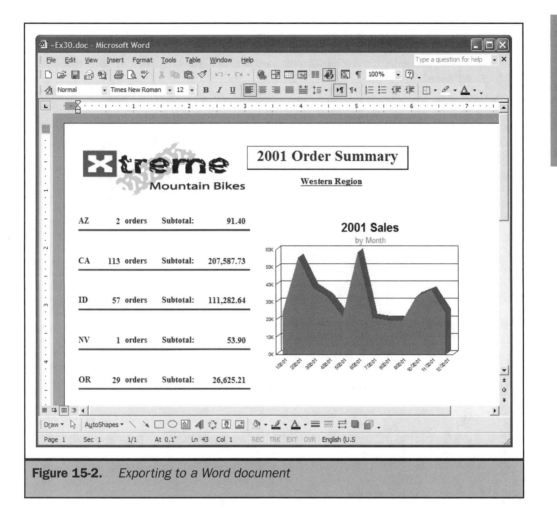

Figure 15-2.   *Exporting to a Word document*

Note   *In previous versions of Crystal Reports, the Word export was unable to convert the drop shadows around the report and chart titles, or the underlay feature of the chart section. In Crystal Reports 9, exporting of graphic elements and formatting is much improved for Word, Excel, and Acrobat Reader formats. However, you'll still find that some of the Crystal Reports formatting doesn't translate to other file formats. You should export to your ultimate destination format throughout your report design process to make sure everything you want to include will be exported correctly.*

If you drill down on a report, a different report "view" will appear inside the drill-down tab. Only the material inside the open drill-down tab will be exported. The main Preview tab won't be included. Exporting the Idaho (ID) drill-down tab will result in a Microsoft Excel file, shown in Figure 15-3.

Depending on the file format you choose, you may receive an additional dialog box prompting you for the page range to be included, and/or other extended information about the export. If, for example, you choose one of the Excel formats, a dialog box will allow you to choose more customized information when exporting to Excel.

Excel Format Options

Column width
- Column width based on objects in the : Whole Report
- Constant column width (in points) : 36.0

☑ Export Page Header and Page Footer
☐ Create page breaks for each page
☐ Convert date values to strings

Page range
- All pages
- From: 0 To: 0

OK   Cancel

Exporting to various text file formats, such as Character Separated Values, will present additional dialog boxes prompting you for, among other things, the characters to surround and separate fields.

Exporting to an Adobe Portable Document Format, or *PDF,* file may be the most effective way to export a report that contains complex formatting and graphics, including underlain sections, as shown in Figure 15-4. First introduced in Crystal Reports 8.5, the PDF export features offer improved resolution and clarity in Crystal Reports 9.

Exporting and Launching an Application

If you choose Application in the Destination drop-down list, Crystal Reports will export the file to a temporary folder and immediately open the file in the corresponding application. If you choose a file format for an application that isn't installed on your computer, you may be presented with a dialog box asking you to choose an application to open the file with. If there is an alternative application that will open that file type, choose it from the list.

Note *The temporary files that Crystal Reports creates will be located in the Windows temporary folder (typically, \Windows\Temp) and may not automatically be deleted when you close the application. If you wish to periodically "clean out" your Windows temporary folder, use Disk Cleanup or another appropriate utility or measure to remove temporary files.*

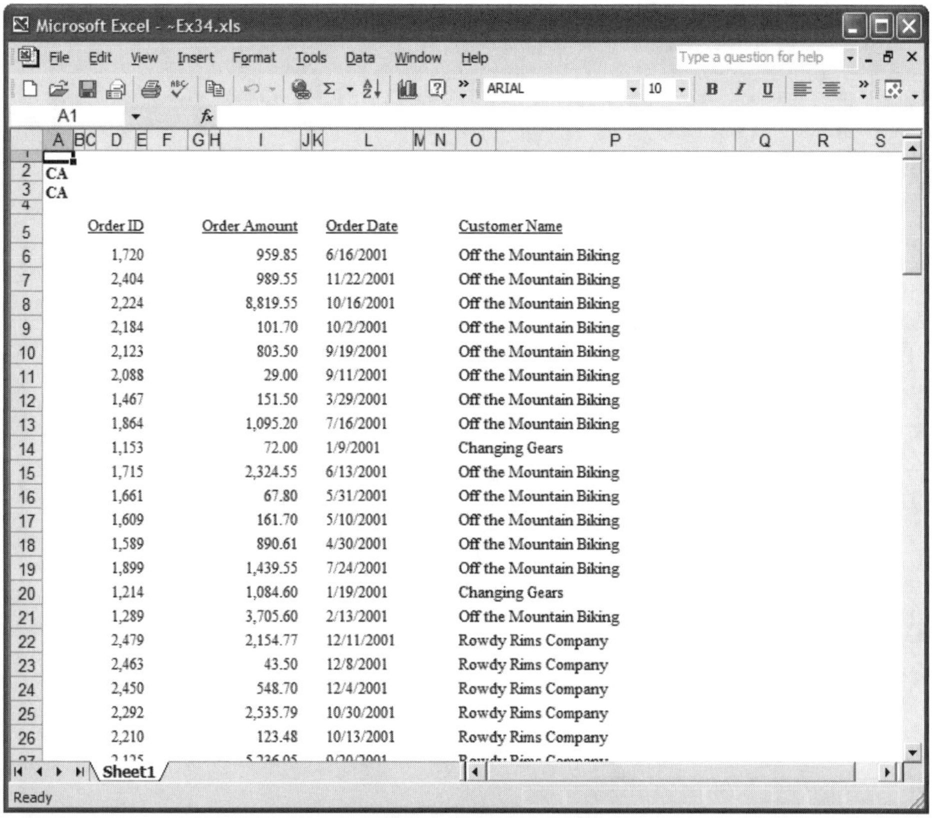

Figure 15-3. *Drill-down tab exported to Excel*

Exporting to an ODBC Data Source

You can export a Crystal Report to an ODBC data source, such as a Microsoft SQL Server or Oracle database. Typically, you'll want to do this with a simple columnar details report that you might be using to transport data from a PC database to a client/ server database.

Note *You cannot create a new ODBC data source inside Crystal Reports. Use the ODBC icon in the Windows Control Panel to modify or create ODBC data sources.*

To export to an ODBC data source, choose the data source you want to export to in the Format drop-down list. You'll then be asked to supply a table name, which Crystal Reports will create in the database referred to by the data source. If the data source refers to a secure database, you will be asked to supply a database logon user ID and password before the export starts. And if the data source does not contain a specific database reference, you may be asked to choose a database in addition to the table name.

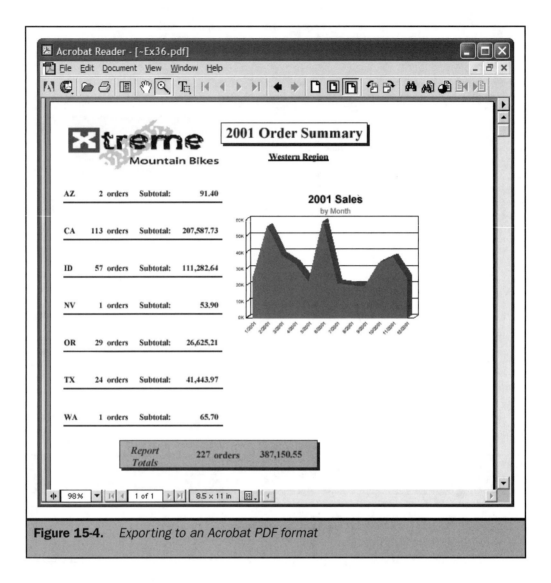

Figure 15-4. *Exporting to an Acrobat PDF format*

Crystal Reports will create a new table in the ODBC database and define fields to hold data from the exported report. If you want to change field names or the layout of the table, you need to use a utility specific to the ODBC database that you exported to.

Caution *ODBC is "picky" about the organization of data you export. You may need to modify the report (perhaps removing groups or changing the formatting of parts of the report) to get the report to export without ODBC errors.*

Creating a Report Definition File

When you create reports, you may want to keep documentation that details the report design, such as the tables that are included, what formulas you've created, and what objects are contained in the report sections.

The Export dialog box in Crystal Reports provides a Report Definition format in the Format drop-down list. When you choose this format, Crystal Reports will save a text file containing a great deal of helpful information about the makeup of the report. You may wish to create and keep these text files in a central location to document the design of your reports. You may also open the text files in a word processor and reformat them to look more appealing.

```
~Ex2B.txt - Notepad

File  Edit  Format  View  Help

        Crystal Report Professional v9.2 (32-bit) - Report Definition

1.0 File Information

        Report File:
        Version: 10.2

2.0 Record Sort Fields

3.0 Group Sort Fields

4.0 Formulas

4.1 Record Selection Formula
        {Orders.Order Date} = {?Date Range} and
{Customer.Region} = {?Region}

4.2 Group Selection Formula


4.3 Other Formulas

5.0 Sectional Information

5.1 Page Header Section
        Hidden, Keep Together

5.2 Page Footer Section
        Visible, New Page After, Keep Together, Print At Bottom of Page

        PageNofM
                String, Visible, Left Alignment, Top Alignment,
                Keep Together, Using System Default Formatting, Word Wrap
```

Exporting to XML

Crystal Reports provides the capability of exporting to Extensible Markup Language, or *XML*. XML, which is an extension of Hypertext Markup Language (HTML—the original "language" of the World Wide Web), and is gaining more acceptance as a method of data exchange among disparate organizations and companies. XML describes the data that it encompasses with a set of descriptors, or *tags*, similar to HTML. These tags format the report content according to standardized language rules established (and still under development) by a consortium of technology and business organizations. XML files can vary in content from very simplified data output to formatted definitions of hierarchically organized data. Each element in an XML file is identified by tags, which define the name of the element, the type of element, and additional optional attributes.

Crystal provides two basic XML output format options: the Crystal ML Schema, which provides a standard set of tags and structure that includes extensive formatting content, and the Custom Format, which allows the user to suppress elements, change the names of elements, and add attributes to elements.

The Crystal ML Schema is the default XML output when you select the Export to XML format. The resulting XML file can be viewed by a Web browser, but will not be interpreted/formatted by the browser the way an HTML file would be. Figure 15-5 shows the XML file output from a simple columnar Orders report (similar to the one

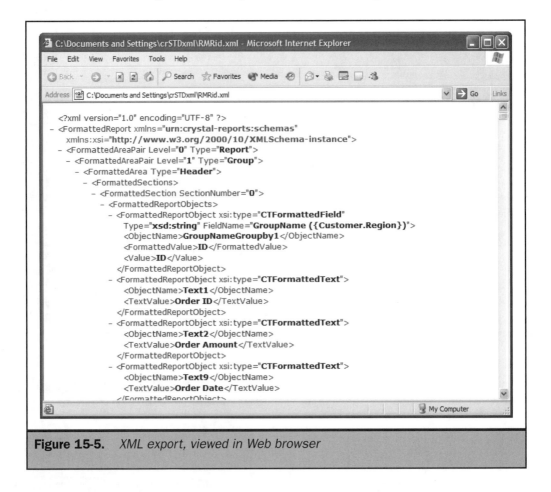

Figure 15-5.   *XML export, viewed in Web browser*

in Figure 15-3), using Crystal ML Schema. This schema is published at http://
www.crystaldecisions.com/xml/schema.xsd.

Note that this XML file includes format-oriented tags for each section of the report
as well as the data elements.

If you wish to customize the XML output format or request an external schema
validation file to accompany the XML file to document the tag conventions used in
the XML file, you'll want do it before exporting your report. To customize the format,
choose Report | XML Expert from the Crystal Reports pull-down menus. When the
XML Format dialog box is displayed, click the Options tab.

On the Options tab, you can select XSD if you want an external schema document to
accompany your Crystal ML Schema file, and also enter any custom text you want to insert
after the header in the XML file to further define the output. Or, if you want to customize
the XML output (perhaps to limit the file to data fields rather than formatted section
tags), click the Custom Format radio button.

Tip *Selecting Custom Format also allows the creation of a Document Type Definition external
document, or DTD; this option creates a short DTD file, but also changes the XML
output itself, eliminating most of the formatting elements and leaving data field elements.*

On the Options tab, after selecting the Custom Format radio button, click the Format tab to display your customization options, as shown in Figure 15-6.

To limit the XML file to just data elements, rather than report/formatting elements, you'll want to suppress some or all of the report section parent elements, such as ReportArea:Report Area and Detail:Detail. To do this, select the desired parent element or section and click the Suppress XML Tag check box beneath the tree. You can use the Suppress All Children check box when you don't want to produce XML tags for *any* subsets of a section/element. However, you would not use the Suppress All Children check box for any of the Details area elements, as it would also suppress tags for the data layer of the Details section. When an element is suppressed, the element can no longer be customized.

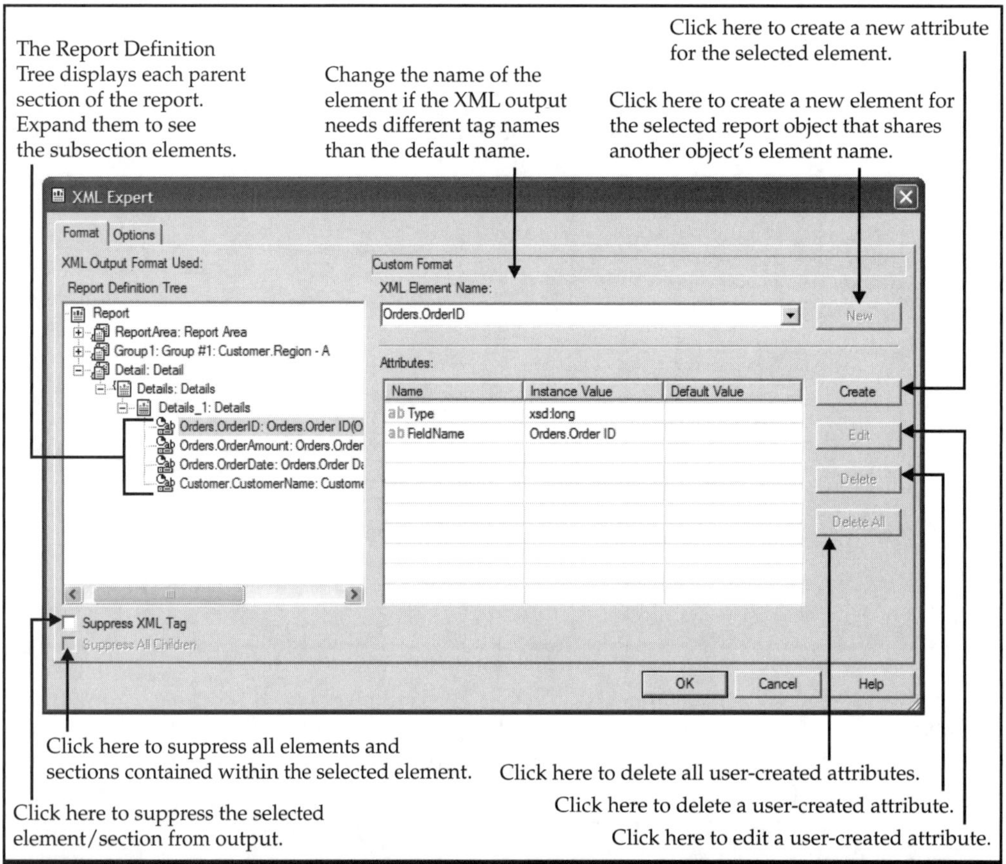

Figure 15-6. *XML Format dialog box*

To customize attributes or element names, select the element you wish to customize. The element name and the attributes of the element are displayed on the right side of the dialog box. In the example illustrated in Figure 15-6, the selected element is the data field containing the order ID. If desired, the name of the element (Orders.OrderID) can be changed for output purposes by simply entering the modified name in the XML Element Name field. By default, Crystal has assigned two attributes to each data field element: Type and FieldName. The gray "ab" designation beside the attribute name indicates that these cannot be changed or deleted. However, additional attributes can be created, changed, and deleted as needed according to the XML output required. For example, if you need to add a "use" attribute to this field, you can click the Create button to produce the XML Attribute Dialog box seen in Figure 15-7.

For this example, supplying an attribute of "use" and text of "required" will result in the standard XML field use attribute being inserted into the OrderID data element tag:

```
<Orders.OrderID FieldName="{Orders.Order ID}"
use="required">1128.00</Orders.OrderID>
```

Figure 15-8 shows the XML file exported from the Orders report with all report section areas suppressed, all data element names changed to eliminate the table name, and a use=required attribute added to the OrderID and OrderAmount elements.

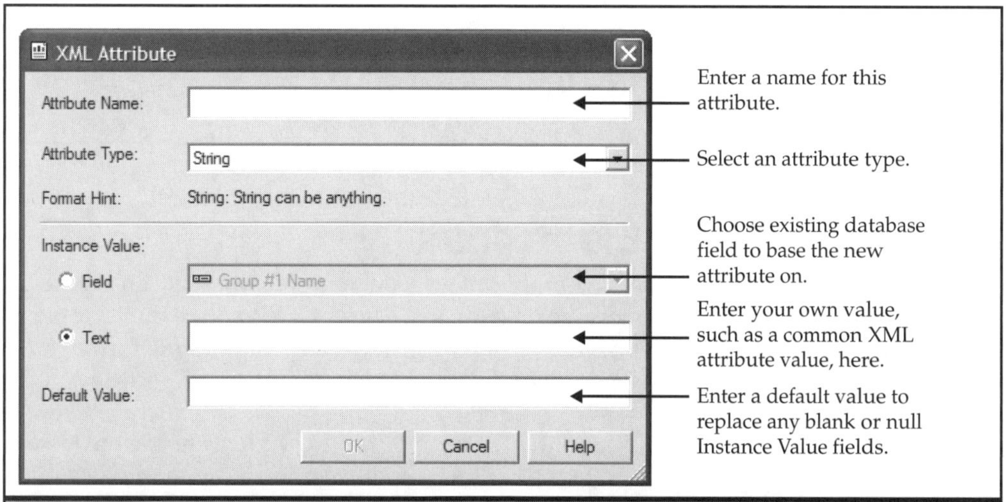

Figure 15-7. *XML Attribute dialog box*

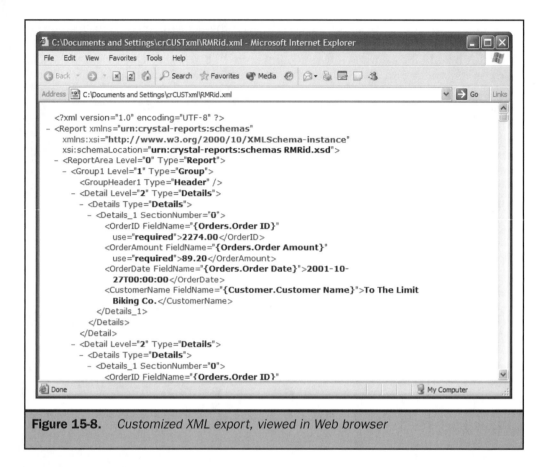

Figure 15-8. Customized XML export, viewed in Web browser

Sending Reports Electronically

In addition to exporting reports to office applications, you may want to create an exported report and attach it to an e-mail message or put it in a Microsoft Exchange public folder. You might expect to have to do this in two steps: export to your chosen file format and then run a separate e-mail package to send the file. However, Crystal Reports lets you do it all in one step.

Display the Export dialog box, and in the Format drop-down list, choose the format you want the report exported to. From the Destination drop-down list, choose the e-mail system you wish to send the report with. Choosing Lotus Notes Database will place a report on the Lotus Notes Desktop; choosing Exchange Folder will add the report to a Microsoft Exchange or Outlook Folder; and choosing Microsoft Mail (MAPI) will use a Microsoft-compatible e-mail program, such as Microsoft Outlook, to attach the report to an e-mail message. Note that you need to have the appropriate "client" software installed on your PC for this to work.

> **Tip** *Although you can choose File | Print | Mail, the same dialog box will be displayed as with the Export toolbar button or menu command. Just choose the correct e-mail type from the Destination drop-down list to electronically send your exported report.*

If Microsoft Outlook is installed on your PC and you choose Microsoft Mail (MAPI) as the destination, the following dialog box will appear.

Specify the e-mail address or addresses you want the message to go to, along with the message you want to appear in the e-mail body. The message will be sent with the report file attached (in the format you specified).

Chapter 16

Reporting from SQL Databases

A s newer leading-edge database applications are released, fewer and fewer make use of PC-style databases. The performance and capacity limitations of local PC databases often limit their usefulness for larger, performance-dependent applications. Instead, most newer applications rely on *client/server* database systems. A client/server system includes two parts: a *client*, typically a PC running software such as Crystal Reports or a data-entry application, and a *server*, typically a larger, high-end PC running Windows NT/2000, or a midrange or even a mainframe computer. The server maintains the database, and the client makes requests of the server for database access. Many different client/server databases exist, with Microsoft SQL Server, Oracle, Sybase, Informix, and IBM DB2 being among the more popular ones.

> **Caution** *Some SQL databases can be used only with the Professional, Developer, or Advanced editions of Crystal Reports 9. The Standard Edition reports only on a limited set of databases. If you want complete database flexibility, you should probably purchase the Professional, Developer, or Advanced edition.*

It's important to understand and contrast the differences between a client/server database system and a PC-style database system that is installed on a shared local area network (LAN). For reporting purposes, in particular, a LAN-based database system presents a much more serious performance hurdle than a client/server database. Figure 16-1 shows a PC reporting on two database environments. The first depicts a Microsoft Access database on a LAN server. The second depicts the same database on an SQL Server system.

The LAN-based scenario places heavy burdens on both the network and the PC making the reporting request. In this scenario, the PC must read the entire 100,000-record Access database across the network, picking and choosing the records that meet the report-selection criteria. This requires large amounts of data to be passed across the network, and the PC has to perform all the selection logic itself.

The client/server environment is much more efficient. The client PC simply makes a request to the database server via a Structured Query Language (SQL) request. The database server, presumably a larger, high-powered PC, Unix computer, or mainframe, runs database software designed to process such queries very efficiently. It directly queries the 100,000-record database and sends only the required 1,000 records back across the network. This places less demand on the client and the network, and the whole process typically takes less time.

Logging On to SQL Databases

The first step to creating a Crystal Report is to select the SQL database that you want to base your report on. There are three general communication methods you can use to connect to a client/server database with Crystal Reports: direct database drivers, ODBC, and OLE DB (pronounced oh-LAY-dee-bee).

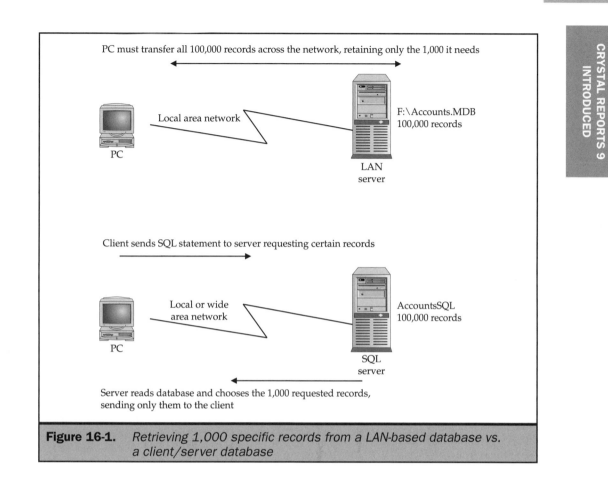

Figure 16-1. *Retrieving 1,000 specific records from a LAN-based database vs. a client/server database*

Direct Database Drivers

Crystal Reports provides direct database drivers that work with many industry-standard client/server databases, including, among others, Oracle, and IBM DB2 (the Microsoft SQL Server Direct Database driver has been eliminated from Crystal Reports 9, however). A direct database driver uses the native communication methods provided by the server vendor to communicate with the database server. This typically requires installing the specific client software provided by the database vendor on the PC. Examples of these packages include SQL*Plus for Oracle.

Crystal Reports will recognize the existence of these packages and provide a direct database driver to connect to the database. In addition, Crystal Reports provides other direct drivers to allow you to report from Microsoft Outlook folders, Microsoft Exchange folders, Lotus Notes databases, Internet Web server activity logs, and the Windows NT/ 2000/XP event log. You can even write reports based on the *local file system*, which consists of the file and directory structure of your C drive or a network drive. More details on these specialized types of reports can be found in Chapter 19.

Using direct database drivers to connect to the database server has two general advantages:

- Because fewer layers of communications protocols are being used, there may be a slight performance improvement when reporting.
- The direct database driver may allow more flexibility for creating server-specific SQL statements or other query features for reporting.

ODBC

Although many companies standardize on database servers that Crystal Reports provides direct database drivers for, many other database systems and specialized data systems exist that you may want to report on. Some standard method of communication is needed to connect standard PC clients with the myriad specialized servers and systems that exist. Microsoft designed open database connectivity (ODBC) to accomplish this communication.

As a general rule, any server or proprietary data platform that is ODBC-compliant can be used with Crystal Reports. If the database or system vendor provides a Windows ODBC driver for its system, Crystal Reports should be able to report against that server or system. Because it has been accepted as an industry standard, ODBC is in widespread use.

| Tip | *Crystal Reports installs ODBC automatically. In addition, it installs some generic ODBC data sources for common database files and formats, including an ODBC data source for using the sample XTREME.MDB database. Before you can use Crystal Reports to report against other ODBC data systems, you must set up an ODBC data source. Use the ODBC Administrator from Windows Control Panel to set up the data source.* |

OLE DB

Microsoft has introduced OLE DB to extend its previous universal data connectivity method, ODBC. OLE DB provides data access in much the same manner as ODBC. A *data provider* acts as an interface between disparate client and server systems. Data providers are available not only for typical relational database systems, but also for more nontraditional data sources, such as spreadsheets, Web servers, and multidimensional OLAP data sources.

Crystal Reports supports OLE DB data sources that are installed on your client PC. Various client applications, such as OLAP client software, will automatically install OLE DB data providers.

Choosing the Database

When you first start Crystal Reports, you can immediately choose and log on to a client/server database before you open an existing report or create a new report. If you don't log on but open a report based on a client/server database, you will be prompted to log on as soon as you try to refresh the report or choose any other function that requires the database to be read.

If you want to create a new report based on a client/server database, you can use a report wizard or the Blank Report option. If you use a report wizard, the first section of the wizard will display your database connection choices.

If you chose the Blank Report option to create a new report, the Database Expert will appear immediately.

The Database Expert is new in Crystal Reports 9, replacing the Data Explorer in previous versions. The Database Expert combines in one place all data sources, including direct database drivers, ODBC, and OLE DB. You may choose from one of these connection types from several places, depending on whether you've used data sources in the past (recently used data sources will appear in the History category), whether you're already logged in to a data source from using another report (currently connected data sources will appear in the Current Connections category), or whether you've added a database connection to the Favorites folder. To maintain connections in your Favorites folder through the Database expert, simply drag and drop a database into the folder or right-click and select Add to Favorites.

Also new to Crystal Reports 9 is the repository, where you can choose a SQL Command as a data source (SQL Commands are covered later in this chapter). Click the plus sign next to the category that you wish to choose from.

If you don't see the data source you wish to connect to in any of these categories, you can create a new connection to a database by clicking the plus sign next to the Create

New Connection category. This will display an additional set of database categories that you can choose from. Again, click the plus sign next to the desired category to create a connection using that connection type. Particular categories that you'll probably use to connect to standard client/server databases include ODBC, OLE DB, and More Data Sources.

> **Tip** *As if ODBC and OLE DB aren't enough "alphabet soup" in the Database Expert, you now are presented with the abbreviations "RDO" and "ADO" after the ODBC and OLE DB categories. These are abbreviations for yet more Microsoft standards for database connectivity. RDO (which stands for Remote Data Objects) and ADO (which stands for ActiveX Data Objects) are technical terms to describe the internal method Crystal Reports uses to connect to ODBC and OLE DB data sources.*

Clicking the plus sign next to the ODBC will display a separate dialog box listing all the predefined ODBC data sources (use the ODBC Administrator from Windows Control Panel to add a data source if you don't see the desired data source here). Choose the desired data source and click the Next button in the dialog box. Depending on the data source you've chosen, as well as the database type it connects to, you'll probably see additional dialog boxes asking you to supply valid logon credentials.

Clicking the plus sign next to the OLE DB category will also launch a separate OLE DB dialog box. You'll initially see a list of installed OLE DB *providers,* or database-specific connection drivers, that have been installed on your PC. Choose the provider you wish to use and click the Next button. As with ODBC, the remaining options in the OLE DB dialog box, such as those to choose a specific database and supply logon credentials, will vary according to the provider you choose.

OLE DB (ADO)

OLE DB Provider
Select a provider from the list or select a data link file.

Provider:

Microsoft Jet 4.0 OLE DB Provider
Microsoft OLE DB Provider For Data Mining
Microsoft OLE DB Provider for DTS Package
Microsoft OLE DB Provider for Indexing Serv
Microsoft OLE DB Provider for Internet Publi:
Microsoft OLE DB Provider for ODBC Drivers
Microsoft OLE DB Provider for Oracle
Microsoft OLE DB Provider for Outlook Sear
Microsoft OLE DB Provider for SQL Server
Microsoft OLE DB Simple Provider

Use Data Link File:

Microsoft Data Link File:

< Back   Next >   Finish   Cancel   Help

If you wish to use a direct database driver, click the plus sign next to the More Data Sources category. This will expand the Database Expert with yet another level of subfolders. Look for a description that matches the type of direct driver you wish to use, such as "IBM DB/2" or "Oracle" (other non-SQL data sources will appear in this category as well—these other data sources are covered in more detail in Chapter 19). As with other connection methods, the direct database driver will provide a database-specific dialog box asking you to provide logon credentials.

If the entry "no items found" appears below the chosen direct driver folder, it may be that you haven't properly installed necessary database client software on your PC. For example, you may see this message underneath the Oracle category if you haven't installed the Oracle SQL Plus client software on your PC.

> **Tip** *Not all direct database drivers will be installed by default when you install Crystal Reports 9. The first time you choose one of these data sources in the Database Expert, you may be prompted to insert the original Crystal Reports CD to install the specific driver. Also, if you add additional data source from Crystal Reports Setup, you'll often see an additional related category appear within the Create New Connection category.*

Once you've successfully logged on to the database, the Database Expert will expand the folder you originally selected and display a list of tables, views, or stored procedures available in the database. Figure 16-2 shows the Database Expert with a list of available SQL Server database tables with two tables already having been added to the report.

Select the table, stored procedure, or view that you want to include in your report, either by double-clicking it or by selecting it and clicking the single right arrow. You can also CTRL-click on more than one table and add them at once with the right arrow. And if you want to add all the tables to the report (probably not a very common occurrence), you can click the double-right arrow. As you add tables, they will appear under the Selected Tables list on the right side of the Database Expert. If you accidentally add the wrong table or tables, you may highlight them in the Selected Tables list and remove them with the left arrow. You may remove all previously added tables with the double-left arrow.

> **Tip** *You may also right-click different entries in the Available Data Sources list to display a pop-up menu to perform many of the operations discussed in this section.*

If you don't see all the tables you expect, or you wish to limit the set of available tables to a certain database owner or certain table name pattern, right-click while pointing to the Available Data Source list and choose Options from the pop-up menu. This will display the Database Options dialog box (discussed later in the chapter under "Changing SQL Options"). After choosing options in this dialog box, you may then choose from any additional entries that appear in the Available Data Sources list. Once you've added the desired tables to the report, click the Links tab in the Database Expert to link the tables together on common fields (more detailed information on linking fields is found in the "Linking Tables" section later in this chapter). Once you've chosen and linked tables, close the Database Expert by clicking the OK button.

Keep in mind that once you log on to a SQL database from the Database Expert, you remain connected to that database even if you close any reports that are based on that database connection. If you then begin a new report and display the Database Expert, the database you are already connected to will appear in the Current Connections category of the Database Expert. If you don't want to use these tables in your report, you need to log off the original server first, either by closing and restarting Crystal Reports or by using the Log On/Off Server option. If you have a report open, choose Database | Log On/ Off Server. If you don't have a report open, choose File | Log On/Off Server. In either case, choose the database you wish to log off from in the Current Connections category and click the Log Off Server button.

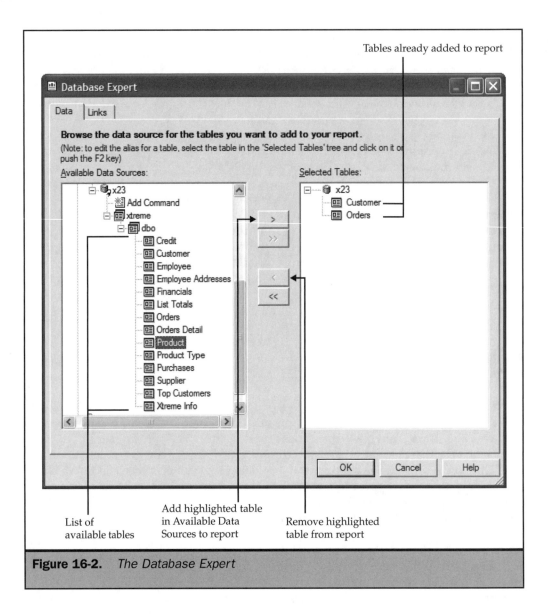

Tables already added to report

List of available tables

Add highlighted table in Available Data Sources to report

Remove highlighted table from report

Figure 16-2. *The Database Expert*

Changing SQL Options

Depending on the data source you choose, you may not see all the database elements you're looking for in the Database Expert. In particular, if your database supports *SQL stored procedures* (precompiled SQL statements that may contain parameters) or *views* (virtual tables that may combine several actual database tables together into one group), you will want to make sure you can see these in the Database Expert. Or, you may want to limit the tables that you see in the Database Expert to only the table names that match a certain pattern or that are owned by a certain database user.

To make these choices, right-click anywhere in the Available Data Sources list on the left side of the Database Expert. Choose Options from the pop-up menu. The Database Options dialog box will appear, as shown in Figure 16-3.

Tip   *You may also make changes to this dialog box when the Database Expert isn't being displayed. Choose File | Options from the pull-down menus and make changes to the Database tab of the Options dialog box.*

The Show area of this dialog box lets you limit the tables that appear in the Database Expert when you log on to a database. Check the table types (Tables, Views, Synonyms, Stored Procedures, and System Tables) to determine the types of tables you want to appear. You can also add a table name or table owner *pattern* to limit the list of tables to those that are named like the pattern or owned by a database user who matches a pattern.

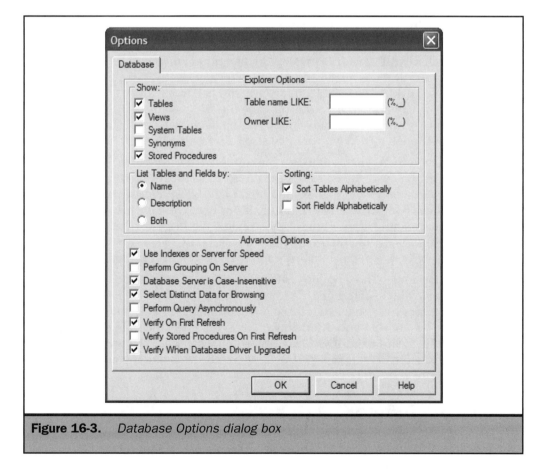

Figure 16-3.   *Database Options dialog box*

The List Tables and Fields By section lets you determine how tables and fields appear in the Database Expert and Field Explorer. You have several choices for how you want table and field names sorted, such as the ability to list tables in the Database Explorer and fields in the Field Explorer alphabetically.

Advanced options determine various database behaviors, depending on the type of database you're using and how you want it to behave. These advanced options are:

- **Use Indexes or Server for Speed**   Choose this option to use index files for PC-style databases (such as Microsoft Access and Paradox), and use a SQL WHERE clause with SQL databases. In most cases, choosing this option dramatically improves reporting performance.

- **Perform Grouping On Server**   Choose this option to have Crystal Reports "push" as much of the subtotaling and aggregation as possible to the database server, to improve reporting performance. Certain conditions required to take full advantage of this feature are discussed later in the chapter under "Enabling Server-Based Grouping."

- **Database Server is Case-Insensitive**   Choose this option to ignore case when doing record selection with a database.

- **Select Distinct Data for Browsing**   This option will continuously read the database until it has retrieved the first 500 *unique* values of a field when you browse the field in the Field Explorer or Formula Editors. If you leave this option turned off, Crystal Reports reads only the first 500 records in the table, even if there are a few (or no) unique values. Although you'll have bigger browse lists with this option turned on, you may also suffer from slower performance.

- **Perform Query Asynchronously**   This option allows you to stop a query from processing on the database server before report records are returned to Crystal Reports. In some cases, queries submitted to the SQL database can take minutes (sometimes hours) to run. By selecting this option, you can click the Stop button (the black square) at the right of the Preview tab to cancel the query on the database server. Note that this option applies only to certain databases and database drivers—not all databases and drivers support this option.

- **Verify Options**   These options determine when Crystal Reports reads the database layout to determine if additional fields have been added, field names or data types have changed, and so forth. If database fields have changed, a message will appear and the Field Explorer will reflect the changes once you respond to the message. If you leave these options turned off, you must manually verify from the Crystal Reports Database pull-down menu if you want database changes to be recognized.

Changing to a Different Database

You may initially create a report based on a PC-style database, such as Microsoft Access, and then decide later to convert the report to use a similarly organized SQL database. Perhaps the Access database has been upsized to SQL Server, or you may initially be developing reports against a test database in Btrieve, but the reports will eventually have to run against an identical Oracle database. Or else you may encounter other situations in which you initially develop a report against a specific database type, such an ODBC database, which now needs to be "pointed" to an alternate ODBC database.

In any case, Crystal Reports 9 has improved the way you change the source database for your report. The two previous Crystal Reports functions (Set Location and Change Database Driver) have been replaced with a single, streamlined choice for choosing a different database. Choose Database | Set Datasource Location from the pull-down menus, which will display the Set Datasource dialog box, shown in Figure 16-4.

If you wish to replace a single table with a new table, select the particular table you wish to replace in the Current Data Source List. Or, you can replace an entire database, including all its tables, by selecting the actual database name above the Properties and individual table entries. Then, expand the database category in the Replace With list

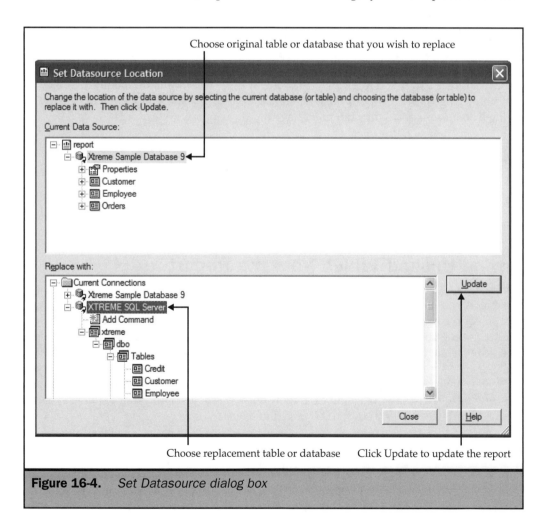

Figure 16-4. *Set Datasource dialog box*

where the new database or table resides. Select a like object type (if you selected the entire database above, select a database name below—if you chose a single table above, select a single table below). If you choose a database in the Replace With list that requires logon credentials, supply proper credentials. Once you've chosen the desired tables or database, click the Update button.

If table or field names have changed in the new database, you'll be prompted to remap old fields to their new names. This is covered in more detail in Chapter 17.

Adding Additional Tables to the Report

Once you've initially chosen and linked tables and continued with report design, you will often find that you need to add and link additional tables to your report afterward. To do so, click the Database Expert toolbar button in the Expert Tools toolbar, or choose Database | Database Expert from the pull-down menus. The Database Expert will return, where you can add additional tables from the Available Data Sources list. Once you've added the additional tables, click the Database Expert Links tab to link the tables together (linking is discussed in detail later in the chapter under "Linking Tables").

Any tables that you've previously added to your report will already appear in the Selected Tables list. If you attempt to add one of these existing tables again, you'll be prompted to give the second occurrence of the table an *alias*, because each table used in the Database Expert Links tab must have a unique name.

Tip   *You may want to intentionally add the same table to a report more than once. If, for instance, you have a common lookup table that is used with several master or transaction tables, you won't be able to retrieve lookup information by linking all the transaction or master tables to the same lookup table. You'll need to add the lookup table to the report multiple times, using a different alias each time. You can then link each transaction or master table to the different aliased versions of the lookup table.*

Removing Unused Tables from the Report

You may inadvertently add too many tables to your report, or you may no longer need tables that you used earlier in the report design process. If the Database Expert is displayed, just select the table you want to remove from the Selected Tables list and click the left arrow. If you want to remove all tables from the Selected Tables list and start table additions over from scratch, click the double-left arrow. If any of the tables you attempt to remove are in use on the report, you will be so notified and prompted to confirm their removal.

If you have proceeded to report design and are currently working in the Design or Preview tabs, redisplay the Database Expert with the toolbar button or Database menu option and delete tables from the Selected Tables list.

| **Caution** | *Make sure you really want to remove the table before you click the left arrows and close the Database Expert. You can't undo a table removal. Also, if you remove a table that is referenced in any formulas, the formulas will no longer work after the table is gone. If you remove a table by mistake, redisplay the Database Expert to re-add and link the table. Or, if you had a known good copy of the report saved on disk, you may wish to close the existing report without saving changes and open the known good copy.* |

Linking Tables

Although you may have rare instances in which you design a report based on just one database table, you usually need to use at least two, and often more, tables in your report, because most modern relational databases are *normalized*. Database normalization refers to breaking out repetitive database information into separate tables in the database for efficiency and maintenance reasons. Consider the following Employee table:

Employee Name	Department Name	Salary
Bill	Information Technology	50,000
Karen	Human Resources	32,500
Renee	Information Technology	37,500
John	Executive	85,000
Carl	Mail Room	24,000
Jim	Information Technology	48,000
Julie	Executive	87,000
Sally	Mail Room	23,500

Although this makes for a simple reporting environment, because you don't need to choose more than one table to print an employee roster or paycheck, it becomes more difficult to maintain. Notice that department names repeat several times throughout this small table. (Think about this same scenario for a 50,000-employee company!) This not only takes up a large amount of storage space, but if a department name changes, much work has to be done to make the change in this table. For example, if the Information Technology department changes its name to Information Systems, a search-and-replace function must be performed through the entire Employee table, replacing every occurrence of the old name with the new name.

Contrast this single-table layout with the following database environment:

Employee Table

Employee Name	Department Number	Salary
Bill	25	50,000
Karen	17	32,500
Renee	25	37,500
John	8	85,000
Carl	13	24,000
Jim	25	48,000
Julie	8	87,000
Sally	13	23,500

Department Table:

Department Number	Department Name
8	Executive
13	Mail Room
17	Human Resources
25	Information Technology

Here, you can see that the database has been normalized by placing the department information in its own lookup table. In this environment, much less storage is used by the Employee table, because only a department number is stored for each employee, not the entire department name. And if the Information Technology department's name changes, only one record in the Department table has to be changed in the entire database.

Database Expert Links Tab

Using multiple tables complicates the reporting environment, because you need more than just the Employee table to print an employee roster or paycheck. In the preceding example, you not only have to include the two tables in your report, but must also link them together with a common field. *Linking* tables (often also known as *joining* tables) consists of choosing the common field that will allow the second table to follow the main table as the main table is read record by record. You link tables in Crystal Reports with the Database Expert Links tab, illustrated in Figure 16-5.

The Database Expert Links tab appears if you initially choose two or more tables when you first create a report, or whenever you choose additional tables within the Database

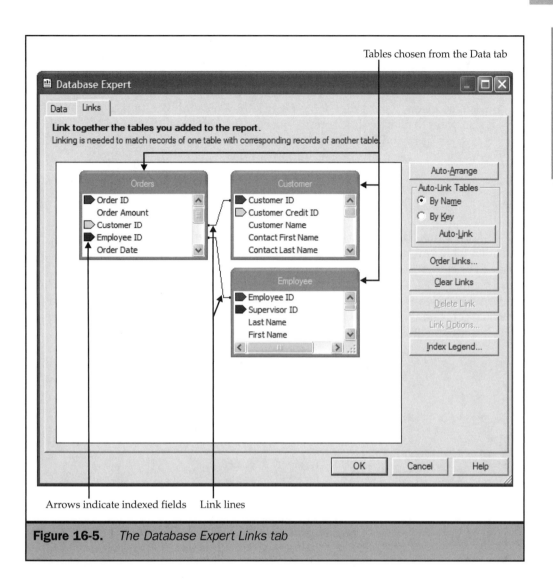

Figure 16-5. *The Database Expert Links tab*

Expert later in the report design process. If you want to work with database links at other times, simply display the Database Expert by clicking the Database Expert toolbar button or by choosing Database | Database Expert from the pull-down menus (as discussed earlier in the chapter). Then, click the Links tab.

You are free to move the individual tables around in the Links tab if you wish to see them in a different organization. You can also resize each table window to make it taller, shorter, narrower, or wider. If you wish to have Crystal Reports automatically rearrange the tables according to the way they're linked, click the Auto-Arrange button.

The Database Expert Links tab have already chosen links between the tables. If you see lines with arrows connecting fields in the tables, the Database Expert Links tab has already automatically linked the tables for you (automatic linking is discussed later in the chapter). You may need to delete these existing links if they are incorrect, or add new links yourself.

To delete a link, click the line connecting the two tables. The link line, along with the fields it connects, will be highlighted. Click the Delete Link button or press the DEL key. If you want to change link options, such as the join type (discussed later in the chapter under "Join and Link Types"), the index used by the link, or multiple-table link behavior, click the Link Options button or double-click the selected link.

Tip *You may also make choices from a pop-up menu by right-clicking on a selected link line.*

To draw a link, click a field in the table you want to link from, drag your mouse to the other table you want to link, and then drop onto the field you want to link to. A link line will be drawn between the two tables.

If Crystal Reports detects no potential problems with the link you've drawn, the link line simply appears and you see no messages. If, however, Crystal Reports detects a potential problem with the link, such as mismatched field types, you'll receive a warning message and the link may not be created.

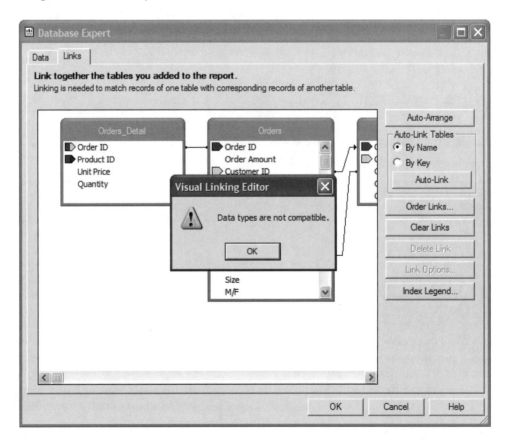

Significance of the Index Arrows

In previous versions of Crystal Reports, only PC-style databases, or other particular databases accessed via direct or "native" database drivers, would result in the display of the colored index arrows in the linking display. Crystal Reports 9, however, is much more adept at determining which fields in a table are indexed, regardless of the connection type. These indexed fields are indicated by colored arrows.

An *index* is a special setting that the database designer creates to speed up access to a table. Searching for specific records from that table will be much faster when the search is based on an indexed field. The different colors of the index arrows indicate that different indexes have been created by the database designer for the table. To display a key to the index arrow colors, click the Index Legend button. The window will appear showing the different colors and their indexes.

Index Legend
Linking TO a table on one of its indexed fields is faster.
▶ 1st Index
▷ 2nd Index
▶ 3rd Index
▶ 4th Index
▶ 5th Index
▶ 6th Index
▶ 7th Index
▷ 8th Index
▷ Index > 8
▶ Multiple Indexes
OK   Help

Previous versions of Crystal Reports also included an inherent requirement that if you saw index arrows in the Visual Linking Expert (the predecessor to the Database Expert Links tab), you had to link *to* one of the indexed fields. In most cases, in Crystal Reports 9 that requirement has been eliminated. However, for performance reasons, you may still want to try to link to indexed fields anyway. You may see improved record retrieval speeds.

So, Which Tables and Fields Should I Link?

You'll quickly figure out that you have to be very familiar with the database you are reporting against to accurately link tables and fields. You have to know the layout of the tables and the data that the common fields contain to successfully link them. This task is complicated even further by database designers who insist on protecting their jobs by creating confusing and cryptic table and field names.

Probably the most expeditious approach is to consult with someone who either designed the database or is familiar with its layout and contents. Barring that, you may be able to discern the proper tables and fields to link if they are named logically. If nothing else, you can browse individual fields in the Database Expert Links tab by right-clicking a field name and choosing Browse Field from the pop-up menu. By looking for similar data types and sample data that seems to match up in both tables, you can find good candidates for links.

Always make sure you test your report and verify that correct data is being returned once you've linked tables. It's *very easy* to create an incorrect link that displays no error message but doesn't return the correctly matched data to the report.

Link Order

When you add tables to the report and then display the Links tab, Crystal Reports makes an assumption about the order in which you wish to link tables (this assumption is made only if Crystal Reports automatically links tables, which it will often do). If you are only linking two tables together, this will not be an issue, as there is only one link between two tables.

However, if you link three or more tables (tables A, B, and C in this example), Crystal Reports will link the tables in a certain order: perhaps first linking table A to table B on one field, and then linking table A to table C on another field. If the database you've used in the report is based on the SQL language (discussed in more detail later in the chapter), you'll be able to view the SQL query that Crystal Reports sends to the database and see the order in which these links will occur.

In most cases, the link order won't be significant and you won't need to change it. However, in certain situations with certain types of table structures and database systems or connection drivers, you may notice a difference in the resulting data if you choose an "an A to C, then A to B order" instead of the "A to B, then A to C order." If this is significant, you can change the order by clicking the Order Links button. Clicking this button will display the Order Links dialog box.

Select the link that you want to move up or down in the order and click the up or down arrow at the top of the dialog box. Click the Link Ordering is Enforced check box to ensure that Crystal Reports reorders the link statements in the SQL query being sent to the database.

Using Multiple Database Types in the Same Report

Crystal Reports doesn't limit you to using just one type of database per report. You may, for example, wish to get the main transaction table for your report from a client/server database using a direct access database driver, one smaller lookup table from a Microsoft Access database on a shared LAN drive, and another lookup table from a Microsoft Excel spreadsheet on your C drive via ODBC or OLE DB.

To accomplish this, simply choose all the different tables from different categories of the Database Expert when you first create the report. Or, to add additional tables (even from different database types) after you've already started designing a report, simply redisplay the Database Expert using the toolbar button or pull-down menu options discussed earlier. After choosing the additional table or tables, click the Links tab and link them appropriately.

In general, this type of mixed reporting is perfectly acceptable. However, because connections to the different database types cannot be accomplished with a single SQL query (this is because a SQL query, by its nature, can't cross database boundaries), Crystal Reports will link the tables itself. In limited cases, this may require you to only link on string fields. Most often, however, mixed database usage will result in a warning message that your report contains more than one database type and that you can't use SQL Expressions or server-based grouping (both topics are discussed later in this chapter).

Database Warning   [X]

(i)   More than one database driver has been used in this report. If you want to change the database drivers use
      Database/Set Location. Also, please make sure that no SQL Expression is added and no server-side group-by is
      performed.

                                [OK]

Join and Link Types

When you link two tables, you must consider carefully what records will be returned from both tables. Consider a slight modification to the normalized table structures illustrated earlier in this chapter.

Employee Table:

Employee Name	Department Number	Salary
Karen	17	32,500
Renee	25	37,500
John	8	85,000
Carl	13	24,000
Denise	32	125,000

Department Table:

Department Number	Department Name
8	Executive
13	Mail Room
17	Human Resources
4	Finance
25	Information Technology

Does Crystal Reports 9 Automatic Linking Work?

When you initially add tables to a report, Crystal Reports will attempt to link the tables automatically. The result will often be link lines appearing in the Links tab when you first display it, even before you draw any manual links in yourself. This is a feature with good intentions, but it is often more trouble than it's worth. This linking automatically links fields in two adjacent tables if the fields meet these criteria:

- The field names are exactly the same.
- The data types are identical.
- In the case of string fields, the field lengths are the same.

In an ideal setting (such as the XTREME.MDB sample database provided with Crystal Reports), automatic linking works perfectly. In the real world, however, things are usually quite different.

Consider, for example, a report that includes a Vendor table and a Customer table. Both tables contain fields named Address, City, State, and Zip_Code. It's perfectly conceivable that these fields have identical data types and field lengths. Automatic linking will dutifully link the two tables together on all four fields. But, these aren't the proper fields with which to link these two tables together.

Another type of automatic linking that Crystal Reports will attempt is linking by key. In this scenario, Crystal Reports attempts to determine a "primary key/ foreign key" relationship between tables by reading the internal database structure provided by the database driver. You must typically choose this form of automatic linking yourself by clicking the "By Key" radio button, and then clicking the Auto-Link button in the Link tab. If the specific set of primary key/foreign key settings can't be found by Crystal Reports, you'll receive a message indicating that key linking can't be performed and asking if you wish to link via the field name scenario.

You'll probably find that automatic linking, either by key or by field name, often results in incorrect link lines being drawn. You then are forced to delete the incorrect links and draw in the correct ones. In Crystal Reports 9, you must just "deal with" this inconvenience—the ability to turn the automatic linking option off has been removed from version 9 (Auto Smart Linking could be turned off in previous versions).

A quick glance at these two tables reveals two inconsistencies: Denise has no matching record in the Department table, and the Finance department has no employees in the Employee table. These two tables are said to lack *referential integrity*—a fancy computer term that simply means the two tables don't completely match up. Fancy term or not, this will be *very* important to you as a report designer. You have to decide how you want to deal with a lack of referential integrity.

Many databases can enforce referential integrity, so the situation described previously will never happen. If the database designer chooses to enforce referential integrity between these two tables, an employee cannot be given a department number that doesn't exist in the Department table, and a department record can't be deleted from the Department table if any Employee table records still contain that department. However, enforcing referential integrity often introduces other complexities in the database, and there are many times when the basic function of the database will not allow referential integrity to be enforced. The database designer or administrator should be consulted if you have questions about the way your database is designed.

A situation in which you would be very concerned about referential integrity is if you were designing a report to print paychecks for employees. Consider the tables previously shown as the basis for your paychecks. If you wish to have the employee's department printed on the check stub to help in check distribution, you would need to link the Employee and Department tables together on the Department Number field. It's a fair assumption that your paycheck run would get at least this far:

The big question for you, the report designer, is "What happens to Denise?" (the last employee in the Employee table). Considering that she's a highly paid employee, at least from most viewpoints, she will probably be very interested in being paid, regardless of referential integrity. Another interesting question is "Will any checks print for the

Finance department?" The answers to your questions are dependent upon which *join type* you use when linking these two tables together.

The following are the two join types that you will be concerned with most of the time:

- **Inner join (sometimes referred to as an *equal join*)**   Includes records from both tables *only when the joining fields are equal.*

- **Left outer join (sometimes simply referred to as *outer join*)**   Includes *all* records from the left table, and records from the right table only when the joining fields are equal.

Even though Denise probably doesn't know what a left outer join is, she probably will be much happier if you choose it. This will result in her receiving a paycheck that simply doesn't have a department name printed on it. This is particularly important in Crystal Reports, because the default join type for SQL databases is an equal join.

Two other types of joins that you may use less frequently are the following:

- **Right outer join**   Includes *all* records from the right table, and records from the left table only when the joining fields are equal.

Denise would be as displeased with this choice as she would with an equal join. You would also get a wasted paycheck with the Finance department on the pay stub, but no employee or salary printed on it.

- **Full outer join**   Includes all records from *both* tables, whether the joined fields are equal or not.

Denise wouldn't mind this joint type—she'd get paid. However, you'd also have a wasted check for the Finance department with no employee information on it.

Choosing the Join and Link Type in the Database Expert Links Tab

Choose the join type in the Database Expert Links tab by double-clicking the link line between the two tables you are interested in, by right-clicking on the link line and choosing Link Options from the pop-up menu, or by selecting the link and clicking the Link Options button. The Link Options dialog box, shown in Figure 16-6, will appear. Select the desired join type from the left side of the dialog box.

Note   *If tables are linked by more than one field, choosing a join type for any of the links will set the same join type for all the links. You cannot have different join types for multiple links between the same tables.*

Although most typical business reporting can be accomplished with inner joins and left outer joins, you may have occasion in specialized reporting situations to use these other join types.

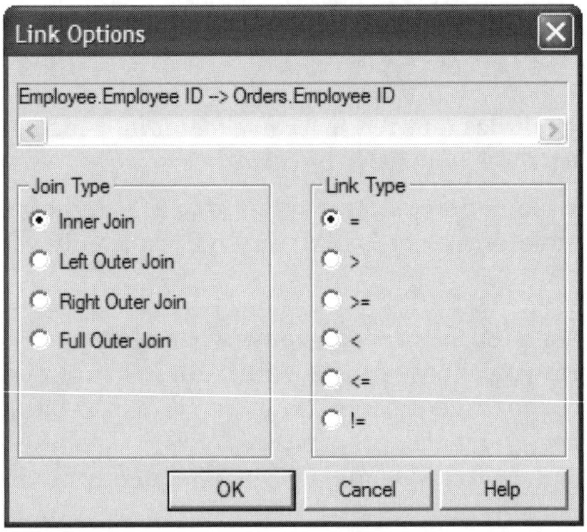

Figure 16-6. *Link Options dialog box*

Crystal Reports 9 Link Types In previous versions of Crystal Reports, you made a choice of a *combined* join and link type. For example, you could choose a Left Outer join or a Less Than join, but not both—any "comparison-type" joins, such as less than, would result in an Inner Join with the chosen comparison operator used between the joined fields. In Crystal Reports 9, you have the additional choice of a *link type* that can be chosen along with a join type.

- **Equal (=)** Returns records from the tables, matching records from the right table every time the joining field in the left table *is equal to* the joining field in the right table.

- **Greater than (>)** Returns records from the left table, matching records from the right table every time the joining field in the left table *is greater than* the joining field in the right table.

- **Greater than or equal (>=)** Returns records from the left table, matching records from the right table every time the joining field in the left table *is greater than or equal to* the joining field in the right table.

- **Less than (<)** Returns records from the left table, matching records from the right table every time the joining field in the left table *is less than* the joining field in the right table.

■ **Less than or equal (<=)** Returns records from the left table, matching records from the right table every time the joining field in the left table *is less than or equal to* the joining field in the right table.

■ **Not equal (!=)** Returns all combinations of records from the two tables where the joining fields *are not equal.*

Various combinations of join and link types can return very interesting combinations of data. For example, choosing an Inner Join but a Less Than link type will return a much larger set of records than an Inner Join with an Equal link type. However, it still won't return records where there is no match at all between link fields. But if you choose a Left Outer Join and a Less Than link type, you'll receive a larger number of matching records, as well as records from the left table that have no match in the right table.

You can choose Database | Show SQL Query from the pull-down menus to see how the combination of join and link types will affect the SQL Query. If you are familiar with the structure of the SQL query, you'll notice that the combination of join and link types will change different portions of the query. For example, an Inner Join with an Equal link type will create this type of query:

```
FROM    "xtreme"."dbo"."Employee" "Employee" INNER JOIN
"xtreme"."dbo"."Orders" "Orders" ON
"Employee"."Employee ID"="Orders"."Employee ID"
```

And, a Left Outer Join using a Less Than link type will return this type of query:

```
FROM    {oj "xtreme"."dbo"."Employee" "Employee" LEFT OUTER JOIN
"xtreme"."dbo"."Orders" "Orders" ON
"Employee"."Employee ID"<"Orders"."Employee ID"}
```

Of course, the exact format of the SQL query and where the joins are performed (the FROM clause in some cases, the WHERE clause in others) is dependent upon the database type and driver being used. Also, you'll see *very* different sets of returned data for the different join and link types you choose. If you aren't extensively familiar with join and link types, you'd be best advised to stick with tried and true Inner or Left Outer join types and Equal link types. In any event, you are well advised to validate the results of your report against your original data source to ensure that all the proper data is being returned by the report once you make join and link choices.

Note *Some join and link types won't be available, depending on the types of databases you have chosen for your report. In those cases, the unavailable join and link types will be dimmed in the Link Options dialog box.*

Which Should Be the Left "From" Table, and Which Should Be the Right "To" Table?

When you use the Links tab, you begin to draw a link by clicking a "from" table. You then drop the link onto the desired field in the "to" table. Initially, you may not be able to tell which table was dragged from and which table was dropped onto. In many cases, Crystal Reports 9 won't indicate this if you are using the default Inner Join and Equal link types.

However, if you change to alternate join or link types, or you use certain databases or database drivers, you'll be able to determine which table is the "from" and which is the "to" by looking carefully at the link line—the "from" side of the line will display a small block, while the "to" side will display an arrow.

This begs the question, "Does it make any difference which is the 'from' and which is the 'to' table?" The answer, again, relates to the join and link types you choose. Generally speaking, if you select an Inner Join and an Equal link, it doesn't make a great deal of difference. However, if you use any other join or link types, it makes a great deal of difference, because the "from," or left table, and the "to," or right table, determine how records are returned.

A relationship between tables is often referred to as a *one-to-one relationship* or a *one-to-many relationship*. If there is always only one matching record in both tables, it doesn't matter which table is the "from" and which is the "to"—it's a one-to-one relationship. However, if there are many matching records in one table for each record in another table, the direction of the link is significant. For example, if a table containing many orders placed by the same customer is linked to a table containing only one matching customer record, you will want to link *from* the Orders table (the "many" table) *to* the Customer table (the "one" table).

If you're concerned that the link may be in "reverse" order, and you'd like to switch the "from" and "to" tables, you can simply delete and redraw the link, or right-click the link and choose Reverse Link from the pop-up menu.

Viewing the SQL Query

Because Crystal Reports works with SQL databases, it must eventually translate the tables, fields, links, sorting, and grouping that you've used to design your report into SQL. You can view the SQL statements Crystal Reports creates by choosing Database | Show SQL Query from the pull-down menus.

Consider the following report Design tab that uses data from the XTREME sample database, converted from Microsoft Access to Microsoft SQL Server, accessed via ODBC. This report uses the Orders and Customer tables, linked with a left outer join and equal link on Customer ID. The Select Expert is limiting the report to U.S.A. customers only. Notice the fields that have been placed in the details section. Also, notice that a group based on Customer.Region has been created.

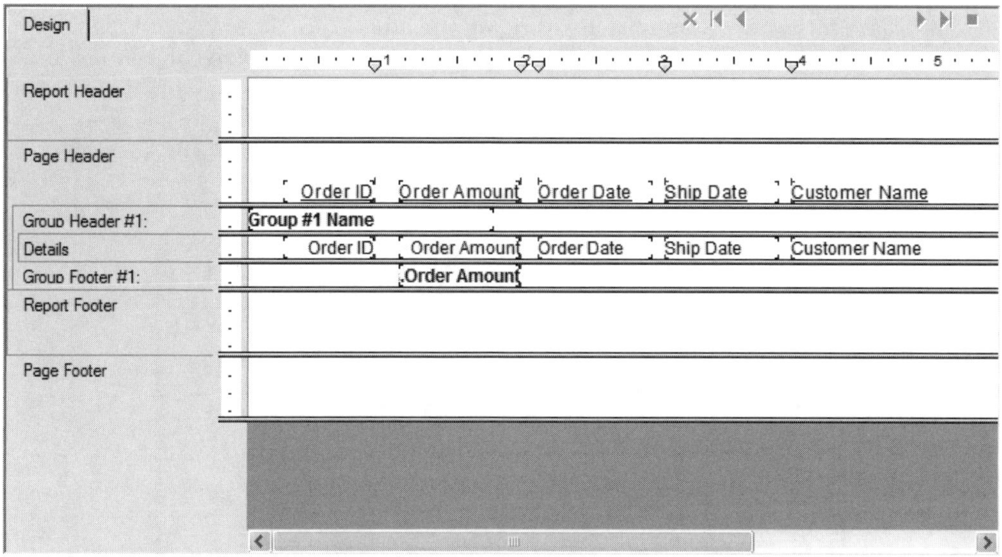

To view the SQL statement that Crystal Reports creates to query the database, select Database | Show SQL Query. You will see the dialog box illustrated here.

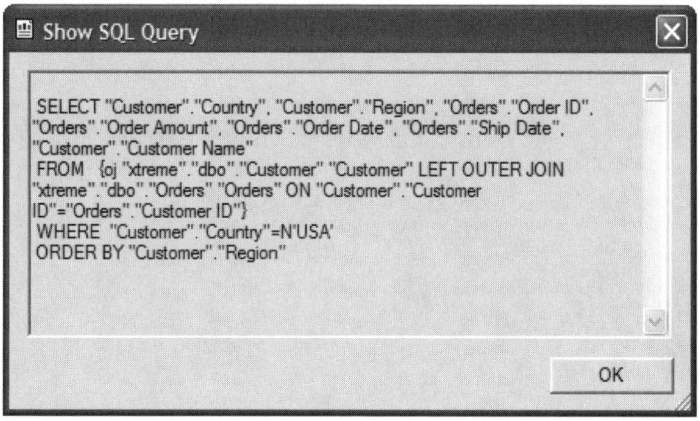

```
SELECT "Customer"."Country", "Customer"."Region", "Orders"."Order ID",
"Orders"."Order Amount", "Orders"."Order Date", "Orders"."Ship Date",
"Customer"."Customer Name"
FROM  {oj "xtreme"."dbo"."Customer" "Customer" LEFT OUTER JOIN
"xtreme"."dbo"."Orders" "Orders" ON "Customer"."Customer
ID"="Orders"."Customer ID"}
WHERE  "Customer"."Country"=N'USA'
ORDER BY "Customer"."Region"
```

Notice the different parts, or *clauses*, of the SQL statement:

■ **SELECT**   Matches the database fields that your report needs (for the details section, formulas, grouping, and so on).

■ **FROM**   Chooses the tables to use and specifies the join type for table linking.

■ **WHERE**   Supplies record selection to the server.

■ **ORDER BY**   Requests that the SQL server sort records in Customer.Region order (for the Region group) before sending them back to the client.

The SQL syntax may change, depending on the type of database you are reporting against and whether you're using ODBC or direct database drivers to communicate with it. You'll also see different syntax for joining tables. And, you may see the actual table join appear in either the FROM or WHERE clause.

Here is the exact same Show SQL Query dialog box using an OLE DB connection to Microsoft SQL Server (notice the slight difference in the JOIN syntax):

and, for the Microsoft Access version of the XTREME.MDB sample database via ODBC (notice no "N" character in the WHERE clause):

Although you may not consider yourself a database expert and might not make a habit of writing huge SQL statements off the top of your head, there is one advantage to being able to see the SQL query that Crystal Reports is sending to the server: this is useful if you are experiencing performance problems or other peculiarities when running the report. In particular, you want to ensure that as much as possible, if not all, of the report's record selection is translated into a WHERE clause in the SQL query. This will maximize the work performed by the database server and minimize the amount of data and amount of processing left for Crystal Reports to deal with once data is returned from the server. More details on performance considerations can be found later in the chapter under "Performance Considerations."

| Note | *In previous versions of Crystal Reports, you could directly modify every SQL clause except SELECT right in the Show SQL Query dialog box. This ability has been removed from Crystal Reports 9. However, you have complete control over the SQL Query when creating a SQL Command, discussed next.* |

Crystal Reports SQL Commands

As mentioned previously, Crystal Reports 9 has eliminated the ability to make direct adjustments to the SQL query in the Show SQL Query dialog box. While this may be an inconvenience, a new way of directly manipulating the SQL query has been added to version 9: *the SQL Command.*

SQL Commands use the same database driver as the previously available Crystal SQL Designer (now a "legacy" application that can be downloaded from the Crystal Decisions Web site—it's no longer included with Crystal Reports). SQL Commands allow you to create a "pass-through" SQL statement that performs more database-specific query processes on the database server, such as aggregate functions, UNION queries, or sub-SELECT queries.

Once you've created a SQL Command, you can base a report on it (it looks like a table) or add it to the Crystal Repository so that other report designers sharing the same repository can base their reports on it.

Creating the SQL Command

Before you can create a SQL Command, you must log on to the database that the Command will be based on. When first creating a report, you can log on to a database from the Database Expert as described earlier in the chapter. Or, if you want to create a SQL Command after you've already commenced report design, redisplay the Database Expert with the toolbar button or Database | Database Expert menu option.

Once you've logged on to a database, notice the "Add Command" option that appears above the tables, views, and stored procedure categories of the Database Expert. Double-click the Add Command option to display the Add Command to Report dialog box, shown in Figure 16-7.

Begin by typing the SQL statement you wish to use for the command in the appropriate box. Note that there is no "Expert" or "Build" functionality in this dialog box—you're on your own for typing correctly formatted SQL particular to the driver or database connection you're using. If you are unsure of proper SQL syntax, you may wish to develop the SQL in another tool provided by your database vendor. Once you've debugged the SQL query in that tool, copy the SQL code to the Windows clipboard and paste the statement into this dialog box.

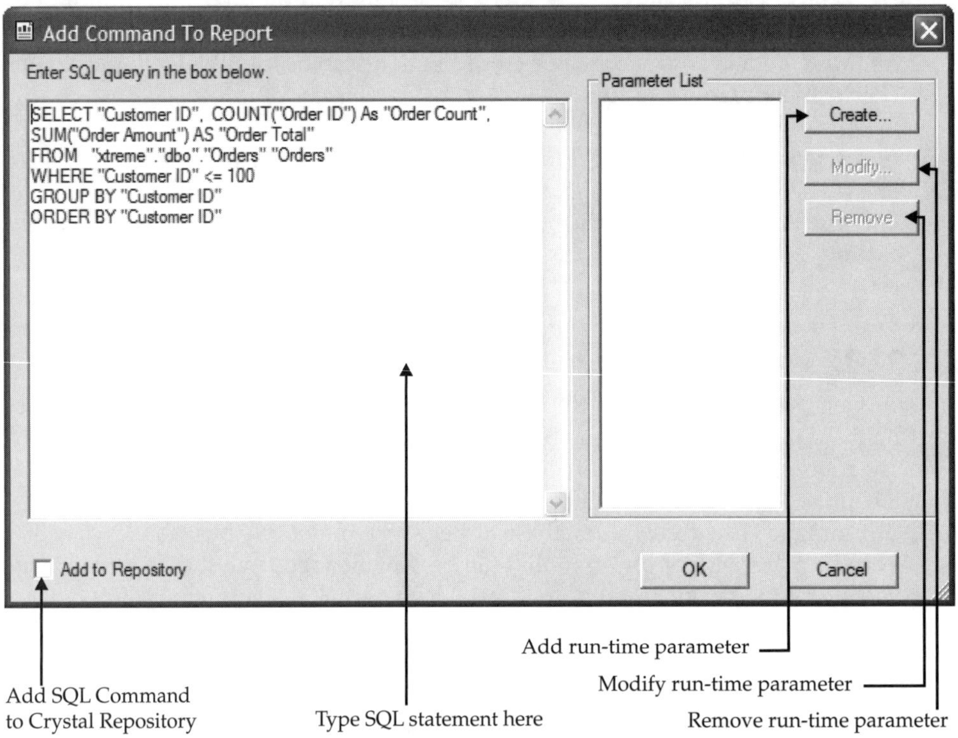

Figure 16-7. *Add Command to Report dialog box*

When you click OK on the Add Command to Report dialog box, Crystal Reports will submit the command to the database to be checked for proper syntax. If you have made an error, the database driver will return a message indicating the particular problem with the SQL statement submitted. The Add Command to Report dialog box will then return, where you may correct the SQL statement and click OK again. Once you've submitted a correct SQL statement, the dialog box will close and "Command" will appear as a table name on the Selected Tables side of the Database Expert. If you wish to give your SQL Command a more descriptive name, select it in the Selected Tables list and then hold your mouse button down for a few seconds. This will place the command name into edit mode, where you may replace the word "Command" with a new name.

If you wish to view or edit the contents of a command you've created previously, select the command in the Selected Tables list and then right-click. Choose View or Edit from the pop-up menu. Both options will display the SQL Command in the same dialog box it was created with. If you chose View, the command will not be editable—Edit will allow the command to be changed; parameters to be added, changed, or deleted; and the command to be added to the Crystal Repository.

Caution *To delete a command that you no longer wish to use, select the command in the Selected Tables list and click the left arrow. Be aware: this is a permanent deletion. The command won't move to the left side of the Database Expert where you can add it back to the report. It will be permanently deleted.*

Adding a Parameter to the Command

As with reports, you may wish to have the SQL Command prompt a viewer for one or more variable pieces of information when it's submitted to the database. This will allow, for example, the SQL Command to run for a specified department, date range, or sales level threshold. You may accomplish this by creating a parameter in the Add Command to Report dialog box, and then placing that parameter within the SQL statement.

To add a new parameter, click the Create button next to the parameter list. The Command Parameter dialog box will appear, as shown in Figure 16-8.

Supply desired options in this dialog box. You must, at least, choose a name for the parameter and a value type. The other two choices, prompting text and default value, are optional. Type a name for the parameter that hasn't been used by any other parameters in the SQL Command. And, ensure you choose a data type that matches the use you have in mind for the parameter—if you are going to use it to compare to a numeric database field, choose Number as the value type for the parameter. Once you've made these choices, click OK. The parameter will be added to the Parameter List.

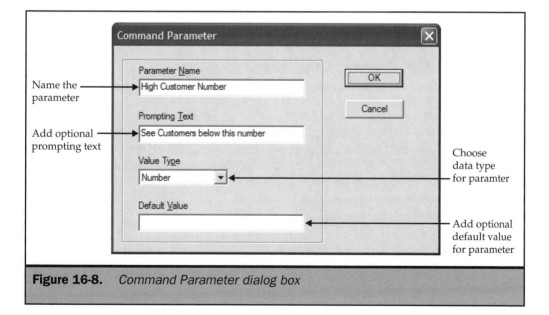

Figure 16-8. *Command Parameter dialog box*

If you later wish to modify or delete a parameter, select the parameter in the Parameter List that you wish to work with. Then, click the Modify or Delete button. Delete will simply remove the parameter from the list (make sure you also remove any references to the parameter from the SQL statement). Modify will redisplay the Command Parameter dialog box, where you may change any of the parameter elements.

Once you've created the Parameter, you must now reference it somewhere in the SQL statement for it to have any effect. For example, if you wish to replace a hard-coded number in the WHERE clause with the parameter, edit the SQL statement and replace the hard-coded number with the name of the parameter. You can either type the parameter name in directly (including curly braces around the parameter name and a question mark preceding the name) or simply place the cursor where you want the parameter name to be placed and then double-click on the parameter in the Parameter List.

Thus, a previous WHERE clause with a hard-coded number:

```
WHERE "Customer ID" <= 100
```

can be replaced with a parameter-driven version:

```
WHERE "Customer ID" <= {?High Customer Number}
```

Once you've added one or more parameters to the SQL Command, click OK. You will then be prompted to supply values for any parameters, and again, the command will be submitted to the database to check for proper SQL syntax. Any errors generated by adding the parameter will appear in an error message, and you'll be returned to the Add Command to Report dialog box, where you may fix the problem. If the command is syntactically correct, the Database Expert will reappear.

Adding the SQL Command to the Repository

Once you've created the SQL Command and clicked OK, it will appear in the Selected Tables list of the Database Expert and will be treated as a table when you continue with report design. After you save the report, the SQL Command will still be in the Database Expert the next time you open that one particular report. However, if you want to use the same SQL Command in other reports, or if you want to share it with other report designers in your organization, you must add it to the Crystal Repository.

To add a SQL Command to the current repository, check the Add to Repository check box when you initially create the SQL Command, or edit it later. Once you click this check box and click OK, the Add Item dialog box will appear, as shown in Figure 16-9.

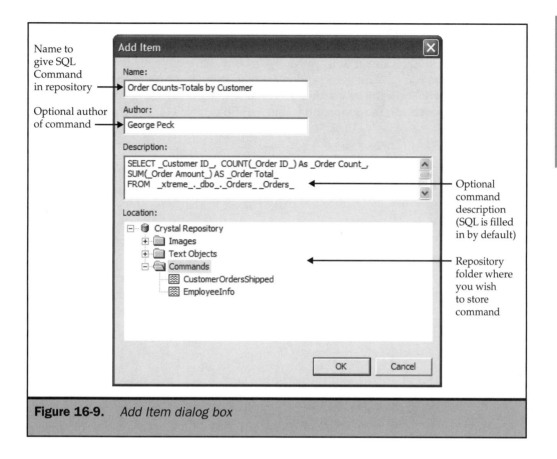

Name to
give SQL
Command
in repository ──▶

Optional author
of command ──▶

Optional
command
description
(SQL is filled
in by default)

Repository
folder where
you wish
to store
command

Figure 16-9.   *Add Item dialog box*

Type the name you want the SQL Command to have in the repository in the first text
box. The author and description entries are optional—they will be filled in with your
name and the SQL statement that makes up the command. You may change these if you
choose. Then, choose the location in the repository where you wish to place the command.
The location can be the root level of the repository (select the name of the repository at
the very top of the list), or a subfolder within the repository, if folders have been added.
If you click the plus sign to open a particular folder, you'll see any existing SQL Commands
that have been added to that folder. If you select just the folder itself, the command will
be added to that folder. If you select an existing command within a folder, it will be
replaced with the command you are currently adding.

Once you've added the command to the repository, you'll notice that it displays differently in the Database Expert. In particular, the name you originally gave the command when you created it will appear as an item below a higher-level item, which displays the name you gave the command in the repository. You'll also notice a small icon next to the "barrel" indicating that the SQL Command is connected to the repository—you won't be able to edit the command while it's still connected.

The SQL Command will now be available to use in other reports—both by you, and by anybody else who is connected to the same repository (information on how to use the repository-supplied command follows later in the chapter). If, however, you wish to change the command in the repository to reflect some change in requirements, you must first *disconnect* the command from the repository before you can change it.

To disconnect a SQL Command from the repository, right-click on the command itself (right-clicking on the higher-level "barrel" object won't provide the proper option) and choose Disconnect from Repository from the pop-up menu. The small icon next to the barrel will disappear, indicating that the command has been disconnected from the repository. You may now edit the command by choosing the Edit command from the same pop-up menu.

Once you've made changes to the command, don't forget that the changes will reside only on the current report—you must replace the command in the repository with the updated command on your report. To replace the repository command, just click the Add to Repository check box in the Modify Command dialog box. The Add Item dialog box (shown earlier in Figure 16-9) will reappear. Just choose the existing SQL Command you wish to replace in the folder list to replace the repository command with the updated command on your report.

| **Tip** | *More information on the Crystal Repository, including how to set up the repository, create folders, and so forth, can be found in Chapter 7.* |

Using a SQL Command in a Report

Once you've created a SQL Command, it will appear in the Selected Tables list of the Database Expert just like a "native" table from a database. Once you close the Database Expert, any fields that the SQL Command returns will appear in the Field Explorer— just drag and drop them onto the report as you would any other database field.

You can even link a SQL Command to another database table in the Database Expert before you proceed to report design. And, you can add an additional table to the report later, linking it to the existing SQL Command on one or more common fields. If you link additional tables to the SQL Command, be aware that you'll be limited in your join and link type choices, as described earlier in the chapter under "Using Multiple Database Types in the Same Report."

Using a Parameter-Based SQL Command

If you added one or more parameters to your SQL Command, you'll find that the command will prompt you for parameter values as you create the command, and later when you refresh a report based on the command. Notice, also, that the parameter will appear in the Field Explorer as though you added it to the report (Chapter 14 discusses report-based parameter fields).

When you refresh the report, you'll be prompted to choose whether to rerun the report with existing parameter values or to specify new parameter values. If you choose to specify new, the familiar parameter prompt will appear asking for values for the SQL Command parameters. You can even place the parameters you added to the command right on the report, or use the command parameters in report formulas.

| **Caution** | *When you create a SQL Command–based parameter, you don't have the choice of advanced parameter types, such as multivalue or range. However, if you edit the resulting parameter from within the Field Explorer, you may be able to make such choices. Be careful, as some changes you make in the Field Explorer parameter dialog box won't be compatible with SQL Command–based parameters. The result may be an error message from the command, or no records returned to the report. You can, however, supply a pick list of default values, set length limits or an edit mask for string parameters, or set range limits for number or date parameters. See Chapter 14 for more information on these options. You can even rename a command-based parameter in the Field Explorer the same way you would rename a regular parameter field (although this won't change the name of the parameter in the SQL Command).* |

Using a SQL Command from the Repository

If you've added a SQL Command to the repository using steps described previously in the chapter, the command will be available to other reports you design, as well as to others who are connected to the same repository. When you initially display the Database Expert, simply open the Repository category of the Available Data Sources list. Navigate to the desired folder. Only SQL Commands will appear within the folder— other repository objects such as text objects and bitmap images won't appear. Choose the SQL Command you wish to add to the report and click the right arrow. The command will appear in the Selected Tables list. You may now add and link other tables, or click OK to close the Database Expert and add the repository-based command to the report.

Using SQL Stored Procedures

Most SQL database systems include the capability to use stored procedures. A *stored procedure* is a SQL query that has been evaluated, or "compiled," by the database server in advance and is stored on the server along with regular database tables. Because the stored procedure is compiled in advance, it often performs faster than a SQL query submitted on the fly. Stored procedures can be created by the database designer or administrator for specific queries that will be run on a frequent basis.

To enhance flexibility, stored procedures can contain one or more stored procedure *parameters* that prompt the user to enter a value. The stored procedure then uses the value to run the query. For example, if you have a stored procedure that returns several fields from linked tables, based on Country and Order Date parameters, you'll be prompted to enter a particular country and order date when the stored procedure runs. The procedure will then return a result set containing only records matching the two-parameter values you supplied.

Choosing Stored Procedures

Crystal Reports treats stored procedures almost identically to regular database tables. Stored procedures appear in the Database Expert and are used in a report just like regular database tables. The only difference is that a stored procedure may have parameters associated with it. However, you do have a choice of whether or not stored procedures will appear in the Database Expert in the first place. The quickest way to ensure that they show up is to right-click in the Available Data Sources portion of the Database Expert and choose Options from the pop-up menu. Then, check the Stored Procedure check box in the Database Options dialog box (shown earlier in Figure 16-3). You may also make the change permanent for all new reports in the future by checking the same option on the Database tab after choosing File | Options from the pull-down menus.

Now, when you open a SQL database, you'll see stored procedures appear along with regular database tables.

> **Tip**   *Crystal Reports 9 allows you to link other database tables to Stored Procedures. Just be aware of limited join and link types, as discussed earlier in the chapter under "Using Multiple Database Types in the Same Report."*

Working with Stored Procedure Parameters

After you choose a stored procedure to report on, you are prompted to supply any values for any stored procedure parameters in the Enter Parameter Values dialog box. This dialog box is identical to the one that prompts for report parameter fields, discussed in Chapter 14.

Type your desired parameter values, and click OK. You can then simply continue your report design process normally. The stored procedure will supply a list of fields you can use in your report, just like a normal database table.

Stored procedure parameters behave almost identically to Crystal Reports parameter fields. The stored procedure parameters will appear in the Parameter Fields category of the Field Explorer. You can edit a stored procedure parameter by selecting it and clicking the Edit button, typing CTRL-E, or right-clicking the parameter and choosing Edit from the pop-up menu. As with SQL Command–based parameters (discussed earlier in the chapter), you may be able to make advanced choices, such as Multi-Value or Range, in the Field

Explorer. Be careful, as some changes you make in the Field Explorer parameter dialog box won't be compatible with Stored Procedure–based parameters either. The result may be an error message or no records returned to the report.

You can, however, supply a pick list of default values and set length limits or an edit mask for string parameters, or range limits for number or date parameters. See Chapter 14 for more information on these options. You can even rename a stored procedure parameter in the Field Explorer the same way you would rename a regular parameter field (although this won't change the name of the stored procedure parameter on the server).

When you refresh the report, you receive the same prompt as when using parameter fields.

You can choose whether to use the existing values for the stored procedure parameters or to prompt for new values. When you prompt for new values, the server will run the stored procedure with the new values and return a new result set to Crystal Reports.

Using SQL Expression Fields

Sometimes you'll want to have the database server actually perform some calculations for you, sending the already calculated field back with the database result set. This is accomplished with SQL expression fields, which can be created right from the Field Explorer. A *SQL expression* is like a formula, except that it's made up entirely of database fields and SQL functions that are supported by the language of the particular SQL server that you're working with. Sometimes there are advantages to using a SQL expression instead of a Crystal Reports formula. The expression is evaluated on the server, not by the client, which can often improve performance.

A particular advantage involves calculations or other specialized functions that are used in record selection. If you use a Crystal Reports formula in record selection, the database server typically won't be able to perform the selection, because it doesn't understand the Crystal Reports formula language. However, when you create a SQL expression and use that in record selection, the SQL server will fully understand the expression, and the record selection will be performed by the database server.

Creating SQL Expressions

The first prerequisite for using SQL expressions is that you must be using a SQL or ODBC database. If you're using a PC-style database that doesn't utilize a SQL-based interface, SQL expressions don't apply and you won't even see the SQL Expression category in the Field Explorer. However, when you are using a SQL database, the Field Explorer includes an additional category labeled SQL Expression Fields. Click the Field Explorer button in the Standard toolbar, or use View | Field Explorer from the pull-down menus to display the Field Explorer. Then, click the SQL Expression Fields category and click the New button in the Field Explorer toolbar, type CTRL-N, or right-click on the SQL Expression Fields category and choose New from the pop-up menu.

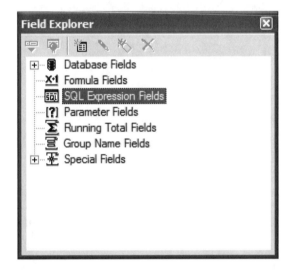

Caution *You can't use SQL expression fields with SQL Commands or stored procedures. If your report is based on either of these connections, the SQL Expression Fields category won't even appear in the Field Explorer.*

Creating a SQL expression is very similar to creating a Crystal Reports formula (discussed in detail in Chapter 5). You first are asked to give the SQL expression a name. As with formula names, you should make the SQL expression name reasonably short and easy to understand. You may include spaces as well as upper- and lowercase letters in the name. The name you give the SQL expression will also be the column heading if you place the SQL expression in the report's details section.

After you give the SQL expression a name and click OK, the SQL Expression Editor appears, as shown in Figure 16-10.

Note the similarities between the SQL Expression Editor and the other Crystal Reports formula editors. Creating SQL expressions is essentially the same as creating other formulas: you can type the expression directly into the Formula text box, or double-click in the top three boxes to help build the expression. Notice that, as when dealing with formulas, parameter fields, and running total fields, Crystal Reports appends a special character to the beginning of the SQL expression's name. The percent symbol (%) is used to denote SQL expression fields.

The functions and operators available in the SQL Expression Editor change, depending on the database and database driver in use. If you look at the Function Tree box in Figure 16-10, you'll notice a certain set of available SQL functions. This example is for a report using Microsoft Access via ODBC. If you use another method to connect to the same database, or another type of database, the SQL Expression Editor will show a completely different set of SQL functions. For this reason, you will probably have to edit or modify some SQL expressions if you change your report from one database to another using Set Location from the Database pull-down menu. To get detailed descriptions of the different built-in SQL functions for your particular database or driver, consult documentation for that database or driver.

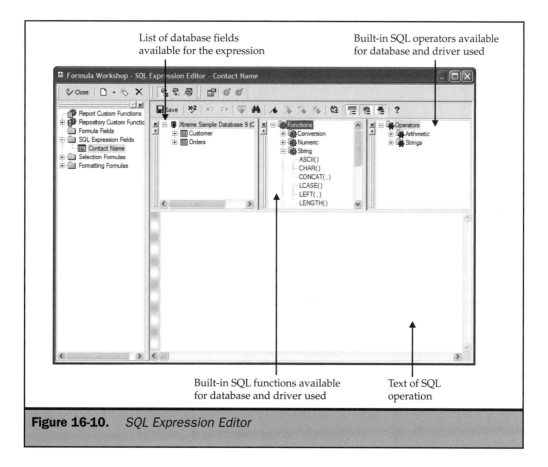

Figure 16-10.   *SQL Expression Editor*

For example, you may want a report viewer to be able to specify with just one parameter field a full or partial contact name to search for. If a customer exists whose contact matches what's entered, the customer will be included on the report. In the Customer table of the XTREME sample database that's included with Crystal Reports, the contact information is actually split into separate first and last name database fields. Without using a SQL expression, you have two choices for setting up this search:

- Create two parameter fields—one for first name and one for last name—and try to compare those to database fields.

- Create a Crystal Reports formula that combines the contact's first and last names, and compare the formula to the parameter field.

There are problems with both approaches, however. If you choose the first option, it's much harder for the viewer to simply type a full or partial contact name, such as "Chris" (to find both Christopher and Christine, for example), because some additional logic will be necessary to ignore the last name parameter field if the viewer just wants to search for full or partial first names. Or, if the viewer wants to see everyone whose last name is "Jones," regardless of first name, then similar logic will have to apply for the first name parameter field. It would be much simpler for the viewer to be able to type **Chris*** or ***Jones** to search for their desired customers.

If you choose the second option, the full or partial searches mentioned in the previous paragraph will work, but because the first and last names are combined in a formula, the record selection will not take place on the database server (remember that most Crystal formulas can't be converted to SQL, so the client will perform record selection).

By using a SQL expression, you can have the best of both worlds. The first and last names can be concatenated into one object and compared to the parameter field. But because the concatenation takes place on the database server, it will still perform the record selection, sending only the resulting customers back to the client, not all customers.

The SQL expression to accomplish this is surprisingly similar to a Crystal Reports formula:

```
`Customer`.`Contact First Name` + ' ' +
`Customer`.`Contact Last Name`
```

Notice that a couple of differences exist, however:

- There are no French or "curly" braces around the field names.

- The literal string that separates the first and last name fields must use apostrophes—quotation marks won't work.

Once this SQL expression has been created, it can be dropped onto the report just like a database field, formula field, or other object. It can also be used inside regular report formulas or in conditional formatting formulas. Notice the change to the SQL query (viewed with Database | Show SQL Query) after placing this SQL expression in the details section:

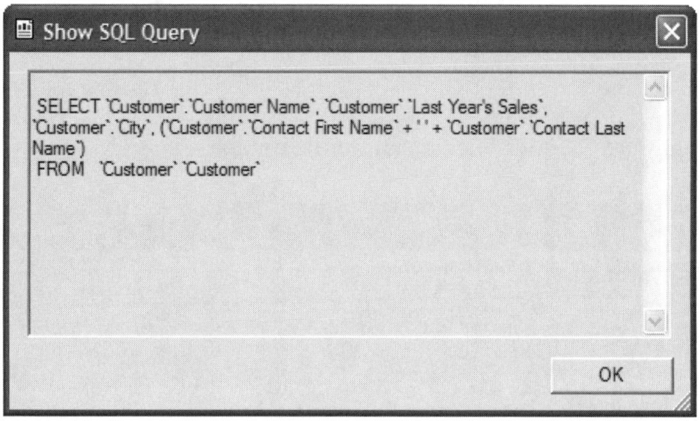

Even though the SQL expression field was given a name in the report, Crystal Reports just adds the SQL expression formula itself right into the SQL statement. The name is simply used by Crystal Reports in the Select Expert or elsewhere on the report.

To now use this SQL expression in record selection, you use the Select Expert's Like operator to allow a wildcard search on the combined first and last names of the contact. If you have already created a string parameter field called {?Contact Prompt}, the Select Expert will look like this:

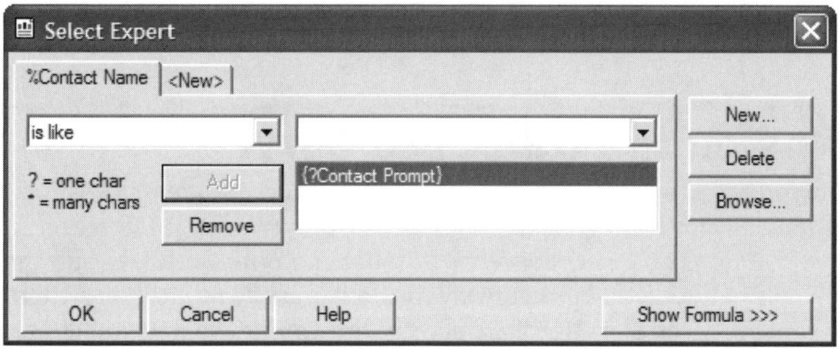

When you refresh the report and are prompted for the Contact Prompt parameter field, entering the Chris* wildcard will return the following records:

Customer Name	Contact Name	Last Year's Sales	City	Region
City Cyclists	Chris Christianson	$20,045.27	Sterling Heights	MI
Pathfinders	Christine Manley	$26,369.63	DeKalb	IL
Orléans VTT	Christophe Jolicoeur	$6,655.90	Troyes	Champagne-Ardenne
The Bike Cellar	Christopher Carmine	$30,938.67	Winchester	VA

Now, look at the SQL query being sent to the database server:

```
SELECT 'Customer'.'Customer Name', 'Customer'.'Last Year's Sales',
'Customer'.'City', ('Customer'.'Contact First Name' + ' ' + 'Customer'.'Contact Last
Name')
FROM  'Customer' 'Customer'
WHERE ('Customer'.'Contact First Name' + ' ' + 'Customer'.'Contact Last Name')
LIKE 'Chris%'
```

Notice that the WHERE clause includes the SQL expression formula text and a SQL comparison operator that allows wildcard searches. The end result: the flexibility of Crystal Reports formulas with the speed of server-based record selection.

Grouping on the Database Server

Another powerful feature of SQL database servers is server-side processing, or server-based grouping. *Server-based grouping* refers to the ability of the SQL server to perform aggregate calculations on groups of records, returning only subtotals, summaries, and other aggregates to the client. If you are creating a summary report (very often the case), this server capability can significantly decrease the amount of data being passed over the network. Also, the summary calculations can be performed on the server rather than on the client.

Consider the following simple Sales by Region report:

Customer Name	Last Year's Sales	City
AL		
Psycho-Cycle	$52,809.11	Huntsville
Benny - The Spokes Person	$6,091.96	Huntsville
The Great Bike Shop	$15,218.09	Huntsville
3 customers	Subtotal: $ 74,119.16	
AR		
Bikefest	$5,879.70	Little Rock
1 customers	Subtotal: $ 5,879.70	
AZ		
Bicycle Races	$659.70	Tempe
Biking and Hiking	$65.70	Phoenix
2 customers	Subtotal: $ 725.40	

This is the beginning of a report that simply shows all U.S.A. customers, grouped by region, with a customer count and sales subtotal for each group. Because the details section is shown, the database server will need to send all customers in the U.S.A. to Crystal Reports. Crystal Reports is actually calculating the subtotal and count for each group on the client machine as the report processes. This is confirmed by looking at the SQL query for this report:

```
Show SQL Query                                    [X]

SELECT 'Customer'.'Customer Name', 'Customer'.'Last Year's Sales',
'Customer'.'City', 'Customer'.'Region', 'Customer'.'Country'
FROM  'Customer' 'Customer'
WHERE 'Customer'.'Country'='USA'
ORDER BY 'Customer'.'Region'


                                            OK
```

Notice that this fairly simple SQL statement just selects database fields and limits records to the U.S.A. The only server feature used here that helps with grouping is the ORDER BY clause, which presorts the result set into Region order before sending it to the client.

To create a summary report, simply hide the details section by right-clicking in the gray details area in the left of the Design tab, and choose Hide (Drill-Down OK) from the pop-up menu. The report will now show just the summary data, with no individual customers appearing on the report.

Customer Name	Last Year's Sales	City
AL		
3 customers	Subtotal: $ 74,119.16	
AR		
1 customers	Subtotal: $ 5,879.70	
AZ		
2 customers	Subtotal: $ 725.40	
CA		
6 customers	Subtotal: $ 211,479.24	
CO		

However, if you look at the SQL query, even after refreshing the report, you'll notice that it hasn't changed, because server-based grouping is turned off by default. The server is still sending all customers in the U.S.A. to Crystal Reports, and Crystal Reports still has to cycle through the individual customer records to calculate the customer count and sales subtotals. Database fields in the details section are hidden, but the database returns them anyway.

Enabling Server-Based Grouping

There are several ways to turn on server-based grouping:

■ To turn it on for the current report only, choose Database | Perform Grouping on Server from the pull-down menus. You can also choose File | Report Options from the pull-down menus and check Perform Grouping on Server. And, you can choose the same option when you right-click in the Available Data Sources area of the Database Expert and choose Options from the pop-up menu.

■ To turn it on for all new reports you create from this point forward, choose File | Options from the pull-down menus and check Perform Grouping on Server on the Database tab.

Once this option is enabled, the report should look the same. There will be some significant changes to the SQL query, however.

```
Show SQL Query                                          [X]

SELECT `Customer`.`Region`,  SUM(`Customer`.`Last Year's Sales`),
COUNT(`Customer`.`Customer Name`)
FROM  `Customer` `Customer`
WHERE `Customer`.`Country`='USA'
GROUP BY `Customer`.`Region`
ORDER BY `Customer`.`Region`



                                                    [ OK ]
```

You will see that the SELECT clause now includes only the group field (in this case, Region) and two *aggregate functions* that perform the sum and count functions right on the database server before data is sent to the client. You will also see a new GROUP BY clause that you have not seen before. This new SQL function tells the server to group database records and perform the summary calculations all on the server. Only the summary totals will be sent to the client.

What's Required to Use Server-Based Grouping

Your report must meet certain criteria and be designed in a certain way to use server-based grouping. When you think about the way the server groups and summarizes records, you'll begin to realize why your report must meet these requirements, shown in Table 16-1.

Requirement	Reasoning
There must be at least one group on the report.	For the GROUP BY clause to be added to the SQL query, there needs to be at least one group defined on the report.
The details section must be hidden.	If the details section is visible, no grouping will occur on the server, because the server must send down individual database records to show in the details section.

Table 16-1. *Server-Based Grouping Requirements*

Requirement	Reasoning
Include only the group fields or summary fields in group headers and footers.	If you include any other database fields (or formula fields that contain anything other than group fields or summary fields), the server will have to send detail data to the client to properly display the report.
Don't group on Crystal Reports formulas.	Because most Crystal Reports formulas can't be converted to SQL, they must be calculated on the client before the report can group on them. Because of this requirement, the server has to send detail records to the client. This is another reason you may want to use SQL expressions as an alternative to formulas, as SQL expressions can still be used for server-based grouping.
Running totals must be based on summary fields.	If running totals (described in Chapter 5) are based on detail fields, Crystal Reports needs the detail data to calculate them as the report processes. This prevents grouping from being done on the server.
The report cannot contain Average or Distinct Count summaries or Top *N* values.	Crystal Reports can't convert these particular functions to SQL. Therefore, the grouping will be performed by the client if these functions are used.
Report groups can be sorted only in ascending or descending order. Specified-order grouping won't work.	Since Crystal Reports bases specified-order grouping on its own internal logic, it needs detail records to properly evaluate what specified groups to place them in. This requires detail records to be sent by the server.

Table 16-1. *Server-Based Grouping Requirements* (continued)

Effects of Drill-Down

When Crystal Reports is performing its own grouping, the concept of report drill-down is fairly straightforward. Even though the details section or lower-level group headers and footers aren't being shown, Crystal Reports is still processing them and storing the data they create. When a viewer double-clicks to drill down on a group, Crystal Reports simply opens a new drill-down tab and displays the data it had previously not displayed.

However, when you enable server-side grouping, there is no detail data to display when a viewer drills down—only the summary data has been sent to the client! Crystal Reports still enables drill-down, however; it just sends another query to the SQL server whenever a viewer drills down. This second query requests just the detail data for the group that was drilled into by adding additional criteria to the WHERE clause. This method provides the benefits of server-based grouping, while still allowing the powerful interactivity of drill-down. The price a viewer pays is the additional time the SQL server may take to process the drill-down query.

Look at the following example. Notice that a viewer has drilled down on a particular region. A new drill-down tab appears, showing detail data for that region. Notice the new SQL query that was created on the fly.

You can view drill-down SQL queries by choosing Database | Show SQL Query when viewing the drill-down tab. If you return to the main Preview tab and show the query, you'll once again notice the GROUP BY clause.

Performance Considerations

SQL databases (or PC-style databases accessed via ODBC) present a very different set of performance considerations than do PC-style databases. As has been discussed throughout the chapter, one of the main benefits of SQL databases over PC databases is the ability of the database server to perform record selection and grouping locally as soon as a SQL query is received from Crystal Reports. Only when the database server has performed record selection or grouping itself will it return the result set back to Crystal Reports.

Let the Server Do the Work

As a general reporting rule, you want to always have the database server perform as much of the processing as possible. Database server software is designed and tuned to perform just such operations, and server software is often placed on very high-end hardware platforms to enhance this performance even further. Any glitch that might cause the database server to send back every record in its database (million-plus-record SQL databases are not at all uncommon) to be selected or summarized locally by Crystal Reports will often result in unsatisfactory performance.

To see how much (or if any) of the query is being evaluated on the database server, view the query by choosing Database | Show SQL Query from the pull-down menus. Look at the SQL statement for the WHERE clause. If you don't see one, no selection at all will be done on the server—every record in the database will come down to the PC, to be left to Crystal Reports to sort through. This can be *very* time-consuming!

Look for an ORDER BY clause if you are sorting or grouping your report. If you see this clause, the database server will presort your data before sending it to Crystal Reports. This can speed the formatting of your report. If you don't see an ORDER BY clause but you specified grouping or sorting in your report, the server will send records to Crystal Reports unsorted, and the client will have to sort the records.

If you wish to use server-based grouping, make sure you see a GROUP BY clause in the query. This ensures that the server is grouping and aggregating data before sending it to Crystal Reports. If you don't see this clause, check back to the server-based grouping requirements earlier in this chapter.

To ensure record selection occurs on the server, Crystal Reports must convert your record-selection formula to a SQL WHERE clause. Several rules of thumb help to ensure that as much record selection as possible is converted to SQL and that it is done on the server:

■ Don't base record selection on formula fields. Crystal Reports usually can't convert formulas to SQL, so most record selection based on formula fields will be passed on to Crystal Reports.

■ Don't use the Crystal Reports formula language's built-in functions, such as ToText, in your selection criteria. Again, Crystal Reports usually can't convert these to SQL, so these parts of record selection won't be carried out on the server. You may be able to find a similar function in a SQL Expression field and use the expression in record selection.

■ Avoid using string subscript functions in record selection. For example, {Customer.Contact First Name}[1 to 5] = "Chris" cannot be converted to SQL, so record selection will be left to Crystal Reports. Create a SQL expression instead, perhaps using a SQL LEFT statement, such as LEFT(Customer.Contact_First_Name, 5). Then use it in record selection.

Use Indexed Fields

In Crystal Reports 9, you'll typically see colored arrows in the Links tab of the Database Expert indicating fields that have been indexed by the database designer. Although you aren't typically required to link only on indexed fields (some PC-style databases in earlier Crystal Reports versions had that requirement), you may want to attempt links on indexed fields if possible anyway. Depending on the database system that you're using, linking to nonindexed fields or performing record selection on nonindexed fields can prove detrimental to the performance of your report. Most SQL database systems have indexing capabilities that the database designer probably considers when designing the database.

If at all possible, work with the database designer to ensure that indexes are created to solve not only your database application needs, but your reporting needs as well. Try to use indexed fields as much as possible as "to" fields in linking, and for record selection.

Also, it may improve performance to select records using as many fields as possible from the main or driving table. For example, you may have a main transaction table that is linked to five lookup tables, and you may want to use the descriptions from the lookup tables in record selection. Instead, consider using the fields in the *main* table for record selection (even if you have to use the codes in the main table, and not the descriptions from the lookup table). Again, if these fields in the main table are indexed, you'll probably see a performance improvement.

Chapter 17

Accommodating Database Changes and Field Mapping

489

There are many situations in which the database you initially developed a report against will change. Perhaps the database is in a state of flux and will be changing dynamically as your report design proceeds. Or, you may develop a report against a test database and then change the report to point to a production database later. Possibly the database has been moved to a different server for network efficiency. Or, you may determine that a different database driver should be used to connect to the database. For true flexibility, you need to be able to accommodate these changes easily so that you don't have to re-create any features or functions of your report just because the database has changed.

With some of these database changes, the database designer or administrator may rename fields. When Crystal Reports detects these changes, it gives you the opportunity to change the field references inside your report, so the new field names can be automatically associated with the previous field names. This field mapping prevents you from having to add fields to the report again or modify formulas that refer to changed fields.

In addition to the Database Expert, which is discussed in Chapter 16, Crystal Reports provides three functions for efficient management of database changes:

- Verifying the database
- Setting the Datasource location
- Mapping fields

When you use either of the first two functions, and Crystal Reports detects changes that it is unable to resolve, such as field name changes or deletions, the field mapping function is automatically displayed.

Recognizing Database Changes

If the database layout changes (field names change, data types are altered, and so forth), if the database is moved to a new location, or if you want to point your report to a different database than it was originally designed with, you need to use Crystal Reports' functions to recognize these changes.

Verify Database

If the database your report is based on changes (perhaps the database designer adds new fields, deletes old fields, or gives existing fields new names or data types), your report won't automatically recognize these changes when the report is opened. Even if you refresh the report, Crystal Reports won't detect the changes, unless a specific field used in the report no longer exists in the database (it has been removed or renamed). To detect changes to the database the report is based on, you must verify the database.

Choose Database | Verify Database from the pull-down menus. If the database has not changed, you'll see a dialog box indicating so:

However, if the database has changed, you'll receive a message like this:

When you click OK at this prompt, Crystal Reports will read the database structure and make any changes to table names, field names, and data types. When you display the Field Explorer, you'll notice the changes. And if you have previously linked tables together and table structures have changed significantly, you may need to relink tables in the Database Expert, as discussed in Chapter 16. If field names have changed, you will see the Map Fields dialog box (discussed later in the chapter).

Verify on First Refresh

If the database changes and you don't verify the database thereafter, your report may show incorrect data if fields have been moved or renamed, or it may display an error message if tables have been removed or renamed. Be very careful when working with a database that may be changing. You'll want to verify the database often to catch any changes.

One way to accomplish this is to select File | Report Options | Verify on First Refresh from the pull-down menus. When you check this menu option, Crystal Reports will verify the database the first time the report is refreshed in any given report session. The on/off state of Verify on First Refresh will be saved with the report—if it was turned on when a particular report was saved, it will be turned on when that report is opened. If you wish to change this choice for all new reports you create in the future, you may modify the same check box on the Database tab after choosing File | Options.

Using Set Datasource Location

Crystal Reports 9 provides a single menu function for changing the connection to the database (database driver), changing the physical location of a database or table, or changing the actual database to be used. Regardless of which of these changes is desired, it is modified through the Set Datasource Location function, and the same process is used to identify the old and new information.

Choose Database | Set Datasource Location from the pull-down menus. The Set Datasource Location dialog box will allow you to select your database or table in the Current Data Source and then explore the Replace With list to identify the replacement data source.

If the desired replacement data source is not displayed in the Replace With list, it may not have had a data source created yet. You can select Make New Connection under the appropriate category and follow the prompts to create a new connection to the desired database, including database logon information, if needed.

When the replacement data source is successfully displayed in the Replace With list, you can select the database or table in both the Current and Replace With lists:

Select current table or database
that needs to change

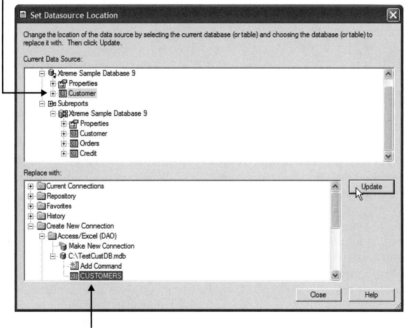

Select the table or database
the report will be pointed to

The streamlining of this function in Crystal Reports 9 means that you can select any replacement data source to make the type of change you need. If you are simply changing database drivers, e.g., from an ODBC connection to an OLE DB connection, you select the current (ODBC) connection in the Current list and browse to or make the new OLE DB connection, to the same database, in the Replace With list. If your database has physically changed locations, you will browse to or create a new connection to the same database on the new server/directory, under the same database driver category in the Replace With list. And if you are actually changing databases, you will browse to or make a new connection to the new database, under the appropriate database driver category in the Replace With list.

When you click Update, Crystal Reports will log on to the identified replacement data source. If the database name is different on the replacement, the database will be verified (as discussed previously in this chapter), and you may see the Map Fields dialog box (discussed in the "Mapping Old Fields to New Names" section later in this chapter). But as long as the database names match, Crystal Reports assumes that the databases are the same and does not prompt for further input; it simply makes the change. The new data source is now displayed in the Current Data Source list, and you can click Close on the Set Datasource Location dialog box or make other data source location changes.

If you also need to change data sources for the subreport(s) in this report, you can select them in the Set Datasource Location lists. If you need to set data sources for individual subreports, perform Set Database Location from the design or preview tab of that subreport.

> **Tip**   *Unlike in previous versions of Crystal Reports, if you change the data source for one subreport, you will not be asked if you wish to propagate the data source change across the other subreports.*

To make the same data source location change for all the subreports that share the same current data source, perform Set Database Location from the main report. You'll see a single Subreports node on the Set Datasource Location list in the main report. Any change made to the elements within that Subreports node will be applied to all subreports sharing that data source.

After you close the Set Datasource Location dialog box, if you have previously linked tables together and the table structures have changed significantly, you may need to relink tables in the Database Expert, in the main report, and/or in any subreports whose data source changed.

Not only will this process allow you to point your report from one database of a particular type (SQL Server, Informix, etc.) to another of the same type, but you may also change database types in the process. For example, if you've built a report based on a test Microsoft Access database, you can use Set Datasource Location to point the report to a production database hosted on Microsoft SQL Server.

> **Note**   *The Set Datasource Location process will allow you to mix different database drivers for individual tables or for multiple databases. However, this may introduce limitations in linking and connections, as Crystal Reports won't be able to create a single, unified SQL statement to get data for the entire report. If this is the case, you will receive an informational warning message not to add SQL Expressions or use server-side grouping.*

Three special features in Set Datasource Location apply only to reports based on PC-style data source connections (such as the Access/Excel DAO connection type). They provide quick ways to identify and modify the name, local directory, and/or network path for a database. Click the plus sign by the PC database in the Current Datasource box to view the elements of the database; then expand the Properties element. Most of the properties are display-only, but the Database Name element, which includes the full path of the database location, can be modified. By right-clicking the Database Name element, you produce a pop-up menu with three options.

Editing Database Name

The Edit option allows you to change the path to the PC-style database used in the report. If the location or name of the database has changed, or will be different for the person to whom you are sending the report, you can change the path here. Changing the database filename in this path tells Crystal Reports to point to a database with the new name.

Same As Report Option

The Same As Report function will remove any drive letter and path name from the PC-style database location. From that point forward, Crystal Reports will look for the database on the same disk drive and in the same folder as the report.

This allows you to create and save a report for distribution to other report viewers. The other viewers can place the report on any drive and in any folder that they choose. As long as the database the report is based on is in the same folder as the report, the report will be able to find it.

Converting to a UNC Name

The Convert To UNC function will change the hard-coded drive letter and path name for the PC-style database to a Uniform Naming Convention (UNC) name that can easily be found by any computer on the network, regardless of its drive mapping. UNC is a way of pointing to a file on a network disk drive without using a drive letter. Consider the following scenario:

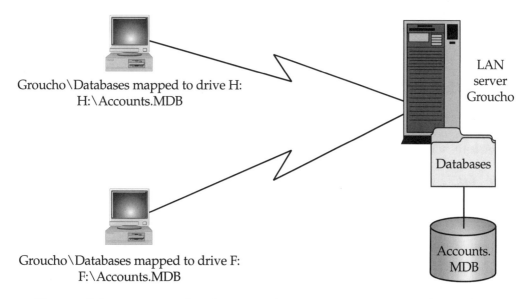

Groucho\Databases mapped to drive H:
H:\Accounts.MDB

LAN
server
Groucho

Databases

Accounts.
MDB

Groucho\Databases mapped to drive F:
F:\Accounts.MDB

The two PCs are connected to the same LAN server, but are using different drive letters to reach the server. If the first PC creates a report based on Accounts.MDB, the report will have the drive letter and filename H:\Accounts.MDB hard-coded into it. When the second PC opens the report, the report will fail—the database won't be found on drive H.

To avoid this kind of problem, you can use a UNC name to replace the drive letter. A UNC name appears in the following format:

\\<*Server Name*>\<*Share Name*>\<*Path and Filename*>

- *Server Name* is the actual name of the computer or server where the file is located (in this case, Groucho). Two backslash characters precede the server name.

- *Share Name* is a name that the LAN administrator has given to a particular group of shared files and folders on the server. When a PC maps a drive letter to a LAN server, the drive letter is mapped to a particular share name (in this case, Databases). A single backslash character separates the *Server Name* from the *Share Name*.

- *Path and Filename* are similar to path names and filenames used on a local PC hard drive, except they are located on the LAN server. In this case, the Accounts.MDB file is in the root of the Databases share name. A single backslash character separates the *Share Name* from the *Path and Filename* (and this path may contain additional backslash characters).

Based on these rules, the corresponding UNC name for the Accounts.MDB file will be as follows:

```
\\Groucho\Databases\Accounts.MDB
```

Notice that the drive letter has been removed. Now, any PC on the network can find the file based on the UNC name—the PC doesn't have to have a drive letter mapped to the LAN server.

Note *In Crystal Reports 9, the Database | Set Alias function has been eliminated. If you need to change the current Alias for a table, you can use the Database Expert: the name of the table is editable in the Selected Tables list of the Data tab.*

Mapping Old Fields to New Names

Database changes can cause a mismatch of field names in your report. For example, your original report may be developed against a Microsoft Access database that includes a field named "Account Number" (note that the space between the words is significant to Crystal Reports). You may need to eventually have the same report work with a SQL Server database where the field is known as "Account_Number" (notice that the space has been replaced with an underscore).

Whenever Crystal Reports detects these kinds of database changes, it can't be sure which new database field the old report object should be associated with. By using Field Mapping, you can point the old object to the new database field. Field mapping simply allows you to change the field name that a report refers to so that, for example, all

Table Names vs. Aliases

When you first create a new report based on certain database tables, you'll notice that the actual name of the table you originally chose shows up in the Field Explorer, the Database Expert, and other places in the report. Although it may appear that Crystal Reports must refer to a database table by its physical name, this name is actually an *alias* automatically assigned, by default, as the table name, and the alias points to the database you selected. When you change a data source location, you're changing where the alias points.

You also have the flexibility to change the alias Crystal Reports uses to refer to this table. Changing an alias name is performed in the Database Expert in Crystal Reports 9. This replaces the previous Database | Set Alias function.

If a database designer or administrator changes the name of a table in the database, the next time you try to refresh your report, you will receive an error indicating that the table can't be found. Unfortunately, refreshing the report or verifying the database will not solve this problem—the message will persist and the report will not print properly.

To solve this problem, perform the following simple steps:

1. Use the Set Datasource Location function as described in this chapter to connect to the new data source (this may be as simple as contracting and re-expanding the category of the Database Expert where the original database was). Select the old table name in the Current Data Source list and the new table name in the Replace with list. Click Update. This will correctly point the report to the new table name. However, the table will still be referred to by the old name in the report.

2. If you want the new name to appear throughout the report, use the Database Expert to change the alias of the old table to the new table name. This will change the name of the table as well, avoiding confusion as to which physical table is actually being used.

objects that used to be associated with "Account Number" will now be associated with "Account_Number." No formulas have to be changed, no old objects have to be removed, and no new objects need to be added.

The Field Mapping function cannot be chosen from a menu. It is triggered when Crystal Reports detects any field name changes in the source database. Crystal Reports will check for these changes whenever you verify the database or use the Set Datasource Location function to change the database or data source connection. When Crystal Reports detects that fields in the report are no longer in the database, it displays the Map Fields dialog box, as shown in Figure 17-1.

The Map Fields dialog box is divided into four boxes or lists. The upper-left Unmapped Fields list shows report fields that don't match up to any field names in the new database.

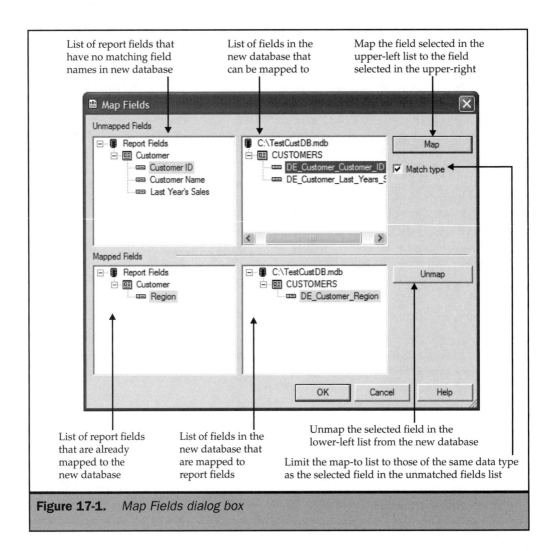

List of report fields that have no matching field names in new database

List of fields in the new database that can be mapped to

Map the field selected in the upper-left list to the field selected in the upper-right

List of report fields that are already mapped to the new database

List of fields in the new database that are mapped to report fields

Unmap the selected field in the lower-left list from the new database

Limit the map-to list to those of the same data type as the selected field in the unmatched fields list

Figure 17-1. *Map Fields dialog box*

The upper-right list shows a choice of fields in the new database that you can map the report fields to. To map the report field to the new database field, select the report field you want to map in the upper-left box, select a matching database field in the upper-right box, and then click the Map button. The fields will be moved from the upper boxes to the lower boxes.

The list of database fields will change according to whether or not you click the Match Type check box on the right side of the dialog box. If the box is checked, only fields of the same data type (string, number, date, and so forth) as that of the selected report field will show up. This helps to ensure that you're making the correct match of fields, by not inadvertently mapping a string field on the report to a number or date field in the new database (although you may want to do this sometimes). There may be times that you won't see the field you want to map to in the right list, however, because of data type mismatches. For example, if you're remapping fields originally from a Microsoft Access database to a SQL Server database, you may not find any SQL Server field that matches a currency field in the Access database. In this situation, uncheck Match Type and look for the field to map to.

When the Map Fields dialog box first appears, some fields probably will already be present in the lower two Mapped Fields boxes. The lower-left list shows report fields that already have a matching field in the new database. And once you've mapped fields from the upper lists, they will be moved to the lower lists as well. If existing mapping was assumed by Crystal Reports (because of identical field names), or you mistakenly mapped fields that don't belong together, you can select a field in the lower-left or lower-right list. The mapped field will appear highlighted in the other box. You can then click the Unmap button to unmap the fields and move them back to the top lists.

Once you have finished mapping fields, click the OK button to close the Map Fields dialog box. Crystal Reports will now associate the mapped fields with the new database. The Design tab, as well as any formulas, will reflect the new field names. If additional tables have mismatched fields, you'll be presented with the Map Fields dialog box for each subsequent table.

Caution   *Any fields that no longer exist in the source database must be remapped to new fields. If you don't map old field names to new fields, the old fields and objects they're based on will be deleted from your report!*

Chapter 18

Reporting from OLAP Cubes

Relational database systems provide the vast majority of the data analysis and reporting capabilities that most organizations need. However, a smaller segment of many organizations can benefit from more flexible and sophisticated analysis tools. In many cases, an organization's higher-level analysts are still using spreadsheet tools in combination with relational databases to make strategic company decisions.

Online analytical processing (OLAP) is a newer analysis technique that provides much more flexibility in analyzing company data. Crystal Reports supports most standard OLAP tools and enables you to create reports based on these database systems.

What Is OLAP?

Most typical company data is viewed in two dimensions, whether it is viewed by a reporting tool such as Crystal Reports or a spreadsheet program such as Microsoft Excel. In the case of a spreadsheet, the rows and columns constitute the two-dimensional analysis. You may be viewing product sales by state, salesperson volume by product category, or customer totals by demographics. In each of these cases, you typically can see only two dimensions at any one time, even though you actually may prefer to analyze a combination of three or more of these factors.

Region

Product

	USA	CAN	UK
PROD 1	534	212	231
PROD 2	45	21	12
PROD 3	321	324	112
PROD 4	204	120	40
PROD 5	78	43	31
PROD 6	32	12	2
PROD 7	786	512	49
PROD 8	123	23	17

Online analytical processing is a leading-edge analysis approach that allows data to be analyzed and viewed in multiple dimensions in real time. With a typical OLAP tool, you may initially be presented with a spreadsheet-like view that shows information using two dimensions, such as product sales dollars by state (or perhaps by country or region, allowing drill-down to the state level).

Even though only two dimensions are visible, additional dimensions are available "behind the scenes" to control the two dimensions you are viewing; you can limit dollars by state by using other dimensions. Perhaps you want to see dollars by state limited to just certain sales reps, certain customer demographics, or certain product categories— you still see the original Dollars and State dimensions, but the numbers are *filtered* by the other dimensions. You may also want to quickly see sales by product category, demographics by state, or some other combinations of dimensions. Using an OLAP analysis tool, "slicing and dicing" through the different dimensions is typically as easy as dragging and dropping one dimension on top of another. Figure 18-1 shows the multidimensional "FoodMart" database included with Microsoft SQL Server 7.0 OLAP Services or Microsoft SQL Server 2000 Analysis Services.

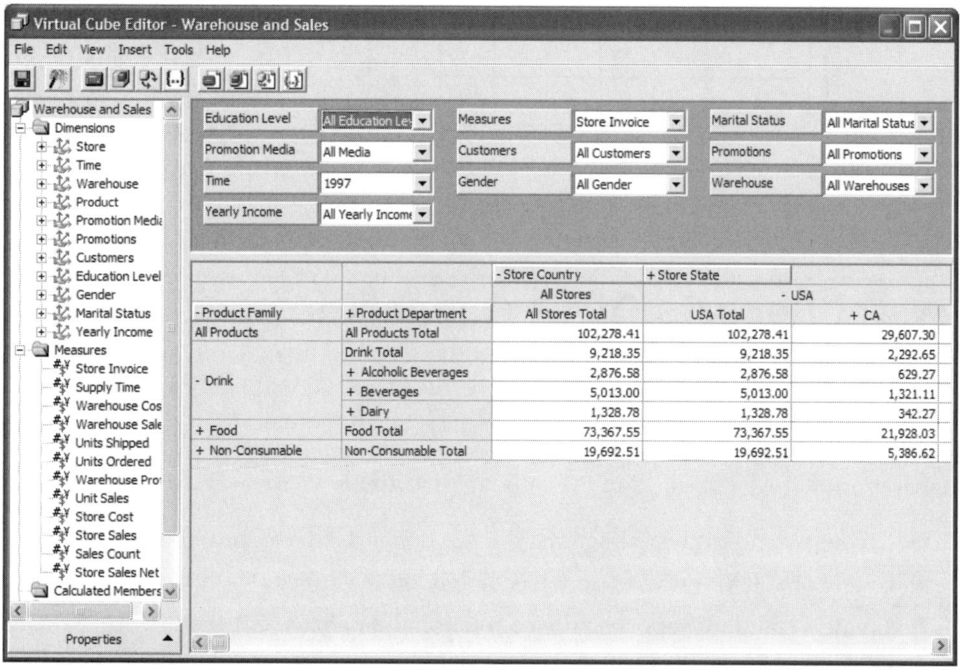

Figure 18-1. *SQL Server Analysis tool viewing OLAP cube*

Whereas relational databases represent data in a two-dimensional, row-and-column (or field-and-record) structure, OLAP databases utilize a multidimensional structure known as a *cube* (which, despite its name, is capable of storing more than three dimensions of data). Often, cubes are built on the basis of regular relational database systems—the relational database is populated using typical data-entry or data-import techniques, and a cube is built that is based on the relational database. Cubes can be refreshed or repopulated on a regular basis to allow multidimensional, real-time analysis of the data in the relational database.

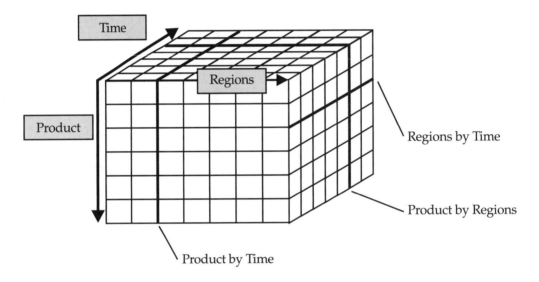

Crystal Reports OLAP Capabilities

You might ask, "Where does Crystal Reports fit into all of this?" Crystal Reports, obviously, can report on the data stored in the two-dimensional relational database. However, Crystal Reports also allows reporting against many industry-leading OLAP cubes. In fact, Crystal Reports can combine reports that are based on both relational databases and OLAP cubes, all in the same report. You have several choices:

- Create a standard report against the relational database the cube is based on.
- Create an OLAP-only report based solely on the cube.
- Create a standard report against a relational database (either the same database the cube is based on or an entirely different database) *and* include an OLAP report based on a cube inside the standard report.
- Create several *different* OLAP reports based on the same, or different, cubes. These OLAP-based reports can exist individually, or be included together inside a standard report based on a relational database.

Supported OLAP Systems

While OLAP technology has been somewhat fragmented and proprietary until recently, industry standards are starting to emerge. Crystal Reports will work with leading proprietary OLAP databases, as well as with the emerging *Open OLAP* standard. Thus, Crystal Reports 9 can create OLAP reports based on the following tools:

- Hyperion Essbase
- Crystal Holos
- IBM DB2 OLAP Server
- Microsoft SQL Server 7.0 OLAP Services or SQL Server 2000 Analysis Services via OLE DB
- OLE DB for OLAP sources (or other "Open OLAP" sources)
- SAP BW
- Crystal Analysis Professional (.CAR file)

Tip *The Standard Edition of Crystal Reports 9 does not support OLAP. The OLAP-related functions will be inactive on all screens.*

OLAP Report Creation Methods

There are several ways Crystal Reports can be used to report on your OLAP data. While all OLAP reporting in Crystal Reports will be based on the same type of object (the OLAP grid), there are several ways to create it. An *OLAP grid* is very similar in appearance and functionality to a cross-tab object (discussed in detail in Chapter 11). An OLAP grid displays one or more cube dimensions in rows and columns on the report. As with a cross-tab, you may format individual rows and columns to appear as you wish. You may also easily swap, or *pivot*, the rows and columns to change the appearance of the OLAP grid. And with Crystal Reports 9, you can launch the *OLAP Analyzer*, an interactive viewer similar to Crystal Decisions Crystal Analysis product, to conduct real-time "slice and dice" analysis of your OLAP data right from within Crystal Reports.

Creating reports with OLAP cubes is straightforward and very similar to creating reports with regular relational databases. You may either use the OLAP Report Creation Wizard right from the Report Gallery or add an OLAP Grid object to a report you've already created using a standard relational database. The OLAP Wizard leads you step by step through choosing the cube and dimensions you want to use in the row and column of your report. It will then create a report containing an OLAP grid. If you add an OLAP grid object to your report manually, you can make similar choices to that of the OLAP Report Creation Wizard to construct the OLAP grid (this is similar to creating a cross-tab object).

Using the OLAP Report Creation Wizard

The OLAP Report Creation Wizard is available from the Report Gallery that appears whenever you create a new report. Just click the OLAP button to use the expert.

The Data dialog displays first in the Report Creation Wizard, to allow you to identify the OLAP cube you wish to base your OLAP report on.

```
┌─────────────────────────────────────────────────────────────────┐
│ ▣ OLAP Report Creation Wizard                              [×]    │
│                                                                    │
│  OLAP Data                                                    ▛▖   │
│                                                                    │
│ ──────────────────────────────────────────────────────────────── │
│                                                                    │
│   Choose the data to be your On Line Analytical Processing (OLAP) source │
│   Choose an OLAP Server type then select the Cube that contains the data. │
│                                                                    │
│                                                                    │
│              ┌─────────────────┐   ┌─────────────────┐            │
│              │  Select Cube... │   │ Select CAR File...│           │
│              └─────────────────┘   └─────────────────┘            │
│                                                                    │
│       Cube: ┌──────────────────────────────────────────┐          │
│             └──────────────────────────────────────────┘          │
│       Type: ┌──────────────────────────────────────────┐          │
│             └──────────────────────────────────────────┘          │
│     Server: ┌──────────────────────────────────────────┐          │
│             └──────────────────────────────────────────┘          │
│                                                                    │
│                                                                    │
│                                                                    │
│         ┌──────┐ ┌──────┐ ┌──────┐ ┌────────┐ ┌──────┐            │
│         │<Back │ │Next >│ │Finish│ │ Cancel │ │ Help │            │
│         └──────┘ └──────┘ └──────┘ └────────┘ └──────┘            │
└─────────────────────────────────────────────────────────────────┘
```

Click the Select Cube button to display the Crystal OLAP Connection Browser, where you can choose from the OLAP cube connections available. If you wish to report on a Crystal Analysis Professional .CAR file, you can click the CAR button; CAR files are found through the standard Open dialog, rather than the OLAP Connection Browser used for most OLAP connections.

Use the OLAP cubes explorer tree to navigate to the OLAP cube you want to report on, then select it and click the Open button, or simply double-click the OLAP cube. If you don't see the desired OLAP cube, you may need to click the Add Server button to browse, log on to, and add a new OLAP server in the New Server dialog.

Depending on the type of cube and location of the OLAP database, complete the fields in the Add Server dialog box. If you are using a Microsoft Analysis Services cube with SQL Server 2000, choose the Microsoft OLE DB Provider for Olap Services 8.0 server type. If you are using Microsoft OLAP Services with SQL Server 7, choose the Microsoft OLE DB Provider for OLAP Services item. In either case, you'll then need to specify the server name, user ID, and password in the following three fields. If you have been provided with an Analysis Services local cube (.CUB) file, select the Local Cube file radio button and type in or navigate to the .CUB file. Or, if you've been instructed to connect to the Analysis Services server via HTTP (the standard Internet protocol), select the HTTP Cube radio button and type in the URL to the server, along with your user name and password.

If you choose other OLAP Server Types, appropriate options will appear in the New Server dialog box for connecting to the associated cube. If you are unsure of how to connect to your particular cube type, consult with the administrator of your OLAP database.

Tip

If your OLAP server doesn't appear in the Server Type drop-down list, you may need to install client software specific to your particular OLAP system, such as a cube-viewing application, on your PC. After you install this software, restart Crystal Reports and try creating the report again.

Once you've successfully logged on to and connected to the proper cube, you'll be returned to the OLAP Connection Browser and the cube will appear in the OLAP Cubes list—you won't have to go through the Add Server process again, as the cube will remain in the list from this point on. If you made errors in the connection process in the New Server dialog box and the cube can't be connected to, right-click the cube definition in the list and choose Remove Server from the list. The server will be removed and you can click the Add Server button to add the server again (you can also rename the server from this pop-up menu, as well as adding individual cubes within the server to the Favorites entry in the browser).

Once you've selected the desired cube in the OLAP Connection Browser, the Data dialog of the Report Creation Wizard redisplays, and the Cube, Type, and Server fields on the Data tab of the Expert will be filled in.

After you make these choices, click the Next button to show the Rows/Columns section, shown in Figure 18-2, to choose the dimension or dimensions you want to include in the rows and columns of your report.

Note

Crystal Reports 9 includes a sample Holos OLAP cube for the Xtreme Mountain Bike company that you can use to experiment with OLAP reporting. XTREME.HDC can be found below the Crystal Reports program directory in \Samples\en\Databases\Olap Data. However, the examples in this chapter are based on the sample Foodmart OLAP cube provided with Microsoft SQL Server Analysis Services.

Dimensions defined in cube   Dimension(s) to appear as rows in OLAP report   Dimension(s) to appear as columns in OLAP report

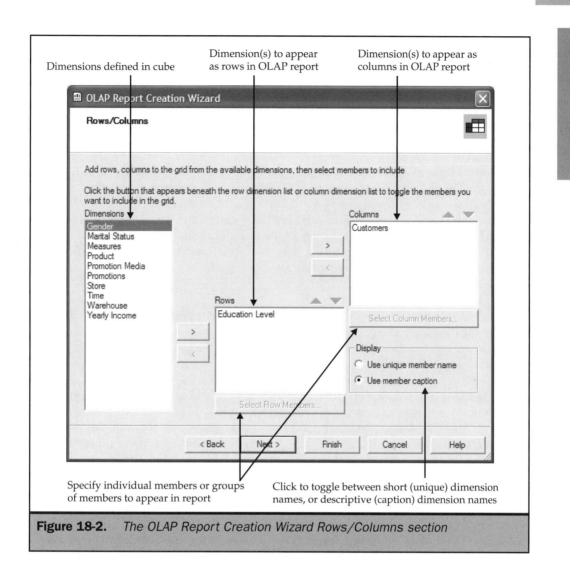

Specify individual members or groups of members to appear in report

Click to toggle between short (unique) dimension names, or descriptive (caption) dimension names

Figure 18-2.   *The OLAP Report Creation Wizard Rows/Columns section*

If the default dimensions already in the Rows and Columns list aren't correct, choose from the Dimensions list the dimension that you want to appear as the row in your OLAP report. Then, simply drag and drop it into the Rows box or click the right arrow next to the Rows box.

Use the same drag-and-drop method to add to the Columns box the dimension you want to appear as the column in your OLAP report. Or, select a dimension and click the right arrow next to the Rows or Columns list.

You aren't limited to placing just one dimension in the Rows and Columns boxes. If you add multiple dimensions, Crystal Reports will "group" the dimensions in the OLAP report. For example, if you add a State dimension, followed by a Customer dimension, Crystal Reports will print states and show customers broken down within each state. If you place the dimensions in the Rows or Columns box in the wrong order, you can simply drag and drop the dimensions into the correct order within the Rows or Columns box. Alternatively, you can select the dimension you want to move, and use the up and down arrows above the Rows and Columns boxes.

If you wish to remove a dimension from the Rows or Columns box, drag the dimension back to the Dimensions list. Or, you can select the desired dimension and click the left arrow (you won't be allowed to leave a row or column empty).

Select the Use Member Caption radio button if you want Crystal Reports to use the "long name" or "alias" in the OLAP report, instead of the short code contained in some cubes. For example, by choosing this option, the OLAP report might show spelled-out state names instead of two-letter state codes. If you prefer the smaller codes, select Use Unique Member Name.

Note   *The behavior of the member name/caption option is dependent on the OLAP database and cube you are using. If you see abbreviated code-like material in your OLAP report, ensure that this option is checked. However, if the OLAP database or cube isn't designed with long field names or aliases, selecting this option will have no effect or different results.*

Depending on the cube you choose for your report, you may find dimensions that contain many levels or members. A *member* (sometimes referred to as a generation) is a lower level of information that breaks down the higher level above it. For example, a Products dimension could contain several members: product type, product name within product type, and size within product name. Each member further breaks down the information shown by the member above it, creating a hierarchy for data in the dimension.

By default, if the dimension you choose for your OLAP report contains multiple members, Crystal Reports will show only the highest member in a group hierarchy when it displays the dimension. While this may be the way you want the report to appear, it may actually display a data level that is too high. Often, you'll add dimensions to a report's Rows and Columns boxes, only to have the OLAP report show just one number at the intersection of one row and column. If you need to increase the number of members shown inside a dimension that appears on the report, you can use the Select Members buttons to select the additional members that you want to see. First, select the dimension in the Rows or Columns list that you wish to work with, and then click the Select Row Members or Select Column Members button. You may also just double-click a dimension in the list. When you do either, the Member Selector will appear, as shown in Figure 18-3.

The Member Selector dialog box shows the dimension members in a hierarchy, with pluses and minuses to the left, much like the display of folders and files in Windows Explorer. You can expand the hierarchy to see lower members by clicking the plus signs

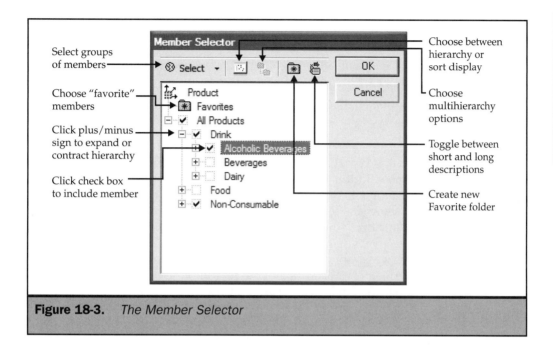

Select groups of members

Choose "favorite" members

Click plus/minus sign to expand or contract hierarchy

Click check box to include member

Choose between hierarchy or sort display

Choose multihierarchy options

Toggle between short and long descriptions

Create new Favorite folder

Figure 18-3.   *The Member Selector*

next to the members. If you want to see just the higher-level members, click the minus sign to collapse them.

Once you've expanded the dimension's members sufficiently, you can simply click the check box next to individual members to select or deselect them. Those that are checked will be included in the report—those that aren't won't. If you want to select multiple members at the same time, you may CTRL-click or SHIFT-click on multiple member names to highlight them (multiselect or range-select, respectively), and then click one check box. All the members that are highlighted will be selected.

If you want to be more systematic in member selection, particularly for very large hierarchies, click the down arrow attached to the Select button in the Member Selector's toolbar to display a pull-down menu (you can also right-click a member name to get the same menu). You'll see various options for selecting groups of members (such as all top-level members, all base members, children, parents, and so forth). Notice that once you choose one of the options in the select menu, the Select button will display an icon similar to the choice you made from the menu. By just clicking the Select button, you can repeat that selection without displaying the menu again.

You can also control other aspects of the Member Selector by choosing other toolbar buttons:

- **Select Display Mode** will change from viewing members in a hierarchy to sorting them in ascending or descending order.

- ■ **Select Hierarchy** will provide additional options if the particular dimension you've chosen encompasses more than one hierarchy.
- ■ **New Favorite Group** will add an additional category underneath the Favorites folder where you may drag "favorite" members.
- ■ **Toggle Descriptions** will toggle between short and long member names (if your cube makes a distinction).

After you choose the members you want included in the report, click OK. You won't notice any difference in the Rows/Columns tab—you'll need to double-click the dimension or click the Select Member button again to see what members you've chosen.

Once you've chosen dimensions and members, click the Next button to advance to the Slice/Page section, shown in Figure 18-4, to determine how the remaining dimensions included in the cube will affect your OLAP report.

In the Slice/Page section, you'll see all the other dimensions in the cube that you didn't include in the Rows or Columns boxes. You can use these dimensions to either slice or page your OLAP report. *Slicing* (similar to filtering) the OLAP report limits the report to certain occurrences of data in these dimensions. *Paging* the OLAP report is very similar to setting up report grouping. Like the grouping of other reports, discussed in Chapter 3, this creates a new section of the OLAP report showing a different OLAP grid every time the value of the chosen dimension changes. Each resulting OLAP report section will contain data just for that one member.

To *slice* the report according to a dimension, look at the Slice part of the dialog box. You'll notice that each dimension displays a filter criterion, such as Store = All Stores. Typically, this default value will be either All or a particular general value that was set as the default when the OLAP cube was defined. Either double-click the dimension you want to slice, or select the dimension and click the Select Slice button. The Member Selector dialog box, described earlier, will appear, in which you can choose a particular value to limit the OLAP report. After you make your choice and click OK, the criterion in the Filter list will change to indicate the value you picked. The OLAP report will now be limited to only values that are included in the dimension you chose.

| Tip | *Unlike the previous example with the Member Selector dialog box, you can choose only one value in the box here. Selecting a new value deselects the preceding value.* |

To *page* the OLAP report according to a dimension, select the desired dimension in the Slice list and either drag it to the Page list or click the right arrow. Once again, the Member Selector dialog box appears, in which you can again select any combination of members (using options from the Select menus, if you'd like). After you make your choices, click OK to close the Member Selector dialog box. The dimension you chose for paging will appear in the Page list at the right of the Slice/Page section. If you wish to later change the members you chose to page the report, return to the Slice/Page section and double-click the dimension in the Page list, or select the dimension and click the Select Page Values button.

CRYSTAL REPORTS 9
INTRODUCED

Limit view to particular member of dimension   Dimensions not included in row or column

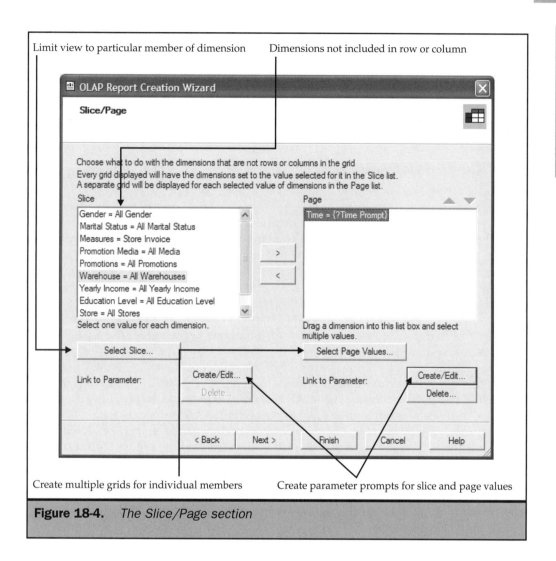

Figure 18-4. *The Slice/Page section*

You can add more than one dimension to the Page list. If you do so, you can change the order in which Crystal Reports will group the OLAP report, by selecting one of the dimensions and clicking the up or down arrow. If you want to remove one of the Page dimensions, select it in the Page list and click the left arrow button or drag the dimension back to the Slice list.

A new feature in Crystal Reports 9 is the ability to base slices and pages on parameter fields. To do this, select the slice or page dimension that you want to create a parameter field for and click the Create/Edit button. The Create Parameter Field dialog box will appear, where you may choose options to prompt the report viewer when the OLAP report is refreshed. Then, the value that the viewer supplies to the parameter field will be passed to the slice or page dimension to control how the OLAP report appears. Once you've added a parameter to a dimension, you'll notice the parameter field to the right of the equal sign in the Slice or Page list. If you later want to edit the parameter field, click the desired dimension and then the Create/Edit button. To delete the parameter and return to a fixed value or values chosen in the Member Selector, choose the desired dimension and click the Delete button.

Tip *More detailed information on creating parameter fields can be found in Chapter 14.*

Once you've made any slicing and paging choices, you're ready to display the OLAP report if you're satisfied with the default formatting Crystal Reports will apply. Click the Finish button if you're ready to view the report. However, you have additional choices in the OLAP Report Creation Wizard if you wish to choose them. You may choose from a set of preformatted *styles* for the OLAP report, as well as adding charts to show data plotted in your OLAP report.

To customize the formatting of the *OLAP Grid objects* the Wizard will create (very similar to the cross-tab object discussed in Chapter 11), click Next to display the Style section of the Wizard. Choose from one of the predefined grid styles to apply to the OLAP report.

You may then click the Finish button to display the report, or click Next to create a chart based on your OLAP data. There is a minimal set of charting choices on this section (more detail on charting on OLAP grids is discussed in Chapter 12).

Click the Finish button in the OLAP Report Creation Wizard to run the report and show it in the Preview tab. Depending on any page dimensions you chose, you'll see a few simple objects on the report, such as the print date and the report title. You'll also see one or more OLAP grid objects, plus any report sections and groups that were created to accommodate the page dimensions.

 If you need to make changes to the Rows/Columns or Slice/Page values in the OLAP cube, you can rerun the Report Creation Wizard by clicking the OLAP Report Settings button in the Expert toolbar or by choosing Report | OLAP Report Settings from the pull-down menus.

Alternatively, to display the full OLAP Expert with all possible options (discussed in the next section, "Adding an OLAP Grid to an Existing Report"), you can select the OLAP grid object by clicking in the blank area of the object's upper-left corner (if there is more than one, select the particular one you want to change). Then, right-click and select OLAP Expert from the pop-up menu.

Adding an OLAP Grid to an Existing Report

You probably will encounter situations in which you want to create a standard database report that includes one or more OLAP grids. By choosing the Blank Report option or other wizards from the Report Gallery, you have more flexibility in creating this type of report. Simply create the base report using the techniques discussed elsewhere in the book.

You may even find it useful to base the main report on some fields from your OLAP database. To use the OLAP database for the main report, choose the OLAP entry under the Create New Connection category of the Database Expert. The OLAP Connection Browser (shown earlier in the chapter) will appear, where you can choose an OLAP cube. You can add as many of these cubes or tables as necessary for the report. Depending on the type of OLAP database you've chosen, the Field Explorer will show the dimensions and members for your chosen cubes, or the fields in the chosen tables. You can add these fields to your main report as you would a regular database field. You may need to try some experimentation to determine which dimensions or fields can be used—OLAP data often doesn't behave the same as relational database data. Once the main part of your report is finished, you can add the necessary OLAP grid objects.

| **Caution** | *Even though you can access the OLAP cube by using the Blank Report option, you won't be able to actually include any cube values in any report sections. You'll only be able to include and manipulate dimension names. The only way to actually include the numeric values from the cube is to create an OLAP grid object.* |

Adding an OLAP Grid Object

To create an OLAP grid on an existing report, click the OLAP grid toolbar button in the Insert Tools toolbar or choose Insert | OLAP Grid from the pull-down menus. The OLAP Expert appears.

OLAP Expert

OLAP Data | Rows/Columns | Slice/Page | Style | Customize Style | Labels

Choose the data to be your On Line Analytical Processing (OLAP) source
Choose an OLAP Server type then select the Cube that contains the data.

Select Cube...

Cube: Xtreme

Type: Holos HDC Cubes (Local client)

Server: C:\Program Files\Crystal Decisions\Crystal Reports 9\Sample

<< Back | Next >> | OK | Cancel | Help

The tabs in the OLAP Expert behave almost identically to the same sections in the OLAP Report Creation Wizard, described earlier in the chapter. Follow the same steps for the Data and Rows/Columns tabs to choose the cube and dimensions for your OLAP grid. You may also use the Style and Customize Style tabs to format the OLAP grid, similar to formatting a cross-tab object (covered in detail in Chapter 11). Three of the tabs deserve more discussion, however: the Slice/Page tab, the Customize Style tab, and the Labels tab.

Slice/Page Tab

Notice that the Page dimension list and the Parameter field buttons that appear with the OLAP Report Creation Wizard are unavailable here, and a note suggests that you use the Wizard if you want to use these features. If you want to have several cubes work as pages, you can either re-create the report using the Wizard or add multiple OLAP grids to your report, specifying a different slice for each grid to mimic the Paged dimension process discussed in the Wizard portion of this chapter.

Customize Style Tab

This tab is identical to the same tab used to format cross-tab objects (see more information on this tab in Chapter 11). Options you choose on this tab change formatting options, such as background color, grid line formatting, and "Alias for Formulas," which lets you give a shorter, more meaningful name to a column or row for use in conditional formatting.

OLAP Labels

Many OLAP cubes of even moderate complexity often contain many dimensions. However, unlike a "slice and dice" OLAP analysis tool, the OLAP grid object that initially appears in the Preview tab or appears when you print or export the report doesn't offer a high level of interactivity (although the OLAP Analyzer, discussed later in the chapter under "The New OLAP Analyzer," does provide high interactivity). Accordingly, you'll probably use only a few (if not just one) dimensions for a row and column. The remainder of the dimensions not actually appearing as a row or column (often called *qualified dimensions*) can simply be ignored, used as Slice dimensions, or used as Page dimensions. Of particular interest is how the report viewer will know what settings have been made for Slice dimensions: if the OLAP grid is limited to just one product, one gender, and one store, how will this be known? The answer is *OLAP labels*.

When you create an OLAP grid object either with the OLAP Wizard or by inserting an OLAP grid manually, OLAP labels are added to the OLAP grid by default, as shown here:

All Customers   All Education Lev All Marital Status Profit   All Media
All Promotions   All Stores   All   All   1997
All Yearly Income

		All Gender		
		F	M	
All Products	Drink	14,706.27	14,652.70	29,358.98
	Food	122,100.72	123,664.15	245,764.87
	Non-Consuma	31,641.74	32,845.31	64,487.05
		168,448.73	171,162.17	339,610.90

Notice that any Filter dimensions, such as 1997, are listed. Otherwise, the All designations appear. This indicates to the report viewer what limits have been placed on the OLAP grid. You may choose to limit the set of OLAP labels that appear—perhaps to just the ones that are used as a Filter dimension. Or, you may want to otherwise customize the way the OLAP labels appear. To do this, click the Labels tab, shown in Figure 18-5.

By default, all qualified dimensions (those that are in the cube, but not included as a row or column on the grid) are placed in the right Labeled Dimensions box. You can change the order in which they will appear next to the OLAP grid by selecting a label and using the small arrows above the box to move it up or down in the list. If you don't want a particular label to appear with the grid, select it and click the left arrow to move it to the Unlabeled Dimensions box.

You can also customize the amount of white space Crystal Reports will place between the labels by specifying a new value in the Vertical Gap and Horizontal Gap text boxes. You can choose to place the entire set of labels on the top or left side of the OLAP grid (or not have the labels show up at all). And finally, you can check the Display Dimension Name check box to replace the "All <value>" label with "<Dimension> = <value>" for labels.

After you make your desired choices in the OLAP Expert, click OK. An outline of the OLAP grid object will be attached to the mouse cursor. Drop the object in the desired section of the report.

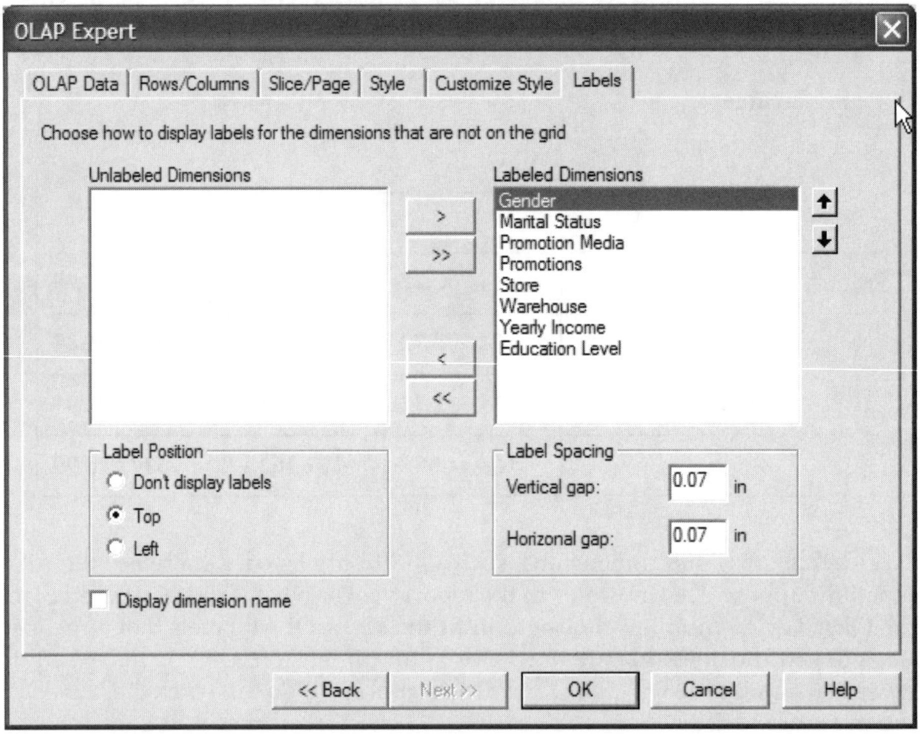

Figure 18-5. The Labels tab

You may make changes or additions to the OLAP grid object by selecting it and then formatting the OLAP grid by using pull-down menu options, the Format button in the Expert Tools toolbar, or format options from the right-click pop-up menu. You can also format individual parts of the OLAP grid, as discussed later in the chapter under "Controlling OLAP Grid Appearance."

Changing the OLAP Database Location

An OLAP grid "points" to a specific OLAP cube location on a server. If that location changes, or if you want to report on a different cube without redesigning the entire OLAP grid, you need to change the location of the OLAP database that the grid refers to.

Select the OLAP grid you want to change by clicking its upper-left corner. Right-click and choose Set OLAP Cube Location from the pop-up menu, or choose Database | Set OLAP Cube Location from the pull-down menus. The Set OLAP Cube Location dialog box appears.

Set OLAP Cube Location

OLAP Server

Server Type: Microsoft OLE DB Provider for Olap Services 8.0

Server: x23

Cube: Warehouse and Sales

Select...

OK   Cancel

Choose the new OLAP cube or new server location for the associated OLAP database. Then click OK.

Controlling OLAP Grid Appearance

An OLAP grid organizes cube information in a row-and-column format, much as a cross-tab object does. In fact, formatting and changing OLAP grid appearance is essentially identical to formatting a cross-tab object:

- Make choices on the Style or Customize Style tab in the OLAP Expert. You can choose from built-in formatting styles on the Style tab or perform more detailed formatting of individual elements on the Customize Style tab.

- Select individual fields that make up the OLAP grid, and resize or format them individually. When you resize an individual field, the row or column that the field is in will change accordingly. You can change field font face, font size, and color. And if you're formatting numeric information, such as the OLAP grid value fields, you can choose rounding, decimal places, currency symbols, and other formatting that applies to the type of field you're formatting.

- Perform conditional formatting on values in the OLAP grid, using the actual numeric data contained in the cells, or using the Row or Column field of the cell.

- Format OLAP Grid labels, either individually or as a group. Select an individual label and use typical formatting options. Or, you may click on the edge of the label area and select all the labels as a group (you'll see OLAP Grid Labels appear in the status bar at the bottom of the screen). You actually have selected the border around all the labels, and you can add a border, drop shadow, or other "border-oriented" formatting options. You can also suppress the labels on the Format Editor common tab if you don't want to see them (this can be done conditionally, as opposed to making as similar choice in the OLAP Labels tab of the OLAP Expert).

Tip	*Formatting OLAP grids is virtually identical to formatting cross-tab objects. Refer to Chapter 11 for a thorough discussion.*

Interacting with the OLAP Grid

Although you don't have quite the "slice and dice" flexibility with Crystal Reports that you may have with your particular OLAP analysis tool, you might be surprised by how easy it is to rearrange the appearance of an OLAP grid object (especially in Crystal Reports 9—this functionality is much improved). When you first create the OLAP grid, you choose which dimensions you want to use as rows and which you want to use as columns. If you choose multiple row or column dimensions, the order in which you add them determines the grouping order for the rows or columns.

You may want to change the order of the OLAP grid's row or column grouping, or you may want to swap or *pivot* the rows and columns, drill down on higher-level dimensions, and so forth. There are a large number of new manipulation choices in Crystal Reports 9 (many of these options are only available when viewing the OLAP grid in the Preview tab—limited options exist in the Design tab):

- **Pivot the rows and columns**   Select the OLAP grid. Then, right-click and choose Pivot OLAP Grid from the pop-up menu. You can also choose Format | Pivot OLAP Grid from the pull-down menus.

- **Reorder dimensions**   Simply click the row or column heading of the dimension you want to reorder. As you hold down the mouse button, you will notice a little "piece of paper" icon appear on the mouse pointer. This indicates that the dimension can be dragged and dropped below or above another dimension to reorder the dimensions. You can even drag and drop a dimension from a row to a column, or vice versa, provided that at least one dimension will be left in the row or column of the OLAP grid.

- **Drill down and drill up (new in version 9)**   Double-click a higher-level member. This, in essence, is the same as rerunning the OLAP Expert and using the Select Row Members option to show the next level of the hierarchy. You can then drill down on the lower levels that you just exposed, until there are no more lower levels to show. To drill up (hide the lower levels you already showed), just double-click the higher-level member again—the lower-level members will disappear. You can also select the member name, right-click, and choose Expand Member or Collapse Member from the pop-up menu.

- **Total columns or rows (new in version 9)**   Select any row or column member (you can't total when you've selected an individual number "cell") and right-click. Choose Automatic Totals from the pop-up menu. A submenu will appear giving you totaling choices.

- **Add custom calculations (new in version 9)**   You may add one or more additional rows or columns (members) based on a calculation. These additional calculated members can consist of such calculations as contribution, growth,

ranking, variance, or other statistical calculations that you can create using the
MDX query language derived from Microsoft Analysis Services.

To create the calculated member, select the member row or column heading
that you want to use as the basis for your calculation. Right-click, and choose
Add Calculated Member from the pop-up menu. The Calculated Members
dialog box will appear.

There are two choices: the Calculation Expert tab and the Calculation tab.
The Calculation Expert limits you to a few common calculations, allowing you
to pick members to include in the calculation, the type of calculation you want to
perform, which other dimension you want the calculated member to relate to, and
so forth.

The Calculation tab will either show you the "long" version of the calculation
you created in the Expert or allow you to create a more complex calculation from
scratch using the MDX calculation language.

Once you've finished your calculation, an additional member will appear
in the grid showing your calculation. To edit or delete the calculated member,
select the member name at the left or top of the grid, right-click, and choose
Edit or Delete options from the pop-up menu.

Note *For more in-depth coverage of OLAP calculations and MDX calculations, consult Crystal Reports online help, or documentation with your online OLAP analysis tool, such as Microsoft Analysis Services books online.*

■ **To create "on-the-fly" filters (new in version 9)** Even though you may have limited your OLAP grid by using a Slice, you can further filter the OLAP grid interactively while you're viewing it. Your filter, based on the "numbers" rather than on the member hierarchy, can consist of a comparison to the numbers, or a top or bottom "N" or percentage.

To add a filter, select the member name column or row that you want to use as a filter (you can't click a number in a cell—it has to be at the edge of a column or row, and only a member name that shows some "filter-able" numbers—not all rows or columns—can be filtered), and right-click. Choose Add Filter from the pop-up menu. The Define Filter dialog box will appear.

Define Filter ☒

Use filters to remove data which is not important, or to define what data you want to see. For example, you may not want to see variances which are below 6%.

Filter Type

Filter the displayed data by: | Top / bottom n ▾ |

Filter Definition

○ Exclude columns
● Display columns

which are in the | top ▾ | | 5 | of the member: All Products

| OK | | Cancel | | Help |

Once you've applied your filter, you'll see a reduced set of rows or columns in the grid, with the filter limiting what appears. You'll know you've added a filter to a row or column if you point to it and your mouse pointer changes to an X. If you want to modify or remove the filter, right-click on the column or row again and choose Edit Filter or Remove Filter from the pop-up menu.

■ **Sort the rows or columns by numeric values (new in version 9)** Normally, rows and columns are ordered according to the member name at the top of the column or the left of the row. However, you can sort the rows or columns by "the numbers" if you choose. To do this, select the row or column member name you want to sort (you can't click a number, and the row or column you choose must be "sort-able"—not all columns or rows will offer the option), right-click, and choose Add First Sort from the pop-up menu. A submenu will appear with sorting options. Choose your desired sort option. Notice that the selected row or column is now sorted by the numbers. Also notice that you'll see a double-arrow cursor appear when you point to the row or column member name, indicating that a sort exists.

If you have duplicate values in a row or column and you wish to add a second level of sorting, click the next column or row member name that you want to sort, right-click, and choose Add Next Sort. Choose similar options.

To change or remove an existing sort, select a row or column member name (one with the double-arrow cursor, indicating an existing sort), right-click, and choose Change Direction of Sort or Remove Sort.

The New OLAP Analyzer

If the new interactivity options discussed previously in the chapter aren't enough, Crystal Reports 9 introduces even more new OLAP interactivity with the OLAP Analyzer. The *OLAP Analyzer* is actually largely based on Crystal Decisions' Crystal Analysis Pro OLAP Analysis tool, providing a great deal of "slice, dice, swap, and analyze" interactivity right in Crystal Reports.

To display the OLAP Analyzer, select the desired OLAP grid object in the Preview tab (you can't launch the OLAP Analyzer in the Design tab). Then, right-click and choose Launch Analyzer from the pop-up menu. The OLAP grid will be displayed in an additional tab in Crystal Reports labeled Cube View, as shown in Figure 18-6.

Once you've launched the OLAP Analyzer, you may return to the report's regular Design or Preview tabs by just clicking them, and then return to the Cube View tab by clicking it. To close the Cube View tab and return to a regular report view, click the red x to the left of the page navigation buttons.

Interactivity in the OLAP Analyzer is somewhat similar to that of the OLAP grid in the preview tab discussed earlier in the report. There is also additional functionality to swap and nest dimensions.

These are among the highlights of OLAP Analyzer interactivity:

- Click plus or minus signs to drill down or drill up (expand or compact members).

- To "drill through" to base relational database data that makes up an individual cell number, right-click on the cell and choose Drill Through from the pop-up menu (only limited OLAP cube servers provide this functionality, so this option may not be available).

- Right-click a member name (row or column name) to choose options from the pop-up menu. Many of these options are similar to those discussed earlier in the chapter relating to the OLAP Grid. Some notable additions to the pop-up menu include formatting options, including the Highlighting Exception option, which will color cells that fall within selected numeric ranges.

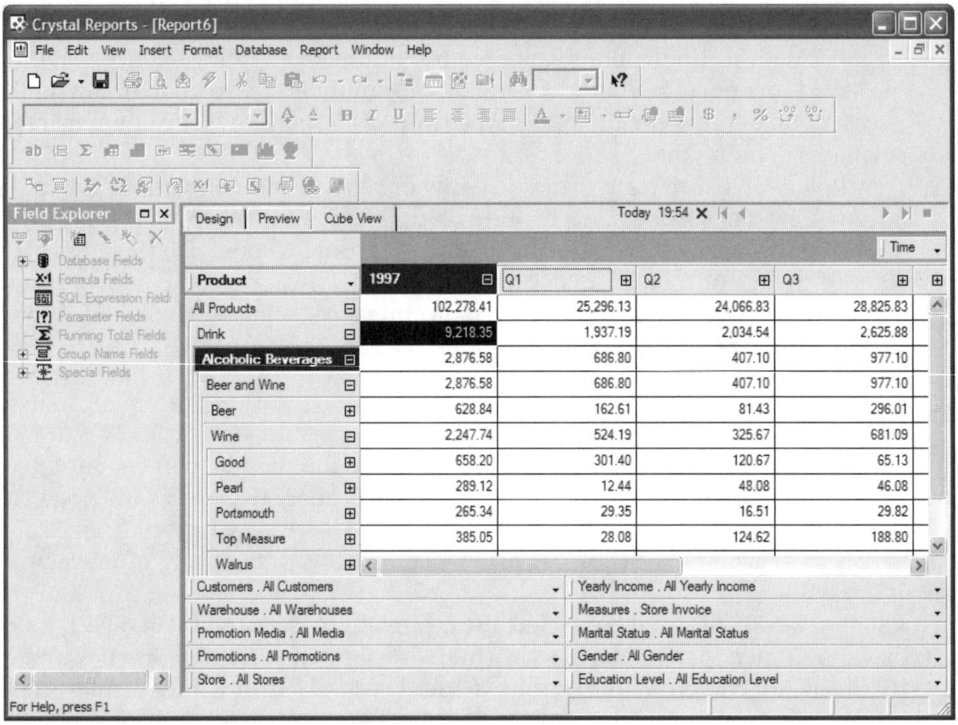

Figure 18-6. *OLAP Analyzer Cube View tab*

■ Click down arrows next to a dimension to launch the Member Selector (Figure 18-3 earlier in the chapter) where you can choose to display individual members of the hierarchy in the grid, or slice the grid (if you choose a dimension at the bottom of the grid).

Note *In the initial Crystal Reports 9 release, you may need to move the Member Selector window once it's been displayed to fully form the window. Otherwise, you will be unable to click the upper right-hand X to close the window.*

■ To swap a row or column dimension with another row or column dimension, or a filter dimension (at the bottom of the Cube View tab), click the dimension name that you wish to swap. Then, drag the dimension to the other dimension that you wish to swap with. When you see the double-arrow, release the mouse button.

■ To nest or "stack" dimensions (add an additional row or column dimension *within* another dimension), click the dimension name that you wish to nest. Then, drag the dimension to the existing row or column dimension that you wish to nest it under. Look very carefully for the *single* arrow. When you see it, release the mouse button.

■ To move a dimension back to the bottom of the Cube View tab (there must be at least two or more nested dimensions to move one of them to the bottom), click the dimension name that you want to move. Drag the dimension to the bottom of the Cube View tab *between* the rows or columns of existing dimensions. Look very carefully for the single arrow (a double arrow will swap the dimensions). When you see it, release the mouse button.

Caution   *In the initial release of Crystal Reports 9, you'll receive an error message if you press* F1 *while working with the Cube View tab. However, you can display regular Crystal Reports help and look for "Cube View" in the help Index tab.*

Chapter 19

Reporting from Proprietary Data Types

Crystal Reports is best known as the "reporting tool of choice" for use with any standard corporate database. "Standard" databases might generally be thought to include Microsoft Access or SQL Server, Sybase, Oracle, Informix, IBM DB2, and others that are well known in the mainstream of corporate database technology.

But, what do you do if your data is contained in some other form of database or data file? Well, if the database or data file system is *very* proprietary and out of the mainstream, and the vendor doesn't provide an ODBC (open database connectivity) driver for the database, then you may be, quite simply, out of luck. However, many proprietary databases can be accessed via ODBC, which Crystal Reports will work with. You can also create reports against regular ASCII-delimited text files and against XML files that conform to certain standards, but you'll need to use a supplied ODBC driver to accomplish this. And, Crystal Reports 9 supports other data types directly, without even requiring an ODBC driver. You can create reports based on Microsoft Exchange Server and Systems Management Server databases, Symantec's ACT! contact manager, Microsoft Outlook, Windows NT/2000/XP event logs, and Web server activity logs.

The general approach for creating reports against these proprietary types of data sources is similar, regardless of the data source:

1. Ensure that the Crystal Reports Data Access driver you wish to report from is installed. If you're unsure, rerun Crystal Reports setup and expand the Data Access area to ensure that proper drivers have been installed. If you haven't done this in advance, you may be prompted to insert the Crystal Reports 9 CD when you initially try to create a report based on a certain type of data.

2. Ensure that the software you want to report from (such as Microsoft Outlook), or the vendor's "client" application to access data (such as Oracle SQL Plus) is installed on the same PC as Crystal Reports. Crystal Reports automatically detects these software packages and will list them when you choose a data source.

3. Create a new report using either the report wizards or the Blank Report option. Using either a wizard or the Blank Report option, expand the Create New Connection category of the Database Expert. Then, look for the type of data you want to report against. So, if you want to write reports against a Microsoft Exchange server, choose one of the Exchange data types in the Create New Connection category, such as Exchange Folders/Address Book, Message Tracking Log, or Public Folder Admin.

4. Follow any prompts specific to the data source, such as choosing an Exchange server and profile. You'll then see a list of tables and/or fields that are specific to that data type. Use them in your report just as you would use other database tables and fields.

Although Crystal Reports supports many popular data types, most of this chapter will focus on four of the most often used: Microsoft Outlook, the file system data (basically, the disk directory on a PC or network disk drive), the Windows NT/2000/XP event log, and standard Web server activity logs.

In addition, the chapter also focuses on reporting from an XML data source, which is handled through an ODBC driver provided with Crystal Reports 9. And, you'll also find an example of connecting to "Active" Data Sources, such as COM (Component Object Model) data provided by custom-written applications.

Reporting from Microsoft Outlook

Microsoft Outlook has become a popular standard on office desktops, because it smoothly integrates e-mail, contact management, and calendar maintenance in one package. Outlook's folder metaphor is handy for organizing your office affairs, and it's also handy for reporting.

The first requirement for creating a Crystal Report based on your Outlook folders is rather obvious—you must have Outlook installed on your PC. More specifically, you must have Outlook installed on the same computer on which you will be running Crystal Reports. Crystal Reports won't report on any other Outlook systems on the network—just your own.

To report on your Outlook data, start a new report just as you would for a standard database. You can use the report wizards or the Blank Report option. In either case, expand the Create New Connection category and then expand the Outlook folder. If you have not reported from Outlook before, or there is more than one Outlook Profile on your system, you'll be presented with the Choose Profile dialog box, and will need to select your profile (or the default Microsoft Outlook profile) from the drop-down list and click OK. Then you'll be presented with the Choose Folder dialog box, showing the folder hierarchy of your Outlook data. Choose the folder that you want to report on and click OK.

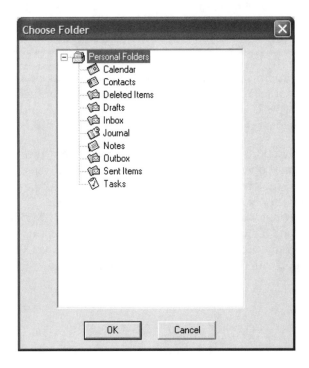

Caution *You cannot report on the Notes folder. You'll receive an error message if you try to select it.*

After you choose the folder and click OK, a "table" will appear in the Available Data Sources list. Select and add the folder just as you would any database table. When you close the Database Expert or advance to the next wizard area, the list of Outlook fields you can report from will appear in the expert or in the Field Explorer.

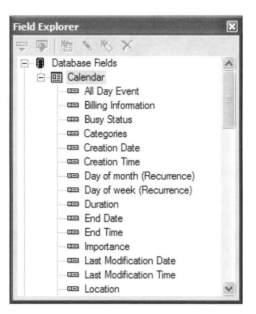

Use the Outlook fields just like other database fields to create your report. You can sort, group, and format the report as you normally would. You can also create formulas, if necessary, to calculate or modify the way Outlook material appears in the report. Figure 19-1 shows a sample report based on the Calendar folder from Outlook.

Note *The field names you see in the Crystal Reports Field Explorer may not always match the field names you see in Outlook. If you don't see the field you expect, look for a reasonable alternative field name. Also, you may need to add other Outlook folders (such as the Contact folder and the Inbox folder) and link the two together to get all the data you expect. Make sure you link on correct fields—Auto Linking typically won't pick the correct fields to perform an Outlook link.*

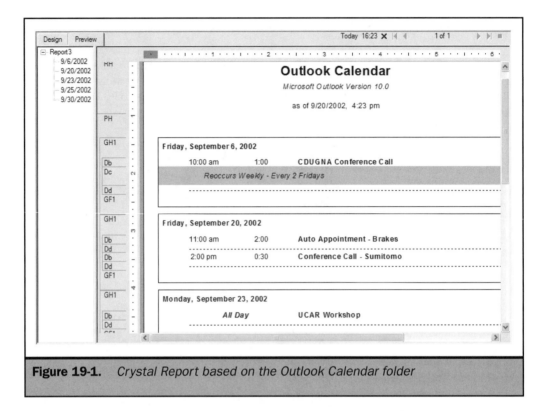

Figure 19-1. *Crystal Report based on the Outlook Calendar folder*

Reporting from the File System Data

You are probably familiar with Explorer, the Windows application that helps you view the hierarchy and layout of your local and network drives, as well as locate one or more particular files you may be looking for. However, if you want a more powerful reporting-type tool to search or report on drive contents, you need another software solution.

Crystal Reports provides the *file system data* option, allowing you to write powerful reports against any local or network drive on your PC. By choosing a drive and folder or directory, as well as specifying some detailed criteria (if you choose), you can create reports that select and sort files and folders with the complete power and flexibility of Crystal Reports.

To report on your file system data, start a new report just as you would for a standard database. You can use the report wizards or the Blank Report option. When choosing a database, expand the File System Data folder in the Create New Connection category.

You'll be presented with the File System Data dialog box, shown in Figure 19-2. If you simply want to supply a drive or path name, you can either type it or click the ellipses button to navigate to the desired drive and directory. You may also add some additional criteria to narrow down the files and directories you want to see.

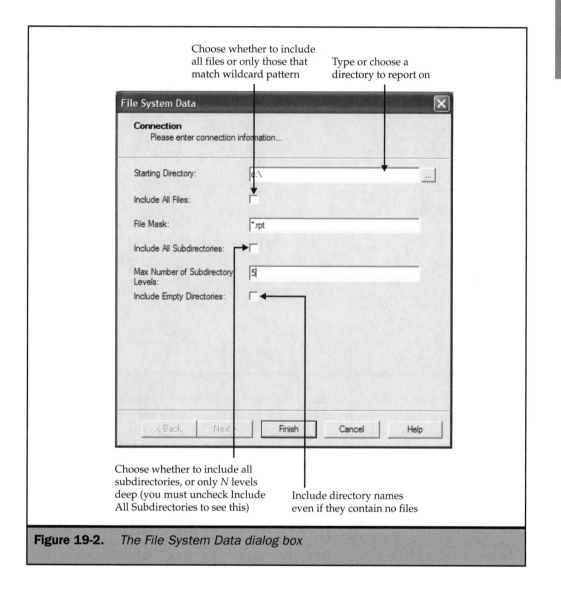

Choose whether to include all files or only those that match wildcard pattern

Type or choose a directory to report on

Choose whether to include all subdirectories, or only *N* levels deep (you must uncheck Include All Subdirectories to see this)

Include directory names even if they contain no files

Figure 19-2. *The File System Data dialog box*

Make your choices and click Finish. A table entry in the Database Expert Available Data Sources list will appear, showing the directory you chose. Add it to the Selected tables list to proceed.

The Field Explorer will expose many different fields containing information you might not have previously been familiar with. Some fields apply only to certain types of files, such as .EXE or .DLL files. Others apply only to files that belong to certain applications (for example, Number of Words generally applies only to Word or other word processing documents). Use these file system fields just like other database fields to create your report. You can sort, group, and format the report as you normally would. You can use the fields to create flexible selection criteria to narrow down your report. You can also create formulas, if necessary, to calculate or modify the way file system material appears in the report. Figure 19-3 shows a sample report based on a local C disk drive.

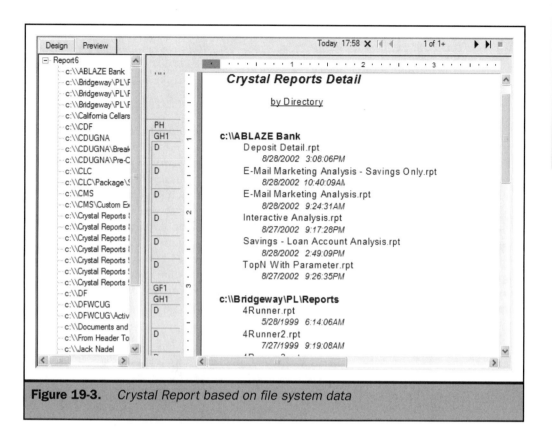

Figure 19-3.   *Crystal Report based on file system data*

Reporting from the Windows NT/2000 Event Log

Windows NT, 2000, and XP have traditionally been the powerful big brothers of desktop operating systems, such as Windows 95 and Windows 98. However, with the advent of more powerful computer hardware available for ever-falling prices, Windows NT and 2000 are finding their way to more and more desktops. And Windows XP builds even further on Windows NT technology.

An integrated part of the Windows NT, 2000, and XP operating systems is the *event log*, a series of files that document events that occur during the general operation of Windows. Several different types of event logs are available, and different types of entries are placed in the event logs as users log on and off, and programs start, stop, and operate. Crystal Reports includes the capability to create flexible reports on these event logs.

Note *Although designing reports against the event logs won't harm the computer containing the log, you probably won't find the information returned to be of much use if you're not generally familiar with Windows NT/2000 and its components. This Crystal Reports capability will probably be most useful to system administrators and other technical personnel.*

To report on event logs, start a new report just as you would for a standard database. You can use the report wizards or the Blank Report option. In either case, expand the NT Current Event Log folder in the Create New Connection category to report on current active event logs on Windows NT/2000/XP computers. Or, you can click the NT Archived Event Log folder to display an Open File dialog box in which to search for archived (.EVT) event log files. If you use this option, upon selecting an event log you will be presented with the Select Archived Event Log dialog box, and you must identify the type of event log you selected (System, Security, or Application).

If you choose the NT Current Event Log folder, you'll see the Select Current Event Log dialog box, shown in Figure 19-4. This allows you to select an event log on a remote computer—it doesn't have to reside on the computer that you are running Crystal Reports on. You can include event logs from more than one computer in your report, if you choose.

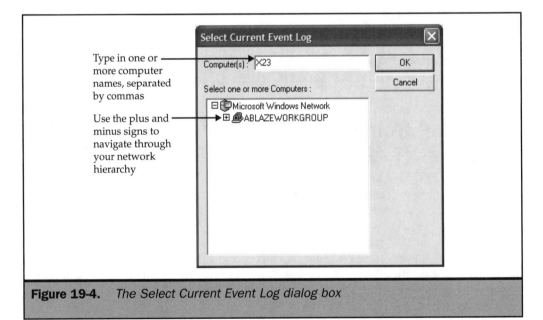

Figure 19-4. *The Select Current Event Log dialog box*

If you know the domain and computer name, you can simply type it in the Computer(s) text box at the top of the dialog box. If you include more than one computer name, separate the names with commas. If you're not sure which computers to include, you can use the Explorer-like hierarchy to select the computers you wish to use. When you see the computer list, you can select one or more computers.

Make your choices and click OK. A new level in the Database Expert will appear for the computer you've chosen, showing the three event logs that are available as tables: Application, Security, and System.

Depending on the types of events you want your report to be based on, choose the appropriate log. If you'd like a better idea of what types of events are contained in each log, use the Event Viewer application from the Control Panel in Windows NT, 2000, or

XP to view the different event-log entries. Once you've made your log choice, the list of event log fields you can report on will appear in the expert or in the Field Explorer.

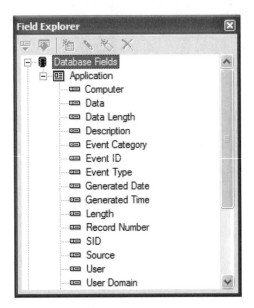

Use these event log fields just like other database fields to create your report. You can sort, group, and format the report as you normally would. The Event Viewer application can help you identify what some of the available fields contain. You can use the fields to create flexible selection criteria to narrow down your report, and you can also create formulas, if necessary, to calculate or modify the way event-log material appears in the report. Figure 19-5 shows a sample report based on a Windows NT application event log.

Reporting from Web Server Logs

It's now a given that most organizations need to document what pages Web users are pointing their browsers to, as well as when and from where. Most Web servers, such as those from Microsoft, Netscape, and others, keep various amounts and levels of data about Web site visits. What better tool to create Web activity reports than Crystal Reports?

There are several types of Web server logs that you may encounter, depending mostly on the Web server that you are using. Most Web server logs are standard delimited ASCII files (a term you don't necessarily need to be familiar with, but it is a common denominator for data-file formats). However, the layout of fields in the files and the information they contain can vary from server to server. There are several "standard" types of log files,

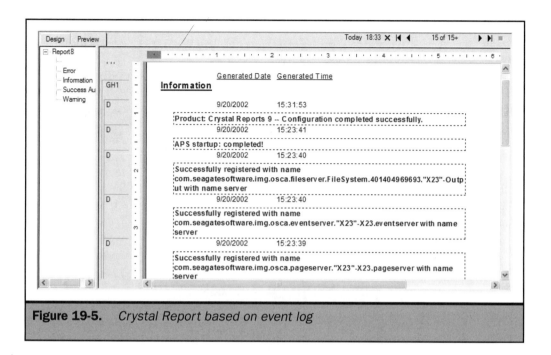

Figure 19-5.   *Crystal Report based on event log*

including a file type simply known as Standard, and another known as the NCSA Standard, defined by the National Center for Supercomputing Applications for its original Web server. Other Web server developers have adopted both standards. In addition, if you are using Microsoft Internet Information Server (IIS), you'll find additional types of log files available, such as Microsoft's extended log format. When you configure IIS, you can choose the type of log file that is generated, as well as the fields that are kept in the log file.

As a general rule, Web servers will create a new log file every day, adding statistics to the daily log file as they occur. The filenames consist of variations of the date on which they were created, with a standard file extension. For example, you may see a file named EX020719.LOG, indicating a Microsoft extended-format log for July 19, 2002. These files will be located in a standard directory, such as \WinNT\System32\LogFiles\W3Csvc1 (this is the default location for Microsoft IIS versions running on Windows NT/2000).

To report on Web server logs, start a new report just as you would for a standard database. You can use the report wizards or the Blank Report option. In either case, expand the Create New Connection category of the Database Expert to proceed. You'll see two categories that may interest you: MS IIS/Proxy Log Files and Web/IIS Log Files.

MS IIS/Proxy Log Files will report on "standard" formats, the various Microsoft IIS formats, and Web proxy and Winsock Proxy formats. The Web/IIS Log Files folder will simply report on "standard" and NCSA formatted logs.

Regardless of whether you're using a wizard or the Blank Report option, the rest of the prompts will be consistent. If you choose the more generic Web Log option, you'll simply be prompted to choose a drive and directory where the standard or NCSA Web logs are located. You can type or browse to select a local or network drive and directory. If you choose the IIS option, you'll see the Select Log Files And Dates dialog box, as illustrated in Figure 19-6.

Choose the type of log file your Web server uses (look for files in a standard location with the .LOG extension to help determine this). You can also choose the format your Web server uses when writing log files, based on how often it creates a new log file. And, if you prefer to limit Crystal Reports to using only log files within a certain date range, make that selection as well.

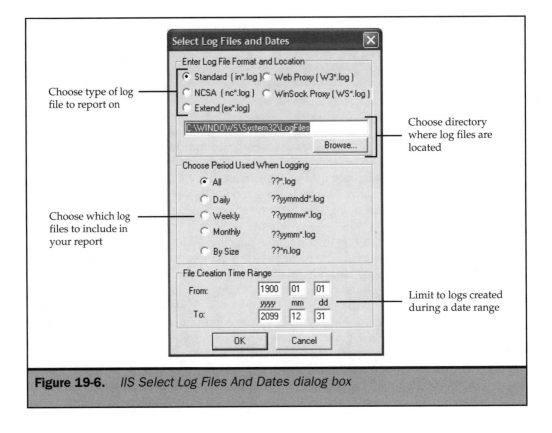

Figure 19-6.   *IIS Select Log Files And Dates dialog box*

When you're finished with your choices, click OK. A new database entry will appear in the Available Data Sources list of the Database Expert showing the directory name of the log files. Underneath this category, a table-type entry will appear, showing a somewhat cryptic entry for the log files you just chose. Add this table to your report (by double-clicking on the table name, dragging it to the Selected Tables list, or selecting the table name and clicking the right arrow) and close the Database Expert. The list of Web server log fields you can report from will appear in the wizard or in the Field Explorer.

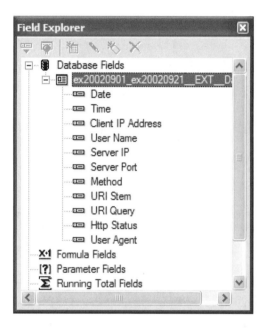

Note   *The log fields you see here will vary, depending on the Web server you are using and the log settings you've chosen for that web server. If you're using Microsoft IIS with NT Server or Windows 2000, you can configure the server to include a variety of helpful statistical fields.*

Use these Web server log fields just like other database fields when creating your report. You can sort, group, and format the report as you normally would. You can use the fields to create flexible selection criteria to narrow down your report. You can also create formulas, if necessary, to calculate or modify the way Web server log material appears in the report. Figure 19-7 shows a sample report based on a Windows 2000/IIS 5 Web server log.

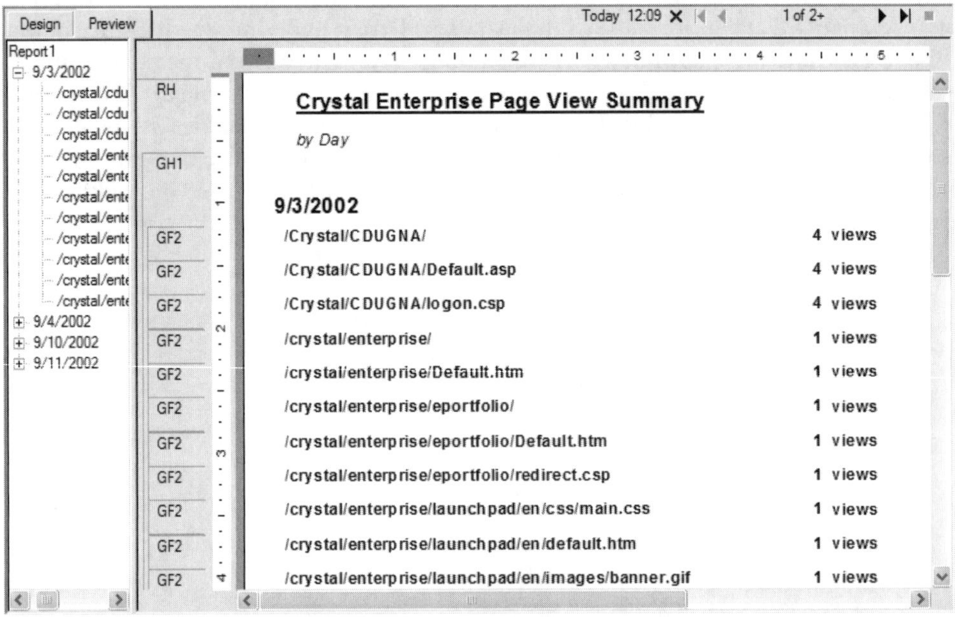
Design
Preview
Today 12:09
1 of 2+
Report1
9/3/2002
9/4/2002
9/10/2002
9/11/2002
RH
GH1
GF2
Crystal Enterprise Page View Summary
by Day
9/3/2002
/Crystal/CDUGNA/ 4 views
/Crystal/CDUGNA/Default.asp 4 views
/Crystal/CDUGNA/logon.csp 4 views
/crystal/enterprise/ 1 views
/crystal/enterprise/Default.htm 1 views
/crystal/enterprise/eportfolio/ 1 views
/crystal/enterprise/eportfolio/Default.htm 1 views
/crystal/enterprise/eportfolio/redirect.csp 1 views
/crystal/enterprise/launchpad/en/css/main.css 1 views
/crystal/enterprise/launchpad/en/default.htm 1 views
/crystal/enterprise/launchpad/en/images/banner.gif 1 views

Figure 19-7. *Crystal Report based on IIS Web server log*

Crystal Reporting with XML

The strong expansion of Internet commerce and the proliferation of proprietary data types are combining to produce an increasing need for platform-independent data transfer. A few years ago, a consortium of organizations began collaborating on developing a standard language called Extensible Markup Language, or *XML*. XML is a format for defining, transmitting, validating, and interpreting data across the Internet, or through electronic file transfers, among independent systems and industries.

While XML has similarities to HTML (Hypertext Markup Language, used widely for Internet applications), it has significant differences and advantages. HTML stores static information and presents it in a static format. XML files can contain a data set, but they also can contain or be accompanied by instructions on how to interpret the file content so that the end user or application can choose how to utilize it. Predictably, several different groups are now working to establish a dominant, widely accepted

XML standard, and several standards are emerging. Some standards are focused on certain industries, such as banking or retail, while other standards are intended to be industry independent.

An XML file usually either contains data interpretation instructions (in a "prolog" between the file header and the data content) or is accompanied by an instruction document that defines the XML file content. Generally, these instructions are referred to as a *schema*, though some of the types of schema also use "Schema" in their name to confuse the issue. The three most common types of instructions are the following:

- The Document Type Definition (DTD), developed early on primarily for validation of XML file data rather than formatting; DTD instructions can reside within the XML file or as a separate .DTD file; they use a different language syntax than XML.

- The XML Schema, developed by the World Wide Web Consortium (W3C) as an international standard. XML Schema instructions reside in an .XML file and use XML syntax.

- The Extensible Stylesheet Language (XSL), which has begun to replace DTD due to its broader format-oriented syntax. XSL instructions can reside within the XML file or in a separate .XSL file.

To use an XML file as a source for a report, Crystal Reports 9 includes updated ODBC drivers. Crystal Reports automatically sets up the CRXML ODBC data source using an updated version 4 driver, which allows you to connect to different types of XML files for reporting.

Note *This XML ODBC driver, which is a Merant DataDirect product, has some limitations that may preclude connecting to your XML file. For more information about these limitations, as well as general information about this ODBC driver, see "XML data, accessing" in Crystal Reports online help.*

Figure 19-8 shows an ADO 2.5 persisted format XML file (one format supported by the Merant driver), to which the CRXML ODBC driver can connect. The file consists of a simple data set of book title data, with tags identified in the file header and prolog.

Crystal Reports 9's new CRXML ODBC data source will probably need to be configured properly before creating your first report based on XML data. Configure this data source by using the ODBC Data Source icon in Windows Control Panel. Once you've chosen various options particular to your environment, such as locations for the XML data files and schemas they conform to, you can return to Crystal Reports and begin the report design process.

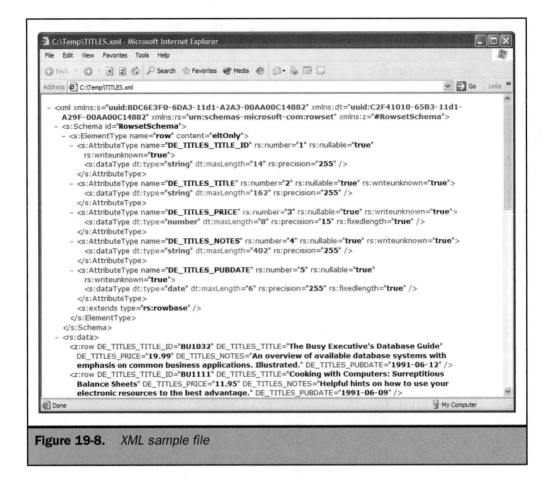

Figure 19-8. *XML sample file*

To report on a supported XML file, start a new report just as you would for a standard database. You can use the report wizards or the Blank Report option. Expand the Create

New Connection section of the Available Data Sources list, and then expand the ODBC (RDO) entry. From the Data Source Selection dialog box, choose the CRXML data source name (or other data source name that you defined for XML reporting). The ODBC XML Driver Connection dialog box appears. If you specified a user ID and password requirement when you defined the ODBC data source, specify them on this dialog box.

Once you've completed this dialog box, the Database Expert will return with a new database entry appearing under the ODBC category. If you expand the database and subsequent entries, you'll eventually see a "table name" that corresponds to the XML data that the ODBC data source refers to.

Caution	*Depending on how you set up the ODBC Data Source, you may see multiple XML tables listed. However, they will not necessarily return valid data to Crystal Reports if they are not organized in a supported XML format.*

Select the desired XML file from the list and add it to the report (by double-clicking the table name, by dragging the table name to the Selected Tables list, or by selecting the table name and clicking the right arrow) and close the Database Expert. The list of fields you can report from will appear in the expert or in the Field Explorer.

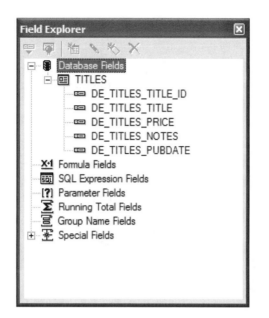

New Crystal Reports 9 Active Data Sources

Crystal Reports 9 had added additional capabilities to base reports on Active Data Sources, which are a departure from typical relational databases, such as Microsoft Access or Oracle. *Active Data Sources* are often used to provide data to Crystal Reports from another program that's running separately on your PC. Such separate programs might be connecting to real-time instrumentation (such as measuring devices). Or, you may be designing a report to integrate within a custom Windows program and wish to connect to a data source exposed by the application.

These new active data sources appear in the Database Expert:

- **COM Connectivity**   This connectivity method allows your report to get data (in a typical table "field and record" fashion) from a program or automation server that conforms to Microsoft's COM (Component Object Model) standard. These programs can be developed in any COM-compatible language, such as Visual Basic or Visual C++.

- **Crystal Data Object**   This connectivity method allows your report to get data (in a typical table "field and record" fashion) from a program that is actually generating the data "on the fly." Custom Windows programs can use the Crystal Data Object to create a "field and record" structure necessary for Crystal Reports entirely within their internal logic.

- **Java Beans Connectivity**   This connectivity method allows your report to get data (in a typical table "field and record" fashion) from a Java-based program that exposes a set of Java classes that use a "Java Data Provider."

Note *These new Active Data Sources are available only with Crystal Reports 9 Advanced Edition.*

To connect to an active data source, begin a new report as you normally would with a relational database. You may use a wizard or the Blank Report option. In either case, expand the Create New Connection category of the Database Expert to proceed. You'll see entries for each of the new active data sources. Click the plus sign next to the desired data source.

If, for example, you choose COM Connectivity to connect to an exposed COM automation server, you'll be presented with a dialog box asking you to specify the *Program ID* of the automation server. Type in the exact name of the COM data source (that you either specified when you developed the program that exposes the automation server, or the name given to you by the program's designer).

COM Connectivity

Connection
Please enter connection informaion...

Program ID: CrystalActiveData.COMData

< Back   Next >   Finish   Cancel   Help

Once you've supplied the proper Program ID, click Finish. The Database Expert will return with a new entry in the Available Data Sources list (record sets returned by active data sources will often appear similar to SQL stored procedures). Select the data source or sources you wish to base the report on and add them to the Selected Tables list. If a data source requires a parameter value to be supplied, you'll be prompted for it much as you are prompted when using a parameterized stored procedure.

Supply any necessary parameters and click OK. Once you've added the active data source, close the Database Expert. Fields exposed by the active data source will appear in the Field Explorer as with any other standard data source.

Tip   *For more information on Active Data Sources, including sample code to create programs that expose data in this fashion, consult the online Technical Reference from the Crystal Reports CD.*

The Complete Reference

Part II

Crystal Reports 9 on the Web

The Complete Reference

Crystal Reports 9

Chapter 20

Crystal Reports Web Alternatives

553

So far, this book has discussed many techniques for creating sophisticated reports with the Crystal Reports 9 designer. Part III of the book discusses methods for integrating those reports into your custom Windows applications with Visual Basic and Visual Studio .NET. However, business organizations, both large and small, continue to turn to Web-based technology for both internal corporate intranets and the Internet. Accordingly, providing a way to display your reports in a Web browser is crucial.

Crystal Reports 9 continues in this Web-based direction. While Crystal Reports 8.5 included an "introductory" version of Crystal Enterprise, Crystal Reports 9 Professional, Developer, and Advanced Editions include yet a newer permutation of Web-based reporting called the Report Application Server (or *RAS*). RAS is the preview of the next version of Crystal Enterprise, version 9 (not available as of the printing of this book).

The original release of Crystal Enterprise has also undergone an upgrade since being originally introduced with Crystal Reports 8.5 (as Crystal Enterprise 8.0). Crystal Enterprise 8.5 (the current version as of this book's publication) adds additional features beyond its initial 8.0 release.

Although Crystal Decisions recommends moving Web-based reporting projects to RAS, a new version of the COM-based Report Designer Component (RDC) is included with Crystal Reports 9 Developer and Advanced Editions, which can be used to run existing RDC-based Active Server Pages applications developed with Crystal Reports 8.5 or earlier.

These different options give you even more choices than before on how to place a Crystal Report on the Web—either on your internal corporate intranet or on the entire Internet:

- **Export static reports to HTML format (covered in this chapter)** In this case, you just export your report to one of several different HTML formats, much as you would export a Word or Excel file. Viewers can simply open the HTML file in their browser, or the file can be placed on a Web server for viewing.

- **Use the Report Application Server (RAS) with Microsoft Active Server Pages (covered in Chapter 21) or Java Server Pages** This method, new to Crystal Reports 9, which requires installing the Crystal Reports RAS SDK on your Web server, provides a high level of Web integration for reports and is the "entry point" into Crystal Enterprise report integration. This method offers several advantages over older Web integration methods, such as the ability to separate the RAS SDK and RAS Server onto two separate machines for more efficient report processing, and the ability to create or modify reports on the fly in Web pages and then save the resultant .RPT files on disk (this last capability exists only with Crystal Reports Advanced Edition).

- **Use Visual Studio .NET with Web Forms (covered in Chapter 26)** Visual Studio .NET (VS.NET) incorporates a special version of Crystal Reports as its included reporting tool. The VS.NET object model exposes Crystal Reports functionality similar to that of the Report Designer Component, allowing complete control of reports at run time in a Web browser. Crystal Reports 9 expands on VS.NET functionality in two ways: (1) by adding additional capabilities and features to the base VS.NET Crystal Report functionality, and (2) by providing a VS.NET connection to the RAS SDK to allow multitier report processing and entry into the Crystal Enterprise object model.

- **Use the Report Designer Component (RDC) with Microsoft Active Server Pages**   This method, which is the state-of-the-art method in previous versions of Crystal Reports, provides a high level of Web integration for reports, virtually identical to the level of flexibility allowed with Visual Basic. This method, however, does not take advantage of the multitier, shared processing capability of Crystal Enterprise or RAS. Despite Crystal Decisions' advice to migrate from the RDC to RAS, converting existing RDC Web applications to RAS requires a fair amount of redesign, so you may still consider using this method.

- **Using Crystal Enterprise (covered in Chapters 22, 23, and 24)**   Crystal Enterprise provides a rich, multitier/multiserver method of hosting real-time and automatically scheduled Crystal Reports on the Web. You can use the standard "out of the box" user interface provided by Crystal Enterprise, or you may completely customize the user interface using HTML and new Crystal Server Pages. Be aware, however, that Crystal Reports 9 has changed the internal format of its .RPT files. This new format is not compatible with Crystal Enterprise 8.0 or 8.5; you'll need to install Crystal Enterprise 9 (not available at time of this book's publication) to fully support Crystal Reports 9.

Crystal Reports Web Alternatives Compared

Each of the Crystal Reports Web approaches listed in the preceding section has advantages and disadvantages, depending on your level of Web-development expertise, corporate development standards, the sophistication of your reports, how fluid the data you want to present is, the number of users you want to serve, and your budget. It's helpful to examine your reporting requirements, expertise level, and hardware and software environment before you decide on a particular Web reporting direction. Choosing one method won't necessarily preclude you from switching later. For example, it's perfectly acceptable to design a simple report that you initially just export to HTML, and then later decide to give Web viewers real-time access to it via RAS, the RDC, or Crystal Enterprise. However, if you design a very interactive report with drill-down capabilities, you won't achieve the desired level of interactivity with a simple HTML export—you'll need to use RAS, the RDC, or Crystal Enterprise.

If you just want to occasionally allow a simple, noninteractive report to be viewed in a Web browser, you may consider simply exporting to HTML right from Crystal Reports (discussed later in this chapter). This simple approach won't allow interactivity with your report (drill-down, on-demand subreports, or use of the group tree) and won't show data in real time. But, a simple detail or summary report that can be viewed in a few pages can easily be opened directly in a Web browser. A viewer simply uses File | Open (Internet Explorer) or File | Open Page (Netscape Navigator/ Communicator) to view the HTML file directly from a local or network drive without a Web server, or they can click a link or enter the correct URL to view the exported file from a Web server.

If you want to provide more interactivity, or your report viewers need access to "live" real-time reporting, you need to choose between the remaining methods (RAS, RDC, VS.NET, or Crystal Enterprise). By using RAS, the RDC, or VS.NET, you can achieve a very high level of report control from a Web page. Because the object models exposed by these options are very robust, you can control almost every aspect of the report at run time, including section formatting, setting formulas, and changing fonts, colors, and other formatting from within your code. Then there's the full version of Crystal Enterprise (version 8.5 is the latest version as of this writing). This option takes Web reporting to yet another level with multitier, multiserver capabilities and automated scheduling and maintenance. While there's a benefit to having more choices than ever, there's potentially a higher level of confusion as well. The question that may very well arise: "Which of these methods should I use?"

If you already have an existing RDC-based Web application in place with a Microsoft Web server, you may simply wish to continue to use it with the new version of the RDC and updated version 9 reports. While Crystal Decisions recommends that you update these applications to RAS, you will need to undertake an additional learning curve to convert your RDC ASPs to RAS—they don't run under RAS as-is.

If you are developing new applications or want to take advantage of new RAS features (such as moving the report processing server to another computer separate from your Web server, or developing interactive "design reports on the fly" applications), you'll probably lean toward a RAS solution. Understand, however, that the edition of RAS included with Crystal Reports is an entry-level version that doesn't provide the scalability or expansion capability of the full versions of Crystal Enterprise. Your RAS development efforts won't be lost, though, as you can migrate your RAS applications to higher levels of Crystal Enterprise 9 should the need arise.

Caution   *Just remember—not all features of RAS are available in Crystal Reports 9 Professional or Developer Edition. For example, the "design on the fly" features are available only in Crystal Reports Advanced Edition. Check to ensure that the version you are purchasing will provide the functionality that you ultimately need.*

The new RAS option in Crystal Reports 9 offers the ability to go beyond the single-tier limitations of the RDC/Active Server Page methodology. By having the option of separating the Web server from the computer that actually processes reports, you gain the ability to support larger and more complex reports without degrading the performance of your Web server (which, in general, is designed to serve up Web pages, not to process large database queries). Crystal Enterprise goes even further, by allowing more granular separation of the various report processing and viewing steps (Crystal Enterprise Professional can take this separation of components to a possibly absurd level). Different computers on the network can be tasked with formatting reports, running database queries, managing report caches to send already generated report pages to the Web browser, and so forth.

If this "sharing of the reporting load" methodology isn't enough benefit, Crystal Enterprise also allows automatic scheduling, e-mailing, or file transfer of reports. This enhanced concept in Crystal Reporting has been taken from Crystal Decisions' lesser-known product, Seagate Info. This feature allows you to schedule reports to run either on a one-time basis or on some recurring basis, such as once a day, once a week, and so on. With Crystal Enterprise 8.5 and later, the result can be viewed in a Web browser, exported to an alternate file format (such as Acrobat. PDF, Excel, or Word), and attached to an e-mail message or sent to an alternate location via File Transfer Protocol. When viewers launch Crystal Enterprise in their browsers, they can look at a report's history and view any of the previously scheduled reports without requiring a database query to be run.

And finally, Crystal Enterprise includes its own Software Development Kit based on Crystal Server Pages, or CSP. This spin-off of Microsoft's Active Server Pages implementation allows you to completely customize the Crystal Enterprise user interface, access Enterprise's scheduling capabilities, and control report customization at run time. And, you can even add more Crystal Enterprise functionality by implementing RAS "report design or modification on the fly" with larger Crystal Enterprise implementations.

If you have an existing RDC-based Web reporting environment that suits you well and is not overburdened by excessive use, you may want to consider continuing to use this solution (especially if any new features of RAS won't be justified by the time and effort required to convert). If you have established Visual Studio .NET as your new corporate standard, you'll obviously want to look at the additional features that Crystal Reports 9 Advanced Edition provides, as well as exploring use of the RAS SDK from within VS.NET. But, if you want to automate report scheduling, support a larger number of users on an Enterprise basis, or automatically export reports to different file formats and deliver via e-mail or FTP, you'll want to explore the fuller versions of Crystal Enterprise.

| Note | *Complete information on Crystal Enterprise 8.5 Professional Edition (the current version as of this writing), including detailed information on Crystal Enterprise usage, implementation, and customization, can be found in Chapters 22, 23, and 24.* |

Exporting to Static HTML

More and more, organizations are looking to distribute Crystal Reports to a large audience in a Web format, through a company intranet or the Internet. To provide this capability, you need to convert your report to Hypertext Markup Language (HTML) format—the "markup language" understood by Web browsers. If you've decided to provide only static, noninteractive reports in a Web browser, you simply need to export the report from Crystal Reports, just as you'd export to a Word document or an Excel spreadsheet.

Caution *Be aware of Crystal Broadcast Licensing. This licensing requirement affects organizations that generally want to supply online reporting access to more than 50 users. If you are placing your exported reports on a Web server that can reasonably be expected to be available to 50 or more users, consult the Crystal Reports license agreement to ensure that you comply with this new requirement.*

Simply start Crystal Reports and open or create the report you want to export to HTML. Remember that whatever is visible on your screen is what will be exported to HTML. If you want to export the main report, make sure the Preview tab is clicked. If you want to export just a drill-down tab, select the correct drill-down tab before exporting. Then, choose File | Export from the pull-down menus, or click the Export button in the Standard toolbar. Figure 20-1 shows a sample report, consisting of a report containing a title surrounded by a border on all four sides and a drop shadow, and an underlain "watermark" graphic.

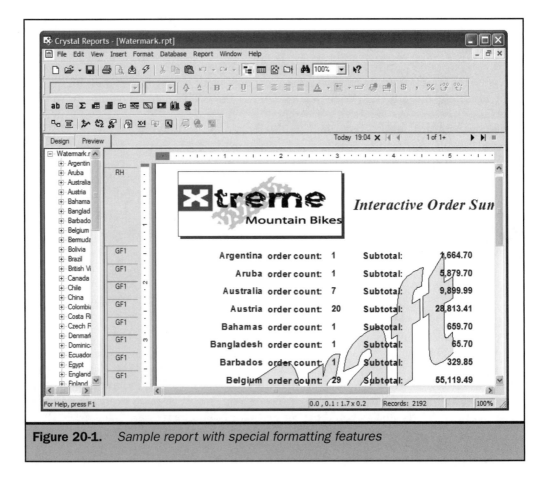

Figure 20-1. *Sample report with special formatting features*

When you choose the Export command, the resulting dialog box allows you to choose the format and destination of your report. You'll be concerned with the two HTML format options available in the Format drop-down list: HTML 3.2 and HTML 4.0. The different versions refer to the different extensions of the HTML language that Crystal Reports can use. To determine which version of HTML you want to use, experiment with your own exports and the browsers that your report viewers will use. Typically, version 4 (Dynamic HTML) will better represent the actual formatting of the report in the Web browser. However, you'll need newer versions of a Web browser (Internet Explorer or Netscape Navigator/Communicator Version 4 or later) to use DHTML. If you're using an older version of these browsers, you may see better results with HTML 3.2.

Note | *Remember that with HTML, particularly HTML 3.2, some "fancy" report formatting (such as drop shadows or special fonts) may not export to HTML properly. You'll want to try some test exports and view the resulting reports in the Web browser that will be used by the majority of your report viewers. That way, you can see what your reports will ultimately look like.*

No matter what destination you ultimately choose from the Destination drop-down list, Crystal Reports must write the HTML code and any associated graphics files (for charts, maps, and bitmaps) to a disk folder. You will be asked to make several choices about how and where you want your report exported, as illustrated in Figure 20-2.

Crystal Reports will create a whole new directory to contain the HTML and graphics files that will make up your report. The drive and folder boxes will let you choose an existing directory *under which* a new directory will be created. Type the name of the new directory in the Directory Name box (Crystal Reports will name the new directory HTML by default). If you wish to place the HTML in a specific folder referred to by a Web "home" page, make sure you export to the predetermined folder on the Web server referred to by the page. Crystal Reports will place the name of the report into the Base File Name box by default. You may want to change this filename to something your Web server expects (for example, DEFAULT.HTM) if you are exporting to a Web server folder.

You may also use the Page Navigator and Separate HTML Pages check boxes (which typically are helpful only with reports that are more than one page in length). If you check Separate HTML Pages, Crystal Reports will export sequentially numbered HTML pages, one for each page in the report. For example, if you're exporting a drill-down tab that consists of four pages, and you choose DEFAULT.HTM as the base filename, the first page of the report will be exported to DEFAULT1.HTM, the second to DEFAULT2.HTM, the third to DEFAULT3.HTM, and the fourth to DEFAULT4.HTM. If you don't check this box, all three report pages will be combined into one larger DEFAULT.HTM.

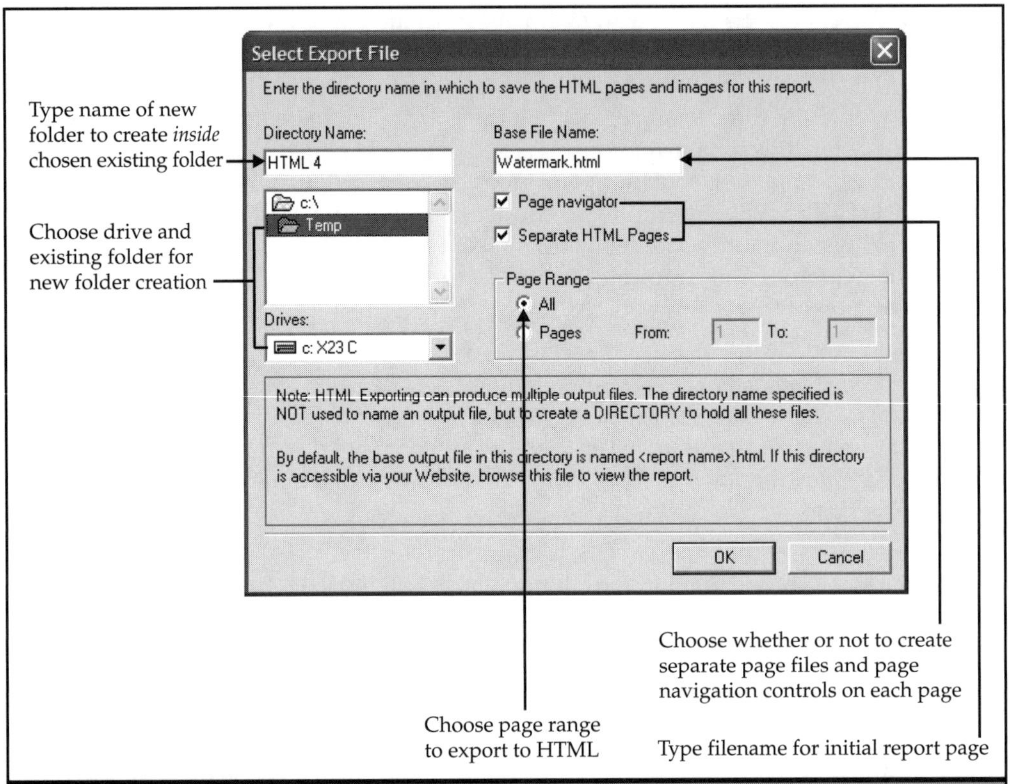

Type name of new
folder to create *inside*
chosen existing folder

Choose drive and
existing folder for
new folder creation

Figure 20-2.   *Export To HTML dialog box*

Choose whether or not to create
separate page files and page
navigation controls on each page

Choose page range
to export to HTML

Type filename for initial report page

Caution   *This numbering behavior has changed in version 9. Previously, the initial page would not be numbered. Keep this behavior in mind if your Web server expects a default filename, such as DEFAULT.HTM. If so, you'll have the limited choices of changing your Web server's default page name to include the number "1" or else manually renaming the first page to eliminate the number and modifying the "first page" hyperlink every other HTML page to point to the unnumbered first page.*

If you check Page Navigator, Crystal Reports will place First, Next, Previous, and Last navigation hyperlinks at the bottom of each page that is exported. If you export to separate HTML pages, these links will navigate to the proper separate HTML page.

If you don't export to separate HTML pages, the navigation links will still appear inside the one large HTML page, simply moving the viewer to different locations within the one HTML page.

Once you've specified all export options, click OK. If the folder you specified doesn't exist, Crystal Reports will automatically create it. If the folder already exists and contains an HTML file with the same name as you specified, you'll be prompted to overwrite the existing file. In addition to the HTML report file, Crystal Reports will create uniquely numbered .PNG graphics files—one for each bitmap, chart, or map contained in the report.

When you point your browser to the folder and view the HTML file, you'll see the exported report in the browser window, as shown in Figure 20-3.

Notice that not all Crystal Reports formatting options are properly converted to HTML version 3.2. You'll see that the drop shadow on the logo did not export properly. And while the watermark graphic did appear underneath some text, it pushed other text aside. Even HTML 4.0 doesn't always perform perfect exports, but you'll often find a much better rendition of your original report formatting. It's a good idea to try sample exports as you're developing your report, to make sure you don't depend on any features that may not export properly. If your organization has standardized on Adobe Acrobat format files, you can also export to .PDF in the same manner. You'll typically find that Acrobat files exhibit a very accurate representation of your original report formatting.

Don't forget that reports exported to HTML are static. They will simply show database information as it existed when the report was exported. The only way to update the HTML reports is to refresh the report in Crystal Reports and export again. Also, drilling down and using group trees won't work with exported HTML reports. If you want viewers to be able to refresh reports on their own, as well as interact with the report by drilling down and using the group tree, use other Crystal Reports Web options, such as RAS, the RDC, Visual Studio .NET, or Crystal Enterprise. And, giving Web users the ability to print reports on their local printers with accurate pagination also becomes a challenge. The options that best provide this capability are PDF export, or the ActiveX or Java report viewers (available with RAS, the RDC, or Crystal Enterprise).

Hyperlink Capabilities

Crystal Reports 9 provides hyperlink capabilities so that you can build hyperlinks into your reports. Virtually any objects on your report, such as text objects, database fields, charts, maps, or bitmap objects, can be linked to Web pages, e-mail addresses, other Crystal Reports, or other Windows programs. When you point to an object with an attached hyperlink, your mouse cursor turns into the now-familiar pointing finger. Click, and your Web browser will launch the Web site, your e-mail program will launch a new message window, or the Windows program or file that is specified will be launched.

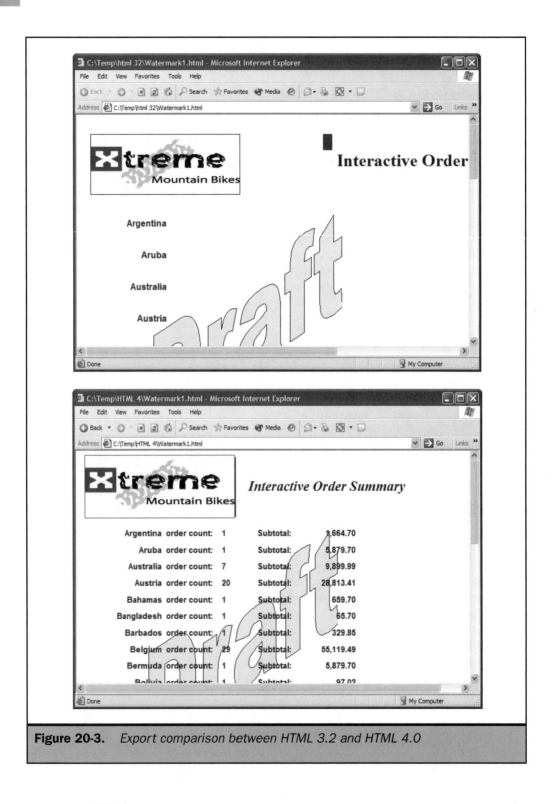

Figure 20-3. Export comparison between HTML 3.2 and HTML 4.0

Hyperlinks are created right in the Crystal Reports designer. In either the Design or Preview tab, select the object you want to create the hyperlink for. Then, choose Format | Hyperlink from the pull-down menus, right-click, and choose Format Field (or a similar format option) from the pop-up menu, or click the Hyperlink toolbar button from the standard toolbar. The Format Editor will appear. If it's not already selected, click the Hyperlink tab, shown in Figure 20-4.

Choose the type of hyperlink you'd like to create:

- **No Hyperlink**   If a hyperlink has already been assigned to this object, clicking this radio button will clear the hyperlink.

- **An E-Mail Address**   Click this radio button and add the e-mail address you want the hyperlink to send e-mail to in the Hyperlink Information text box after the mailto: text. If you'd like to create a conditional string formula to customize the hyperlink according to a database field or conditional value, click the conditional formula button next to the text box.

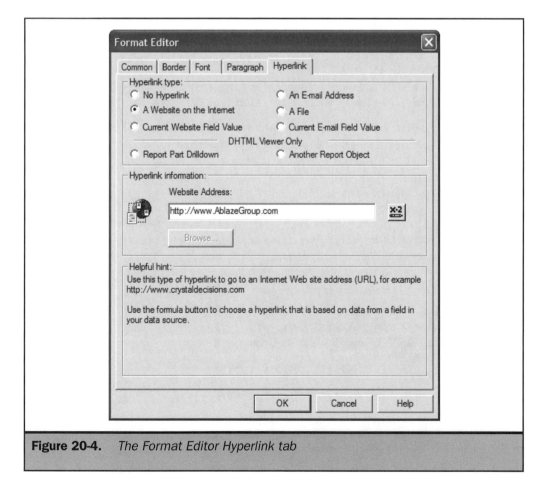

Figure 20-4.   *The Format Editor Hyperlink tab*

- **A Website on the Internet**   Click this radio button and add the Web site URL you want the hyperlink to launch in the Hyperlink Information text box after the http:// text. If you'd like to create a conditional string formula to customize the hyperlink according to a database field or conditional value, click the conditional formula button next to the text box.

- **A File**   Click this radio button and add the path and filename of the file you want the hyperlink to launch or the command you want to execute in the Hyperlink Information text box. Type the same command or path/filename you'd type after choosing Start | Run in Windows. If you'd like to create a conditional string formula to customize the hyperlink according to a database field or conditional value, click the conditional formula button next to the text box.

- **Current Website Field Value/Current E-mail Field Value**   These options are available only if you've chosen a string database or summary field on the report. In this case, the hyperlink will simply be the value of text from the database. To correctly use this option, the database field must return a complete Web site URL (including the http:// prefix), or an e-mail address, depending on which option you've chosen.

| **Note** | *The "DHTML Viewer Only" options in this dialog box are new to Crystal Reports 9 and are used to control Guided Navigation and Report Part viewing. More details can be found later in this chapter under "Navigating and Viewing Report Parts."* |

To further benefit the report viewer, you may wish to click the Common tab on the Format Editor and add a tool tip indicating what the hyperlink does. Either type the tool tip into the text box directly, or click the conditional formula button next to the text box and enter a string formula that will display when the viewer moves his or her mouse over the object.

Once you've specified all necessary information, click OK to close the Format Editor. When you preview the report in Crystal Reports, you'll see the mouse cursor change to a familiar pointing finger hyperlink cursor when you point to the object. If you added a tool tip, it will appear in a small yellow box. When you click your mouse button, the hyperlink will launch the Web page, e-mail Send dialog box, or Windows file.

After you create a hyperlink, follow the same steps you used to create it to modify or remove it. If you are modifying your report in the Preview tab, you may find it difficult to select an object that you've defined a hyperlink for. If you point to it with your mouse, your mouse cursor will change to a hyperlink cursor and you'll actually execute the hyperlink if you click. If you need to select an object in the Preview tab that has a hyperlink associated with it, SHIFT-click or right-click on the object to select it.

> **Tip** *Hyperlinks aren't applicable only to reports exported or viewed on the Web. When you view reports in the Crystal Reports Preview tab, or view a report integrated with a VB program, hyperlinks will work as you expect. Just remember that a viewer who is using Crystal Reports needs a network connection to your corporate intranet or the Internet to successfully use Web or e-mail hyperlinks.*

Cascading Style Sheet Support

If you are a Web developer, a new option on the Format Editor Common tab may catch your eye. The CSS Class Name text box/conditional button allows you to specify a Cascading Style Sheet (CSS) class name for most any object on the report (boxes and lines are notable exceptions). By specifying a CSS class name for the object, you can control formatting "globally" from a style sheet in an HTML document that includes the report.

Either type a CSS class name directly into the text box, or click the conditional formula button. A conditional formula editor will appear, where you may type in a string formula that can dynamically set the CSS class name according to database fields, formula functions, and so forth.

> **Note** *CSS class names specified in the Format Editor will be exposed in the HTML report viewers from RAS, but not when exported to HTML, as outlined earlier in the chapter.*

Navigating and Viewing Report Parts

Crystal Reports 9 has added several new features that enhance Web-based reporting, particularly when using RAS (discussed in more detail in Chapter 21) and the follow-on version of Crystal Enterprise 9 (not available at time of this writing). Previously, Crystal Reports "on-line" Web viewers, such as the HTML Page viewer, DHTML Frames viewer, the ActiveX viewer and Java viewer, supported standard Crystal Reports drill-down capabilities (discussed in detail in Chapters 3 and 10). And, they supported hyperlinks to standard "Web" items, such as Web pages and e-mail addresses. However, these capabilities were always limited to drilling down within groups in the same report or using other Web resources as hyperlink targets. While these standard capabilities remain in Crystal Reports 9, two new features provide more flexibility for drill down and navigation.

The first improvement is known as Guided Navigation (or just *Navigation* for short). Navigation allows you to designate certain objects on your report, such as charts, summary fields, and so forth, to act as hyperlinks to **other** objects on a report—either the same report where the original object resides, or an entire separate report. The second improvement is *Report Parts*, the ability to display just certain portions of a report in a Web page, rather than the entire page of a report. Navigation gives you much more flexibility to navigate through reports—you are no longer limited to hyper linking to Web pages or e-mail addresses. And, by using report parts, you can develop Web applications that show just specific parts of a report that you may be interested in, such as a single chart or a single grand total in a portal application.

Using Navigation

Navigation can be used in several ways in the new RAS DHTML-based report viewers (you cannot use the feature in older viewers, such as the ActiveX viewer). By using navigation, you can set up two types of hyperlinks:

■ **Report Part Drilldown**   A hyperlink to another part of the same report. Only the object or objects that you choose as the destination of your hyperlink will appear when you drill down—not the entire report. This option is only available when using the Report Part viewer, and is discussed later in the chapter in the Displaying Report Parts section.

■ **Another Report Object**   A hyperlink to another report object, either in the same report as the calling object, or in a completely separate .RPT file. If you use this option with the Report Part viewer, only the object or objects you choose as the destination of your hyperlink will appear when you click. If you use one of the page-oriented DHTML viewers, the entire report will appear when you click, but the object you choose as the destination will be navigated to and highlighted.

First, if you will be hyper linking from one report to another, it's helpful to begin the process by opening **both** reports in the Crystal Reports designer. This comes in handy when you need to reference the destination object in the Format Editor Hyperlink tab of the source object. If you are only hyper linking within the same report, you need only have one report open.

1. Select the object that you wish to be the destination of the hyperlink. For example, if you wish to click on a group name field in one report to display related detail data from another report, select the object in the detail report that you wish to navigate to.

2. Right-click on the destination object and choose Copy from the pop-up menu. While you will actually be able to paste a copy of the object onto the Design tab if you choose, if you "paste" the object into the Hyperlink tab of the Format Editor, a *reference* to the object will be pasted.

3. If you are working with multiple reports, use the Window menu to choose the report that will contain the original hyperlink. If you are hyper linking from the same report, you can obviously skip this step.

4. Select the object that you wish to act as the hyperlink. Right-click on the object and choose Format *<object type>* from the pop-up menu, choose Format | Format

<object type> from the pull-down menus, or click the Format button in the
Expert Tools toolbar.

5. When the Format Editor appears, click the Hyperlink tab. Click the Another
Report Object radio button in the DHTML Viewer Only section.

6. Right-click in the Select From text box and choose Paste from the pop-up menu.
The reference to the object you copied previously (not the object itself) will appear
in the Select From, Object Name, and Data Context text boxes.

Format Editor [X]

| Common | Border | Font | Date and Time | Hyperlink |

Hyperlink type:
- ○ No Hyperlink
- ○ A Website on the Internet
- ○ Current Website Field Value
- ○ An E-mail Address
- ○ A File
- ○ Current E-mail Field Value

DHTML Viewer Only
- ○ Report Part Drilldown
- ◉ Another Report Object

Hyperlink information:

Select From: `Xtreme Orders Detail (Navigation).rpt` **X·2**   ☐ Latest Instance

Object Name: `Text1`

Data Context: `/Order Date[1/2001]`   **X·2**

Helpful hint:
This type of hyperlink will link you directly to the specified object(s) and data
context within the same report or another report. This feature is most effective
when utilized within the Crystal Enterprise environment. For all other
implementations it is highly recommended that all reports navigated to and from
reside in the default RAS report directory. This will ensure that the linked reports
can be easily migrated to a Crystal Enterprise environment.

This type of hyperlink is active only in the DHTML viewers. If you are viewing the
object(s) as report parts, only the specified objects will be displayed.

[OK]   [Cancel]   [Help]

While the method described above will work most of the time, you may find
situations where you need to complete some or all of the fields in the Hyperlink tab
yourself. The Select From box references the report you wish to navigate to (if you'll
be navigating to the same report, this can be left blank). While the dialog box makes
reference to Crystal Enterprise reports, you can enter an .RPT file name outside of
Crystal Enterprise to navigate to directly (including the complete drive and pathname).
The Latest Instance check box will be dimmed if you do this—Latest Instance is only
relevant when pasting a Crystal Enterprise report into the dialog box.

The Object Name box should contain the name of the object that will be appear and
will be highlighted when you click the hyperlink. To find the name of the object, check

the Object Name text box on the Format Editor common tab. You may wish to give relevant objects more logical names (TopProductsChart instead of Chart1) when preparing them to act as hyperlink targets. You may also find it helpful to use the Report Explorer (discussed in Chapter 1) to determine object names.

Data Context indicates the location in the destination report that will initially be displayed. For example, if you preview a report and, in the preview tab, click on a group name field displaying "1/2001," you'll notice a data context string similar to /Order Date[1/2001] when you paste the object reference into the Hyperlink tab. Data Context strings require some getting used to. The best approach is to experiment with various permutations of "copy and paste" operations to see the resulting Data Context strings. You may, for example, see different results if you paste an object reference you copied when displaying the design tab as opposed to an object you copied when displaying the preview tab—the preview tab paste will often include extra material in the Data Context string to navigate to a particular group or record.

You may also use the conditional formula button to the right of the field to customize the data context string to the field being used as the hyperlink. For example, to customize the "1/2002" hard-coded date given in the earlier example, you might use the following conditional formula for the Data Context string:

```
"/Order Date[" & GroupName ({Orders.Order Date}, "quarterly")
& "]"
```

In this example, the group name field from the originating report will be passed as part of the Data Context string, allowing different targets to be chosen, based on which group name field is clicked.

Tip   *More details on Data Context strings can be found in Crystal Reports online help. Search for "Navigation" and select the subcategory "Data Context formats."*

Displaying Report Parts

In previous Crystal Reports versions, reports were always displayed a full page at a time. While the "page on demand" architecture that's familiar to most Crystal Reports users is very effective at displaying only the currently required page of the report, an entire page is always displayed. And, for the most part, this behavior remains the norm in Crystal Reports 9. However, there is an additional choice now available to those who use RAS as their Web reporting method. The *Report Part Viewer* allows individual objects on a particular report page (such as charts, summary fields, cross-tabs, text objects, and so forth) to be specifically chosen as report part targets. When you use this new viewer, only those objects specifically chosen as Report Part hyperlink targets will be shown in the viewer.

For example, a report shown using the HTML Interactive Viewer (one of the new full-page Viewers supplied with the Report Application Server) will appear similar to Figure 20-5.

By simply changing the viewer choice from HTML Interactive Viewer to Report Part Viewer, the same report will appear similar to the one shown in Figure 20-6.

The difference is that the chart shown in the latter example was specifically chosen as the initial report part object for the demonstrated report. Had no initial report part object been selected, the Web page would have been blank when using the Report Part Viewer to view the report.

The general idea in using report parts is to show only limited sets of report objects in a Web browser (perhaps inside a larger Web application, such as a portal) and allow those limited sets of objects to act as hyperlinks to other limited sets of objects. The

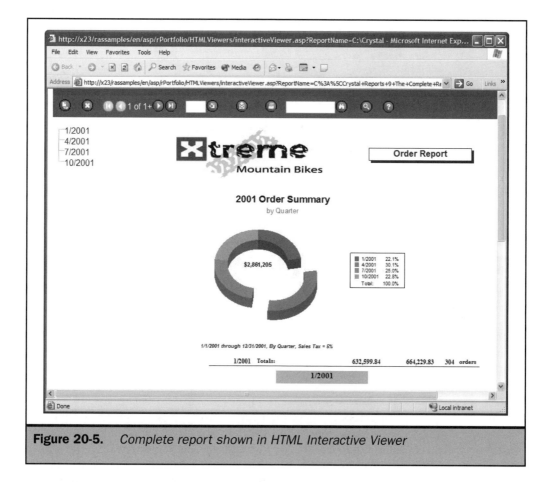

Figure 20-5.   *Complete report shown in HTML Interactive Viewer*

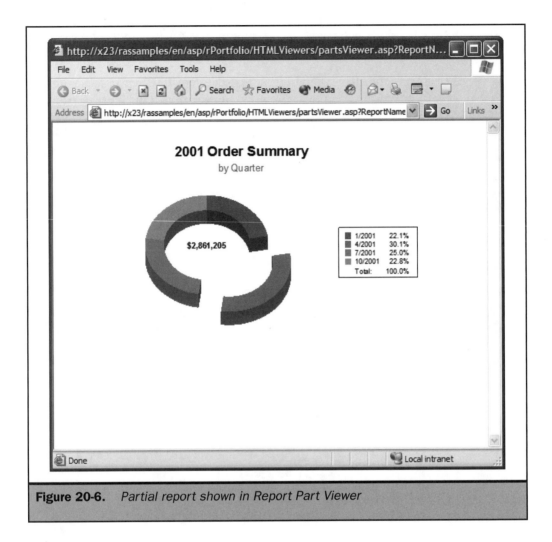

Figure 20-6. *Partial report shown in Report Part Viewer*

stark difference between the Report Part Viewer and the other DHTML viewers is that the other viewers all maintain the "whole report page at a time" approach, whereas the Report Part Viewer can now display just individual objects on a report.

Initial Report Part Setting

The first step in setting up a report to use the Report Part viewer is selecting initial report part settings. These indicate what specific object or objects will initially appear when you view a report in the Report Part viewer. If you don't specify these, the report will appear as an empty Web page when you attempt to view it. Initial report part settings are chosen in the Report Options dialog box. Choose File | Report Options from the pull-down menus to display this dialog box.

Complete the Object Name and Data Context fields with appropriate report object names and data context strings (discussed earlier in the chapter). If you choose, you may use the same "copy and paste" approach to place an object reference in these fields. If you wish to initially display more than one object in the Report Part Viewer (perhaps a chart along with a text object describing the chart), separate each object name in the Object Name field with a semicolon. As discussed previously, you may find it helpful to give report objects more meaningful names in the Format Editor before using them, as well as using the Report Explorer to locate specific objects.

Note   *It's important to remember that you can only display objects in the same report section when working with the Report Part Viewer. For example, if you want to display a chart and text object side by side in the Report Part Viewer, they must be in the same section of the originating report—the chart can't, for example, be in the report header if the text object is in a group header. This limitation also pertains to Report Part Drilldown, discussed in the following section.*

Report Part Drilldown

While showing an initial limited set of objects in the Report Part Viewer may be sufficient for simple applications, the drill-down capabilities of the Report Part Viewer give you tremendous flexibility in controlling how end users navigate through your report. While the page-oriented viewers use the grouping hierarchy of your report to determine drill-down logic, you can more closely control individual objects that appear when you drill down with the Report Part viewer.

This is accomplished by setting up a specific drill-down "path" in your report. For example, you may choose to have a group chart contained in the report header be the initial report part object that appears when you first view the report. If a viewer then clicks on a particular pie wedge or bar in that chart, your drill-down path will take them to a lower level summary field or advanced chart that appears in a lower group level. In this situation, you are mimicking the regular drill-down capabilities of the page viewer, but you are completely controlling the specific objects that appear when the user drills down.

Once you've defined your initial report part object, you may then further define your path by creating a Report Part Drilldown hyperlink for this object. For example, if you select a chart to display as your initial report part object, format that chart and choose the Hyperlink tab of the Format Editor. Click the Report Part Drilldown radio button in the DHTML Viewer Only section. You'll then be presented with a single Object Name list box where you can either type an object name in directly, or choose an object from the drop-down list.

Note *Report Part Drilldown is only available if you've chosen a group chart or map or a summary field. You may also choose a field in a group header or footer—other objects will not allow a Report Part Drilldown to be chosen.*

In the Object Name list box, type the name or choose the object that you want to be the target of the drill down. If you want to display multiple objects side by side (perhaps a lower-level chart and associated text object or group name field), type in multiple object names, separated by semicolons. As a general rule, you'll need to choose objects that are in a lower report "level" than the originating object. For example, you won't be able to choose a chart in a group header and hyperlink to a chart in the report header.

Once you've made these choices, view the report in the Report Part Viewer (perhaps add the report to the folder referred to by ePortfolio lite, discussed in Chapter 21). Notice that the initial report view shows only the object or objects that you chose in the initial report part settings. If you then click the initial object (assuming you've defined a Report Part Drilldown for the object), only the resulting objects for that Report Part Drilldown will appear in the browser.

For example, if you set a Report Part Drilldown hyperlink for the initial chart shown in Figure 20-6 to navigate to a lower-level advanced chart, along with a group name field, the following might appear in the Report Part Viewer when you click the "1/2001" wedge in the original chart.

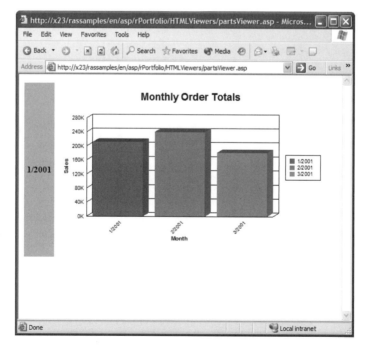

Tip *While you may "hard code" report part and navigation information in Crystal Reports, you can also control these properties from within your code when designing custom RAS Web applications. See Chapter 21 for information on RAS coding, and online Developer's Help for specific information on navigation in the RAS SDK object model.*

Chapter 21

Crystal Reports and Microsoft Active Server Pages

A s discussed in Chapter 20, there are several general ways to integrate real-time Crystal Reports in a Web page. In addition to Crystal Enterprise (discussed in Chapters 22, 23, and 24), you can integrate Crystal Reports into your Web pages using Microsoft Active Server Pages (ASP) and the Report Designer Component (RDC). And, Crystal Reports 9 Professional, Developer, and Advanced Editions feature a brand-new technology known as the Report Application Server, or RAS. Custom RAS applications can be developed using Microsoft Active Server Pages, as well as Java Server Pages on non-Microsoft Web servers.

This chapter will discuss using both the RDC and RAS to integrate Crystal Reports into your Microsoft Active Server Page applications. To sum up other Chapter 20 discussions, RAS is new technology using a very different object model than the RDC. If you have a large investment in RDC applications, you'll want to think carefully about converting them to RAS—it will involve a significant amount of recoding. If, however, you are looking to develop new from-the-ground-up applications and you want them to be fully "Crystal Enterprise–ready," then you'll want to look seriously at RAS and your integration method of choice.

And, remember that Crystal Enterprise 8.5 (the current version as of this printing) contains its own set of object models and its own ASP-like coding language (CSP or Crystal Server Pages) that also allow you to customize Web applications (CSP coding is discussed in Chapter 24).

> **Note** *Crystal Reports is also supported for integration with Web-based Visual Studio .NET applications. Chapter 26 discusses both Windows and Web Crystal Reports integration using VS.NET.*

Active Server Pages and VBScript Overview

The original language of the Web, Hypertext Markup Language (HTML), can be used to create attractive, hyperlinked pages with graphics, various font sizes, and (with the advent of newer HTML extensions, such as dynamic HTML) more interactivity and multimedia features. However, being a "markup language" instead of a true procedural or event-driven development language, HTML falls far short of providing all the flexibility you may need to create full Web-based custom applications. To help fill this void, the industry has moved toward *scripting* languages that allow browsers to perform much more sophisticated and intricate procedures. Two scripting languages are established: *JavaScript* is a scripting language based on Java, and *VBScript* is a scripting language based on Microsoft's Visual Basic for Applications (VBA). JavaScript is supported by both major browser vendors, Microsoft and Netscape. VBScript, generally, is limited to versions of Microsoft Internet Explorer (IE).

JavaScript and VBScript are *client-side* scripting languages—both being interpreted by the browser after being downloaded in a Web page. The scripts are not compiled into machine-executable code and generally cannot make database connections to a corporate database. And because these scripts execute on a browser that can be affected by any number of client-side variables, a developer cannot always expect consistent results.

To provide more flexibility and offer connectivity to corporate databases, Microsoft also implements *server-side* scripting on its Internet Information Server for Windows NT Server, Windows 2000, and Windows XP Professional. In this instance, the scripting language is interpreted by the Web server instead of the Web browser client. The results of the server-executed script are then sent to the Web browser as HTML. Because the script is executed on the server, you can create much more robust and flexible applications that are browser-independent—all that is sent to the browser is HTML. Microsoft's implementation of server-side scripting is called *Active Server Pages (ASP)*. When a Web server has ASP support installed, pages scripted with ASP are given a file extension of .ASP instead of .HTM. The Web server will then scan the .ASP file for server-side script and execute any it finds, sending the results of the script to the browser.

To enhance ASP even more, Microsoft extends the Component Object Model (COM), which is discussed in more detail in the Visual Basic chapters in Part III of this book, to its Web server platform. Because of this, the RDC and RAS can both be integrated with server-side scripts to create extensive reporting flexibility in Web applications. By using the full VBA power of ASP, combined with the ability of the RDC and RAS COM object models to control almost every aspect of a report at run time, you can create VB-like applications that integrate reports in a Web browser.

Note *RAS introduces support for Java Server Pages on Java-oriented, non-Microsoft Web Servers. And, both VBScript and JScript (Microsoft's version of JavaScript) can be executed in ASP on a Microsoft Web server. However, only VBScript within Microsoft ASP is discussed in this book.*

Web Integration with the Report Designer Component

The "legacy" choice for Active Server Page integration of Crystal Reports is the RDC. The RDC, originally introduced as an add-on to Crystal Reports 7, is a Component Object Model (COM)–compliant set of objects that expose virtually every feature of a report to a COM-compliant development environment, such as Visual Basic or ASP. While Crystal Decisions urges Web-based developers to move toward RAS, the RDC is still a very valid development choice for ASP-based applications—an updated version of the RDC in Crystal Reports 9 supports many of the new features introduced in this Crystal Reports version.

Crystal-Supplied Sample ASPs

When you install Crystal Reports 9 Developer or Advanced Editions (the RDC is not included with Standard or Professional Editions), the RDC is installed and registered automatically. Also, some Crystal Decisions–supplied ASPs are installed for your use. Look in Program Files/Crystal Decisions/Crystal Reports 9/Samples/<*language*/ Code/ Web/Report Designer Component. This supplied set of core ASPs needs to be called from your own ASPs to display a report in the desired report viewer (viewer choices are discussed later in this chapter).

However, Crystal Decisions no longer supplies sample ASP applications that demonstrate ASP integration methods (probably in an effort to prod developers toward RAS). If you wish to see sample applications using the RDC, you may visit the Crystal Decisions support site (support.crystaldecisions.com) for samples, as well as visiting this book's companion Web site (www.CrystalBook.com) for an RDC sample.

Once you've created any necessary virtual directories and copied the sample applications, you may use Visual InterDev, Notepad, or another editor to view the HTML and ASP code in these applications.

What Is RPTSERVER.ASP?

As you look through ASP example files, you'll notice that ASP Web reports are displayed in one of several Crystal Report Viewers. Note that the report viewers are always pointed to another file, called RPTSERVER.ASP. This Crystal-supplied ASP is a very important part of Crystal Reports' integration with the RDC (it is no longer required for use with RAS, however).

When you integrate a report with the RDC and Visual Basic (as covered in Chapter 25), you use the separate Report Viewer ActiveX control to show the report in a VB window. However, because integrating with the Web means your eventual display target is a Web browser, you need to consider some other viewing alternatives when using ASPs. The available Web report viewers—ActiveX, Java for Browser JVM, Java Plug-In, Netscape Plug-In, HTML Frames, and HTML Page—can all be used with ASPs. In fact, the report viewer for ActiveX is the same CRVIEWER.DLL module used to display reports with the RDC in Visual Basic.

Because these viewers use Crystal Reports' page-on-demand architecture, they expect report pages to be fed to them by the RDC's PageEngine object. This rather complicated logic and interaction is handled by RPTSERVER.ASP. Although you might be able to write your own ASP code to replace the function of RPTSERVER. ASP, one look at the ASP code in this file will probably convince you that it won't be worth the effort.

The RDC Object Model in ASPs

Because Active Server Pages support COM automation servers, you can implement Crystal Reports integration in ASP in much the same way as you do in Visual Basic. The complete RDC object model is available for you to use in your Active Server Pages. You can set properties and execute methods for different objects to customize report behavior. Typically, you'll use controls your user has completed on a form, or perhaps values your ASP is retrieving from a database, to control report appearance at run time.

The Application and Report Objects

As with Visual Basic, two base-level objects must be initially declared in your Web project: the Application object and the Report object (the Application object is used in VB only if you are integrating an external .RPT file). The Application object needs to be declared only once, at the beginning of a project. The Application object is then used to open a Report object; it is generally not used again throughout the rest of the project. Because these objects must remain in scope throughout the project and all associated ASP files, they are declared as *session* variables, which retain their values and remain in scope throughout an entire ASP project. Here's sample ASP code to declare them:

```
' CREATE THE APPLICATION OBJECT
If Not IsObject (session("oApp")) Then
    Set session("oApp") = Server.CreateObject("CrystalRuntime.Application")
End If

' CREATE THE REPORT OBJECT
reportname = Path & "Xtreme Orders.rpt"
'Path must be physical path, not virtual path
If IsObject(session("oRpt")) then
    Set session("oRpt") = nothing
End If
Set session("oRpt") = session("oApp").OpenReport(reportname, 1)

' Disable error prompts on the Web server
 session("oRpt").EnableParameterPrompting = False
```

A few notes about this sample VBScript code:

- Variables don't need to be identified with DIM or declared before use. In VB terms, no Option Explicit statement has been executed. While this may seem to ease your coding requirements, you need to remember that this means that all variables used in this fashion are variants. Some RDC methods require that variables be passed with a specific data type. In those cases, use VBScript typecasting functions, such as CStr and CInt, to correctly cast variables when passing them.

- The report file has been preceded with a Path variable, which is assigned in previous VBScript not shown here (the Request.ServerVariables "PATH_TRANSLATED") value can be queried for an actual physical pathname to the current ASP). The path must be the physical path to the report file (for example, C:\REPORTS) because the RDC can't resolve Web server virtual paths. If you know that the .RPT file will be in a fixed, known location, you can skip this entire section of code and simply supply a physical path and filename to the OpenReport method.

- The Application object is declared only once. If this section of VBScript is executed again, the previous declaration of oApp will remain. However, if there is a previous declaration of the Report object (presumably for a different report that may have been processed in a previous pass through this code), it will be set to Nothing before being set to the new report with the Application object's OpenReport method.

- The EnableParameterPrompting property of the Report object is set to false. This reduces the chances of any prompts appearing on the Web server if not supplied by your code. If the RDC displays a prompt on the Web server screen while a browser is waiting for a report request, the Webmaster likely won't be sitting by, waiting to respond to the Web server message. The browser session will hang, or eventually time out, if this happens.

Manipulating the Report Object

Once the Report object has been assigned to an .RPT file, you can use your user interface elements, such as controls on the calling form, to customize the way the report behaves. Use objects, collections, methods, and properties for the Report object to control report behavior. You can also pass logon information for the report (using the new RDC version 9 connection "property bag" properties) from within your code.

Here are some examples:

```
' Log On to report database connection

Session("oRpt").Database.Tables(1).ConnectionProperties("User ID")_
    = "DBReader"
Session("oRpt").Database.Tables(1).ConnectionProperties("Password")_
    = "DBPassword"
```

This code supplies logon information to the first table of the report (if there is more than one table, you'll need to supply logon information to each table within the tables collection). This makes use of the new ConnectionProperties collection added to version 9 of the RDC. An individual member of this collection is known as a "property bag," which can contain variable numbers and types of properties, depending on the particular database connection used for that particular table.

Tip *More information on connection information property bags can be found within the "What's New in the RDC" category of Crystal Reports 9 Developer's Help.*

```
session("oRpt").DiscardSavedData
session("oRpt").RecordSelectionFormula = _
    "{Orders.Order Amount} < " & CStr(Request.Form("value"))
```

This code first discards any saved data records that may exist within the .RPT file. It then sets the Report object's RecordSelectionFormula property to limit the report to orders over the amount supplied by the user in a control named "value" on the calling form. Notice that the CStr function is used just to make sure that the entire value being submitted to the RecordSelectionProperty is a string.

The following sample code is used to pass a value to a report parameter field:

```
session("oRpt").ParameterFields(1).AddCurrentValue _
CInt(Request.Form("txtTaxRate")))
```

Again, this code is passing the value from the calling form object "txtTaxRate" to the AddCurrentValue method. This method applies to a member of the ParameterFields collection of the Report object. Again, note that you should use a type declaration function (such as CInt) to ensure that the proper data type is being passed to the RDC.

> **Tip** *These are just a few examples of how to manipulate the Report object within your code. For more specific information on the RDC's object model, methods, and properties, refer to Chapter 25, or look through the CrystalDevHelp help file located in Program Files\ Crystal Decisions\Crystal Reports 9\Developer Files\Help\<language>\.*

After you set all necessary properties for the report object and are ready to process the report, you may need to execute the Report object's ReadRecords method to actually populate the report with data from the database. If the report is based on a PC-style database or an ODBC connection that the Web server can reach during the report process, this step may not be necessary. However, if you've used the DataBase object's SetDataSource method to change the data source of the report to an ADO recordset or some other data source that's only in scope in the current VBScript procedure, you need to execute ReadRecords so that the report won't fail. If you don't, and the Report object is used in another VBScript procedure (such as RPTSERVER.ASP) when the recordset is no longer in scope, the report won't be able to read records from the recordset. Here's sample code to execute ReadRecords:

```
On Error Resume Next
session("oRpt").ReadRecords
If Err.Number <> 0 Then Response.Write _
   "A server error occurred when trying to access the data source"
```

The PageEngine Object

The RDC exposes a PageEngine object that you normally don't need to worry about in Visual Basic applications because of the report viewer's ViewReport method. However, since you need to pass the Report object to RPTSERVER.ASP to page out to a Crystal Report Viewer, you need to declare the PageEngine object so that RPTSERVER.ASP can use it to communicate with the report viewers. If you look at RPTSERVER.ASP, you'll be able to get an idea (probably after a significant amount of poking around, though) of how the PageEngine works. Declare it with code similar to the following:

```
If IsObject(session("oPageEngine")) Then
    set session("oPageEngine") = Nothing
End If
Set session("oPageEngine") = session("oRpt").PageEngine
```

Caution   *Because RPTSERVER.ASP is the ultimate ASP that processes the report, you need to think about it when you declare session variables. It expects three session variables to be declared with specific names: session("oApp"), which is the Application object; session("oRpt"), which is the Report object; and session("oPageEngine"), which is the PageEngine object. Don't use alternative variable names for these session variables, or RPTSERVER.ASP will fail.*

RDC Report Viewers

As discussed in Chapter 20, one of the main benefits of using the RDC and RAS instead of just exporting reports to HTML from the Crystal Reports designer is that the RDC and RAS can offer full report interaction, such as drill-down and group-tree manipulation. The trick, though, is how to fully implement this interaction in a Web browser. One of the continual challenges faced when "Web-izing" Crystal Reports is supporting all the formatting and interaction options that Crystal Reports provides (and Crystal Decisions' approaches to these challenges get more creative with each successive version of Crystal Reports).

The options with the most cross-platform support are, as you might expect, HTML-based. While more flexibility and interactivity is added with each new revision of HTML (DHTML 4 has some, but very few, formatting limitations from a Crystal Reports perspective), it still has inherent limitations that make reproducing every element of a Crystal Report difficult. And, dealing with interactive options, such as drill-down and group tree navigation, introduce even more challenges.

To deal with these limitations, Crystal Decisions developed several "thin-client" report viewer applications (as opposed to the "zero-client" HTML viewers) that can be used with most common Web browsers. The *Report Viewer for ActiveX* is a Microsoft-compatible ActiveX control that can be viewed in Internet Explorer 3.02 or greater. The *Report Viewer for Java with Browser JVM* and the *Report Viewer for Java with the Java Plug-In* are Java-based viewers that can be viewed in 32-bit versions of Netscape Navigator 2.0 or greater, Internet Explorer 3.02 or greater, or other Java-compatible browsers. The Browser JVM version uses your particular browser's Java Virtual Machine, whereas the Java Plug-In version uses the Sun Java 2 Runtime Environment. The *Report Viewer for Netscape Plug-In* views a report inside Netscape Navigator.

These viewers implement almost all the features and functionality of the regular Crystal Reports Preview tab, although there are some visual differences. Both enable you to drill down on group headers and footers, charts, and maps, and both offer full interaction with the group tree. The thin-client viewers maintain most font and object formatting, and they allow you to print reports in their "native" paginated format on an attached printer.

There are still situations, however, for which an ActiveX control, Java applet, or the Netscape plug-in cannot be used. Perhaps there are security restrictions in your company, performance concerns about network traffic, or noncompatible browsers being used. For these situations, there are two HTML-based alternatives:

- **Report Viewer for Standard HTML with Frames**   Requires a browser that can support JavaScript and DHTML 4.0. Frames allow more than one scrollable window to be displayed within the browser at one time; this feature is used to mimic the group tree as closely as possible in a separate frame on the left side of the browser.

- **Report Viewer for Standard HTML**   If your browser doesn't support frames, you can use this alternative, which displays the entire report without a group tree in a single browser window.

Report Viewers Compared

Each of the various report viewers has advantages and disadvantages, in terms of several factors. The ActiveX, Java, and Netscape plug-in viewers offer more features but also place a higher burden on the Web server and network because of their size; they also have higher browser requirements. The HTML viewers have fewer browser requirements, but they may make some formatting compromises and offer less functionality than the ActiveX or Java viewers. Table 21-1 compares the different viewers and their advantages and disadvantages.

As a general rule, you should use the report viewer that provides the highest level of user functionality for your particular browser and network environment. If your users are all on a 100-megabit intranet with fast PCs and the latest version of Microsoft IE, there can't be too many arguments made against using the Report Viewer for ActiveX. If you have a mix of Netscape and Microsoft browsers, the Report Viewer for Java will work with both. But, if you are providing reports on your extranet that can potentially be accessed by any number of unknown browsers using 28.8 Kbps modems, you may want to use either of the Report Viewers for HTML to streamline performance and support the widest variety of browsers.

One thing should always be kept in mind: When you design reports to be distributed over the Web, take your target audience's report viewer choices into serious consideration when you design your reports. If your ultimate goal is that reports look good on a printed page, you need to make serious changes to report formatting and layout if your audience will be using HTML-based viewers instead of the ActiveX or Java viewers. If your reports

Report Viewer	Advantages	Disadvantages
ActiveX Netscape Plug-in	Provides highest mirror-image level of original report and most flexibility, including full group tree and drill-down interactivity, and accurate printing of reports on your local printer.	Only works with 32-bit versions of Microsoft IE 3.02 or greater, or with newer 32-bit versions of Netscape Navigator. Requires extra time and increases network strain when downloaded to browser.
Java with Browser JVM Java Plug-In	Provides good mirror-image level and high flexibility, such as group tree and drill-down interactivity, and ability to print reports on your local printer. Works with any Java-compatible browser.	Requires extra time and increases network strain when downloaded to browser. Won't work with earlier browsers that don't support Java. Windows XP support may required download of separate JVM plug-in.
HTML Frames	Will work with browsers that just support frames and JavaScript (such as earlier 16-bit browsers)—ActiveX and full Java capabilities aren't required. Mimics group tree with faster initial response, and no control or applet download is required.	Makes some formatting compromises because of HTML limitations. Only prints what's in the current browser window—original report pagination and layout are not preserved. Drilldown on charts and maps isn't supported. No Export button on toolbar.
HTML Pages	Works with even the simplest browsers that don't support frames, while still allowing "pseudo" drilldown by creating links in group headers. Faster initial response, and no control or applet download is required.	Makes some formatting compromises because of HTML limitations. Only prints what's in the current browser window—original report pagination and layout are not preserved. Drilldown on charts and maps isn't supported. No Export button on toolbar.

Table 21-1. *RDC Report Viewers Compared*

rely heavily on group-tree and drill-down interactivity (detail sections are hidden, lots of charts are included, and so on), don't realistically expect satisfactory results with the HTML-based viewers. And, don't forget that Crystal Reports includes many formatting options, such as drop shadows, underlaid sections, and object and section background shading, that may not convert properly to HTML when displayed in the HTML viewers. Always test your reports and make sure you're getting the results you expect in your target report viewer.

Choosing and Customizing Report Viewers

You'll need to determine which of the report viewers you want to provide to your viewer's Web browser. You can include commonly available VBScript code to query the browser for its type. If you encounter Internet Explorer, you can automatically provide the ActiveX viewer. If you encounter Netscape, you can provide the Netscape Plug-In or a Java viewer. Or, you can create a control on a Web page (perhaps a combo box) that allows the viewer to make the choice.

Crystal Decisions provides some intermediate ASPs that you may include in your ASP code to choose the desired report viewer. You'll find SmartViewerActiveX.ASP, ActiveXPluginViewer.ASP, SmartViewerJava.ASP, JavaPluginViewer.ASP, and HTMStart.ASP supplied with Crystal Reports 9 (look in Program Files/Crystal Decisions/Crystal Reports 9/Samples/*<language>*/Code/Web/Report Designer Component). There are also some companion .ASPs that some of these ASPs call (such as FramePage.ASP and Cleanup.ASP). You can just copy and paste the code from one of the ASPs into your own file, or use the HTML *#include file* statement to bring in the proper report viewer code. If you've set up a control on your application form that allows the user to choose a report viewer (similar to the viewer variable in the following example), you might use code similar to this to set the chosen report viewer:

```
viewer = Request.Form("Viewer")
If cstr(viewer) = "ActiveX" then
%>
<!-- #include file="SmartViewerActiveX.ASP" -->
<%
ElseIf cstr(viewer) = "Netscape Plug-in" then
%>
<!-- #include file="ActiveXPluginViewer.ASP" -->
<%
ElseIf cstr(viewer) = "Java using Browser JVM" then
%>
<!-- #include file="SmartViewerJava.ASP" -->
<%
ElseIf cstr(viewer) = "Java using Java Plug-in" then
```

```
%>
<!-- #include file="JavaPluginViewer.ASP" -->
<%
ElseIf cstr(viewer) = "HTML Frame" then
    Response.Redirect("htmstart.ASP")
Else
    Response.Redirect("rptserver.ASP")
End If
```

The Crystal-supplied report viewer ASPs for Java and ActiveX set certain viewer parameters to default settings. When you view the ASP code in these files, you'll notice parameters, such as group-tree display, toolbar button display, enabling of drill-down, and so forth, set with PARAM tags. You may modify this report viewer behavior if you so desire. If you want to make permanent changes to these options, simply change the Crystal ASP to use your new desired options (perhaps you don't want to offer a Print or Export button to your users at any time). If you want to hard-code a change only for a particular application, while others still use the Crystal defaults, you need to copy the code from one of the Crystal files into your own ASP file and change the parameter in your own file, or set session variables and modify the Crystal-supplied ASPs to look for them.

Look at the following sample code:

```
<%
If session("GroupTree") = "ON" Then
    %>
    <PARAM NAME="DisplayGroupTree" VALUE=1>
    <%
Else
    %>
    <PARAM NAME="DisplayGroupTree" VALUE=0>
    <%
End If
%>
```

The <% and %> characters in the preceding code indicate separation of the server-side ASP script from the actual HTML text to be submitted to the browser. Because the parameters are part of the report viewer Object tag, they need to be returned to the browser, while the If-Then-Else statement will execute on the server. This separation of server-side script from client-side HTML is the basic premise of Active Server Pages.

What Is CleanUp.ASP?

CleanUp.ASP is a Crystal Decisions–supplied ASP that "cleans up" the three necessary session variables required by RptServer.ASP. By setting the three session variables to "Nothing," resources on the Web server are released. CleanUp.ASP is called by an HTML BODY tag's ONUNLOAD event (via a JavaScript function), executing its code when a browser window containing the report viewer closes.

Web Integration with the Report Application Server

Crystal Reports 9 introduces the Report Application Server, or *RAS*, as the newest method of Crystal Reports integration into Web applications. RAS, which was originally introduced as a "build a report wizard in a Web browser" add-on to Crystal Enterprise 8.0, is included with Crystal Reports 9 Professional, Developer, and Advanced Editions.

Crystal Decisions encourages developers to move toward RAS and away from the Report Designer Component. There are several reasons you should consider this option:

- **Multitier processing capabilities**   RAS provides the ability to move report processing off the Web server to another dedicated computer (the RDC requires the Web server to perform all report processing).

- **Adoption of a Crystal Enterprise–centric object model**   Code developed with RAS is Crystal Enterprise 9–ready, requiring little additional effort to move to a full Crystal Enterprise environment (Crystal Enterprise 9 was not released as of this book's printing).

- **On-the-fly report design capability**   (Crystal Reports Advanced Edition only) The initial purpose of RAS was solely to provide the ability to design a report from scratch using a Web-browser-based "wizard." While the RDC also features the ability to create new reports from scratch, this was the initial purpose of RAS, and the RAS capability is well developed.

While these capabilities are considerable, you still may wish to stay with the RDC in certain circumstances.

- **A considerable amount of existing RDC code**   Converting RDC code to RAS is not simple—the object models are quite different. You'll face a significant conversion hurdle.

Note	*Crystal Reports Advanced Edition includes a more robust RAS in two respects: it accepts more user processing requests in a "queue and wait" mode than do the Professional and Developer Editions, which will reject excess requests with user error messages. Also, Crystal Reports Advanced Edition supports RAS applications that can create new reports on the fly, whereas other editions support only integrating existing reports.*

Basic RAS Operation

RAS ships with Crystal Reports on a separate CD. When you install it, a default Launchpad page is installed. Browse to http://<*Web server*>/rassamples to view it. The Launchpad will be displayed.

ePortfolio Lite

Several sample applications that are installed with RAS can help you get a feel for the new object model and new approach to report integration. The most familiar to existing

Crystal Enterprise users is *ePortfolio Lite.* This application offers the same look and feel as the out-of-the-box Crystal Enterprise user interface called ePortfolio.

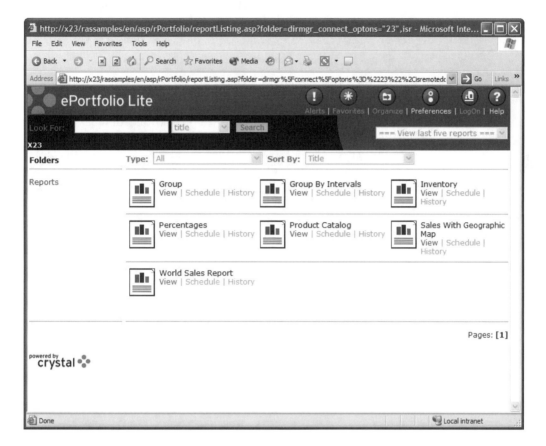

This "peek" at Crystal Enterprise 9 technology provides a basic interface to view existing reports in a browser. You'll immediately notice lots of dimmed controls that are functional in previous full versions of ePortoflio. These features aren't implemented in the RAS version of ePortfolio Lite (in fact, if you click the Preferences link, you'll find an option to turn these features off).

And, if you view the source file for ePortfolio Lite (either the HTML returned to the browser, or the original ASP source file), you'll find a liberal use of JavaScript and very little use of the RAS object model. ePortfolio Lite doesn't use RAS object model features to their fullest capabilities. In fact, all the report "view" links on the ePortfolio Lite screen simply link to one of the supplied viewer ASPs, providing the physical path and filename of the report as a URL parameter.

This use of the supplied viewer ASPs demonstrates RAS integration in its simplest form (this particular usage is substantially simpler than RDC integration and is largely

CRYSTAL REPORTS 9
ON THE WEB

similar to older Web Component Server or Web Access Server integration in Crystal Reports 8 and earlier, where a simple .RPT filename could be passed within a Web server URL). Accordingly, you might design a Web page link as simple as:

```
<A HREF=InteractiveViewer.ASP?ReportName=C:\Reports\Sample.rpt>
Display Sample Crystal Report
</a>
```

In this instance, you are linking to InteractiveViewer.ASP, an ASP supplied by Crystal Decisions in Program Files\Crystal Decisions\Report Application Server 9\Samples\<*language*>\ASP\rPortfolio\HTMLViewers (the previous anchor tag example assumes that InteractiveViewer.ASP is in the same folder as the HTML file with the tag). InteractiveViewer.ASP contains a few lines of code to instantiate one of the COM report viewers and pass the physical pathname and filename of the report to the COM object model. The COM report viewer can read the .RPT file directly, prompting the user for any necessary parameter fields or logon information, before displaying the report right in the browser.

While this method doesn't make any use of the RAS object model to modify report properties at run time, it is a very "quick and dirty" way to add RAS functionality to your Internet or intranet site in a very short period of time.

Web Report Design Wizard

As discussed earlier, the version of RAS included with Crystal Reports 9 Advanced Edition includes the capability to design new reports on the fly right from within a Web browser (using a Wizard approach). An example of this capability is installed with RAS and can be started from the RAS Launchpad.

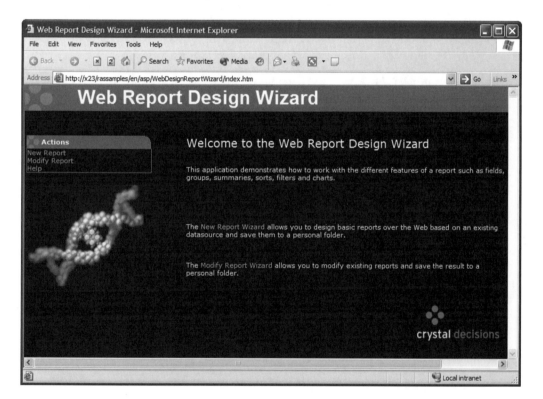

When you launch the Web Report Design Wizard, you'll be presented with two choices: create a new report or modify an existing report. Each choice will launch a separate browser window that takes you through a report design process via a "Next/ Back" wizard interface—this is not the interactive drag-and-drop report design that you're familiar with in Crystal Reports. Both processes make use of the RAS capabilities to create a new report or modify and save an existing report entirely within the RAS object model. The beginning file for the Web Report Design Wizard, ChooseReport.ASP, can be found in Program Files\Crystal Decisions\Report Application Server 9\ Samples\

<language>\ASP\WebDesignReportWizard. By following this ASP, and the subsequent ASPs that it calls, you'll get a good idea of this level of RAS integration.

The RAS Configuration Manager

While RAS exposes a much simpler version of the multitier, multiprocessor architecture of the full Crystal Enterprise product, it does have a small set of "configurable" items that you may need to adjust, depending on your particular environment. Many of these items can be changed with the RAS Configuration Manager, a Windows program that's installed on the same computer as the RAS Server. To launch the RAS Configuration Manager, choose it from the Tools submenu of the main Crystal Enterprise 9 program menu that appears when you install RAS. The main window appears in Figure 21-1.

For many situations, the default settings in this dialog box still suffice. However, if you wish to customize certain RAS behavior, make changes as follows:

- **Max Number Of Records**   If you choose the Records Limited To radio button, you may specify the maximum number of records you wish RAS to send to a Web browser. You may wish to specify a finite number to avoid large amounts of data being sent over your network.

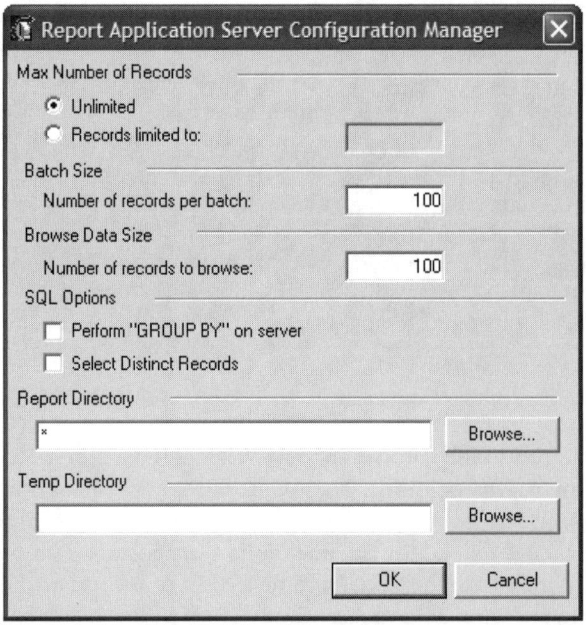

Figure 21-1.   *RAS Configuration Manager*

■ **Batch Size**   RAS communicates with the database in record batches. Depending on the database you are using and your network environment, you may see improved performance by enlarging or reducing the size of the record batch.

■ **Browse Data Size**   RAS features the ability to request a batch of sample data to be returned from the database (much as Crystal Reports does). This setting allows you to specify the number of distinct values that will be returned from the database for the browse. Adjusting this number may improve browse performance.

■ **SQL Options – Perform "GROUP BY" On Server**   This option, similar to that provided in Crystal Reports, will attempt to "push" as much report processing as possible to the database server by using a SQL Group By clause with aggregate functions. This may improve processing time for reports that meet certain criteria. Note that this option will apply only to new reports created with RAS. An existing report will make use of the option saved with that report.

■ **SQL Options – Select Distinct Records**   This option will add a "DISTINCT" keyword to the SELECT clause used in a report. This will return only unique combinations of values from the database, excluding any records that contain exact duplicate data when compared to other records. Note that this option will apply only to new reports created with RAS. An existing report will make use of the option saved with that report.

■ **Report Directory**   By default, RAS will access only reports in a certain directory, and any directory below that directory. This is provided as a security measure. Set the top-level directory with this option. To be able to process reports from any directory on the machine, place an asterisk (*) in this field.

■ **Temp Directory**   RAS creates temporary files as part of normal operation. If you wish to specify a particular location for these files, place a pathname in this field.

Note   *Changes made in the RAS Configuration Manager will take effect only when the RAS Server NT Service has been stopped and restarted. This can be done with the Services icon in the Windows Control Panel.*

Customizing RAS at Run Time with the RAS SDK

While ePortfolio Lite or passing an .RPT filename to one of the viewer ASPs may be adequate for simpler integration requirements, you may wish to take fuller control of your Web-based integration, much as you may have done with the RDC. The RAS Software Development Kit (SDK) provides a very involved object model to allow this. Just be aware: If you are used to the RDC object model, give yourself some extra time to adjust to the new approach the RAS SDK object model requires.

RAS SDK Model/View/Controller Architecture

The RAS SDK object model differs substantially from the RDC in both architecture and syntax. The first substantial difference is the way objects are organized and exposed. While the RDC is relatively "flat," exposing only a few high-level objects, such as the Application object and the Report object, RAS takes a different view of object orientation by introducing a *Model/View/Controller* (or MVC) architecture. MVC is a design paradigm often applied to application or development environments that separates application elements into three parts: Model, View, and Controller.

When attempting to fit the RAS SDK into this architecture, you can consider the three members of MVC to approximate to RAS in this way:

- **View**   The end-user view of the report, this is designed by you (the developer) and presented to the end user in the user's browser.

- **Model**   All possible properties of a report, generally available in a read-only mode. The model exposes the names of fields, groups, formulas, report objects and sections, and so forth.

- **Controller**   All report objects that can be deleted, added, or modified. For the most part, however, you cannot query a controller to find out the *existing* status of a report object.

To put the MVC architecture in more of a real-world perspective for the RAS developer, the *View* is the custom application, the *Model* is where you get existing report properties, and the *Controller* is where you change report properties. Probably the most important point here is that you must use a Controller to *modify* report properties—you can't do it with the Model.

To further define the RAS SDK architecture, look at Table 21-2. This table breaks down the object models in the RAS SDK and their associated controllers. As you begin to work with RAS, you'll soon discover the relationship between each as you modify reports at run time: get an existing value from the object model, make some changes to it, then pass it to a controller to actually modify the report. Or, in the case of adding new report objects, create a new object, set its properties, then add it to the report via a controller.

In greatly simplified form, then, you could retrieve the second formula object in an existing report with

```
DataDefinition.FormulaFields(2)
```

and you could update the contents of the same formula with

```
DataDefController.FormulaFieldController.Modify 2, NewFormula
```

Types of Report Items	Object Model	Controller
Database connections, tables, links	Database Object	DatabaseController
Database fields, groups, record selection (filters), and so forth	DataDefinition Object	DataDefController
Report areas, sections, charts, cross-tabs, and so forth	ReportDefinition Object	ReportDefController
Unformatted "flat" data within the report	Rowset Object	RowsetController

Table 21-2. *RAS SDK Object Models and Controllers*

The ObjectFactory

While perusing sample applications included with RAS, or the sample application from this book's Web site (www.CrystalBook.com), you will encounter reference to the ObjectFactory, which you have not seen previously with the RDC or even with earlier versions of Crystal Enterprise. The ObjectFactory is simply a "wrapper" around other RAS objects that appends a version number onto any objects you create from within it. This is an innovative approach to version control that will help you immensely when upgrading to later versions of RAS, or when working with multiple versions of RAS on the same computer.

Typically, when newer versions of Crystal Decisions tools have been installed on a computer, they *replace* any previous versions that may have existed—it's often been difficult, if not impossible, to support multiple versions of the same Crystal Decisions product on the same computer. Not only does Crystal Reports 9 share a computer nicely with an earlier version, but the RAS SDK is designed to allow easy version changes in just one place, the declaration of the ObjectFactory.

Compare the following two pieces of sample RAS code:

```
Set rptAppSession = _
    CreateObject("CrystalReports.ReportAppSession.2")
```

This piece of code creates a new object called rptAppSession using the Prog ID of "CrystalReports.ReportAppSession.2." This gets the object definition from one of the RAS object libraries, in particular, the "version 2" library. Contrast this with

```
Set objFactory = CreateObject("CrystalReports.ObjectFactory.2")
Set rptAppSession = _
objFactory.CreateObject("CrystalReports.ReportAppSession")
```

Initially, you'd think the first option would be more efficient, as it requires only one line of code. However, if you subsequently need to create many additional objects throughout the remainder of the project, you can use the objFactory CreateObject method to create them, rather than creating them with direct Prog IDs from the RAS libraries. The result: when RAS version 3 is released, you need only change *one* reference in the code (the original CreateObject function that instantiates the original objFactory object). All remaining object creation statements may be left as is, and they'll automatically be adjusted to the new version of RAS!

ReportAppSession

If you've developed applications with the RDC, you're probably familiar with the Application object, which is the first object that you must declare in the RDC. RAS has a similar requirement to use the ReportAppSession object. This object establishes a session with the actual Report Application Server itself (remember from earlier discussions that the RAS SDK and Report Application Server can reside on separate computers). The ReportAppSession object establishes a connection with the RAS Server prior to opening an existing report or creating a new report.

Examine the following sample code:

```
Set rptAppSession = _
    objFactory.CreateObject("CrystalReports.ReportAppSession")

' RAS Server name is taken from clientSDKOptions.XML,
' or can be specified by setting ReportAppServer property
' rptAppSession.ReportAppServer = "AblazeServer"

rptAppSession.Initialize
```

A rptAppSession object is created, using the Object Factory's CreateObject method. Optionally, the rptAppSession object's ReportAppServer property can be set to "point" this particular session to a specific RAS server computer. If this property is not set within your code (notice that the line is commented out in this sample), then the RAS SDK uses the RAS server specified in the file clientSDKOptions.XML located in the folder \Program Files\Crystal Decisions\Report Application Server 9 to determine which RAS server to use. The file looks similar to this:

```
C:\Program Files\Crystal Decisions\Report Application Server 9\clientSDKOptions.xml - Microsoft Internet Explorer
File   Edit   View   Favorites   Tools   Help
Back   ·        ·            Search      Favorites      Media                
Address    C:\Program Files\Crystal Decisions\Report Application Server 9\clientSDKOptions.xml         Go   Links »

- <CrystalReports.ClientSDKOptions xmlns:xsi="http://www.w3.org/1999/XMLSchema-instance" version="2"
    xsi:type="CrystalReports.ClientSDKOptions">
  - <ServerInfos version="2" xsi:type="CrystalReports.ServerInfos" id="1">
    - <ServerInfo version="2" xsi:type="CrystalReports.ServerInfo" id="2">
        <Server>X23</Server>
        <Adapter>TCPIP</Adapter>
      </ServerInfo>
    </ServerInfos>
  </CrystalReports.ClientSDKOptions>

Done                                                                    My Computer
```

You may edit this file with a text editor, changing the value between the <Server> and </Server> tags. Also, if you wish to connect to the RAS server via something other than the default TCP/IP port, you may add a colon, followed by the port number, after the server name within these tags.

By separating the RAS server computer from the Web server (where the RAS SDK libraries are typically located), you can generally improve overall performance by eliminating the report processing tasks from the Web server (a limitation imposed by the RDC).

Once you've declared the rptAppSession object, execute its Initialize method to actually commence communications with the RAS server before proceeding.

ReportClientDocument

Continuing the comparison to the RDC, the RAS also establishes an initial object to refer to a specific report object that you will use throughout the remainder of your application. The report object can be either an existing .RPT file that already exists on disk or a new report object definition that you will continue to build as your application proceeds (don't forget that the ability to create a new report from within your custom application is available only if you've purchased Crystal Reports Advanced Edition).

This object is known as a ReportClientDocument object, as is created using the following example:

```
'Create a new ReportClientDocument object for this reportAppSession
Set oClientDoc = _
rptAppSession.CreateService("CrystalClientDoc.ReportClientDocument")
```

The ReportClientDocument is created with the ReportAppSession's CreateObject method, with the prog ID "CrystalClientDoc.ReportClientDocument" supplied as the argument.

Once this object has been created, however, you must execute a method that it exposes to either open an existing report or create a new report. Examine the following:

```
Dim ReportName

' Turn virtual directory into physical pathname
ReportName = MID(request.ServerVariables("PATH_TRANSLATED"), 1, _
             (LEN(request.ServerVariables("PATH_TRANSLATED"))-18))

' Append report name to it
ReportName = ReportName & "Last Year's Sales.rpt"

'Open the report
oClientDoc.Open ReportName
```

This code uses the ReportName variable to initially store the physical pathname to the calling ASP. In the preceding example, the calling ASP is "LastYearsSales.ASP," the name of the ASP being 18 characters long. By using the PATH_TRANSLATED member of the Request object's ServerVariables collection, you can obtain the actual physical path to LastYearsSales.ASP. By using Mid and Len functions, the preceding sample "strips off" the rightmost 18 characters, returning just the physical pathname. The actual .RPT filename is then appended to the ReportName variable to derive the entire physical path/filename for the report. This, in turn, is supplied to the ReportClientDocument (oClientDoc) open method to actually open the Crystal Report.

Tip *The entire process of deriving the physical pathname is unnecessary if you have a fixed location for your reports, such as C:\Reports. In that case, simply provide the actual physical path/filename to the Open method, as in:*
oClientDoc.Open "C:\Reports\Last Years Sales.rpt"

Because of the multiserver nature of RAS, the possibility exists that the report file you are trying to open may be on a different computer than the actual RAS Server itself. By default, the ReportClientDocument object Open method will open the report on the RAS Server machine. If the RAS Server and RAS SDK are being run on the same single computer, this is a straightforward process.

However, if you've separated the two portions of RAS on two separate computers, you may need to think carefully about where the report .RPT file actually resides. Crystal Decisions recommends storing .RPT files on the computer that is operating as the RAS Server. Since this computer is the machine to actually process the report, including making the database connection, it is more efficient to have the report file reside on this machine. However, if for some reason or another this isn't practical, you can store .RPT files on the RAS SDK computer. When you execute the ReportClientDocument Open method, the .RPT file will be copied to the RAS Server machine prior to report processing (this copy operation is where the efficiency issue comes into play).

To indicate that the report file is located on the RAS SDK computer, preface the report filename argument with the characters rassdk:// (note that this prefix is case-sensitive—don't use uppercase letters). Thus, the previous Open method example would look like this, if the report file were located on the RAS SDK computer:

```
oClientDoc.Open "rassdk://C:\Reports\Last Years Sales.rpt"
```

Controlling General Report Behavior with the RAS SDK

The sample application available on this book's Web site (visit www.CrystalBook.com to download the application) provides a moderate level of report customization at run time. By gathering several items from the end user in an initial Web form and passing them to the report at run time, the application demonstrates how to customize a report from within a RAS application, much as a similar application (discussed earlier in the chapter, and also available from the book's Web site) performs customization with the RDC. Some of the more common report customization procedures follow.

Report Database Login

If you've designed a report against a secure database, either you or your report user must provide login credentials before the report will process. You may either do this within your code or let the chosen Crystal Report viewer prompt the user directly.

In many cases, you may have already gathered login credentials from the user earlier in your application, or they are provided as an internal part of the application automatically. In either of these cases, you'll probably not want to pester the user again by allowing the report viewer to prompt for login credentials. While there are several ways to supply this information from within RAS, one of the simplest is the DatabaseController's logon method, demonstrated here:

```
'Logon to database, if necessary
oClientDoc.DatabaseController.Logon "DBReader", "DBReader"
```

This simple method takes two parameters: a user ID and a password. The Logon method will pass this logon information to every table in the report (with the assumption that all tables came from the same database with the same login credentials). If you need to supply individual login credentials for certain tables, use the DatabaseController's SetConnectionInfos or ModifyTableConnectionInfo methods.

Record Selection

One of the major features of integrated Crystal Reporting, no matter what the method or environment, is controlling report record selection from within your application. You'll often want to change report record selection according to some object on a Web form, or according to some other logic within the application. As such, one of the first RAS processes you'll want to learn about is controlling record selection.

If you've used the RDC in the past, you'll discover that changing record selection at run time isn't nearly as straightforward with RAS as it was with the RDC. As opposed to simply modifying the record selection property of the Report object, RAS requires a more complex approach, based on the concept of *filters* and *primitive expressions*.

Take, for example, the following common Crystal Reports record selection formula in Crystal syntax:

```
{Customer.Country} = "USA" and {Orders.Order Amount} >= 1000
```

If this selection formula has already been added to the report before being opened, the report is considered by RAS to contain the following objects:

A *FieldRangeFilterItem* containing the following properties:

- **RangeField**   The Customer.Country database field object
- **Operation**   The number 1 (for Equal To)
- **Inclusive**   False (not applicable to an Equal To operator)
- **Values**   Another collection of individual Value objects—in this case, a single ConstantValue object with the Value property containing "USA"

Another FieldRangeFilterItem containing the following properties:

- **RangeField**   The Orders.Order Amount database field object
- **Operation**   The number 4 (for Greater Than)
- **Inclusive**   True, indicating the "or equal to" addition to the greater-than operator
- **Values**   Another collection of individual Value objects—in this case, a single ConstantValue object with the Value property containing 1000

Both of these FieldRangeFilterItem objects are included in the DataDefinition Object's FilterItems collection. Each is said to represent a "primitive expression," or a Field- Operator-Value expression.

In addition, the collection contains a third element known as an *OperatorFilterItem* object (in actuality, this item is the second element in the collection, between the two FieldRangeFilterItem objects). The OperatorFilterItem ties the two FieldRangeFilterItem objects together (in this case, the "And" which connects the two primitive expressions in the selection formula). The OperatorFilterItem's Operator property can be set to the string AND, the string OR, a left parenthesis, or a right parenthesis. In the case of the previously discussed record selection formula, the property equates to AND.

RAS proceeds through a process of *parsing,* or "picking apart" the various pieces of the record selection formula set in the report and loading the FilterItems collection with the combinations of primitive expressions and OperatorFilterItem objects. If the record selection formula is too complex to parse (it contains complex built-in Crystal Reports formula functions, or similar items), the FilterItems collection won't be populated and the original record selection formula will appear in the Filter objects FreeEditingText property.

If you think that this entire process unduly complicates the record selection process (especially when compared to the previous single RecordSelectionFormula property of the RDC's report object), you may be right. This new architecture is no doubt the result of the redesigned Query Engine in Crystal Reports 9. However, with some examination of sample code and some experimenting, you'll eventually be able to navigate this rather complex object model to control record selection within your RAS code.

Examine the following:

```
'Create a new filter object
Set NewFilter = objFactory.CreateObject("CrystalReports.Filter")

'FieldRangeFilterItem is used to store the filter info
Set NewFilterItem = _
    objFactory.CreateObject("CrystalReports.FieldRangeFilterItem")

'ConstantValue object is used by the FieldRangeFilterItem
'to store the comparison value
Set NewConstantValue = _
    objFactory.CreateObject("CrystalReports.ConstantValue")

'Build the NewFilterItem object
NewFilterItem.RangeField = _
oClientDoc.Database.Tables.Item(0).DataFields.Item(12)
'Customer.Country is the 13th field in the first table
NewConstantValue.Value = CStr("USA")
```

```
NewFilterItem.Values.Add NewConstantValue

NewFilterItem.Operation = 1 'Number 1 is Equal To

'The completed NewFilterItem object is added into
'the NewFilter object
NewFilter.FilterItems.Add NewFilterItem

'The new filter is assigned to the Report Document
oClientDoc.DataDefController.RecordFilterController.Modify NewFilter
```

The purpose of this entire block of code is to add the {Customer.Country} = "USA"
filter to a report at run time (this code fragment is from the sample application on this
book's Web site and is based on a control on the original Web form). In this example,
there is no reason to get the existing contents of the record selection formula, so it is
not initially retrieved from the DataDefinition Object. Instead, new objects representing
a Filter, a single FieldRangeFilterItem, and ConstantValue are defined. Then, the
FieldRangeFilterItem object's RangeField property is set to Customer.Country (the
twelfth field in the report), the Operation property is set to 1 (for Equal To), and
the ConstantValue object's Value property is set to the string USA. The ConstantValue
object is then added to the FieldRangeFilterItem object's Values collection (there can
be more than one member of this collection, in the case of many "One Of" values, for
example). Then, the FieldRangeFilterItem object is added to the Filter object's FilterItems
collection. Since there is only one primitive expression in this situation, no additional
FieldRangeFilterItems objects, or any OperatorFilterItem objects, are added. Finally,
two controllers are used to modify the existing filter in the report with this new one.

Again, be patient when you attempt to follow this logic and object model approach
to record selection—it takes time to make complete sense of it.

Controlling Groups

You may also find a need to change, remove, or add report grouping within your RAS
code. This is a fairly straightforward process (at least once you've mastered the general
Model/View/Controller approach of "get the existing information from the Model,
update it, and update the report via a Controller").

Examine the following sample code:

```
'Create a new group
Dim NewGroup
Set NewGroup = oClientDoc.DataDefinition.Groups(0).Clone
```

First, declare an object to hold a single object from the DataDefinition object's Groups collection. The Clone method can then be used to copy an existing group object, including all its current properties and values, from the report.

Next, add the new field you wish to base the group on:

```
'Set the field that will define how data is grouped.
NewGroup.ConditionField = _
oClientDoc.Database.Tables.Item(0).DataFields.Item(12)
'Customer.Country is the 13th field in the first table
```

The group object's ConditionField property is set to the field that you wish to now base that group on. Note that additional information about the group, such as Specified Order and Date grouping information, is specified with SpecifiedGroupOptions and DateGroupOptions objects.

Somewhat new in RAS is the closer connection between grouping and sorting. If you wish to change the sort direction of the group (from ascending to descending), you must actually make this specification in a separate Sorts collection within the DataDefinition object.

In this example, you can now remove the existing group and add the newly defined group object in its place, using controllers:

```
'Remove the existing group
oClientDoc.DataDefController.GroupController.Remove 0

'Add the new group to the end of the groups collection
oClientDoc.DataDefController.GroupController.Add -1, NewGroup
```

The Remove method removes an existing group, taking one parameter: the zero-based index of the group to remove. Then, the Add method is executed to add the new group to the report. The Add method takes two parameters: the location in the Groups collection where you wish the new group to be placed (–1 adds to the end of the collection, making it the innermost group) and the group object to add.

Caution   *At the time of this book's printing, the GroupController's Modify method did not operate properly, requiring that an existing group be removed and a new group added in its place (as the preceding code illustrates). While this does, in fact, change the grouping, it also removes any summary or subtotal objects from the group footer, as well as the group name field from the group header. When the process is complete, you have a properly grouped report, but no objects in the group header or footer. While you could take this approach and then programmatically add new objects into these sections, you may find an alternative way of changing grouping without destroying all group header/footer objects to be more palatable. The sample RAS application from www.CrystalBook.com instead modifies a formula that the report group is based on.*

Modifying Parameter Fields

Probably one of the most common requirements of integrating Crystal Reports into custom applications is supplying parameter field values from within your code. Again, following the "get data from the model, update, change the report with controller" approach, this is straightforward.

Examine the following code gleaned from the sample application from www.CrystalBook.com:

```
'Copy existing parameter to NewParam object
Set NewParam = oClientDoc.DataDefinition.ParameterFields(0).Clone
```

Use the DataDefinition object's ParameterFields collection to get the value and properties (data type, and so on) of an existing parameter field. This is accomplished with the Clone method, which creates a "mirror-image" object from the desired parameter field.

Depending on the type of parameter field (discrete value, range value, multivalue), you'll need to create an additional object to hold the parameter field's value, as in:

```
'Create new "DiscreteValue" object to hold new parameter's value
Set NewValue = _
objFactory.CreateObject("CrystalReports.ParameterFieldDiscreteValue")
```

In this case, a discrete (single) value is required for this parameter field, which is used to calculate a sales tax rate within the report. The NewValue object is created by calling the Object Factory's CreateObject method.

Then, you need to supply the actual value to the NewValue object.

```
If Trim(Request.Form("txtTaxRate")) = "" Then
    NewValue.Value = 0
Else
    NewValue.Value = CDbl(Request.Form("txtTaxRate"))
End If  'Request.Form("txtTaxRate") = ""
```

In this example, an If-Then-Else construct is used to set the Value property of the DiscreteValue object, based on a control on the originating Web form.

Tip   *Notice how VBScript's CDbl typecast function is used when setting the Value property of the NewValue object. It's important in RAS to ensure that data is properly typed when supplying it to RAS properties. Use VBScripts typecasting functions, such as CStr and CDbl, to ensure this.*

Before actually updating the report with the new parameter field, you must add the DiscreteValue object to the actual parameter field object, as in:

```
'Set the new value for the parameter
NewParam.CurrentValues.Add(NewValue)
```

Execute the parameter field object's CurrentValues collection's Add method, supplying the parameter field value object created earlier (it may be a discrete value, a range value, or a multivalue object, depending on how it was originally defined).
Then, actually update the report with the new parameter field object.

```
'Modify the first parameter field with the NewParam object
oClientDoc.DataDefController.ParameterFieldController.Modify 0, NewParam
```

As in previous examples, you must use a controller to actually modify the report. In this case, the ParameterFieldController's Modify method will, in essence, replace the parameter field specified in the first argument with the parameter field object supplied via the second argument.

Changing Report Formulas

Another way of performing many run-time modifications to a report, in addition to or instead of using parameter fields, is modifying report formulas within your code. RAS continues the "get from model, update, modify with controller" approach to formula modifications.
Examine the following sample code:

```
'Copy the first existing Formula
Set NewFormula = oClientDoc.DataDefinition.FormulaFields(0).Clone

'Set text of new formula
NewFormula.Text = chr(34) & SelectionText & chr(34)

'Update first formula in report with new formula
oClientDoc.DataDefController.FormulaFieldController.Modify 0, NewFormula
```

Much as with parameter fields, an existing formula is extracted from the DataDefinition object FormulaFields collection using the Clone method. The new formula field object's Text property is changed to reflect the new desired formula (in the case of the preceding code, a variable set earlier in the code that simply contains literal text, surrounded by quotation marks). In this case, everything else about the formula remains as it was when originally cloned (field heading, syntax, and so on). If you wish to change these items, or if you are creating a new formula from scratch, you'll find other FormulaField object properties you can set, such as Syntax and HeadingText.

Viewing the Report

Once you've finished manipulating the ReportClientDocument, you need to display it to the viewer in the viewer's Web browser. As with the RDC, there are several viewing options available to you, depending on how much interactivity you wish to provide to the viewer, whether you'll be showing the entire report or just "report parts," and whether you still need the "completely integrated" solution provided by the ActiveX thin-client viewer.

Available RAS Viewers

As when using the Report Designer Component, you can use the "legacy" ActiveX and Java thin-client viewers with RAS. And in some cases, you'll find the best combination of performance, "true format" report viewing, and integrated functionality with these viewers. However, Crystal Decisions has been very creative in maximizing the use of DHTML (Dynamic Hypertext Markup Language) and a new COM object model in Crystal Reports 9 and RAS. This creativity, along with new Crystal Reports 9 "report part" capabilities, Office XP smart tags, and the advent of wireless Web technology (in Web-enabled cell phones and Personal Digital Assistants) has led Crystal Decisions to offer new HTML-based report viewers with RAS.

> **Note** *The terms "thin client," "thick client," and "zero client" are often confused when referring to an application's footprint. In the case of the RAS report viewers, this book refers to HTML-based viewers as "zero client" and ActiveX- or Java applet-based viewers as "thin client." This contrasts with "thick client," which the book considers to be a full-fledged, PC-based Windows application.*

Available report viewers for use in Active Server Pages include the following:

- **COM Report Page Viewer** This HTML-based viewer provides good "basic" report viewing capabilities, including the ability to export to another file format and print paginated text to your local printer, via a downloaded Portable Document Viewer file.

- **COM Interactive Viewer** This HTML-based viewer largely duplicates the features of the Report Page Viewer, while also adding a new "Boolean search" capability that allows a user to display a search "wizard" to apply sophisticated searching against the data in the report.

- **COM Report Part Viewer** This new HTML-based subset of the Report Page Viewer provides new "Report Part" capabilities to show only certain parts of a report (such as charts, text, and fields) in a browser. The Report Part Viewer is helpful when integrating Crystal Reports into portal applications when you desire only a specific part of a report to appear in a portal page. The Report Part Viewer can be further enhanced with special drill-down capabilities to allow a fuller view of a report part to be displayed when the report part is clicked.

■ **ActiveX Viewer**   A "legacy" report viewer also available with the RDC, this viewer displays "native" Crystal Reports formatting in a thin-client ActiveX control. The control allows exporting and printing to the locally attached printer without an intermediate .PDF file download. This viewer requires an ActiveX-capable browser, such as Microsoft Internet Explorer.

■ **Java Viewer**   Another "legacy" report viewer also available with the RDC, this viewer displays "native" Crystal Reports formatting in a thin-client Java applet. The applet allows exporting and printing to the locally attached printer without an intermediate .PDF file download. This viewer requires a Java-capable browser, such as Netscape Navigator, or a locally installed Java Virtual Machine.

| Tip | *Look at the online Developers Guide or the COM Viewer SDK Help file installed with RAS for a more complete comparison of individual capabilities of each of these browsers.* |

Passing a Report to the Viewer

There are several ways of viewing a report with one of the available report viewers. For example, you may wish to refer back to the beginning of this RAS section of the book for an example of a simple Crystal Decisions–supplied ASP that accepts a report filename as a URL parameter for viewing. Also, Crystal Decisions supplies some simple viewing ASPs that can be "redirected to" from your ASP code to view reports. Look for these ASPs (such as CrystalReportInteractiveViewer.ASP) in Program Files\ Crystal Decisions\Report Application Server 9\Samples\<*language*>\ASP\Migration.

Using one of these supplied viewer ASPs, viewing a report object that you've modified with the RAS SDK is as simple as the following code (and even simpler if you don't choose to control display of the Group Tree):

```
'Call the viewer to display the new report
Session("GroupTree") = Request.Form("chkGroupTree")
Set Session("oClientDoc") = oClientDoc
Response.Redirect("CrystalReportInteractiveViewer.ASP")
```

In the preceding code fragment, a session variable is set that copies the value of a control on the original HTML form indicating whether the end user wants to see the group tree or not. A session object variable is next created to contain the ReportClientDocument that has already been manipulated as described earlier in the chapter. Then, control is redirected to the CrystalReportInteractiveViewer.ASP file, which follows:

```
'Define ObjectFactory
Dim ObjectFactory
```

```
Set ObjectFactory = CreateObject("CrystalReports.ObjectFactory.2")

'Call the viewer to display the new report
Set HTMLViewer = _
ObjectFactory.CreateObject("CrystalReports.CrystalReportInteractiveViewer")
```

The first step (as described earlier in the chapter) is to declare an ObjectFactory object to control "versioning" of subsequent object definitions. This ObjectFactory capability extends to the COM Viewer SDK, as well as the RAS SDK. Then, a new object is created via the ObjectFactory CreateObject method, using the CrystalReportsInteractiveViewer class from the COM Viewer SDK. This is the instance of the COM Interactive Viewer described previously.

The Interactive Viewer includes the capability of providing a sophisticated search option to the end user. To provide this, an additional BooleanSearchControl object must be created and defined, as demonstrated in this code fragment:

```
Set BoolSearchControl = _
ObjectFactory.CreateObject("CrystalReports.BooleanSearchControl")
BoolSearchControl.EnableSelectFieldsPage = true
BoolSearchControl.EnableFormulaBuildPage = true
BoolSearchControl.ReportDocument = Session("oClientDoc")
HTMLViewer.BooleanSearchControl = BoolSearchControl
```

Here, the ObjectFactory is once again used to create a BooleanSearchControl object (another class available in the COM Viewer SDK). Several properties of this object are set, and then the object is supplied to the Viewer object's BooleanSearchControl property.

Finally, the report is viewed with the following code:

```
With HTMLViewer
    .ReportSource = session("oClientDoc").ReportSource
    .Name = "Crystal Reports Preview"
    If session("GroupTree") = "ON" Then
        .IsDisplayGroupTree = True
    Else
        .IsDisplayGroupTree = False
    End If'session("GroupTree") = "ON"
End With

Response.Write(HTMLViewer.ProcessHTTPRequest(Request, Response, Session))
```

The Viewer object's ReportSource property is set to the ReportClientDocument session object variable that was set in the calling ASP. The Name property is used to differentiate between multiple Viewer objects in the same HTML page. And, the session variable indicating the user's desired group tree visibility is used to conditionally set the Viewer object's IsDisplayGroupTree property. Finally, a Response.Write statement routes the Viewer object's ProcessHTTPRequest method to actually render the report in HTML and return it to the browser. The three parameters being passed to this method are standard Active Server Page Request, Response, and Session objects. The resulting report looks similar to this inside a Web browser.

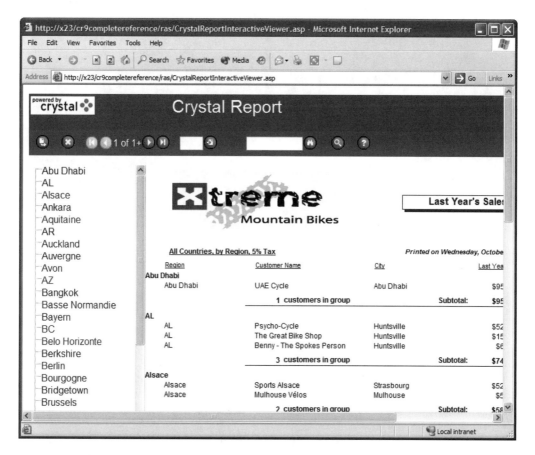

Because the COM Interactive Viewer was chosen and a BooleanSearchControl object was defined and supplied, an additional capability is available once this report has been viewed. By clicking the "Show/Hide Advanced Search Wizard" link at the top of the viewer (you'll often need to scroll the bottom scroll bar all the way to the right to see this button), you are presented with the Advanced Search Wizard (enabled with the BooleanSearchControl object).

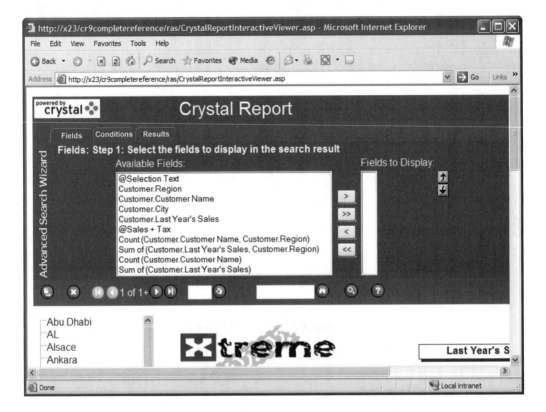

This wizard is designed to perform an additional detailed query on the data contained in the report. The wizard consists of three tabs: Fields, Conditions, and Results.

On the Fields tab, choose the result fields from the report that you wish to see in the query's resulting display. One or more fields can be selected by CTRL-clicking on the desired fields and then clicking the single right arrow (or all fields can be added with the double right arrow).

The Conditions tab is where the "Boolean" part of the search comes into play. Choose a particular field you wish to use to filter the report's data. Then, choose the search criterion in the Filter Type list. Finally, type in a value for the comparison in the Value text box. You may add more than one criterion by clicking the Add More Filters button, as well as typing in a Crystal Reports selection formula directly by clicking the Free Form button.

Once you've completed the Fields and Conditions tabs, click the Results tab. The resulting subset of the report data will appear in a small row/column grid at the top of the Interactive Viewer.

Chapter 22

Introduction to Crystal Enterprise

The Crystal Reports 8.5 release marked the introduction of a new Web-based report distribution system named Crystal Enterprise. Since that time, the new framework has gained wide acceptance as organizations large and small realize the benefits of Crystal Enterprise's scalability, security, and customization possibilities.

Caution	*As of the publication date of this book, Crystal Reports 9 does not work with the most recent release of Crystal Enterprise, version 8.5. In order to take advantage of Crystal Enterprise, you'll have to stick with Crystal Reports 8.5. Therefore, all material in this chapter refers to Crystal Reports 8.5 only. However, Crystal Reports 9 includes a "sneak preview" of some of the upcoming features of Crystal Enterprise 9. For more information on these features, and other Web delivery options with Crystal Reports 9, see Chapter 20.*

Crystal Enterprise Defined

As the World Wide Web has become not only a more integral part of consumer computing, but an important consideration for business computing platforms as well, Crystal Reports has continued to offer more and more Web-based reporting solutions as each new version is released. Version 7 featured the Web Access Server (WAS) for running reports in Web pages. Version 8 introduced a more robust version of the same feature called the Web Component Server (WCS). And, while Crystal Reports 8.5 eliminated the Web component server as a Crystal Reports–only Web solution, Active Server Pages and the Report Designer Component (discussed in Chapter 21), as well as basic HTML exports (discussed in more detail in Chapter 20) remained as Crystal Reports–only Web options. Crystal Reports 9 also includes new Web-based reporting features (such as the Report Application Server) to provide further Web-based reporting options. All of these options allow end users who wish to view reports to do so from within their Web browsers. A stand-alone copy of Crystal Reports or a custom Windows application integrating Crystal Reports is not required on each of the workstations. And, the workstations don't all have to have connectivity to the corporate database.

However, there was an increasing demand for more enterprise-oriented, high-capacity Web-reporting capabilities. As larger organizations looked more and more toward Web-based solutions, Crystal Decisions needed to move beyond the limited-user, Web-server-centric tools it had offered in the past for real-time Web reporting. Companies needed a reporting solution that would scale to potentially support hundreds, or even thousands, of Web-based report viewers.

While Crystal Decisions' existing Seagate Info multitier reporting tool does include a Web-based interface that can be used, Crystal Decisions elected to move toward one unified, enterprise-oriented reporting and analysis architecture. Crystal Enterprise was the first example of the new Crystal Decisions direction.

The Two-Tier Web Reporting Method

Crystal Reports 7.0 and 8.0 included a limited Web server–based reporting system that could be described as *two-tier architecture* (and the Version 9 ASP/RDC solution described in Chapter 21 still adheres to this architecture). The basic premise of this architecture is to route the report viewing audience through a Web browser and Web server, rather than placing an individual copy of Crystal Reports or a Crystal Reports–based custom application on each user PC. Only the Web server requires connectivity to the corporate database for ad hoc reporting. This architecture is illustrated in Figure 22-1.

Note *Yes, the argument could be made that the architecture being described here is in fact a three-tier architecture—Web browser to Web server to database. However, by basically moving all of the previous client-based processing to the Web server and transforming clients to simple viewer status, the previous two-tier client/server architecture is just being moved around. It can still be argued that in the typical database/query client/server model, the Web server has become the client and the database remains the server.*

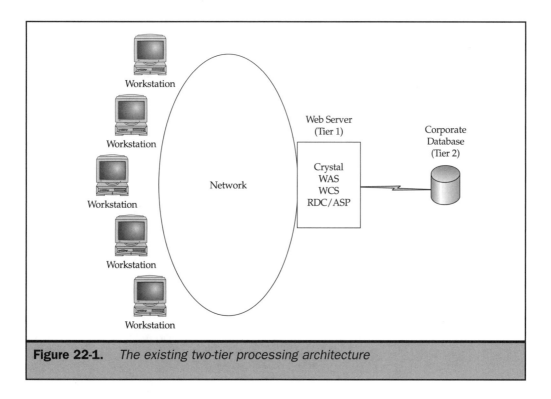

Figure 22-1. *The existing two-tier processing architecture*

By centralizing this approach via the Web, much reduced software maintenance on client-side computers is required. Not only do new versions of reports or reporting systems not require any new software to be installed on individual client computers (only the Web pages that compose the application need to be updated on the Web server), but the application can now support multiple computing platforms, such as Windows-based PCs, Apple Macintosh, and Unix and Linux workstations. As long as a compatible Web browser can be used, Crystal Reports can be viewed on a computer or workstation.

Crystal Enterprise Multitier Reporting Method

While the existing architecture just described is an overall improvement beyond the classic client/server computing model of an application on a client with a network connection to a server, there are still bottlenecks and disadvantages that limit this architecture's capacity for large reporting environments. In particular:

■ The Web server suddenly becomes a concentrated reporting and query client instead of the Web page distribution server it's designed to be. Every request for an ad hoc report requires the Web server to send a query to the database, wait for a result set, and format the result set before sending the report back to a Web browser.

■ The network connection between the Web server and the database can become overloaded, depending on the types of queries and reports that the Web server submits to the database and the size of the return result sets.

■ There is limited sharing or caching of report requests (particularly for ad hoc real-time reports). If 25 users request the same report, the Web server oftentimes will have to submit the report's query to the database 25 times.

■ Earlier Crystal Reports Web systems do not allow reports to be automatically scheduled to run at regular intervals, such as once per day, once per month, and so on.

The answer to these inherent limitations of existing Crystal Web reporting alternatives lies in the new Crystal Enterprise multitier report processing architecture, as illustrated in Figure 22-2. Built largely on the existing multitier structure of the Crystal Decisions Seagate Info reporting product, this multitier structure is new to the Crystal Reports user. By creating multiple software functions and creating the ability for them to be rolled out or "scaled" to multiple processors, Crystal Enterprise immediately offers a dramatic improvement in reliability, load capability, and fault tolerance. The Web server can return to its core requirement to serve up Web pages. Additional components now work together to run ad hoc report and query requests, schedule automatically recurring reports, convert completed reports pages to "page-on-demand" viewing files, handle security, and cache recently reviewed report pages for delivery to the next report viewer. The result is a completely scalable multitier structure that dramatically improves the capabilities and capacity of Web-based reporting.

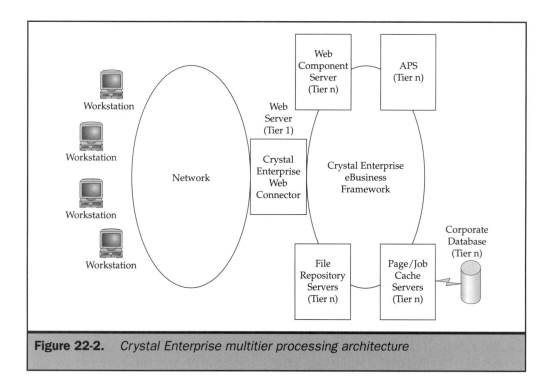

Figure 22-2. *Crystal Enterprise multitier processing architecture*

CRYSTAL REPORTS 9
ON THE WEB

Note *Complete discussions of the different server components shown in Figure 22-2 are found in the "Crystal Enterprise Architecture" section later in this chapter.*

Standard Edition 8 Versus Professional Edition 8.5

Comparing versions of Crystal Enterprise can be a challenge, especially with the introduction of Crystal Reports 9 and the Report Application Server. Crystal Enterprise was initially included as a "free bundle" with Crystal Reports 8.5. As of this publication, Crystal Enterprise (which was initially released at Version 8.0) is available in two versions: Crystal Enterprise 8 Standard Edition and Crystal Enterprise 8.5 Professional Edition. If you received the Crystal Enterprise CD bundled with your copy of Crystal Reports 8.5, you received Crystal Enterprise 8 Standard Edition. Standard Edition is designed to handle a low-capacity, simple Web-based reporting environment. It might be considered a "light" version of the full Crystal Enterprise product, limited in expandability and capacity. While you can purchase additional user licenses for Crystal Enterprise Standard, you'll need to upgrade to Crystal Enterprise Professional 8.5 to gain the full benefit of Crystal Enterprise's multitier scaled server technology. But be prepared—the upgrade pricing is steep, and you'll most likely find yourself working to justify the investment. (To upgrade, you'll need to contact Crystal Decisions or a limited set of key resellers, as Crystal Enterprise is not for sale in the same retail channel as Crystal Reports.)

There are several significant differences between the features offered in Standard Edition versus Professional Edition. These differences revolve around several core feature areas:

- User capacity
- Security capabilities
- Fault tolerance
- Server scaling

User Capacity

Crystal Enterprise Standard is limited to a five-user concurrent licensing structure. This basically means that any five users can be using the tool at the same time. The sixth user that attempts to log in will receive a message indicating all licenses are in use. While you can purchase additional Standard Edition licenses, Crystal Enterprise Professional, on the other hand, features a wide array of licensing options that you may choose. You may purchase combinations of concurrent licenses, named-user licenses, or processor licenses.

Additional concurrent user licenses allow any user to log in to the system, provided that the total number of users logged in at any one time doesn't exceed the concurrent user limit. Named user licenses allow users with specific user IDs that belong to them to log in at any time, regardless of how many other users are currently logged in. And, processor-based licenses are dependent upon the number of computers or "processors" that are required to implement a Crystal Enterprise system. The proper type and number of licenses will depend entirely on how many users you need to support, what capabilities they need to have, and how often and how long they'll need to use Enterprise. Study and consider these varying options carefully, so you'll have the proper number of licenses for all potential user combinations, without undertaking extra expense that may be incurred for an "overkill" license structure.

Security Capabilities

Crystal Enterprise Standard supports only two user IDs: Administrator and Guest. The Administrator user should be limited to the person(s) in charge of maintaining the system and publishing reports (the Guest user account can't publish reports). The Guest account is for shared use among all the concurrent users (again, of which any five can be connected at the same time). All Guest users will have the same privileges and will be able to see the same folders and reports. And, Crystal Enterprise Standard will not integrate with the Windows NT or Windows 2000 security system, or with an LDAP security scenario—it maintains its own security separate from any existing operating system or network security.

Crystal Enterprise Professional allows creation of as many user IDs as necessary (based on named-user licenses that are purchased). In fact, the Professional Edition even allows users to create *their own* accounts by clicking a link in ePortfolio (discussed in Chapter 23).

In the Professional Edition, users may be assigned to varying *user groups,* each of which is given varying rights and capabilities. Certain groups, for example, can be given the right to publish reports to ePortfolio or schedule reports on a recurring basis. Other groups, however, may only be able to view reports that have already been published and scheduled by others.

Crystal Enterprise Professional 8.5 allows three choices of user security: Enterprise Authentication, Windows NT/2000 Authentication, or LDAP Authentication. With Enterprise Authentication, separate user IDs and passwords are maintained in the Enterprise system database. When a user logs in with Enterprise Authentication, that user must specify a separate user ID and password from any existing ID/password combination he or she may have already used to log in to Windows. However, the Professional Edition allows creation of a specific Windows NT/2000 account group that will interface directly with the Enterprise system database. A user's Windows NT/2000 user ID and password can then be automatically checked against this account group to verify Crystal Enterprise authority. This negates the need for users to specify a separate user ID and password from those they've already used to log in to Windows—they may simply supply their Windows domain name and user ID at the sign-on prompt. Finally, LDAP Authentication may also be used. Crystal Enterprise supports several of the major directory servers "out-of-the-box" (including iPlanet Directory Server, Novell Directory Server, Domino Directory Server and IBM SecureWay), while others are supported with custom mapping into Crystal Enterprise.

| Tip | *Another feature of Crystal Enterprise Professional is Windows NT/2000 Single Sign-On. This allows users to connect directly to the Crystal Enterprise ePortfolio without having to specify any additional user ID or password at all—the user's Windows NT/2000 ID and password are passed on automatically by their Web browser. This feature requires that users connect to Crystal Enterprise through a Microsoft Internet Information Server (IIS) Web server, as well as requiring use of Microsoft Internet Explorer as their Web browser. Get more information on the particular procedures for enabling this feature by viewing the Crystal Enterprise Administrator's Guide (available from the Crystal Enterprise Launchpad). Click the Index tab and search for "NT Single Sign On, setting up."* |

Fault Tolerance

Crystal Enterprise Standard does not allow the creation of fault-tolerant server platforms. Only a single set of components can reside on a single computer. Should the Enterprise computer fail, the entire Crystal Enterprise system will be inaccessible. However, this eliminates one of the major benefits of the Crystal Enterprise architecture—its multitier, multiserver technology.

Crystal Enterprise Professional restores this capability, in particular the ability to set up multiple Automated Process Scheduler (APS) machines that back each other up and provide processing scalability (the APS is described in more detail in the Crystal Enterprise Architecture section of this chapter). Should one APS machine fail, the remaining machines will pick up the extra load and continue to process Crystal Enterprise requests. And, when a large processor load is required, multiple APS machines will share that load as necessary, enabling a very large user base to be supported. The *clustering* of APS computers is provided only by Crystal Enterprise Professional.

Server Scaling

As described previously, one of the main benefits of Crystal Enterprise over the previous single-server approach of the Crystal Reports Web component server is the ability to spread the processing load across multiple "tiers." Instead of one computer having to process all report and query processes, report formatting, and HTML page generation, Crystal Enterprise Professional allows these functions to be spread over several computers. Crystal Enterprise Standard, while adhering to this multitier software structure, still requires that all these software components reside on a single physical computer. The only exception is that the Web connector (described in more detail in the architecture section of the chapter) can reside on a Web server separately from the remaining Crystal Enterprise components.

Crystal Enterprise Professional Edition, however, allows each software component or "tier," or any combination of components, to reside on separate personal computers on the network. In a very large Enterprise environment, it might be desirable to have each individual software component—such as the APS, the input file repository server, the output file repository server, the cache server, the page server, and the Web component server—reside on a separate computer on the network. In a high-volume implementation, you might even need to set up multiple computers that share the same responsibility (multiple physical APS machines in a cluster, for example), to satisfy the load requirements of your particular Crystal Enterprise system.

Crystal Enterprise Architecture

Crystal Enterprise is a monumental change from the previous single-server approach of the Crystal Reports Web component server. As discussed previously in this chapter, one of the huge benefits of Crystal Enterprise over earlier tools is its multitier, multiserver approach to Web reporting. By spreading the processing load over multiple software and hardware layers, much higher numbers of users and much better sustained performance can be expected.

If you are an end user of Crystal Enterprise, there are several software components that you may encounter as you view reports. Depending on your particular Enterprise implementation, you may also be required to design, publish, and schedule reports as well. You'll want to be familiar with the different components that are required to use Enterprise in these various ways. If you are a Crystal Enterprise administrator who is responsible for installing, maintaining, and supporting Crystal Enterprise, you'll not only want to be familiar with the end-user tools available to your user community, but also the particular server components, communications methods, and administrative tools available for your use.

End-User Components for Reporting

As a Web-based reporting tool, Crystal Enterprise provides interaction almost entirely within a Web browser. If you are using a Windows PC, an Apple Macintosh, or a Unix/ Linux workstation, all you need to work with the majority of Crystal Enterprise features is a standard Web browser (a newer browser that supports HTML Version 4 and JavaScript is required). The only exception to the Web browser rule is for designing reports—Crystal Reports 8.5 is used to design reports and must run in a Windows environment. And, there are several ways of publishing reports to Crystal Enterprise. One way, the Crystal-supplied Crystal Publishing Wizard, is also a Windows-only program.

Caution   *Crystal Reports 9 is not compatible with Crystal Enterprise 8.0 or 8.5. The new .RPT file format of version 9 cannot be read by older Enterprise versions. You'll need to use techniques discussed in Chapters 20 and 21, or wait for the release of the next version of Crystal Enterprise to make use of Crystal Reports 9 reports in Crystal Enterprise.*

As an end user, you'll normally start using Crystal Enterprise from one of two places: the Crystal Launchpad or ePortfolio. Both are Web pages that can be viewed by pointing your browser to a standard location specified by your Crystal Enterprise administrator. Because Crystal Enterprise is Web-based, it's entirely possible to customize the Web interface to it. Your organization may still use the standard locations for Enterprise pages (but may have customized the pages), or it may have created an entirely customized interface (such as an internal intranet or portal) that interfaces with Crystal Enterprise.

If you wish to add newly designed Crystal Reports to ePortfolio, you can use either the Crystal Management Console (discussed in the "Server and Maintenance Components for Administrators" section later in this chapter) or the Windows-based Crystal Publishing Wizard.

Crystal Launchpad and ePortfolio

The Crystal Launchpad is the beginning point for Crystal Enterprise usage. It is simply a home page where you may navigate to other portions of Crystal Enterprise—there are no functional capabilities on the Launchpad itself. From the Launchpad, you may click links to online documentation, to ePortfolio, to the Crystal Management Console, and to Developer Samples that demonstrate customized Crystal Enterprise pages.

You may click the ePortfolio link on the Launchpad, or type in the location (known in Web parlance as a Universal Resource Locator, or URL) of ePortfolio to display the actual starting point for Crystal Enterprise report viewing.

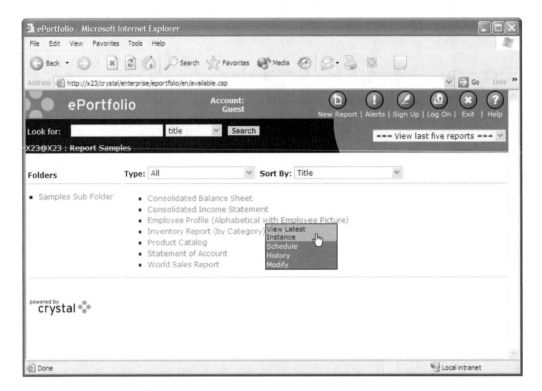

From ePortfolio, you can create a new user account, log on as a different user, navigate through report folders, view reports and report alerts, and schedule reports to run on a recurring basis. ePortfolio may appear identical to the preceding illustration, or it may have been modified to more closely align with your organization's standard Web look and feel.

Customized Web Interface

ePortfolio is a Crystal Decisions–designed interface to Crystal Enterprise. Based on Crystal Server Pages (discussed in detail in Chapter 24), all ePortfolio source code is provided for perusal and modification. You may modify the existing ePortfolio to more closely match your standard Web interface, or create a completely new set of Web pages to expose Crystal Enterprise features. If a customized intranet page or portal has been created, your administrator may give you a completely different URL to launch your Crystal Enterprise system.

Crystal Publishing Wizard

Depending on how responsibilities for maintaining your Crystal Enterprise system are divided within your organization, you may need the ability to post reports you've designed with Crystal Reports 8.5 to your Crystal Enterprise system. There are two ways to accomplish this: using the Crystal Management Console (discussed in the "Server and Maintenance Components for Administrators" section of this chapter) or the Crystal Publishing Wizard (outlined in Chapter 23).

The Crystal Publishing Wizard provides certain advantages over the Crystal Management Console and is designed to be easier to use overall. This is a Windows program that does require installation on your individual computer from a Windows Setup routine.

Note   *More detailed information on connecting to and using the Crystal Launchpad, ePortfolio, and Crystal Publishing Wizard can be found in Chapter 23.*

Server and Maintenance Components for Administrators

Crystal Enterprise's multitier architecture lends itself to a much more flexible, higher-capacity system for Web reporting. It also lends itself to more complexity when it comes to initial setup, operation, and administration. This increased complexity comes, in large part, from the increased number of components that make up the server portion (or "back end") of Crystal Enterprise. While an Enterprise end user simply sees Web pages that allow scheduling and viewing of reports, there are many separate components working together to provide this capability to the user.

Crystal Enterprise has two general types of components that a Crystal Enterprise administrator will be concerned with: back-end servers and administrative tools. The various server components that make up Crystal Enterprise share the overall processing requirements of Enterprise, passing information among themselves as required. The administrative tools (both Web-and Windows-based) are used by administrators to control and customize Crystal Enterprise behavior.

Servers

Administrators of Crystal Decisions' other multitier reporting system, Seagate Info, will see many similarities between Crystal Enterprise server architecture and Seagate Info server architecture—Crystal Enterprise architecture was borrowed from Seagate Info. However, if you are in charge of administering Enterprise and this is your first experience with a multiserver configuration, there is much to learn about how all these different server components work together and pass information back and forth.

In order for Crystal Enterprise to potentially support up to thousands of Web users, a great deal of processing power must be available for peak processing loads. The idea behind the Enterprise multiserver architecture is to spread that processing load around. Different server components have limited functionality—some are designed to run reports against a corporate database, and others have as their sole purpose to keep track of already viewed report pages, while others keep track of security and report scheduling. Determining how many different computers to use for back-end processing and which components to place on those computers is largely dependent on your individual system and where you think the largest processing loads will be. By studying the remainder of this chapter, by consulting documentation accompanying Crystal Enterprise, and by pure experimentation, you'll eventually be able to determine the proper delineation of server resources. And, you may always move components around or "scale out" if you need to—you may initially start with all components running on one physical computer, but later split servers out to multiple processors as your capacity needs increase.

Note *Don't forget that Crystal Enterprise Standard Edition included with Crystal Reports 8.5 is a low-volume solution designed for small production implementations or for evaluation prior to a Crystal Enterprise Professional upgrade. Crystal Enterprise Standard requires all back-end server components to reside on a single physical computer (the only exception being the ability to place the Web connector on a Web server separate from the remaining server components). To gain full flexibility in loading server components on separate physical computers, you'll need to upgrade to Crystal Enterprise Professional.*

APS   The Automated Process Scheduler, or APS, is the heart of Crystal Enterprise. Every other component communicates through the APS (the APS acts as a name server, keeping track of the locations and statuses of the other server components). The APS also acts as the central security point for Crystal Enterprise login—all user IDs, passwords, and rights lists are maintained on the APS. And, the APS also keeps track of report scheduling. If a report is scheduled to automatically run every day at midnight, the APS sets the report processing cycle in motion at the prescribed time.

Because the APS is so critical to the operation of Crystal Enterprise (the entire system is completely "dead in the water" without it), Enterprise provides for fault tolerance and increased processing capacity with *APS clustering*. With APS clustering, multiple physical computers can run as APS servers. Sharing a common system database hosted on a standard server platform, such as Microsoft SQL Server, Oracle, or Informix, all APS machines appear as one *logical* APS to the entire Crystal Enterprise system. They share processing load, sending processing requests to the least-busy machine in the cluster. If one machine should fail, the remaining APS machines pick up the load and continue to operate—the end user will not even know that one of the APS machines has failed.

Web Component Server/Web Connector   The Web component server, or WCS, bears little functional resemblance to the component with the same name in Crystal Reports 8.0. The WCS is the "front line" component of Crystal Enterprise, intercepting all initial requests for Enterprise Web pages and reports from the Web Connector and Web server. The WCS also processes the Crystal Server Page scripting language (covered in detail in Chapter 24) to allow complete customization of the Crystal Enterprise user interface in a Web browser.

The Web Connector is the actual Crystal Enterprise component that resides on the Web server. By moving other Crystal Enterprise components to their own servers and leaving the Web server to its preferred task of communicating with Web browsers, Crystal Enterprise can achieve much higher levels of performance without bogging down the Web server. The Web Connector passes information to and from the WCS, which then communicates among other Enterprise servers to process Web page display, Crystal Server Page script interpretation, report viewing, and other Enterprise functions.

The other benefit Crystal Enterprise derives from placing a very small demand on the Web server is cross-platform Web server support. By minimizing the software footprint on the Web server, Crystal Decisions has been able to support many popular Web servers running on both Windows NT and Unix platforms. While the other back-end servers require Windows NT/2000 to run, there are several Web Connectors that expand Web server support to other platforms.

The following Web Connectors are included with Crystal Enterprise:

- Microsoft Internet Information Server (IIS) running on Windows NT/2000
- Netscape Enterprise or Fast Track Server running on Windows NT/2000
- Lotus Domino running on Windows NT/2000

- Apache, Linux, Solaris (and other servers compliant with Apache Dynamic Shared Objects) running on Unix

- Any Common Gateway Interface (CGI) Web server running on Windows NT/2000 or Unix

Tip   *Complete descriptions and installation steps for all Web Connectors can be found in the online or printed Crystal Enterprise Installation Guide.*

File Repository Servers   As Crystal Enterprise reporting is based on Crystal Reports, procedures for handling the Crystal .RPT files that are published, scheduled, and viewed must be established. This is where the file repository servers come in. These servers store .RPT files that can be viewed on demand and .RPT files that are to be scheduled on a regular basis (perhaps every night, every week, and so on), as well as the finished copies of scheduled reports—the .RPT files with saved data that can be viewed after they've successfully run.

There are actually two different file repository servers (and there can be only one of each in Crystal Enterprise—you can't have multiple copies of these servers running in one Enterprise system). The *input* file repository server is where Crystal Report .RPT files are stored after they've been published with Crystal Reports 8.5, the Crystal Publishing Wizard, the Crystal Management Console, or the Crystal Import Wizard.

When a request is received to view a published report on demand, or when the APS runs a scheduled report on a regular basis, the input file repository server is queried for a copy of the .RPT file to run.

The *output* file repository server keeps all the finished .RPT files with saved data (known as report *instances*) that result from reports that are scheduled by the APS on a regular basis. When an end user wishes to view a report instance, the other Crystal Enterprise components query the APS, which keeps track of report instances in the output file repository server. The .RPT file with saved data is transferred from this server to other components for caching and HTML formatting, eventually appearing in the end user's Web browser.

Job Server and Page Server   Of all the servers that compose a Crystal Enterprise system, only two actually require connectivity to the corporate database: the job server and the page server. Both of these servers need to connect to the database to actually run Crystal Reports that have been published. The difference between the job server and the page server is the group of .RPT files each is dedicated to running.

The job server is dedicated to running reports that are scheduled by the APS. Only reports that run on a regular basis (every day, every week, the first day of the month, and so forth) are submitted to the job server. When the APS needs to schedule a report to run, it passes the request on to the job server. The job server obtains the .RPT file to run from the input file repository server, actually connects to the database to run the report, and sends the completed report instance (an .RPT file with saved data) to the output file repository server.

The page server is dedicated to two tasks: creating EPF files and running on-demand .RPT files. This first task comes into play whenever an end user requests to view a completed report. The page server communicates with the cache server and may be asked to create individual page image files (known as encapsulated page files, or EPF files) that are stored by the cache server and delivered to the end user one page at a time. This "page-on-demand" architecture has been a cornerstone of Crystal Reports performance for several versions. This way, if a report actually encompasses several hundred pages, only the page requested by the viewer will be sent across to the Web browser.

The other task given to the page server is the processing of *on-demand* reports. On-demand reports differ from reports scheduled by the APS on a regular basis, which are handled by the job server. While the automatic scheduling of reports is a very powerful feature of Crystal Enterprise, certain reporting environments require near-instantaneous access to a current set of data. In these situations, the page server is used to run reports against the database whenever a user requests them. By utilizing both on-demand and scheduled reports (and by dedicating servers to each), Crystal Enterprise can satisfy a broad mix of regular production reporting needs versus on-demand ad hoc reporting needs.

Tip *Depending on how your Crystal Enterprise system will be used, you may find processing bottlenecks occur on the job server or page server. If you schedule a great number of large reports to run on a regular basis, and many of these scheduled reports run at the same time, you may find the need to add additional job servers to your Enterprise system. However, if your primary crunch is on-demand reports, or viewing a large number of reports (which requires a large amount of EPF generation), you'll want to consider adding additional page servers to your Enterprise system.*

Cache Server   As discussed earlier in the chapter, one of the benefits of Crystal Enterprise (and of several versions of Crystal Reports before it) is page-on-demand architecture. This approach to delivering report pages to the end user's Web browser significantly improves performance, especially with larger reports that comprise many pages. The page-on-demand process will deliver only the page of a report that a viewer currently needs to see. When a report is first viewed, only page 1 is delivered to the viewer. If, for example, the viewer then clicks an entry in the group tree that requires page 210 of the report to be delivered, only page 210 is sent to the browser—pages 2–209 are ignored.

As discussed previously, part of this page-on-demand process is the creation of EPFs, which is handled by the page server. The other very important part of this process, however, is storing already-viewed EPFs for later reuse (known as "caching"). This process is handled by the cache server. The cache server and the Web component server communicate very closely with each other. When the Web component server requests that a particular report page be sent to the browser, the cache server keeps track of pages that may have already been viewed (and that are already cached). If the cache server can find an already generated EPF, it simply sends it for viewing.

If the cache server needs the EPF to be generated (a user, for example, has asked for a report page that hasn't been viewed previously), it asks the page server to generate the EPF, which it then caches and sends to the Web component server.

Event Server   Crystal Enterprise 8.5 Professional Edition brought with it the debut of a new server designed to offer more powerful and integrated scheduling. Previously, reports could be scheduled to run at specific times on specific days. The Event Server makes it possible to generate a report upon a particular event such as the creation of a file, the completion of another report run, or the manual clicking of a button.

The Event Server manages the creation, maintenance, and monitoring of the various events. There are three types of events: a file event, which is triggered upon the creation or modification of a specific file; a schedule event, which is triggered upon the completion of a report run; and a custom event, which may be triggered manually by an administrator in the Crystal Management Console.

These events can be used in combination to create very sophisticated scheduling. For example, an organization may want to make sure the data is ready before running a group of reports, which would then need to be run as efficiently as possible. A mainframe database synchronization job could be set up to create a specific file at the end of the script. A file event could be set up to trigger an event when that file is created. The first report to be processed would wait for that event, then run. A schedule event could also be set up to trigger upon the completion of that report's processing, whether it succeeded or failed. That in turn could trigger the processing of the second report, and so on and so forth through all of that night's reports.

Note	*All Crystal Enterprise server components, with the exception of the Web Connector (which can run on certain Unix Web servers as well as Windows NT/2000 Web servers), run only on Windows NT or 2000 platforms as "NT services." While you can view reports from within any Web browser on any Windows platform (or other platforms that supply Web browsers), you cannot use Windows 9x or ME to run any of the Crystal Enterprise server components. Also, Crystal Enterprise 8.5 Professional has introduced Sun Solaris support for most "back-end" server components. You may now mix and match Solaris and Windows NT/Windows 2000 computers to implement your Crystal Enterprise system.*

Crystal Management Console

The Crystal Management Console is the first of several administrative software interfaces to Crystal Enterprise. Because the Crystal Management Console is Web-based, you can run it on any computer on the network that has a Web browser. You don't need to run it on any of the physical components that make up Crystal Enterprise. You can even run it in a remote location from the Internet, provided your internal network security allows an outside browser to navigate to the proper location.

What Is the Crystal eBusiness Framework?

As you peruse marketing materials and documentation for Crystal Enterprise, you'll see frequent referrals to the *Crystal eBusiness Framework.* While you may have reached your limit of technological terms that start with the letter *e*, Crystal Decisions has elected to bestow this name upon its new communications infrastructure first introduced with Crystal Enterprise.

In general terms, the Crystal eBusiness Framework is the common communications structure that ties all the Crystal Enterprise components together. All the back-end servers described in this chapter communicate with each other through the eBusiness Framework. Custom Crystal Server Pages script used to create custom Web pages that expose Crystal Enterprise features includes software "hooks" to allow connection to the eBusiness Framework (Crystal Server Pages are covered in detail in Chapter 24). And, related software products that work in tandem with Crystal Enterprise, such as Crystal Reports 8.5 and Crystal Analysis Professional, all connect to the eBusiness Framework to publish reports, analyze data, or provide extra services and functions to existing Crystal products.

In technical terms, the Crystal eBusiness Framework is a communications layer based on the Transport Control Protocol/Internet Protocol, or TCP/IP (the network protocol that originated with the Internet and that has become the de facto networking standard for most corporate networks). Furthermore, the way servers are named and communicate within Enterprise revolves around the Common Object Request Broker Architecture, or CORBA.

This open standard for network communication is useful from several perspectives, the least of which is cross-platform support. The ability for Crystal Enterprise Windows-based components to work with Web Connectors on Unix is part of the CORBA benefit. The other benefit is ease of communications throughout the corporate network. Crystal Decisions' other multitier product, Seagate Info, doesn't use a CORBA communications framework. As such, difficulty often arises when one Seagate Info server needs to communicate with another inside a Windows network. If network security is not set up to support all the possible server communications paths, the system fails. The CORBA-based Crystal eBusiness Framework has eliminated many of these Windows-based security problems.

The Crystal Management Console can be chosen as a link from the Crystal Enterprise Launchpad, or navigated to directly with the following URL:

```
http://<web server>/crystal/enterprise/admin
```

The first step to take after starting the Crystal Management Console is to log in to the APS. Although most users will be able to successfully log in to the Crystal Management Console, only those with administrative privileges will be able to perform many of the functions offered by the tool. If they choose to perform a function that they're not authorized to complete, an error message will result.

After successfully logging in, you'll be presented with the main Crystal Management Console screen.

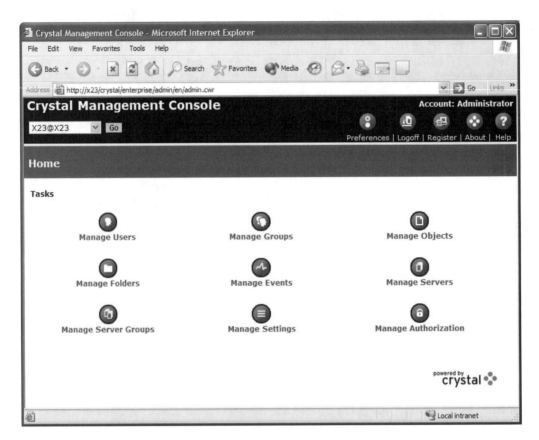

Here, administrative personnel can add and edit user IDs; organize users into user groups; change passwords and grant and deny rights to users; manage back-end servers; add, remove, and modify folders to logically organize reports; and add and remove reports in existing folders.

Tip   *More detailed information about all Crystal Management Console functions and capabilities can be found in the online or printed Crystal Enterprise Administrator's Guide.*

Upgrading to Crystal Enterprise Professional Edition

As described earlier in this chapter, many features of Crystal Enterprise are eliminated or "crippled" in the Crystal Enterprise Standard Edition that's included with Crystal Reports 8.5. To expand Crystal Enterprise beyond its initial limits, such as the inability to place back-end servers on multiple machines or create additional user IDs, requires an upgrade to Crystal Enterprise Professional Edition.

One of the places you'll probably discover the Standard Edition's limitations fairly quickly is when working with the Crystal Management Console. For example, because Crystal Enterprise Standard only allows the two default user IDs already included (Administrator and Guest), you'll immediately run into a limitation if you attempt to add or modify an additional user by clicking the Users link in the left frame of your browser window.

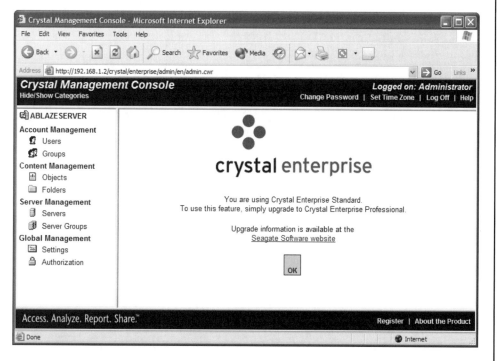

Contact Crystal Decisions or selected "Enterprise-authorized" resellers for pricing and options for Crystal Enterprise Professional. Once you have purchased the upgrade, you'll need to install the Enterprise 8.5 software from CD and add a new Professional Edition keycode.

Crystal Configuration Manager

Administrative tasks in Crystal Enterprise are split between the Web-based Crystal Management Console (discussed previously) and the Windows-based Crystal Configuration Manager. When you install a Crystal Enterprise component on a back-end server, you'll generally want to install the Crystal Configuration Manager on that machine as well (although you can connect to another server remotely with the Crystal Configuration Manager).

While some administrative tasks or viewing of certain server information can be accomplished from both the Crystal Management Console and Crystal Configuration Manager, more "global" management tasks, such as dealing with user IDs, folders, and reports, are accomplished with the Web-based Crystal Management Console. More technical administrative tasks, such as adjusting startup parameters, changing network port numbers, and migrating the APS system database to a SQL server to enable APS clustering, are accomplished with the Crystal Configuration Manager.

To start the Crystal Configuration Manager, click the Windows Start button and choose Crystal Configuration Manager from the Crystal Enterprise group. The Crystal Configuration Manager will appear.

To modify properties of any of the servers listed, double-click the desired server, highlight the server in the list, and click the Properties button in the toolbar. Or, you may right-click the name of the server and choose Properties from the pop-up menu. When you do so, a tabbed properties page for that server will appear.

As well as changing server properties, the Crystal Configuration Manager allows you to add additional servers to the Crystal Enterprise system, stop and start servers, disable particular servers, and configure Web Connectors.

> **Tip** *Many options for servers shown in the Properties dialog boxes can't be changed while the servers are running. First, stop the desired server using the Stop button in the Crystal Configuration Manager toolbar. Make changes to the server properties, and then restart the server. Of course, you'll want to make sure no critical processes or users are connected to the server before you stop and reconfigure it.*

Crystal Web Wizard

As mentioned earlier in this chapter, the Crystal Enterprise ePortfolio is the standard end-user Web interface to Crystal Enterprise. ePortfolio is designed entirely using standard HTML in conjunction with the Crystal Enterprise scripting language, Crystal Server Pages (CSP). Your organization may prefer to modify the existing ePortfolio to more closely match the standard look and feel of your company intranet. Or, you may wish to design a completely new user interface separate from the "out of the box" ePortfolio.

While you can write all necessary CSP code from scratch, Crystal Decisions has included the Windows-based Crystal Web Wizard to create a basic set of CSP pages based on responses to a few simple dialog boxes within the wizard. By using the Crystal Web Wizard, you can get a quick jump-start on custom Crystal Enterprise Web pages without tedious amounts of CSP coding. The Crystal Web Wizard is discussed in more detail in Chapter 24.

Crystal Import Wizard

If you are a user of Crystal Decisions' previously released multitier reporting system, Seagate Info, you may be considering a migration to the new Web-based Crystal Enterprise. Or, you may have set up an initial test version of Crystal Enterprise but wish to copy the existing set of user IDs, the same report and folder structure, and other characteristics to a newer production, Enterprise APS.

To prevent an administrator from having to manually reenter all Seagate Info or Crystal Enterprise information into a new Crystal Enterprise system, Crystal Decisions supplies the Crystal Import Wizard. The Crystal Import Wizard reads the contents of an existing Seagate Info version 6 or 7 APS database, or an existing Crystal Enterprise 8.0 or another 8.5 APS database.

It will then allow an administrator to choose which users, user groups, folders, and reports to automatically transfer to a new Crystal Enterprise APS database. When completed, the Crystal Import Wizard will have created a new Crystal Enterprise system that closely mirrors that of the previous Seagate Info or Enterprise system.

The Crystal Import Wizard is a Windows-based program that must be installed from the original program CD. Once it is installed, you may start the Crystal Import Wizard by clicking the Windows Start button and choosing Crystal Import Wizard from the Crystal Enterprise group. Perform the following basic steps to migrate an existing Seagate Info or Crystal Enterprise system to a new Crystal Enterprise APS:

1. Choose the existing APS that you wish to import from (you'll need to specify an Administrator user ID and password on the existing APS).

2. Then specify an Administrator user ID and password on a new Crystal Enterprise APS that you wish to migrate the existing system into.

3. Choose whether you want to import user IDs and user groups, as well as whether you want to import folders and reports.

4. If you chose to import users and groups, you'll be presented with a user group/user ID "Explorer-like" structure where you may choose the users and groups that you want to migrate.

5. If you chose to import folders and reports, you'll be presented with a folder/report "Explorer-like" structure where you may choose the folders and reports that you want to migrate.

6. Once you've specified all the desired information, click Finish. The migration will occur and a log listing will appear detailing the status of the migration.

Note *For complete information on the Crystal Import Wizard, including descriptions of how users and reports may be affected by a migration, display the Administrator's Guide online help and search the index for "import from Info/Enterprise."*

Chapter 23

Using the Crystal Launchpad and ePortfolio

635

The Crystal Launchpad is the starting point for most end-user interaction with Crystal Enterprise. The primary function of the Launchpad is as a launch point for ePortfolio and the Crystal Management Console; the Launchpad also provides links to additional resources for Crystal Enterprise users, administrators, and developers.

- **ePortfolio** is a desktop-style browser environment designed to allow end users to view, schedule, and monitor reports on Crystal Enterprise. As discussed in Chapter 24, your organization might opt to develop a custom Enterprise environment for your users, or modify ePortfolio, rather than use the standard ePortfolio covered in this chapter. However, many of the functions will be similar.

- **The Crystal Management Console**, also run from the Launchpad, is designed to allow administrators to manage the organization, storage, and accessibility of reports through the maintenance of folders, users, and system settings. This chapter discusses only the report publishing function of the Crystal Management Console. Other functions of the Crystal Management Console are discussed in Chapter 22 of this book and in the online Crystal Enterprise Administrator's Guide.

Tip	*Both the Crystal Management Console and ePortfolio (or any substitute Enterprise environment) can be called directly from your Web browser, by typing a URL into the address line. Therefore, you might not end up using the Launchpad at all.*

Several differences between Crystal Enterprise Standard and Crystal Enterprise Professional (discussed in Chapter 22) will directly affect the options available to you in ePortfolio, or your custom environment. The main difference regarding ePortfolio is that Crystal Enterprise Standard allows only two user accounts: Guest and Administrator. Up to five users can log on as Guest at the same time. Furthermore, with Crystal Enterprise Standard, only the Administrator user may publish reports for others to view and schedule.

In contrast, Crystal Enterprise Professional allows the Administrator user (and any other users configured with sufficient security levels) to add and manage users, groups, and folders in accordance with Windows NT security structures; in fact, NT users and groups can be mapped to Crystal Enterprise Professional if desired. Then, users can log on with their own NT identities to use ePortfolio—and all users with sufficient access rights can publish reports to Enterprise Professional.

There are several ways to publish Crystal Reports for use in Crystal Enterprise, whether you are an administrator on Crystal Enterprise Standard or a user on Crystal Enterprise Professional. Publishing methods and options also are discussed in this chapter.

Navigating the Crystal Enterprise Launchpad

To open the Launchpad, select Crystal Launchpad from the Crystal Enterprise program group. If you have not installed any Enterprise components on your computer, you may reach the Launchpad by pointing your browser to http://<*web server*>/crystal/ enterprise. The Launchpad will appear in your Web browser, similar to the view in Figure 23-1.

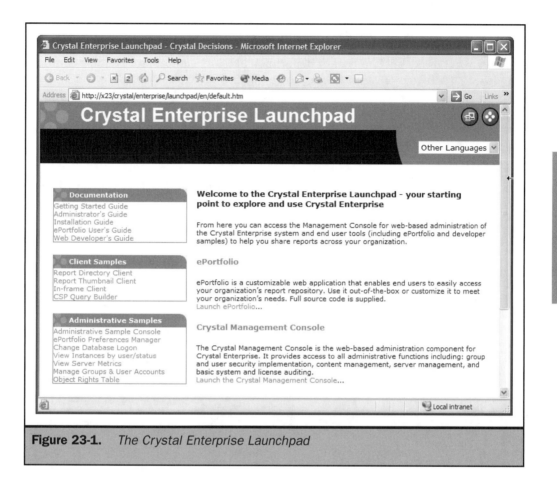

Figure 23-1.   *The Crystal Enterprise Launchpad*

On the Launchpad, you'll find links to many useful pages, including online documentation and tools that reside with Crystal Enterprise; Internet Web sites for support, tools, and samples; and the primary components of Crystal Enterprise: the ePortfolio and the Crystal Management Console. Also available is the Crystal Offline Viewer tool, which, after a one-time setup, allows you to view reports that have been downloaded to your workstation, even when your connection to your Web or network server is unavailable.

Navigating the Launchpad consists entirely of clicking the item you want to see. If the link is unavailable, or you don't have security access for it, you'll receive a descriptive message stating this.

Using the Crystal Enterprise ePortfolio

To start the ePortfolio, the end-user interface to Crystal Enterprise, click the Launchpad link to ePortfolio, or point your browser directly to the URL provided by your administrator. The default page for ePortfolio is loaded as seen in Figure 23-2, with the Guest account automatically logged on. In the example in this figure, the Crystal Enterprise environment has not yet had user or departmental folders and reports published to it for viewing, so there is only one folder showing in the Folders list, called Report Samples.

Note   *If the Guest account has been disabled in order to require all users to log on individually, you will see the logon screen prior to the main ePortfolio screen.*

ePortfolio Elements

The main page of ePortfolio is divided into several basic functional areas that provide other ePortfolio navigation links, search functions, and search result display areas. The page itself can be considered a "view" into the reports, folders, and functions

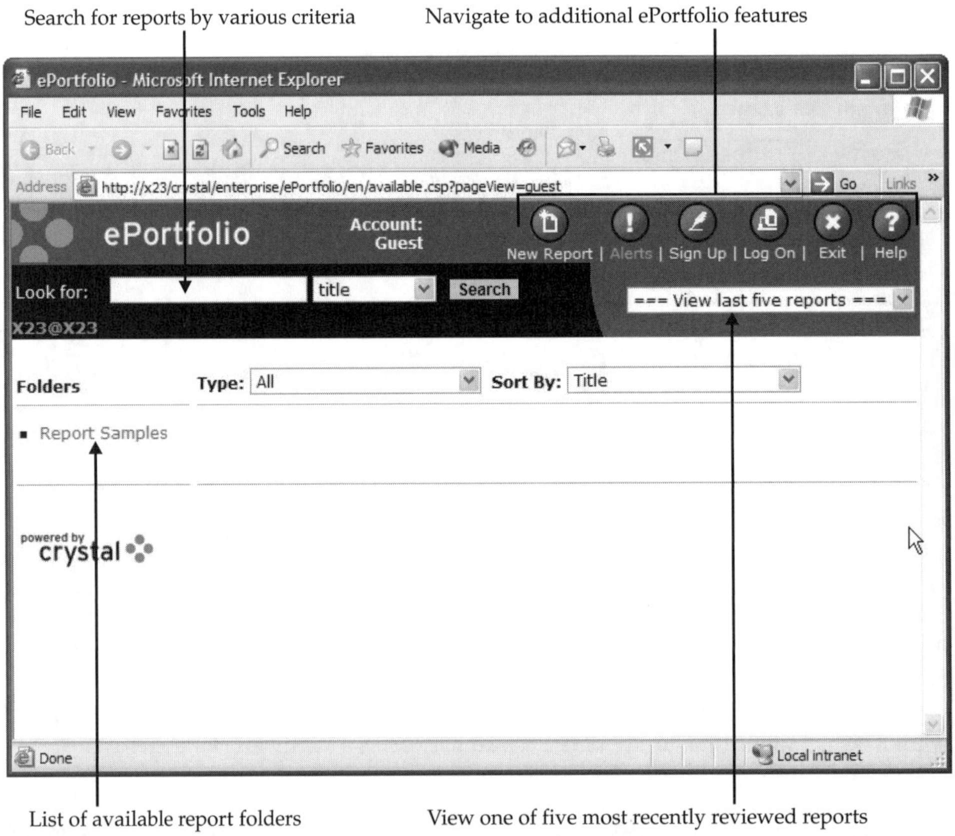

Figure 23-2.   *ePortfolio default page with Guest account logged on*

that the logged-on user has access to. The precise appearance of the page, or view, depends on who is logged on, and how the active view has been customized by the user or the administrator. Views are discussed in more detail later in this chapter. Also be aware that the page will appear and behave slightly differently depending on what Web browser you are using. For example, when you roll the cursor over clickable elements on the page, they change color if you are using Microsoft Internet Explorer, but otherwise they may not.

Header Bar Functions

The header bar displays the logged-on user, along with functions and navigation options, which vary depending on whether you are using Crystal Enterprise Standard or Professional, and whether you are logged on as a guest, a named user, or the administrator (who is essentially a named user in either edition of Crystal Enterprise).

Options available to *all* users, and both editions of Crystal Enterprise, include:

- **Alerts** Opens a screen listing any alerts activated by report instances within your viewing rights.

- **Sign Up** Allows Guest to create a new, named user account (this option is available only to a *Guest* user with CE Professional, and only if the administrator has set the "Guest users can create their own Enterprise accounts" option).

- **Log On** Allows logged-on user to log on as different user.

- **Help** Opens online help system.

- **Exit** Exits ePortfolio and returns to the Crystal Launchpad.

The following options are available to the administrator with both editions of Crystal Enterprise, and to named users with CE Professional:

- **Favorites / Public** Toggle between Favorites view and Public view.

- **Organize** Create and organize folders in Favorites view.

- **Preferences** Customize the appearance of the ePortfolio views, including how much information is displayed about each report, color scheme, time zone, and other preferences. Also provides access to Account Settings for password changes and so forth.

- **Log Off** Log off Enterprise, returning to the Guest account or to the logon screen.

Note   *The New Report button is new in Crystal Enterprise 8.5. However, the button (which can be used to launch the Report Application Server, or RAS) does not provide any functionality "out of the box," unless RAS has been installed and properly configured. You'll receive a "not found" message if you click it.*

The Search Bar

This second section of the ePortfolio allows you to search through your viewable folders for specific reports or folders. Search functions include:

- **Text search**   Search for objects by report title, report description (summary info), folder title, or all fields.
- **Most recent reports**   Shows the five most recently viewed reports.

Navigation Bar

Below the search bar you will see the folder path and the name of the folder or view you're currently in. Roll your cursor over the path to see that you can navigate directly to any folder in the path.

Folder and Report Display Area

Depending on the ePorfolio "view" that has been chosen with the Preferences link, the main area of ePortfolio will have varying looks. The Folders column on the left lists any folders within the folder or view you're in. The right column shows a list of reports in the open folder. Additional information besides the name of the report may appear (depending on your view). However, the default "out-of-the-box" view shows only report names, as shown in Figure 23-3. This figure shows an administrator's view of the Report Samples folder with one of the reports selected. (Also note the different navigation options in the title bar.) Hovering over a report capsule produces a pop-up text box containing further information about the report, including the report's description. Clicking a report capsule produces a pop-up menu with options to view the report, view the latest instance of the report (if available), schedule the report, or see a history of the report's instances.

Page Navigation

If there is more than one page of report summaries to display, page navigation elements will appear at the bottom right of the ePortfolio.

On the main ePortfolio view, the Type drop-down box over the report summary display column enables you to limit the display to only reports generated by the Crystal Report Designer, or only reports generated by Crystal Analysis Professional. The default setting includes all types of reports. And the Sort By drop-down box allows you to change the report display sort order to Title or Owner.

Searching for Reports

The primary function of the ePortfolio is to search for, view, schedule, and monitor reports. Therefore, navigation and search capabilities are both key to the efficiency of the tool. As outlined in the preceding section, there are several ways to find the reports you're looking for.

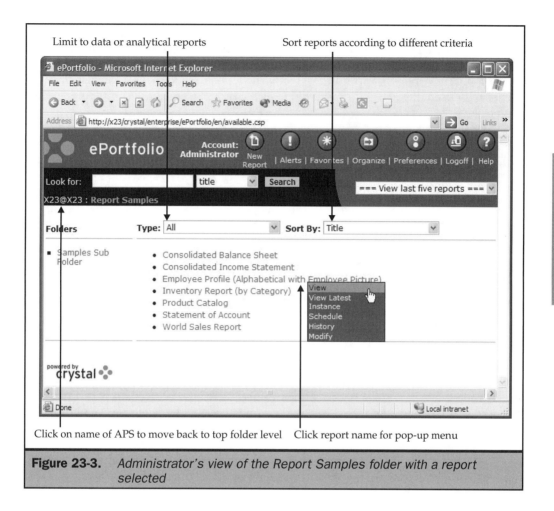

Figure 23-3. *Administrator's view of the Report Samples folder with a report selected*

Navigating to Your Report

The basic organization of the ePortfolio page is such that it's easy to navigate through folders to get to the one you need by simply clicking the folder names in succession until you have drilled down to the correct folder and your report is displayed. You'll find that ePortfolio behaves much the same as Web pages do when viewed in your Web browser. You can even use the browser's Back button to return through previous folders. In addition, you can navigate directly to a particular folder within the path you've followed by clicking the folder name in the navigation path bar.

Searching for Your Report

If you have specific information about a particular report, you can go directly to it by using one of the searches—if you have a text string that you know is part of a report or folder title or is even contained within the report description field (created with the Crystal Reports File | Summary Info menu option), you can enter the text in the search box, select the fields you want to search, and click the Search button.

As in many Windows applications, including Crystal Reports, you can also always see recently used files. The ePortfolio displays the five most recently run reports in the search bar.

> **Note** *Only public reports that you and other users have viewed, and favorites that you have viewed, will be displayed in the Last Five Reports list. You will not see nonshared recent reports.*

Once you have located the report you need, simply click the desired report title. Up to four action options—View, View Latest Instance, Schedule, and History—appear in a pop-up menu and can be used to process the report.

> **Note** *The Modify option that may appear on the pop-up menu will result in a "File Not Found" message, unless the Report Application Server has been properly installed and configured.*

Viewing and Running Instances and Reports

For most users of ePortfolio, there are four potential actions to take on a report: View, View Latest Instance, Schedule, and History. View and Schedule are both actions that involve actually running the report, either immediately or at a specified time. (When a report is run, it loads the report instructions and accesses the database, then formats and displays the report.) So, your administrator must have granted you appropriate rights to a report to perform either the View or the Schedule task in the action list.

The History and View Latest Instance actions also require certain rights be granted you by the Enterprise administrator. With certain rights combinations, you aren't allowed to run (load and process) the report, but you are allowed to view copies, or instances, of the report saved from when other users did run it. Every time an authorized user schedules a report to be run, the system saves what the data looked like at run time and stores it as an *instance* of the report. These instances are saved for a period of time so that users can view them without having to reaccess and process data.

No matter which of the actions you take, when a report is finally displayed it will be in a new Web browser window, formatted according to the Format and Viewer options selected by you (or your administrator) in your Preferences screen. These settings are discussed later in this chapter.

The View Option

When you ask to "view" a report, it is considered on-demand viewing—you are asking it to run immediately. For an on-demand view request, if a copy of the same report has been run recently, it will be displayed. If you need a fresher view of the database the report is based on, you can refresh the report once it is shown to you in a report viewer.

If there is not a recent copy, Enterprise accesses the database and then creates and displays the report. Several things affect view options and behavior:

- You can view only reports to which you have appropriate rights.

- You can view and/or refresh a report only if you have access to the database. A database logon screen will appear if you view or refresh a report requiring database logon.

- If the report has parameters that must be completed at run time, you will be prompted for this information in your Web browser before the report can display.

- On-demand report copies are retained on the server for a period of time controlled by the administrator—usually 10 to 20 minutes. When the period has expired for an on-demand report, it is cleared from the server and fresh requests will reread the database.

To view a report, locate a report you're authorized to run and click the title or thumbnail. Select View from the pop-up menu. The report is loaded and run, and a new Web browser window appears with a view of the report or a request for any further information required. If additional information is required, such as the database logon ID and password, or a Crystal parameter field, you'll be so prompted.

Crystal Report Viewer - Microsoft Internet Explorer

The report you requested requires further information.
When you are done, click View Report.

[View Report] [Help]

Crystal Parameter Field(s)

You can provide a single range of values for this parameter. Enter a lower and an upper limit to describe the range of values you want to include.

Date Range

Choose Order Date

This parameter is range limited and requires a value between DateTime (1998, 1, 1, 0, 0, 0) and DateTime (1998, 12, 31, 12, 0, 0).

Range of values between:

`DateTime(yyyy,mm,dd,hh,mm,ss)`

☑ Include this value ☐ Range has no lower limit
and

`DateTime(yyyy,mm,dd,hh,mm,ss)`

☑ Include this value ☐ Range has no upper limit

If you are not familiar with Crystal Reports' parameter behavior, you can click the Help button for additional information. When you have successfully completed any requested further information, using the on-screen prompts, the report is displayed in your Web browser, as seen in Figure 23-4.

When you view a report, the toolbars and buttons will vary depending on your Viewer and Format settings. You will always have a Web browser toolbar with whichever tools apply to your viewer (Back, Stop, Refresh, Favorites, and so forth). You will also have an application toolbar for whatever format you've asked to view the report in. If you are viewing a report in Crystal Reports format, you will have a Crystal Reports

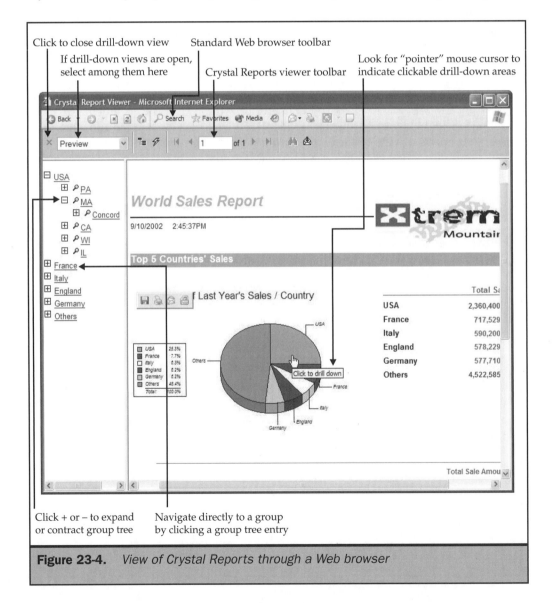

Figure 23-4. *View of Crystal Reports through a Web browser*

toolbar limited to those tools available to report management in the chosen Web viewer. When you've requested another application format, such as Microsoft Word or Excel, the application toolbar will offer some of the common tools for those applications rather than Crystal Reports tools.

The tools that may be available when viewing in Crystal Reports format are discussed in the following list. If your chosen viewer doesn't support a tool, it won't be offered. For a complete list of the tools supported by each viewer, see "Report Viewers" in Crystal Enterprise Online Help.

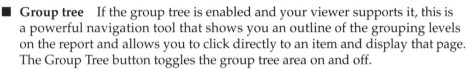 ■ **Page navigation**   All viewers let you click to the first page, previous page, next page, or last page, or else to a specific page number.

■ **Group tree**   If the group tree is enabled and your viewer supports it, this is a powerful navigation tool that shows you an outline of the grouping levels on the report and allows you to click directly to an item and display that page. The Group Tree button toggles the group tree area on and off.

 ■ **Drill-down and close drill-down**   If the report has further detail supporting some of the data on the report, you may be able to drill down to the detail by clicking on the summary information on the report. The cursor will change when it is rolled over clickable areas, just as it does when rolled over a link on a Web page. When you double-click on a drill-down area, a drill-down page opens in the browser. You can then toggle between the main Preview page and any open drill-down pages by either selecting them in the current view drop-down box (some browsers) or clicking the drill-down tab. To close a drill-down page, click the red X button when the drill-down page is the current view.

■ **Refresh**   Refresh an older instance or a recent view to reflect the latest data. You can refresh a report only if you have run rights to it and have access to the database. If you try to refresh it without those rights, you will receive an error message in the browser.

■ **Zoom control**   Some browsers allow you to specify a standard or custom screen magnification value for viewing, in percentages or in relative terms such as page width.

■ **Find**   All browsers provide for searching in the report for certain text or data content. Some browsers have the search text box in the toolbar, and others prompt for the text string after you click the Find button.

■ **Print**   A print request will generate the Print dialog box with such options as printer choice, page range, paper layout, number of copies, and so forth. The options and defaults provided depend on the way the report was saved and the operating system and viewer you're using. Check the default values carefully to see that they are what you want.

 ■ **Export**   You have the option to export a report from the viewer to several different file formats, including Crystal Reports, Microsoft Excel, Microsoft Word, Rich Text Format, and Adobe Acrobat. When you click the Export button, you're prompted with a dialog box allowing you to enter a filename, select the file type, and browse to the location you want to store the new file.

When you have finished viewing, printing, and/or exporting the report, you can close the report's browser window or leave it open. If your user settings dictate that subsequently viewed reports open in the same window, the next report you view will display in place of this one.

Schedule Instances

When you schedule a report, you are setting a time to run the report—either once or on a recurring schedule. You can schedule a report to run immediately, if desired; the difference between doing this and viewing on demand is that Crystal Enterprise saves the "instance" of the report when it is run, and makes it available to other users. Unlike the temporary copy that's available only to you for a little while, after you view a report, the Schedule action puts the report instance in history, and these instances are typically available for a much longer time. As with viewing on demand, you must have run rights to a report in order to schedule it. However, the resulting report instances can be seen by users who have only view-level rights to the report.

Using scheduled reports has several advantages:

■ Scheduling instances can optimize server performance by avoiding excess server and database requests.

■ The scheduling function provides the ability to enter embedded parameter values, database logon, report format, and/or selection criteria so that the users don't have to be prompted for these values.

■ Scheduling instances can significantly reduce the time it takes to support a large group of users requesting reports.

So, scheduled instances are flexible and informative while still protecting databases from uncontrolled access and protecting the database servers from unnecessary hits.

To schedule a report, click a report you're authorized to run, and select schedule from the pop-up menu. Figure 23-5 shows the resulting Schedule dialog page after the "run once" option has been chosen.

In order to schedule a report, you must provide information about when to run it, what database logon to use if needed, any parameter values applicable, and any selection criteria you want. You may also select the file format for the instance, as well as the destination (such as e-mail or FTP). Depending on how the report was saved, there may be default values provided and you might not have to go through these options. However, you'll often have to at least provide a database logon or a different run time.

To review and/or change the default options, select each category from the drop-down box titled Customize Your Options.

You can click the Schedule link in the title bar to proceed with processing the instance, whenever you've completed the desired options.

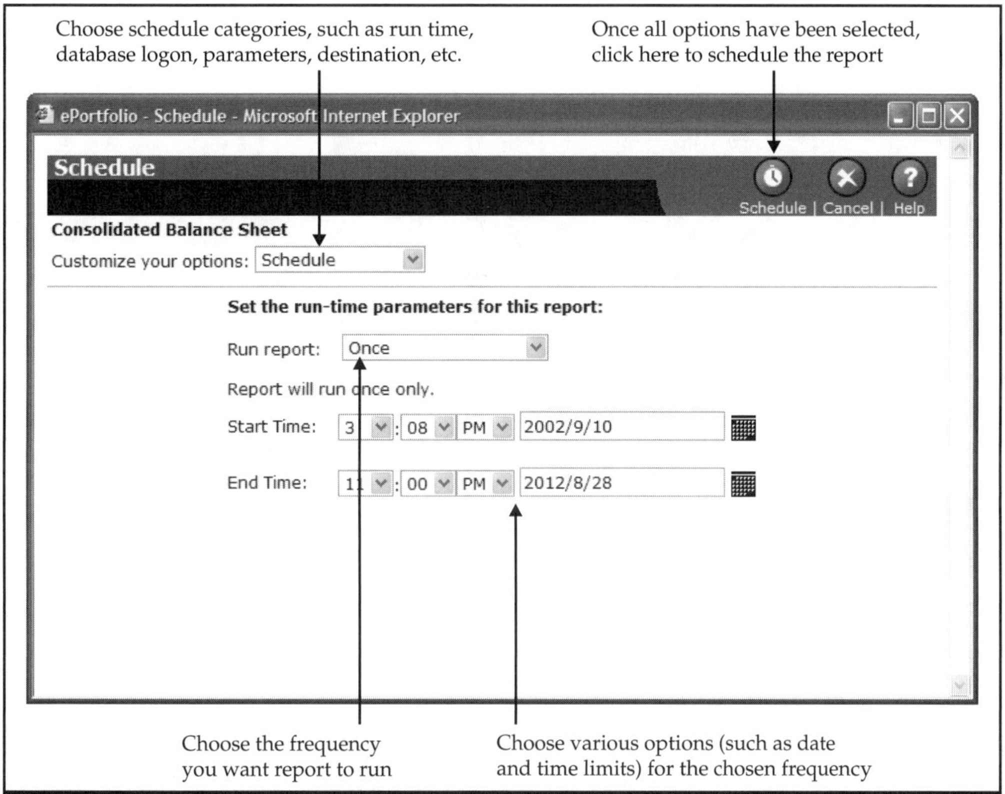
Choose schedule categories, such as run time, database logon, parameters, destination, etc.
Once all options have been selected, click here to schedule the report
ePortfolio - Schedule - Microsoft Internet Explorer
Schedule
Schedule | Cancel | Help
Consolidated Balance Sheet
Customize your options: Schedule
Set the run-time parameters for this report:
Run report: Once
Report will run once only.
Start Time: 3 : 08 PM 2002/9/10
End Time: 11 : 00 PM 2012/8/28
Choose the frequency you want report to run
Choose various options (such as date and time limits) for the chosen frequency

Figure 23-5. *Schedule dialog page with run-time options displayed*

Run-Time Options The Schedule page always opens with the run-time options displayed. These values determine how often and at what time a report instance will be created. The default option is "Now," meaning the report will run immediately. The second option, "Once," means it will run only once—at the time specified and within 24 hours. It defaults to the current time, so accepting the defaults provides an immediate run. The other options run it regularly at the time specified. Options include:

- Run report: Now, Once, Hourly, Daily, Weekly, Monthly, Nth Day of Month, First Monday of Month, Last Day of Month
- Start Time: Exact hour, minutes, am/pm

Complete the desired options and click the Schedule link in the title bar, or change the Customize category if you need to change other options.

Database Logon Options   To display the database logon options, select Database Logon from the Customize list.

The four fields on the Database Logon page provide a way for the report to access any secure databases when the scheduled instance is being processed. If these fields are not completed, a scheduled instance will fail:

- **Data Source(s)**   Lists all data sources used by the report, with the first one highlighted.
- **Database**   Lists the path to the highlighted database.
- **User**   Requires a valid user name with access to this database.
- **Password**   Requires the password applicable to this user, if any.

If there is more than one database, be sure to click each and complete the user information for each. To finish the process, click the Update button.

Parameters Options   If this report uses Crystal Reports parameters, which normally prompt the user to make choices about what to include on the report, those parameter values need to be provided in order for an instance to run successfully. Most reports will have default values for parameters, and those defaults may be acceptable to you; if they are, you won't have to change them before scheduling the report. However, if you need different values for this instance, you'll need to complete the Parameters page. To display any parameters active on this report, select Parameters from the Customize list.

CRYSTAL REPORTS 9
ON THE WEB

The parameters displayed will vary, depending on what types of parameters exist on the report you're scheduling. Generally, you'll see each parameter listed with its user prompt, and beneath that you'll see an area for adding values for that parameter.

If a pick list has been provided, you can select the value you want from the drop-down list and then click the Add button. If the value you want is not in the drop-down list, you can type the value in the text box and click Add. If multiple values or ranged values are allowed for a parameter, you will be able to add those values. Be sure to click the Update button when you are done entering parameter values.

Filters   You can modify any existing selection formula this instance uses (either record selection or group selection), and you can add any. To display any selection criteria in use, or to enter a new one, choose "Filters" from the Customize list.

Make any desired changes to either selection formula and click Update.

Caution   *You must enter correct Crystal Reports selection formula syntax or the scheduled instance will fail to run. Syntax is not validated during scheduling.*

Destination   Newly added to Crystal Enterprise 8.5 is the Destination option. At the end of report processing, Crystal Enterprise can send the instance to a number of destinations. The Destination drop-down allows you to choose Default, Unmanaged Disk, Email (SMTP), FTP, or Printer. ("Printer" is available only when the format is set to "Report.") The "Default" choice signals Crystal Enterprise to keep the instance in the internal database without sending it elsewhere. The remaining options all produce a set of additional options related to that particular destination such as the name of the printer if you select Print.

When all of the information is complete, click the Update button.

Format   Also new to Crystal Enterprise 8.5 is the Format choice. Instances can be created in a variety of formats. The Format drop-down includes Crystal Report, Excel, Word, Acrobat, and five different plain text formats. Once you've selected the desired format, there is no Update button to click, so you may simply select a different customization section or finalize the schedule.

Finalizing a Schedule   When you are finished setting all of the customization options, click the Schedule link in the title bar. The History page is displayed, with the requested instance showing as pending. See the history discussion that follows for further instructions.

View Instances: History and Latest

When you need to view a report, and either you don't have view rights or you need to view a scheduled instance, one or two options are available to you when you click on the report on your public or favorites page. For any report that has a processed instance currently on file, View Latest Instance will be available in the pop-up menu. For all reports, the History action is always available to display and select from all scheduled instances.

> **Note** *How long a successfully processed instance remains accessible depends on administrative settings and on server resources—instances that expire and instances that don't get used are automatically deleted if the system needs the space.*

History When you select History from the action options for a report, or when you schedule a report to run once right now, the History page opens in your Web browser, similar to Figure 23-6. It displays a list of any scheduled instances on file for this report. The history display includes the following important elements:

- **Instance Time** Click the instance date/time to view an instance of this report if its status is Success.
- **Run By** Name of user who scheduled each instance.
- **Parameters** Any parameter values added during scheduling.
- **Format** The file format of the instance.
- **Status** Instance status may be Waiting, Recurring, Pending, Running, Stopped, Failed, or Success. "Failed" can be clicked to see reason for failure.

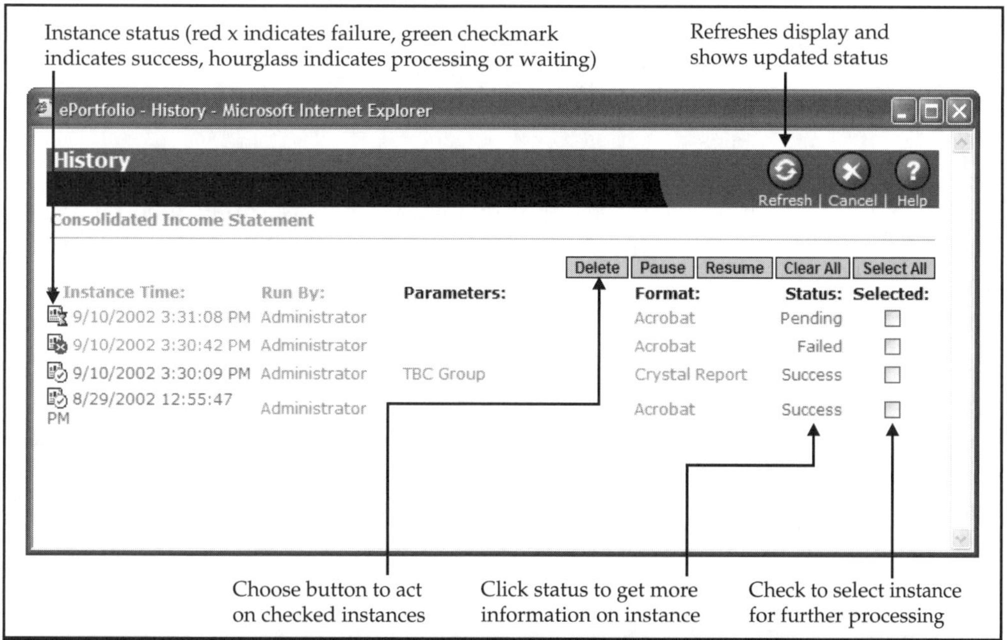

Figure 23-6. *History page for report*

If the status of the instance you wish to view is Success, you can click the date/time for that instance and be taken to the view of the report.

If the status is Pending or Running, you can click the Refresh button periodically to update the status, or you can close the History page and reopen it later to see if the instance has processed successfully. If the status is Failed, you can't view this report instance, but can you view the reason for failure by clicking the Failed status.

When you click the date/time of a successful instance, the report opens in a new Web browser according to the format and view settings on your user account. It is the same view you see if you are viewing the report on demand, or viewing the latest instance.

If you have sufficient rights, you can control instance processing, such as pausing or resuming a pending instance. You can also delete instances manually. To make these choices, check the Selected box for the instance or instances that you wish to control. Then, click one of the associated buttons above the instance list, such as Pause or Resume.

View Latest Instance   When you ask to view the latest instance, the most recent successful instance opens in a new Web browser according to the format and viewer settings on your user account, just as if you were viewing a report on demand or from a scheduled instance in the History list.

Note   *Only successfully scheduled instances will show up as "latest instances." If you have viewed a report on demand, that instance won't be the latest instance (but it will show up in the Last 5 Reports list, in the search bar).*

Guest Versus User Account

As discussed earlier, the default Guest account may allow you a certain amount of flexibility in using Crystal Enterprise. However, having a named user account will further enable you to publish reports to the network, and to customize and maintain your ePortfolio folders and views. In order to log on as a named user, you must first have a user account.

Sign Up Page

If users are not allowed to create their own accounts on your system, you will need to contact the administrator to obtain a named user account for yourself so that you can log on as that user in the future. If you are allowed to create the account yourself, open ePortfolio as the default guest user and click Sign Up.

---

ePortfolio - Sign Up Page - Microsoft Internet Explorer

File   Edit   View   Favorites   Tools   Help

Back   ·   ·   Search   Favorites   Media

Address   http://x23/crystal/enterprise/eportfolio/en/signup.csp   Go   Links »

ePortfolio

Log On | Cancel | Help

Sign Up

Profile Information

Full Name:

Account Information

User Name:

Password:

Confirm Password:

[Sign Up] [Clear Form]

Done   Local intranet

> **Note**   *This is available only if the administrator has activated "Guest users can create their own Enterprise accounts" in the Crystal Management Console.*

Complete the fields as desired to create your user identity and click the Sign Up button. If you are not sure you have completed it correctly, click the Clear Form button and begin again, or click the Cancel link in the title bar.

> **Note**   *You will automatically be logged on when you complete the sign up, and the Favorites view for your user account will display with no folders yet organized in it. For more information on the next steps, see "Favorites Versus Public Folder Views" later in this chapter.*

Logon and Logoff Functions

Opening ePortfolio from the Launchpad automatically logs the user on as a guest, and if you are using Crystal Enterprise Standard, there is no need to use either logon or logoff unless you are the administrator. If you are using Crystal Enterprise Professional and are a named user (or the administrator), you will use the logon and logoff functions to access and protect your existing account.

On the Logon page, fill in the user name and password information for your account. If you are using Crystal Enterprise Professional, make sure that the Authentication drop-down box displays the correct security mode in use on your network—if Enterprise is operating with an independent security structure, leave the default (Enterprise). However, if the administrator has implemented another security model that you should use, choose the alternate security method (such as LDAP or Windows NT) in the drop-down list.

If you don't have an individual account yet but believe you're allowed to set one up, use the Sign Up title bar link or the "Sign me up now!" link at the bottom of the screen, and refer to the earlier Sign Up page discussion.

You can always cancel out of the Logon screen by clicking the Cancel title bar link or the "Continue as 'Guest' user" link at the bottom of the screen.

Note	*The APS field will be active only if you are on Crystal Enterprise Professional in an installation with multiple APS servers. Otherwise, it simply displays the one applicable APS machine name.*

When you have finished your session with ePortfolio, be sure to use the Logoff function. It will confirm that you wish to log off and will automatically return the screen to the Guest view.

Caution	*If your network license includes a limited number of guest users as well as named users, be sure to exit ePortfolio after logging off. Leaving the ePortfolio page logged on to Guest will tie up a user license and potentially prevent other guests from logging on.*

If you are logged on but leave the workstation idle for a period of time, Crystal Enterprise may log you off. This period of time is controlled by the administrator. If you have been logged off and you request activity, you will receive a logon screen at that time.

Favorites Versus Public Folder Views

The ePortfolio is a view or window into the reports that are available to you on your company's Crystal Enterprise system. There are two basic view types:

- **Public view**   Whether you are a guest user or a named user, you have a view of all the shared (public) reports and folders, and you can also see any other folders your account has the rights to view. You can temporarily narrow your Public view to certain reports by choosing to limit the type of report displayed, or by searching for specific folder or report criteria. If you are a named user (including the administrator), you can also customize the *appearance* of your Public view through the Settings function. But the *contents* of the public view will still be similar to the Public view of other users, because it's a window into the same shared folder structure.

- **Favorites view**   If you are a named user or the administrator, you can toggle back and forth between your Public view and a personal, customizable Favorites view. The Organize function in the title bar is used to customize the *contents* of the Favorites view, adding folders and copying reports and folders into your Favorites view for easy access. Also, most custom settings selected on the Settings page apply to the *appearance* of both your Public and Favorites views.

Organizing the Favorites View   The Organize function allows you to create folders for your own Favorites view in ePortfolio. You can create folders to hold reports, and you can store copies of reports or report shortcuts (links) into those folders, in whatever organizational structure you prefer. You may also use the Organize function to organize other folders in your environment.

When you are logged on as a named user or the administrator, you can click the Organize link in the title bar to open the Organize Favorites page.

The top drop-down box on the screen displays the reports folders at the top level, including the Favorites folder. Below is a list box with all of the folders and reports in the currently selected folder.

To the right, there are action buttons:

- ■ **Expand**   Allows you to expand a selected folder in the list.
- ■ **Copy**   Allows you to copy a report from the one folder to another (see further details later in this section under "Copying and Moving Folders and Reports").
- ■ **Move**   Allows you to move reports and folders around.
- ■ **Shortcut**   Allows you to create a shortcut, or link, in your Favorites view to a report in the public folders (see further details later in this section under "Creating Shortcuts to Reports").
- ■ **Rename**   Allows you to rename any folder.
- ■ **Delete**   Allows you to delete a folder or report.

In order to activate the action buttons, you have to select a folder or report first. Each of these selections brings a dialog box prompting you for complete information on the action you wish to take.

You can navigate through the folders by double-clicking a folder to open it, by clicking a folder and clicking Expand, by selecting another folder from the drop-down box, or by clicking the Up-Folder button. When you see the report or folder you want, select it and then click the desired action button to the right.

 Creating Folders   Usually, the first thing you'll want to do when organizing favorites is create a few folders to hold different categories of reports for logical access. To create a new folder in the Favorites view, select the Favorites folder and then click the New Folder button on the upper-right side of the Organize Favorites page. The Add New Folder dialog box is displayed.

Type the desired folder name in the text box and click the Add button. The folder is added to whichever folder is currently selected. If the resulting location is not at the correct hierarchical level, use the Move function to adjust it.

Copying and Moving Folders and Reports   If you want to copy or move a folder or report to another location, select the item and click Copy or Move. The appropriate dialog box is displayed.

Copy - ePortfolio - Microsoft Internet Explorer

Copy   ← ?
                                                                           Cancel | Help

Selected Items: Click the button below to apply   **Folders:** Select the folder where you want to place
the action to all listed items to the selected folder.   the listed items.

Drill Down   X23@X23

                                                             .\Report Samples

Copy   Expand

Done   Local intranet

The selected item is displayed on the left side. The folder structure appears on the right. Clicking the Copy or Move button on the lower-left side will copy or move the item into whatever folder is currently open on the right. Therefore, before clicking Copy or

Move, navigate through the folders on the right until the folder name displayed in the drop-down box is the folder into which you wish to copy or move this item. The new folder organization is now displayed on the Organize Favorites page.

Creating Shortcuts to Reports   The whole purpose of the Favorites view is to organize your reports into efficient locations. Now that you have folders in which to store them, you can add reports. Obviously, one way to do this is to publish reports and save them there (covered later in this chapter under "Publishing Crystal Reports to Crystal Enterprise"), but what if there are already some useful reports in the public folders? You don't have to toggle to the Public view every time you want one if you make them accessible from your Favorites folders.

Crystal Enterprise provides a much better way to deal with this situation. The Shortcut option creates a shortcut, or link, to a public report, so when you run it, the instances you create are accessible in the History lists in the public folders for other users. And when other users run the report, you will see those instances in the history from your Favorites folder because you are really viewing the public copy.

Caution   *Though it may be tempting to have your own copy of every report you run, it is not efficient if you and other users run your own copies of reports that could have been shared. If other instances of a report might suffice for your needs, it is better to use a linked (shared) report to minimize server workload.*

To copy or link to a report, select the report and click the Shortcut button. When you click Shortcut, a dialog similar to the Copy and Move dialogs appears. On the right side, select the folder for the new shortcut, then select the Link To button on the lower-left side.

Note   *You can use standard Windows keyboard tools to select multiple items—for example, select a report and hold down the SHIFT or CTRL key while clicking additional reports.*

The new shortcut will be created with the words "Shortcut to" and the report name in the destination folder. Remember that if you later organize the destination folder, you can safely delete the "Shortcut to" report without deleting the original report in the original folder.

Renaming or Deleting Reports or Folders   If a report name is too long, or you have a more meaningful name for it, you can select the report and use the Rename function to give the report a new name. A dialog box will appear where you can type in the new name of the report. The Rename function can also be used for folders.

If you do not need a particular folder or report, you can select it and click the Delete button. You will receive a message asking you to confirm the action.

Caution	*If you delete a folder, all of its contents, including instances in the history, will also be deleted; there is no additional warning about this. If the folder contained only links and copies of public reports, it can be re-created (minus the history). But if it contained reports you published directly to an Enterprise Favorites folder, these will be lost.*

Customizing Preferences for Public and Favorites Views   If you are logged on as a named user or as the administrator, you can use the Preferences option on the title bar to customize the desktop/browser appearance and behavior of ePortfolio. Most of the settings, such as color scheme, apply to both your Public view and your Favorites view. Most of the settings are self-explanatory, and you can experiment to see which ones you prefer. These are a few settings of particular note:

- **Initial view...**   This setting determines the first folder to be displayed when you enter ePortfolio. If you've set up your Favorites, you will probably want to select that for your initial view.

- **On my desktop, show me...**   This setting changes the format of the report capsules displayed in ePortfolio. The Thumbnail and List views are most similar, as they both generated the pop-up menus discussed previously in the chapter. The Action view dispenses with the pop-up menu by placing links directly on the page.

- **View my reports using the...**   If you are viewing your reports in Crystal Reports format, this setting dictates which of the many Web-based viewers you need to use. The default is either DHTML (which will work for almost all Web browsers), or a viewer your administrator has deemed more effective for your system. You can choose one of the other viewers if recommended by your administrator. For a complete discussion of the features of each viewer, see "Report Viewers" in Crystal Enterprise Online Help.

When you finish making changes to your user settings, click the Apply link in the title bar or at the bottom of the page.

Changing Your Password   If you are logged on as a named user or the administrator, you can change your password. From the Preferences page, click the My Password link in the title bar to obtain the Change Password dialog box. You must enter the old password as well as the new password before clicking the Submit button to make the change.

Publishing Crystal Reports to Crystal Enterprise

The main purpose of Crystal Enterprise is to provide a secure, flexible way of distributing reports to people who don't necessarily have or need the full Crystal Reports designer, and who may not even have access to the reported databases. But how do you get reports into the Crystal Enterprise environment, where they can be managed and viewed?

There are three basic ways to publish a report so that it is stored in and recognized by Crystal Enterprise:

- **Publish from Crystal Reports 8.5** If you have the Crystal Reports 8.5 program, you can choose to publish (save) a report to folders in Crystal Enterprise from the Crystal Reports 8.5 application. You can't determine a schedule or modify other run-time criteria, but it gets the report into Crystal Enterprise, where it can be viewed and scheduled. The administrator determines whether users are allowed to save reports from Crystal Reports using this method.

- **Crystal Publishing Wizard** Crystal Enterprise comes with this tool for publishing reports into new or existing Enterprise folders. It can identify and publish multiple reports at a time, and it allows you to establish report properties, scheduling, database logons, and parameters. The administrator determines whether this tool is accessible to users.

- **Publishing with the Crystal Management Console** The administrator can use the Crystal Management Console to publish an existing report into the Enterprise system of folders. It can be used remotely and has the most comprehensive set of control options, including all of the ones Crystal Publishing Wizard allows plus user rights and selection criteria. However, it can't publish multiple reports at a time.

Each of these methods is discussed under "Publishing with Crystal Reports 8.5." Keep in mind that the functions offered to you will depend on what rights you've been given by the administrator. Disallowed options will not display, or may display but be disabled (grayed out).

| Caution | *As of this publication, Crystal Reports 9 .rpt files cannot be published to Crystal Enterprise 8.5 using any of these methods. If you wish to publish reports to Crystal Enterprise 8.5, you must supply an .rpt file created in an earlier version of Crystal Reports. Only Crystal Enterprise 9 and above (not released as of this publication) can accept Crystal Reports 9 .rpt files.* |

Publishing with Crystal Reports 8.5

To publish or distribute a report from within Crystal Reports to Crystal Enterprise so that you and/or other users can access it from ePortfolio and other Web-based Enterprise tools, you must open the report in Crystal Reports 8.5.

While the report is open, think about how it will be used by Enterprise end users. Will they need any parameter fields for selective viewing? Should you create or modify any selection criteria? Should you activate the Save Preview Picture feature so that a thumbnail can be activated? Remember that most end users won't have access to the Crystal Report Designer, so you need to provide as much flexibility as you can.

When you are ready to publish the report, select the File | Save As menu function from the toolbar in Crystal Reports.

In the Save As dialog box, your default folder (probably a documents folder) is displayed. Click the Enterprise Folders button in the left column under Save As. You must be logged on to Crystal Enterprise to give you access to the Enterprise folders.

The Connect To APS dialog box appears. If you have already logged in to Crystal Enterprise during this Crystal Reports session, your user name and the APS name will be filled in. If not, you'll need to supply these items, along with your password. Once you've supplied the necessary information, click OK.

If the information you enter is not recognized, the Save As dialog box redisplays with the original defaults.

When your logon information is recognized, the Save As dialog box redisplays with all Enterprise folders available to you (see Figure 23-7).

Browse to the folder you want to place this report in. If you choose a shared public folder, all other Enterprise users will be able to access the report. If you choose your Favorites folder, only you will see the report from within the Enterprise system.

When the correct folder is displayed in the Save In box at the top, verify that the File Name is correct, then click the Save button.

Caution   *When you browse to subfolders within the Enterprise directory, the filename (which will be the name of the report when saved) may change to match the name of the folder you're browsing to. Be sure to change it to the desired report name.*

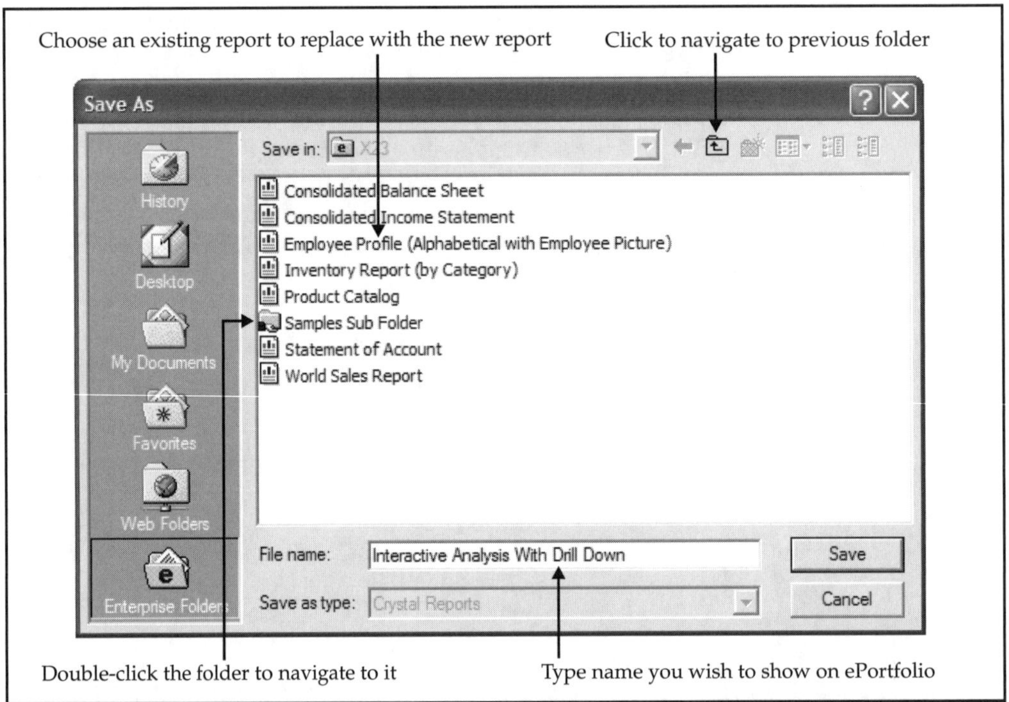

Choose an existing report to replace with the new report   Click to navigate to previous folder

Double-click the folder to navigate to it   Type name you wish to show on ePortfolio

Figure 23-7.   *Save As dialog box with Enterprise folders*

When the report is saved, the Crystal Reports screen is redisplayed with the report still open. Continue working, or exit Crystal Reports. When you next view your folders in ePortfolio, or your custom Enterprise end-user environment, you will see the report.

Note   *Crystal Enterprise 8.5's internal structure requires an update to Crystal Reports 8.5 before reports can be published from the Save As dialog box. Install this update on each copy of Crystal Reports 8.5 that you wish to use to publish in this manner. The update can be found on the Crystal Enterprise 8.5 CD in the \Updates\Crystal Reports folder.*

The Crystal Publishing Wizard

The main tool provided for end users to publish Crystal Reports into the Enterprise environment is the Crystal Publishing Wizard. This is a Windows-based program that must be specifically installed from the Crystal Enterprise program CD—it can't be accessed from a Web browser. If it has been properly installed, it will be found in the Crystal Enterprise program group from the Start button.

The Publishing Wizard allows you to identify one or more existing reports and publish them (move copies of them) into existing Enterprise folders on your APS, and it enables you to create and organize Enterprise folders if needed. It also prompts you to complete any desired scheduling, database logon, and default parameter prompts and values needed, in order for users to view and/or run the reports.

As with all such wizards, the Publishing Wizard walks you through a logical sequence of dialog screens to complete all the information needed, and you can at any time click the Back, Cancel, or Help button if you are not ready to go to the Next screen.

To begin, click the Next button. The Select A File dialog box is displayed, with the option to browse to a report file.

Select a File or Add Multiple Reports

If you are publishing only one report, enter the path to the file in the File field, or click the Find File button to browse to the report location. When the report file path is correctly identified, you can click the Next button.

Otherwise, if you wish to publish more than one report at this time, check the Add Multiple Reports box. Additional prompts appear in the dialog box that allow you to identify a directory containing reports, add those reports to a list of reports to publish, and then modify the list.

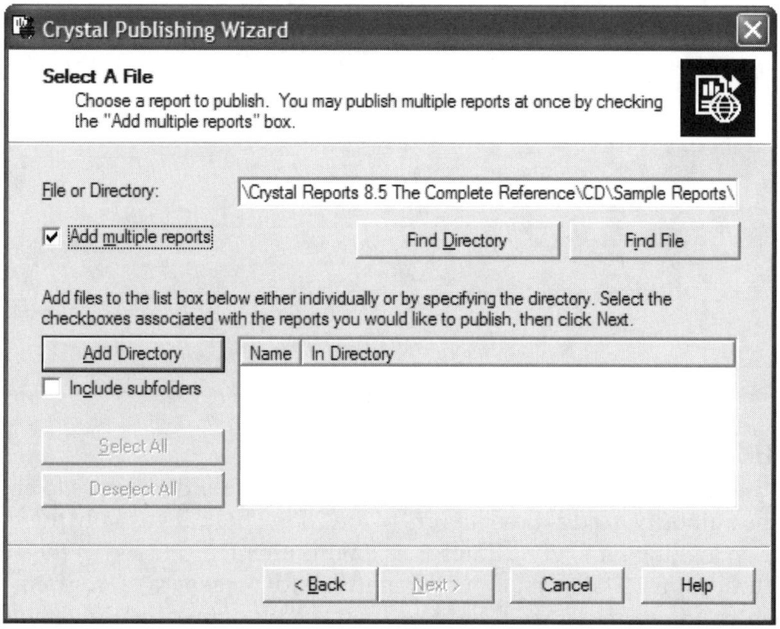

In the File Or Directory field, enter the path to the directory (folder) that contains reports you want published, or click the Find Directory button to browse to the folder.

Once you've identified the path to the folder, you can click the Add Directory button to bring all the reports from that directory to the list of potential reports to publish in the center of the dialog box. If the directory has subfolders that also contain reports you might want, check the Include Subfolders box *before* clicking Add Directory. If you aren't sure whether there are reports you want in any subfolders, check the box, and if there aren't any to add, a message will tell you so.

Use the check box beside each report to select the ones you do want. If you want most or all of them, click the Select All button. This checks them all, and you can uncheck the ones you don't need. If necessary, use the Deselect All button to start over with selection.

Click the Next button to continue when you've checked all the reports you want on the list. The Select An APS dialog screen is displayed.

```
┌─────────────────────────────────────────────────────────────┐
│  🖳 Crystal Publishing Wizard                             [X] │
│                                                               │
│   Select an APS                                         ┌───┐ │
│     Before users can access your report through the     │📥🌐│ │
│     Crystal framework, it must be added to a Crystal APS.└───┘ │
│  ─────────────────────────────────────────────────────────── │
│                                                               │
│        Enter the name of your Crystal APS. You also need to   │
│        specify your user name and password.                   │
│                                                               │
│        Authentication:   [Enterprise            ▼]            │
│                                                               │
│        APS:              [X23                    ]            │
│                                                               │
│        User Name:        [Administrator          ]            │
│                                                               │
│        Password:         [                        ]           │
│                                                               │
│  ─────────────────────────────────────────────────────────── │
│              [ < Back ]  [ Next > ]  [ Cancel ]  [ Help ]     │
└─────────────────────────────────────────────────────────────┘
```

Select an APS

Complete the Authentication, APS, User Name, and Password prompts to ensure that you have the authority to add these reports to the APS. These are usually the same values you use when logging on to your Enterprise environment, discussed in the ePortfolio section of this chapter. The Crystal Publishing Wizard is a separate program, so you have to identify yourself as a valid Enterprise user. This allows the Publishing Wizard to find your folders and access rights for Enterprise.

Click the Next button to begin creating objects for the report(s) you're publishing. If you're publishing only one report, or if your reports all come from one directory, you'll go straight to the APS Folder dialog box to determine where you want your report(s). However, if you're adding multiple reports from more than one folder/subfolder, you will be prompted with the Folder Hierarchy screen.

If you see this screen, you must decide whether to duplicate the folder hierarchy of the reports you chose for the APS:

- **Yes**   The system will copy the folder names and structure from the local reports directories you've chosen into the existing Enterprise folder system.

- **No**   The system assumes you want to arrange all the reports yourself in the existing Enterprise folder structure or create different folders there, and the originating folders won't be copied.

Click the Next button to display the APS Folder dialog screen.

APS Folder (Enterprise Folders)

The APS Folder dialog screen displays the folder structure in your existing Enterprise environment. It displays only folders to which you're authorized full rights. The purpose of this screen is to let you identify or create a destination folder for the report(s) you're publishing. This is just the top-level folder for your reports—you'll still be able to create subfolders for some of the reports in a later step, if desired, as well as move folders and reports around within the structure. If you chose to duplicate an existing outside folder hierarchy, the reports and folders in the original directory will all be copied into the folder you select on this screen.

Find and Select Existing Folder   If the folder you want is showing, click it and then click Next. If the folder you want exists but is not showing, expand the top-level folders (click the + beside them) to find the desired destination folder. Select it and click Next.

 Create New Folder, or Rename or Delete Folder   If you need to create Enterprise folders, click the folder in which you want the new folder to reside and then click the New Folder button. Then type a name for the folder. You can also rename folders you've created by clicking in the name field and typing over the old name.

Note   *Folders you create are green to show that you can rename and delete them. Folders created by the system can't be deleted or renamed here.*

If needed, you can delete folders you create by pressing DEL or clicking the Delete button (the X) when a green folder is selected.

When it's created and named as desired, click the destination folder for the report(s) you're adding and then click Next. The Location Preview screen appears, with your report(s) listed under the folder you selected.

Crystal Publishing Wizard

Location Preview
Preview folder location of reports.

Move the objects to different folders using the up and down arrows or by dragging them to the desired folder.

Folder preview: Show file names

- Report Samples
  - Samples Sub Folder
    - ABLAZE Bank
      - Deposit Detail Report
      - E-Mail Marketing Analysis
      - E-Mail Marketing Analysis - Savings Only
      - Interactive Analysis
      - Savings/Loan Account Analysis
      - Top Depositor Report

< Back   Next >   Cancel   Help

CRYSTAL REPORTS 9
ON THE WEB

Location Preview

This screen allows you to arrange all the new reports and folders to suit your needs. The reports you added are displayed by title, but you can click the Show Filenames button to display the original file paths and names if it helps you identify them. (You will have an opportunity later to change the titles, if desired.)

Move Report or Folder   To move a report, or a green folder, click it and click the Up or Down Arrow button. The report or folder moves through the folder hierarchy. You can also click and drag the report or folder directly to the folder desired.

Create, Rename, or Delete Folder   You can create new folders on this screen, and you can rename and delete your new folders (shown in green) if needed, using the same buttons and methods discussed for the previous screen.

Note   *You have to move all reports out of a folder before you'll be allowed to delete it.*

When you've identified the correct location for your new report(s), you're ready to start defining the run-time qualifications and properties that the report(s) will exhibit in the Enterprise environment. Click Next. The Schedule Interval dialog box is displayed.

Schedule Interval

The purpose of this screen is to identify how and when each report will be run. The area on the left lists the report(s) you're publishing; on the right are three choices: Run Once Only, Let Users Update The Object, and Run On A Recurring Schedule.

The default scheduling option is Let Users Update The Object. If you do not make any selections on this screen before clicking Next, this option will apply to all the reports in the list.

The first report in the list is highlighted. You can highlight different reports and select a different option for each, or can hold down the SHIFT or CTRL key on your keyboard while you highlight several at once, and have the selected option apply to all.

Depending on the option you select for a report, you may receive additional prompts.

Run Once Only   The Run Once Only option produces an additional prompt asking you to choose whether to run the report as soon as the wizard finishes or at a specified date and time.

Let Users Update the Object   Letting users update the object means the report is not scheduled at all at this time but will be available for users to view and/or schedule at their convenience.

Run on a Recurring Schedule   If you ask for a recurring schedule, you'll need to click the Set Recurrence button that appears. It provides additional prompts:

- **Occurs**   Choose between Daily, Weekly, or Monthly. The Runs prompt area, below Occurs, changes depending on which option is selected.

- **Starting at**   Set a time that the report will run each recurrence.

- **Daily**   If the report occurs daily, choose between Every N days or Every N hours and X minutes.

- **Run weekly**   If the report occurs weekly, choose the day or days of the week.

- **Run monthly**   If the report occurs monthly, choose the Nth calendar day (for example, the first of every month) or choose the Nth weekday (for example, the last Friday of every month).

When you have set any specific scheduling desired for each report, click Next. The Change Default Values dialog box is displayed. The question posed on the Change Default Values screen is whether you wish to review and modify report properties before the final publishing step, including parameters, database logons, report titles, and descriptions.

If you choose Publish Reports Without Modifying Properties, you'll be advanced directly to the final publishing screens (see the "Final Publishing Dialogs" section later in the chapter); the system does check the reports for complete default information and may issue additional messages, which are discussed in that section.

If you choose Review Or Modify Report Properties, the system displays a progress message as it reads the report file(s) to establish the qualities of each report. Then, the Review Report Properties dialog box appears.

Review Report Properties

Similar to the Scheduling screen, this dialog box lists the report(s) being published on the left, with the first report highlighted. On the right are any existing properties of the highlighted report, including the path to the report filename, text entry areas for the title and description of the report, and a Generate Thumbnail check box.

- ■ **Title**   In the Enterprise environment, reports are listed by their titles, if they have titles (if not, they are displayed by report filename).

- ■ **Description**   The description will display in tool-tip text in the Enterprise desktop every time the user points to the report. It helps viewers understand the purpose of the report.

- ■ **Generate thumbnail image**   If activated, the thumbnail shows a tiny picture of the first page of a report on the Enterprise desktop.

Note

Generate thumbnail is available only for reports that were saved with the Save Preview Picture feature activated. If the thumbnail check box is grayed out, the report doesn't have a preview picture to generate.

You can set all or several reports to Generate Thumbnail by selecting a report, holding down your CTRL key, and selecting other reports. Then check the Generate Thumbnail check box. Other values are grayed out, showing that they will not be affected by this global change.

When each report is updated as desired, click Next. The Database Logon dialog box should appear.

Caution

If any of your reports use a file-based data source (for example, MS Access, FoxPro, and so forth) rather than an ODBC or SQL connection to those tables, you will receive a warning indicating that those reports may not be accessible to users in Enterprise. The reports are listed, with the instruction to modify those reports (in Crystal Reports) to use an accepted data source and then republish them through the wizard or another publishing method. This warning will appear at any point that the wizard is verifying data-source choices, which could be here (before the Database Logon dialog box) or could be after choosing to skip report properties altogether.

Database Logon Information

The area on the left displays your report(s). Click the + beside a report to see the database(s) it uses, then click the database. This activates the fields on the right, for entering default database, logon user name, and logon password applicable to that database.

If you want Enterprise users to have to log on to the database any time they run the report, leave the User Name and Password fields blank. Otherwise, if the report will be scheduled rather than run on demand, or if the users who can run it don't have a database user ID and password available to them, complete the screen for the report.

Be sure to highlight each report and its database(s) and complete the information.

To simplify publishing a large number of reports that all use the same database, complete the information and then check the box that allows you to apply this information to all reports requiring a logon for that database.

When all database logons are correct, click Next to review the report parameters.

Set Report Parameters

If any reports have parameters, the reports appear on the left, with the parameters that apply to the highlighted report on the right. You may wish to set some default values for parameters, or you may wish to leave them blank.

If each Enterprise user should be allowed to enter different parameters when running this report on demand, do not fill in default values for the report. However, if the report is being scheduled without user intervention, you'll need to provide the parameter values that you want for the scheduled instance(s).

Highlight the report you want, and click the Edit Prompt button.

The Set Parameter Values dialog box appears, and allows you to set up default values for each of the parameters for that report. The options provided will vary according to what type of parameter is being updated. You may be allowed to enter single values, multiple values, or ranged values, for example. When you have established values for all desired parameters on a report, click OK on the Set Parameter Values box to close it.

When you have set parameters on all desired reports, click the Next button on the Set Report Parameters screen. This takes you to the Schedule Format screen.

Schedule Format

Crystal Enterprise can produce instances of reports in several different formats. This selection sets the default format for the reports. Once you've selected the desired format, click the Next button to go to the final publishing dialog screens.

Final Publishing Dialogs

When you've been through all the report identification, location, and properties dialogs, or have opted to skip some of them, the Crystal Publishing Wizard lists all the report objects for you and gives you the opportunity to review your settings and choices before committing to the final publishing steps. At this point, you can use the Back button to check your choices, if desired. This is also your last chance to cancel the publishing process, if needed.

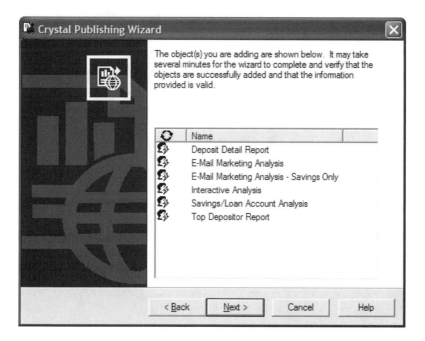

CRYSTAL REPORTS 9
ON THE WEB

When you click the Next button, the system reviews the report object(s) to ensure all required values and properties are complete. If there are any problems, you will receive a message, such as the file-based data-source issue discussed earlier.

When all properties and values are adequate, the Committing Objects progress screen will display report names as they are being committed to publishing. When the commitment process is complete, the final Crystal Publishing Wizard screen appears. The reports and folders you've added are listed, with a Details area for displaying any comments about that object. Normally, the details say, "Object committed to APS successfully." Unusual activity will be marked by a yellow exclamation sign over the object's report or folder icon, and if you click the object, you'll see a comment describing the unusual event. For example, if you copied folders that contained duplicate reports, the comment will indicate that the object was committed to the APS with a "(2)" after the filename.

You can't click Back or Cancel at this point, because the reports have actually been published. Click Finish. The Crystal Publishing Wizard application closes.

Publishing with the Crystal Management Console

This method of publishing is useful for the administrator who is managing several aspects of Enterprise and has one or two reports to publish as well. It's also useful when your local machine has no access to the Crystal Publishing Wizard or the Crystal Report Designer, because you can use the Console remotely.

Also, you can set or modify selection criteria, a feature that is not available through either of the other publishing methods.

This chapter assumes that you have some familiarity with the Crystal Management Console, and does not explore every option on each page. It is a review solely of the steps needed to publish a report.

There are two ways of adding a report after launching the Crystal Management Console.

- Select Manage Folders. Then, navigate to the folder you want to add the new report to. Then, select the Reports tab at the top to display any existing reports in that folder. Then, click the New Report button.

- Select Manage Objects. This will show you all reports in the system, with the folder each is in displayed next to the object name. Click the New Report button.

In either case, the New Report dialog will appear.

New Report

The first step is to identify the report you want to publish and choose a folder to put it in. Enter the path to the desired report, or click the Browse button to browse to it. Click the Generate Thumbnail check box, if available. If activated, the thumbnail shows a tiny picture of the first page of a report on the Enterprise desktop.

Note   *Thumbnail is available only for reports that were saved with the Save Preview Picture feature activated.*

If you wish to identify a destination folder different than the current folder, you must click a folder in the Destination list and then click Show Subfolders until the folder you want is in the Destination drop-down box.

Click OK to add the report to the system. A new page is generated for the report, with a tab for reviewing each of the publishing options on the report. Some tabs may be grayed out and inaccessible if those features (for example, parameters) aren't present on or applicable to the report. You do not have to go to every tab. When you do make a change on a tab, be sure to find and click the Update button to save your changes before looking at another tab. Although you can view the tabs in any order, it makes sense to go to the Schedule tab last, because an update to that tab creates any scheduling requests with all the information updated on other tabs.

Properties Tab

The Properties tab allows you to update the title and description of the report, and request a thumbnail if you didn't do so on the previous page.

- **Title** In the Enterprise environment, reports are listed by their titles—if they have titles (if not, they are displayed by report filename).

- **Description** The description will display in tool-tip text in the Enterprise desktop every time the user points to the report. It helps viewers understand the purpose of the report.

- **Show thumbnail** If activated, the thumbnail shows a tiny picture of the first page of a report on the Enterprise desktop.

Note   *Thumbnail is available only for reports that were saved with the Save Preview Picture feature activated.*

The Properties tab also allows you to set the processing server options for the report. This will be of concern only in a multiple-server environment, and even then will be necessary only when servers are set up differently in order to handle specific tasks or specific sets of reports. There are two sets of options: one for scheduling and one for viewing. Each set of options includes Use the first available server (the default), a radio button and drop-down for selecting a "preferred" server group, and a radio button and drop-down for selecting a "use only" server group.

When Properties are correct, click the Update button (at the bottom). Go to another tab or click Home (above the report name in the blue title bar) if you're finished publishing the report.

History Tab

This tab displays all existing (scheduled and historical) instances for a report. For a new report, there are no instances, so instructions on running the report are inserted in place of the list.

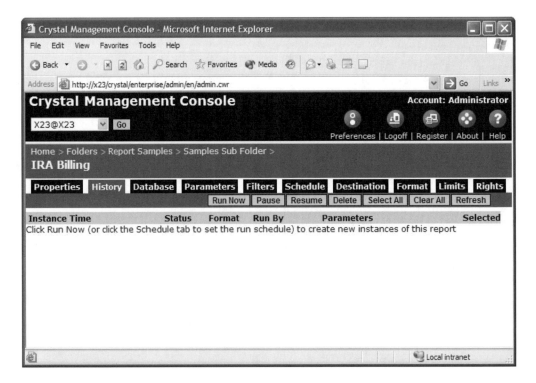

If you do wish to create an instance immediately, rather than scheduling future or recurring instances, click Run Now (above the instructions, below Parameters tab name). This places an instance in the display area immediately. Note that the instance created will use the information from all the other tabs (Parameters, Format, etc.) as they are currently set.

From this tab, you can go to other tabs or click Home (above the report name in the blue title bar) if you're finished publishing the report.

Database Tab

In order for instances of the report to be run or viewed by users who don't have database logon information or access, complete information must be provided for any required database logon.

If the Database tab is grayed out, then the information is not needed by the report object (for example, the report was saved with data).

If the Database tab is active, it displays the data source(s) in the report object on the left and the path to the highlighted database in the Database box to the right. You can change the database a data source points to if there is a different but identical database that should be used; otherwise, leave the database path intact and complete the user Logon Name and Password information if you want it provided for users or for scheduled instances. If you still want users to have to enter valid logon information, check "Prompt the user for new value(s) when viewing."

After you have completed the prompts for each data source in the report, click Update (bottom right) before going to other tabs.

Parameters Tab

This tab will be active only if there are parameter fields active in the report. If you do not complete any default values for parameters, users trying to run the report on demand will be prompted for parameter values. Users who are scheduling instances are also offered a parameters page. But if there is a standard data set you'd like to generate for users who have only view rights, you should enter the appropriate parameter values here before scheduling instances for those users.

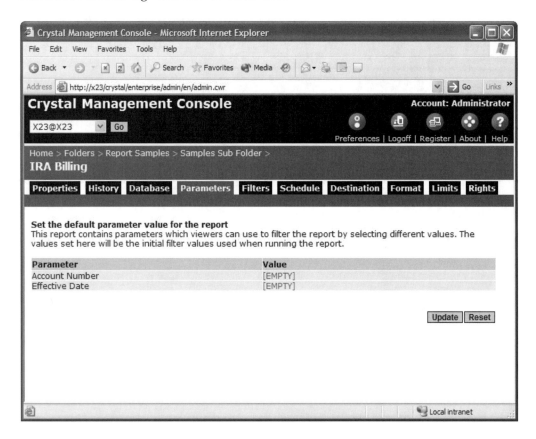

Each parameter in the report is listed, with currently set values displayed. A newly added report normally shows EMPTY in the Values column. Click the word EMPTY to obtain the dialog box for setting initial values for that parameter.

The Set Initial Values dialog options vary according to the way the parameter was created in the report, allowing for single, multiple, and/or ranged parameter values. When you have set the initial values for a given parameter field, click OK to save these values and return to the main Parameters tab.

When you have established values for each parameter desired, click Update (bottom right) before looking at other tabs.

Filters Tab

You can create or modify existing record and group selection formulas on this tab. If users have the rights to schedule a report, they will be able to modify these, but all other viewing methods will run the record and group selections exactly as entered here.

Caution   *The Crystal Management Console does not check for correct Crystal syntax in the selection formula. If you update an incorrect formula, the resulting report instances will not run successfully.*

You can also add processing extensions to the report on this tab. A list of available processing extensions is on the left, and the list of processing extensions to be used for this report is on the right. The left and right arrow buttons are used to include and exclude processing extensions, while the up and down arrow buttons are used to specify the execution order for the included processing extensions.

Be sure to click Update (bottom right) to save all of your changes before viewing other tabs.

Note   *Processing Extensions are a new Crystal Enterprise 8.5 feature that allows custom-designed processing to be performed on a report when it is run. Your organization must have designed or purchased processing extensions, and installed them properly, to make use of these options.*

Schedule Tab

This tab offers scheduling options similar to those in either the Crystal Publishing Wizard or the scheduling page of ePortfolio. You can schedule instances to run on a regular calendar basis, or you can indicate that the report will be available for on-demand viewing.

Note   *When you use this tab to schedule a report, it uses the values currently set in the other tabs. For example, if you would like to schedule a report to be produced in Excel format, you must first use the Format tab to set the report format before completing the Schedule tab. So be sure to set your database logon information, parameters, filters, destination, and format before scheduling a report.*

Each calendar option, when selected, provides additional prompts for further defining the schedule. In all cases (except for the "Now" option), you will be asked for a Start Date, which is the date and time you want to run the report, as well as an optional End Date, which is the date and time past which you would not want the report run. You will also have the option to select "with events." This combines with the scheduling information to delay processing until a specific event or events have been triggered. For example, a weekly report could be scheduled to run every Friday night at 11:00 P.M. but only after an event is triggered that signifies that the database synchronization has been completed. Events may also be set up to trigger upon the completion of the report processing.

On Demand   Choose On Demand if you do not wish to schedule any recurrent instances at this time. This allows users with run rights to view and schedule the report on demand from their Enterprise environment.

Once Choose Once to run the report immediately or at a specific time in the future.

Daily Choose Daily to see three suboptions:

- Once each day
- Every X hour(s), N minute(s)
- Every X day(s)

Weekly The Weekly option allows scheduling on any combination of the seven days. Check boxes are provided for easy selection. For example, three clicks could schedule a report to run on Monday, Wednesday, and Friday of each week.

Monthly Choose Monthly to see five suboptions:

- On the Nth day of the month   For example, on the fifteenth of every month.
- On the Nth X of the month   For example, on the second Friday of every month.
- Every N months
- On the first Monday of the month
- On the last day of the month

When you have established any recurrent or on-demand scheduling, click Update (bottom right).

> **Tip** *If you created a recurrent schedule, you can view the resulting instance on the Instances tab.*

Destination Tab

Crystal Enterprise can "send" a completed report instance to a number of destinations. This tab starts with a drop-down to select the destination. All of the options except "Default" produce more form elements to provide the details for that particular destination.

The destination choices for a report instance file are

- **Default**   Kept on the Crystal Enteprise server and managed by the APS.
- **Unmanaged disk**   Written to any accessible disk location.
- **FTP**   Transferred via FTP to any accessible FTP server.
- **Email (SMTP)**   Attached to an e-mail message and sent via SMTP.
- **Printer**   Written directly to a printer.

Once you've selected your destination, click Update (bottom right).

Format Tab

As in Crystal Reports, Crystal Enterprise can save a report instance in a variety of formats. This tab has a single drop-down to select the desired format.

- Crystal Report   The only way to provide the group tree and drill-down.
- Excel
- Excel (Data Only)   Can be particularly useful for users who want to further manipulate the data.
- Word
- Acrobat   More commonly known as Adobe PDF format.
- Rich Text
- Plain Text
- Paginated Text
- Tab-Separated Values
- Character-Separated Values

Once you've selected your format, click Update (bottom right).

Limits Tab

This tab defines the rules for limiting the number of instances kept in the system. There are two basic rule types for deleting instances: delete excess instances when there are more than N instances and delete instances after N days. These two types of rules may be applied for users and/or groups, as well as globally. For example, a global rule may be to delete excess instances over 100, and a specific rule may be to delete any instances more than seven days old for a specific management group.

To add rules, click the appropriate Add/Remove button on the right side. The resulting page has three possible modes: Add/Remove Groups, Add Users, or Remove Users. Use the arrow buttons in the middle to move the desired groups and/or users into or out of the report's list box. When you are finished, click the OK button. Any users or groups added will now have a line on the limits tab so that you may fill in the numbers to complete the rule.

CRYSTAL REPORTS 9
ON THE WEB

Rights Tab

On this tab, you can define what access other users will have to this report. Only users and groups with rights set at a higher level are displayed here, with their net rights to this report (inherited rights based on the folder it's in) listed on the far right. You can change a user or group's explicit rights to this report by selecting a different rights level from the drop-down box.

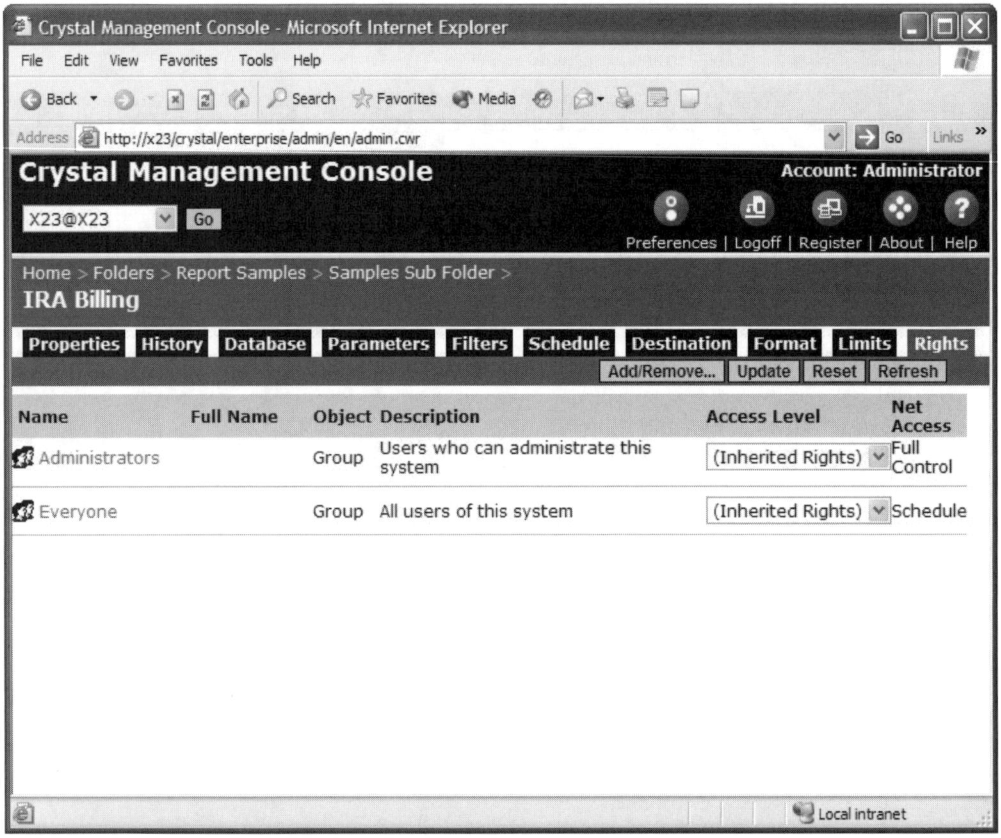

You can also add or remove users and groups by clicking the Add/Remove button on the upper-right side. The resulting page has three possible modes: Add/Remove Groups, Add Users, or Remove Users. Use the arrow buttons in the middle to move the desired groups and/or users into or out of the report's list box. When you are finished, click the OK button. Any users or groups added will now have a line on the rights tab so that you may select the desired rights.

The available rights levels are

- **No Access**   User or group cannot see the report at all.
- **View**   User or group is allowed to view scheduled instances, through History and View Latest Instance; cannot run (View or Schedule) the report.
- **Schedule**   User or group is allowed all viewing and running functions, including View and Schedule.
- **View on Demand**   User or group is allowed to preview the report.
- **Full Control**   User or group is allowed all viewing and running functions and can also move, rename, or delete the report.
- **Advanced...**   This option produces a page where much more granular rights may be either explicitly granted or explicitly denied. For example, a single user may be granted the right to refresh the report's data.

> **Tip**   *The report must be in a shared public folder in order for users to find it easily. If the report was published into a single user's Favorites folder, and that folder is not shared, then users with access to the report can find it through the search functions but will not see the folder it's in.*

When you've adjusted the rights to the report, click Update (this time on the upper-right side) before going to another tab.

When you have reviewed all the desired tabs and updated any changes on each tab, you can close the report by navigating to another function or page in the Crystal Management Console, or you can close the Console.

Reports and report instances you've published through any of the publishing methods are now visible in ePortfolio and the Enterprise environment.

Chapter 24

Customizing Crystal Enterprise ePortfolio

693

C rystal Enterprise comes "out of the box" with its own user interface, ePortfolio. This Web-based application is the default method for users to interact with Crystal Enterprise when you first install it.

Caution *As of the publication date, Crystal Reports 9 does not work with the most recent release of Crystal Enterprise, version 8.5. In order to take advantage of Crystal Enterprise, you'll have to stick with Crystal Reports 8.5. Therefore, all material in this chapter refers to Crystal Reports 8.5 only. For more information on Web delivery options with Crystal Reports 9, see Chapter 20.*

While ePortfolio is fairly complete in the Enterprise feature set that it exposes, it is obviously not designed to mirror your existing corporate intranet or Internet look and feel. As ePortfolio is entirely Web based, and because Crystal Decisions provides completely open source code for ePortfolio, you have complete flexibility to customize ePortfolio to your exacting requirements. In fact, the included Crystal Enterprise Software Development kit, or *SDK*, allows you to completely design and code your own custom Crystal Enterprise user interface.

Note *If you wish to just use the standard ePortfolio without any customization, you can find detailed information about its features and options in Chapter 23.*

Customization Overview

While the unmodified ePortfolio that comes with Crystal Enterprise may be appropriate for many Enterprise installations, you may have a desire to customize its appearance to more closely match the look and feel of your standard corporate Web site. Perhaps you already have a corporate intranet or portal in place that you wish to match ePortfolio to. Or, you may have an Internet site that will benefit from the scheduling or report presentation capabilities of Crystal Enterprise. These are just a few of the many possible instances where you'll find the ability to customize ePortfolio to be of immense value in your overall Web development direction.

Tip *You should make it a practice to always make copies of any Crystal-supplied images, HTML pages, CSP pages, and JavaScript code before you make your own modifications. If you experience technical problems with modified files, you can revert to the Crystal-supplied files to see whether the problems go away.*

There are several directions you may take to customize the appearance and behavior of ePortfolio, from simple replacement of bitmap images with those more appropriate for your existing Web standards, to a complete redesign of the Crystal Enterprise user interface (in essence, *replacement* of ePortfolio) utilizing the full capabilities of the Enterprise SDK. The direction you choose will be based on a combination of factors:

- The extent to which you want to change the look and feel of the standard ePortfolio
- The level of Web development and coding expertise in your organization
- The amount of time available for completing the customization

As you might expect, you can generally expect to require less time and less expertise to perform simpler customizations. However, if you prefer to largely redesign the basic look and feel of ePortfolio, or perhaps even design your own from-the-ground-up user interface using the Enterprise SDK, expect larger time and expertise requirements.

Simple Customization

Relatively simple customization of ePortfolio can consist of merely replacing some of the included bitmap images with your own, or performing simple customization to the existing CSS, HTML, and JavaScript code already supplied by Crystal Decisions. This customization can be as simple as replacing the default logo for ePortfolio with your own custom logo.

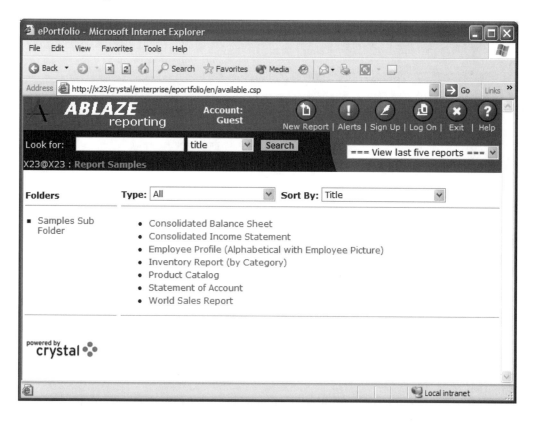

Another easy customization can be performed by editing the default CSS file. With just a few changes, you can significantly alter the fonts and colors of ePortfolio.

You may also perform modifications to existing JavaScript code (provided you have a basic knowledge of JavaScript) or modify other graphical elements of ePortfolio by modifying other .GIF files that are shipped with the product.

Complete Customization

Crystal Decisions also includes a complete Software Development Kit (SDK) to allow you to either customize ePortfolio in larger scale or completely replace ePortfolio with your own custom-designed interface to the core Crystal Enterprise components.

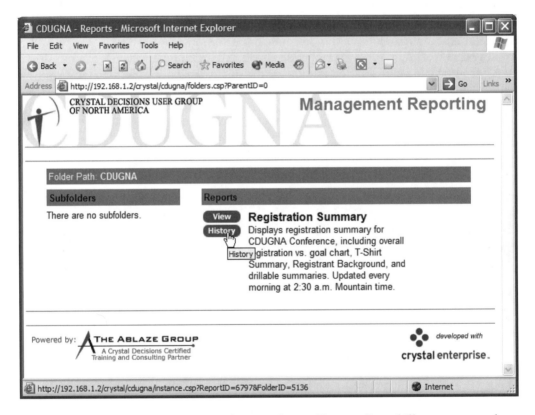

Utilizing your existing HTML and Active Server Page coding skills, you can make use of Crystal Server Pages (CSP) to gain access to the core Crystal Enterprise components, such as folders, reports, and report instances. You may then build your own user interface around these elements, displaying reports inside a Web browser utilizing one of the provided report viewers.

Crystal Enterprise even includes the Crystal Web Wizard, an interactive Windows application that generates a basic set of CSP code automatically, on the basis of the parameters you supply to the Web Wizard.

Tip	*Crystal Decisions provides extensive documentation for different customization options, as well as sample custom applications. After installing Crystal Enterprise, point your Web browser to http://web server/crystal/enterprise and click the Web Developer's Guide and Developer Samples links.*

Simple Modifications

As discussed earlier in this chapter, if you have minimal customization requirements for your particular Web environment, there are many places you can turn to provide a custom look to ePortfolio without having to undertake a large customization project. Since ePortfolio consists primarily of images, Cascading Style Sheets, and Crystal Server Pages (JavaScript and HTML) that are completely open and available for your modification, you may make relatively simple changes to the standard ePortfolio offering with limited effort.

By simply replacing some .GIF image files provided by Crystal Decisions, you may replace the standard ePortfolio logo with your own company logo. And by making some simple changes to a .CSS file, you may quickly change the colors and fonts for the entire ePortfolio application. While a specific Crystal Enterprise user can choose between all the available Web-based report viewers, the Guest account is restricted to the DHTML report viewer by default (the differences among report viewers is discussed later in the chapter in "Changing Defaults for the Guest Account"). By performing simple modifications to a single Crystal Server Page, you may change this default to a preferred report viewer. Other defaults may be set at the same time to further tune ePortfolio to your application. And if you do plan on relying largely on the DHTML report viewer, you may easily customize its top toolbar frame by replacing .GIF image files with those more appropriate to your environment.

Tip	*Depending on how you've installed Crystal Enterprise, you may need to search on separate computers to find files necessary for customization. If you've installed both the Web Connector and the Web Component Server on your Web server, look on this single computer for the pathname \Program Files\Crystal Decisions\Web Content\Enterprise\ ePortfolio\en\. You'll find mostly JavaScript (JS) and Crystal Server Page (CSP) files in this folder. In the images folder below, you'll find .GIF files, and in the css folder, you'll find Cascading Style Sheet files. If you have installed the Web Component Server on a computer separate from your Web server, most image and JavaScript files will reside on the Web server, but CSP files will reside on the Web Component Server. You'll need to coordinate modifications on both computers.*

Adding Your Own Company Logo

One very simple customization can be undertaken if the general look and feel of ePortfolio meets your needs and you merely wish to customize the product with your own company logo. Locate the file eportfolio_default.gif in the \Program Files\ Crystal Decisions\Web Content\Enterprise\ePortfolio\en\images folder. This image appears in the upper left-hand corner of many ePortfolio pages; by replacing this file with your own company logo, you can easily add your own identity to ePortfolio. If you are allowing users to change their color schemes, you will also want to replace the four alternate-color logos: eportfolio_gold.gif, eportfolio_green.gif, eportfolio_purple.gif, and eportfolio_red.gif. To maintain proper appearance, you'll want to ensure that your replacement files are named the same, and are the same horizontal and vertical size as the original files you are replacing.

One other change you may want to make is to eliminate the "powered by Crystal" image. There are two ways to do this: eliminate the image tags from the available.csp and logonform.csp files, or simply replace the pb_blue_sml.gif image with a white or transparent image. The crystaldecisions.com hyperlink may also be eliminated or replaced by looking through each of these CSPs for the line containing www.crystaldecisions.com. The line may be commented out with a JavaScript comment (//) or replaced with your own desired URL.

Changing Colors and Fonts

Another simple customization that can further match ePortfolio to your company's look and feel is to change the basic color scheme and fonts. This can be accomplished by editing a Cascading Style Sheets file and replacing a couple of simple .GIF images.

The CSS file to edit is \Program Files\Crystal Decisions\Web Content\ Enterprise\ ePortfolio\en\css\default.css. To edit the file, you can use any text editor, such as Notepad, or an editor specially made to edit CSS files, such as TopStyle or the CSS editor in Visual InterDev.

Note *It is beyond the scope of this book to get into the details of Cascading Style Sheets. There are many sites on the Web with tutorials, samples, and references. One great place to start is http://www.w3.org/Style/CSS/.*

To change the color scheme of the application, you must edit the CSS file and replace a couple of image files. To change the main blue color everywhere, perform a search-and-replace; search for "#006699" and replace it with your desired RGB color value, such as "#FF0000" or "red." There are many other colors defined in the CSS file, too, defined both as RGB values (such as "#6699FF") and color constants (such as "black"). You may change any and all of these color values to customize font colors, background colors, link colors, etc. To complete the color change, you must change two image files: menu_dot_bg_default.gif and small_dot_default.gif. These two graphics produce the rounded separators in the header areas. You could eliminate these graphics altogether by changing the HTML embedded in the CSP files, but it is a lot easier to use graphic editing software (such as Photoshop) to produce new images that match your color scheme.

To change the font across the entire application, search for "verdana" and replace it with your desired font, such as "arial." You may also want to make some of the fonts a bit larger, replacing "9pt" with "10pt," and then replacing "8pt" with "9pt," for example.

If you know more advanced CSS techniques, you may make other changes to the existing CSS classes to further affect the look and feel of the application.

Changing Defaults for the Guest Account

Several important defaults for ePortfolio can be set quite easily by editing \Program Files\Crystal Decisions\Web Content\Enterprise\ePortfolio\en\globals.csp.

Default Viewer

As with the Web Component Server supported by earlier versions of Crystal Reports, as well as with the Crystal Report Designer Component and Active Server Pages, Crystal Enterprise supports multiple browser-based viewers for displaying reports on the Web. The default viewer for all Crystal Enterprise accounts is the DHTML frames viewer, as shown in Figure 24-1. This viewer takes advantage of the latest HTML standard (Dynamic Hypertext Markup Language, or HTML 4) to provide very accurate report formatting in a simple HTML frames display.

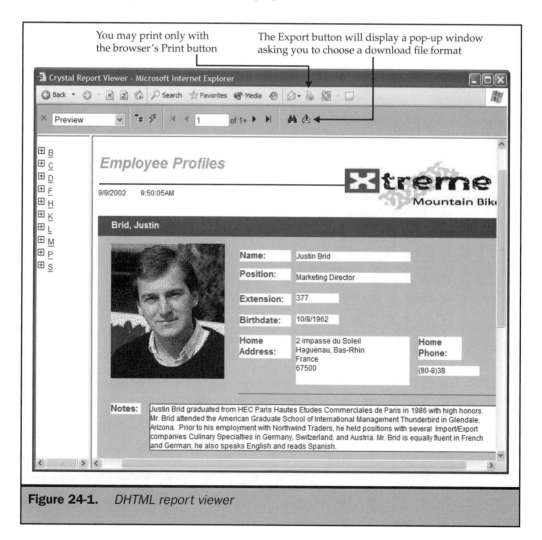

Figure 24-1.   *DHTML report viewer*

While this viewer does an admirable job of reproducing most Crystal Reports formatting accurately, there are certain functions (such as printing fully paginated reports to an attached printer) that this viewer does not provide. For this reason, there may be a desire to use one of the available alternate report viewers. For example, the ActiveX viewer (designed for the Microsoft Internet Explorer browser) or one of the Java viewers (designed for Internet Explorer, Netscape Navigator, and other Java-capable browsers) includes a more robust print function, as well as a more seamless export file option. The ActiveX viewer is illustrated in Figure 24-2.

When you log on to Crystal Enterprise as a named user, you will have the ability to choose the report viewer that you'd like to use by clicking the Preferences link on ePortfolio main page (Chapter 23 discusses ePortfolio usage in more detail). However, the default account that ePortfolio initially presents to a user is the Guest account, which does not have a Preferences option and does not allow a customized viewer choice.

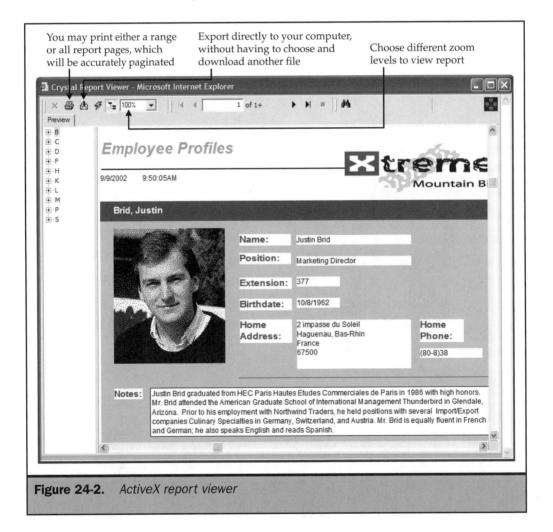

Figure 24-2. *ActiveX report viewer*

The choice of the DHTML viewer as the Guest account default has been hard-coded into the globals.csp file. You are free to change this choice should you prefer to present an alternate viewer to the Guest account and to users when they first log in. To make this change, find the line that has var DEF_VWR = 1 and simply change the 1 to any of the following:

0   ActiveX viewer

2   HTML page viewer

3   Java viewer (using the browser's built-in Java Virtual Machine)

4   Java plug-in viewer

5   Navigator plug-in viewer (provides same functionality as ActiveX viewer, but in Netscape Navigator)

 Look in Chapter 21 under "Report Viewers Compared" for a description of available viewers and a comparison of their features.

Menu Style

The style of the menu in the upper-right corner can be set in globals.csp. Find the line with var DEF_MENU = MENU_BUTTONS_AND_TEXT, and choose from the menu types of MENU_BUTTONS_AND_TEXT, MENU_BUTTONS_ONLY, and MENU_TEXT_ONLY.

Reports per Page

The number of reports displayed on a single ePortfolio page can be set by finding var DEF_RPP = 39 and replacing the 39 with the desired number of reports.

Others

There are several other defaults available in globals.csp, such as Report View Mode, Data View, and Report Listing. With further tweaking of these defaults, you can create a version of ePortfolio that is better tuned for your application.

Tip *Another way you can change the default preferences for the Guest account is to use the ePortfolio Preferences Manager sample application, which is available from the Crystal Enteprise Launchpad page. By selecting that sample and logging on as the Administrator to Crystal Enterprise, you can get a listing of all the listed user accounts in Crystal Enterprise, including the Guest account. By selecting the Guest account and clicking on preferences, you can get and set the Guest user preferences you would normally see if a user logged on to ePortfolio with a defined account and chose their own preferences. This method enables the change of Guest user preferences without the requirement of any code changes. This also protects from those changes being lost should the user apply a modified version of ePortfolio, such as might be received through a Crystal Decisions patch.*

Customizing the DHTML Viewer Toolbar

While there are certain advantages to using the ActiveX and Java report viewers, you also gain an advantage if you use the default DHTML report viewer. Not only do you negate the need to download an ActiveX control or Java applet to the browser, potentially reducing network bandwidth and avoiding any related security issues, but you have more control over how the DHTML viewer appears inside the target Web browser. In particular, you have the ability to customize the appearance and behavior of the toolbar that appears as part of the DHTML report viewer.

A simple approach to this customization is to reorder the appearance of the elements in the toolbar, (for example, placing page navigation buttons before other elements in the toolbar and so forth) or change the bitmap images that make up the toolbar elements. You may edit the existing HTML that creates the toolbar by opening \Program Files\ Crystal Decisions\Viewers\html\en\toolbar.html.

You'll notice a large amount of JavaScript code, which implements what Crystal Decisions calls the *HTML Frame API*. While it's arguable that this is really an application programmer interface, or API, in the true sense of the acronym, it does expose a set of JavaScript functions that you can call from your customized toolbar HTML to manipulate the report contained in another browser frame.

Once you've opened toolbar.html, you can make modifications to the order in which elements appear or eliminate elements you may not wish to provide to your end users. Another option is to leave the toolbar basically intact as Crystal Decisions has provided it, but to provide your own image files for such toolbar elements as page navigation buttons, the Refresh button, and other toolbar elements. You can either change references to the provided .GIF files in toolbar.html to refer to your custom images, or you may replace the supplied .GIFs with new files with identical filenames. You'll find toolbar images in the \Program Files\Crystal Decisions\Viewers\html\ en\images folder. Just make sure you provide properly designed replacement graphics. You'll typically notice that three images are required for each toolbar element: an enabled button image (for example, refresh.gif), a "grey" disabled button image (refreshgrey.gif), and a "mouse over" button image (refreshover.gif).

Should you wish to completely redesign the toolbar frame to match your own intranet or Internet site, you may engage in a more complex from-the-ground-up design. In this scenario, you should perform the following high-level tasks:

- Create a main CSP that creates a frameset for at least two frames: the report frame and the toolbar frame. You may want to consider creation of additional frames for other window elements specific to your desired user interface.

- Create a separate HTML page that includes your custom toolbar code. You'll need to include the Crystal-supplied htmlviewer.js JavaScript code so that your custom toolbar HTML can call appropriate HTML Frame API functions to move among report pages, refresh the report, export the file, and so on.

Complete Customization with Crystal Server Pages

While the procedures discussed previously in this chapter provide you a certain amount of customization capability to the out-of-the-box ePortfolio, you may have a greater need than these techniques satisfy. For example, you may have a radically different intranet or Internet user interface that can't be matched by simple ePortfolio customization. Or, you may have developed a completely customized portal for your employees or customers that requires only limited pieces of Crystal Enterprise to be exposed. Potentially, for as many different Web interfaces that exist, there are options for integrating Crystal Enterprise.

Creating these higher levels of customization and integration will require greater effort on your part, as well as greater knowledge of more base-level Crystal Enterprise interfaces. In particular, you'll need to become familiar with Crystal Server Pages, or *CSP*, as well as the programming interface exposed by the Crystal Enterprise Software Development Kit, or Enterprise *SDK*. As discussed earlier, ePortfolio is based largely on CSP and is a good place to look when you're first starting to explore this programming interface.

CSP Overview

Crystal Server Pages can be most closely compared to Microsoft Active Server Pages (ASP), Microsoft's server-side scripting language for their Internet Information Server Web server. Like ASP, CSP can support both VBScript and JavaScript code, as well as embedded HTML and calls to Component Object Model (COM) objects. If you're familiar with ASP, making the transition to CSP should be a fairly straightforward process. CSP supports almost all the language functions of ASP, and it also includes additional calls to the Enterprise SDK to allow you to interact with the Automated Process Scheduler (APS), the central "brain" of Crystal Enterprise.

Like ASP, CSP operates as a *server-side* development tool—that is, the code is actually processed on the server, not on the Web browser. While you may write fairly extensive CSP code to create your custom interface to Crystal Enterprise, only the resulting HTML or JavaScript will be returned to the end-user Web browser—you may have a 250-line CSP script that ultimately returns only 20 lines of HTML and/or JavaScript to the Web browser.

Examine the following CSP code, which has been saved on a Web server set up to run Crystal Enterprise:

```
<HTML>
<BODY>

<%@ Language="VBScript" %>
```

```
<%
Dim DayNumber
DayNumber = WeekDay(Date)
If DayNumber = 1 or DayNumber = 7 then
  Response.Write "<B>Have a nice weekend on this " & _
  WeekDayName(DayNumber) & ".</b>"
Else
  Response.Write "Today is " & WeekDayName(DayNumber) & "."
End If
%>
<BR>
</BODY>
</HTML>
```

Notice, in particular, the text between the <% and %> symbols. This text is the server-side script that will be evaluated by the Web Component Server. Only after this script has been evaluated will the actual results of the Response.Write statement be sent back to the Web browser. All text outside of these special symbols will be sent directly to the Web browser as standard HTML. As a result, the following HTML will be returned to the browser, if the system clock on the Web Component Server is set to a Saturday (the WeekDay of the week is 7):

```
<HTML>
<BODY>




<B>Have a nice weekend on this Saturday.</b><BR>
</BODY>
</HTML>
```

The preceding example actually shows standard VBScript that would work just as well when saved as a Web page with an .ASP extension as it would with a .CSP extension. However, there are two immediate stark differences between ASP and CSP code. Unlike ASP, which is evaluated on the Web server (and that Web server *must* be Microsoft

Internet Information Server), CSP is evaluated on the Crystal Enterprise Web Component Server. This difference gives you more flexibility with Crystal Enterprise, in that you are not required to use CSP with a Microsoft Web server. You may use CSP with a variety of Web servers, including Netscape Web servers and "plain" CGI Web servers, as well as certain UNIX Web servers. Also, CSP exposes additional software interfaces beyond ASP that can be used to interact with Crystal Enterprise components—in particular, the Crystal Enterprise ASP.

Note   *There are other subtle differences between ASP and CSP. For details, look in the Enterprise Web Developer's Guide, or search the Crystal Decisions support site at http://support.crystaldecisions.com.*

You will typically find there to be much more to a CSP page than the simple example given previously. Here's a small fraction of the code belonging to a relatively small CSP that simply extracts the list of folders from the Crystal Enterprise APS:

```
Folder.csp - Notepad
File  Edit  Format  Help

'Retrieve the parent's ID for the current folder.
Result = RetrieveParentID(IStore,CurrentFolderID,ParentID)

'Check to see if the query was successful.
If Result = TRUE Then

'If this is not the top level of folders display the Up A Level option and just-opened fol
        If Not IsEmpty(ParentID) And (CurrentFolderID<>0) Then
                Result = RetrieveFolderName(CurrentFolderID, CurrentFolderName)
                Response.Write "<tr><td valign=""center""><img src='UpALevel.gif'><A HRef=
                Response.Write "<img src='Folderopen.gif'> "
                Response.Write "<b>" & Server.HTMLEncode(CurrentFolderName) & "</b></td></
        End If

        'If there are sub-folders display a link to them.
        If Not isEmpty(FolderNames) Then
                Dim k
                For k = 1 to UBound(FolderNames)
                        Response.Write "<tr><td valign=""center""><img src=""Folderclosed.
                        Response.Write "<a href='home.csp?FolderID=" & FolderIDs(k) & "' t
                        Response.Write Server.HTMLEncode(FolderNames(k)) & "</a></td></tr>
                Next
        End If
Else
        Response.Write "There was an error trying to retrieve the parent folder."
End If
```

The resulting HTML is very small—simply showing a few .GIF files and the names of the retrieved folders:

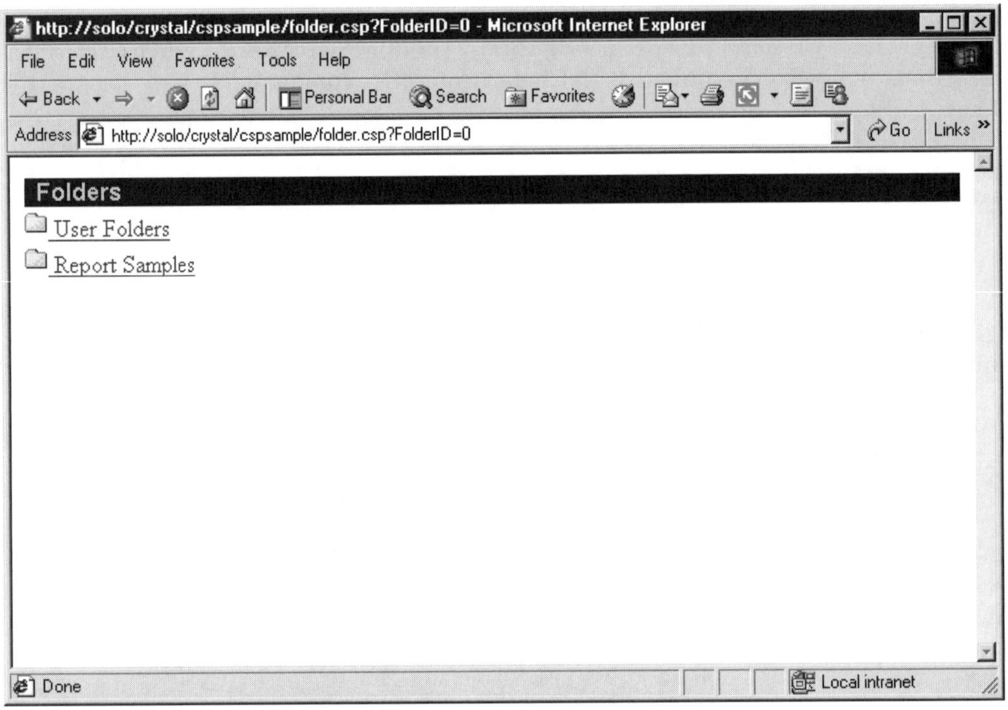

In order for CSP functionality to operate with diverse Web servers, specific Web page file extensions are "flagged" for special handling on the Web server when a Crystal Enterprise Web Connector is installed on the server. In particular, the following Web page file extensions are automatically routed to the Web Component Server when encountered by the Web server:

CSP	Crystal Server Page
CWR	Crystal Web Request
RPT	Crystal Reports File
CRI	Crystal Reports Image File

As such, any URL containing any of these three extensions will not be processed on the Web server—the file will be routed by the Web server to the Crystal Enterprise Web Component Server, which will process the file according to Enterprise's predetermined processing cycle. The results of that processing cycle (standard HTML and/or JavaScript from a CSP or a report viewer from a CWR or RPT) will then be sent back to the Web server for return to the Web browser originating the URL.

> **Note**   *For more information on Crystal Enterprise Architecture and a discussion of different Enterprise components, such as the APS and Web Component Server, refer to Chapter 22.*

Creating Crystal Server Pages

Once you decide to undertake a CSP project (either modification of an existing system or creation of a new ground-up application), you'll have several choices available to you when it comes to code creation. Considering that your custom application will probably make at least minimal use of Crystal Enterprise functionality, be prepared for a fairly code-intensive process. One look at the supplied ePortfolio CSPs will give you an idea of the amount of code required to make even moderate use of Crystal Enterprise features (one of the main ePortfolio files, available.csp, contains over 2,000 lines of code). The choice of your ultimate coding method will depend on a number of factors:

- Your coding skills
- Availability of an existing application you can modify
- The complexity of the application
- Whether Crystal-supplied tools can create a close enough starting point

You have several choices available, much as you do when creating Active Server Pages. You can use HTML authoring tools, such as Microsoft FrontPage; Web-application development tools, such as Visual InterDev; and even simple text editors, such as Notepad. Crystal Decisions provides some supplementary tools to make CSP creation easier. The Crystal Web Wizard is available to help you create a "starting application" using a simple "expert" interface. You'll also find the CSP Query Builder to help you create SQL-like queries to retrieve data from the APS. And the sample applications (available on the Enterprise Launchpad) show various ways to embed Crystal Enterprise functionality into a variety of applications.

Manual Creation with an HTML Tool or Text Editor

If you are familiar with Active Server Pages, you're aware of various tools used to create them. In general, the development community appears to be evenly divided between a development tool such as Visual InterDev, a "fancy" text editor such as Microsoft FrontPage, and a plain text editor such as Notepad (Microsoft's new development environment, Visual Studio.NET, stands ready to offer a much better alternative to these existing methods). You'll find a similar set of options for Crystal Server Pages. While CSPs are plain ASCII text files, you may want to look for a more robust editing tool—at least one that will highlight different syntax elements inside the VBScript or JavaScript code your CSP is based on. While none of the aforementioned tools will specifically recognize particular Crystal Enterprise CSP syntax elements, you will gain the benefit of at least denoting standard VBScript of JavaScript code included in the CSP.

Note	*You may need to set options for Microsoft Visual InterDev or FrontPage to set the tools to properly recognize the .CSP file extension. Look at online documentation for these tools to get more information on adding additional file extensions. Or, you may wish to rename your .CSP files with an .ASP extension for editing, and then rename them back to .CSP before testing.*

You may also be satisfied with the text-editing capabilities of a simple text editor such as Notepad. While you won't see particular VBScript or JavaScript syntax, a simple editor requires no special configuration to recognize file types and can simply be left open side by side with a Web browser to perform an edit-save-refresh type of development and debugging process.

No matter which method you use to create or modify CSPs, you will need to keep a reference of CSP objects, properties, and syntax close at hand, particularly when you first begin developing your application. While a comprehensive discussion of all Enterprise SDK options is beyond the scope of this Crystal Reports–oriented book, the Enterprise Web Developer's Guide (available from the Crystal Enterprise Launchpad) provides a complete reference to the CSP object models and syntax. You'll also find a complete set of tutorials in this help file, including sample CSP code you can copy to your own editor for use in developing your custom application.

The Crystal Web Wizard

As discussed earlier in this chapter, even a moderately simple Crystal Enterprise custom application can become very code intensive very quickly. You will want to eventually develop good knowledge of the individual elements of the Enterprise SDK to maximize your coding flexibility. However, you may appreciate a Crystal Decisions–supplied tool that makes initial creation of custom CSP code as simple as using an expert-like interface to specify simple requirements for your initial application. The *Crystal Web Wizard* is available as a stand-alone Windows program.

The Crystal Web Wizard will present you with a series of screens allowing you to choose particular options for your Crystal Enterprise application. First, you'll have the choice of either creating a new project or creating an Admin project. A new project will create a generic user interface, including logon information and a folder/report list. You will then be able to modify the CSP created by the wizard to more closely match your desired look and feel. Choosing an admin project will produce an application for managing users and groups.

The Crystal Web Wizard is a Windows application that must be specifically chosen when you install Crystal Enterprise. If you click your Windows Start button and don't see a Crystal Enterprise menu option or don't see the Crystal Web Wizard option within this menu, you'll need to rerun Crystal Enterprise setup from the program CD-ROM and ensure that the Web Wizard is chosen as an option.

To use the Crystal Web Wizard, perform the following steps:

CRYSTAL REPORTS 9 ON THE WEB

1. Start the Crystal Web Wizard from the Windows Crystal Enterprise Start button menu. The Web Wizard initial screen will appear.

2. Choose Create a New Project or Create an Admin Project. Then, click the Next button.

3. If you choose to create a new project, you'll next be given the opportunity to determine the logon method you wish to present to your end user when the application first runs. Choose Crystal Enterprise Authentication if you want to provide only Crystal Enterprise–based security (no NT security option will be available). Choose Logon (All Options) if you want to provide a choice of authentication methods (Enterprise or Windows NT) to your end user. Or, choose Windows NT Authentication to provide only Windows NT–integrated security to your end user. Then, click the Next button.

4. You'll then be presented with a choice of content templates to control the display of folders, reports, and report instances. Each of the four choices (Classic Report Listing, Directory Listing, Large Icon View, and Report Listing) will display folders and reports in a different fashion. A thumbnail view of the way the page will appear shows in the preview area when you select each option. Make your desired choice and click the Next button.

5. You'll now be given a choice of a style sheet for the display of your Crystal Enterprise application. As with the content template type, you'll be given choices in a drop-down list, with a matching thumbnail appearing in the preview area when you choose different options. Make your choice of a style sheet and click the Next button.

6. The last screen in the Web Wizard will allow you to select a drive and directory where the CSP, HTML, GIF, and other files should be copied. Either type in a pathname directly or click the Browse button to choose a directory from a directory list.

7. You may choose any pathname you wish (the default being the standard inetpub\wwwroot root directory for Microsoft Web servers). However, you'll probably want to choose a pathname that can be referenced via a Web server virtual directory. If the pathname you choose can't be referenced by a Web server virtual directory, you'll need to map the pathname you specify here to a virtual directory with your Web server administration tools before you can successfully view your completed Enterprise application.

8. After you've specified the location to save the files, click the Finish button. The files composing your Crystal Enterprise application will be created and placed in the pathname you specified.

You may now modify any of the wizard-created CSPs to more closely match your desired intranet or Internet standards. To view the completed custom application, simply point your Web browser to the virtual directory where you save the application.

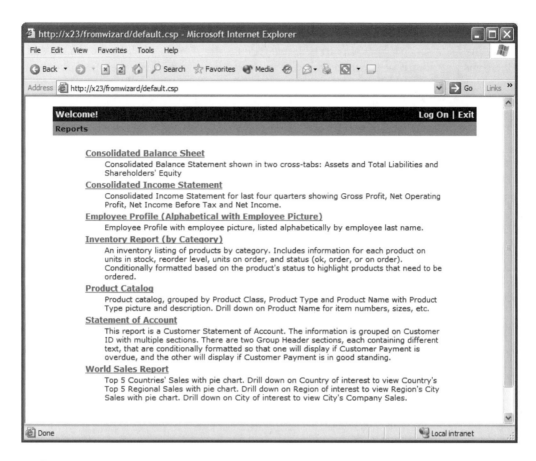

Using the CSP Query Builder

Part of the basic requirement for accessing Crystal Enterprise reports, folders, scheduled objects, and instances from within your CSPs is the ability to submit queries to the SDK's "InfoStore" object (an object-oriented interface to the Enterprise APS system database). This process is undertaken using a query language that's very similar to standard Structured Query Language, or SQL.

For example, to retrieve a list of reports in a particular folder to display in a secondary report frame, you might execute CSP code similar to the following:

```
query = "Select SI_NAME, SI_ID From CI_INFOOBJECTS Where "
query = query & "SI_PROGID='CrystalEnterprise.Report' "
query = query & "And SI_INSTANCE=0 AND "
query = query & "SI_PARENT_FOLDER=" & CStr(CurrentFolderID)


'Query the server
Set ObjectResult = IStore.Query(Query)
```

An entire section of the Web Developer's Guide is dedicated to this query syntax, including a reference to all the objects that can be returned and tested. However, Crystal Decisions provides a Web-based tool to allow you to create and execute these queries outside your CSP code. This tool serves several useful purposes—allowing you to see another Web-based example of how to interact with the Enterprise SDK, facilitating a query of the APS database with a stand-alone tool, and giving you an expert-like way of exploring the syntax for InfoStore queries.

To use the Query Builder, choose the CSP Query Builder from the Developer Samples link on the Crystal Enterprise Launchpad, or point your browser to http://*web server*/crystal/enterprise/websamples/en/query. The CSP Query Builder will appear in a Web browser, as shown in Figure 24-3.

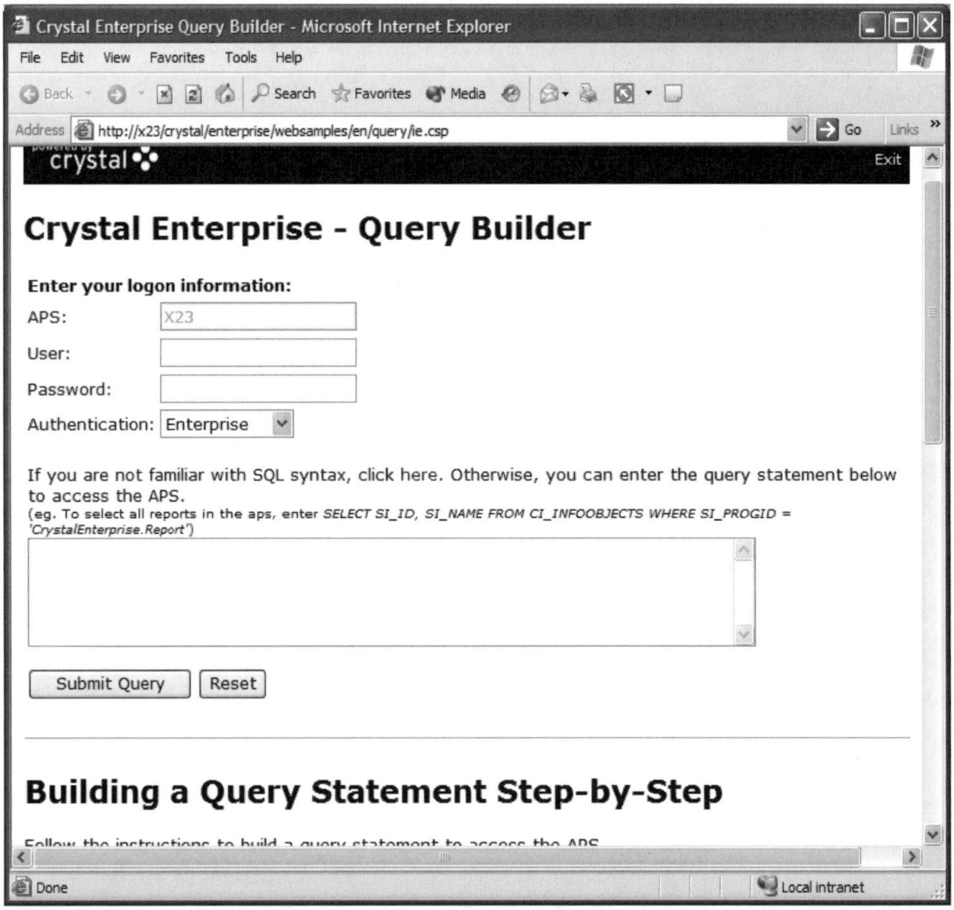

Figure 24-3. *Crystal Enterprise CSP Query Builder*

This Web-based tool allows you to enter an SDK-formatted SQL statement directly into the text box below the login information, or use a simpler step-by-step process of building "rules." Once you've built rules, you may click the Finish button to create a SQL statement at the top of the Query Builder window. When you click the Submit Query button, your query will be submitted to the APS and a result set of folder, report, or object data will appear in your browser. You may then use the query that you built interactively in the Query Builder right inside your CSP code. You may simply copy and paste the query that was displayed from the Query Builder into your text editor, or retype it using the same syntax.

| Tip | *You'll notice that many objects and properties exposed by the Enterprise SDK begin with the letters "SI," while some begin with "CI." This indicates that the Enterprise SDK actually had its beginnings in other Crystal Decisions products—Seagate Info and its predecessor, Crystal Info. You'll notice some of these properties are documented as being unavailable in Crystal Enterprise Standard or Professional Editions. This indicates that these properties are "left over" from Seagate Info and are not supported in this release of Crystal Enterprise.* |

Sample Applications

The Crystal Launchpad contains links to several sample applications that feature a variety of Crystal Enterprise functionality. All of the source code for these applications is available for research, modification, or copying-and-pasting. Depending on your needs, it may be possible to use a sample application as the starting point for your own application.

When first viewing the Crystal Launchpad, examine links to the samples on the left side of the screen under "Client Samples."

The
Complete
Reference

Crystal
Reports 9

Part III

Developing Custom
Window Applications

The Complete Reference

Crystal Reports 9

Chapter 25

Integrating Crystal Reports 9 with Visual Basic

717

I f you've read even a bit of Part I of this book, you've seen some of the power and flexibility of Crystal Reports. By making the vast array of corporate databases accessible with its simple, straightforward user interface, Crystal Reports has established itself as a valuable tool simply by virtue of its reporting and querying capabilities. Part II explored the myriad ways to integrate Crystal Reports with the World Wide Web. But there's a whole other side of Crystal Reports that has yet to be explored.

Because database reporting and querying is a large part of many standard business applications, you'll often need to include these features in custom applications that you create for your own use. If you develop custom applications for Microsoft Windows in any of the popular Windows development tools, you'll probably soon need some type of database reporting functionality inside the application. While you can develop your own routines to step through the database record by record to generate your own internal reporting mechanism, all the intricacies of formatting, font management, graphics, and other Windows-related printing issues can create a significant, if not impossible, coding challenge.

Crystal Reports has featured developer interfaces for virtually all of its Windows versions. Version 9 offers some improved developer integration features that make it an even better choice for inclusion in custom Windows applications. Microsoft Visual Basic 6 (VB) developers, as well as other developers using a development tool compatible with Microsoft's Component Object Model, will appreciate improvements to the Report Designer Component (RDC). In Visual Basic and later Microsoft Office Developers editions, this interface allows both report design and flexible report integration to occur entirely in the VB integrated development environment (VB IDE). You'll never have to leave Visual Basic to perform any report development or integration tasks!

If you're looking toward Microsoft's significantly updated Visual Studio .NET tool for Windows or Web application creation, you'll find Crystal Reports is an integral part of this new development environment as well. Much like the Report Designer Component with Visual Basic 6, Crystal Reports for Visual Studio .NET is fully integrated with the development environment, allowing complete report development right inside Visual Studio .NET. Finished reports can be made available in both Windows and Web applications, as well as being published as Web services. And, Crystal Reports 9 Advanced Edition adds even more functionality to your existing .NET environment.

Furthermore, Crystal Decisions provides flexibility when it comes to distributing your custom applications. While you are not allowed to redistribute the Crystal Reports design components (such as the Crystal Reports design program itself), your custom programs that merely manipulate and customize existing reports can be distributed without charge. You receive a royalty-free license to distribute the Crystal Report Designer Component and associated files, such as associated database and exporting .DLL files. You may purchase a single copy of Crystal Reports, develop your custom application, and distribute the run-time files with as many copies of your application as you like, at no additional charge. If you elect to use newer report creation functions or the embedded Report Designer control that is available in Version 9, you will need to purchase a run-time license from Crystal Decisions.

Note *Don't forget that Crystal Reports 9 is available in four different editions. The Developer or Advanced Edition will be of interest to you if you plan on using any Windows development features. To use any of the developer interfaces discussed in this section of the book, you need to purchase the Developer or Advanced Edition—the other editions don't provide necessary components for custom Windows integration. If you want to make use of new Crystal Reports 9 additions to Visual Studio .NET, you need to purchase the Advanced Edition.*

Development-Language Options

Crystal Reports developer interfaces have been designed to work with most popular Windows development tools that support Microsoft's standard Component Object Model (or COM). Previous Crystal Reports versions also included "legacy" interfaces that could be used with non-COM environments, such as those that integrated via Windows API calls or Visual Basic ActiveX (.OCX) controls. While some of these older interfaces may still be supported with Crystal Reports 9, they have been given the dubious distinction of "legacy status," indicating that they don't contain newer features that the COM options provide.

And finally, Crystal Decisions Software provides a Java-capable interface with Crystal Reports 9. The Crystal Reports Java Bean Viewer allows you to integrate a report into your Java applet or Web application. The Java Bean Viewer exposes a similar set of properties and methods as the Crystal viewer control for non-Java development tools.

Which Development Language Should I Use?

Which development language you should use is a question that cannot be answered simply in this book. It obviously depends largely on your experience level with particular developer tools. Also, your company may standardize on certain development tools that limit your choices. However, if your project will depend heavily on built-in reporting, you may want to consider an alternative tool if the tool you are familiar with doesn't support Microsoft's COM-standard interface.

With Crystal Reports 9, there is no more question about Crystal Decisions' intended direction with developer interfaces. Previous interfaces, such as the Report Engine API, have been relegated to "legacy" status—a separate help file exists to document these interfaces (Legacy.CHM is located in Program Files\Crystal Decisions\Crystal Reports 9\ Developer Files\Help\<*language*>). Since most common Windows languages work with Microsoft's COM, chances are good that you'll be able to program Crystal Reports applications using this method.

Overall, you need to balance your corporate standards, your knowledge level, the size and speed you want your application to maintain, and the reporting demands of your application when making a development-tool choice. While Crystal Decisions still provides several different interfaces, it is now "Crystal Clear" (pun intended!) that the COM-based Report Designer Component is the integration direction of choice.

> **Tip**
>
> *The best source of developer-related information from Crystal Decisions is a Windows Help file that ships with Crystal Reports. Use Windows Explorer to navigate to the CrystalDevHelp.CHM file in Program Files\Crystal Decisions\Crystal Reports 9\ Developer Files\Help\<language>. You'll find complete documentation for the Report Designer Component, sample code that you can copy from the Help file, and references to sample applications that are installed along with Crystal Reports. You can also find several helpful online documents in Adobe Acrobat PDF format on the product CD-ROM. While DevGuide.PDF provides a higher-level overview of integration options, TechRef.PDF provides much of the same detailed information as CrystalDevHelp.CHM.*

Different VB Reporting Options

One of the big reasons for Crystal Reports' popularity is that it seems to automatically show up whenever you install a great number of other applications. It has been bundled with Visual Basic since version 3 and is also included with some other Microsoft development tools and over 150 other general and specific off-the-shelf applications. This, combined with the inclusion of Microsoft's Data Report Designer in VB 6, may beg the question: "Why should I upgrade to the full Developer or Advanced Edition of Crystal Reports if I can use the Data Report Designer or already have a bundled version of Crystal Reports with Visual Basic?"

Crystal Reports Versus the Microsoft Data Report Designer

In VB versions prior to 6, the only reporting options you had "out of the box" were excruciatingly painful record-by-record coding options, or the various bundled versions of Crystal Reports. Visual Basic 6 introduced the Microsoft Data Report Designer, as well as continuing to include a bundled version of Crystal Reports. Whereas Crystal Reports was typically installed automatically with VB in versions prior to 6, you have to dig for it with VB 6. Microsoft automatically installs its own Data Report Designer instead.

However, a peek at the Microsoft offering will quickly give you an idea of where you may want to turn for report design. While the Data Report Designer is fairly well integrated with Visual Basic (using the VB Data Environment), it quickly runs out of steam. And Microsoft obviously didn't think that highly of its report designer either— it has been eliminated from Visual Studio .NET to make way for Crystal Reports!

Bundled Crystal Reports Versus the Stand-Alone Version

Even with Microsoft's Data Report Designer included in VB 6, Crystal Reports is *still* bundled in the VB package—you just have to install it separately. VB 4 and 5 also included bundled copies of Crystal Reports. The versions that are included with VB differ dramatically from off-the-shelf Crystal Reports 9 Developer, however.

In VB 5 and 6, Crystal Decisions bundles a version of Crystal Reports known as Version 4.6. This is interesting, because Crystal Decisions never released an off-the-shelf Version 4.6 of Crystal Reports—stand-alone Crystal Reports versions progressed from 4.5 to 5.0, and then 6.0, 7.0, 8.0, 8.5, and now 9. Why the version of Crystal Reports that's bundled with VB goes so far back is a question for someone who understands software company marketing and upgrade strategies. But for you, the developer, the differences between the 4.6 bundled version and off-the-shelf Crystal Reports 9 are vast and significant:

- Bundled Crystal Reports was brought to market before Microsoft's COM became a standard. It doesn't contain any of the newer programming interfaces, such as the RDC.

- Crystal Reports 5 and later introduced many new usability enhancements, such as conditional formatting, multiple sections, and subreports. Accordingly, many capabilities will be severely limited if you choose to use the bundled Visual Basic 6 version.

- The bundled version contains absolutely no Web-reporting capabilities. If your VB apps will ever get *near* the Web, you'll appreciate the stand-alone version's Web-reporting features, such as RAS and Crystal Enterprise (discussed in Part II of this book).

Visual Basic Developer Interfaces

Crystal Decisions provides several methods for you to use Visual Basic to create a custom reporting application. Your choice of a programming interface will depend on several factors, such as your experience level and the particular functions that you need to include in your application.

As mentioned previously, the Report Designer component is, without a question, Crystal Decisions' tool of choice for VB integration—and with good reason. The RDC provides a good mix of functionality and ease of use. With its object-oriented interface, you can accomplish any sophisticated report customization that you require without having to get down and dirty with Windows API calls. The RDC also provides report design capabilities right inside VB. And, while the ActiveX control is a great way to integrate a report in simpler applications, you will soon find that it doesn't offer sophisticated features that you will need later on, when your application grows. This is especially true considering that it has not been updated with new features since Crystal Reports Version 6.

Part III Does Not Teach You Visual Basic!

The rest of Part III assumes you have a beginning-to-intermediate working knowledge of Visual Basic. It's not practical to try to teach you VB at the same time you're learning how to integrate reports. You'll need to have a fundamental knowledge of how to create VB forms and how to respond to events. There are many good texts (including several from Osborne/McGraw-Hill), training programs, and interactive tutorials available to teach you these fundamental skills.

Also, this section assumes that you have gleaned report design knowledge from Part I of this book. Crystal Reports features, such as selection criteria, parameter fields, and object and section formatting, will be covered. If necessary, refer to Part I to brush up on these report design topics.

One thing to keep in mind when making your choice of a VB interface is that you must choose one option for each individual application. You can't use more than one approach in the same application. For example, if you add the ActiveX control to your application and then try to make direct API calls, errors will result. Evaluate your needs and skills. Then, choose a method and stick with it. Changing an interface in midstream will require you to do significant recoding.

Note *Due to Crystal Decisions' continuing movement toward the Report Designer Component (RDC) as its single developer interface of choice, the remainder of this book section will concentrate on the RDC only. Chapters covering the older "legacy" integration methods, such as the ActiveX control and Report Engine API, are available for reference on this book's companion Web site at www.CrystalBook.com.*

The Report Designer Component

Continuing along the direction set with Crystal Reports 8.5, Crystal Reports 9's premier programming integration method is the Report Designer Component, or *RDC*. While there aren't major revisions to Version 9 of the RDC, there are some notable changes that can make your development activities easier:

- Connection Information "property bags" are part of the new core Crystal Reports query engine. This approach provides a complete set of properties for each table in your report that can be read or written at run time.

- Support for embedding database, formula, or special fields inside text objects. While this has been supported in the Crystal Report designer for some time, it is now available programmatically to you within your app.

- Additional exporting, printing, and charting options. Many new Crystal Reports 9 capabilities related to these features are now exposed by the RDC.

There are some additional new features not mentioned here as well—look at the beginning of CrystalDevHelp.CHM for more details. What's probably most blatantly absent from the version 9 RDC is repository support. Arguably, the repository is the most notable new feature in the Crystal Reports 9 designer. However, the ability to add, remove, or update objects in the repository is not provided with the initial release of the version 9 RDC.

Note *The RDC is available only with Crystal Reports 9 Developer or Advanced Edition—it isn't included with the Standard or Professional Edition. If you're using Visual Basic with the RDC, you must use Visual Basic 5 or later. The RDC can also be used with other languages that support standard Microsoft COM Libraries.*

RDC Object Model Architecture

The RDC conforms to Microsoft's COM. As such, it can be used in any COM-compatible development environment that supports a COM Library (formerly known as an "OLE server"), such as Visual Basic, Visual C++, Delphi, and Microsoft Visual InterDev for Web page development (Web integration with the RDC is covered in Chapter 21). While an in-depth discussion of COM is better left to Microsoft documentation, you can consider COM to be a set of standards that allows one software environment to utilize the functions of another software environment by way of objects, properties, methods, and events.

COM development falls under the category of object-oriented programming (OOP). An *object hierarchy* is exposed by the RDC. This hierarchy begins with high-level objects that contain lower levels of objects. These second-level objects can contain lower levels of objects, and so on. If it sounds like the levels of objects can get "deep," they sometimes do. Some objects in the RDC are four or five layers deep in the object hierarchy.

Objects can contain not only additional single objects below them, but also collections of objects. A *collection* is a group of related objects contained inside the parent object. For example, a Report object will contain a collection of Section objects (an object for the report header, page header, and so on). Each of these Section objects itself contains its own collection of Report objects, such as fields, text objects, formulas, lines, boxes, and so on. If the details section of a report has ten database fields, four formulas, and a line drawing, the Details Section object will contain an object collection consisting of 15 *members*—one member for each of the Report objects in the section. And, if a report simply contains the five default sections that are created with a new report, the report's Sections collection will contain five members—one for each section.

If you aren't using the RDC's internal ActiveX report designer but instead are integrating an external .RPT file, the highest level in the object hierarchy is the Application object—everything eventually "trickles down" from it. Although you do need to declare the Application object in your VB code, you will rarely (if ever) refer to it again, or set any properties for it, once it's declared. As a general rule, the highest level of object you'll regularly be concerned with is the *Report* object, created by executing the Application object's OpenReport method (or automatically created if you are using the RDC's internal ActiveX designer). You will then manipulate many of the Report object's properties (such as the RecordSelectionFormula property), as well as work with many objects below the Report object (such as report sections, as just discussed).

Because the RDC is a tightly integrated COM component, you will benefit from Visual Basic's *automatic code completion* when you use it. When you begin to enter code into the VB code window for the Report object, the properties, methods, and built-in constant values become available to you from automatically appearing drop-down lists. If you've used Visual Basic 5 or 6, you're probably already familiar with this feature. You'll enjoy the benefit it provides with the RDC, as well.

Whereas older Crystal Reports integration methods required you to develop the report's .RPT file in the Crystal Reports design tool and *then* integrate it into your VB application, the RDC gives you the choice of actually designing the report right inside VB, as well as integrating existing .RPT files. Not only will you find most of the same design capabilities available from within the RDC that are available in regular Crystal Reports, but virtually all the fields, formulas, text objects, sections, and other parts of the report will be exposed to VB as objects (but, alas, the repository is not supported inside the VB designer). Like VB forms and controls, Report objects have properties and methods that can be set at both design time and run time. And, if you still choose to use an external .RPT file, the RDC exposes several COM interfaces, allowing sophisticated object-oriented report integration with both external .RPT files and the RDC's built-in report designer.

The Xtreme Mountain Bike Sample Reporting Application

The sample application used in this chapter, as well as on the book's companion Web site (www.CrystalBook.com), is a sample orders report for Xtreme Mountain Bike, a fictional company used throughout this book. The data for the report comes from the XTREME.MDB Microsoft Access sample database that's included with Crystal Reports 9 (connected via ODBC). The application will present a user-friendly, graphical user interface for end users who want to print an Xtreme order report.

This report contains several special features you'll want to enable for your end users in the VB application:

- A user-specified sales tax rate that is used in the "Order + Tax" formula.

- The ability to group by calendar quarter or customer name, based on user selection.

- A prompt for a highlight value to set orders over a certain amount apart. This value will be passed to a report parameter field.

- An order-date range that will limit the report's record selection.

- A label in the page header of the report indicating the choices the user has made.

- The choice to show detail data, or to just group subtotals and summaries for drill-down. The report contains two different page header sections and two different group header sections, containing column headings that are suppressed and shown according to the summary/detail choice.

- Destination options to preview the report in a window, print the report to a printer, or send the report as a Portable Document Format (.PDF) file, attached to an e-mail message.

If the report is grouped by quarter, given a 5 percent tax rate, and restricted to orders from January 1 through December 31, 2001, and if the parameter field to high-light orders is given a value of $5,000, the report will appear as illustrated here:

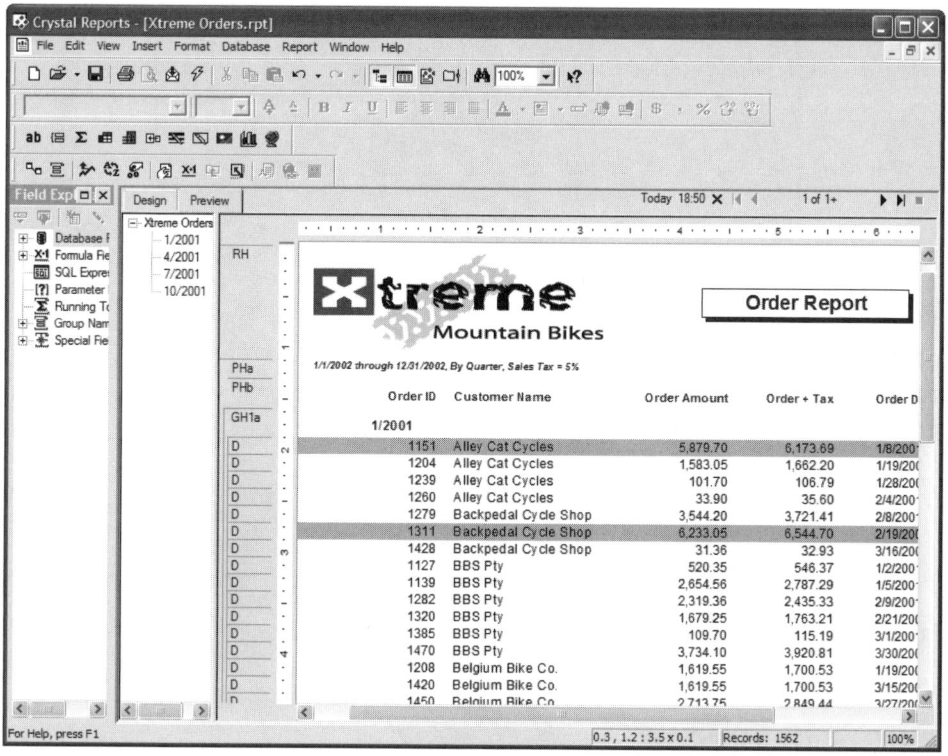

DEVELOPING CUSTOM WINDOW APPLICATIONS

The VB application that will be used to integrate this report is a simple, single-form dialog box that gathers data from the user via text boxes, a combo box, radio buttons, and a check box. When the user clicks OK, the report is previewed, printed, or e-mailed, depending on the selections made. The main form from the application looks like this:

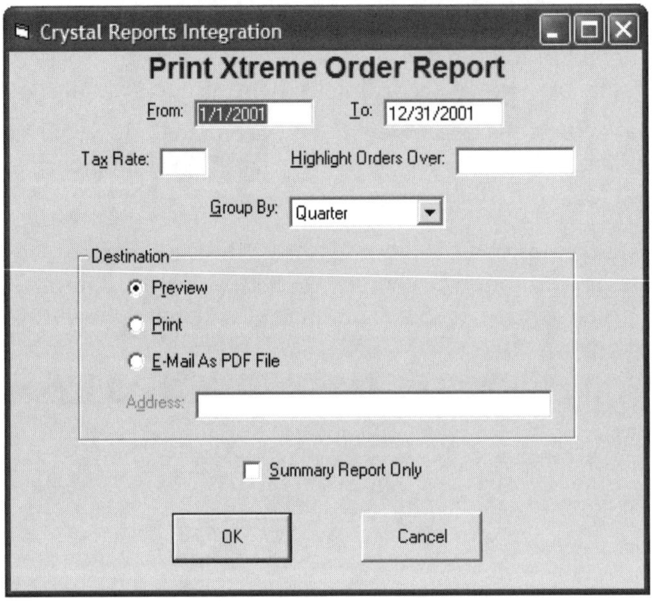

To correctly accomplish the integration, you need to programmatically modify the following report properties from within your VB application:

- Record selection formula
- Report formula
- Parameter field
- Output destination
- Report section formatting (suppress and show)

Tip *You can find the completed VB application on this book's companion Web site. Download the application from www.CrystalBook.com.*

Different RDC Pieces

The entire RDC actually consists of several parts that work together. In particular, it has four separate pieces:

- **ActiveX designer**   Enables you to actually create and modify reports inside the Visual Basic IDE.

- **Run-time Library**   After you create the report, the RDC exposes a set of powerful properties, methods, and events via a COM library.

- **Report Viewer**   Because the RDC doesn't include its own built-in preview window, you use another ActiveX component, the Report Viewer, to view reports on the screen. The Report Viewer also exposes a large set of properties, methods, and events, enabling you to have complete control over how your application users can interact with your report in the viewer window.

- **Embeddable Report Designer**   This feature allows you to place an ActiveX control on your VB form to allow end users to interactively design reports using features almost identical to the report designer available inside the VB IDE. Once users have finished their report design, the Embeddable Report Designer returns a report object that can be further modified and controlled with the run-time library.

The ActiveX Designer

The first part of the RDC is an *ActiveX designer,* an interface that works with Visual Basic 5 and 6, and Microsoft Office Developer's Edition (using VBA 6). Whereas other ActiveX controls and libraries generally extend the capabilities of the Visual Basic language, an ActiveX designer actually extends the capabilities of the Visual Basic IDE. Some common examples are the User Connection Designer and the Data Environment Designer, both of which are ActiveX designers for connecting to remote databases that are available with Visual Basic 6.

The designer portion of the RDC allows you to create a complete report right inside Visual Basic. You no longer need to use the iterative process of creating or editing a Crystal Reports .RPT file, working with it inside your VB code, going back to Crystal Reports to make changes to the .RPT file, and going back to VB to make changes in the code. The RDC looks similar to the Crystal Reports design screen, with multiple report sections, lists of database fields, formulas, parameter fields, and so on. You interact with the RDC via toolbar buttons and pop-up menus.

What the RDC designer features that Crystal Reports doesn't offer is a complete object model for every report section and every object you place in any report section. Every field, text object, formula, parameter field, or any other type of object has its own set of properties that appears in the property sheet, and many of those properties can be set at run time. With the RDC, you can customize formulas, text objects, section formatting, and most other aspects of report behavior and formatting by using VB coding. By creatively using text objects, you can even create report formulas using the Visual Basic language instead of the Crystal formula language so that the text objects will be under complete VB control at run time. Of course, any Crystal formulas you create will still work, and they can still be modified on the fly from within your application, just as with other integration methods.

The Run-time Library

The second part of the RDC is the RDC runtime library. This component can accept either a report designed with the RDC ActiveX designer or an external .RPT file created with Crystal Reports 9. The RDC then exposes a large number of properties and methods that can be used to completely customize reporting behavior at run time.

The Report Viewer

The RDC Design Time or Run-time components don't include their own built-in preview window for previewing reports on the screen. Therefore, report previewing is provided by yet another ActiveX component that is available with the RDC, the Report Viewer. This ActiveX control is added to a form, where it exposes a large number of properties in the Properties box displayed in the VB IDE that can be set at design time. When your program is run, the viewer is supplied with a Report object from the RDC Library, which it then displays in its window according to the selections you made at design time.

Not only can many of these properties also be set at run time, but the viewer contains its own COM library, which exposes a large number of other properties, methods, and events that let you completely control report behavior and interaction. You can open drill-down tabs right from within your code, trap a button click in the viewer toolbar, or respond to a drill-down click on a group footer or header. The viewer is versatile enough that conceivably you can design your own container for the Report Viewer window, creating all of your own controls and logic for report interaction.

| Tip | *The RDC's run-time library and Report Viewer also can be used to develop "thin-client" applications that require only a Web browser. Both modules can integrate reports using Microsoft Active Server Pages. Chapter 21 provides complete details of this use of the RDC.* |

The Embeddable Report Designer

Not only can you modify existing reports at run time from within your code, but Crystal Reports 9 offers a fully interactive report design ActiveX control that can be added directly to a VB form. With this control, end users have full interactive capabilities to design new reports or edit existing reports from within your VB application. By providing an already defined Report object to the Embeddable Report Designer, you can allow users to modify an existing report interactively. Or, simply allow an end user to use the Embeddable Designer to create a complete report from scratch, much as you would using the RDC ActiveX designer inside the VB IDE. In either case, when the end user has completed his or her report design process, the Embeddable Report Designer simply returns another Report object that can be further manipulated before being printed, exported, or displayed in the Report Viewer.

When Are Royalty Payments Required?

Crystal Reports has always maintained a tradition of a royalty-free, run-time license for developers. In the past, you could freely distribute run-time Crystal Reports modules, such as CRAXDRT9.DLL (the RDC run-time library), without having to notify, or pay royalties to, Crystal Decisions. As report integration capabilities have become more robust, however, your free distribution options have been reduced.

However, this isn't necessarily cause for concern. Quite simply, all *run-time* report modification functions (that make changes to existing reports, either designed in the Crystal Reports designer or VB's integral designer) can still be included in your custom applications without requiring any royalty payments to Crystal Decisions. However, functionality that allows an application to create a *new* report from scratch, as well as use of the Embeddable Report Designer, *does* require a separate license and royalty payments to Crystal Decisions.

This new arrangement has a fairly straightforward explanation. In previous versions of Crystal Reports developer interfaces, you had to design a report in advance (either with the Crystal Reports designer or the RDC ActiveX designer) to include with your application—your application could not create and save an external .RPT file. Well, the Crystal Reports 9 RDC enables you to do this entirely from within your application at run time. And, the Embeddable Report Designer allows users of your custom application to create and save their own reports, which your application can save as .RPT files.

Because of this functionality, Crystal Decisions understandably is concerned about the potential for competing products to its flagship Crystal Reports product (in fact, their license agreement specifically forbids "competitive products"). Accordingly, developers who use the Report Creation RDC calls or Embeddable Report Designer must make licensing arrangements and pay royalties to Crystal Decisions. However, if you *don't* use these report-creation calls, you are still free to distribute the run-time components free of charge and without the need to notify Crystal Decisions.

Crystal Decisions also continues use of the *Broadcast License,* which is a potential trap you need to watch out for when creating an "automated distribution system" that can distribute reports to 50 or more users. This may potentially involve additional licensing requirements for you if you're developing a system to automatically distribute reports (even if you export them to an alternate file format, such as .PDF, .DOC, or .XLS).

When you are developing applications inside Visual Basic, either you'll receive a dialog box notification if you use a property or method that requires special licensing, or VB may throw a trappable error (Crystal Reports 9 is stricter about what you can't do at design time). More information about licensing options, the new Crystal Reports License Manager application, and pricing for add-on licenses can be found at http://www.crystaldecisions.com/products/crystalreports/licensing.

Adding the RDC to Your Project

The first step in using the RDC is to add it to your project. After installing Crystal Reports 9 Developer or Advanced Edition, the RDC should be properly registered on your system and ready for use.

1. Start Visual Basic and create a new project, or open the existing project with which you wish to use the RDC.

2. Choose Project | Components from the pull-down menus, or press CTRL-T. The Components dialog box will appear.

3. Click the Designers tab. You'll see a list of ActiveX designers registered on your system. Ensure that the Crystal Reports 9 designer is selected and then click OK.

4. Using the Project pull-down menu, choose the Add Crystal Reports 9 option (it may appear on the More ActiveX Designers submenu in VB 5). The RDC will be added to Visual Basic, and the Report Gallery dialog box will appear, as shown in Figure 25-1.

> **Tip** *Crystal Reports 9 attempts to add the RDC directly to the Project menu automatically when it's installed. If you need to add it manually with Project | Components, it will "stick" from that point forward. You won't have to add it each time you want to use the RDC with a new VB project.*

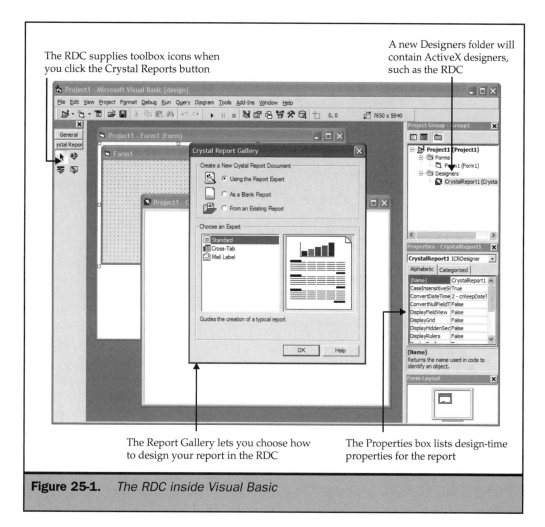

The RDC supplies toolbox icons when you click the Crystal Reports button

A new Designers folder will contain ActiveX designers, such as the RDC

The Report Gallery lets you choose how to design your report in the RDC

The Properties box lists design-time properties for the report

Figure 25-1.   *The RDC inside Visual Basic*

The RDC begins by displaying its own version of the Report Gallery. The RDC Report Gallery is very similar to the Report Gallery that appears when you create a new report in the Crystal Reports program, with a few changes. For example, there isn't an OLAP report option here, and the From An Existing Report option has been added. Your initial choices in the Report Gallery determine how your main report is designed inside the RDC.

Importing an Existing Report

If you've created an .RPT file in Crystal Reports 9 or an earlier version and you want to use that report in the RDC, click the From An Existing Report radio button and click OK. A File Open dialog box will appear, in which you can choose the .RPT file that you wish to import. Once you've chosen the report file, you are prompted to add the Report Viewer to your project.

Here, you can determine whether you want the Report Viewer added to a new form in your project and, if you do, decide whether you want the Report Viewer form to be set as the startup form. If you need to preview the report in a window from within your VB application, you need to add the Report Viewer. Although you can do it later if you need to, the RDC will offer to add it automatically, along with some simple code to tie the report to the viewer. If your report will be used strictly for exporting, e-mailing, or printing to a printer, you don't need to add the Report Viewer control because it won't be used.

If you import a report and add the Report Viewer to a new form, your screen will look something like the one shown in Figure 25-2.

You'll notice that the RDC design window looks quite similar to the regular Crystal Reports design window—many of the features and report design steps apply equally to both environments. There are several ways of carrying out functions in the RDC design window: by using toolbox and toolbar buttons, by choosing items from the Field Explorer at the left of the report, and by right-clicking in the design window and choosing options from the pop-up menus. As with the regular Crystal Reports designer, you can select objects in the RDC design window and then move, resize, format, or delete them. Steps for these functions are basically the same as they are for regular Crystal Reports (with the exception that all RDC functions must be chosen with toolbar buttons and right-clicks— there are no pull-down menus here, as there are in regular Crystal Reports).

Remember that when you import an .RPT file into the RDC, the RDC simply copies the contents of the .RPT file into the design window and then completely disregards

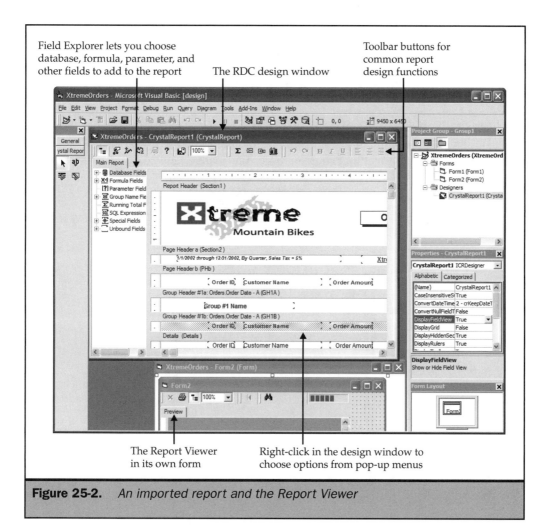

Field Explorer lets you choose
database, formula, parameter, and
other fields to add to the report

The RDC design window

Toolbar buttons for
common report
design functions

The Report Viewer
in its own form

Right-click in the design window to
choose options from pop-up menus

Figure 25-2.   *An imported report and the Report Viewer*

any changes that may later be made to the original .RPT file. Also, if you make any
changes to the report inside the RDC, there will be no effect on the original .RPT file.
You are not creating a real-time link to the .RPT file.

> **Tip**   *If you want to save the contents of the RDC designer to an external .RPT file to use for
> other purposes, you may do so. Right-click in the design window and choose Report |
> Save To Crystal Reports File from the pop-up menu.*

While the RDC design window may not provide any particular functional advantage over the regular Crystal Reports designer (except that you don't have to exit VB to use it), the real benefit is the object model that it opens for report contents. When you select an individual Report object, such as a database field or text object, or a report section, such as the report header or details section, you'll see design-time properties in the Properties box. Also, by using the internal report designer, your report design is saved as a .DSR file along with .FRM, .BAS, and other files that make up your VB project. When you compile the project, the report design is embedded in the application's .EXE file—there are no external .RPT files that your end users may inadvertently (or purposely) change.

Properties - SubHeading	☒
SubHeading ITextObject	▾

Alphabetic	Categorized

Height	199
HorAlignment	1 - crLeftAlign
KeepTogether	True
Left	480
LeftIndent	0
LeftLineStyle	0 - crLSNoLine
MaxNumberOfLines	0
Name	SubHeading
RightIndent	0
RightLineStyle	0 - crLSNoLine
Suppress	False
SuppressIfDuplicate	False
TextColor	▉ &H00000000&
TextRotationAngle	0 - crRotate0
Top	0

Name
Gets or sets object name.

As you can with properties for a combo box, radio button, form, or other regular VB control, you can set properties at design time for any of these report elements as well. The Properties box and pop-up menu options, such as the Format Editor, interact with each other. For example, you can select a date field, right-click it, and choose Format from the pop-up menu. On the Date tab of the Format Editor, you might choose a spelled-out month and four-digit year, showing no day at all. When you click OK to close the Format Editor and then look in the Properties box, you'll notice that the Day Type property has changed to 2 – crNoDay, the Month Type property has changed to 3 – crLongMonth, and the Year Type property has changed to 1 – crLongYear. The opposite behavior is also true—changes you make in the Properties box will be reflected elsewhere in the RDC dialog boxes.

Tip *Depending on how you plan to integrate your report and how much customization you want to perform at run time, you may want to rename some of the default names given to objects by the RDC. When you begin looking through report objects in your VB code, recognizing what SubHeading represents is easier than recognizing what Text25 represents. This is improved in Crystal Reports 9, as any name you give an object on the common tab of the Format Editor in the regular Crystal Reports designer will remain when the report is imported into the RDC.*

After you modify your report as necessary, save the report design the same way you save changes to a form, module, or project file from within VB. Just click the Save button on the toolbar, right-click the Designer object in the Project Explorer window, and choose Save from the pop-up menu, or just close the project or VB. You'll be prompted to choose a filename for the RDC designer, just as you would for a form or module. Choose a path and filename for the designer file—the default file extension for ActiveX designers is .DSR. When you next open the VB project, the .DSR file will load with the rest of the project files, and all properties and characteristics of the report design window will reappear.

Creating a New Report

Although the ability to import an existing .RPT file into the RDC is an excellent way to integrate an existing .RPT file into a Visual Basic application, you may prefer to maximize the power of the RDC and design the report entirely inside the Visual Basic IDE from scratch. The RDC allows you to do this with one of the Report Gallery choices that appear when you first add the RDC to your project.

If you choose one of the report experts, you'll be led section by section through the expert dialog box, much as you are when you use the report wizards inside regular Crystal Reports (refer to Chapter 1 for more information). If you choose the Empty Report option, you are presented with an empty report design window in which you need to choose database connections, tables, and fields individually to add to the report. Start by right-clicking in the window and choosing Database | Database Expert from the pop-up menu.

Choosing a Report Data Source

When you import an existing .RPT file into the RDC, the report inside your VB application will use the same data source as the imported report did (such as ODBC or a native database driver). These data sources are all provided by Crystal Reports functionality, separate from any database-connectivity features within Visual Basic.

However, when you create a new report from scratch using a report expert in the RDC, you have several choices for how your report will "connect" to a database. Because the RDC is so tightly integrated with Visual Basic, you may want to consider using a database connection that can easily be manipulated from within your VB code. In particular, the RDC can connect to data using various Microsoft data-access methods provided by Visual Basic. These include Data Access Objects (DAO), Remote Data Objects (RDO), and ActiveX Data Objects (ADO). In addition, you'll be able to connect directly to an existing data environment that you may have already defined in your VB application (consult the VB documentation for more information on the Data Environment).

When you're ready to choose a data source, the Database Expert will appear, as shown in Figure 25-3.

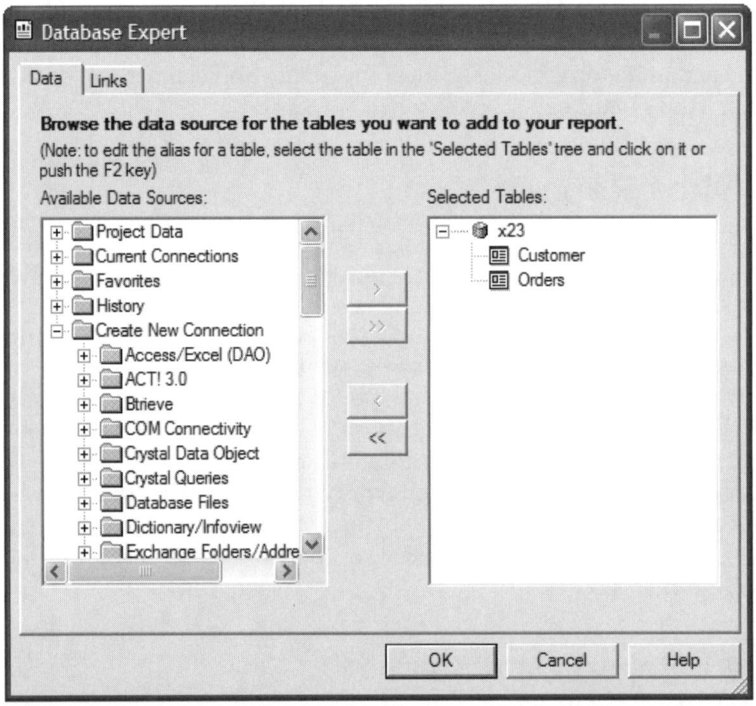

Figure 25-3. *Database Expert*

The Data Environment category will have entries in it only if you've already added and defined a Visual Basic 6 Data Environment (which is another example of an ActiveX designer) in your project. When you expand this category, the set of connections and commands in the Data Environment will be available to be chosen for your report.

The remaining items in the Database Expert are identical to those displayed in the regular Crystal Reports designer, described in more detail in Chapter 16. Open the desired category, supply logon credentials (if required), and add one or more tables to the Selected Tables list. You can also create new Crystal Reports 9 SQL Commands in the Database Expert (also discussed in Chapter 16).

Make note of "VB-oriented" data sources that appear in the Database Expert, such as COM Connectivity, Crystal Data Object, and Field Definitions Only. These "Active" data sources are designed to allow you to connect to nondatabase data sources that you may have created from other Visual Basic or programmatic options.

Note	*The data definition file options are included here for backward compatibility. The Unbound Fields feature of the RDC is a much more elegant way to accomplish the same thing: creating a generic report that doesn't connect to a database at design time. This is discussed in detail later in the chapter.*

If you add more than one table, you must link the tables before proceeding to report design. Click the Links tab of the Database Expert (it will appear only if you add more than one table). Once you've properly linked tables (discussed in detail in Chapter 16), click the Database Expert's OK button to proceed with report design.

Adding Objects

If you are using one of the report experts, you'll design the report by using the simple sectioned dialog box. Since this approach is virtually identical to the technique discussed in Chapter 1, you should refer to that chapter if you're unfamiliar with designing a report with an expert.

If you chose the As A Blank Report option (or if you've already closed the report expert but want to add additional objects to the report), use the Field Explorer on the left side of the RDC design window to add objects to the report. For example, to add a field from the database, click the plus sign next to the database fields category to display the data source(s) the report is based on. Click the plus sign next to the data source to see the fields contained in it. Then, just drag and drop the fields you want to the desired section of the report design window.

To create new formulas, parameter fields, running totals, or SQL expression fields, right-click their category in the Field Explorer and choose New from the pop-up menu. When the new object has been added, you can drag and drop it on the report. Special fields can also be added to the report by dragging and dropping them from their area of the Field Explorer.

After you add objects, you can select them and move or resize them just as you would in regular Crystal Reports. You can format an object that you've selected by right-clicking and choosing the appropriate choice from the pop-up menu. And, don't forget that you also have Visual Basic properties for every object or report section in the report. Select the object or report section and make design-time property choices in the Properties box—that's the power of the VB-integrated RDC.

> **Tip**   *There are many capabilities and design techniques available that you can apply to the RDC, as you do with regular Crystal Reports. Look at the chapters in Part I of this book for ideas and techniques for designing sophisticated reports.*

The RDC Object Model

As discussed at the beginning of the chapter, the RDC actually consists of four different main components that exist in your Visual Basic application: The ActiveX designer, the Run-time Library, the Report Viewer, and the Embeddable Report Designer. When you actually process a report in VB, you design the report within the ActiveX designer window or allow the user to create it with the Embeddable Report Designer and eventually pass a *Report object* to the Report Viewer. The Run-time Library, in essence, appears in the middle to control report customization.

Using the ActiveX Designer Report Object

The first step is to assign the design-window report definition to a Visual Basic object variable, as demonstrated in the following sample code:

```
Public Report As New dsrXtreme
```

In this code, from the modXtreme module in the sample application, *dsrXtreme* is the name given to the ActiveX designer object in the Property Pages dialog box. *Report* is the name of the object that will "point" to the report. Because this object is declared to be Public in a module, it will remain in scope and be accessible throughout the entire application. Then, when the report is going to be viewed in the Report Viewer, the Report object is passed to the Report Viewer's ReportSource property. The following code is from the sample application's Viewer Form_Load event:

```
CRViewer91.ReportSource = Report
```

In this code, CRViewer91 is the default name of the Report Viewer (and it hasn't been changed to another name). The Report object is given to the ReportSource property so that the Report Viewer knows which report to show.

What the RDC Library does between defining the Report object and assigning it to the Report Viewer is the "meat" of RDC integration programming. After you assign the designer to the Report object variable, an entire object model becomes available to you for modifying and customizing the report. By using the RDC's object model, consisting of objects, collections, properties, methods, and events, you have extensive control over your report behavior at run time.

When you add the RDC to your report, the CRAXDRT (Crystal Reports ActiveX Designer Run-Time) Library is added to your project automatically. This COM interface provides a complete set of properties and methods that you can set at run time. To see the objects, collections, properties, and methods that are exposed by this Library, use Visual Basic's *Object Browser.* The Object Browser can be viewed in Visual Basic any time your program isn't running. Press F2, or choose View | Object Browser from the pull-down menus. Then, choose CRAXDRT in the first drop-down list to see the object library exposed by the RDC.

Although an extensive explanation of COM and its general approach to an object model and object hierarchy is better left to Microsoft documentation, navigating the RDC object model will soon become second nature to you. The highest level in the object hierarchy is the Application object—everything eventually falls below it. In general, throughout the RDC, the Application object is assumed by default, so you don't need to explicitly refer to it (unless you use the RDC without the RDC ActiveX designer report design window). The highest level of object you'll need to be concerned about is the Report object.

Tip   *If you are using the Embeddable Report Designer to give your end user interactive report design capability, you'll want to use the combined design-time/run-time library, CRAXDDRT. Look up this library in the Object Browser to explore its objects, collections, properties, and methods. The Embeddable Report Designer is discussed in more detail later in this chapter.*

Using an External .RPT File

One of the main benefits of the RDC is the ability to design a report entirely from within the Visual Basic IDE. When you save this internal report design, the designer specifications are saved in a .DSR file along with the rest of your Visual Basic project. When you compile the project, all of the report design specifications are saved in the compiled modules—there are no external report files to be accidentally deleted or modified (either accidentally or otherwise).

However, sometimes you may want to use the flexibility of the RDC and Report Viewer with an external .RPT file, similar to older Crystal Reports integration methods. This is entirely possible, and quite straightforward. Examine the following code module from a VB form.

```
Project1 - Form2 (Code)                                        _ □ ×
Form                          ▼   Load                            ▼
    Dim Application As CRAXDRT.Application
    Dim Report As CRAXDRT.Report

    Private Sub Form_Load()
    Screen.MousePointer = vbHourglass
    Set Application = CreateObject("CrystalRuntime.Application")
    Set Report = Application.OpenReport(App.Path & "\Xtreme Orders.rpt")
    CRViewer1.ReportSource = Report
    CRViewer1.ViewReport
    Screen.MousePointer = vbDefault

    End Sub


    Private Sub Form_Resize()
    CRViewer1.Top = 0
    CRViewer1.Left = 0
    CRViewer1.Height = ScaleHeight
    CRViewer1.Width = ScaleWidth

    End Sub
```

Notice the code that's very similar to the standard code the RDC automatically adds to your project. Notice a couple of differences, however. Rather than declaring and creating one Report object, consisting of an instance of the ActiveX designer (CrystalReport1), this code declares and assigns two objects: the Application object and the Report object.

The Application Object When you use the built-in RDC ActiveX designer, you needn't worry about the Application object. However, if you choose to use an external report instead of the built-in designer, you'll need to declare and assign a single instance of the Application object, the highest-level object in the RDC's object hierarchy. Don't forget to fully qualify the Application object by preceding the object type with CRAXDRT (or CRAXDDRT if you're using the combined design-time/run-time library).

Assign the Application object by using the CreateObject method. The ProgID for the RDC CRAXDRT Library is CrystalRuntime.Application.

The Report Object The Report object is crucial. You'll use it to perform almost all run-time customization to your reports. You need to declare and assign a Report object for each report you want to have "open" at the same time within your application. For example, if you want to have three separate reports all appearing in their own preview windows simultaneously, you need to declare and assign three different Report object variables. However, if you'll have only one report in use at a time, you can merely declare and assign a single Report object variable, setting it to Nothing and reassigning it as necessary inside your code. Don't forget to fully qualify the Report object when declaring it with the Dim statement by preceding the object type with CRAXDRT or CRAXDDRT, depending on which library you're using.

Assign the Report object by using the Application object's OpenReport method. Supply the external report's filename, including the full path name, as the argument.

Caution	*If you decide to use the RDC with an external .RPT file and don't use the Add Crystal Reports 9 option from the Project menu, you need to ensure that the RDC Run-time Library (or combined Design-time/Run-time Library) and, optionally, the Report Viewer are added to the project. In order for the proper library to be available, choose Project	References and ensure that the proper library is chosen (either Crystal Reports 9 ActiveX Designer Run-Time Library or Crystal Reports 9 ActiveX Designer Design and Run-Time Library). To use the Report Viewer, choose Project	Components and ensure that the Crystal Report Viewer Control 9 option is selected (setting this option in Project | References won't be sufficient for the Report Viewer).*

An Introduction to the RDC Object Model

While the Report object has many properties of its own (such as the RecordSelectionFormula property), it contains many objects and collections of objects that fall below it. One available Report object collection is FormulaFields, which contains a set of FormulaFieldDefinition objects, one for each formula defined in the report. Each of these objects contains all the properties for that particular formula, such as the formula name, the text of the formula, the data type that it returns, and other properties.

When you're dealing with a collection of objects, you need to identify which member of the collection you wish to manipulate, by using an index pointer to the appropriate member. In the RDC, indexes are "one-based." That is, the first member is numbered 1, the second is numbered 2, and so on. This is in contrast to the ActiveX control and other VB object models, which often expose "zero-based" indexes. The RDC typically numbers the collection members in the order in which they were added to the report.

For example, to print the formula text from the first formula in the Xtreme Orders sample application, you can type the following code into the Immediate window while the program is in break mode:

```
? Report.FormulaFields(1).Text
```

Here, the object hierarchy is being "navigated" to reveal the Text property of the first member of the FormulaFieldDefinitions collection (referred to simply as FormulaFields) of the Report object. Since the Text property is a read/write property, you not only can retrieve what the formula already contains, but also replace it by setting the Text property to a string value, as in the following:

```
Report.FormulaFields(1).Text = "{Orders.Order Amount} * 1.1"
```

Manipulating Collection Indexes by Name Instead of Number

Unlike the Report Engine Automation Server, which preceded the RDC as Crystal's initial COM-based integration method, the RDC will allow you to use string indexes to refer to members of only certain collections, but not all of them. For example, the RDC requires you to set the contents of a formula with

```
Report.FormulaFields(1).Text = "{Orders.Order Amount} * 1.1"
```

while the Report Engine Automation Server allowed you to use

```
Report.Formulas("Order + Tax").Text = "{Orders.Order Amount} * 1.1"
```

You sometimes need to do some experimenting to find the actual member of a collection that you wish to manipulate.

Wouldn't it be nice if, instead of using the numeric index to set the value of a formula, you could use code like this:

```
If SetFormula("Order + Tax","{Orders.Order Amount} * 1.1") Then
    MsgBox "Formula Changed"
Else
    MsgBox "Incorrect Formula Name Supplied"
End If
```

Examine the following function code:

```
Public Function SetFormula(FormulaName As String, _
                           FormulaText As String) As Boolean
Dim intCounter As Integer
For intCounter = 1 To Report.FormulaFields.Count
  If Report.FormulaFields(intCounter).FormulaFieldName = FormulaName Then
     Report.FormulaFields(intCounter).Text = FormulaText
        SetFormula = True
        Exit Function
  End If  'Report.FormulaFields(intCounter).Name = FormulaName
Next intCounter
SetFormula = False
End Function
```

If you examine this code closely, you'll see that the FormulaFields collection can be cycled through using a For loop, looking for the formula that has the same name as the passed FormulaName argument. Once it's found, the value of the passed FormulaText argument is used to set the value of the formula. If a formula with the same name isn't found, the subroutine returns a false value that can be tested for.

If you have a large number of formulas, parameter fields, SQL expressions, or other objects that may be easier to manipulate by name rather than by index number, use this type of logic to make your coding life easier!

Also, a new method has been added to various RDC collections (of particular interest are the FormulaFieldDefinitions and ParameterFields collections) that allow you to retrieve an object by name rather than index. Examine the following code for an example of the GetItemByName method.

```
Dim FormulaField As CRAXDRT.FormulaFieldDefinition
Set FormulaField = Report.FormulaFields.GetItemByName("Order + Tax")

FormulaField.Text = "{Orders.Order Amount} * 1.1"
```

In this example, a new object variable is declared to hold a formula. It is then set to an existing formula in the report by calling the FormulaFields collection's GetItemByName method, using the actual name of the formula as an argument. The method returns an actual formula field object, which can then be manipulated by reading or setting properties.

Note that the formula or parameter field name you supply as the GetItemByName argument cannot contain the @ sign, ? sign, or curly braces—just the formula field or parameter field name should be supplied, without any extraneous punctuation. If you supply an invalid name, the RDC will throw a trappable error to VB.

Because the RDC is a tightly integrated COM component, you will benefit from *automatic code completion* (Microsoft refers to it as *IntelliSense*) when you use the RDC with Visual Basic. When you begin to enter code into the VB code window for the Report object, the properties, methods, and built-in constant values will become available to you from automatically appearing drop-down lists. If you've used Visual Basic 5 or 6, you're probably familiar with this feature. You'll enjoy the benefit it provides with the RDC.

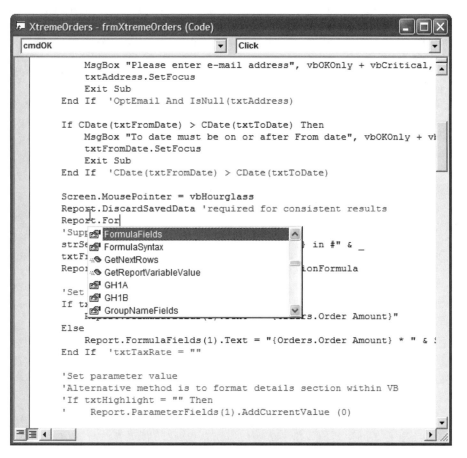

Providing Database Login Credentials

Many reports you integrate using the RDC will be based on secure databases, requiring a user ID and password to be supplied before the report can retrieve data. In many cases, you will have already established a secure connection with the database through your application before report processing ever begins. In these cases, you'll probably want to pass these credentials directly to the report from within your code. This is particularly important to RDC developers, as the Report Viewer control included with the RDC *will not* prompt the user for login credentials if they have not been previously provided—the viewer will simply throw an error when attempting to process the report. This is in contrast to RAS (discussed in Chapter 21), which will automatically prompt users for login credentials if the code doesn't provide them.

Depending on how the report is designed, you may need to approach supplying the user ID and password to the report from several different perspectives. The simplest way to do this is to provide a single user ID and password to the entire report. Even if the report makes use of several database tables, you can supply a single user ID/password combination that will apply to all tables. If, however, you have created a report that mixes tables from separate databases, or you have included subreports in your main report, you may need to perform extra steps to provide login credentials to individual tables in the main report, or to the subreport.

To supply an all-encompassing user ID/password combination that will apply to all tables originating from the same database, navigate through the RDC object hierarchy to the Database object within the Report object. The LogOnServer method will log in to the database, providing a secure connection to all tables within that database. LogonServer syntax is

```
LogOnServer <databaseDLL>, <Server>, <Database>, <UserID>, <Password>
```

The following code fragment shows how to log in to a Microsoft SQL Server database via ODBC. The ODBC Data Source Name is Xtreme SQL Server, the database name is XTREME, the user ID is DBReader, and the password is DBPassword. No matter how many tables have been added to the report from this database (the main report only—not subreports), this will satisfy login requirements for all of them.

```
' Login to entire database for main report
Report.Database.LogOnServer "PDSODBC.DLL", _
   "XTREME SQL Server", "XTREME", "DBReader", "DBPassword"
```

If you need to supply different sets of credentials to individual tables (or you just want a more robust way to retrieve and set database properties in general), version 9 of the RDC introduces *Connection Information Property Bags*. A "property bag" is a collection of properties that exist for a certain object. The number of members and names in the collection can change, however, depending on the type of object. In the case of Connection Information property bags, varying sets of properties exist within the DatabaseTable object's ConnectionProperties collection, depending on the particular database DLL being used for a particular table.

Crystal Decisions' "new" way, then, of supplying login credentials to an individual report table looks like this:

```
' Login to individual database tables
Report.Database.Tables(1).ConnectionProperties("User ID") = "DBReader"
Report.Database.Tables(1).ConnectionProperties("Password") = "DBPassword"
```

In this example, two property bag properties from the ConnectionProperties collection (User ID and Password) are set for the first table in the database.

Logging In to Subreports

While the requirement to potentially provide different login credentials to individual tables in the main report is one consideration, logging in to subreports is another. Because subreports contain unique database connections separate from the main report, you will need to provide login credentials to each of them separate from the main report. The RDC object model deals with subreports in a fashion that requires a bit of extra coding.

Because a subreport is, in essence, a "report within a report," it possesses its own unique set of properties, methods, and events. Therefore, in order to completely control it, a separate RDC Report object must be declared and assigned to each subreport. Then, that subreport's properties (such as the Database object ConnectionProperties collection) can be manipulated from within their own Report object.

Examine the following sample code:

```
' Login to database for subreport
Dim Top5ProductsSub As CRAXDRT.Report
Set Top5ProductsSub = Report.Subreport1.OpenSubreport
Top5ProductsSub.Database.LogOnServer "PDSODBC.DLL", _
"XTREME SQL Server", "XTREME", "DBReader", "DBPassword"
```

In this example, an additional Report object is declared, using the fully qualified object type of CRAXDRT.Report. It is then "set" to the subreport by navigating to the subreport within the main report object. The subreport object's OpenSubreport method is executed, which creates another RDC Report object (named Top5ProductsSub) just for the subreport. Then, the Database object's LogOnServer method, or ConnectionProperties collection, can be used to supply login credentials.

Tip *More information on working with subreports can be found later in this chapter under "RDC Subreports."*

DEVELOPING CUSTOM WINDOW APPLICATIONS

Controlling Record Selection

One of the main benefits of Visual Basic's integration with Crystal Reports is the ability to control report record selection on the fly, based on your user's interactions with the VB application. You can design the exact user interface you need for your application and build the report record selection formula to match how your user interacts with it. Because VB has such powerful user-interface features (such as the VB date picker and other custom controls), you have much more flexibility using VB controls than you do using Crystal Reports parameter fields.

Because the record selection formula you pass to the RDC must still conform to Crystal Reports syntax, you need to be familiar with how to create a Crystal Reports formula. If you are used to using the Crystal Reports Select Expert for record selection, you need to familiarize yourself with the actual Crystal Reports formula that it creates, before you create a selection formula in your VB application. A Crystal Reports record selection formula is a Boolean formula that narrows down the database records that will be included in the report. For example, the following record selection formula will limit a report to orders placed in the first quarter of 2001 from customers in Texas:

```
{Orders.Order Date} In #1/1/2001# To #3/31/2001#
And {Customer.Region} = "TX"
```

Tip	*For complete discussions of Crystal Reports record selection and how to create Boolean formulas, consult Chapters 5 and 6.*

Use the RecordSelectionFormula property of the Report object to set the record selection formula for the report. You can set the property to either a string expression or a variable. Here's the code from the sample application to set record selection, based on the contents of the user-supplied From Date and To Date text boxes:

```
'Supply record selection formula based on dates
strSelectionFormula = "{Orders.Order Date} in #" & _
    txtFromDate & "# to #" & txtToDate & "#"
Report.RecordSelectionFormula = strSelectionFormula
```

Record Selection Formula Tips

You need to consider several important points when building a Crystal record selection formula within your application. Specifically, some tricks are available that you can use to make sure that your string values are formatted properly, and that as much of the SQL database query as possible is performed by the database server rather than by the PC.

The string value you pass must adhere *exactly* to the Crystal Reports formula syntax. This includes using correct Crystal reserved words and punctuation. The preceding example shows the necessity of including the pound sign (#) around date values in the selection formula.

Also, it's easy to forget the required quotation marks or apostrophes around literals that are used in comparisons. For example, you may want to pass the following selection formula:

```
{Customer.Region} = 'TX' And {Orders.Ship Via} = 'UPS'
```

If the characters TX and UPS are coming from controls, such as a text box or combo box, you might consider using the following VB code to place the selection formula in a string variable:

```
strSelectionFormula = "{Customer.Region} = " & txtRegion & _
" And {Orders.Ship Via} = " & cboShipper
```

At first glance, this appears to create a correctly formatted Crystal Reports record-selection formula. However, if you supply this string to the RecordSelectionFormula property, the report will fail when it runs. Why? The best way to troubleshoot this issue is to look at the contents of strSelectionFormula in the VB Immediate window, by setting a breakpoint or by using other VB debugging features. This will show that the contents of the string variable after the preceding code executes as follows:

```
{Customer.Region} = TX And {Orders.Ship Via} = UPS
```

Notice that no quotation marks or apostrophes appear around the literals that are being compared in the record selection formula, a basic requirement of the Crystal Reports formula language. The following VB code will create a syntactically correct selection formula:

```
strSelectionFormula = "{Customer.Region} = '" & txtRegion & _
"' And {Orders.Ship Via} = '" & cboShipper & "'"
```

If your report will be using a SQL database, remember also that RDC will attempt to convert as much of your record selection formula as possible to SQL when it runs the report. The same caveats apply to the record selection formula you pass from your VB application as apply to a record selection formula you create directly in Crystal Reports. In particular, using built-in Crystal Reports formula functions, such as UpperCase or ToText, typically causes record selection to be moved to the client (the PC) instead of to the database server. The result can be very slow report performance. To avoid this situation, take the same care in creating record selection formulas that you pass from your application as you would in Crystal Reports. Look for detailed discussions on record selection performance in both Chapters 8 and 16.

DEVELOPING CUSTOM
WINDOW APPLICATIONS

You may also choose to create the SQL statement that the report will use right in your VB application, and then submit it to the report by setting the Report object's SQLQueryString property.

Setting Formulas

The RDC gives you an extra level of flexibility by allowing you to control the contents of Report objects as each record is processed by the report (see "Changing Text Objects at Run Time" and "Conditional Formatting and Formatting Sections" later in the chapter). Using these techniques, you can actually have objects on your report show the results of Visual Basic calculations and procedures. However, it still may be more straightforward to simply modify the contents of Crystal Reports formulas dynamically at run time. This will be useful for changing formulas related to groups that can also be changed from within your code, for changing a formula that shows text on the report, or for changing a formula that relates to math calculations or conditional formatting on the report.

Setting formulas at run time is similar to setting the record selection formula at run time (described in the preceding section). You need a good understanding of the Crystal Reports formula language to adequately modify formulas inside your VB code. If you need a refresher on Crystal Reports formulas, review Chapter 5.

The RDC provides a FormulaFields collection in the Report object that can be read or written to at run time. This collection returns multiple FormulaFieldDefinition objects, one for each formula defined in the report. Although a great deal of information may be gleaned from the FormulaFieldDefinition object, the simplest way to change the contents of a formula is simply to set the Text property for the particular member of the collection that you want to change. The collection is one-based, with each member corresponding to its position in the list of formula fields.

In the Xtreme Orders sample application, the Order + Tax formula is modified according to the user's completion of the Tax Rate text box. The formula is changed using the following code:

```
'Set @Order + Tax formula
If txtTaxRate = "" Then
   Report.FormulaFields(1).Text = "{Orders.Order Amount}"
Else
   Report.FormulaFields(1).Text = "{Orders.Order Amount} * " &_
   Str(txtTaxRate / 100 + 1)
End If  'txtTaxRate = ""
```

You needn't change the property for all formulas in the report—just the ones you want to modify at run time. Remember that you can't specify the formula name directly as the collection index argument—you must use a one-based index number. This is determined by where the formula is in the formula list in the RDC design window—

the first formula will have an index of 1, the fifth, 5, and so on. Review the sample code earlier in the chapter if you wish to refer to formulas by name instead of index number.

The Text property requires a string expression or variable, correctly conforming to Crystal Reports formula syntax, that contains the new text you want the formula to contain. Take care when assigning a value to the formula. The Order + Tax formula is defined in Crystal Reports as a numeric formula. Therefore, you should pass it a formula that will evaluate to a number. If the user leaves the text box on the form empty, the VB code assumes no additional sales tax and simply places the Order Amount database field in the formula—the formula will show the same amount as the database field.

If, however, the user has specified a tax rate, the VB code manipulates the value by dividing it by 100 and then adding 1. This creates the proper type of number to multiply against the Order Amount field to correctly calculate tax. For example, if the user specifies a tax rate of 5 (for 5 percent tax), the VB code will change the value to 1.05 before combining it with the multiply operator and the Order Amount field in the formula.

If you've used other integration methods from earlier Crystal Reports versions, such as the ActiveX control or the Report Engine API, you've probably used a formula modified at run time to show some form of text on the report, such as the report criteria that have been supplied by the user. Although this can also be accomplished with a formula here, the RDC's capability of manipulating text objects at run time gives you the opportunity to approach this from another angle. Therefore, a formula is not used to accomplish this in the Xtreme Orders sample application with the RDC. The following section explains how this is accomplished by using a text object.

| Tip | *Crystal Reports 9 features two formula syntaxes: Crystal syntax, which is compatible with Crystal Reports 7 and earlier, and Basic syntax, which was introduced in Crystal Reports 8. If you need to know which syntax an existing formula is based on, execute some code to access the formula, such as retrieving the Text property. Then, retrieve the Report object's LastGetFormulaSyntax property to determine the syntax of the formula you retrieved before. If you want to assign a specific syntax to a certain formula, set the Report object's FormulaSyntax property first. Then, set the formula's contents by passing formula text in the correct syntax to the Text property.* |

Changing Text Objects at Run Time

With older integration approaches, changing textual information on the report, such as a company name or a description of the report's selection criteria, must be done with a formula. Typically, the formula simply contains a text literal (a text string surrounded by quotation marks or apostrophes) that is then changed at run time. While this will still work with the RDC, the RDC permits a new approach that can potentially give you much more flexibility.

Remember that when you add any object to the report (a field, formula, text object, or other object), the object can be manipulated by VB. It has properties that can be set on the Property Pages dialog box at design time, as well as being modified at run time. If you add a text object to the report, a TextObject object becomes available from within the overall Report object. The TextObject object exposes many properties (you can see most of them in the Properties dialog box) that can be set at run time.

You can access the actual contents of the text object with a property and a method. The Text property can be read during code execution to see what the text object contains. To change the contents of a text object, you need to use the TextObject SetText method at run time.

In the Xtreme Orders sample application, a text object has been placed in the report header and given the name SubHeading. The following code indicates how to set the contents of the text object to indicate what choices the user has made on the Print Xtreme Orders form. This code assumes that the strSubHeading string variable has been declared elsewhere in the application. You'll also notice references to the text object and combo box controls on the form.

```
'Set SubHeading text object
strSubHeading = txtFromDate & " through " & txtToDate
strSubHeading = strSubHeading & ", By " & cboGroupBy
If txtTaxRate = "" Then
    strSubHeading = strSubHeading & ", No Tax"
Else
    strSubHeading = strSubHeading & ", Sales Tax = " & txtTaxRate & "%"
End If   'txtTaxRate = ""
Report.SubHeading.SetText (strSubHeading)
'Note: parentheses around argument to SetText method are optional
```

If you have used other integration methods in the past, you may want to change the general approach that you have used for custom formulas. Because you can change the contents of a text object from your VB code, you can essentially create "VB formulas" in your report by using the RDC. Each section of the report will fire a Format event when it is processed at report run time. You can use the SetText method inside this Format event to change the contents of text objects for each report record (in the details section Format event) or for group or report headers or footers (in their respective Format events). More information on the Format event and conditional section formatting is provided later in this chapter.

The RDC limits some of this ease of individual object control to only reports created with the RDC's internal ActiveX designer. If you use an external .RPT file with the RDC Library, you must sometimes navigate much deeper down the object hierarchy to perform this type of customization. For example, if you have just set up Application and Report objects that point to an external .RPT file (there is no ActiveX designer in your project), and you wish to set the contents of a text object, you'll need to execute code similar to this:

```
Report.Sections("PHb").ReportObjects(1).SetText "Order #"
```

This code will set the contents of the first text object in Report Header b to "Order #." This is accomplished by navigating into the Sections collection (one of the RDC collections that allows string indexes to be used, in addition to numbers). Within the Page Header b section, the first member of the ReportObjects collection (the text object) is being changed by executing the SetText method.

Tip *Version 9 of the RDC now allows you to manipulate embedded fields inside text objects. Using the TextObject object's FieldElements collection, you can add, remove, or query for embedded fields inside text objects.*

Passing Parameter-Field Values

If you are importing an existing .RPT file into the RDC or using an external .RPT file, the report may contain parameter fields that are designed to prompt the user for information whenever the report is refreshed. If you simply leave the parameter fields as they are, the application will automatically prompt the user for them when the report runs. Obviously, one of the main reasons to integrate the report into a VB application is to more closely control the user interface of the report. You'll probably want to alter the mechanism for gathering this data from the user, and then have the application supply the appropriate values to the parameter fields from within the application code.

Because you can control both report record selection and report formulas at run time from within your VB application, there may not be as much necessity to use parameter fields with an integrated report as there might be for a stand-alone report created with regular Crystal Reports. However, if you are using RDC to "share" an external .RPT file with other Crystal Reports users who are not using your custom application, you may need to set the values of parameter fields from within your code.

In this situation, use the Report object's ParameterFieldDefinitions collection to manipulate the parameters. As with formulas, there is one ParameterFieldDefinition object in the collection for each parameter field defined in the report. And as with formulas, the proper member of the collection is retrieved with a one-based index determined by the order in which the parameter fields were added to the report. You can't retrieve a parameter field by using its name as the index (unless you use the looping technique or GetItemByName approaches discussed earlier in the chapter for use with formula fields).

The RDC approach for setting the value of a parameter field being passed to a report is to use the ParameterFieldDefinition object's AddCurrentValue method. This passes a single value to the report parameter field. Because a report can contain multiple-value parameter fields, you can execute the AddCurrentValue method as many times as necessary (for example, in a loop that looks through a list box for selected items) to populate a parameter field with several values.

Although the report included in this sample application (available at www.CrystalBook .com) uses a direct format of the details section during its Format event (discussed later in the chapter) to change section color, this is an example of where a parameter field could be used. If this were the desired approach for conditional formatting, the following code would correctly pass the value to the parameter field:

```
'Set parameter value
'Alternative method is to format Details section within VB
If txtHighlight = "" Then
    Report.ParameterFields(1).AddCurrentValue (0)
Else
    Report.ParameterFields(1).AddCurrentValue (Val(txtHighlight))
End If  'txtHighlight = ""
```

Here, the value is set to 0 if the text box is empty. This is important to note because the actual parameter field in the report is numeric. Passing it an empty string might cause a run-time error when the report runs. Also, because the AddCurrentValue method is executed at least once, and a value has been passed to the parameter field, the user will no longer be prompted for it when the report is run.

Tip *The RDC object model exposes all the features of Crystal Reports 9 parameter fields, such as range values, multiple values, and edit masks. Look in online help to find the "ParameterFieldDefinition Object" entry. There, you'll find a complete description of the object, as well as all the methods available for manipulating parameter fields.*

Manipulating Report Groups

One of the requirements for the Xtreme Orders report is that the user be able to specify how the report is grouped. A combo box exists on the Print Report form that lets the user choose between Quarter and Customer grouping. In the RDC design window, this is normally accomplished by using the Change Group option from a pop-up menu to change the field a group is based on, as well as the sequence (ascending or descending) that you want the groups to appear in. If the group is based on a date field, such as Order Date, you may also specify the range of dates (week, month, quarter, and so on) that make up the group. To familiarize yourself with various grouping options, refer to Chapter 3.

By being able to change these options from within an application at run time, you can provide great reporting flexibility to your end users. In many cases, you can make it appear that several different reports are available, depending on user input. In fact, the application will be using the same Report object, but grouping will be changed at run time according to user input.

Manipulating groups in the RDC object model requires a bit of navigation "down the object hierarchy." Ultimately, the database or formula field a group is based on is specified by the GroupConditionField property of the Area object. A report contains an Areas collection consisting of an Area object for each area in a report. Consider an "area" of the report to be each individual main section of the report, such as the page header, details section, group footer, and so on. If there are multiple sections on the report, such as Details a and Details b sections, they are still part of the overall details *area*, and there is only one member of the Areas collection for them. The Areas collection has one advantage not shared by most other collections exposed by the RDC—the index used to refer to an individual member of the collection can be a string value or a numeric value. This allows you to specify RH, PH, GH*n*, D, GF*n*, PF, or RF as index values, or use the one-based index number. Using the string values makes your code much easier to understand when working with the Areas collection, and you don't have to write extra looping code, like that shown earlier for formula manipulation.

Note *The Areas and Sections collections are similar, but not identical. As shown in an example earlier in this chapter in the section "Changing Text Objects at Run Time," the Sections collection can also accept a string index; but this collection exposes individual sections, with indexes such as PHa for Page Header a and PHb for Page Header b. The Areas collection contains only one member for the Page Header area (referenced with a string index of PH), even if there are multiple page header sections, such as Page Header a and Page Header b.*

However, once you navigate to the specific Area object to specify the GroupConditionField property, you are faced with another peculiarity of the RDC object model. With older integration methods (the ActiveX control, in particular), you may supply a string value containing the actual field name (such as {Orders.Order Date} or {Customer.Customer Name}) to indicate which field you wish to base a group on. The RDC doesn't make life this simple. You must specify a DatabaseFieldDefinition object to the GroupConditionField property—you can't just pass a string containing the field name.

The DatabaseFieldDefinition object is found quite "deep" in the object hierarchy—there is one of these objects for each field contained in the DatabaseFieldDefinitions collection in a DatabaseTable object. And, multiple DatabaseTable objects are contained in the DatabaseTables collection of the Database object, contained inside the overall Report object. To make things even more complex, none of the collections just mentioned will accept a string index value—you must specify a one-based index value. You can use the previously-mentioned GetItemByName method with the DatabaseFieldDefinitions collection, but not with the DatabaseTables collection.

Although this sounds confusing and hard to navigate, you'll eventually be able to travel through the object hierarchy fairly quickly to find the database table and field you want to provide to the GroupConditionField property. Look at the following code from the Xtreme Orders sample application:

```
'Set grouping
If cboGroupBy = "Quarter" Then
    Report.Areas("GH").GroupConditionField = _
```

```
            Report.Database.Tables(1).Fields(5) 'Orders.Order Date
        Report.Areas("GH").GroupCondition = crGCQuarterly
    Else
        Report.Areas("GH").GroupConditionField = _
            Report.Database.Tables(2).Fields(3) 'Customer.Customer Name
        Report.Areas("GH").GroupCondition = crGCAnyValue
    End If  'cboGroupBy = "Quarter"
```

In this example, notice that the grouping is based on the user choice for the
cboGroupBy combo box. In either case, the GroupConditionField property of the GH
member of the Areas collection (the group header) is being set. If the user chooses to
group by Order Date, the property is set to the fifth member of the Fields collection in
the first member of the Tables collection. This indicates that the fifth field (Order Date)
in the first table (Orders) will be used for grouping. If the user chooses to group by
Customer, the third field (Customer Name) in the second table (Customer) will be used
for grouping. As with other collections that don't allow string indexes, you can use quick
Print statements in the Immediate window to search through different members of the
collection. You can also look at the Database section of the Field Explorer view in the
RDC design window to determine which index numbers to use to point to the correct
tables and fields. The GetItemByName method can be used. Or, you can write a function
that uses looping logic, described earlier, to search through the collections until you
find a matching name value.

In addition to choosing the database field you want to use for the group, you may
have to choose how the grouping occurs, particularly if you use a date or Boolean field
as the group field. This is accomplished by setting the Area object's GroupCondition
property, which can be set to an integer value or an RDC-supplied constant (see the
explanation for the Area object in the online Help for specific constants and integer
values). In the sample code shown previously, the group is set to break for every calendar
quarter if Order Date grouping is set (hence, the crGCQuarterly constant that is provided).
If Customer Name grouping is chosen, the crGCAnyValue constant is supplied, indicating
that a new group will be created whenever the value of the group field changes.

Conditional Formatting and Formatting Sections

You'll often want to present your RDC reports in the Report Viewer to allow report
interaction in an online environment, instead of having them printed on paper. The
Report Viewer provides complete interactive reporting features, such as drill-down,
that are invaluable to the application designer. Having control over these capabilities
at run time provides for great flexibility.

The Xtreme Orders sample application gives the user the opportunity to specify whether or not to see the report as a summary report only. When this check box is selected, the VB application needs to hide the report details section so that only group subtotals appear on the report. In addition, you need to control the appearance of the report's two page header sections (Page Header a and Page Header b), as well as the two Group Header #1 sections (Group Header #1a and Group Header #1b). This is done to accommodate two different sections of field titles that you wish to appear differently if the report is presented as a summary report instead of a detail report. If the report is being displayed as a detail report, the field titles should appear at the top of every page of the report, along with the subheading and smaller report title. If the report is displayed as a summary report, you want the field titles to appear in the group header section of a drill-down tab only when the user double-clicks a group. Since no detail information will be visible in the main report window, field titles there won't be meaningful.

And finally, you'll want to show Group Header #1a, which contains the group name field, if the report is showing detail data. This will indicate which group the following set of orders applies to. However, if the report is showing only summary data, showing both the group header and group footer would be repetitive—the group footer already contains the group name, so showing the group header as well will look odd. However, you will want the group header with the group name to appear in a drill-down tab. Therefore, you need to control the appearance of four sections when a user chooses the Summary Report option. Look at Table 25-1 to get a better idea of how you'll want to conditionally set these sections at run time.

Section	**Detail Report**	**Summary Report**
Page Header b (field titles)	Shown	Suppressed (no drill-down)
Group Header #1a (group name field)	Shown	Hidden (drill-down okay)
Group Header #1b (field titles)	Suppressed (no drill-down)	Hidden (drill-down okay)
Details (detail order data)	Shown	Hidden (drill-down okay)

Table 25-1. *Section Formatting for Different Report Types*

You'll notice that, in some cases, sections need to be completely suppressed (so they don't show up, even in a drill-down tab) as opposed to hidden (they show up in a drill-down tab, but not in the main Preview tab). There is a somewhat obscure relationship among areas and sections that make this determination. Specifically, only complete areas (such as the entire Group Header #1) can be hidden, not individual sections (for example, Group Header #1a). However, both areas and sections can be suppressed. To further explain this concept, if you look in the Properties dialog box after you've selected a section in the design window, you'll see a Suppress property but no Hide property.

This presents a bit of a coding challenge for the Xtreme Orders sample application. First, you need to determine the correct combination of area hiding and section suppressing that sets what appears in the Preview window and in a drill-down tab. If an area is set to Hide, none of the sections in it will appear in the main Preview window. And when the user drills down into that section, you will also want to control which sections inside the drilled-down area appear in the drill-down tab. Then, you must find where to set the Hide property for a particular area. You must also find where to set the Suppress property for sections inside the hidden area, or other sections that aren't hidden.

Since the Hide property is available only for an entire area, you need to set the HideForDrillDown property for the appropriate member of the Areas collection. Since the Suppress property needs to be set for individual sections, you can just refer to the individual sections in the RDC design window by name, setting the Suppress property for them as needed. Consider that the Page Header b section has been given the name PHb in the Properties dialog box (it was named Section 3 when the report was imported). Other sections have been given more descriptive names in the RDC design window, as well. Group Header #1a is named GH1A, and Group Header #1b is named GH1B.

Keeping in mind the preceding discussion and the hide and suppress requirements outlined in Table 25-1, look at this code from the sample application:

```
'Hide/show sections
With Report
    If chkSummary Then
        .Areas("D").HideForDrillDown = True
        .PHb.Suppress = True
        .Areas("GH1").HideForDrillDown = True
        .GH1A.Suppress = False
        .GH1B.Suppress = False
    Else
        .Areas("D").HideForDrillDown = False
        .PHb.Suppress = False
        .Areas("GH1").HideForDrillDown = False
```

```
        .GH1A.Suppress = False
        .GH1B.Suppress = True
    End If   'chkSummary
End With   'Report
```

Notice that both Area objects for the details and Group Header #1 areas are being formatted, as well as individual sections. The areas must be formatted from their collection, whereas sections can be manipulated directly below the Report object by name.

> **Note** *You can navigate deeper into the object hierarchy and actually set the Suppress property for members of the Sections collection inside the Area object. Although this is a little more code intensive, it is required if you are using an external .RPT file, which doesn't expose individual section names as does the RDC ActiveX designer.*

The Format Event

Another benefit that only the RDC provides to developers (only with reports supplied by the ActiveX designer) is the Format event. This event is "fired" every time the processing of an individual report section begins. Consider the way the first page of a report might be processed. First, the overall report is "prepared"; then the page header prints, followed, in order, by the report header (since this is the first page of the report), the first group header, all the details sections in that group, the first group footer, and so on. Each time any of these sections begins to print (including when the report is "prepared"), its respective Format event fires.

You can intercept these formatting events and change the behavior of the section, or of objects within the section. This gives you complete Visual Basic functionality when it comes to conditional formatting or section formatting. In older integration methods that use .RPT files (including using an external .RPT file with the RDC), you must use Crystal Reports conditional formulas or the Highlighting Expert to set background colors for sections, highlight fields over a certain value, and perform other formatting based on certain conditions. While the RDC continues to support that flexibility, you can now base individual section and object formatting on VB code.

To add code for any Format event, simply double-click a section in the RDC design window. This displays the Format event in the code window for the particular section you double-clicked. You can also right-click the designer in the Visual Basic Project Explorer and choose View Code from the pop-up menu. In either case, each report section appears in the object drop-down list in the upper-left corner of the code window. The only available procedure for each report section is Format, which will appear in the procedure drop-down list in the upper-right corner.

You have all the power of VB at your disposal to control the appearance and formatting of sections and objects, or the content of text objects, while the report is being formatted. This allows you to write VB code to determine how to format a field in the current section being formatted (perhaps to set the background or font color of an object according to some VB code). You can also change the formatting of the entire section, as demonstrated in the following code from the Xtreme Orders sample application:

```
Private Sub Details_Format (ByVal pFormattingInfo As Object)
    If Val(frmXtremeOrders.txtHighlight) > 0 And _
    Report.fldOrderAmount.Value > Val(frmXtremeOrders.txtHighlight) Then
        Report.Details.BackColor = &HFFFF00
    End If  'Report.fldOrderAmount > Val(txtHighlight)...
End Sub
```

Tip	*The pFormattingInfo argument that is passed into the module is an object that exposes three read-only properties that return true or false: IsEndOfGroup, IsStartOfGroup, and IsRepeatedGroupHeader. You can read the contents of these properties to help determine how to handle logic in the Format event.*

This code is contained in the Format event for the details section (notice that the report section has been renamed Details from its default name of Section 6). Every time the details section begins to format, this event fires. At that time, the contents of the Highlight text box on the Print Xtreme Orders form are checked for a value. If the user has supplied a value, and the fldOrderAmount database field from the report is greater than the value the user supplied, the background color of the details section is set. This logic replaces the parameter field and conditional formatting used in many other similar reporting situations.

Obviously, many other flexible and complex types of formatting and manipulation can occur during the Format event. A common use of this manipulation is to replace formula fields on the report with text objects and to use the SetText method to change the contents of the text objects from within the Format event. Essentially, this extends the complete power of the Visual Basic language to objects you place your report.

The RDC exposes some additional events to the report-processing cycle. Not only can you trap the Format event for every report section, but the Report object itself fires several events as it processes. An event of particular interest is NoData. Look at this code fragment:

```
Private Sub Report_NoData(pCancel As Boolean)
    MsgBox "There is no data in this report. " & _
    "Supply different selection criteria"
    pCancel = True
End Sub
```

If the report contains no data when it processes, the NoData event will fire. You may trap this event and perform special handling. In particular, by setting the pCancel value to true, you can cancel the remainder of report processing. Be aware, though, that canceling report processing won't stop the Report Viewer from appearing—you need to add a global variable or some other flag to indicate that the Report Viewer should not be displayed in this event.

As you search through RDC documentation, you may see references to "Formatting Idle" or other processing time references. Certain object properties can be set only during certain times when the report is processing. This is mostly significant when writing code in the Format event. If you attempt to set a property that can't be set during that particular report-processing time, you'll receive either error messages or unexpected results. Look for a discussion of formatting modes by searching the online Help for "Format event."

DEVELOPING CUSTOM
WINDOW APPLICATIONS

> **Caution**   *Formatting events may fire more often than you might expect because of the multiple passes Crystal Reports must make as it processes the report. This may happen, for example, when the RDC encounters a Keep Together section option at the end of a page. If you place code to accumulate values in the Format event without accounting for these multiple passes, your accumulations will be inaccurate. The RDC includes a feature called Report Variables that can keep track of these reporting passes. If you use Report Variables instead of your own variables, values will accumulate only when an actual "logical" change occurs to a report section. Search the online Help file for "Report Variables" to get complete details.*

Choosing Output Destinations

If your users will have a choice of output destinations (as the user does in the Xtreme Orders sample application), you need to create appropriate code to handle the user's choice. In the Xtreme Orders sample application, radio buttons and a text box allow the user to choose to view the report in the preview window, print the report to a printer, or attach the report as a .PDF file to an e-mail message. If the user chooses e-mail as the output destination, an e-mail address can be entered in a text box. Based on the user's selection, you need to set the output destination in your VB code.

If the user chooses to view the report on the screen, you need to activate the Report Viewer. In the sample application, this simply entails displaying the form that contains the Report Viewer control, by executing the form's Show method. The Form_Load event of this form will pass the Report object to the Report Viewer and execute the Report Viewer's ViewReport method.

As mentioned earlier, use of the Report Viewer is completely optional—you are free to answer No when you are prompted about whether or not to add it when first adding the RDC to your project. However, if one of the output options will be to the screen (as in the Xtreme Orders sample application), make sure that the Report Viewer is eventually added to your project.

If you respond Yes to the RDC's "Do you want to add the Report Viewer" prompt, the RDC automatically adds the Report Viewer for you. It will create a new form, place the Report Viewer in the form, and automatically add rudimentary code to supply the Report object to the Report Viewer and resize the Report Viewer to be the same size as the form. If the RDC adds the Report Viewer automatically, you can leave this default behavior as is, move the Report Viewer object to another form, or build additional elements into the form that the RDC created automatically. You can also manually add the Report Viewer to your project later and supply code to pass the Report object to the Report Viewer.

If you wish to print the Report object to a printer, execute the Report object's PrintOut method. The syntax is as follows:

```
object.PrintOut Prompt, Copies, Collated, StartPage, StopPage
```

In this statement, *Prompt* is a Boolean value indicating whether or not to prompt the user for printer options, *Copies* is a numeric value indicating how many copies of the report to print, *Collated* is a Boolean value indicating whether or not to collate the pages, and *StartPage* and *StopPage* are numeric values indicating which page numbers to start and stop printing on. The parameters are optional—if you want to skip any in the middle, just add commas in the correct positions—but don't include the parameter.

If you wish to export the report to a disk file or attach the report to an e-mail message as a file, use the Report object's Export method. The syntax is as follows:

```
object.Export PromptUser
```

In this statement, *PromptUser* is a Boolean value indicating whether you want to prompt the user for export options. If you choose not to prompt the user for export options, you need to set properties of the report's ExportOptions object. The ExportOptions object contains many properties that determine the output destination (file or e-mail), file format (Word, Excel, PDF, XML, and so on), filename, e-mail address, and more. Many of these properties accept integer values or RDC-supplied descriptive constants. If you choose MAPI as the destination, the user's PC needs to have a MAPI-compliant e-mail client installed, such as Microsoft Outlook or Eudora Pro. Look for all the available ExportOptions properties by searching the online Help for "ExportOptions object."

In the Xtreme Orders sample application, the following code is used to choose an output destination, as well as to specify a file type and e-mail information, based on user selection:

```
'Set output destination
If optPreview Then frmViewer.Show
If OptPrint Then Report.PrintOut (True)
If OptEmail Then
    With Report
        .ExportOptions.DestinationType = crEDTEMailMAPI
        .ExportOptions.MailToList = txtAddress
        .ExportOptions.MailSubject = "Here's the Xtreme Orders Report"
        .ExportOptions.MailMessage = _
"Attached is a PDF file showing the latest Xtreme Orders Report."
        .ExportOptions.FormatType = crEFTPortableDocFormat
        .Export (False)
    End With  'Report
End If  'optEmail
```

Caution *If you use the Report object's Export method to export or send the report attached to an e-mail message, make sure you specify all the necessary ExportOptions object properties. If you fail to specify necessary properties or specify them incorrectly, an error may be thrown. Or, the user may be prompted to specify export options, even though you specifically add a false argument to the Export method. If the export takes place at an unattended machine, your application has to wait for a response, even though no user is available to respond.*

Changing the Data Source at Run Time

Obviously, one of the main benefits of integrating a Crystal Report in a Visual Basic program is the ability to tie the report contents to a data set or result set that the program is manipulating. This allows a user to interact with your application and then run a report that contains the same set of data that the user has selected.

One way to accomplish this is to create a Crystal Reports record selection formula or a SQL statement based on your user interface. The formula or SQL statement can then be passed to the report, as discussed elsewhere in this chapter. This allows the user to interact with a data grid, form, or other visual interface in the application and create a report based on its contents.

However, you may encounter situations in which you prefer to have the contents of an actual Visual Basic record set from one of Visual Basic's intrinsic data models act as the data source for a report. The RDC provides for this with the SetDataSource method. Using SetDataSource, you can initially design the report using a particular database or data source, or using a field-definition file (discussed in the online Help). Then, you can pass a Visual Basic DAO, RDO, or ADO record set, snapshot, or result set to the report at run time. The RDC will use the current contents of the VB data set to populate the report.

The syntax for SetDataSource is as follows:

```
[form]Object.SetDataSource data, DataTag, tableIndex
```

In this statement, *Object* is the RDC Database object (residing below the Report object) that you want to supply data to; *data* is the DAO, ADO, or RDO data set that you want to supply data to the report; and *DataTag* and *tableIndex* are parameters indicating, respectively, the type of data and the index of the table that you want to change the data source for. The *DataTag* parameter should always be specified as 3, with *tableIndex* being set according to the table you wish to "point" to the new data source.

Thus, if you have created an RDC report and named the Report object "Report," and you have identified an ADO Resultset object elsewhere in your VB application with the name "ADOrs," the following code will pass the contents of the result set to the report. When the report is printed, exported, or passed to the Report Viewer, the contents of the result set will be used by the report's Database object to populate the report.

```
Report.Database.SetDataSource ADOrs,3,1
```

Notice that the last two parameters to the SetDataSource method are 3 and 1, indicating the only allowable data tag (3), and the first table in the database (1).

There are actually two forms of the SetDataSource method available with the RDC. The method described previously applies to the entire Database object, requiring the third argument indicating a table index. There is also a SetDataSource method available for the DatabaseTable object. The syntax is almost the same—the only difference is that a table-index parameter is not required, because the method applies only to a single Table object.

If you use SetDataSource to change the data source for a database table, make sure the data source you pass to the report remains in scope whenever the report runs. For example, you may define a Report object that's global to your application (by declaring it at the module level). But if you pass it a data source that was declared at the form level, and then try to run the report in another form, the data source will be out of scope and the report will fail. The ReadRecords method is available for reading the contents of the data source into the Report object, if maintaining scope for the data source isn't practical. Search the Developer's Help for information on "ReadRecords."

Tip *The RDC provides two other methods available from the Database object (underneath the Report object) that are similar to SetDataSource. AddOLEDBSource will add an OLE DB table and make its fields available to the report. AddADOCommand will add and pass an ADO record set as a table to the report through an ADO connection and command.*

Unbound Fields

Depending on the reporting application you are designing, you may choose to create a very basic generic report layout that doesn't connect to any particular database at the time you design it. This might be appropriate, for example, for an application that allows a user to choose from a list of database fields and drag and drop them to a pseudoreport outline in your application. When the report is actually printed, your code would need to match the chosen fields to actual field locations on a Crystal Report. Or, you may design one report that a user can choose to connect to either a test database or a production database. Although the SetDataSource method, described previously, may be a good alternative for this example, you may also want to manually assign database values to fields on the report.

The RDC provides capabilities to make this type of customized reporting much easier. *Unbound Fields* can be added to your report in the ActiveX designer just like database fields, formula fields, and so forth. The only difference is that the fields don't actually connect to any particular database table or field. This assignment is made at run time, using automatic or manual binding (discussed later in the chapter).

Adding Unbound Fields to a Report

The first step in using Unbound Fields is to add them to the report in the RDC designer. You'll notice the additional Unbound Fields category in the Field Explorer that you don't see in the regular Crystal Reports designer. When you click the plus sign next to this category, you'll see a list of Unbound Field data types. Drag and drop the desired data types to the report just as you would other Field Explorer objects. Figure 25-4 shows Unbound Fields being placed on a report.

The RDC will apply default object names to the Unbound Fields you drag and drop. Depending on how you're planning ultimately to bind the fields to your data source, you may leave the default names if you so choose. But, it probably makes sense to at least give the Unbound Fields meaningful names, to help you remember what you're binding when you begin to write the binding code. And, if you plan to use the RDC's automatic binding method (discussed in the next section), you need to give them names identical to the field names in the data source that you will be binding to them.

Binding Fields to the Data Source

Once you've created the report with your complement of Unbound Fields, it's time to bind them at run time. First, declare and assign any necessary objects. In the following sample code, a Report object is defined to contain the ActiveX designer report, and an

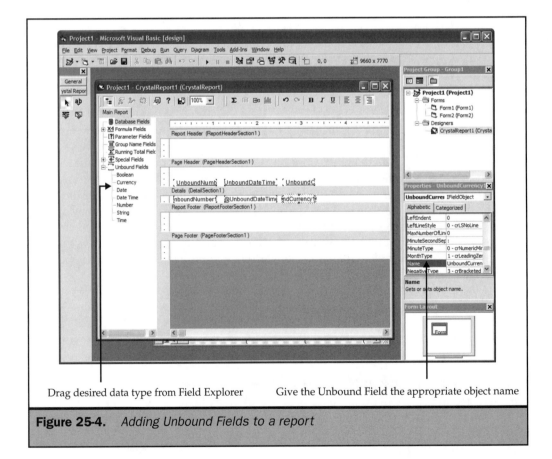

Drag desired data type from Field Explorer   Give the Unbound Field the appropriate object name

Figure 25-4.   *Adding Unbound Fields to a report*

ADO record set is created. Fields from this record set will be bound to the Unbound Fields created in the report.

```
Dim Report As New CrystalReport1
Dim rs As New ADOR.Recordset
rs.Open "select * from orders", "xtreme sample database 9"
Report.Database.AddADOCommand rs.ActiveConnection, rs.ActiveCommand
```

Remember that even though the Unbound Fields you added to the report aren't "connected" to any particular database fields, the Report object itself must be connected to your desired data source before you can bind any fields to it. This is accomplished with AddADOCommand, AddOLEDBSource, or some similar method.

After you make the data connection, there are two ways of actually binding the Unbound Fields to a database field: automatic binding and manual binding.

Automatic Binding   *Automatic binding* uses the Unbound Field's data type and, optionally, object name to bind to actual data fields in the data source. To use automatic binding, execute a single line of code similar to this:

```
Report.AutoSetUnboundFieldSource crBMTNameAndValue
```

By supplying the crBMTNameAndValue constant to the AutoSetUnboundFieldSource method, you assure that the RDC will use both the name and data type of the Unbound Field to try to match to a data source field. If you want to base this object-to-field matching on name only, supply the constant crBMTName. The RDC will then attempt to match Unbound Fields to data source fields solely on the basis of name, regardless of data type.

Manual Binding   If you have disparate data sources that won't always match field names with the names you've given your Unbound Fields, you can assign data source fields to the Unbound Fields one by one. Examine the following code fragment:

```
Report.OrderID.SetUnboundFieldSource "{ado.Order ID}"
Report.OrderDate.SetUnboundFieldSource "{ado.Order Date}"
Report.OrderAmount.SetUnboundFieldSource "{ado.Order Amount}"
Report.ShipVia.SetUnboundFieldSource "{ado.Ship Via}"
```

In this example, individual Unbound Fields are matched to data source fields using the field object's SetUnboundFieldSource method.

Customizing the Report Viewer

If you've added the Report Viewer ActiveX component to your project, you have a great deal of flexibility in customizing the way the Report Viewer appears and behaves. By default, the RDC will add the Report Viewer to its own form and add a small amount of code to supply the Report object to the Report Viewer and resize the Report Viewer whenever the form is resized.

This default behavior uses just a fraction of the Report Viewer's capabilities. The viewer has many options, exposed by its own library, which will meld it more tightly into your application. You can customize how the Report Viewer looks, what controls and toolbar buttons are available, and the Report Viewer's size. You may even perform all the functions from within code that the built-in toolbar buttons would accomplish. This allows you to make the Report Viewer show virtually no controls but the report itself, if you prefer. You can design a completely separate user interface for page control, zoom levels, printing, exporting, and more.

In addition, the Report Viewer contains a flexible event model that will "fire" events as the Report Viewer performs various functions, or as a user interacts with it. You can trap button clicks, drill-down selections, changes in the zoom level, and other events. You can execute extra code when any of these events occurs, or intercept the events and cancel them if you wish to not have the Report Viewer complete them.

When you add the Report Viewer to a form (or when it's added automatically by the RDC), you'll see the outline of the Report Viewer appear as an object inside the form. When you select the Report Viewer object, you'll see a large number of design-time properties appear in the Properties box in VB. This is illustrated in Figure 25-5.

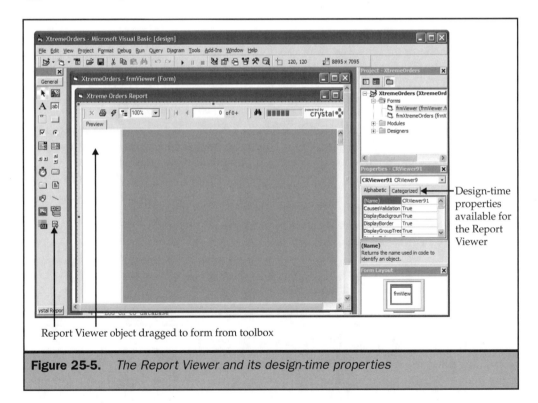

Report Viewer object dragged to form from toolbox

Figure 25-5. *The Report Viewer and its design-time properties*

If you want the Report Viewer to exhibit consistent behavior during the entire application, you can change properties for the Report Viewer at design time, such as which toolbar buttons are shown, whether a report group tree is displayed, whether a user can drill down, and so on.

Most of these properties can also be set at run time by supplying the appropriate values to the Report Viewer object's properties. Because the Report Viewer object actually adds its own COM library to your project, you can get an idea of the object model, properties, methods, and events that are available by looking at the Object Browser. Press F2, or choose View | Object Browser from the Visual Basic pull-down menus. Then, choose CRVIEWER9LibCtl in the library drop-down list to see the object model exposed by the Report Viewer's Library.

Here's some code from the Xtreme Orders sample application that customizes several Report Viewer behaviors. The Print button is turned off on the Report Viewer by setting the EnablePrintButton property to false. The Help button is displayed on the Report Viewer by setting the EnableHelpButton property to true. The Crystal Decisions logo animation control is turned on by setting the EnableAnimationCtrl property to true. And, the EnableDrillDown property determines whether or not a user can double-click a group in the Report Viewer to drill down (if the user chooses to show a detail report, drill-down isn't of benefit).

```
CRViewer91.EnablePrintButton = False
CRViewer91.EnableHelpButton = True
CRViewer91.EnableAnimationCtrl = True

If frmXtremeOrders.chkSummary Then
    CRViewer91.EnableDrillDown = True
Else
    CRViewer91.EnableDrillDown = False
End If  'frmXtremeOrders.chkSummary
```

Trapping Report Viewer Events

The Report Viewer library, in addition to offering a good selection of properties and methods, exposes a large number of events that allow you to trap button clicks, report-processing cycles, and drill-down attempts. These events can be used to modify the behavior of the Report Viewer, to execute some additional supplementary code when a certain event occurs, or potentially to modify report contents while it is being viewed.

A section of CrystalDevHelp.CHM covers programming the Report Viewers. You'll find complete information about which events are available for custom coding. You may also look at the Object Browser. Or, just open the code window for the Report Viewer object and look at the procedure drop-down list in the upper-right corner of the code window.

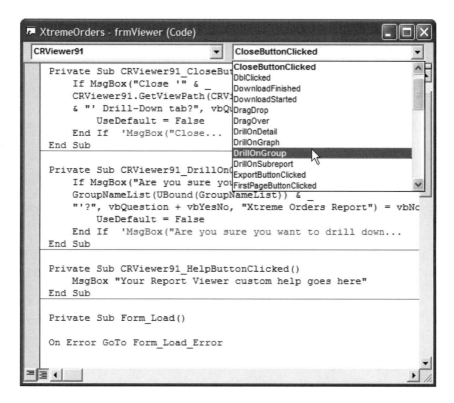

Because you can trap many events that occur during report processing and user interaction with the Report Viewer, you have tremendous power to customize your reporting application. The Xtreme Orders sample application has only three simple examples of these capabilities. If the user clicks the Help button in the Report Viewer, a message box appears indicating "Custom Help Goes Here." When the user drills down on a group, a confirmation message box appears, asking the user to confirm the drill-down. If the answer is Yes, the drill-down will occur. If the answer is No, the drill-down will be canceled. And, after a user drills down and clicks the Close View button (the red X) in the Report Viewer, another confirmation message box appears, asking the user to confirm the closure. As with the original drill-down, the drill-down tab will be closed only if the user answers Yes. Otherwise, the event will be canceled.

One of the more complex parts of these examples is actually determining which group will be affected when the drill-down or drill-down tab closure occurs. Understanding this is crucial for fully exploiting the power of the event model—trapping these events is probably of little use if you can't determine which group is actually being manipulated. The Report Viewer DrillOnGroup event makes this task easier by passing the GroupNameList parameter into the event function. This zero-based array contains an element for each group that has been drilled into previously, with the current group that is now being drilled into being the last element of the array.

If your report contains only one level of grouping (as does the Xtreme Orders sample report), the GroupNameList will always contain just element 0—the group that was drilled down to. However, if your report contains multiple levels of grouping, you'll have the extra benefit of determining how deep and which groups are included in the group that is currently being drilled down to. For example, if your report is grouped on three levels—Country, State, and City—a user may first drill down on Canada. This will fire the DrillOnGroup event, and the GroupNameList array will contain only element 0, Canada. Then, in the Canada drill-down tab, the user might double-click BC. This will again fire the DrillOnGroup event, and the GroupNameList array will now contain two elements, Canada in element 0 and BC in element 1. Then, if the user double-clicks Vancouver in the BC drill-down tab, yet another DrillOnGroup event will fire. Inside this event, the GroupNameList array will contain elements 0, 1, and 2—Canada, BC, and Vancouver.

If you are concerned about only the lowest level of grouping, just query the last element of the GroupNameList array by using the VB UBound function. Even though the Xtreme Orders report contains only one level of grouping (thereby always allowing GroupNameList(0) to be used to determine the group), the UBound function has been used for upward compatibility.

The other argument passed to the DrillOnGroup event is UseDefault. This Boolean value can be set to true or false inside the event to determine whether the drill-down actually occurs. If UseDefault is set to true (or left as is), the drill-down will occur. If it is set to false inside the DrillOnGroup event, the drill-down will be canceled and no drill-down tab will appear for the group in the Report Viewer.

Here's the sample code from the Xtreme Orders application. Note that the actual group being drilled on is included in the message box and that the results of the message box determine whether or not the drill-down occurs.

```
Private Sub CRViewer91_DrillOnGroup(GroupNameList As Variant, _
ByVal DrillType As CRVIEWER9LibCtl.CRDrillType, UseDefault As Boolean)
    If MsgBox("Are you sure you want to drill down on '" & _
    GroupNameList(UBound(GroupNameList)) & _
    "'?", vbQuestion + vbYesNo, "Xtreme Orders Report") = vbNo Then
```

```
        UseDefault = False
    End If  'MsgBox("Are you sure you want to drill down...
End Sub
```

The other Report Viewer event that is used in the Xtreme Orders sample application is CloseButtonClicked. This event fires whenever a user clicks the red X in the Report Viewer to close the current drill-down tab (known in the Report Viewer object model as the *current view*). Again, the sample application simply displays a confirming message box asking whether or not the user really wants to close the drill-down tab. By setting the UseDefault parameter inside the event code, the drill-down tab is closed or not closed, based on the user's choice.

As when drilling down, the actual drill-down tab that's being closed needs to be known inside the event (it's just being included in the message box in this example). Because the CloseButtonClicked event doesn't pass a GroupNameList or similar parameter into the event, a little more sleuthing has to be done to determine what the current view is. This is where both the Report Viewer's GetViewPath method and its ActiveViewIndex property come into play.

The ActiveViewIndex property simply returns an integer (one based) indicating which drill-down tab is the currently selected tab. While this is helpful, it doesn't return the actual string containing the group name of the tab being viewed. This must be accomplished by using the GetViewPath method of the Report Viewer object. This method accepts one argument, a numeric index indicating the tab in the Report Viewer window for which you want to see the view path. The method returns a one-based string array that includes the actual views (or group names) that are included in the drill-down tab whose index is provided as the argument to GetViewPath. As with GroupNameList, you can then determine the actual name of the current tab being closed by accessing the last element (using the UBound function) of the array.

Examine the following code closely:

```
Private Sub CRViewer91_CloseButtonClicked(UseDefault As Boolean)
    If MsgBox("Close '" & _
CRViewer91.GetViewPath(CRViewer91.ActiveViewIndex)
(UBound(CRViewer91.GetViewPath(CRViewer91.ActiveViewIndex))) _
    & "' Drill-Down tab?", vbQuestion + vbYesNo, _
        "Xtreme Order Report") = vbNo Then
        UseDefault = False
    End If  'MsgBox("Close...
End Sub
```

Note   *Due to width restrictions in the book, the line of sample code in the preceding example that demonstrates the CRViewer91.GetViewPath command is broken after the first right parenthesis. If you look at the sample application, you'll notice that this is a continuous line, which is required for proper VB interpretation of the line.*

Notice that GetViewPath is supplied with the ActiveViewIndex property. This will return a string array containing all the groups that are included in the current drill-down tab. Even though the Xtreme Orders report contains only one level of grouping, the UBound function is still used to retrieve the last element of the array returned by GetViewPath. This provides upward compatibility if you ever choose to add multiple groups to the report.

The RDC provides additional Report Viewer support for the familiar Crystal Reports Select Expert and Search Expert, as well as a Text Search feature. Buttons for these tools can be enabled or disabled at design time or run time. And, you can programmatically perform both formula-based and text-based searches with the Report Viewer's SearchByFormula and SearchForText methods.

Caution   *If you are integrating an external .RPT file with the RDC, and you wish to trap drill-down events from within the Report Viewer, ensure that the Create Group Tree option is checked from File | Report Options in Crystal Reports. If you don't specifically set this option, you may get an error when the Report Viewer attempts to trap drill-down events.*

Error Handling

You need to set up error-handling code for all aspects of RDC programming. As you manipulate the Report object itself (setting properties and executing methods), you need to plan for the possibility that errors may occur. And if you use the Report Viewer in your application, it can also throw errors for any number of reasons. Add error-handling logic accordingly.

All Report object and Report Viewer errors will appear as regular Visual Basic run-time errors. These need to be trapped with an On Error Goto routine. The hard part is trying to figure out what error codes to trap. Unfortunately, Crystal Decisions has yet to provide comprehensive documentation for the errors that either the Report or Report Viewer objects might throw. In many situations, you'll see typical VB-type error codes for report-related errors. For example, supplying a string index argument to a Report object collection that accepts only integer arguments won't generate an RDC-specific error; instead, Subscript Out of Range will be returned. However, certain error messages that are Report- or Report Viewer–specific generally throw errors that start with –2147 and are followed by six other numbers.

You'll simply have to test your application thoroughly and create error-handling code appropriately. Try intentionally creating any Report- or Report Viewer–related errors that have even a remote chance of occurring. You can then determine what corresponding error codes the Report or Report Viewer objects throw, and add code to trap those specific errors. Here's sample code from the Xtreme Orders application that traps potential errors when setting Report properties at run time:

```
cmdOK_Click_Error:
Screen.MousePointer = vbDefault
Select Case Err.Number
   Case -2147190889
       MsgBox "Report Cancelled", vbInformation, "Xtreme Order Report"
   Case -2147190908
       MsgBox "Invalid E-Mail address or other e-mail problem", _
             vbCritical, "Xtreme Order Report"
       txtAddress.SetFocus
   Case Else
       MsgBox "Error " & Err.Number & " - " & Err.Description, _
             vbCritical, "Xtreme Order Report"
End Select   'Case Err.Number
```

Other RDC Properties and Methods

This chapter has covered many RDC procedures for handling most common report-customization requirements, but several other areas of RDC functionality deserve some discussion. In particular, RDC functions that pertain to handling SQL database reporting, as well as dealing with subreports, should be addressed. In addition, the RDC DiscardSavedData method for "resetting" or clearing the contents of properties that may have been set in previous VB code should be explored.

The DiscardSavedData Method

If you find yourself displaying a Report object in a viewer, or performing some other output mechanism with the same Report object over and over, you will want to take steps to ensure that any "left over" settings from a previous report process are reset when you run the next report. While you can set the Report object to Nothing and instantiate it again, you may instead want to use the Report object's DiscardSavedData method if you will be running a report multiple times without the Nothing setting.

The Xtreme Orders sample application provides a good example of where this is helpful. The Report object is declared in a global module, and the Print Xtreme Orders form stays loaded during the entire scope of the application. Every time the OK button is clicked, the application sets Report properties based on the controls on the form and then either prints or exports the report, or else displays the form containing the Report Viewer.

The issue of clearing previous settings comes into play when a user runs the report more than once without ending and restarting the application. Because the Report object is never released and reinstantiated, all of its property settings remain intact when the user clicks OK subsequent times. If the Visual Basic code doesn't explicitly set some of these previously set properties, the report may exhibit behavior from the previous time it was run that you don't expect. Executing the Report object's DiscardSavedData method clears many properties of settings from any previous activity, returning them to the state they were in when designed.

Simply execute the DiscardSavedData method for any Report objects that you want to "clean up," as shown in the following sample from the Xtreme Orders sample application:

```
Report.DiscardSavedData 'required for consistent results
```

You may wonder about the significance of DiscardSavedData with the RDC, particularly when you're integrating a report that you designed in the ActiveX designer that does not have a Save Data With Report option. If you are using an external .RPT file that has been saved with File | Save Data With Report turned on, you'll probably want Visual Basic to discard the saved data at run time and refresh the report with new data from the database. Because the RDC is integrating a report that is contained entirely within the VB IDE (even if an .RPT file was imported, its saved data is not imported with it), you may be confused as to how DiscardSavedData applies. The RDC, in essence, "saves" data in the Report object when it is viewed in the Report Viewer, printed, or exported (or when the ReadRecords method is executed). That saved data remains a part of the Report object until it's discarded or the object reference is destroyed.

SQL Database Control

Many corporate databases are kept on client/server SQL database systems, such as Microsoft SQL Server, Oracle, and Informix. Many Visual Basic applications provide front-end interfaces to these database systems and need to handle SQL reporting as well. The RDC contains several properties and methods that help when integrating reports based on SQL databases.

Probably the most common interaction with SQL databases is providing login credentials. This is discussed elsewhere in this chapter under "Providing Database Login Credentials."

Retrieving or Setting the SQL Query

When you submit a record selection formula, as discussed earlier in the chapter, the RDC automatically generates a SQL statement to submit to the database server. However, if the record selection formula contains a Crystal Reports formula or other "complex" characteristics that prevent the RDC from generating a WHERE clause in the SQL statement, report performance can be dramatically and negatively affected. You may, therefore, want to create the SQL statement the report uses directly in your VB application.

As part of this process, you may find it helpful to retrieve the SQL statement that the RDC is generating automatically.

The Report object provides a read/write SQLQueryString property that can be read or written to at run time. By examining the contents of this property, you can see what the SQL query is that the RDC is generating. You can then make necessary modifications to the query, depending on the state of your application and the database on which the report is based. Then, pass the modified query to the SQLQueryString property to be submitted to the server when the report runs.

It's important to note that you can't modify the SELECT clause in the SQL query. Only FROM, WHERE, ORDER BY, and GROUP BY can be modified. However, you must still include the SELECT clause when you return an updated SQL statement to the report, and it must not be changed from the original clause the RDC created. Also, if you create ORDER BY or GROUP BY clauses, you must separate them from the end of the WHERE clause with a carriage return/line feed character sequence. Use the vbCRLF constant to add the CR/LF sequence inside the SQL query.

> **Tip**   *Crystal Reports 9's new SQL Command capabilities are included in the RDC. One option you have for complete database control is to base your report entirely or partially on SQL commands, rather than manipulating the SQL Query from within your code.*

Reading or Setting Stored Procedure Parameters

If your report is based on a parameterized SQL stored procedure, you will probably want to supply parameter values to the stored procedure from within your code, much as you will want to respond to any RDC parameter fields that may have been created.

With the RDC, SQL stored procedure parameters are treated identically to Report parameter fields. The Report object contains the ParameterFieldDefinitions collection, containing one ParameterFieldDefinition object for each Report parameter field *or* stored procedure parameter contained in the report. The ParameterFieldDefinition object's ParameterType property will indicate whether the parameter is a Report parameter or a stored procedure parameter.

By executing the ParameterFieldDefinition object's AddCurrentValue method, you can pass a value to a stored procedure parameter from within your code. More detailed information on interacting with parameter fields can be found earlier in this chapter.

RDC Subreports

The RDC brings all the flexibility of Crystal Reports subreports to Visual Basic. If you import an .RPT file that contains subreports into the RDC, the subreports will be imported along with the main report. And, you can add your own subreports to the RDC design window at any time by right-clicking a blank area of the report and choosing Insert | Subreport from the pop-up menu (see Chapter 11 for more information on creating subreports).

DEVELOPING CUSTOM WINDOW APPLICATIONS

The unique part of the RDC is the way a subreport fits into the object model. When you are displaying the main report in the RDC design window, a subreport will appear as an object outline, just as it does in regular Crystal Reports. However, if you click the subreport object, it has a set of properties that appears in the Properties box, just like other objects on the report. Figure 25-6 illustrates this.

You can set several design-time properties for the Subreport object, the same way you can for other objects on the report. One of the properties you may want to set as a matter of habit is the subreport name. By giving the subreport a descriptive name, you'll be able to more easily identify and work with it as you write code for your application.

After you add the Subreport object to the main report, it's treated just like a text object, field, line, box, or other object that appears on the main report in the main Report object model. But because the subreport contains its own set of fields and objects that are separate from the main report, the object model can expose them in a number of ways. Subreport objects (fields, formulas, sections, lines, and others) actually appear as part of the main Report object. The RDC precedes the object names with the name of the subreport and an underscore.

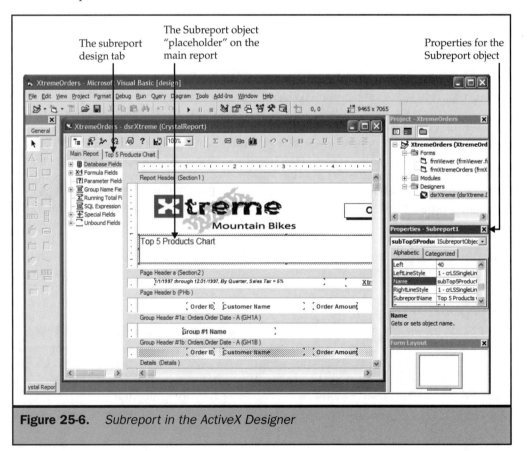

Figure 25-6.   *Subreport in the ActiveX Designer*

Consider a main report that contains several database fields that haven't been renamed since the report was created (Field1, Field2, and so on). The main report also contains a subreport that you've named subTop5Products. The Subreport objects actually become part of the main report. You can now set properties for the Report object named Field1, which will refer to the first field on the main report. If you then set Report properties for an object named subTop5Products_Field1, you are setting properties for the first field on the subreport.

Also, the main report exposes a SubreportObject object for every subreport "placeholder" contained on the main report. This object exposes a variety of properties that can be read and written to at run time to control the appearance and behavior of the placeholder (although not the actual subreport itself). Consider the following code:

```
'Set subreport object borders to blank
Report.subTop5Products.TopLineStyle = 0
Report.subTop5Products.LeftLineStyle = 0
Report.subTop5Products.BottomLineStyle = 0
Report.subTop5Products.RightLineStyle = 0
```

Here, the SubreportObject object is being manipulated from the Report object (referred to with the subreport name subTop5Products). The four line-style properties are all being set to 0, indicating that the border around the Subreport object will be invisible at run time.

Despite this tricky way of sharing objects and setting properties for the subreport placeholder, not all subreport properties, methods, and events are available from the main Report object. And if you're using an external .RPT file, these options won't be available either. Because the subreport is, in essence, an additional report that appears only on the main report, you need a way to control the behavior of the subreport using the same object model as the main report.

To accomplish this, you must declare an object of type Report from the CRAXDRT or CRAXDDRT libraries (the libraries the RDC exposes). You then use the main report's OpenSubreport method to create another Report object variable to contain the subreport. You can then set properties, execute methods, and trap events for the main report using its original object variable, and for the subreport using its own object variable. The following code fragment demonstrates this approach:

```
Dim Subreport as CRAXDRT.Report
...
...
'Put subreport in its own object
Set Subreport = Report.subTop5Products.OpenSubreport
```

```
'Set record selection formula for subreport
Subreport.RecordSelectionFormula = "{ado.Unit Price} > 1000"
```

Note   *You may also have to supply login credentials for databases in any subreports, separate from databases in the main report. Examples of how to do this appear earlier in the chapter under "Providing Database Login Credentials."*

Creating New Reports at Run Time

One of the main benefits touted by Crystal Decisions in Crystal Reports 9 is RAS, with its ability to create new reports "on the fly." In fact, the RDC has had this capability for several versions now. Version 9 of the RDC continues the capability to actually create a new .RPT file from scratch. The *Report Creation API,* as Crystal Decisions refers to this feature, allows your VB code to create a new report entirely from scratch, including tables and fields, report sections, and Report objects. After you create the base report structure, you can further manipulate report sections or format Report objects using code. You can even add the Embeddable Report Designer to your application to allow end users to interactively modify the report, virtually identically to the report design capabilities you have with the RDC's internal ActiveX report designer.

And, once all the code-based design and user manipulation is complete, not only can you view the report in the Report Viewer, or print or export the report, but you can save the completed report as an .RPT file, ready to be opened in Crystal Reports or another custom application. Because of the RDC's ability to create a report from scratch, Crystal Decisions considers this a potential threat to its flagship Crystal Reports designer. For this reason, you must enter into a license agreement and pay royalties to Crystal Decisions if you wish to distribute an application that uses these calls. Also, note that Crystal Decisions' license agreement specifically forbids you from using these report design techniques to create "competitive products."

Caution   *In previous versions of the RDC, you were given "nag" messages inside VB when you tried to use a Report Creation API call, but the function still worked. In version 9, the RDC is less forgiving. You'll receive a trappable error if you attempt to use a creation API call without the proper developer license. You must now purchase a specific license and use Crystal Decisions License Manager to add the key code (discussed in more detail in Appendix A) before making use of these API calls in your development environment. Information on licensing can be found on Crystal Decisions Web site at www.crystaldecisions.com/products/crystalreports/licensing.*

There are two general approaches to creating a report at run time:

■ Creating all report elements entirely within code

■ Using the new Embeddable Report Designer within your VB application to allow an end user to create the report interactively

Creating a New Report with Code

Creating a report with code requires the same basic steps that creating a report interactively in the RDC ActiveX designer or in stand-alone Crystal Reports requires:

1. Create a new report.

2. Choose database tables and link them, if necessary.

3. Add fields, text objects, bitmap images, and other objects to various report sections.

4. Add any desired groups.

5. Add subtotals and grand totals.

6. Format objects for desired appearance.

7. View the report in the Report Viewer, print it, or save it as an external .RPT file.

The RDC object model exposes methods and properties to accomplish each of these steps. Initially, you must add the RDC Report Creation library to your application, using Project | References. Check the Crystal Reports 9 ActiveX Designer Design and Run-Time Library (CRAXDDRT9.DLL). And, if you will be viewing the completed report in the Report Viewer, add it with Project | Components.

Tip   *You may download a Report Creation API sample application from this book's companion Web site, www.CrystalBook.com. The sample code in the remainder of this chapter is taken from this sample application.*

Declare Application and Report objects as you do with applications that use existing reports. Consider this sample code:

```
Public Application As New CRAXDDRT.Application
Public Report As CRAXDDRT.Report
```

Note references to the combined design-time/run-time library (CRAXDDRT). This is in preparation for using the Embeddable Report Designer (described later in the chapter). If you will not be using this designer, but just creating a report entirely within code, you may use the run-time–only library, CRAXDRT9.DLL.

The first new step involves assigning an object to the Report object variable. Previously, you've either assigned an existing ActiveX designer object to this variable or used the Application object's OpenReport method to assign an external .RPT file. Now, however, you will be creating a new report from scratch. The Application object exposes the NewReport method to accomplish this:

```
' Create a new empty report
Set Report = Application.NewReport
```

Tip   *This will be the first place where you may encounter an error message if you have not purchased the proper license for design-time development.*

As when creating a new report from scratch in the ActiveX designer or Crystal Reports, you must choose a data connection method and database tables for the report. The Report Creation API requires the same steps. The following sample code illustrates how to assign an ADO connection to the Report object, using the Orders table from the Xtreme Sample Database ODBC data source. The ADO connection string makes this connection (assume that the Microsoft ActiveX Data Objects library has been added to the project, and theADOConnection and ADOCommand objects have been declared earlier in the Declarations section):

```
' Open the data connection
Set ADOConnection = New ADODB.Connection
ADOConnection.Open "Provider=MSDASQL;Persist Security Info=False;
Data Source=Xtreme Sample Database 9; Mode=Read"

' Create a new instance of an ADO command object
Set ADOCommand = New ADODB.Command
Set ADOCommand.ActiveConnection = ADOConnection
ADOCommand.CommandText = "Orders"
```

```
ADOCommand.CommandType = adCmdTable

' Add the data source (the XTREME Orders Table) to the report
Report.Database.AddADOCommand ADOConnection, ADOCommand
```

Note *Width limits of this book require that the argument to the ADOConnection.Open method be broken in the middle of the line. Note that the actual sample application maintains the string argument for the Open method all on one line.*

You now have the beginnings of a report, including an assigned Report object with a data connection. Were you to open this report in the Crystal Report designer or supply the Report object to the Embeddable Report Designer at this point, you'd find an empty report, but the Field Explorer would be populated by fields from the Xtreme Sample Database Orders table. You would then drag and drop desired fields into various sections of the report. The next requirement of your Report Creation application is to add objects to different report sections. Examine the following code fragments from the RDC Report Creation sample application:

```
Report.Sections(1).AddPictureObject "Xtreme.bmp", 1000, 75
Report.Sections(1).AddTextObject "FedEx Order Detail", 6000, 400
```

The first line of code adds a bitmap picture to the report header (Section 1) of the report, placing it 1,000 twips from the left side of the section and 75 twips down from the top of the section. The next line adds a text object containing the text "FedEx Order Detail" to the report header, at position 6,000/400. Both of these lines of code use methods several levels deep in the RDC object hierarchy. The AddPictureObject and AddTextObject methods are available below an individual Section object within the Sections collection (in this case, the first member in the Sections collection) below the Report object.

Note *If you look at the sample application from www.CrystalBook.com, you'll actually find more involved logic than just demonstrated to add the text object and format it. For simplicity, this code is not demonstrated in the book text.*

The sample application proceeds to add four database fields to the details section of the report:

```
' Add fields to details section
' Note that the Sections collection can be accessed via
' number or string index
```

```
Report.Sections("D").AddFieldObject "{ado.Order ID}", 750, 5
Report.Sections("D").AddFieldObject "{ado.Order Date}", 3150, 5
Report.Sections("D").AddFieldObject "{ado.Order Amount}", 5500, 5
Report.Sections("D").AddFieldObject "{ado.Ship Via}", 8850, 5
```

RDC object-hierarchy navigation in the details section is similar to that used to add objects to the report header. The AddFieldObject method used adds a database field, requiring the database field, left position, and top position as arguments. Note that the Sections collection can be accessed via either a numeric or a string index.

If you wish to create groups, there are methods exposed in the object hierarchy to allow complete flexibility with group creation. There are also options to create both group summary fields and report grand totals. The RDC Report Creation sample application creates a grand total of Order Amount in the report footer (Section 4) with the following code:

```
' Create and format Order Amount Grand Total in report footer
Dim AmountTotal As CRAXDDRT.FieldObject
' Creating a separate object variable avoids deep navigation
' down the hierarchy when formatting
Set AmountTotal = Report.Sections(4).AddSummaryFieldObject _
(Report.Sections(3).ReportObjects(3).Field.Name, crSTSum, 6000, 750)
With AmountTotal
     .Width = 1500
     .Font.Bold = True
End With    'AmountTotal
```

Note several important points about the preceding code fragment:

- ■ A separate object to hold the grand total field was declared and assigned. Note that this wasn't done previously for the bitmap graphic, text object, and field objects. While it is possible to create lots of objects, as shown in the preceding example, this requires extra coding and keeping track of all the additional objects. The purpose in this example is to make formatting easier by eliminating navigation into the object hierarchy to set the Width and Font.Bold properties.

- ■ You can apply every conceivable kind of formatting to objects once they have been added to the report. Note that the grand total has been widened from its default size and given a bold formatting attribute. A glance through the sample application reveals the UseOneSymbolPerPage formatting attribute being applied to the Order Amount field, so only one dollar sign will appear at the top of each page:

```
' Format the Order Amount to have one dollar sign per page
Report.Sections(3).ReportObjects(3).UseOneSymbolPerPage = True
```

At this point, a basic report design has been created and is contained in the Report object. Additional RDC methods and properties that you are probably more familiar with can be applied to the Report object as well. For example, the sample application limits the report to orders shipped via FedEx with the following, now familiar approach:

```
Report.RecordSelectionFormula = "{ado.Ship Via} = 'FedEx'"
```

Now, you're ready to proceed to view, print, export, or perform other familiar functions with the Report object. You can also now supply the partially designed Report object to the Embeddable Report Designer to allow the end user to interactively modify the report you've already started to design in code.

Assuming you've added the Report Viewer to a form, the following code will now display your report in the viewer:

```
CRViewer91.ReportSource = Report
CRViewer91.ViewReport
```

Saving the Report

As discussed earlier in the chapter, the ultimate result of your application can be a saved .RPT file that can be opened in stand-alone Crystal Reports or other applications or custom programs that utilize .RPT files. The RDC exposes a Report object method to accomplish this:

```
Report.SaveAs "Sample.RPT", crDefaultFileFormat
```

Executing the SaveAs method will save the contents of the Report object to the filename supplied as the first argument. The second argument uses an RDC-provided constant to determine what Crystal Reports file format the file is saved in. If the file already exists when SaveAs is executed, it will be overwritten without a warning or any Visual Basic error being thrown. If this is of concern to you, execute additional code prior to SaveAs to check for the existence of the file.

Caution *Online help indicates that the file format argument can be either a Crystal Reports 8 or Crystal Reports 7 format. This is an error in the document. While these arguments will not throw an error (for backward code compatibility), the version 9 RDC will always save a file in version 9 format, unable to be opened by earlier versions of Crystal Reports. The crDefaultFileFormat constant will also save the report in version 9 format.*

The Report Creation Wizard

In addition to the RDC Report Creation API, Crystal Decisions has provided an additional COM library to assist you in developing custom report creation applications. The *Report Creation Wizard* is available to lead your application user step by step through a report creation process. In fact, the Report Creation Wizard object library is the same library used by Crystal Reports 9's Microsoft Access and Microsoft Excel add-ins.

This tool allows an end user to create a report with an expert-type interface, complete with Next and Back buttons. If you're comparing the Report Creation Wizard to the Embeddable Report Designer (described later in the chapter) from a Crystal Reports perspective, you might consider the Report Creation Wizard to be a "Report Wizard" and the Embeddable Report Designer to be the "Blank Report" option.

Since the Report Creation Wizard is a separate library, you must add the library to your VB project. Choose Project | References and check the Crystal Report 9 Standard Wizard Library option. And, as with other COM components, you must declare an object variable to hold the wizard object:

```
Dim CRWizard As New CrystalReportWizard.CRStandardWizard
```

If you view the CrystalReportWizard library in the Object Browser, you'll notice that it exposes only the single CRStandardWizard object with one property and one method. The CrystalReport property is used to assign the wizard a partially defined Report object for the wizard to use as a starting point:

```
Set CRWizard.CrystalReport = Report
```

For the wizard to be of any use, the Report object you supply must already have a data source and tables defined, because the wizard doesn't include any capabilities for the user to choose a data source or choose and link tables. This must be done prior to running the Report Creation Wizard. Also, the wizard does not contain any record selection capabilities. You need to provide your own user interface for record selection and set the RecordSelectionFormula property prior to or after running the wizard. If the Report object already has fields and groups created, the wizard will recognize them and place them in their appropriate locations in the wizard dialog boxes.

Once you've supplied the Report object, display the Report Creation Wizard to the user by executing the DisplayReportWizard method:

```
CRWizard.DisplayReportWizard
```

The Report Creation Wizard appears as an application-model dialog box on top of any existing forms your application may be displaying.

Your user may now progress step by step through the report creation process, clicking the Next button to move to each successive step. These steps can include choosing fields to include on the report; adding groups; creating subtotals, summaries, and grand totals; choosing TopN grouping; and choosing from the usual predefined report styles. When the user clicks the Next button in the Style box, they will be given a choice of what to do next.

Because the Report Creation Wizard is a completely self-contained object, it will launch Crystal Reports with no further coding required on your part. It will also view the resulting report in the Report Viewer, even if you haven't added it to your project. And, it will save an external .RPT file with no further coding required. Although you might prefer that the wizard merely return the modified Report object to your code to allow you to control what happens next, you have no choice—the options to edit and save are built into the wizard and can't be disabled.

But, once the wizard *does* finish what it's doing, it will return the modified Report object to your application, where you may print, save, or export the report, or supply the Report object to the Report Viewer to be viewed.

Using the Embeddable Report Designer

One of the more usable features of the RDC is the *Embeddable Report Designer*. This ActiveX control, when added to a VB form, allows an end user complete interactive report design and modification capabilities, virtually identical to the capabilities provided by the ActiveX report designer that appears in the Visual Basic IDE when the RDC is first added to a VB project. The end result from the Embeddable Report Designer is a Report object, identical to the Report object that's been discussed earlier in the chapter. It can be further manipulated from within your VB code, supplied to the Report Viewer, exported with the Export method, printed with the PrintOut method, or saved to an .RPT file with the SaveAs method.

For all the interactive power it gives to your end users, the Embeddable Report Designer is surprisingly simple to implement inside your VB application. To enable the Embeddable Report Designer in your VB application, several general steps are required:

1. Add proper references and components from the Project menu.

2. Add the Embeddable Designer to a form.

3. Supply a Report object to the Embeddable Designer.

4. Do any necessary further manipulation to the Report object, such as printing, exporting, saving, or showing in the Report Viewer.

Begin by choosing Project | Components from the VB pull-down menus. You'll see the list of all registered ActiveX controls on your computer. In particular, you'll want to check the Embeddable Crystal Reports 9 Designer Control. This will place a Crystal Reports icon on the VB toolbar. You may optionally want to choose the Crystal Report

Viewer control as well, if you will be providing an online viewer for your reports within your application.

You must also add a reference to the Crystal Reports 9 combined design-time/run-time library. Choose Project | References from the VB pull-down menus and check the Crystal Reports 9 ActiveX Designer Design and Run-time Library.

Note *This combined design- and run-time library (CRAXDDRT9.DLL) is one of two RDC libraries you can use. The run-time–only RDC library (CRAXDRT9.DLL) is available as well. When you distribute applications, you'll want to include the combined library if and only if you will be including the Embeddable Report Designer in your application. If you will not require this designer, distribute the run-time–only library (CRAXDRT9.DLL).*

Once you've added the proper components and references from the Project menu, you'll notice a new Crystal Reports icon for the Embeddable Report Designer in the VB toolbox. Simply add this control to a form as you would any other VB control. When you do so, you'll see the outline of the designer in your form, along with the designer's design-time properties in the VB Properties box.

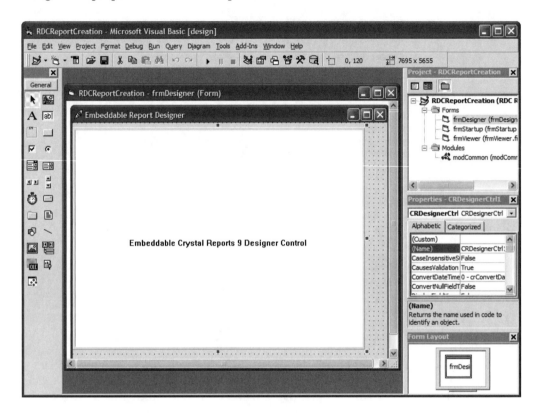

Enabling the designer is as simple as supplying an existing Report object to the designer's ReportObject property, as in the following code:

```
CRDesignerCtrl1.ReportObject = Report
CRDesignerCtrl1.DisplayToolbar = True
CRDesignerCtrl1.EnableHelp = False
```

This code assumes that the Embeddable Designer object has been left with its default name of CRDesignerCtrl1 and that an already declared Report object named Report is in scope within the current procedure. If you wish the end user to modify an existing report, you will have obtained this Report object by using the OpenReport method of an application object, or perhaps used the application object's NewReport method and programmatically added a database connection, fields, text objects, and other items (as in the sample application from this book's accompanying Web site). Note, however, that the Embeddable Report Designer features the capability of displaying the Database Expert with a right-click menu option, so you may provide a completely "empty" report object to the designer if you choose. Your end user will be able to add tables and fields as they wish.

You'll also notice that the designer's EnableHelp property has been set to false. This property setting will hide the Help button from the designer's toolbar, as well as from pop-up menus. In fact, the Embeddable Report Designer exposes an entire set of properties, a single method, and a few Windows-standard events as part of its own library. Most of the report-specific customization of the designer is accomplished by setting properties at design time in the Properties box or at run time in code. A complete description of these properties can be found in the developer's Help file by opening the "Embeddable Crystal Reports Designer Control Object Model" category from the table of contents.

| **Tip** | *If you don't disable the online Help button in the Embeddable Designer by setting EnableHelp to false (either in the Properties box or at run time), users will receive a "Help File not found" error message if they attempt to get online help. Information for creating a Windows .HLP file and using it with the Embeddable Designer is available in CrystalDevHelp.chm. Look in the Help file contents and open the "Embeddable Crystal Reports Designer Control Object Model" category. Then, choose "Distributing the Embeddable Designer."* |

Once this code has been executed and the form is displayed, you'll note a report designer identical to the designer that appears in the VB IDE when you first begin using the RDC. Users may use the Field Explorer on the left to add fields, create formulas, and so on. They may select objects and format them with right-click pop-up menus or toolbar buttons. The main differences between the Embeddable Report Designer and actual Crystal Reports is that all interaction must be with toolbar buttons, the Field Explorer, and pop-up menus—there are no pull-down menus in the designer. Figure 25-7 shows the Embeddable Report Designer and some of its interface elements.

Once the user has finished interacting with the report, he or she may simply close the window containing the designer, or use some other user interface element you've built into the form, such as a command button or tab control. However, the designer itself *doesn't* contain the Preview tab familiar to Crystal Reports users—you'll have to facilitate viewing of the modified report in your own code.

The designer simply returns the same Report object to your VB code that you initially supplied with any changes the end user made. You may now pass the modified Report object to a Report Viewer control, export it to a file, e-mail it, or execute the Report object's PrintOut method to print it to a printer. These capabilities are discussed earlier in this chapter.

Use the Field Explorer to add fields, create
formulas, and use other elements of the
regular Crystal Reports Field Explorer

Use toolbar buttons to perform commonly
required report design functions

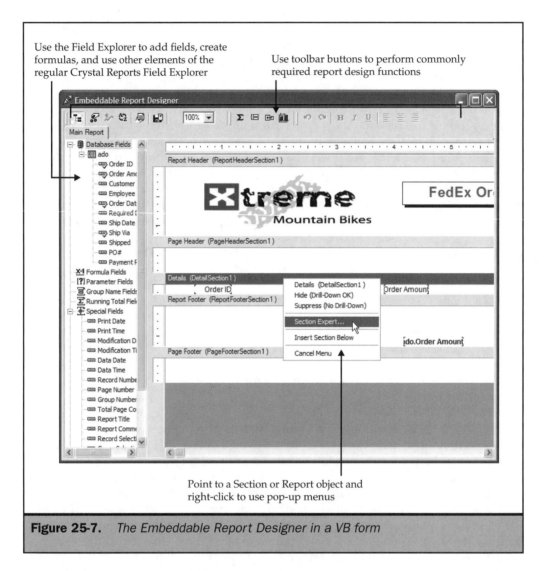

Point to a Section or Report object and
right-click to use pop-up menus

Figure 25-7.   *The Embeddable Report Designer in a VB form*

Distributing RDC Applications

After you create an RDC application that integrates Crystal Reports, you'll want to compile
and test the application. This process is unchanged with Crystal Reports 9. Unless you're
using the application only for yourself, you also need to set up a distribution mechanism
to pass your application to your intended audience: the application users.

Because you are distributing Crystal Reports features and components with your VB application, some distribution issues come into play. This section of the chapter discusses both the general points you want to keep in mind when creating your distribution package and specific areas that concern certain reporting features you may want to include or exclude from your application.

Distribution Overview

The days of creating a single .EXE executable file that can be easily copied to a single floppy disk are long gone. Standard Visual Basic projects already consist of the main program executable file, run-time files, and a host of support files. Introducing Crystal Reports into the mix adds a fairly large burden to this process. Because Crystal Reports is designed in a very modular fashion, it's easy to add functionality and upgraded features to the tool. However, this modularity also complicates the distribution process because so many different files are involved in the overall Crystal Reports product.

If you prefer to integrate external .RPT files with your RDC application, rather than using the ActiveX designer within the VB IDE, you must include those .RPT files in your distribution package. A variety of support files also are required, depending on several issues such as the database connections the report uses and the export capabilities that the project entails. The best part is that this is all handled pretty much automatically if you use Visual Basic distribution tools to create your distribution package.

In addition to available third-party distribution products, such as InstallShield and Wise, Visual Basic 6 includes the Package and Deployment Wizard, and Visual Basic 5 includes the Application Setup Wizard. All of these tools are designed to gather all the necessary executable and support files required for a project, compress them into a smaller space, and add them to a setup program. When the setup program is run from floppies or a CD-ROM, run from a network share, or downloaded from a Web server, all the necessary files are decompressed and installed in the proper locations.

| Note | *Specific instructions for using these distribution tools can be found in the documentation accompanying them—this chapter will not teach you how to distribute VB applications. Examples in the chapter are based on the Visual Basic 6 Package and Deployment Wizard.* |

Distribution tools, such as the Package and Deployment Wizard, look through your VB project file and attempt to determine all the necessary files that must be distributed with the project. Depending on the different RDC libraries and modules you have chosen for your application, a different set of files needs to be included in the distribution process. Having a fundamental understanding of this process will help you tailor your project's distribution, based on its individual needs.

Most tools use *dependency files* to determine what files to include in your distribution package. These files consist of the same base filename as the file used to provide Crystal Reports integration, but contain a .DEP extension. For example, the dependency file for the combined design-time/run-time RDC library (CRAXDDRT9.DLL) is CRAXDDRT.DEP. The dependency file is a straight ASCII text file that you can open with Notepad, containing a list of all related DLLs or other files that the "base" file is dependent upon. The distribution package uses the dependency file to include all necessary files (and, in most cases, several that are unnecessary) when the VB application is packaged. If you create VB projects on a regular basis, you may want to customize the appropriate .DEP files to include additional files or exclude files that your applications don't need.

If you let your distribution tool work with default options, you most probably will include necessary files for your application. Simply taking the default options has two potential disadvantages, though:

- More files than you actually need may be included, which likely is a minor inconvenience, eating up a bit more disk space than you really need to use.

- Necessary files may not be automatically detected, which means the application won't work correctly.

By reading on, you'll learn how to selectively remove unnecessary files that are included automatically. However, only by carefully considering your individual application, and the files that it ultimately requires, will you avoid the second problem. In all cases, the rule of thumb is to test and then test again—always try installations on a "clean" machine (similar to what your end users will have in place) to ensure that all files are being installed correctly. Simply installing the package on your development PC (which already has a complete copy of Crystal Reports Developer or Advanced Edition on it) won't be a sufficient test—you won't detect any missing elements that may be required on a user machine without Crystal Reports already installed.

The RDC is unique among integration methods in that it doesn't use external .RPT files, unless you specifically choose to use them over the internal ActiveX report designer. Report definitions are actually contained in the ActiveX designer (.DSR) files that are added to the project. Because these are an integral part of your application, VB will compile the .DSR files and include them automatically in the project's executable. In addition, the other COM components that make up the RDC will be included in the project.

In particular, the CRAXDRT.DEP or CRAXDDRT.DEP dependency files will include all necessary COM components for the RDC libraries. If you are using the ActiveX Report Viewer to view your reports in a form, CRVIEWER.DEP will be used to include its necessary components. While you probably won't have to worry about including external .RPT files, make sure any required database files are included in your package. You may also want to remove some unnecessary database or export-support files to save disk space.

If your RDC application uses external .RPT files, make sure to add them to your distribution package

| Tip | *Crystal Decisions includes an online Help file that contains a complete discussion of run-time file requirements. Open the RUNTIME.CHM file from Program Files\ Crystal Decisions\Crystal Reports 9\Developer Files\Help\<language>.* |

DEVELOPING CUSTOM
WINDOW APPLICATIONS

Database Considerations

The databases that your reports use must be considered when you are deploying your VB application to end users. Obviously, you need to ensure that each end user is able to connect to the database that the reports require. This may be a PC-style database distributed along with the application, a database shared on a common LAN drive, or a client/server database accessed through either a native Crystal Reports database driver or ODBC. You also need to include only the .DLL files specific to the database and access method being used by your reports. Although it won't necessarily hurt to include database driver DLLs for Microsoft Access in your project, even if your reports all connect to an Informix database via ODBC, you can save disk space by eliminating any unnecessary database drivers.

Direct Access Databases

If your reports use a PC-style database, such as a Microsoft Access .MDB file or a dBASE for Windows .DBF file, you'll want to make sure that the reports will be able to locate the database when the application is installed. If these files were installed on the C drive when you designed the report, but will reside on a network F drive when the end user runs the application, you need to make sure the reports can still find the file. You can either execute calls inside your VB application to change the data-source location of the reports, or use the Crystal Reports Database | Set Datasource Location command in either Crystal Reports or the RDC ActiveX report designer to point to a different database before distributing the application. You may prefer using the Same As Report option from the Set Datasource Location dialog box to have the report look in the same drive and directory as the report for the database. In this scenario, you need only ensure that the database and reports reside in the same place, regardless of drive or directory, for the reports to be able to locate the database.

You may be able to save disk space by including only the necessary database drivers for your particular Direct Access database. If, for example, you are using only reports that connect directly to a Microsoft Access database, you don't need to include all the other database drivers in your distribution package. Look in the RUNTIME.CHM file to determine the core set of database drivers required for the particular method your reports use to connect to the database. If you exclude other database drivers, make sure you test your installation on a machine similar to those found in your end-user environment, to make sure all necessary drivers are being included.

ODBC Data Sources

As a general rule, ODBC is used to connect to centralized client/server databases (although some desktop databases you distribute with your application still may use ODBC as the connection method). Therefore, you probably won't have to worry about distributing the actual database with your application. However, you need to make sure that an ODBC data source is set up so that the report will be able to connect to the database from your end user's machine. Your VB application may take care of this automatically if the application itself will be accessing the same ODBC data source. Also, if your report will be using the Active Data driver to connect to a Data Access Objects (DAO) or ActiveX Data Objects (ADO) record set in the application, special provisions probably won't need to be made.

If your report is the only part of the application that will be using a particular ODBC data source, make sure that the setup application creates the correct ODBC data source. You may even need to install ODBC as part of your setup program, if there's a possibility it won't already be installed on the end user's machine.

You also save disk space if you eliminate other Crystal Reports database drivers that won't be used in your application. Look in the RUNTIME.CHM file to determine which ODBC drivers will be required for the particular ODBC data source and database your reports use. Once you exclude other database drivers, make sure you test your installation on a machine similar to those found in your end-user environment, to make sure all necessary drivers are included.

File Export Considerations

The Xtreme Orders sample application that is used in this chapter allows three output destinations to be used: the preview window, the printer, and a .PDF file attached to an e-mail message. Both exporting the report to a .PDF file and selecting e-mail as the output destination create additional file requirements when you distribute the application. Because Crystal Reports is designed with a modular framework, both the file type (PDF, Word, Excel, HTML, and so on) and output destination (disk file, MAPI e-mail, Exchange public folder, and so on) functions are provided in separate .DLL files. If you are using these export formats and methods, make sure the correct files are included in your application.

Conversely, if you are using only a few output types and destinations, or perhaps none at all, you'll save disk space by eliminating these DLLs from your distribution package. Crystal Reports output destinations are provided by U2D*.DLL files. Output formats are provided by CRXF*.DLL and U2F*.DLL files. There are a few additional requirements for certain picture types when exporting to HTML. Look at RUNTIME.CHM for specifics. You need to include only the formats that you specifically call in your application or wish to have available to your end users if they click the Export button in the preview window.

User Function Libraries

If you use formulas in your report that call for external User Function Libraries (UFLs), don't forget to include the external UFL .DLL files when you distribute your application. An external .DLL file is called anytime a formula uses any functions in the Additional Functions list in the Formula Editor. If you fail to include the .DLL file with your application, the formula will fail when the report runs on the end user's machine.

By default, Crystal Reports installs several UFLs with the rest of the Crystal Reports package. These are all included in the dependency files that Crystal Reports supplies, so you generally don't have to worry about manually including the UFL files in your distribution package. However, if you've created your own UFLs (a supplementary document appears on www.CrystalBook.com describing how to create your own UFLs with Visual Basic), you'll want to either manually add them to your distribution package or modify the .DEP files to include them in all future distributions. You'll also be able to save disk space by removing UFL files that aren't used in any of your formulas.

UFL files generally adhere to the file format U2*.DLL. RUNTIME.HLP contains a description of individual UFL .DLL files and the functions that they provide. If none of the formulas in your report use functions from the Additional Functions list, you can safely remove these UFL files from your distribution package. Again, you should test your installation on a target machine to ensure that your formulas will work properly without the extra UFL files.

DEVELOPING CUSTOM
WINDOW APPLICATIONS

Chapter 26

Crystal Reports with Visual Studio .NET

As of the release of Crystal Reports 9, Microsoft's new Visual Studio .NET (VS.NET) development environment is starting to emerge as a new standard in Windows and Web development tools. This new development environment not only presents a whole new way to develop custom Windows- and Web-based applications, but even introduces a new language—C#—to develop with.

One of the more interesting changes noted in VS.NET is the prominence enjoyed by Crystal Reports. Whereas Microsoft had moved Crystal Reports "out of the way" for its own embedded report developer in Visual Studio 6, you'll notice that Microsoft's offering is gone from Visual Studio .NET, and Crystal Reports has returned as the report designer of choice for Microsoft Windows and Web development. And, Crystal Reports 9 Advanced Edition introduces additional features above and beyond the Crystal Reports version bundled with the initial Microsoft release of VS.NET.

Crystal Reports for Visual Studio .NET Overview

Crystal Decisions has completely retooled its report offering in VS.NET. Whereas the reporting tool bundled with Visual Studio 6 was a slight modification of Crystal Reports 4.5, Crystal Decisions is offering a modified version of Crystal Reports 8 inside VS.NET. And unlike with Visual Studio 6, VS.NET's Crystal Reporting component is an integral part of the VS.NET integrated development environment (IDE), much as is the Report Designer Component when added to Visual Basic 6. And, installing Crystal Reports 9 Advanced Edition after installing VS.NET will add yet more features above and beyond what Microsoft ships.

Similarity to RDC

The Report Designer Component, or *RDC*, has emerged as the preferred direction for integrating Crystal Reports, both with Visual Basic 6 applications (covered in Chapter 25) and Web pages with Microsoft Active Server Pages (covered in Chapter 21). Crystal Reports for Visual Studio .NET picks up largely on the same concept as the RDC:

- Integration of a report designer right inside the VS.NET IDE
- A rich object model that exposes virtually all report properties at run time, allowing complete control over report customization from within the application
- Small-footprint Windows Forms Viewer and DHTML Web Forms Viewer for viewing reports in Windows applications and Web pages

Of course, one of the biggest changes between Visual Basic 6 and VS.NET is the more integrated development environment for creating both Windows and Web applications, as well as the common language run time and common features among different development languages. Crystal Reports fits seamlessly into the entire VS.NET environment, being equally functional in Windows and Web applications, as well as being completely accessible by Visual Basic, Managed C++, and C#.

Note   *Illustrations in this chapter reflect certain additions and changes made to the Visual Studio .NET environment when Crystal Reports 9 Advanced Edition is installed. If you are using the "out-of-the-box" version of VS.NET, your screens may exhibit slightly different behavior.*

Crystal Reports in Windows Applications

For current Visual Basic developers, the existing Report Designer Component provides many features that go far above and beyond the Crystal Reports product bundled with Visual Basic 6. However, to fully enjoy these benefits (especially for the RDC available in Crystal Reports 9), you need to purchase a new copy of or upgrade to Crystal Reports 9 Developer or Advanced Editions. Installing one of these tools will make the newest version of the RDC available to Visual Basic.

The "out of the box" version of Crystal Reports inside Visual Studio .NET is built largely on the same model as the RDC with Crystal Reports versions 8 and 8.5. If you will be creating custom Windows or Web applications with VS.NET, you'll be able to design a report entirely inside the VS.NET IDE without having to purchase a separate copy of Crystal Reports. However, installing Crystal Reports 9 Advanced Edition automatically detects the presence of VS.NET on your machine and installs updated components. However, you don't have to purchase Crystal Reports 9 if version 8.5 "functionality" is sufficient for your current development needs.

Regardless of whether you update your copy of VS.NET with new version 9 features or not, built-in VS.NET reporting capabilities are significant, much as they are with the RDC in Visual Studio 6. For example, the embedded report designer in Visual Studio .NET:

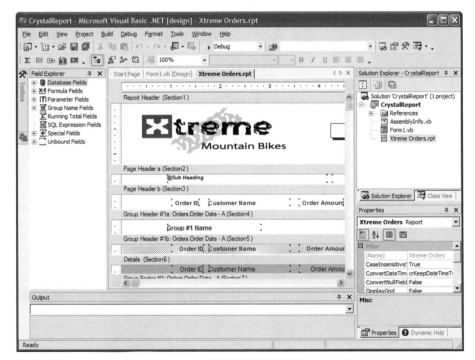

looks very similar to that supplied by the RDC in Visual Basic 6.

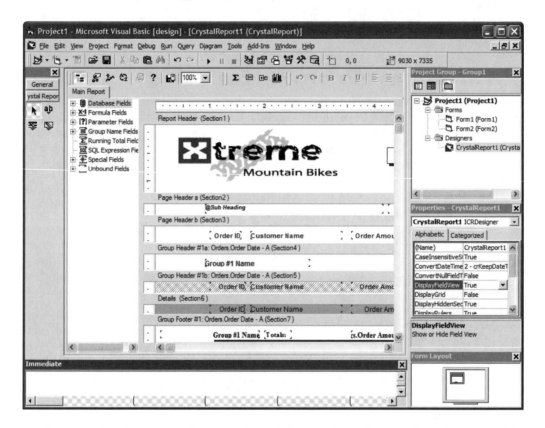

Once you've either created a new report from scratch or imported an existing .RPT file inside the VS.NET IDE, you present the report in your Windows application using a Crystal Report Windows Forms Viewer placed in a Windows form, similar to the ActiveX Report Viewer provided by the RDC in Visual Basic 6.

As you might expect, the Windows Forms Viewer provided in Visual Studio .NET, shown in the following illustration:

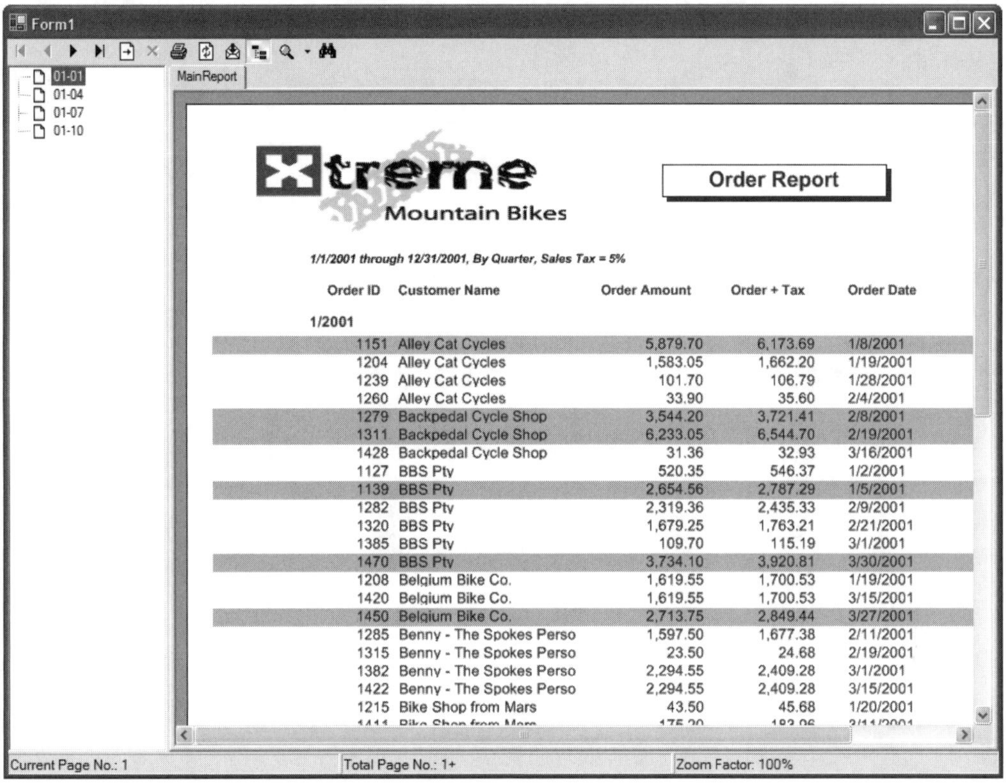

looks similar to the Crystal Reports Viewer supplied by the RDC in Visual Basic 6:

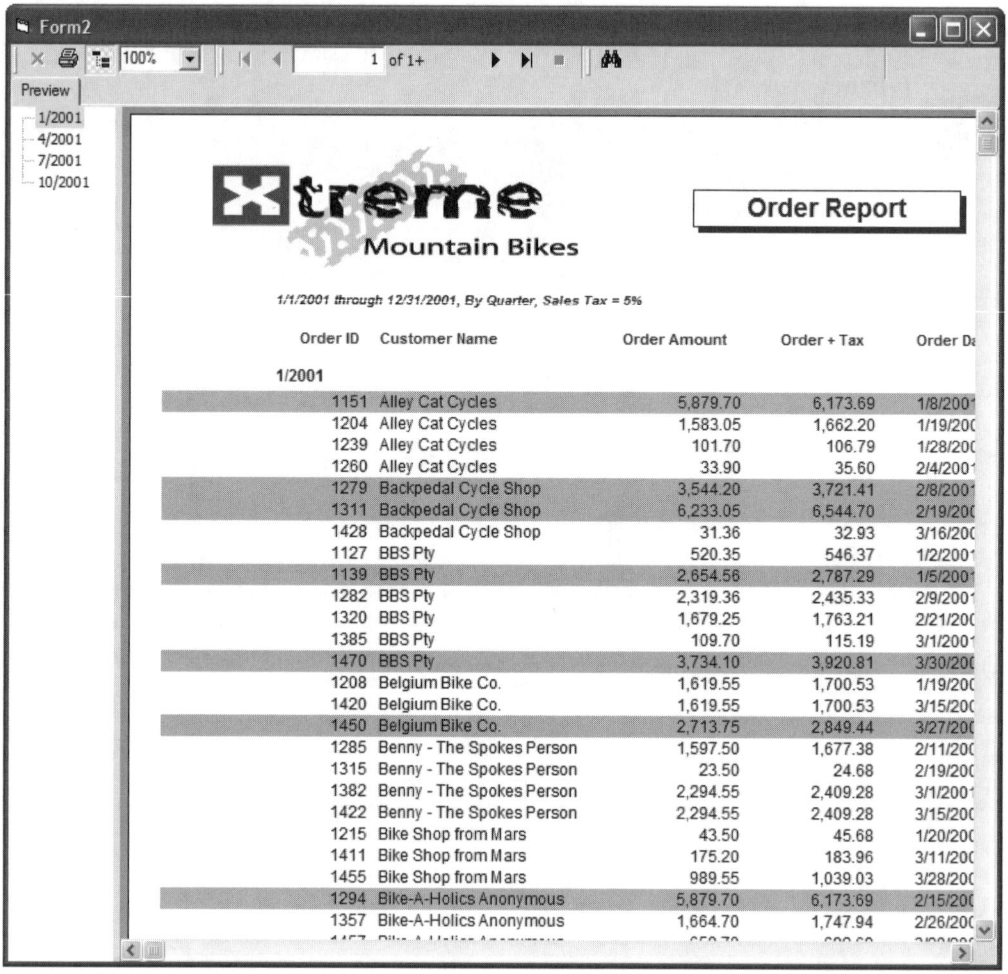

And, as with the RDC and Visual Basic 6, Crystal Reports in VS.NET exposes an extensive object model that not only allows complete report customization at run time from within VS.NET code, but also can trap Windows Forms Viewer events, such as drill-downs, button clicks, and so on. And, you can develop your own user interface elements to replace the standard toolbar in the Windows Forms Viewer, controlling report navigation entirely from within your code.

More information on creating VS.NET Windows applications with Crystal Reports can be found later in this chapter under "Creating Crystal Reports Windows Applications."

Note	*As different versions and capabilities of Crystal Reports have evolved, so have the different licensing scenarios. As such, some server-based applications created using VS.NET require acquisition of Crystal Decisions licenses. Visit the Crystal Decisions Web site at http:// www.crystaldecisions.com/products/crystalreports/licensing for information regarding requirements, procedures, and costs for acquiring additional licenses.*

Crystal Reports in Web Applications

While the RDC with Microsoft Active Server Pages is a very flexible and effective Web reporting method, developing these Web-based applications can be very tedious. In many cases, you gain very little benefit from using previous Microsoft development tools, such as FrontPage or Visual InterDEV, due to limited support for COM objects and the Crystal Reports viewers. In many cases, it is often just as effective to use a plain text editor, such as Notepad, to create Crystal Reports web applications.

The segment of the Crystal Reports developer community probably the happiest with VS.NET is Web developers. As VS.NET creates Web applications with virtually the same ease and speed as it creates Windows applications, and because Crystal Reports works just as seamlessly with Web applications, Crystal Reports Web applications are now infinitely easier to create.

And if the ease of development isn't enough, you gain a whole new level of flexibility with VS.NET Web applications and Crystal Reports. The same type of rich object model available with the RDC and Active Server Pages is fully exposed to VS.NET Web applications for report customization. But, VS.NET raises the bar for the DHTML-based Crystal Reports Web Forms Viewer. This viewer, as do VS.NET Web-based forms in general, actually exposes its own object model that can be controlled from within code, including the ability to trap viewer events such as page navigation button clicks and drill-downs. This new interactivity in a "plain" DHTML Web browser page is one of the major new features provided by Visual Studio .NET.

More information on using Crystal Reports in Web applications can be found later in this chapter under "Creating Crystal Reports Web Applications."

Crystal Reports as VS.NET Web Services

One of the new features of Visual Studio .NET is the *web service*: a server-based "application" that exposes a set of data to other applications using standard Web-based data layouts through standard Web-based communications protocols such as SOAP and XML. The benefit is that any other application, anywhere on the Web (even behind a firewall), can access a Web service. A VS.NET Web service can be written in any of the VS.NET languages, or built using many of the VS.NET-bundled tools such as Crystal Reports.

DEVELOPING CUSTOM
WINDOW APPLICATIONS

When you create a Crystal Reports–based Web service, the layout and appearance provided by the report are available to any Web service client on the Web. A Web service client can be another Crystal Windows Forms Viewer or Crystal Web Forms Viewer away from your own network—reports can be viewed remotely in Windows or Web applications without any additional effort on your part. In fact, consuming a Report Web service can be as simple as setting the URL of the service to the ReportSource property of a viewer control.

More information on creating Crystal Reports Web services is found later in this chapter under "Crystal Reports and Web Services."

Creating Crystal Reports Windows Applications

If you've already made significant use of the Report Designer Component with Visual Basic 6, you should be familiar with most steps in creating a Windows application using Crystal Reports in VS.NET. Because the VS.NET implementation of a Crystal Report is similar to the embedded designer/object model/ viewer component structure of the RDC, the steps to creating a Crystal-based Windows application basically remain the same:

- Create a new application or open an existing application.

- Either create a new report with the IDE report designer, import an existing report into the IDE report designer, or define a report object in code referencing an external .RPT file.

- Manipulate the report object within code, if necessary.

- Supply the report object as the ReportSource of the Windows Forms Viewer for display in a Windows form.

- Design any event-trapping code in the Windows Forms Viewer to handle page navigation button clicks, drill-downs, and so on. Or, design customized code to control behavior of the Windows Forms Viewer from within your own code.

Tip *You may find the information provided in Chapter 25 to be helpful in learning more about the general "object model" approach to report integration.*

Creating or Modifying Reports in the VS.NET Crystal Report Designer

Once you've created a new VS.NET project or opened an existing VS.NET project, you have several choices as to how to add a report reference to the project. If you haven't purchased a copy of Crystal Reports or don't have a predesigned .RPT file that you just want to reference directly in your code, you'll need to add the Crystal Report Designer to your project. From this designer, you can create a new report entirely from scratch or import an existing .RPT file to modify.

To add a report to your project, right-click in the VS Solution Explorer and choose Add | Add New Item from the pop-up menu. You may also use File | Add New Item from the VS.NET pull-down menus. The Add New Item dialog box will appear.

Choose the Crystal Report icon. Then, either accept the default filename given at the bottom of the Add Item dialog box or type a different filename for the report. When you click OK, the familiar Report Gallery will appear, much as it does when you initially create a new report inside Visual Basic 6 with the RDC. You may choose to create a new report using a Report Expert or the Blank Report option.

You may also simply add an existing .RPT file you've already created with Crystal Reports to VS.NET. Perform the same initial steps as described previously with the pop-up menu or File pull-down menu options—except, choose Add Existing Item instead of Add New Item. A file open dialog box will appear (you may need to change the file type to Crystal Reports to see .RPT files in the folder you navigate to). Choose an existing .RPT file to add to your project.

Once you've made your choices (and in the case of using a Report Expert, chosen all necessary items in the various tabs), the Crystal Report Designer will show your report inside the VS.NET IDE, as shown in Figure 26-1.

You may work with the Report Designer inside VS.NET much as you work with the regular Crystal Reports program, as discussed in Part I of this book. You may add report objects, format them, create formulas, add parameter fields, and perform virtually all report manipulation techniques that you would with Crystal Reports. As with other elements of your VS.NET project, such as forms, you can save the results of your report design with the VS.NET toolbar buttons or File menu options.

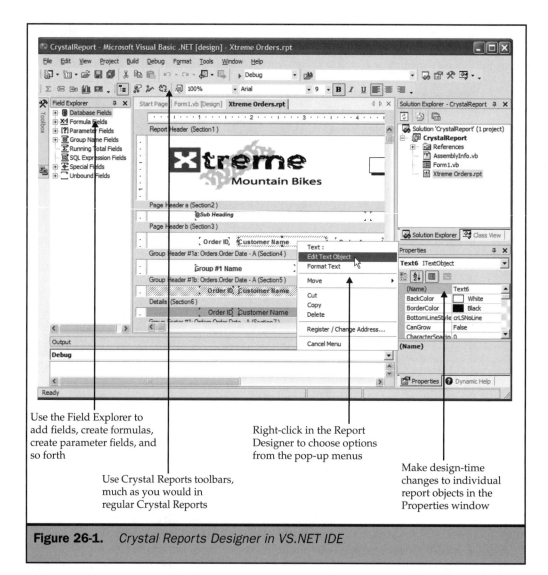

Use the Field Explorer to add fields, create formulas, create parameter fields, and so forth

Right-click in the Report Designer to choose options from the pop-up menus

Make design-time changes to individual report objects in the Properties window

Use Crystal Reports toolbars, much as you would in regular Crystal Reports

Figure 26-1.   *Crystal Reports Designer in VS.NET IDE*

Caution   *Importing an existing .RPT file using either of these methods will make a copy of the report into the folder with the remainder of your VS.NET project files. This copy (along with another .RPT file that will be given a unique filename—not the same filename as the report you imported) will be modified as you work in the Report Designer. Your original .RPT file will be unchanged by modifications you make in your VS.NET project. Also, the .RPT file format in the "original" version of Visual Studio .NET may not be readable in version 8.5 of Crystal Reports. And, if you've installed Crystal Reports 9 Advanced Edition to add additional reporting features to VS.NET, only Crystal Reports 9 stand-alone versions will be able to read the .RPT files.*

You may also add what's known as an *untyped report* to your project. This type of report object doesn't refer to an actual report that uses the Report Designer inside the project. Instead, an untyped report refers to an external .RPT file somewhere on your network. Untyped reports are added via code. Look in the VS.NET online help index for "untyped report components" for information on how to reference an external .RPT file.

Manipulating Reports Inside Code

Once you've added a report to your project, either via the Report Designer in the VS.NET IDE or as an untyped report, you may create a reference to the report object for the purpose of run-time customization. Once this occurs, you have the complete Crystal Reports for VS.NET object model at your disposal. All report objects (such as fields, formulas, parameter fields, and so forth), as well as report sections (such as the Details section, Page Header, and so forth) are available for run-time manipulation via your custom code.

The report object will expose its object model when manipulated in code.

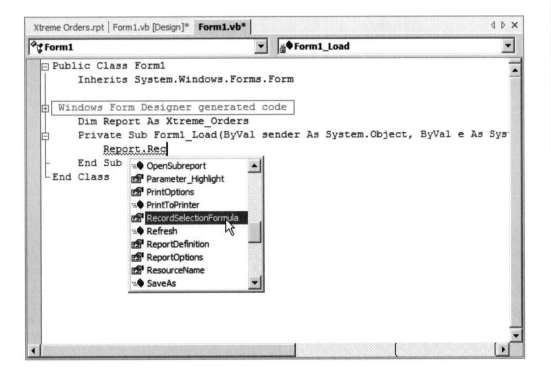

And, you can also display the Object Browser (by pressing the CTRL-ALT-J key combination or by choosing View | Other Windows | Object Browser), where you'll find Crystal Reports objects, properties, and methods.

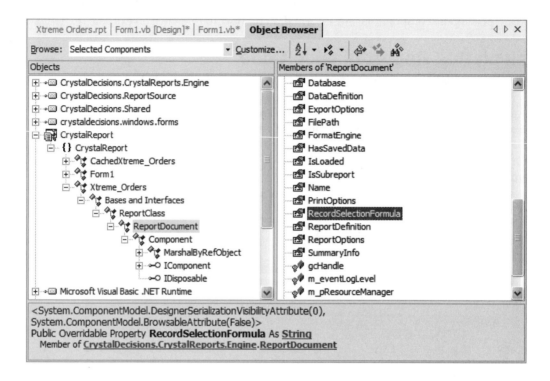

> **Tip**   *Although the examples shown here utilize Visual Basic code, all VS.NET Crystal Reports functionality is also available when using Managed C++ or C# code.*

Using the Windows Forms Viewer

Once you've added a report to your project, you need to facilitate some way to show the report in a Windows Form. As with Visual Basic 6 using the RDC, a Crystal Reports viewer control is available from the toolbox to add to a form. Find the Crystal Report Viewer choice in the toolbox and add it to a Windows Form, as you would any other control. Figure 26-2 shows a VS.NET Windows Form with the Windows Form Viewer added to it.

One of the first steps required after adding the Windows Forms Viewer is connecting it with the desired report object. You may perform this connection at design time utilizing the ReportSource property or the DataBindings properties. Or, you may dynamically assign a report to the viewer from within code. For example, if you've declared an object named Report and set it to a "New" instance of a ReportDocument

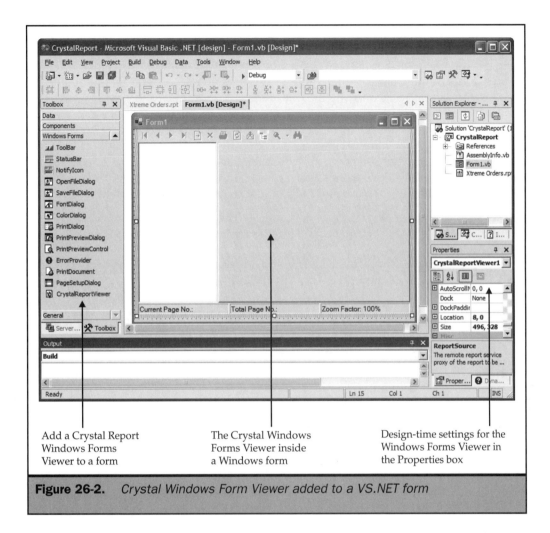

Add a Crystal Report Windows Forms Viewer to a form

The Crystal Windows Forms Viewer inside a Windows form

Design-time settings for the Windows Forms Viewer in the Properties box

Figure 26-2. *Crystal Windows Form Viewer added to a VS.NET form*

object earlier in your code, you can bind it to the Windows Forms Viewer at run time using the viewer's ReportSource property within code like this:

```
CrystalReportViewer1.ReportSource = Report
```

Tip   *There are several different methods for connecting the desired report object to the Windows Forms Viewer in a process called binding. For a thorough description and examples of these different binding methods, search the VS.NET online help index for "Binding Reports."*

You may control many aspects of the Windows Form Viewer at design time from within the VS.NET Properties box. One of the new properties that saves you some coding is the Windows Forms Viewer Anchor property. This allows you to "attach" the viewer to one or more sides of the Windows Form, allowing the report to automatically resize as the form is resized (using the RDC Report Viewer the same way in Visual Basic 6 required code to be placed in the form's Resize event).

The Anchor property, like most for the Windows Forms Viewer, can be set at design time in the Properties window. However, you may also control viewer behavior at run time, as the viewer exposes its own object model. For example, if you wish to control other aspects of the Windows Forms Viewer, such as the end user's ability to drill-down on reports, you may wish to execute code similar to the following at run time:

```
CrystalReportViewer1.EnableDrillDown = False
```

Once you've bound a report to the viewer and added any customization code, running the VS.NET project will render the report in a Windows form.

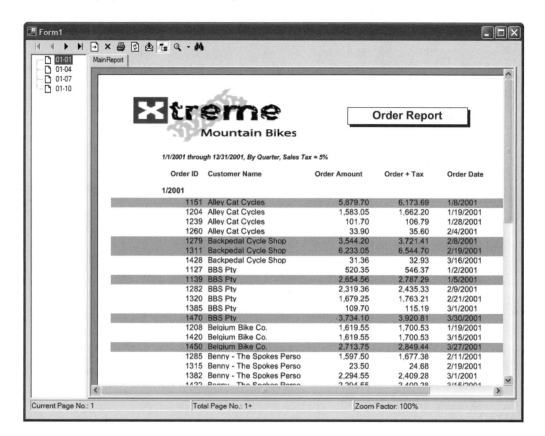

> **Tip**   *There is also a "Dock" property that will allow you to fill the form with the viewer or dock it to either the top, bottom, left or right of the form. It behaves slightly differently than Anchor, in that it retains its height or width when resized, depending on the option selected.*

Responding to Windows Forms Viewer Events

Not only can you control behavior of the Windows Forms Viewer at run time, but you can respond to events that may happen due to user interaction with the viewer. For example, you can trap page navigation button clicks, drill-downs on group headers/ footers, drill-downs on charts, and so on.

Just open the code view of the Windows form containing the Crystal Report Windows Forms Viewer. Choose the viewer in the object drop-down list at the upper right of the code window. Then, look for available events in the right drop-down list. Choose an event to trap and add code to the desired event.

Creating Crystal Reports Web Applications

Of course, one of the biggest improvements of Visual Studio .NET over previous Microsoft developer environments is the very fuzzy line between Windows applications and Web applications. The development environment, languages, and associated SDKs and tools are all as Web-aware as they are Windows-aware. Crystal Reports within VS.NET is no exception.

The steps for adding a report to your Web application are virtually identical to those for a Windows application (see "Creating Crystal Reports Windows Applications" earlier in the chapter). And, steps for customizing the report object with the Crystal Reports Object Model are also identical to those used in Windows applications.

Using the Crystal Web Forms Viewer

The primary difference between Crystal Reports Windows applications and Web applications is the way reports are viewed. While the "internal" coding is similar (and Crystal Reports Web applications use server-side code in VS.NET as they do with the RDC and Active Server Pages), the report must ultimately be displayed in a Web browser as opposed to in a Windows application. As with the Report Designer Component, this requires some creative approaches to render the report in a Web browser with formatting as close as possible to the original report.

The Crystal Web Forms Viewer is provided to show reports in a Web browser. Based on DHTML 4.0, the Web Forms Viewer can be passed as a report object, just like the Windows Forms Viewer. When VS.NET builds the Web application, it includes code to show the report as HTML frames inside the Web page where the viewer has been added.

Add the Web Forms Viewer to a Web form the same way you might add the Windows Forms Viewer to a Windows form—it will be available in the toolbox. Figure 26-3 shows a Web Forms Viewer in a Web form.

As with the Windows Forms Viewer, you must connect the Web Forms Viewer to the desired report object. You may perform this connection at design time utilizing the ReportSource property or the DataBindings properties. Or, you may dynamically assign a report to the viewer from within code. For example, if you've declared an object named Report and set it to a "New" instance of a ReportDocument object earlier in your code, you can assign it to the Web Forms Viewer at run time using the viewer's ReportSource property within code like this:

```
CrystalReportViewer1.ReportSource = Report
```

Note *There are several different methods for connecting the desired report object to the Web Forms Viewer in a process called binding. For a thorough description and examples of these different binding methods, search the VS.NET online help index for "Binding Reports."*

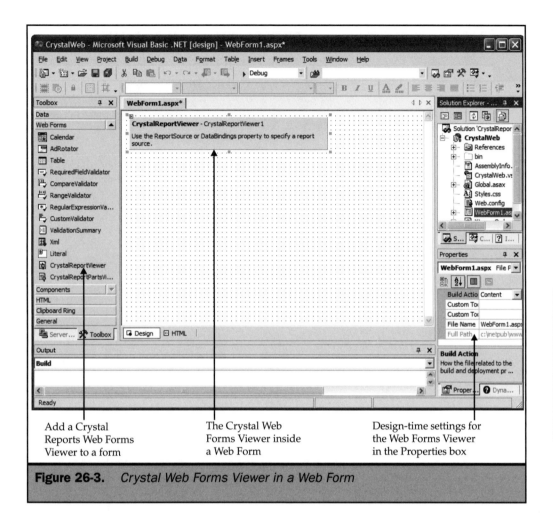

Add a Crystal
Reports Web Forms
Viewer to a form

The Crystal Web
Forms Viewer inside
a Web Form

Design-time settings for
the Web Forms Viewer
in the Properties box

Figure 26-3.   *Crystal Web Forms Viewer in a Web Form*

And as with the Windows Forms Viewer, the Web Forms Viewer exposes an object
model that allows you to control viewer behavior at design time from the Properties
window (which isn't possible with the RDC and development tools prior to VS.NET).
And, you may also set these properties at run time from within code.

Note that one difference between the VS.NET implementation of the Web Forms
Viewer and viewers available in Active Server Pages with the RDC is available choices
of viewers. While the RDC provides not only the HTML 3.2 and DHTML 4.0 viewers,
additional viewers residing in a browser-based ActiveX control or Java applet may be

used. In VS.NET, the Web Forms Viewer is strictly an HTML-based viewer—you cannot provide any browser-based ActiveX control or Java applet to view reports.

Once you've bound a report to the viewer and added any customization code, running the VS.NET project will render the report in a Web browser.

Responding to Web Forms Viewer Events

One of the major new features of Visual Studio .NET is the ability to develop an event-based object model for Web-based applications similar to that for Windows applications. Previously, Windows developers were the only developers generally able to trap user actions, such as resizing windows and so forth. For Crystal Reports developers, the Windows viewer provided by the RDC exposed a large event model. However, Crystal Reports Web developers weren't able to trap report events, such as drill-downs.

With Visual Studio .NET, creative use of client-side script, as well as Web-server interfaces, allows this type of interaction with Crystal Reports viewed in the Web Forms Viewer. As with the Windows Forms Viewer, the Web Forms Viewer exposes a list of events that can be trapped. Just open the code view of the Web form containing the Crystal Report Web Forms Viewer. Choose the viewer in the object drop-down list at the upper right of the code window. Then, look for available events in the right drop-down list. Choose an event to trap and add code to the desired event.

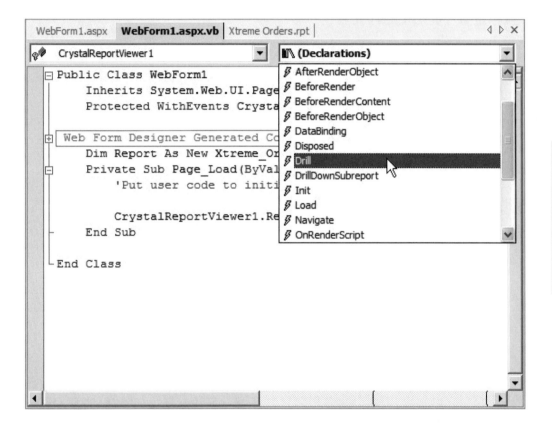

Crystal Reports and Web Services

One of the new features of Visual Studio .NET is the *web service*: a server-based "application" that exposes a set of data based on the Extensible Markup Language, or XML. The Web service exposes its actual data, as well as its data layout (or *schema*), through the Hypertext Transport Protocol, or HTTP. Because the XML data layout is simply an extension of HTML and because HTTP is such a ubiquitous communications protocol, virtually all networks, intranet systems, and Internet connection methods (dial-up, firewalls, and so forth) work with these standards already.

Crystal Reports for Visual Studio .NET fully supports Web services—being able to both create and "consume" Web services. Creating a Web service based on a Crystal Report exposes a report via HTTP to anyone who can consume a Web service anywhere on the Internet. VS.NET also allows you to create projects that use or "consume" published Crystal Report Web services. In this scenario, you create a Windows or Web application, including a Windows Forms Viewer or Web Forms Viewer, which is then bound to the report exposed by the Web service.

Creating a Web Service

Creating a Web service based on a Crystal Report is a very straightforward process—almost identical to creating a Windows or Web application using a Crystal Report. Once you've opened or created your Web service or Web application project, add a Crystal Report the same way you would for another application. You may make any design changes and customization to the report in the Report Designer inside the VS.NET IDE, the same as you would for any other report.

When you're ready to post the report on a Web server as a Web service, simply right-click on the report object in the Solution Explorer that you want to publish. Choose Publish as Web service from the pop-up menu.

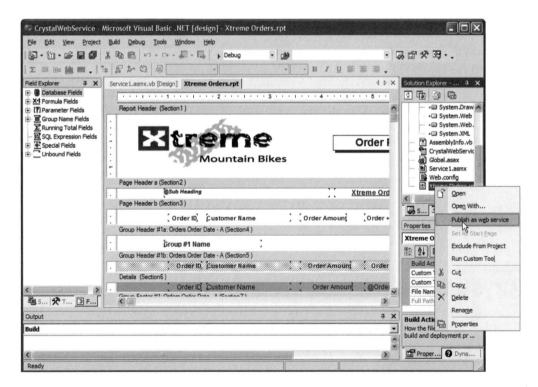

Additional files representing the Web service will be created in the Solution Explorer. To actually post the Crystal Report Web service on the Web server that the Web service project was created on, choose Build | Build Solution from the VS.NET pull-down menus.

Consuming a Web Service

Once a Crystal Reports Web service has been created, you may access the Web service using regular HTTP protocols, similar to a standard Web page. You may create either a Windows or Web application, using the respective Windows Forms Viewer or Web Forms Viewer, to show the contents of the Web service in your application.

Create a standard Windows or Web application with VS.NET. Add a Crystal Report viewer to the form as described in earlier sections of this chapter. Once you're ready to connect the report viewer to the Web service, perform the following steps:

1. Add a reference to the Web service by clicking on the References category of the Solution Explorer. Right-click on the References category and choose Add Web Reference from the pop-up menu. The Add Web Reference dialog box will appear.

2. In the Address line of the Add Web Reference dialog box, type the following URL: **http://<*web server*>/<*project name*>/<*service name*>.asmx?wsdl**. For example, if the project you created the Web service with is "CrystalWebService," and the report you published as a service is Xtreme Orders, then you would use the following URL to reference the service on your local machine:

   ```
   http://localhost/CrystalWebService/Xtreme OrdersService.asmx?wsdl
   ```

3. You may click the View Contract link to see the XML that is exposed by the Web service. Once you are ready to add the Web service to your project, click the Add Reference button. A Web Reference section of the Solution Explorer will appear, followed by the name of the Web server containing the Web service. Within the Web services category, you'll find a reference to the Web service.

DEVELOPING CUSTOM
WINDOW APPLICATIONS

To reference the Web service in the Windows Forms Viewer or Web Forms Viewer, you may execute code similar to the following in the Load event of the form containing the viewer:

```
CrystalReportViewer1.ReportSource = _
New localhost.Xtreme_OrdersService()
```

Alternatively, you can simply provide the URL to the Report Web Service as the ReportSource for the viewer control:

```
CrystalReportViewer1.ReportSource =
http://<servername>/CrystalWebService/Xtreme_OrdersService.asmx
```

When you run the application, the report exposed by the Web service will appear in the form containing the viewer.

The
Complete
Reference

Crystal
Reports

Appendix

Installing and Configuring Crystal Reports Components

821

Installing Crystal Reports is a fairly straightforward process, especially if you are simply installing with a standard set of options on an end-user PC. Some changes have been made to the version 9 setup process, but not a great many of them. Many of the database drivers, along with the Geographical Mapping components, are now set with an "install on first use" option that will, by default, prompt you for the original program CD the first time you attempt to use them. Crystal Enterprise Standard 8.0 has been replaced with the Report Application Server with Crystal Reports 9 Professional, Developer, and Advanced Editions. RAS is included on a separate CD in the box.

<table>
<tr><td>Note</td><td>Crystal Reports 9 is available only in a 32-bit platform. You must be using Windows 98 Second Edition, Windows ME (Windows 95 is no longer supported), Windows NT 4, Windows 2000, or Windows XP to use the software. The minimum memory requirement is 32MB, while 64MB is required if using Windows NT. You'll see better performance if you use at least 64MB of memory with all platforms. You'll also need at least 60MB of hard disk space for a minimal installation, and up to 235MB for a full installation (possibly more for non-English versions of Crystal Reports).</td></tr>
</table>

Installing the Crystal Reports Designer

When you put the Crystal Reports program CD-ROM into a CD-ROM drive, the Setup program starts automatically. If Setup doesn't start automatically (perhaps your CD-ROM drive has Auto-Insert notification turned off), you can choose two different places to start. To choose from several links to release notes, technical resources, and other information, as well as to be given a choice to install Crystal Reports 9, navigate to the root directory of the CD-ROM and double-click CR9_Autorun_ENENT.EXE. To proceed directly to Crystal Reports Setup, navigate to the root directory of the CD-ROM and double-click SETUP.EXE.

Crystal Reports Setup will check to make sure current versions of required base Windows components are installed on your computer. If they're not, Setup will indicate that they need to be installed. Once this is done, Setup will continue. Typical Setup prompts, including a display of the Crystal Decisions license agreement and a prompt for the installation key on the back of the CD-ROM, will appear. Click the Next button after responding to a prompt to continue. Of particular note is the prompt giving you the option to choose a Typical or Custom setup. Typical setup includes most common Crystal Reports components.

As mentioned earlier, however, this choice will leave many database drivers, Geographical Maps, and many exporting options set with an "install on first use" choice. This will cause Crystal Reports to prompt you for the original program CD the first time you try to use these features in Crystal Reports. If you know you want to use certain drivers or choices right away, you'll want to choose the Custom option and specifically choose your desired options. If you choose the Custom option, a Custom Installation Options dialog box will appear, as shown in Figure A-1.

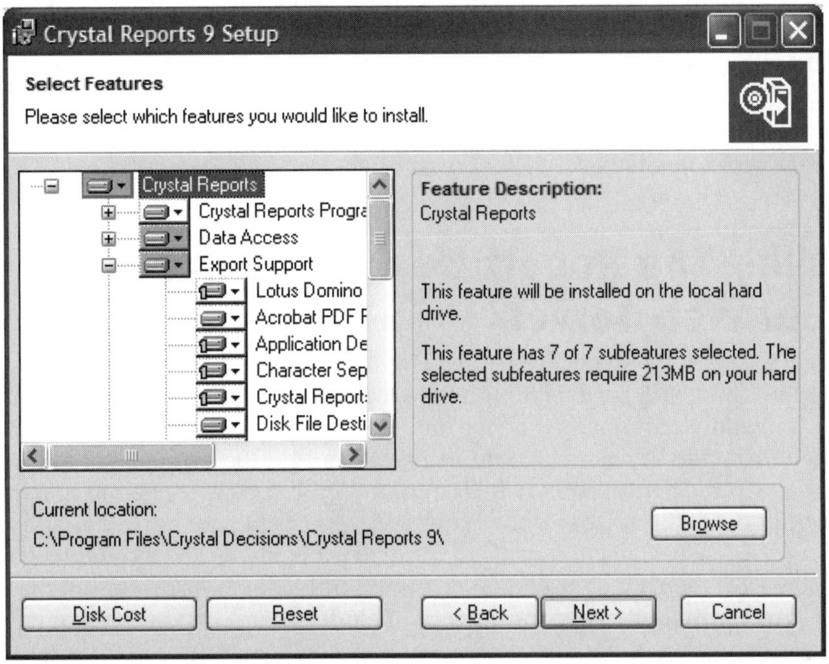

Figure A-1. *Custom Setup option*

You'll see a Windows Explorer–like interface, showing the main Crystal Reports elements that can be customized. A plus sign next to an item indicates that there are subfeatures below it that can be selected or deselected. Click the plus sign to see the subfeature list. If an option is displayed in white with no other graphical element on it, that means that it (and all of its subfeatures, if it has any) will be installed. If the option is displayed in a gray color, it means that *some* of its subfeatures are selected and some aren't. If the option is displayed with a yellow "number 1," it means the feature will only be installed the first time you use it. If the object has a red *X* across it, that means that the item will not be installed.

To change the option, click the down arrow next to it. A menu will appear giving you several choices, such as installing the feature on your hard disk, or possibly running it from the CD-ROM (depending on the chosen feature). If the feature you've selected has subfeatures underneath it, you'll have an option to install the feature and all of its subfeatures. You'll also have the option not to install the feature. Choose the desired option and notice that the color of the feature changes to indicate the choice you've made.

For example, if you're running Setup on your Web server to install the Report Designer Component, you may choose not to install the Crystal Reports programs (although it's a good idea to install them, in case you need to physically troubleshoot reports on the Web server machine itself). Also, you should double-check the Data Access subfeature list to make sure the proper data drivers will be installed for the types of databases you'll be reporting on.

Installing the Report Designer Component on Your Web Server

If you wish to set up the Report Designer Component for use with Active Server Pages (discussed in Chapter 21), run Setup on the Web Server computer. While you may be tempted to install a minimal set of components (perhaps just the Report Designer Component from the Developer Components category), don't forget that many of the other options in the Setup list may be required. You'll certainly need to install Data Access components for databases that your Web reports may require. (Don't leave the Install On First Use option chosen, as no one will probably be around the Web server to put in the CD when a Web user adds a report with a database driver that hasn't been installed!) And, you'll probably want to also include other components that may be of use, such as Exporting options, Custom Charting, and Geographic Mapping.

You should seriously consider installing the complete Crystal Reports package on your Web server. Although it's doubtful (and probably unwise) that you'll want to use a production Web server as a report design computer, installing the complete product will allow you to troubleshoot reporting problems that may occur on the Web. If you encounter a report that won't properly run on the Web server, you can launch Crystal Reports directly on the Web server, open the report, and see whether the report will run within Crystal Reports directly. If not, you can more easily troubleshoot the problem, perhaps tracing it to a security or data connectivity problem.

Note that because the Report Designer Component adheres to Microsoft's Component Object Model (COM), you may use it only with Microsoft Internet Information Server with Active Server Pages—Unix and Linux Web servers can't use the Crystal Reports Web components. And, only Windows NT, 2000, or XP Web servers are supported—you can't use Windows 95 or 98 Personal Web Server.

The Crystal License Manager

As the combination of available Crystal Reports Web-based and server-based licensing possibilities grows, so does the complexity of trying to keep track of purchased licenses and the rights they grant. To help with this complexity, you can download the Crystal Reports 9 *License Manager*. This stand-alone Windows application enables you to view current usage of your Crystal Reports licenses, as well as to add additional license keys (for multiuser additions, Report Creation API licenses, and so forth). Although the License Manager was included with Crystal Reports 8.5, it is not with 9—you need to download it from Crystal's Web site. Download it from www.crystaldecisions.com/products/crystalreports/licensingab.asp.

After downloading License Manager, unzip it to a folder. The License Manager application consists of a single executable file with an associated help document. If you think you will be using this application on a regular basis, you may want to add a shortcut to a Windows program menu for LicenseManager.EXE. Start the License Manager by viewing the folder you unzipped the files to and double-click on LicenseManager.EXE. Or if you added the shortcut to this file, double-click it. The License Manager will appear, as shown in Figure A-2.

In the first drop-down list, choose the product you wish to examine existing licenses for or add new licenses to. If any existing keycodes for the chosen product have already been added, you'll see them appear in the Existing Keycodes list. If you wish to see the specific number of licenses and level of software (such as Standard, Professional, or Developer) provided by a particular keycode, click it in the Existing Keycodes list. The bottom of the License Manager will denote the license granted by that keycode.

In many cases, when you purchase additional licenses, such as more concurrent RDC licenses for your Web server or the Enterprise Broadcast License, you won't receive any additional software CD-ROMs from Crystal Decisions—you'll merely receive a piece of paper containing additional keycodes. To activate your additional licenses, use the drop-down list to choose the product that you wish to upgrade with additional licenses. Then, type the new keycode in the Add Keycode text box and click the Add button. The new keycode will be added to the Available Keycodes list, where you may select it to confirm the additional licenses it has granted you. To remove a keycode (perhaps to transfer the license to another computer), select the desired keycode in the Available Keycodes list and click the Remove button.

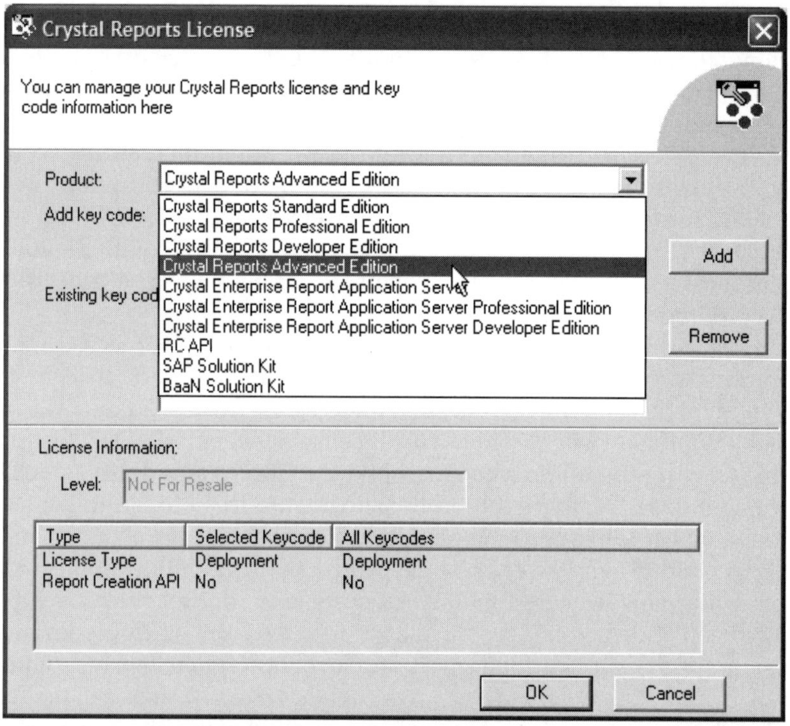

Figure A-2. *The Crystal Reports License Manager*

Installing Report Application Server

If you purchased Crystal Reports 9 Professional, Developer, or Advanced Editions, a separate CD containing the Report Application Server (RAS), discussed in Part II of this book, will be included in the package. When you insert the CD, however, the setup program may not run automatically. If this doesn't happen, simply navigate to the root folder of the CD in Window Explorer and double-click the Setup.EXE program. Setup will then start.

As with Crystal Reports setup, you'll proceed through the typical license agreement and keycode screens, eventually ending up at a screen giving you the choice of a Full or Custom setup. If you are planning on installing RAS all on one computer (the RAS SDK and RAS Server on a single Web server, for example), choose Full. If, however, you wish to take advantage of new RAS multicomputer functionality and install the RAS SDK on the Web server and the RAS Server on a separate computer dedicated to report processing, choose Custom. The Custom setup dialog box will give you choices in the now-familiar explorer-like environment.

Make your desired choices from the various categories of options. As with Crystal Reports setup, you'll find choices to install the option on disk, install on first use, run from CD-ROM, or not install. However, unlike in Crystal Reports 9, none of the options will have a default "install on first use" choice—this isn't a valid choice at an unattended Web server or RAS Server machine!

Make your choices and click Next. The RAS files you chose will be installed on the computer.

Index

INTERNATIONAL CONTACT INFORMATION

AUSTRALIA
McGraw-Hill Book Company Australia Pty. Ltd.
TEL +61-2-9900-1800
FAX +61-2-9878-8881
http://www.mcgraw-hill.com.au
books-it_sydney@mcgraw-hill.com

CANADA
McGraw-Hill Ryerson Ltd.
TEL +905-430-5000
FAX +905-430-5020
http://www.mcgraw-hill.ca

GREECE, MIDDLE EAST, & AFRICA
(Excluding South Africa)
McGraw-Hill Hellas
TEL +30-210-6560-990
TEL +30-210-6560-993
TEL +30-210-6560-994
FAX +30-210-6545-525

MEXICO (Also serving Latin America)
McGraw-Hill Interamericana Editores S.A. de C.V.
TEL +525-117-1583
FAX +525-117-1589
http://www.mcgraw-hill.com.mx
fernando_castellanos@mcgraw-hill.com

SINGAPORE (Serving Asia)
McGraw-Hill Book Company
TEL +65-863-1580
FAX +65-862-3354
http://www.mcgraw-hill.com.sg
mghasia@mcgraw-hill.com

SOUTH AFRICA
McGraw-Hill South Africa
TEL +27-11-622-7512
FAX +27-11-622-9045
robyn_swanepoel@mcgraw-hill.com

SPAIN
McGraw-Hill/Interamericana de España, S.A.U.
TEL +34-91-180-3000
FAX +34-91-372-8513
http://www.mcgraw-hill.es
professional@mcgraw-hill.es

UNITED KINGDOM, NORTHERN,
EASTERN, & CENTRAL EUROPE
McGraw-Hill Education Europe
TEL +44-1-628-502500
FAX +44-1-628-770224
http://www.mcgraw-hill.co.uk
computing_europe@mcgraw-hill.com

ALL OTHER INQUIRIES Contact:
Osborne/McGraw-Hill
TEL +1-510-549-6600
FAX +1-510-883-7600
http://www.osborne.com
omg_international@mcgraw-hill.com

On the Go?